LONGMAN CLASSICS *in* POLITICAL SCIENCE

The Presidential Character

Predicting Performance in the White House

Fourth Edition

JAMES DAVID BARBER

PEARSON

Longman

New York San Francisco Boston
London Toronto Sydney Tokyo Singapore Madrid
Mexico City Munich Paris Cape Town Hong Kong Montreal

For Skiff

Editor-in-Chief: Eric Stano
Executive Marketing Manager: Ann Stypuloski
Supplements Editor: Brian Belardi
Production Coordinator: Scarlett Lindsay
Electronic Page Makeup: Alison Barth Burgoyne
Cover Designer/Manager: John Callahan
Cover Photo: Getty Images
Senior Manufacturing Buyer: Alfred C. Dorsey

Visit us at www.pearsonhighered.com

ISBN-13:978-0-205-65259-4
ISBN-10:   0-205-65259-X

Foreword

In the nearly two generations since James David Barber published the first edition of *The Presidential Character*, it has been one of the most widely read, frequently discussed, and controversial books in political science. Barber's ambitious goal for his book was to develop some clear criteria for choosing presidents. Throughout his career, and in a variety of professional settings, one could observe him asking, "What should we look for in a president?"

Answering this question, he believed, required understanding the whole person, including the personality. Because the presidency is a place of public leadership, the president bears "intense moral, sentimental, and quasi-religious pressures." The president must not allow these pressures to distort his thinking. Sanity is needed in the presidency.

How do we determine who is sane, or less dramatically, best suited to carry the burdens of the presidency? Barber argues that we can identify patterns in a person's character, world view, and style that allow us to anticipate his performance as president (the subtitle of the book is "Predicting Performance in the White House"). Our focus, then, must be on the individual rather than the external influences on the president.

Because personality is so complex, Barber tries to identify those aspects of it that are most relevant to presidential performance. He suggests that character, style, and world view are cognitive handles for assessing presidential personality.

CHARACTER

The core of Barber's analysis, which gives the book its title, is the president's character. Presidential character is the "way the President orients himself toward life." Developed mainly during childhood, this orientation toward experience endures for a lifetime. But how do we determine a president's character?

In just a few paragraphs, Barber lays out a typology based on two observable behavioral dimensions: activity and affect. Activity is the level of energy that a president devotes to the job, and affect is the level of satisfaction the president obtains from it. He divides each dimension into two categories (active-inactive and positive-negative), creating four possible combinations of character-oriented tendencies. Although he discusses much more than character in the biographies that compose the rest of the book, he early declares, "the core of the argument . . . is that Presidential character . . . comes in four varieties. The most important thing to know about a President or candidate is where he fits among these types . . .".

The reason that character type is so critical, according to Barber, is that "the relation of activity to enjoyment in a President . . . tends to outline a cluster of characteristics, to set apart the adapted from the compulsive, compliant, and withdrawn types." In other words, by measuring observable surface behavior, we can identify underlying psychological tendencies.

Some critics found these claims problematic. Barber asserts that his two dimensions tap what is essential and common to most theories of personality, yet he does not show they are grounded in the literature on personality. Although he claims that his four basic character patterns are "long familiar in psychological research," he provides no citations to support his assertion. Thus, critics called for Barber to validate the premise that surface phenomena tap underlying personality characteristics and that the traits Barber attributed to each type go together and only with each other.

For Barber, self-esteem underlies character. The better people feel about themselves, the more likely they will be able to accept criticism, think rationally, and learn on the job. Thus, he maintains that the degree and quality of the president's emotional involvement in an issue are powerful influences on how he defines the issue itself, how much attention he pays to it, which facts and persons he sees as relevant to its resolution, and what principles and purposes he associates with the issues.

The most well-known aspect of Barber's analysis is his argument that active-negative presidents experience a common pattern of *rigidification* resulting from the relationship of a situation they face to their innermost feelings. In other words, these presidents, who are fundamentally insecure, persevere in disastrous policies when opponents threaten their self-esteem, especially their power and rectitude. Always in pursuit of inner phantoms, active-negative presidents respond to threats in ways that Barber finds inappropriate for the objective political situation.

Of the four character types, the active-positive is the one Barber believes is best suited for the presidency. Such a person has the energy needed to do the job and the personal security to deal with the inevitable interpersonal conflicts that result from competing perspectives, interests, policy goals, and ambitions. Thus, they do not need to defend their egos and can concentrate on achieving their policy goals. Although the personalities represented by the other character types may impede presidential performance, perhaps adversely affecting a president's vision, judgment, or actions, the personality of the active-positive presidents allows them to learn from their mistakes and open themselves to a wide range of views.

Because the four personality types are so different, it is essential to place presidents and potential presidents in the correct category of character. Obviously, you cannot predict behavior if you have misclassified a person. Barber acknowledges that that no one fits exactly one of the four character types and that every president is a mixture of the four types. This makes categorization difficult, but Barber resolves the issue by using the dominate tendency of a president. However, he does not resolve the question of identifying the personality characteristics of a mixed character type.

Not everyone agrees with Barber's categorization of individual presidents. Is Dwight Eisenhower a passive-negative type, as Barber claims, or active-positive, as scholar Fred Greenstein concludes?[1] Some also note that liberal Democrats Franklin D. Roosevelt, Harry S Truman, John F. Kennedy, and Jimmy Carter do best in Barber's framework. On the other hand, presidents of whom Barber clearly disapproves, such as Herbert Hoover (for the failure to deal with the Depression), Lyndon Johnson (for the escalation of the war in Vietnam), and Richard Nixon (for just about everything), fall into the active-negative category.

Barber does not fail to provide the appropriate caveats, noting that his categories are somewhat crude and that the impact of personality on performance is a matter of tendencies. He also disavows the reductionist view that character determines everything. Yet his core theory and its use in explanation and prediction of the most important aspects of presidential performance rests upon the special significance he places upon character.

PRESIDENTIAL STYLE

If character forms the inner core of personality, then style is its outer garb. It is a coping mechanism, a means by which people deal with their environment. In Barber's words, "style is how a . . . President goes about doing what the office requires him to do—to speak, directly or through media, to large audiences; to deal face to face with other politicians, individually and in small, relatively private groups; and to read, write, and calculate by himself in order to manage the endless flow of details that stream onto his desk."

---

1. Fred I. Greenstein, *The Hidden-Hand Presidency* (New York: Basic Books, 1982).

Presidents have habitual ways of performing these three political roles, and the balance among the roles varies among presidents. In addition to his basic patterns of style, each president has a unique mode of coping with and adapting to the demands of the office. According to Barber, presidents choose their style in early adulthood with their first independent political success. A confluence of needs, skills, and opportunities shows them what works—and they stick to it.

WORLD VIEW

Each president also has a world view—the "primary, politically relevant beliefs, particularly his conceptions of social causality, human nature, and the central moral conflicts of the time." These views condition their perceptions, their thinking, and their judgment. As with character and style, world views develop early, mainly in adolescence, according to Barber. But, he argues, world view only provides a general indication of the propensities of choice in a decision-making situation.

There is no explicit provision for dealing with world views in the character framework, and Barber handles them in an impressionistic and fragmentary way in the biographies of individual presidents. Nevertheless, his focus sensitizes us to the importance of the president's basic premises in decision making, which commentators frequently overlook in their analyses of presidential behavior. In addition, his descriptions are often provocative, which challenge us to refine our own perceptions of the presidents.

CLASSIFYING THE COMPONENTS

According to Barber, these three psychological components form a pattern of motives, habits, and beliefs that result in behaviors that are evident throughout life. Character is dominant and provides the main thrust and broad direction but does not determine in any fixed sense world view and style. Moreover, these behaviors and the psychological foundation on which they rest do not change easily. Once developed, character, style, and world views tend to persist over time, while issue positions may shift with the public mood and election potential. As a consequence, personality factors may be a better predictor of how people will perform in office than what they say they will do if elected.

The best way to determine character, world view, and style, according to Barber, is to see how they developed early in life. The problem is that the relevant historical information varies in quantity and quality. Often it is sketchy and unreliable. Yet it is essential to classify the three components accurately if we are to use the framework to explain presidential behavior.

EXPLAINING PRESIDENTIAL BEHAVIOR

The critical test for Barber's argument is explaining and predicting presidential behavior. Most of the book is a set of biographies in which he applies his concepts to modern presidents. These essays aim to explain presidential actions, but they also raise important questions for readers.

The president operates at the vortex of many competing forces, ranging from public opinion and the party divisions in Congress to the nation's foreign policy commitments and his own ideological predispositions. Barber typically accords greater weight to personality than to other factors in explaining presidential behavior. Moreover, he usually gives greater weight to character than to style or world view.

This reluctance to consider alternative explanations raises important questions. Was it rigidification or his political philosophy of individualism that discouraged Hoover from aggressively advocating welfare policies? Was LBJ defending his ego against harsh criticism or was he responding to his world view, formed partly by domestic politics and opposition charges of the "loss" of China during the Truman presidency? At the very least, we need to consider such explanations.

Moreover, one could argue that neither Hoover nor Johnson had displayed rigidity in their long careers prior to facing these issues. And what are we to make of Hoover relaxing his views on the federal role in the economy in 1932 and LBJ reversing his escalation of the war in late 1968? Was Richard Nixon rigid regarding the Watergate cover-up, or was he amazingly flexible in his efforts to hide his violation of the law and maintain his office?

In addition, Barber does not consider the possibility of ego controls. Many people learn to control and regulate the expression of their personal needs and anxieties. For example, we are all familiar with people who learn to control their tempers. Such defenses help them to realistically appraise situations and deal with them more effectively. Is it not possible that the disciplined politicians who become president also have some resources of self control?

The most memorable aspect of *The Presidential Character* is Barber's claim that the interaction between character and a particular situation may produce tragedy for active-negative presidents as a result of their rigid response. Yet, how do we know when rigidification will occur? How do we know a trigger when we see it? Barber does not say.

In addition, we need to determine an appropriate test of the model. If tragedies do not appear, Barber asserts the environment was not ripe for producing rigidification. In the first edition of the book, Barber concludes that Richard Nixon was a special variant of the active-negative character type who had avoided tragedy. If even the nonoccurrence of a prediction does not invalidate the theory, what would it take to falsify it? Is the argument tautological?

If a predicted tragedy does occur, Barber can claim that the psychological explanation is valid. Perhaps it is. Or perhaps there is another explanation . . .

CONCLUSION

The Presidential Character raises many important questions about presidential performance. Barber forces us to consider the occupants of the White House as individuals and to contemplate the less visible influences on their behavior. He applies social science concepts to real-world politics in an attempt to be helpful to citizens and scholars alike. And he does all this in an appealing and interesting fashion. It is not surprising that Pearson Longman is reissuing his book.

Barber also engages our analytical faculties as he offers an original approach to understanding politics and seeks to reach generalizations about presidential performance across presidents. To evaluate such an engaging and unique work calls for thinking carefully and critically about analysis of complex behavior in an equally complex environment. The encouragement of analytical rigor alone makes reading *The Presidential Character* a worthwhile endeavor.

Barber's work should encourage us to think about our current president and leaders who might become president. As Barber used to ask, "What should we look for in a president?" What criteria should we apply in evaluating candidates? Do character, world view, and style help us? Can we determine the president's character? In addition, are there other criteria that are important to successful leadership, such as values, commitment, resolution, strength, and resiliency? Barber has begun the conversation, but it is an enduring one in which each generation must engage.

GEORGE C. EDWARDS III

RECOMMENDED READINGS

Alexander L. George and Juliette L. George, *Presidential Personality and Performance* (Boulder, CO: Westview, 1998), chapters 2, 4, 5.

———, *Woodrow Wilson and Colonel House* (Mineola, NY: Dover, 1964).

Fred I. Greenstein, *Personality and Politics* (Princeton, NJ: Princeton University Press, 1987).

Erwin C. Hargrove, "Presidential Personality and Leadership Style," in *Researching the Presidency*, ed. George C. Edwards III, John H. Kessel, and Bert A. Rockman (Pittsburgh, PA: University of Pittsburgh Press, 1993).

Robert Tucker, "The Georges' Wilson Reexamined: An Essay on Psychobiography," *American Political Science Review* 71 (June 1977): 606–18.

Edwin A. Weinstein, James William Anderson, and Arthur S. Link, "A Reappraisal of Woodrow Wilson's Political Personality," *Political Science Quarterly* 93 (Winter 1978–79): 585–98.

Contents

Preface

For better or for worse, who gets to be President of the United States makes a difference for our future. Our strength is democracy, government by consent of the governed, using reason to protect and advance progress for human beings. Our weakness is anarchy, government and politics shredded into fragments, thanks to dreamy public apathy and brainless emotion. History shows that political weakness can degenerate into tragedy: dictatorship, set up to cure confusion. But what if when that temptation looms, we wake up, take part, and find leadership, we can make life, liberty, and the pursuit of happiness actually happen.

Leadership is not sainthood. The President is no god. As Harry Truman reminded us, the President (so far a male) puts his pants on one leg at a time. Fortunately the President stands with is power inside a system with "checks and balances," a system put together after centuries of learning how tragic it turns out to be when a society kneels down and sends its faith to a monarch. By long, hard experience, we finally learned that government—even democracy—is no church. Democracy is a system, a set of conditions, a down-to-earth skeleton put together to host and foster baseline virtues such as justice, freedom, equality, community, and participation, rather than topline virtues such as faith, hope, and charity. So who ought to be picked for the Presidency is a concern we ought to think about not in the context of moral perfection but in the context of basic political leadership in the reality of democracy.

Voting is not the only available mistake. Television dominates the news, so we are tempted to judge candidates by how they look rather than what they decide. Political knowledge declines, popping from argument to slogan, from commitment to gesture, from accuracy to impression. The Presidential contest can come on as a game, shown like T.V. sports, watching who's ahead and who's behind rather than who they are. Who they will be is important to all of us. A ball game ends with the final score. The audience does not then put their power in the hands of the winning team. The campaign for President is different: it sets up a future, a game for the next four or eight years and beyond. We need to treat the campaign game not as a sporty moment but as a tough test based on standards of the Presidency itself.

And what does our President face? Exciting times, because democracies are trying to rise up and hang on all around the world, as humans of wildly different cultures come to recognize their need for the same form of government. And fortunately more and more people recognize that democracy is rights as well as process—requiring a guarantee that the *results* of democracy must never include the bashing of human rights. Think of yourself as becoming President of the United States—the first nation in this world founded on human rights, as the declaration of our revolution and the ultimate passage of our constitution makes clear. What an exciting challenge you would face.

But we also face dark times. Democracy can die. Here inside the United States we have been lazily floating over toward the edge of political disaster. Half of Americans do not bother to vote for a President. Congress fails to debate. Parties are falling apart. Law drifts toward uncertainty, decided too often by a split 5–4 vote in the Supreme Court. Decisions in foreign affairs, including war, slide over into the secret White House, where decisions are made without consent of the governed or even consent of the Congress. National economics is flooded with enormous debt, potential to drown free enterprise and fair taxes. Millions of citizens are poorly educated, worse than in a dozen other countries. Far more thousands get killed with guns in the United States than in countries like Japan and Germany, whose guns once set us to war. Drugs and AIDS and bankruptcy and Americans actually sleeping on the streets are increasing every day. And overseas, despite the excitement for democracy, television shows us starving children but cannot film the quiet and secret spread of nuclear weapons, building the possibility of Chicago as a Hiroshima.

No wonder, then, that we need a President whose character, style, and world view can contribute to a real fix for this country and this country's leadership for the world. To make that happen, we need voters who are into thinking, not just feeling, and talking, not just musing. My hope is that that can happen in political parties, Congress, and journalism—but also in colleges and universities, where advanced rationality can develop and even leadership can emerge.

This strange book includes predictions which were put forth before the public, and the retrospective writing about what I saw as what actually happened afterward. No one shares blame for my mistakes, but over the years scores of scholars, journalists, editors, critics, encouragers, and institutions have helped me with the task, helpers I am very thankful for. As ever, I am specially grateful to the seven Yale graduate students who, at the start, raked through biographies with my instruments and told me what they thought: Richard S. Beth, Father Richard Costigan, S.J., Charles G. Daney, Elizabeth Kodama, Stephen Austin Merrill, Byron E. Shafer, and Robert James Straus. In the past, many readers have given me the benefit of their thoughts. I hope you write to me what you think, especially if you care about politics.

JAMES DAVID BARBER
Cullowhee Spring
Durham, N.C.

The Presidential Character

1

Presidential Character and How to Foresee It

When we citizens vote for a Presidential candidate, we make, in effect, a prediction. We choose from among the contenders the one we think (or feel or guess) would be the best President. We operate in a situation of immense uncertainty. If we have already been voting for years, we can recall time and time again when we guessed wrong. We listen to the commentators, the politicians, and our friends, then add it all up in some rough way to produce our prediction and our vote. Earlier in the game, our anticipations have been taken into account, either directly in the polls and primaries or indirectly in the minds of politicians who want to nominate someone we will like. But we must choose in the midst of a cloud of confusion, a rain of phony advertising, a storm of sermons, a hail of complex issues, a fog of charisma and boredom, and a thunder of accusation and defense. In the face of this chaos, a great many citizens fall back on the past, vote their old allegiances, and let it go at that. Nevertheless, the citizens' vote says that on balance we expect Candidate X would outshine Candidate Y in the Presidency.

This book is meant to help citizens and those who advise them cut through the confusion and get at some clear criteria for choosing Presidents. To understand what actual Presidents do and what potential Presidents might do, the first need is to know the whole person—not as some abstract embodiment of civic virtue, some scorecard of issue stands, or some reflection of a faction, but as a human being like the rest of us, a person trying to cope with a difficult environ-

1

ment. To that task, the candidate brings an individual character, worldview, and political style. None of that is new at campaign time. If we can see the pattern set already for the candidate's political life, we can, I contend, estimate better the pattern this person brings forth to the stresses and chances of the Presidency.

The Presidency is a peculiar office. The Founding Fathers left it extraordinarily loose in definition, partly because they trusted George Washington to invent a tradition as he went along. It is an institution made a piece at a time by successive men (so far) in the White House. Jefferson reached out to Congress to put together the beginnings of political parties; Jackson's dramatic force extended electoral partisanship to its mass base; Lincoln vastly expanded the administrative reach of the office; Wilson and the Roosevelts showed its rhetorical possibilities—in fact every President's mind and demeanor has left its mark on a heritage still in lively development.

But the Presidency is much more than an institution. It is a focus of feelings. In general, popular feelings about politics are low-key, shallow, casual. For example, the vast majority of Americans knows virtually nothing of what Congress is doing and cares less. The Presidency is different. The Presidency is the focus for the most intense and persistent emotions in the American polity. The President is a symbolic leader, the one figure who draws together the people's hopes and fears for the political future. On top of all his routine duties, he has to carry that off—or fail.

Our emotional attachment to Presidents shows up when one dies in office. People were not just disappointed or worried when President Kennedy was killed; people wept at the loss of a man most had never even met. Kennedy was young and charismatic—but history shows that whenever a President dies in office, heroic Lincoln or debased Harding, McKinley or Garfield, the same wave of deep emotion sweeps across the country. On the other hand, the death of an ex-President brings forth no such intense emotional reaction.

The President is the first political figure children are aware of (later they add Congress, the Court, and others, as "helpers" of the President). With some exceptions among children in deprived circumstances, the President is seen as a "benevolent leader," one who nurtures, sustains, and inspires the citizenry. Presidents regularly show up among "most admired" contemporaries and forebears, and the President is the "best known" (in the sense of sheer name recognition) person in the country. At inauguration time, even Presidents elected by close margins are supported by much larger majorities than the election returns show, for people rally round as he actually assumes office. There is a similar reaction when the people see their President threatened by crisis: if he takes action, there is a favorable spurt in the Gallup poll whether he succeeds or fails.

Obviously the President gets more attention in schoolbooks, press, and television than any other politician. He is one of very few who can make news by doing good things. *His* emotional state is a matter of continual public commentary, as is the manner in which his personal and official families conduct themselves. The media portray the President not as some neutral administrator or corporate executive to be assessed by his production, but as a special being with mysterious dimensions.

We have no king. The sentiments English children—and adults—direct to the Queen have no place to go in our system but to the President. Whatever his talents—Coolidge-type or Roosevelt-type—the President is the only available object for such national-religious-monarchical sentiments as Americans possess.

The President helps people make sense of politics. Congress is a tangle of committees, the bureaucracy is a maze of agencies. The President is one man trying to do a job—a picture much more understandable to the mass of people who find themselves in the same boat. Furthermore, he is the top man. He ought to know what is going on and set it right. So when the economy goes sour, or war drags on, or domestic violence erupts, the President is available to take the blame. Then when things go right, it seems the President must have had a hand in it. Indeed, the flow of political life is marked off by Presidents: the "Eisenhower Era," the "Kennedy Years."

What all this means is that the President's *main* responsibilities reach far beyond administering the Executive Branch or commanding the armed forces. The White House is first and foremost a place of public leadership. That inevitably brings to bear on the President intense moral, sentimental, and quasireligious pressures which can, if he lets them, distort his own thinking and feeling. If there is such a thing as extraordinary sanity, it is needed nowhere so much as in the White House.

Who the President is at a given time can make a profound difference in the whole thrust and direction of national politics. Since we have only one President at a time, we can never prove this by comparison, but even the most superficial speculation confirms the commonsense view that the man himself weighs heavily among other historical factors. A Wilson re-elected in 1920, a Hoover in 1932, a John F. Kennedy in 1964 would, it seems very likely, have guided the body politic along rather different paths from those their actual successors chose. Or try to imagine a Theodore Roosevelt ensconced behind today's "bully pulpit" of a Presidency, or Lyndon Johnson as President in the age of McKinley. Only someone mesmerized by the lures of historical inevitability can suppose that it would have made little or no difference to government policy had Alf Landon replaced FDR in 1936, had Dewey beaten Truman in 1948, or Adlai Stevenson reigned through the 1950s. Not only would these alternative President have advocated different policies—they would have approached the office from very different psychological angles. It stretches credibility to think that Eugene McCarthy would have run the institution the way Lyndon Johnson did.

The burden of this book is that the crucial differences can be anticipated by an understanding of a potential President's character, his world view, and his style.[1] This kind of prediction is not easy; well-informed observers often have guessed wrong as they watched a man step toward the White House. One thinks of Woodrow Wilson, the scholar who would bring reason to politics; of Herbert

Hoover, the Great Engineer who would organize chaos into progress; of Franklin D. Roosevelt, that champion of the balanced budget; of Harry Truman, whom the office would surely overwhelm; of Dwight D. Eisenhower, militant crusader; of John F. Kennedy, who would lead beyond moralisms to achievements; of Lyndon B. Johnson, the Southern conservative; and of Richard M. Nixon, conciliator. Spotting the errors is easy. Predicting with even approximate accuracy is going to require some sharp tools and close attention in their use. But the experiment is worth it because the question is critical and because it lends itself to correction by evidence.

My argument comes in layers.

First, a President's personality is an important shaper of his Presidential behavior on nontrivial matters.

Second, Presidential personality is patterned. His character, world view, and style fit together in a dynamic package understandable in psychological terms.

Third, a President's personality interacts with the power situation he faces and the national "climate of expectations" dominant at the time he serves. The tuning, the resonance—or lack of it—between these external factors and his personality sets in motion the dynamic of his Presidency.

Fourth, the best way to predict a President's character, world view, and style is to see how they were put together in the first place. That happened in his early life, culminating in his first independent political success.

But the core of the argument (which organizes the structure of the book) is that Presidential character—the basic stance a man takes toward his Presidential experience—comes in four varieties. The most important thing to know about a President or candidate is where he fits among these types, defined according to (a) how active he is and (b) whether or not he gives the impression he enjoys his political life.

Let me spell out these concepts briefly before getting down to cases.

PERSONALITY SHAPES PERFORMANCE

I am not about to argue that once you know a President's personality you know everything. But, as the cases will demonstrate, the degree and quality of a President's emotional involvement in an issue are powerful influences on how he defines the issue itself, how much attention he pays to it, which facts and persons he sees as relevant to its resolution, and, finally, what principles and purposes he associates with the issue. Every story of Presidential decision-making is really two stories: an outer one in which a rational man calculates and an inner one in which an emotional man feels. The two are forever connected. Any real President is one whole man and his deeds reflect his wholeness.

As for personality, it is a matter of tendencies. It is not that one President "has" some basic characteristics that another President does not "have." That old way of treating a trait as a possession, like a rock in a basket, ignores the universality of aggressiveness, compliancy, detachment, and other human drives. We all have all of them, but in different amounts and in different combinations.

THE PATTERN OF CHARACTER, WORLD VIEW, AND STYLE

The most visible part of the pattern is style. *Style is the President's habitual way of performing his three political roles: rhetoric, personal relations, and homework.* Not to be confused with "stylishness," charisma, or appearance, style is how the President goes about doing what the office requires him to do—to speak, directly or through media, to large audiences; to deal face to face with other politicians, individually and in small, relatively private groups; and to read, write, and calculate by himself in order to manage the endless flow of details that stream onto his desk. No President can escape doing at least some of each. But there are marked differences in stylistic emphasis from President to President. The *balance* among the three style elements varies; one President may put most of himself into rhetoric, another may stress close, informal dealing, while still another may devote his energies mainly to study and cogitation. Beyond the balance, we want to see each President's peculiar habits of style, his mode of coping with and adapting to these Presidential demands. For example, I think both Calvin Coolidge and John F. Kennedy were primarily rhetoricians, but they went about it in contrasting ways.

A President's *world view consists of his primary, politically relevant beliefs, particularly his conceptions of social causality, human nature, and the central moral conflicts of the time.* This is how he sees the world, and what his lasting opinions are about what he sees. Style is his way of acting; world view is his way of seeing. Like the rest of us, a President develops over a lifetime certain conceptions of reality—how things work in politics, what people are like, what the main purposes are. These assumptions or conceptions help him make sense of his world, give some semblance of order to the chaos of existence. Perhaps most important, a man's world view affects what he pays attention to, and a great deal of politics is about paying attention. The name of the game for many politicians is not so much "Do this, do that" as it is "Look here!"

"Character" comes from the Greek word for engraving; in one sense it is what life has marked into a man's being. As used here, *character is the way the President orients himself toward life*—not for the moment, but enduringly. Character is the person's stance as he confronts experience. And at the core of character, a man confronts himself. The President's fundamental self-esteem is his prime personal resource; to defend and advance that, he will sacrifice much else he values. Down there in the privacy of his heart, does he find himself superb, or ordinary, or debased, or in some intermediate range? No President has been utterly paralyzed by self-doubt and none has been utterly free of midnight self-mockery. In between, the real Presidents move out on life from positions of relative strength or weakness. Equally important are the criteria by which they judge themselves. A President who rates himself by the standard of achievement, for instance, may be little affected by losses of affection.

Character, world view, and style are abstractions from the reality of the whole individual. In every case they form an integrated pattern: the man develops a combination which makes psychological sense for him, a dynamic arrangement of motives, beliefs, and habits in the services of his need for self-esteem.

THE POWER SITUATION AND "CLIMATE OF EXPECTATIONS"

Presidential character resonates with the political situation the President faces. It adapts him as he tries to adapt it. The support he has from the public and interest groups, the party balance in Congress, the thrust of Supreme Court opinion, together set the basic power situation he must deal with. An activist President may run smack into a brick wall of resistance, then pull back and wait for a better moment. On the other hand, a President who sees himself as a quiet caretaker may not try to exploit even the most favorable power situation. So it is the relationship between President and the political configuration that makes the system tick.

Even before public opinion polls, the President's real or supposed popularity is a large factor in his performance. Besides the power mix in Washington, the President has to deal with a national climate of expectations, the predominant needs thrust up to him by the people. There are at least three recurrent themes around which these needs are focused.

People look to the President for *reassurance*, a feeling that things will be all right, that the President will take care of his people. The psychological request is for a surcease of anxiety. Obviously, modern life in America involves considerable doses of fear, tension, anxiety, worry; from time to time, the public mood calls for a rest, a time of peace, a breathing space, a "return to normalcy."

Another theme is the demand for a *sense of progress and action*. The President ought to do something to direct the nation's course—or at least be in there pitching for the people. The President is looked to as a take-charge man, a doer, a turner of the wheels, a producer of progress—even if that means some sacrifice of serenity.

A third type of climate of expectations is the public need for a sense of *legitimacy* from, and in, the Presidency. The President should be a master politician who is above politics. He should have a right to his place and a rightful way of acting in it. The respectability—even religiosity—of the office has to be protected by a man who presents himself as defender of the faith. There is more to this than dignity, more than propriety. The President is expected to personify our betterness in an inspiring way, to express in what he does and is (not just in what he says) a moral idealism which, in much of the public mind, is the very opposite of "politics."

Over time, the climate of expectations shifts and changes. Wars, depressions, and other national events contribute to that change, but there also is a rough cycle, from an emphasis on action (which begins to look too "political") to an emphasis on legitimacy (the moral uplift of which creates its own strains) to an emphasis on reassurance and rest (which comes to seem like drift) and back to action again. One need not be astrological about it. The point is that the climate of expectations at any given time is the political air the President has to breathe. Relating to this climate is a large part of his task.

PREDICTING PRESIDENTS

The best way to predict a President's character, world view, and style is to see how he constructed them in the first place. Especially in the early stages, life is experimental; consciously or not, a person tries out various ways of defining and maintaining and raising self-esteem. He looks to his environment for clues as to who he is and how well he is doing. These lessons of life slowly sink in: certain self-images and evaluations, certain ways of looking at the world, certain styles of action get confirmed by his experience and he gradually adopts them as his own. If we can see that process of development, we can understand the product. The features to note are those bearing on Presidential performance.

Experimental development continues all the way to death; we will not blind ourselves to midlife changes, particularly in the full-scale prediction cases. But it is often much easier to see the basic patterns in early life histories. Later on a whole host of distractions—especially the image-making all politicians learn to practice—clouds the picture.

In general, character has its *main* development in childhood, world view in adolescence, style in early adulthood. The stance toward life I call character grows out of the child's experiments in relating to parents, brothers and sisters, and peers at play and in school, as well as to his own body and the objects around it. Slowly the child defines an orientation toward experience; once established, that tends to last despite much subsequent contradiction. By adolescence, the child has been hearing and seeing how people make their worlds meaningful, and now he is moved to relate himself—his own meanings—to those around him. His focus of attention shifts toward the future; he senses that decisions about his fate are coming and he looks into the premises for those decisions. Thoughts about the way the world works and how one might work in it, about what people are like and how one might be like them or not, and about the values people share and how one might share in them too—these are typical concerns for the post-child, pre-adult mind of the adolescent.

These themes come together strongly in early adulthood, when the person moves from contemplation to responsible action and adopts a style. In most biographical accounts, this period stands out in stark clarity—the time of emergence, the time the young man found himself. I call it his first independent political success. It was then he moved beyond the detailed guidance of his family; then his self-esteem was dramatically boosted; then he came forth as a person to be reckoned with by other people. The *way* he did that is profoundly important to him. Typically he grasps that style and hangs onto it. Much later, coming into the Presidency, something in him remembers this earlier victory and re-emphasizes the style that made it happen.

Character provides the main thrust and broad direction—but it does not *determine*, in any fixed sense, world view and style. The story of development does not end with the end of childhood. Thereafter, the culture one grows in and the ways that culture is translated by parents and peers shapes the meanings one makes of his character. The current world view gets learned and that learning helps channel character forces. Thus it will not necessarily be true that compulsive characters have reactionary beliefs, or that compliant characters believe in compromise. This is also true of style: historical accidents play a large part in furnishing special opportunities for action—and in blocking off alternatives. For example, however much anger a young man may feel, that anger will not be expressed in rhetoric unless and until his life situation provides a platform and an audience. Style thus has a stature and independence of its own. Those who would reduce all explanation to character neglect these highly significant later channelings. For beyond the root is the branch, above the foundation the superstructure, and starts do not prescribe finishes.

FOUR TYPES OF PRESIDENTIAL CHARACTER

The five concepts—character, world view, style, power situation, and climate of expectations—run through the accounts of Presidents in the chapters to follow, which cluster the Presidents since Theodore Roosevelt into four types. This is the fundamental scheme of the study. It offers a way to move past the complexities to the main contrasts and comparisons.

The first baseline in defining Presidential types is *activity-passivity*. How much energy does the man invest in his Presidency? Lyndon Johnson went at his day like a human cyclone, coming to rest long after the sun went down. Calvin Coolidge often slept eleven hours a night and still needed a nap in the middle of the day. In between, the Presidents array themselves on the high or low side of the activity line.

The second baseline is *positive-negative affect* toward one's activity—that is, how he feels about what he does. Relatively speaking, does he seem to experience his political life as happy or sad, enjoyable or discouraging, positive or negative in its main effect? The feeling I am after here is not grim satisfaction in a job well done, not some philosophical conclusion. The idea is this: is he someone who, on the surfaces we can see, gives forth the feeling that he has *fun* in political life? Franklin Roosevelt's Secretary of War, Henry L. Stimson, wrote that the Roosevelts "not only understood the *use* of power, they knew the *enjoyment* of power, too. . . . Whether a man is burdened by power or enjoys power; whether he is trapped by responsibility or made free by it; whether he is moved by other people and outer forces or moves them—that is the essence of leadership."

The positive-negative baseline, then, is a general symptom of the fit between the man and his experience, a kind of register of *felt* satisfaction.

Why might we expect these two simple dimensions to outline the main character types? Because they stand for two central features of anyone's orientation toward life. In nearly every study of personality, some form of the active-passive contrast is critical; the general tendency to act or be acted upon is evident in such concepts as dominance-submission, extraversion-introversion, aggression-timidity, attack-defense, fight-flight, engagement-withdrawal, approach-avoidance. In everyday life we sense quickly the general energy output of the people we deal with. Similarly, we catch on fairly quickly to the affect dimension—whether the person seems to be optimistic or pessimistic, hopeful or skeptical, happy or sad. The two baselines are clear and they are also independent of one another: all of us know people who are very active but seem discouraged, others who are quite passive but seem happy, and so forth. The activity baseline refers to what one does, the affect baseline to how one feels about what he does.

Both are crude clues to character. They are leads into four basic character patterns long familiar in psychological research. In summary form, these are the main configurations:

Active-Positive

There is a congruence, a consistency, between being very active and the enjoyment of it, indicating relatively high self-esteem and relative success in relating to the environment. The man shows an orientation toward productiveness as a value, and an ability to use his styles flexibly, adaptively, suiting the dance to the music. He sees himself as developing over time toward relatively well defined personal goals—growing toward his image of himself as he might yet be. There is an emphasis on rational mastery, and on using the brain to move the feet. This may get him into trouble; he may fail to take account of the irrational in politics. Not everyone he deals with sees things his way and he may find it hard to understand why.

Active-Negative

The contradiction here is between relatively intense effort and relatively low emotional reward for that effort. The activity has a compulsive quality, as if the man were trying to make up for something or to escape from anxiety into hard work. He seems ambitious, striving upward and seeking power. His stance toward the environment is aggressive and he has a persistent problem in managing his aggressive feelings. His self-image is vague and discontinuous. Life is a hard struggle to achieve and hold power, hampered by the condemnations of a perfectionistic conscience. Active-negative types pour energy into the political system, but it is an energy distorted from within.

Passive-Positive

This is the receptive, compliant, other-directed character whose life is a search for affection as a reward for being agreeable and cooperative rather than personally assertive. The contradiction is between low self-esteem (on grounds of being unlovable, unattractive) and a superficial optimism. A hopeful attitude helps dispel doubt and elicits encouragement from others. Passive-positive types help soften the harsh edges of politics. But their dependence and the fragility of their hopes and enjoyments make disappointment in politics likely.

Passive-Negative

The factors are consistent—but how are we to account for the man's *political* role-taking? Why is someone who does little in politics and enjoys it less there at all? The answer lies in the passive-negative's character-rooted orientation toward doing dutiful service; this compensates for low self-esteem based on a sense of uselessness. Passive-negative types are in politics because they think they ought to be. They may be well adapted to certain nonpolitical roles, but they lack the experience and flexibility to perform effectively as political leaders. Their tendency is to withdraw, to escape from the conflict and uncertainty of politics by emphasizing vague principles (especially prohibitions) and procedural arrangements. They become guardians of the right and proper way, above the sordid politicking of lesser men.

Active-positive Presidents want to achieve results. Active-negatives aim to get and keep power. Passive-positives are after love. Passive-negatives emphasize their civic virtue. The relation of activity to enjoyment in a President thus tends to outline a cluster of characteristics, to set apart the well adapted from the compulsive, compliant, and withdrawn types.

The first four Presidents of the United States, conveniently, ran through this gamut of character types. (Remember, we are talking about tendencies and broad directions; no individual man exactly fits a category.) George Washington—clearly the most important President in the pantheon—established the fundamental legitimacy of an American government at a time when this was a matter in considerable question. Washington's dignity, judiciousness, his aloof air of reserve and dedication to duty, fit the passive-negative or withdrawing type best. Washington did not seek innovation, he sought stability. He longed to retire to Mount Vernon, but fortunately was persuaded to stay on through a second term, in which, by rising above the political conflict between Hamilton and Jefferson and inspiring confidence in his own integrity, he gave the nation time to develop the organized means for peaceful change.

John Adams followed, a dour New England Puritan, much given to work and worry, an impatient and irascible man—an active-negative President, a compulsive type. Adams was far more partisan than Washington; the survival of the system through his Presidency demonstrated that the nation could tolerate, for a time, domination by one of its nascent political parties. As President, an angry

Adams brought the United States to the brink of war with France, and presided over the new nation's first experiment in political repression: the Alien and Sedition Acts, forbidding, among other things, unlawful combinations "with intent to oppose any measure or measures of the government of the United States," or "any false, scandalous, and malicious writing or writings against the United States, or the President of the United States, with intent to defame . . . or to bring them or either of them, into contempt or disrepute."

Then came Jefferson. He too, had his troubles and failures—in the design of national defense, for example. As for his Presidential character (only one element in success or failure), Jefferson was clearly active-positive. A child of the Enlightenment, he applied his reason to organizing connections with Congress aimed at strengthening the more popular forces. A man of catholic interests and delightful humor, Jefferson combined a clear and open vision of what the country could be with a profound political sense, expressed in his famous phrase, "Every difference of opinion is not a difference of principle."

The fourth President was James Madison, "Little Jemmy," the constitutional philosopher thrown into the White House at a time of great international turmoil. Madison comes closest to the passive-positive, or compliant, type; he suffered from irresolution, tried to compromise his way out, and gave in too readily to the "war-hawks" urging combat with Britain. The nation drifted into war, and Madison wound up ineptly commanding his collection of amateur generals in the streets of Washington. General Jackson's victory at New Orleans saved the Madison administration's historical reputation, but he left the Presidency with the United States close to bankruptcy and secession.

These four Presidents—like all Presidents—were persons trying to cope with the roles they had won by using the equipment they had built over a lifetime. The President is not some shapeless organism in a flood of novelties, but a man with a memory in a system with a history. Like all of us, he draws on his past to shape his future. The pathetic hope that the White House will turn a Caligula into a Marcus Aurelius is as naive as the fear that ultimate power inevitably corrupts. The problem is to understand—and to state understandably—what in the personal past foreshadows the Presidential future.

2

Three Tragic Tales

Lord Acton's aphorism, "Power tends to corrupt; absolute power corrupts absolutely," has been no more true for Presidents than John Adam's view that "the first want of man is his dinner, and the second his girl." Power may corrupt—or ennoble or frighten or inspire or distract a man. The result depends on his propensity for, his vulnerability to, particular kinds of corruption or cleansing—in short, on his character. In the Presidency, power seems to have left George Washington with his pre-Presidential dignity intact, to have lifted Chester Arthur and Harry Truman somewhat above what they were before, to have revealed strengths Lincoln was not thought to have possessed—and to have ruined some good men for other political roles.

Political power is like nuclear energy: available to create deserts or make them bloom. The mere having of it never yet determined its use. The mere getting of it has not stamped into the powerful some uniform shape.

In our peculiar democracy, as Richard Neustadt clarified so effectively, political power is the power to *persuade*. Only very rarely can a President issue definitive commands and expect to see them executed. He is always about the business of persuading people to do what he wants them to do in their own interests. The contradiction of power is that the President, like most actors in the political system, is dependent on his dependents, subject to his subjects, forever in the position of supplicant for renewal of his license to rule. A President can so dissipate his real powers that he has nothing left but the shell of office. The most powerful man in the world is also the man most vulnerable to the complex mix of consent on which his power rests.

This chapter is about three Presidents who seem to have forgotten that power means persuasion. Different as they were in other ways, Woodrow Wilson, Herbert Hoover, and Lyndon B. Johnson came to share in their Presidencies a common pattern: a process of rigidification, and a movement from political dexterity to narrow insistence on a failing course of action despite abundant evidence of the failure. Each of these three helped arrange his own defeat, and in the course of doing that, left the nation worse off than it might have been. Not by accident, these three are the prime twentieth-century examples of the active-negative type. Their political tragedies developed, I will argue, out of inner dramas in which themes of power and themes of conscience struggled for pre-eminence. I think it would have been possible to foresee this development even before these men took office. But first, is it plain that Wilson, Hoover, and Johnson displayed, as Presidents, a pattern of progressive—and politically significant—attachment to a "solution" each could neither sustain nor abandon?

WILSON DEFEATS THE LEAGUE

In many respects Woodrow Wilson was one of the nation's most successful Presidents; certainly he was not the machinelike psychotic some have made him out to be. In a scathing review of the worst Wilson book, a biography in which Sigmund Freud and William C. Bullitt (both intense Wilson-haters) are said to have collaborated, Arthur Link comments: "For a mentally unbalanced person, Wilson had a remarkable career. Somehow he managed to make distinguished contributions to the four separate fields of scholarship, higher education, domestic politics, and diplomacy."[1] The idea of Wilson as a leader totally in the grip of mental disease is obviously false. Far from being paralyzed by his inner conflicts, Wilson was able to draw on extraordinary strengths to produce a political legacy that places him firmly among the "great" Presidents. Not much is to be gained, then, from attempts to assess either the depth of his "psychosis" or the height of his "greatness." We are dealing with neither a patient nor a god but with a man who, trying hard to do the right thing, killed a dream he shared with millions throughout the world. But the story will have to carry its own weight.

The history of Wilson and the League extends far back into Wilson's own history and far out into the world he had to deal with. Perhaps the clearest place to grasp the essentials is the President's return from the Paris Peace Conference in July 1919 with the Covenant of the League of Nations, which required ratification by two-thirds of the Senate, or 64 votes. The situation he faced was as follows:

Republicans controlled the Senate by a majority of two. In the House, the Republicans had a majority of 39. In 1918, Democrat Wilson had taken the unusual step, over the protests of his key advisors and his wife, of asking the people to vote for Democrats for Congress; a

Republican victory, he had said, "would certainly be interpreted on the other side of the water as a repudiation of my leadership." Only five months earlier the wartime President had declared politics "adjourned" for the duration. The election had been a massive defeat for Wilson, resulting in the Republican majorities.

The chairman of the Senate Foreign Relations Committee, Wilson's arch-enemy Henry Cabot Lodge, was responsible for initial consideration of the Treaty. Lodge had stacked the Committee with opponents of the League. Ten of the eighteen members were determined to kill it.

Senator Lodge was also majority leader of the Republican party in the Senate.

Forty-nine Senators had declared themselves, shortly before Wilson's return from Paris, in favor of "reservations" (basically, amendments) to the League Treaty.

Nevertheless, there was strong support both within the Senate and in the country at large for some form of the League. In a preliminary poll by the "League to Enforce Peace," 64 Senators were prepared to vote for ratification, 20 were doubtful, and 12 opposed. And even Senator Lodge confessed that "the vocal masses of the community"—most clergy, professors, editors and so forth—were "friendly to the League."

In other words, the President faced an implacable enemy in Lodge, a very difficult proposition in the Foreign Relations Committee, a near stand-off in the Senate as a whole, and a generally favorable climate of opinion in the "vocal" public. Rarely had there been a situation which called more clearly for the most adroit political leadership by the President of favorably inclined Senators and the most intense efforts at developing the compromises necessary to bring around the waverers. Long before, Wilson himself had advised Presidents in such circumstances to

> be less stiff and offish, [to] himself act in the true spirit of the Constitution and establish intimate relations of confidence with the Senate on his own initiative, not carrying his plans to completion and then laying them in final form before the Senate to be accepted or rejected, but keeping himself in confidential communication with the leaders of the Senate while his plans are in course . . . in order that there may be veritable counsel and a real accommodation of views instead of a final challenge and contest.[2]

Like others of his character, Wilson found this lesson of life easier to expound than to live by.

Before leaving Paris, the President had sent a message to the American people, a message which began, "The treaty of peace has been signed. If it is ratified and acted upon in full and sincere execution of its terms it will furnish the charter for a new order of affairs in the world." He rested only one day after arriving in the United States, then appeared before the Senate to speak on the treaty. But before leaving the White House for the Senate chamber, he held a press conference; to a reporter who inquired whether the Treaty would pass the Senate with "reservations," Wilson snapped: "I do not think hypothetical questions are concerned. The Senate is going to ratify the treaty." However, his speech that day first developed a conciliatory theme:

My services and all the information I possess will be at your disposal and at the disposal of your Committee on Foreign Relations at any time, either informally or in session, as you may prefer; and I hope that you will not hesitate to make use of them. . . .[3]

But his tone changed as his rhetoric rose. The League was "a practical necessity," "an indispensable instrumentality." "Statesmen might see difficulties," he said,

but the people could see none and could brook no denial. . . . The League of Nations was . . . the only hope for mankind . . . the main object of the peace . . . the only thing that could complete it or make it worthwhile . . . the hope of the world. . . . Shall we or any other free people hesitate to accept this great duty? Dare we reject it and break the heart of the world? There can be no question of our ceasing to be a world power. The only question is whether we can refuse the moral leadership that is offered us, whether we shall accept or reject the confidence of the world.

"Accept or reject"—that was the way Wilson posed the question. The Senate was challenged on moral grounds. Putting aside his notes, the President concluded with an image which made clear his view that only one course was available to the Senate:

The stage is set, the destiny disclosed. It has come about by no plan of our conceiving, but by the hand of God who led us into this way. We cannot turn back. We can only go forward, with lifted eyes and freshened spirit, to follow the vision. It was of this that we dreamed at our birth. America shall in truth show the way. The light streams upon the path ahead, and nowhere else.[4]

Wilson's friend William Gibbs McAdoo saw the effect of this speech as "casting pearls before swine, so far as the Senatorial cabal is concerned." Another Senator called it "soap bubbles of oratory and soufflé of phrases," and Senator Warren G. Harding, characteristically, found the speech "utterly lacking in ringing Americanism."

Henry Cabot Lodge began his Committee's deliberations on the treaty by reading aloud its entire text, 268 pages. It took him two weeks; often he read to a clerk alone, as the Committee members drifted away. Lodge's strategy is evident from his correspondence at the time: he hoped to wreck the League, to prevent the Democrats from entering the 1920 election as the party of peace, not by a frontal assault on the treaty but by offering a barrage of "reservations" he thought Wilson would not accept. These covered a variety of restrictions aimed at gaining support from groups skeptical of the League—insuring control of immigration, reaffirming the Monroe Doctrine and the right to withdraw from the League, and, most important, retaining Congressional control over the commitment of American forces. These were questions of substance, but Lodge's letters and statements leave no doubt that he saw them as instruments to defeat the League and that he would keep inventing reservations until the League fell.

Lodge shared this purpose with the Senate "irreconcilables," about fifteen in number. But many other Senators were undecided, somewhat confused, ready to consider possibilities and alternatives. In response, Wilson adopted a peculiar position: he would entertain the possibility of "interpretations" passed simultaneously but separately from the treaty, but would not agree to "reservations" attached to the treaty itself. This issue of the *form* by which the Senate could express its understanding of the treaty's meaning loomed large in Wilson's mind; he stuck to the stance that no word of the treaty could be changed without resubmitting it to the European powers, and to the view that "reservations"—but not "interpretations"—should be rejected because they would change the treaty.

Lodge sought much information from Wilson, but Wilson, despite his generous offer in the Senate speech, refused many of these requests. Lodge pointed to the President's behavior as proof of Wilson's disrespect for the Senate.

A week after presenting the treaty, Wilson called in a group of wavering Senators for a conference at the White House. "He refused to risk a controversy by discussing the merits of the reservations that they proposed." Instead he lectured them for hours on the necessity for approving the treaty as it stood. The press covered this and other conferences thoroughly, the big question being whether any Senators would shift in Wilson's direction. None did. "Almost to a man, these Senators warned Wilson that unless he accepted binding reservations, the treaty would not be ratified."

"I am pondering very carefully," Wilson wrote, "the method of action best calculated to bring about the right results in these difficult days." On July 21, Republican ex-President William Howard Taft, who had long been an effective advocate of the League and a supporter of Wilson's effort, suggested five "interpretations" and one "reservation," explaining later that while he himself would be ready to vote for the League as is, it was necessary "to recognize the exigencies, personal, partisan, and political" and to give leadership to the "mild reservationists" in the Senate who held the key to success. Wilson's Senate leader Gilbert Hitchcock rejected Taft's try as Republican propaganda and said it changed nothing.

On July 30, four Republican moderates told Wilson the treaty could be ratified quickly with reservations, and Senator Frank Kellogg said 37 Republicans would support it with moderate reservations. Wilson did not follow up on this.

On July 31, Wilson told a friend, "I have been talking to some more senators about the treaty," and added, "They are endeavoring to humiliate me."

On August 1, to a Republican Senator who told him the treaty could pass only with "the Lodge reservations," Wilson responded, "The *Lodge* reservations! Never! Never—I'll never consent to adopt any policy with which that impossible name is so prominently identified."

On August 12, Lodge delivered a Senate speech which Wilson's sympathetic biographer Walworth calls "one of the great orations of American history," invoking George Washington, American idealism, free will, and the Constitution. When Wilson heard of it he declared that "if I said what I thought about those fellows in Congress, it would take a piece of asbestos two inches thick to hold it."

On August 15, Senator Hitchcock emerged from a conference with the President to say it was necessary "to remove absolutely any probability of the dotting of an 'i' or the crossing of a 't.'"

On August 19, President Wilson met publicly with the Foreign Relations Committee. He said nothing stood in the way of ratification except certain doubts about the meaning of various provisions and added, "I must frankly say that I am unable to understand why such doubts should be entertained." He reiterated his stand on reservations versus interpretations.

According to McAdoo, Wilson had a political reason for his adamance: he would not be averse to "mild" reservations, but was convinced "that the opponents of the treaty had not advanced them in good faith and the moment there was any indication on his part of a willingness to accept them, partisan opponents would immediately propose other and more objectionable reservations which it would be impossible to consider. They were, he said, determined to prevent ratification at whatever cost; therefore, it was impossible for him to discuss compromise."

"Subsequent events proved clearly," McAdoo continued, "the correctness of his judgment. Lodge and the opponents of the treaty were determined to defeat it, regardless of consequences."

What this line of argument totally ignores is the presence of a large and potentially decisive body of Senatorial opinion held by those Senators ready to vote for the League with a few minor modifications. Indeed, Senator Lodge was out to kill the League by fair means or foul, as his subsequent behavior and correspondence revealed. Wilson could not hope to compromise with Lodge. But the "mild reservationists" were another story. Wilson gave Hitchcock a draft of four "interpretations" which were virtually identical with the four "reservations" being sponsored by the mild reservationists. But he would never drop the distinction. To partisan opposition by the Republicans he added institutional opposition: the Senate was not to "advise and consent" on this treaty except in the most passive way. For many members this was probably a critical point, though one hard to state publicly. If there was to be a dramatic new move for peace after the World War, they wanted to have a hand in it. Wilson slapped them back continually, offering only to "explain," in the style of a schoolmaster.

Wilson often argued that the Allies would not accept reservations, but the biographies do not show that he tried to find out if they would. Later it became clear that the French and British wanted America in, and were not much concerned with what French premier Georges Clemenceau called "a few harmless compromises."

On September 3, 1919, President Wilson left the tangle of Washington politics to launch a nationwide speaking tour for the League of Nations, delivering 40 addresses in 22 days before he collapsed with a stroke in Colorado. Others tried to carry on the work of compromise, but eventually, on March 19, 1920, the

Senate voted to reject the treaty, with Lodge's reservations, by a margin of seven votes. Wilson refused to the end even to free his Senate supporters to vote their own consciences, which would have resulted in the entry of the United States into the League of Nations.

Much later, on Armistice Day, 1923,

> a throng of well-wishers gathered in front of his "S" Street house. Wilson appeared on the balcony and, overcome by emotion, made a brief speech. "I am not one of those that have the least anxiety about the triumph of the principles I have stood for," he concluded. "I have seen fools resist Providence before and I have seen their destruction, as will come upon these again—utter destruction and contempt. That we shall prevail is as sure as that God reigns." (The main headline in the New York Times the day Wilson's remarks appeared read, across three columns, HITLER FORCES RALLYING NEAR MUNICH.)[5]

HOOVER WITHHOLDS RELIEF

Herbert Hoover did not create the Great Depression. Nor was he an ogre who liked to see people suffer, or a witless tool of the big corporations, or even a typical Republican politician in his day. Like Wilson and Lyndon Johnson and most other human beings, Hoover set out to do the right thing, and much more than most, he devoted his whole heart and soul to the struggle. In the Presidency he failed, not because of any wicked moral flaw but because he could not meet one of the extraordinary demands the Presidency places on a man—the demand for confidence.

Long after his Presidency, Hoover got a letter from a schoolgirl asking him "what, in your opinion, constitutes a great leader." Hoover replied, "Certainly these qualifications include integrity, education, administrative experience, specialized information on foreign and domestic affairs, devotion to the American heritage and the American way of life." He made no mention of inspiration, of any *public* quality, nor of the communication of ideas, hopes, or fears. Yet Hoover as President had done his best to make words into weapons against disaster.

Well before the disaster, Hoover saw his own vision in the sky. Accepting the Republican nomination in 1928, he had said that

> We in America today are nearer to the final triumph over poverty than ever before in the history of any land. The poorhouse is vanishing from among us. We have not yet reached the goal, but, given a chance to go forward with the policies of the last eight years, we shall soon with the help of God be in sight of the day when poverty will be banished from this nation.[6]

On Inauguration Day he had "no fears for the future of our country. It is bright with hope."

Then, the week before Halloween, 1929, came the sharp tumble that would become the Crash. There had been a few warning signs in the economy of bricks and potatoes and coin over the counter, but the paper economy of Wall Street wafted upward. General Electric more than tripled its price in a year and a half, reaching 396 in September 1929. Then, starting on October 23, the bottom fell out of the stock market. The next day—"Black Thursday"—the loss of values amounted to nearly as much as the United States had spent on winning the World War. By mid November, the stocks listed on the New York exchange had fallen over 40 per cent in value.

But it was just paper, just the mysterious machinations of the money-changers, many thought. The President reinforced this whistle-in-the-dark attitude the day after the big slide: "The fundamental business of the country, that is, the production and distribution of commodities, is on a sound and prosperous basis." "All of which," he concluded, "indicates a healthy condition."

In November, speaking confidentially, Hoover told a conference of business leaders to "think beyond emergency relief and plan ahead to maintain social order and industrial peace while bringing about orderly liquidation and prevention of panic during a period of readjustment to new ideas of living more in accordance with the heritage of America's founders." He told this select group that a depression was at hand, a severe depression. But the world "depression" did not often escape him in public. On December 3, he said that "a very large degree of industrial unemployment and suffering which would otherwise have occurred has been prevented." "The maximum point of depression," he said soon thereafter, "was about the first of the year." Later, in January 1930, the President announced that the unemployment trend had been reversed, and on March 7 he noted that "employment had been slowly increasing" since December and that "all the evidences indicate that the worst effects of the crash upon unemployment will have been passed during the next sixty days." But unemployment kept rising. Sixty days passed. In May, Hoover found his program had "succeeded to a remarkable degree," the slump "greatly diminished."

"I am convinced," he said, "we have now passed the worst and with continued unity of effort we shall rapidly recover." Later in May he said business would be back to normal by the fall. In June he told a visiting delegation, "The depression is over." Summer 1930 came and went. In October, a year after the crash, Hoover gave Americans this message:

> No one can occupy the high office of President and be other than completely confident of the future of the United States. . . . Perhaps as to no other place does the cheerful courage and power of a confident people reflect as to his office. . . . There are a few folks in business and several folks in the political world who resent the notion that things will ever get better and who wish to enjoy our temporary misery. To recount to these persons the progress of cooperation between the people and the government in amelioration of this situation . . . only inspires the unkind retort that we should fix our gaze solely upon the unhappy features of the decline. . . . This is no time to talk of any surrender, . . . the spirit of this people will never brook defeat.[7]

Meanwhile, out in the countryside, folks were finding life harder and harder to enjoy. From Black Thursday on, unemployment increased steadily, doubling in the year following March 1930. Wage rates began to decline significantly in the last quarter of 1930; during that year only 125 firms reported wage increases, while 900 reported cuts. In 1931, 3,586 concerns cut wages.

In the nation's nineteen largest cities, unemployment increased 149 percent over the nine months ending January 1931. In October 1931, more than 100,000 Americans applied for jobs in the Soviet Union in response to an ad for 6,000 skilled workers. Lacking other accommodations, several hundred women were counted sleeping in Chicago's Grant and Lincoln Parks in September 1931. Chicago's school teachers received no pay for eight of the thirteen months from April 1931 to May 1932. Hunger riots were instigated in early 1931 in Oklahoma City, Minneapolis, St. Paul, and New York. In the summer of 1931, Great Britain went off the gold standard, and seventeen other nations followed suit. That spring, all the mills and factories in Lawrence, Massachusetts, were closed and silent.

By 1932, about one out of four Americans was without adequate income, somewhere between 600,000 and 1,000,000 were wandering across the country looking for work, city after city had totally exhausted relief funds, and thousands upon thousands had had their savings wiped out in bank closures. Homeless men slept in garbage incinerators, families lived on dandelion soup or existed on occasional handouts, and malnutrition spread. In short, a very great many Americans, through no fault of their own, lost their jobs, their homes, their savings, and their dignity; turning in desperation to their government for help, they found relief funds exhausted and no jobs to be had.

A miner in Appalachia told a reporter, "I don't say they can keep the hard times from coming. But they can make us understand the whys and wherefores, can't they? That's all I ask, and everybody in the mine is asking the same thing. You go back to New York and tell 'em the miners want to understand what's going on."

The President's optimistic statements began thinning out after 1930, but many people remembered (erroneously) that he was the one who said prosperity was just around the corner. His complicated explanations had been so often coupled with unfulfilled promises that people doubted both. Hoover sent a telegram to a comedy team saying the country needed some jokes to wash away the Depression and would they think of some. He told Christopher Morley a poem might do it—"something simple enough for a child to spout in school on Fridays." And he said to Rudy Vallee, "If you can sing a song that would make people forget their troubles and the Depression, I'll give you a medal."

The jokes came back at him: Mr. Bones says, "The stock market went up." Mr. Interlocutor asks, "Oh, is Hoover dead?" "Hoover asks Andrew Mellon for a nickel to call a friend. Mellon gives him a dime so he can call all his friends." His very name became a hateful prefix: "not only 'Hoovervilles,' but 'Hoover blankets' (newspapers wrapped around for warmth), 'Hoover wagons' (broken down automobiles hauled by mules), 'Hoover flags' (empty pockets turned inside out), 'Hoover hogs' (jackrabbits)."

Not long after his Presidency began, the Democrats opened up a propaganda shop in Washington to criticize his every move. Quickie books were produced accusing him of all sorts of evil in the past and present. The barrage continued past 1930 when, in the Congressional elections, Democrats won over 50 House seats to gain a majority and the Senate Republicans hung on by a bare 48 to 47. The party balances were deceptive, though, because the lone independent Senator (George Norris of Nebraska) and a sizable number of progressive Republicans opposed Hoover's policies.

Hoover's policies for meeting the Depression were complex and he worked extremely hard in long conferences with innumerable groups to knit them together. His approach was clear in the stance he took and maintained toward relief. By the summer of 1930, social workers could chart with considerable accuracy the decline and fall of households—from the sacrifice of extras to the desperate search for enough to eat. Detroit had a carefully worked out plan for registering the unemployed, developing part-time work, and rotating jobs. But in just seven weeks Detroit went through this process: 86,000 unemployed registered, 11,000 of them were put to work at a cost of $2 million—and the number of unemployed rose to 90,000. In the summer of 1930, a severe drought hit the Southwest; the Secretary of Agriculture called it the worst in our history and recommended a relief fund of $25 million. Congress preferred a bill authorizing $60 million, to which the President responded "prosperity cannot be restored by raids on the public treasury" or by "playing politics with human misery." Millions of farmers went bankrupt. Senator William Borah thundered, as Christmas 1930 approached, "For God's sake, get something done to feed the people who are hungry." The President pressed forward a plan to provide loans for farmers for seed, fertilizer, and cattle feed—but not direct relief, not cash to the hungry, not the dreaded "dole." Committees were formed. Congress finally compromised on $45 million. On into the spring of 1931 the President and his Congressional allies fought off proposals to "put a man on a basis of equality with a mule" by providing food for the hungry farmers to eat as well as to feed their animals. The relief funds were quickly exhausted as farmers borrowed (against who knows what security) some $47 million, or an average of only $150 apiece for some 385,000 borrowers.

The President's philosophy with respect to relief began to emerge in the farm crisis of 1930–31. He turned to the Red Cross and appealed for contributions of $10 million for farm relief. In November 1930 the Red Cross had less than $5 million of uncommitted general funds. By the end of 1930 it had given out some relief to 50,000 families—on the average, ten dollars per family. Instead of approving the $15 million Congress wanted to appropriate for food loans, the President backed the Red Cross drive to raise what was necessary by voluntary contributions. Over the radio he said, "It is unthinkable that any of our people should suffer from hunger or want. . . . It is to the heart of the nation that I am appealing tonight." Support for the drive did not raise the issue of "whether people shall go hungry or cold. It is a question as to whether the American people will maintain the spirit of charity and mutual self-help." But he added, "if the time should ever come that the voluntary agencies of the country are unable to find resources with which to prevent hunger and suffering, I will ask the aid of every resource of the Federal Government." The drive netted some $5 million. According to one careful historian of the period:

> The fight over adding a few millions for food to the drought relief measure cost the President an incalculable loss of prestige. A relief expert with worldwide fame, Hoover could have played a leading role with full popular support.... But Hoover had to make the decision and he feared "wholesale raids on the public treasury." He seemed to forget the long history of federal appropriations to supplement private contributions in disaster relief. He feared that approval of even $15 million for food for drought sufferers would open the way for appropriations to feed victims of the depression.... It was easy for relief advocates to picture the President as being indifferent to human suffering, however unfair such a charge might be. Hoover clung with wonderful stubbornness to the idea that local resources should be able to take care of hunger and misery regardless of their causes.[8]

Not just in agriculture but in the Depression generally, the President clung to his confidence in the nation's "sense of voluntary organization and community service." In the fall of 1930, he appointed an Emergency Committee for Employment, its work to be guided by the principle that unemployment was strictly a local responsibility.

The Committee's chairman drafted a message for the President to submit to Congress calling for public works, slum clearance, low-cost housing, and rural electrification. The Committee also favored Senator Robert Wagner's initiative for public works planning and a national employment service. The President rejected both. In the spring the chairman resigned.

For all Hoover's intense action in "coordinating" national relief efforts, he thought of disbursements from Washington as a last resort and of direct payments to the poor as beyond the pale. In his message to Congress of December 1930, he made his principles clear:

> Economic depression can not be cured by legislative action or executive pronouncement. Economic wounds must be healed by the action of the cells of the economic body—the producers and consumers themselves. Recovery can be expedited and its effects mitigated by cooperative action. That cooperation requires that every individual should sustain faith and courage; that each should maintain his self-reliance ... that the vast majority whose income is unimpaired should not hoard out of fear but should seek to assist his neighbors who may be less fortunate; that each industry should assist its own employees; that each community and each State should assume its full responsibilities for organization of employment and relief of distress with that sturdiness and independence which built a great nation.[9]

Wounded by the accusation that he would feed cattle while men starved, Hoover insisted that a breakdown of the principles of self-help and local responsibility would "have struck at the roots of self-government"; if the day ever came when federal help was the only alternative to starvation, he would be for it, but "I have faith in the American people that such a day shall not come."

The critic Edmund Wilson, responding to the view that hardship strengthens character, commented, "It is a reassuring thought, in the cold weather, that the emaciated men in the bread lines, the men and women beggars in the streets, and the children dependent on them, are all having their fibre hardened."

In that same fall of 1930, Pennsylvania, with one-twelfth of the country's population, had one-sixth of its unemployment. Governor-elect Gifford Pinchot protested that the time for "gentle bedside language" had passed. The states had already discarded Hoover's principled distinction between the dole and indirect relief. "Industry and business are not giving men the chance to work. Nor are they feeding the unemployed. We must feed them if they are to live." And then he said what was so rarely brought forth in these debates: opposition to federal relief came from "fear lest the taxation to provide that relief be levied on concentrated wealth—fear lest the policy of years, the policy of shielding the big fortunes at the expense of the little ones, should at long last be tossed into the discard." At the same time that Congressmen and Governors were pleading for a few more millions in federal relief, Hoover's Reconstruction Finance Corporation, operating in secret to prevent distorting money markets, was disbursing millions of dollars a day in loans to business. Shortly after the RFC director resigned, that body lent banks he headed $80 million. A Congressman noted that "President Hoover has given an outright dole to the railroads. He would give a dole to the building and loan associations. He would come to the aid of banks with frozen assets. He would help foreign countries, but to starving American women and children he wouldn't give a red cent." On the income side of the ledger, taxes on the rich were a sometime thing. Colonel Robert R. McCormick, editor and publisher of the *Chicago Tribune,* paid $1,515 in taxes on a supposed personal property total of only $25,250, while calling on his readers to pay their full taxes. Louis Florsheim of the shoe company paid income taxes of $90, S. J. T. Straus $18. Federal income taxes for Mr. J. P. Morgan, who encouraged workers to contribute to relief ("we must all do our bit"), amounted to zero for the years 1930, 1931, and 1932.

Despite the rising tide of criticism, the President stood firm. "No governmental action, no economic doctrine, no economic plan or project can replace that God-imposed responsibility of the individual man and woman to their neighbors," he said on the radio; and to Congress he said, "I am opposed to any direct or indirect government dole. Our people are providing against distress in true American fashion." Isolated in the White House, existing on three hours of sleep a night, the President said of Congressmen pleading for all sorts of fiat money, public works, doles and the like, "As long as I sit at this desk they won't get by."

After numerous vetoes of relief bills and with the election looming before him, Hoover signed a bill in the summer of 1932. This bill provided that financially exhausted states could borrow from an RFC fund of $300 million for specified purposes. In terms of the public confidence, however, the damage had been done. "If any one attitude lost the election in 1932," writes Harris Gaylord

Warren, "it was Hoover's refusal to use federal resources in direct relief." Whatever he felt in private, Hoover *seemed* uncaring—and adamantly so. "To these ideas Hoover clung with an obstinacy worthy of a better cause. . . . No matter how often he denied it, people were starving in the midst of plenty."[10]

The "Bonus Expeditionary Force" descended on Washington in the summer of 1932 to demand immediate payment of bonuses due veterans in 1945. Some 20,000 strong, the veterans had made it to Washington from all over the country, riding the rails and living on handouts, under the rule of "no panhandling, no drinking, no radicalism." They set up camp and, under the command of Walter W. ("Hot") Waters, maintained a semblance of military order. On June 15, a somewhat nervous House of Representatives passed a bill to grant the bonus; on June 17, the Senate defeated it, and the ex-soldiers gathered outside the Capitol and sang "America." Some went home, but 15,000 stayed on in the sweltering heat hoping that Congress and the President would help them. Hoover said nothing. By mid July the veterans had been encamped in Washington for two months, during which time the President received the heavyweight wrestling champion, delegates of sorority members, and essay contest winners, but no one from the Bonus Army. He did get a bill passed lending money to those willing to go home—the loan to be subtracted from the bonus due them in 1945. On the last day of Congress, the veterans' leader gathered his men on the Capitol steps, saying "We're going to stay here until I see Hoover," who was expected for his traditional adjournment visit. The President stayed in the White House. In April he had said that he was "absolutely opposed" to passage of the bonus bill, which would "irretrievably undermine" the government's credit, and in May he announced that "The Government cannot be dictated to by organized minorities." On July 28, 1932, General Douglas MacArthur and his troops drove the bonus marchers out of Washington, burning their shacks and tents, and killing with tear gas a baby born earlier in the summer at the camp. The B.E.F. News suggested an epitaph for the child: "Here lies Bernard Myers, aged three months, gassed to death by order of President Hoover." The President was satisfied with MacArthur's work: "A challenge to the authority of the United States Government has been met, swiftly and firmly. . . ." "What a pitiful spectacle," said the Washington *News*, "is that of the great American Government, mightiest in the world, chasing unarmed men, women and children with Army tanks. . . . If the Army must be called out to make war on unarmed citizens, this is no longer America." When a delegation of writers called at the White House to protest the attack, the President was too busy to see them. As they left they heard children's voices singing "Happy Birthday to You"—a group of schoolchildren were presenting Mr. Hoover a birthday cake.

In the Presidential campaign of 1932, Hoover's original plan was to give only a few speeches, but by August he was determined to stump the nation. When Henry Stimson suggested that Hoover not use the recovery programs for partisan purposes, Hoover "broke out into a rather impassioned speech in which he said that . . . he was going to use all the machinery to win the election, for he felt that victory was necessary to the country."

A reporter for the *Saturday Evening Post* tried to help "humanize" Hoover for the public, but came away from his interview saying that "I had never seen so much romance buried in the course of a single afternoon." In the campaign Hoover made 200 speeches, mainly defenses of his programs and attacks on the uncertainties of Roosevelt. He began at Des Moines, in his home state, Iowa. In preparation he wrote a draft speech 71 typed pages long and nursed it through 15 redrafts, then sent the printed proofs out to a dozen people for suggestions. The speech ended this way: "We held the Gibraltar of world stability. The world today has a chance. It is growing in strength. Let that man who complains that things could not be worse thank God for this victory." The audience, carefully selected for their loyal Republicanism, responded warmly. Through the campaign such indoor crowds cheered him, but in the streets he met the hatred from which the White House shielded him. In Detroit a mob crying "Hang Hoover!" was held back by armed mounted police. Driving to the stadium where he would speak, "Through block after block they flashed past tens of thousands of men and women utterly silent and grim save for those who could be glimpsed shaking their fists and shouting unheard words and phrases." On Halloween night he made his way into Madison Square Garden through a crowd of thousands shouting "We want bread."

In 1928 Hoover had carried forty states. On November 8, 1932, he carried six. Forty-five percent of factory workers were unemployed.

JOHNSON ESCALATES THE WAR

The ghost of Woodrow Wilson drifts through the careers of the Presidents I call active-negative. Hoover wrote a book about Wilson's ordeal; Nixon had Wilson's desk moved into the White House for his use. And Lyndon Johnson's crucial decision on the war in Vietnam was made in a conversation with another Henry Cabot Lodge. Johnson—who, Eric Goldman thinks, "re-enacted the presbyter-professor Woodrow Wilson"—had a style radically different from Wilson's,[11] yet there is a curious similarity to their histories. Each started out strong and wound up defeated. Each fastened on a particular line of policy and stubbornly pursued it to the end. It is probably not too much to say that each played a crucial role in the disillusionment of a political generation.

In November 1963, immediately after the eulogy for President Kennedy in the Great Rotunda of the Capitol, Johnson, with tears still on his face, met with Lodge. Lodge, then ambassador to Vietnam, reviewed the situation there and said of the hard decisions coming, "Unfortunately, Mr. President, you will have to make them." Johnson replied with feeling, "I am not going to lose Vietnam. I am not going to be the President who saw Southeast Asia go the way China went." Later that day he told his advisors to "increase the pressure and press on." There in the emotional backwash of the assassination began Lyndon Johnson's intense personal commitment to a line of policy that would lead him, his nation, and Indochina to disaster.

To those who attribute the Vietnam disaster to "the system," to some institutional inevitability in the American government, there is a hard question in the Johnson history. What was it in the system that made John Kennedy determined to withdraw from Vietnam after what he hoped would be his reelection in 1964? What in the same basic system led Johnson, in contrast, to increase the number of men in Vietnam by some 2,500 percent, to more than 535,000, and to pour in American money at the rate of some $30 billion per year? The men and money were the President's to command; Johnson commanded and the men and money moved. If any "system" was moving inexorably down the track toward tragedy in Vietnam, it was Johnson's own system—his character—not some structure of government or set of abstractions.

The President, after his retirement, enumerated programs he had launched for young people and then said, "But the statistics are meaningless unless young people feel a basic trust and understanding of the process of their government. Sadly, we've been unable to build that trust."

Lyndon Johnson's escalation of the war in Vietnam was a complex checker game in which the meaning of each little move is hard to unravel. It is easy to get lost in the maze of verbiage, hard to stand back and see clearly what was happening at any given time. But in the end, the result was a series of tremendous losses—of life, health, national spirit, and of confidence in the Presidency. Through it all, Johnson's credibility crumbled as he hewed stubbornly to an increasingly unrealistic line of policy. Three lines of development first ran parallel, and then diverged: Johnson and the public; Johnson as Commander-in-Chief; Johnson and the peace feelers.

With the public, Johnson repeatedly stressed his peaceable ways, his opposition to hawkish opponents, and his desire to turn his hand to the building of America. In the 1960 campaign, he had disdained Richard Nixon: "One of my friends that drinks Pepsi-Cola—a former Vice-President—went out to Vietnam and said we ought to have a little more war. Well, we won't."

As 1964 moved toward election day, "Peaceable" Lyndon thumped more and more on the contrast between himself and his opponent, Senator Barry Goldwater:

August 16, 1964: Some others are eager to enlarge the conflict. They call upon us to supply American boys to do the job that Asian boys should do. They ask us to take reckless actions, which might risk the lives of millions and engulf much of Asia.

August 29: I have had advice to load our planes with bombs and to drop them on certain areas that I think would enlarge the war and result in commiting a good many American boys to fighting a war that I think ought to be fought by the boys of Asia to help protect their own land. And for that reason, I haven't chosen to enlarge the war.

September 25: There are those that say you ought to go north and drop bombs, to try to wipe out the supply lines, and they think that would escalate the war. We don't want our American boys to do the fighting for Asian boys. We don't want to get involved in a nation with seven hundred million people and get tied down in a land war in Asia.

September 28: We are not going north and we are not going south; we are going to continue to try to get them to save their own freedom with their own men, with our leadership and our officer direction, and such equipment as we can furnish them.

October 21: We are not going to send American boys nine or ten thousand miles away from home to do what Asian boys ought to be doing for themselves.[12]

On October 27 Johnson stated categorically, in a speech at Pittsburgh, "There can be and will be, as long as I am President, peace for all Americans."[13]

And the week before the voting, Johnson said in Los Angeles that "The only real issue in this campaign, the only one you ought to get concerned about, is who can best keep the peace. . . . I tell you, as your Commander-in-Chief of the mightiest nation in all the world, we can keep the peace, in the words of the prophet Isaiah, by reasoning together, by responsibility, by negotiation." He won the election by a landslide. He continued, through his term of office, to present himself as the determined seeker after peace. On April 7, 1965, at Johns Hopkins University, the President pulled out all the stops again:

We will never be second in the search for . . . a peaceful settlement in Vietnam. There may be many ways to this kind of peace; in discussion or negotiations with the governments concerned; in large groups or in small ones; in the reaffirmation of old agreements or their strengthening with new ones. We have stated this position over and over to friend and foe alike. And we remain ready with this purpose for unconditional discussions.[14]

He offered one billion dollars for development of Southeast Asia after the fighting stopped. Many times Johnson had left the impression with the public that he set no conditions whatever for negotiations, that he would meet with the Pope and Ho Chi Minh at the North Pole if necessary to make peace. "I will go anywhere anytime to talk peace with anyone." Returning from Konrad Adenauer's funeral in April 1967, he pounded at this theme: "Maybe someday, somehow, sometime, somewhere, someone will want to sit at a table and talk instead of kill, discuss instead of fight, reason instead of murder; and when they do, I will be the first to come to that table, wherever it is." In his fifth State of the Union address on January 17, 1968, the President said, "Our goal is peace, and peace at the earliest possible moment." And so on. The message to the public was a continual barrage of hope and promise, an apparently heartfelt desire for nothing so much as an end of the killing.

Meanwhile, in his role as Commander-in-Chief, Johnson made war with a vengeance. After the Kennedy funeral he had given his pledge not to lose Vietnam; increasingly he saw escalation as the only way to fulfill that pledge. In the spring and summer of 1964, he set in motion the detailed studies of how to heat up the war, as revealed in the leaked "Pentagon Papers" of 1971. Even before that, in February, "an elaborate program of covert military operations against the state of North Vietnam" was started, including U-2 flights over Laos, commando raids, and naval bombardment of the North Vietnamese coast. The

Pentagon drew up a plan calling for full-scale bombing of North Vietnam and the possible use of ground combat forces to protect the air bases. A resolution was drawn up for possible Congressional approval of "wider U.S. actions in Southeast Asia."

The President told Charles Roberts of *Newsweek* that he had actually decided in October 1964 to undertake bombing of North Vietnam after the election. That is a matter of memory; Johnson remembered it differently in 1971. "Decision" is the key word here—did the President "decide" then? Or had his key advisors reached a "consensus" on escalation beyond what the President had "decided"? Or were the extensive proposals for escalation simply "contingency plans" available, supposedly, along with other "options"? The detailed answers were not entirely clear in the 1971 releases of "The Pentagon Papers." But, aside from the details, several larger features of the situation were beyond serious question:

The President in his campaign treated the public to a very strong impression that he was not going to escalate the war. Meanwhile his topmost advisors had been working for half a year to develop plans for exactly that. It is not believable that the President was ignorant of these plans, however distracted by campaigning he may have been.

The United States, under Johnson's leadership, did not stumble accidentally into a "quagmire" in Vietnam by reacting to discrete events on a one-at-a-time basis. The Tonkin Resolution, for example (see below), was ready and waiting in the President's pocket for a suitable incident. However hesitant the President may have been to actually implement each "next step," the precise steps were planned out in advance by top advisors fully aware of what they were doing.

Throughout the deliberations in progress while Johnson was campaigning, the policy-makers had near the fronts of their minds the problem of persuading the public that nothing much was happening, that escalation was simply an extension of past policy. By April 1965 when Johnson ordered a troop increase of 18–20,000 men, additional Marine forces, and a "more active" mission for the Marines in Vietnam, he also ordered that "premature publicity" be avoided by taking all possible precautions. The actions themselves should be taken as rapidly as practicable, but in ways that should minimize any appearance of sudden changes in policy. . . . The President's desire is that these movements and changes should be understood as being gradual and wholly consistent with existing policy." The very day the President made these decisions, he told a press conference that he knew of "no far-reaching strategy that is being suggested or promulgated." Thus the lying to the public was not a matter of the President's reacting in response to criticism, but a carefully thought through part of administration planning.

Johnson's public escalation of the war began in circumstances which seem nearly comic in retrospect. In the first days of August 1964, an American destroyer escorting South Vietnamese ships on a raid against a North Vietnamese island installation (a practice not widely known by the public or by Congress) was approached by three North Vietnamese torpedo boats. The American skipper later said he fired the first shot, then sank two of the PT boats.

On August 4, the President went on television to recount an unprovoked attack on the destroyers *Maddox* and *C. Turner Joy*. Johnson warned, "These acts of violence against the armed forces of the United States must be met not only by alert defense, but with positive reply. . . . That reply is being given as I speak to you. Air action is now in execution against gunboats and certain supporting facilities of North Vietnam which have been used in these hostile operations." He also called upon Congress to pass a resolution he had been carrying around in his pocket for weeks, asserting

> That the Congress approves and supports the determination of the President, as Commander-in-Chief, to take all necessary measures to repel any armed attack against the forces of the United States and to prevent further aggression.
> The United States regards as vital to its national interest and to world peace the maintenance of international peace and security in Southeast Asia. [Consonant with the Constitution and treaty obligations,] the United States is, therefore, prepared, as the President determines, to take all necessary steps, including the use of armed force, to assist any member or protocol state of the Southeast Asia Collective Defense Treaty requesting assistance in defense of its freedom.[15]

The President then had his resolution, a virtual blank check, when the measure passed the Senate 88 to 2 and the House 416 to 0 on August 7. Heading into their own elections, and accustomed to deferring to Presidential judgment in foreign military affairs, Congressmen dashed to his support.

All this arose out of an incident which, as was revealed much later, probably never occurred. The attacking North Vietnamese vessels were later dismissed by a *Maddox* officer as "nothing more than a flock of geese on radar screens." The *Maddox's* captain told reporters, "Evaluating everything that was going on, I was becoming less and less convinced that somebody was there." And a *Maddox* lieutenant confessed, "I had nothing to shoot at. I recall we were hopping around up there, trying to figure out what they [on the *Turner Joy*] were shooting at because we didn't have any targets."

"Hell," Johnson said later, "I think we may have fired at a whale."

The President did not respond to two other incidents which clearly did occur. Three days before the election, the Viet Cong attacked an airbase near Saigon, killing four Americans, wounding 76, and destroying six B-57 bombers. Despite General Maxwell Taylor's insistence on reprisal, Johnson held back. His reasons are unknown but the election was at hand—against "warmonger" Goldwater. On Christmas Eve, Viet Cong soldiers killed two Americans and wounded 63 in a surprise attack on American officers' billets in Saigon. Again the President held his hand; he would be inaugurated on January 20.

Finally, on February 7, Johnson broke through the restraints and began the massive escalation of the air war. The occasion was an attack on Pleiku, an American base 240 miles north of Saigon; seven were killed and 109 wounded. Strangely, "a week earlier the State Department had guessed that Pleiku would be the Viet Cong target." But the enemy infiltrators were able to get through the South Vietnamese guardline and reach the American barracks.

President Johnson received the news of the Pleiku attack at 3:00 P.M., Saturday, February 6, 1965. For months he had been studying aerial photographs of North Vietnam, speculating on targets. That evening at 7:45 he told a meeting of the National Security Council, "I've had enough of this," and explained, "The worst thing we could possibly do would be to let this go by. It would be a big mistake. It would open the door to a major misunderstanding." Apparently he did not ask why the base had not been protected. Secretary of Defense Robert S. McNamara, General Earl Wheeler, and Johnson then picked two targets, and retaliatory raids were ordered. The degree to which such a move was anticipated by Pentagon planning is evidenced by the fact that within twelve hours of the *start* of the Viet Cong attack on Pleiku, 49 American planes from carriers in the South China Sea were dropping bombs on targets 160 miles above the 17th parallel.

The story of the war's escalation from that point on is relatively familiar. At each point the public was reassured that the increase in military activity was not a departure from previous policy. Thus Johnson said in Washington that the raids carried out in response to Pleiku meant "no wider war." In January 1967, he called it "the most careful and most self-limited air war in history." But in 1965, the Air Force had flown 24,570 sorties over North Vietnam. In 1966 the Pentagon reported what looked like a decrease: 23,577 missions. Not many realized that a "sortie" was an individual plane flight and a "mission" normally consisted of *four* planes, making the actual number of sorties some 94,308 in 1966—almost four times as high.

Three days after the Pleiku raids, the President ordered regular, not just retaliatory, bombing of major installations in North Vietnam. "They woke us up in the middle of the night and we woke them up in the middle of the night. Then they did it again, and we did it again," he said. Soon the relationship between stimulus and response was lost. The purposes offered in justification varied. One was to slow down infiltration of men and supplies from the North. Yet in February 1966, McNamara testified that even the total destruction of North Vietnamese industry would have "no measurable effect" on their ability to supply the forces in the South, and as regards morale, he pointed out that massive bombing had not lowered the enemy's will to fight in Japan, in World War II, or in Korea. Another justification was to improve the stability of the South Vietnamese government—an institution that could stand some improvement. In Saigon there were eight heads of state during the Johnson Presidency; in the summer of 1965 the last civilian government fell and Air Vice-Marshal Ky ("People ask me who my heroes are. I have only one—Hitler") took over. Ky closed down newspapers and on July 24 declared that "support for neutralism" would be punishable by death. That same day, 39 "recruits" to the South Vietnamese army seeking to escape from military service jumped from a boat and drowned. In 1966, desertions from the South Vietnamese army numbered 116,858. "After seventeen months of bombing, the White House had to admit that there were 100 percent more North Vietnamese troops in South Vietnam than when the bombings began."

Eventually, then, the war from the air became a turkey shoot, North and South, with villages selected as targets on the "probability" that Viet Cong might be in them and with fire directed at unseen persons in the jungle whose body heat registered on airborne instruments. Millions of people were made homeless, hundreds of thousands killed and maimed by Americans. In 1967 the American chemical industry was producing a record 50 million pounds of napalm per month. The new language of gamesmanship developed by games theorists and systems analysts helped the policy makers obscure from themselves and others the enormity of their actions.

On the ground, Vietnam was more and more crowded with American soldiers, from 15,000 at the start of 1965 to 190,000 in January 1966, to 380,000 a year later. In the first year of escalation, 1,350 Americans had been killed, 5,300 wounded. The war raged on.

Johnson had claimed another purpose for the continuous bombing of North Vietnam: "to force the North Vietnamese into negotiation." Paralleling the history of Johnson as espouser of peace and Johnson as practitioner of escalation is that of Johnson as decliner of diplomatic peace initiatives. The history is complex in the extreme, but again the broad outlines are clear enough. The same President who hewed to his line of negotiations "anytime, anywhere" and continually announced his willingness to enter "unconditional discussions," repeatedly refused to exploit diplomatic opportunities for talks. Indeed, a strong and carefully documented case has been made that the President's behavior showed a "somber, recurring pattern of political exploration cut short by [American] military escalation." In other words, Johnson repeatedly responded to pressures for and possibilities of negotiations by raising the level of killing in Vietnam. This history of these possibilities only slowly got through to the public. A few examples show what was going on.

On July 23, 1964, the same summer Lyndon Johnson was stumping the country whipping Goldwater with his palm branch, Charles de Gaulle called for a new meeting of the Geneva Conference which had originally developed a plan for Indochina peace in 1954. A few days earlier, U Thant, Secretary-General of the United Nations, had issued a similar proposal. Two days after de Gaulle's move, the Saigon government of Nguyen Khanh, who had couped his way into power the previous January and would soon be dumped in the continuing game of musical chairs, "categorically rejected" the de Gaulle-Thant proposal. Meanwhile, the leader of the Viet Cong expressed willingness "to enter into negotiations with all parties, groups, sects, and patriotic individuals, without regard to differences of political points of view or past actions. . . . The NLF," he added, "is not opposed to the convening of an international conference in order to facilitate the search for a solution." That same day the Soviet Union urged the fourteen participants in the 1961–62 Geneva Conference on Laos to reconvene. The Hanoi government responded quickly, asking that the Conference be reconvened "as rapidly as possible . . . to preserve the independence, peace, and neutrality of Laos and to preserve the peace of Indochina and Southeast Asia." On August 4, the government at Peking also announced its support.

Thus, within a two-week period, proposals for a Geneva-type conference on Vietnam, and, more largely, Southeast Asia had emanated from three important sources—U Thant, France, and the U.S.S.R.—and it had been favorably received in Hanoi and Peking. None of these proposals, it should be noted, specified conditions or "preconditions" in urging that a solution be found for the Indo-Chinese crisis.[16]

President Johnson's view was expressed the day after de Gaulle's announcement: "We do not believe in conferences called to ratify terror, so our policy is unchanged." The next day he ordered 5–6,000 additional troops to Vietnam, with the reassurance that this did not signify an extension of the war. And then in early August came the Tonkin incidents—real or imagined, but still minor events—and the new escalations.

That same August, U Thant visited Johnson and came away thinking the President had agreed to U.S.-North Vietnamese talks. In September, Thant told Adlai Stevenson, U.S. Ambassador to the United Nations, that he had convinced Ho Chi Minh to agree to speak privately with an American on preliminary peace talks. Stevenson excitedly reported this to Secretary of State Dean Rusk. There it stopped. Whether Johnson knew of it or not is obscure; later he said he did not— in itself rather a telling testimony to the lack of interest in negotiations he had communicated to his Secretary of State.

U Thant continued his efforts into the autumn of 1964. After several meetings with Soviet Foreign Minister Andrei Gromyko, Adlai Stevenson, and others, Thant arranged to get the Americans and the North Vietnamese together in Rangoon. But on January 30, 1965, Stevenson told Thant the answer was no; the United States was worried that "any rumors of such a meeting might topple the Saigon government." In a much advertised visit, Soviet Premier Alexei Kosygin arrived in Hanoi for talks with Ho Chi Minh on February 6. Early the next day (Vietnam time) the Viet Cong raided Pleiku and Johnson sent the bombers out. Later that year, referring to the post-Pleiku retaliation, Johnson said that "when we began the bombings there was no talk of negotiations." Kosygin later said a North Vietnamese spokesman told him then, "Every time we have agreed to talk to the Americans, Washington has escalated the war."

U Thant, at a press conference on February 24, gave his sad report:

> I am sure that the great American people, if only they knew the true facts and the background to the developments in South Vietnam, will [sic] agree with me that further bloodshed is unnecessary. The political and diplomatic method of discussions and negotiations alone can create conditions which will enable the United States to withdraw gracefully from that part of the world. As you know, in times of war and of hostilities, the first casualty is truth.[17]

Johnson had his Press Secretary tell the press, "The United States has received no proposal from U Thant." And later he said, "Candor compels me to tell you that there has not been the slightest indication that the other side is interested in negotiation." Then he amended that to say that "there are no *meaningful* proposals for negotiations that are before our government." Near the end of the year, the first article on Johnson's "credibility gap" appeared in the *Washington Post.*

Through 1965, opposition to the war continued to rise in the Senate. Mike Mansfield delivered a striking lecture to the President asserting that bombing would not bring peace and concluding that "This is not an American war and the United States must not make it one." On Christmas Eve, 1965, Johnson began a bombing halt that would last 37 days, and dramatically dispatched Averell Harriman, Arthur Goldberg, and McGeorge Bundy to various capitals to bring the North Vietnamese to the negotiating table. But there had been a six-day bombing pause in May; Secretary Rusk sent a secret message to Hanoi saying he would have his eyes open for "significant reductions" in attacks on the South. In those few days, the Hanoi government expressed privately that they would negotiate on the basis of their "Four Points" without prior withdrawal of the Americans. This response reached Washington a few hours after the bombing had been resumed.

The December pause and "peace offensive" did not work for two reasons: the U.S. continued to insist it would not confer with the National Liberation Front, and during the bombing pause itself undertook a radical escalation of the war on the ground. By contrast, the North Vietnamese lay low during the pause—a signal Dean Rusk seems to have missed. Beginning January 27, the U.S. launched "Operation Masher," "the largest amphibious operation by the United States Marines since the 1950 Inchon landing in Korea." Resuming the bombing on January 31, the President and Rusk said that "acts of violence in South Vietnam . . . made it clear [that the] negative attitudes of Hanoi and the Liberation Front" were unchanged.

In February 1966, the Chairman of the Senate Foreign Relations Committee J. William Fulbright began hearings on the war in Vietnam. The story from that point on is too recent to have faded from memory, though pieces of it are still not in place. The rise of Senate opposition, and particularly the increasingly bitter feud between the President and Senator Robert F. Kennedy; Johnson's break with Fulbright; the raids and civilian casualties in Hanoi; the mounting protest at home over American—and, eventually, Indochinese—casualties, all led up to the climactic moment on March 31, 1968, when Johnson announced a partial pause in the bombing of North Vietnam and his own decision not to run for reelection or accept a draft in 1968.

As late as March 16, 1968, Johnson was telling his staff:

> Let's get one thing clear! I'm telling you now I am not going to stop the bombing. Now I don't want to hear any more about it. . . . I've heard every argument. I'm not going to stop it. Now is there anybody here who doesn't understand that?[18]

Over the next two weeks he changed his mind. But, as if to undercut his credibility even at that point, Johnson let himself in for one last wave of disbelief. He claimed to have ordered air and naval forces "to make no attacks on North Vietnam, except in the area north of the demilitarized zone where the continuing enemy buildup directly threatens allied forward positions and where the movements of their troops and supplies are clearly related to that threat." On the very next day, April 1, 1968, American planes struck targets 205 miles north of the demilitarized zone, 70 miles south of Hanoi. In the Senate, Mansfield gave a damning defense of the President: "The President did not lie," he explained. "Technically he is correct."

But the night before Johnson's announcement, the State Department sent out this secret message to American ambassadors in six capitals, instructing them what to tell the allied governments about the bombing limitation:

> You should make clear that Hanoi is most likely to denounce the project and thus free our hand after a short period.
> Nevertheless we might wish to continue the limitation even after a formal denunciation, in order to reinforce its sincerity and put the monkey firmly on Hanoi's back for whatever follows.[19]

There was much to Lyndon Johnson's Presidency besides Vietnam, including the "Great Society," progress in civil rights and a remarkable legislative record. Yet from at least 1966 onward, he and the nation were grappling primarily with a dismal war in the wrong place for the wrong cause. The President became the first clear resigner from that office; even Calvin Coolidge, despite his demurrers, had hopes for 1928. The war contributed its share to the first period in recent national history in which the average American was pessimistic about the future of his country. And Johnson's stubborn insistence, until the failure and death toll had mounted out of all proportion to his purpose, easily matched that of Woodrow Wilson and Herbert Hoover. The "system" was roughly the same for Eisenhower, Kennedy, and Nixon as for Lyndon Johnson. But he seemed in the grip of forces a good deal older, in his experience, than the system itself. "I was born the way I am," he said, "I can't do anything about it."

RIGIDIFICATION

These three stories show a common pattern, the essence of which is this: the President defeated both his own purposes and the nation's purposes by adhering rigidly to a line of policy long after it had proved itself a failure. The problem was not depravity but blindness. In light of the facts, it is simply implausible that President Wilson consciously set out to prevent American entry into the League; that Hoover wanted, in any conscious way, to abandon people to despair and starvation; or that Lyndon Johnson found conscious satisfaction in the oceans of blood he left behind him. *Each meant well.* We are not going to discover the way out of such disasters by identifying, among the Presidential hopefuls, those mythical moral lepers who would plot our downfall—or their own.

The blindness bears on the results of policy. Each of these Presidents had in his mind a theory, a conception of reality and causation, and a set of principles which came to guide his action. Those principles, and even the inferences for action these Presidents drew from them, were plausible at the time, shared by a great many thoughtful people. They were "wrong" in terms of logic and evidence, but they were widely accepted. It takes a special retrospective arrogance, then, to attribute these failures wholly to mistakes in their philosophical beginnings and it takes an incredible faith in the tightness of social causality to suppose that all else followed once the "principles" were set.

What needs explaining is why, in the face of the *facts* of failure, these Presidents held tightly to their courses. For in each of these histories the President appears as a man unable to see what, eventually, nearly everyone else around him sees: that the line of action simply is not working—that, for whatever reason, the costs of persevering in it are far too high.

All that I have hoped to show so far is that in each of these cases the President did in fact freeze onto a line of action and stick to it long after it began to produce terrible trouble for the country and for the man. I think no objective observer can deny that the toll of destruction in Vietnam, the lasting wounds of the Great Depression, and the return to isolationism after the First World War were extremely significant historical developments. We have yet to recover fully from any of them.

I want now to link these events, not just to Presidential decisions, but to the Presidents' own emotional experience. It can be shown that we are not dealing here simply with some cold, computational connection in which the President was intellectually mistaken, but with experiences which touched on his fundamental feelings. These Presidents were, I want to demonstrate, deeply involved in what they were doing. We can see this in the ways they reacted to what they felt they had to do.

WILSON'S INNER STRUGGLE

For Woodrow Wilson the League became a highly personal crusade. He fastened upon the League as *his* League, his unique contribution to history. As early as January 1917, Wilson had come to see himself as *the* leader of an afflicted humanity longing for peace. "Perhaps I am the only person in high authority amongst all the peoples of the world," he said, "who is at liberty to speak and hold nothing back. I would fain believe that I am speaking for the silent mass of mankind everywhere who have as yet had no place or opportunity to speak their real hearts out." He thought in 1918 that if necessary "I can reach the peoples of Europe over the heads of their Rulers."

Both Colonel House and Secretary of State Robert Lansing had advised Wilson not to attend the Paris Peace Conference, to maintain his position above the grubby details, to remain free to play a larger and more flexible role. Wilson would have none of it. Not only would he go, he would preside. His choice of advisors to accompany him raised a storm of protest: all except one aging and inactive Republican were entirely dependent on the President—House, his personal advisor; Lansing, his Secretary of State; and Tasker H. Bliss, a general in his Army. Eminences such as Elihu Root, Charles Evan Hughes, Charles Eliot, and particularly William Howard Taft were left out, for Wilson resented the interference of "butters-in" and "wool gatherers." He failed to include any Senator who could have helped him sell the treaty at home. In Paris, his fellow Commissioners filled their diaries with complaints that they were being excluded. Lansing was left completely in the dark: Wilson had never even shown his Secretary of State his plan for the League Covenant. When Lansing tried to help, Wilson barked that he did not intend to have lawyers drafting the treaty. Lansing, the only lawyer on the Commission (besides Wilson himself), in turn abandoned his work.

Wilson was involved in high drama. On the ship taking him to the Paris Conference he had said, in a pensive tone, "What I seem to see—with all my heart I hope I am wrong—is a tragedy of disappointment." He flabbergasted the wily European diplomats with this question and answer:

> Why has Jesus Christ so far not succeeded in inducing the world to follow his teachings in these matters? It is because He taught the ideal without devising any practical means of attaining it. That is why I am proposing a practical scheme to carry out His aims.[20]

Wilson was ill much of the time at Paris, but he continued day after day, to the point of complete exhaustion, taking only an occasional break for a game of solitaire. He got edgy and angry, calling Clemenceau and Lloyd George "madmen." "Logic! Logic! I don't give a damn for logic!" blurted this champion of reason. He attributed a blinding headache to "bottled-up wrath at Lloyd George." Finally he went to bed with a fever. During his illness he acted strangely, suspecting that the French servants were spies who spoke perfect English, that furnishings were being stolen from the house he stayed in, that the staff was using official automobiles for recreational drives. He kept all his documents in a locked safe near him, had the furniture itemized, and ordered use of the cars restricted to official missions. Back on his feet, he infuriated the Europeans by lecturing at them. "I never knew anyone to talk more like Jesus Christ and act more like Lloyd George," said Clemenceau. Again and again he insisted on going into conferences alone—no secretary, no aides, no advisors.

On Memorial Day, 1919, President Wilson gave a moving address at an American Army cemetery in France; its climax shows Wilson in the role of Martin Luther, compelled by God to do the right:

> If I may speak a personal word, I beg you to realize the compulsion that I myself feel I am under. By the Constitution of our great country, I was the Commander in Chief of these men. I advised Congress to declare that a state of war existed. I sent these lads over here to die. Shall I—can I—ever speak a word of counsel which is inconsistent with the assurance I gave them when they came over? It is inconceivable. There is something better, if possible, that a man can give than his life, and that is his living spirit to a service that is not easy, to resist counsels that are hard to resist, to stand against purposes that are difficult to stand against, and to say, "Here I stand, consecrated in the spirit of the men who were once my

comrades and who now are gone, and who left me under eternal bonds of fidelity."[21]

Over and over in his fight for the League, Wilson reminded audiences of his high calling:

> The facts are marching and God is marching with them. You cannot resist them. You must either welcome them or subsequently, with humiliation, surrender to them. It is welcome or surrender. It is acceptance of great world conditions and great world duties or scuttle now and come back afterwards.[22]
>
> I wish that they could feel the moral obligation that rests upon us not to go back on those boys, but to see the thing through . . . to the end and make good the redemption of the world. for nothing less depends upon this decision, nothing less than the liberation and the salvation of the world.[23]
>
> I am ready to fight from now until all the fight has been taken out of me by death to redeem the faith and promises of the United States.[24]
>
> I know that the whole world will lose heart unless America consents to show the way.[25]

Over and over, Wilson denied that he personally had any self-interest in the League (some of his enemies had said he wanted to be first President of the world): "I would be glad to die that it might be consummated." "I thank God that on this occasion the whole issue has nothing to do with me." And in his last speech before his breakdown and return to Washington: "The chief pleasure of my trip has been that it has nothing to do with my personal fortunes, that it has nothing to do with my personal reputation, that it has nothing to do with anything except great principles. . . ." Worn to the bone, Wilson was at last forced to stop speaking, despite his protest—"No, no, no, I must keep on."

President Wilson, then, demonstrated the most intense personal commitment to the League of Nations treaty throughout his struggle. The incredible energy he poured into the fight, his insistence that he and he alone create it and get it approved, his identification of the League with the will of God, with the will of history, and with his obligation to the dead, and his reiterated insistence that he was completely selfless in pursuing it—all contribute to a pattern of emotional investment far beyond what is ordinary in the making of public policy.

Wilson's commitment is shown from a different angle in the negative side of his fight, particularly his intense aggressiveness against his opponents (increasingly focusing on Lodge) and his rejection of allies who meant to help him (culminating in his break with Colonel House). Wilson came back from Paris spoiling for a fight. The day he landed he made a speech "throwing down the glove of defiance to all Senators and others who oppose the League of Nations," as the *New York Times* saw it. Wilson denigrated "those narrow, selfish provincial purposes which seem so dear to some minds that have no sweep beyond the nearest horizon. I should welcome no sweeter challenge than that. I have fighting blood in me and it is sometimes a delight to let it have scope, but if it is challenged on this occasion it will be an indulgence."

He was up against formidable opposition in the Senate. Lodge ridiculed his scholarship: of the League Covenant he said, "As an English production, it does not rank high. It might get by at Princeton but certainly not at Harvard." He had made a careful assessment of Wilson's "temperament, intentions, and purposes" and decided that "the key to all he did was that he thought of everything in terms of Wilson. . . . Mr. Wilson was devoured by the desire for power."

Once Senator James Watson said to Lodge, "Senator, suppose that the President accepts the treaty with your reservations. Then we are in the League, and once in, our reservations become purely fiction."

Lodge replied, "But, my dear James, you do not take into consideration the hatred that Woodrow Wilson has for me personally. Never under any set of circumstances in this world could he be induced to accept a treaty with Lodge reservations appended to it."

Watson said, "But that seems to me to be rather a slender thread on which to hang so great a cause."

To which Lodge exclaimed: "A slender thread! Why it is as strong as any cable with its strands wired and twisted together."[26]

As we have seen, Wilson returned the sentiment. He worked to contain his aggression. "If I could really say what I think of them," he said of the opposing Senators, "it would be picturesque." And he continued, "The President, if my experience is a standard, is liable some day to burst merely by containing restrained gases. . . . When the lid is off I am going to resume my study of the dictionary to find adequate terms to describe the fatuity of these gentlemen with their poor little minds that never get anywhere but run around in a circle and think they are going somewhere. I cannot express my contempt for their intelligence." He could not be sure, he said, "by what influences they have been blinded," but he had no doubt they were blind. His opponents were acting from "downright ignorance" or some evil "private purpose." The malicious ones would be "gibbeted" in the annals of mankind. The ignorant ones "do not understand English"—and should therefore try French.

To one of his allies who warned that the treaty was in grave danger, he said, "Martin! Anyone who opposes me in that, I'll crush."

In the end, Lodge could say with satisfaction, "We can always count on Mr. Wilson. He has never failed us."

Wilson detested his foes and he progressively sacrificed the friends who tried to steer him to compromise, which left him at last with no independent mind around him. Ex-President Taft was driven away fairly early; Secretary Lansing was excluded and finally fired for meeting with the Cabinet when Wilson was ill. But Wilson's most intimate advisor had for long been Colonel House. House had long shown an "extraordinary capacity for enhancing the President's self-esteem." He kept always in the background, until at Paris he occupied an official position which led him into more and more independent behavior, making suggestions, meeting with the press, treating with the Allied statesmen. All House's energies were devoted to the League cause, but his independence began to irritate Wilson. "Sooner or later," House wrote in his diary, "I suppose I shall get into trouble." He did. He was progressively excluded from

Wilson's deliberations after standing in for the President when he was ill. In June 1919, just before Wilson returned to the United States, House urged him to be conciliatory with the Senate. Wilson replied, "House, I have found one can never get anything in this life that is worthwhile without fighting for it." At that, they separated for good.

At last, everyone seemed to turn against him. Sick and isolated after his collapse, Wilson heard his wife say, "For my sake, won't you accept these reservations and get this awful thing settled?"

> He turned his head on the pillow. He took her hand. "Little girl, don't you desert me; that I cannot stand. Can't you see I have no moral right to accept any change in a paper I have already signed? It is not *I* who will not accept; it is the Nation's honor that is at stake." His eyes were gleaming. "Better a thousand times to go down fighting than to dip your colors to dishonourable compromise."[27]

There is a second level, then, on which Wilson's fight for the League can be understood. Behind all the substantive issues, all the calculations about reservations and interpretations and understandings, was Wilson's own personal struggle—to win out alone, to yield nothing, to meet his binding obligation to his individual values, to crush the enemies who scoffed at him. And perhaps one should add, to die in the attempt.

HOOVER'S INNER STRUGGLE

In contrast to Wilson and Lyndon Johnson, Herbert Hoover was not given to airing his emotions in public—or in private. When we get to a discussion of his rhetorical style, Hoover's penchant for privacy, for the good deed done in the dark, for charity on the sly will come through. Not only was he that way but he believed in being that way. And when he was, as he felt, forced into using rhetoric, the way he used it reflected his inner opinion of it. Part of Hoover's compulsion, then, was a *stylistic* stubbornness. More of that later.

Of Hoover's mood as he ground on through his Presidency there is virtually no disagreement. One afternoon shortly before he left office, he told his secretary that "All the money in the world could not induce me to live over the last nine months. The conditions we have experienced make this office a compound hell." In his marathon conference sessions with business leaders (John Kenneth Galbraith called them "No-business meetings"), Hoover "invariably appeared solemn and sad, an unhappy man, a man without hope. Instead of radiating confidence and good cheer in the presence of the economic crisis, his portraits made one want to sell short, get the money in gold, and bury it." Henry Stimson said that a tête-à-tête with Hoover was "like sitting in a bath of ink."

"By the fall of 1931," writes Gene Smith,

> Hoover while dining would sit in complete silence, sunk in concentration. He was capable of utter silence even when greeted by his closest associates. He

completely ignored the White House servants; his wife's personal maid heard exactly one sentence from him in her life. . . . He did not like seeing the servants in the halls; and so they hid when the White House bells announced his presence, footmen holding trays high in the air as they scurried into hall closets already crowded with maids.[28]

Ike Hoover, the White House major domo (and no relation), remembered that "There was always a frown on his face and a look of worry"; the President "never laughed aloud." When one of his secretaries asked him about his refusal to engage in small talk, he replied with irritation that "I have other things to do when the nation is on fire." Mrs. Hoover called the President's tendency to mumble an "awful habit," and "Foreign ambassadors presenting their credentials were told by State Department officials not to think the President's lack of enthusiasm had any diplomatic significance."

He cut down on his sleep until he was getting only three hours sleep a night. His hands shook. He did not miss one day of grinding work through illness. In 1932, "with whitened hair and drooping shoulders," Hoover "appeared twenty years older than he had been in 1928." When Republican leaders came to tell him how bad things were, he wailed, "If only they would leave me alone and let me work perhaps I could help to change the situation."

And so on, dismal day after day. Near the end of his campaign, as rotten eggs pelted his train, Hoover seemed resigned to his fate: "I see the handwriting on the wall. It is all over." When a delegation of Palo Alto girl scouts presented him with flowers, he finally let the tears go down his face, and a twelve-year-old turned to her mother to ask, "Mommy, what do they do to a President to make a man look like Mr. Hoover does?"

On election night,

When he went down to circulate among the people Mrs. Hoover had invited in, his appearance shocked them. This neighbors had not seen him in four years and could hardly believe this man with the sagging shoulders and whitened hair and stunned look was the man they had known. Nor had the Washington people even seen him look so ghastly. He seemed in a daze as he read the telegrams from all over announcing an unparalleled disaster. Bewildered, he appeared entirely to lose his orientation, so much so that he shook hands with one man three times in a short period. The wife of his old friend Secretary of the Interior Ray Lyman Wilbur thought that the incredible defection of entirely safe Republican states took him entirely by surprise, and that he had fully expected to be reelected. He seemed to her about to collapse.[29]

As President, Hoover's typical response to criticism was "hurt contempt" or "pained disbelief." His chief critic, Charlie Michelson, thought Hoover the thinnest-skinned politician he had encountered. But only rarely, at first, did his anger emerge forcefully. Although he might occasionally "blow off steam" in private, he was "almost always the master of his emotions," his secretary wrote, "however provoked he might be." His responses to those who baited him was that "A man should not become embroiled with his inferior." His stance was that of the martyr. In what Hoover called "the one harsh word that I have uttered in public office," he defended himself against the charge that he had done nothing to ease the pain of the Depression. He said,

> When you are told that the President of the United States, who by the most sacred trust of our nation is the President of all the people, a man of your own blood and upbringing, has sat in the White House for the last three years of your misfortune without troubling to know your burdens, without heartaches over your miseries and casualties, without summoning every avenue of skillful assistance irrespective of party or view, without using every ounce of his strength and straining his every nerve to protect and help, without using every possible agency of democracy that would bring aid, without putting aside personal ambition and humbling his pride of opinion, if that would serve—then I say to you that such statements are deliberate, intolerable falsehoods.[30]

Hoover was bitter but restrained. But as the campaign of 1932 developed, he began to lash out, sometimes at his audiences. When someone yelled, "Oh, raspberries!" during one of his speeches, Hoover said, "If the man who made that remark will step forward I will attend to him." Increasingly he attacked Roosevelt: he would "carry the fight right to Roosevelt. . . . We have got to crack him every time he opens his mouth." He would use the whole machinery of the recovery programs to beat Roosevelt. In Hoover's *Memoirs*, he devotes 129 pages to answering Roosevelt's charges one after another. He could hardly contain his anger when FDR refused to join in reassuring statements or commitments to Hoover programs between the election and inauguration day. The enemy had emerged and Hoover spent a great deal of his own energies in his waning Presidential days answering attacks and warning against the awful results of following Roosevelt's way rather than pointing forward a Hoover way.

As the national crisis deepened into 1932, Hoover became more and more isolated. He hardly seemed to realize the Bonus Army was in town. "Intently studying mounds of bank reports and business statistics on his big desk," Hoover was "barricaded in his study." He worried that others were under attack for his sake: "It's a cruel world," he complained. "My men are dropping all around me." But he would not—probably could not—change his line of action, for to do that would be tantamount to surrendering to "the lure of the rosy path to every panacea," to follow "the easy ways to imagined security"—all of which had to be resisted to the last, however "tempting" they might be. In his own mind, Hoover was out "to save the American people from disaster." "Above all," he said in justification of his policies, "we have maintained the sanctity of the principles upon which this Republic has grown great. . . . Government by the people has not been defiled." And he was up against ultimate evil in Roosevelt, who was offering "the most revolutionary new deal, the most stupendous breaking of precedent, the most destructive undermining of the very safeguard of our form of government yet proposed by a presidential candidate." As with Wilson, Hoover's struggle was not a matter of opinion, not a matter of experiment and compromise in the face of uncertainty, but a war for a principle—that "above all."

Arthur Schlesinger captures in a few sentences the gist of Hoover's character-rooted tragedy:

> In the end, Hoover, dragged despairingly along by events, decided that wherever he finally dug in constituted the limits of the permissible. Doctrinaire by temperament, he tended to make every difference in degree a difference in kind and to transform questions of tactics into questions of principles.
>
> As his term wore on, the ideological obsession grew. . . . His was the tragedy of a man of high ideals whose intelligence froze into inflexibility and whose dedication was smitten by self-righteousness.[31]

Back in 1928, when all but a few observers were finding the country's future "bright with hope," Herbert Hoover had given a powerful clue to the personal depth of the philosophy he insisted on to the end. Responding to the suggestion that he had somehow "earned" the right to be President of the United States, he said:

> My country owes me no debt. It gave me, as it gives to every boy and girl, a chance. It gave me schooling, independence of action, opportunity for service, and honor. In no other land could a boy from a country village, without inheritance or influential friends, look forward with such unbounded hope. My whole life has taught me what American means. I am indebted to my country beyond any human power to repay. . . .[32]

JOHNSON'S INNER STRUGGLE

Even more clearly than Wilson and Hoover, Lyndon Johnson took his tragedy personally. His initial commitment to the war was made in personal terms: "*I* am not going to lose Vietnam. *I* am not going to be the President who saw Southeast Asia go the way China went." By 1965 Johnson was speaking of "my Security Council," "my State Department," "my troops." With a sigh he would excuse himself from dinner saying, "I've got to go to Da Nang." It was *his* war, his struggle; when the Viet Cong attacked, they attacked him. After Pleiku, his response was "I've had enough of this." "Just like the Alamo," he said, "somebody damn well needed to go to their aid. Well, by God, I'm going to Vietnam's aid." Returning from a whirlwind tour of Vietnam, Johnson dictated a statement mentioning himself eleven times in the first few minutes and saying, "Do you know that some of those men had just climbed out of foxholes to be with me, they had just come from battle carrying guns on their backs?" And he would say to startled visitors, "I could have bombed again last night, but I didn't," and "I don't want China to spit in my eye and I don't want to spit in China's eye." The Viet Cong, he said, "actually thought that pressure on an American President would be so great that he'd pull out of Vietnam. They don't know the President of the United States. He's not pulling out!" The one escape Lyndon Johnson rarely used was to pass the buck to someone else. It was his war and he would run

it his way. There was in all aspects of his Presidency an extraordinary person-
alism in Johnson's policy making, but nowhere was this tendency stronger than
with respect to Vietnam.

Not only did he talk that way, but he invested his energies as intensely as
his words. He had always been a fantastically active politician, driving himself
well beyond what those around him could do. "Lyndon acts as if there is never
going to be a tomorrow," his wife said, and this was part of his code: "When you
have something to do, don't just sit there. Do it, and do it fast." In the White
House he developed a system for making two days of every one, the first beginning with a bedroom conference at 6:30 or 7:00 A.M. and ending about 2:00 in
the afternoon with lunch and a nap. By 4:00 he was ready to go again—"It's like
starting a new day," he'd say—and he kept at it until 1:00 or 2:00 in the morning.
No one reported an atmosphere of Coolidgean placidity in the Johnson White
House; "You know I do everything intensively," he said.

He tried playing golf in the spring of 1964, but the game bored him; he
smacked the ball "like he was killing a rattlesnake," according to one of his
companions. He tried bowling, but could never be satisfied unless he made a
strike. He tried swimming in the White House pool but turned each dip into a
political conference; in the pool at his ranch in Texas he had a floating telephone
installed so he could work in the water. Lured to a baseball game, he "ignored
the game completely and talked politics almost nonstop through the nine innings
of play."

Before illness made him quit, he smoked three packs of cigarettes a day.
Then after his heart attack, "As the danger receded, he was like a penned lion
pacing his cage." Gulping his meals as if he were starving, Johnson hurried from
task to task continually driving himself to the point of exhaustion.

"Let's go, let's go"—that was Johnson in the White House.

At least from 1966 on, it was the war in Vietnam that consumed these
immense energies, as Johnson pored over detailed maps to choose bombing
targets and had himself wakened at three in the morning to get reports on air
strikes. And through it all he complained that he was "the loneliest man in the
world," "the most denounced man in the world," for whom "nothing really seems
to go right from early in the morning till late at night," a man who "will never get
credit for anything I do in foreign policy, no matter how successful, because I did
not go to Harvard." "The load is unbearable," he said. "You have to have the
physical constitution of a mule and great dedication."

June 29, 1966, was what Johnson called "the night of the little monks."
His daughter Luci told him he looked tired and Johnson sat her down and told
her "You may not wake up tomorrow. Your Daddy may go down in history as
having started World War III" and he described his restless nights waiting for the
American planes to return to their bases. As the President recalls it, "Luci said,
'Come with me to the monastery and my little monks will pray for you.' So I went
with Luci to her monastery" he tells us, "and I prayed with her little monks.
Then I went back to the White House and slept like a baby."

Mrs. Johnson remarked in 1965, "I just hope that foreign problems do not keep mounting. They do not represent Lyndon's kind of Presidency." But they did keep mounting. "Oh me," the President would wail, "I try so hard. Why do these things have to happen to me?"

He had an answer to that question: his miseries came from the "knee-jerk liberals," "crackpots," and "trouble-makers." By the spring of 1967, Johnson was calling his critics "Nervous Nellies" and "cussers and doubters" in public, and using rather more colorful language in private. "McNamara has gone dovish on me"—that "military genius." The list of Nervous Nellies expanded: Fulbright, Mansfield, Pope Paul. "I can't trust anybody!" he blurted to an aide. "What are you trying to do to me? Everybody is trying to cut me down, destroy me!" He came to see the Russians behind his Senate critics, feeding them material for speeches. FBI checks were instituted for all White House guests, including the Presidential Scholars. Citizens who wrote to the President in support of anti-war demonstrations received answers from the Internal Security Division of the Justice Department.

But the prime villain, for Johnson, became Robert F. Kennedy, the rival he had always called "Sonny Boy." Johnson alternated between rage (Vice President Hubert Humphrey said that when Johnson and Kennedy got together "all sense flies out the window and they become two animals tearing at each other's throats") and despair (his friend Senator George Smathers would "walk in and find him sitting there in his chair with his face all screwed up sadly and a fist against his cheek, and he greets me with a sort of cry: 'Tell me what to do about Bobby, that little blankety-blank'"). Nothing enraged him more than Robert Kennedy's suggestion that an independent commission—including Kennedy—should be formed to develop proposals for ending the war.

The President fought back with hard deeds against the enemy in Vietnam and with a whirlwind of flimflammery against his enemies at home. When his press coverage was favorable, he could say, "I trust the press. I trust you just as much as I trust my wife." But when he felt the press had turned against him he lashed out: "They warp everything I do, they lie about me and about what I do, they don't know the meaning of truth. They are liars and cheats." But it was Johnson himself who came to the White House with a reputation for stretching the truth, as Hugh Sidey recounts in the following incident:

> A former Johnson aide tells how LBJ as a Senator was pointing out the ramshackle cabin on his Texas ranch which he described in Lincolnesque detail as his birthplace. Johnson's mother was along on the ride, and when her son finished she mildly admonished him, "Why, Lyndon, you know you were born in a much better house closer to town which has been torn down." The listener reports that Johnson replied, "I know, Mama, but everybody has to have a birthplace."[33]

Caught in a flood of petty lies—about appointments, about his schedule, about his relationship with Bobby Baker, about his health and finances, about non-existent murder and mayhem in the Dominican Republic, about the polls—Johnson's reassurances concerning Vietnam became less and less believable as he rushed to insist that each new escalation represented no policy change. As the polls in 1967 showed public confidence in him waning fast, he said, "I never used to have trouble with the press. I don't understand it." More cautious in making statements about Vietnam than about most of his doings, the President nevertheless continually communicated to the public two false impressions, which he knew to be false: that the major emphasis of effort in his government was on making peace through negotiations (in fact, he kept the top brainpower in his administration constantly at work on warmaking), and that he was not altering the character of the war as he escalated it (in fact, he transformed a minor military advisory mission into full-scale war).

As Johnson saw it, the cause in Vietnam was of such overriding importance that criticism itself was immoral, even unpatriotic. He had made up his mind: "Appeasement would be disaster." "If we quit in Vietnam," he said, "tomorrow we'll be fighting in Hawaii and next week we'll have to fight in San Francisco." The stakes were no less than everything:

> As long as there are men who hate and destroy, we must have the courage to resist, or we will see it all, all that we have built, all that we hope to build, all of our dreams for freedom—all—all—will be swept away in a flood of conquest. So, too, this shall not happen. . . . We shall stand in Vietnam.[34]

The war was a matter of national honor as well as of national interest. "Where American citizens go, the American flag goes with them to protect them . . . ," he said, and the more Americans he sent the more he wrapped their mission in the flag. The United States would "fight to its last soldier" if necessary.

In the course of his crusade, Johnson slowly whittled his advisors down to those ready to back his course. George Ball had opposed the war from the early days, but Johnson had managed to plug him so firmly into the role of official dissenter that his views were listened to and then easily dismissed. One by one his aides resigned: McNamara, Reedy, Valenti, Busby, Moyers, Jacobson; all departed, leaving six loyal Texans in his top staff of ten. Walt Rostow, the chief pusher of escalation, remained to follow Johnson into retirement at the University of Texas. Near the end, Johnson turned to his old friend Clark Clifford to replace McNamara. When Clifford convinced himself that the war was not working, he put his advice squarely to the President and contributed to Johnson's decision to resign.

But by then it was almost all over. In order to meet the immense manpower needs which the military told him in 1968 it would need to achieve its mission, reserves would have to be called up and wage and price controls might have to be imposed—highly unpopular steps, just at a time when the polls showed Johnson's public support rapidly leaking away and the primaries looking bad. So he stepped down, hoping that if he went away the war would go away, or at least that negotiations could begin in earnest.

Even at the height of his success—at the close of the remarkable first session of the 89th Congress—Johnson complained bitterly, asking

What do they want—what *really* do they want? I am giving them boom times and more good legislation than anybody else did, and what do they do—attack and sneer! Could FDR do better? Could anybody do better? What *do* they want?[35]

By late in the term he had the wish to be "like an animal in the forest, to go to sleep under a tree, eat when I feel like it, read a bit, and after awhile, do whatever I want to do."

THE COMMON STRUGGLE

Each of these three stories—of Wilson and the League, of Hoover and relief policy, of Johnson and Vietnam—is really two stories. The first is external: the facts demonstrate, I have argued, that each of the three Presidents persevered in a destructive line of policy long after it had shown its destructiveness. The results of the policies for society were disastrous: the United States did bow out of world politics and another World War followed, people did starve in the Depression and millions who did not starve suffered severe privation, and Vietnam did come to mean death and maiming for hundreds of thousands of human beings. None of these disasters appeared suddenly; the awful realities revealed themselves gradually, a piece at a time. Yet the power of the Presidency was thrown into the balance against modification, urged at the time, which might well have saved untold lives and fortunes. That is the factual story; the record shows what the President did in each case.

Underlying that is a story of each President's highly personal involvement in the policies he supported. These are not case studies in cool calculation, not neutral histories. Wilson, Hoover, and Johnson *cared*, deeply and sincerely, about what they were doing. They experienced intense anxiety, frustration, and near despair as they clung to their battle flags. Their personalities were engaged—not peripherally, but centrally—in fights against great odds. Their actions cannot be understood apart from the passions each poured into his task.

Even when we focus only upon feelings directly connected with the major policy lines of these three cases, the following themes are evident in all of them:

The Fight Against "Giving In"

The President experiences a sense of temptation. The issue is highly moralized, a matter of principle, not prudence. Therefore to compromise, to move toward any easy "panacea," is seen not only as mistaken but evil. In moral terms the cost of compromise is simply too high for the President as a person: he would have to sacrifice his own integrity, his stance as a being responsible to his conscience. Furthermore, he sees the conflict as one between strength and weakness. He himself, he feels, must be tough—and others should also show their mettle, their fiber, their manhood. The soft way out is closed to him, for his fight against giving in is a double fight, against both sinfulness and weakness.

The Answer in Effort

The President experiences severe depression as the personal implications of his policy unfold. In an attempt to overcome his practical problems he turns to work, which he progressively transforms into grueling labor in which his effort is more and more narrowly focused. He loses himself in his task, concentrates on repetitious plunges into the most difficult labors. Throughout his working, he suffers—and reminds himself, again and again, how much pain and self-sacrifice he is experiencing.

The Lone Struggle

Increasingly as the issue develops, the President feels that the responsibility for success depends entirely on him. The policy becomes his policy, inexorably welded to his person; its defeat means his defeat. The reason he must bear the burden alone is, as he feels it, that others who might help him keep deserting him. In a way he would prefer to welcome them as followers, but bitter experience has taught him not to trust them when the chips are down. The result is a President isolated from independent voices in his own camp.

The Appeal to Faith

The President increasingly uses opportunities for persuasion as opportunities for exhortation. The policy problem is transformed from a matter of calculation of results to a matter of emotional loyalty to ideals. The President appeals for faith in himself as keeper of the nation's promises. Because the cause is so tremendously important, the President concentrates on whatever rhetorical tactics are necessary for his grand strategy; *his* view of reality must be accepted lest the cause fall apart.

The Emergent Enemy

The President experiences intense anger as he meets the frustrations imposed upon him. That anger moves gradually away from him, outward to targets in the environment. The beginnings may be mere irritation kept in the privacy of his staff, but this extends and deepens to include whole categories of weak and immoral people on the outside. As the process of rigidification moves along, the President finds among his enemies an individual who, to him, personifies the threat. That person becomes the focus for the President's aggression; the critical task becomes defined as defeating this emergent enemy at all costs. The alternative is defeat at his hands, surrender.

For the active-negative President, that is the ultimate threat. For him, surrender is suicide, an admission of guilt and weakness. Having invested all his moral capital in the cause, he will—he must—plunge on to the end.

3

The Active-Negative Presidents

The themes discussed in the preceding chapter are plain even when we restrict our attention only to the major line of policy around which each of these active-negative Presidents froze. But these cases tell only part of the story. For the behavior in question was in each case part of a pattern. The President's particular course of action was sustained by the style, the world view, and the character he demonstrated *typically* in the Presidency; it was not some isolated fluke. I want now to explicate these patterns, to show how their parts reinforced one another, and most important, to explore how the President's orientation toward his role might have been anticipated before he became President. Throughout, I will be reaching for themes these three Presidents shared. The purpose is not to characterize each as an individual, but to move beyond special cases to larger cues. Eventually this may enable us to see how to predict, before the man settles into the Oval Office, how he will go about his business there.

For the active-negative Presidents especially, character is the key. Their styles and world views—so different from Wilson to Hoover to Johnson—turn out to be largely at the service of character forces which, in the end, linked with an issue in a direct and compelling way.

WILSON'S STYLE

The core of Woodrow Wilson's Presidential style was rhetoric—especially "oratory"—and he excelled in that beyond any of his near predecessors or followers. Again and again he met opposition and turned to speech-making as the way out.

Would the wily European leaders try to bamboozle him? Then he would take his case to the people of Europe, "over the heads" of their supposed representatives. Was the Senate cabal waiting to trap him on his return? Despite Colonel House's advice, Wilson began his Senate fight with a speech—to the public. His repeated suggestions that the contest be moved from Washington out into the country, in solemn referenda on his policies, meant that he thought he could win if he could speak out to the masses. And in the end, when his most cherished plan for the world faced failure, Wilson took on his last great tour of oratorical performances.

It was no secret to Wilson himself that his style rested on his rhetoric. Shortly after his *Congressional Government* was published, Wilson had written to his dear friend Ellen Axson that he was longing for a political career, one in which he would be able to speak out:

> I have a strong instinct of leadership, an unmistakably oratorical temperament, and the keenest possible delight in affairs; and it has required very constant and stringent schooling to content me with the sober methods of the scholar and the man of letters. I have no patience with the tedious toil of what is known as "research"; I have a passion for interpreting great thoughts to the world; I should be complete if I could inspire a great movement of opinion, if I could read the experiences of the past into the practical life of the men of to-day and so communicate the thought to the minds of the great mass of people so as to impel them to great political achievements. . . . My feeling has been that such literary talents as I have are *secondary* to my equipment for other things: that my power to write was meant to be a handmaiden to my power to speak and to organize action.[1]

Wilson's mind focused most naturally on phrases and images which would inspire an audience. Through his Presidency, by contrast, he had little use for "research." In 1916 he confessed he had not read a serious book in fourteen years. And when he appeared before the Senate Foreign Relations Committee to defend the League Covenant he showed substantial lapses of knowledge about details. "The facts," Wilson said, "are marching and God is marching with them." The role of facts was to march, to persuade, to overcome stupid opposition, not to test a case. While writing *Congressional Government,* a few miles away in Baltimore, Wilson did not trouble to visit the Congress.

Wilson's passion was for *direct* relations with his audience. He intensely disliked the necessity for communicating with the public through the press. As Arthur S. Link puts it, "Few Presidents in American history have better understood the importance of good press relations and failed more miserably to get on with newspapermen than Woodrow Wilson." He opened his first press conference asking for the reporters' assistance and expressing his confidence in them; those were the words, but his chilling manner—"suspicious, reserved, a little resentful," according to a friendly reporter—"utterly failed to get across to those men anything except that this was very distasteful to him; and they, on their part, resented it very, very seriously. They came out of that conference almost cursing, indignant." He was infuriated at press speculations about his Cabinet appointments and personal family affairs. "You gentlemen must learn sooner or later that you must take me at my word," he thundered at reporters in 1912. "I have told you repeatedly that I reached no decisions, and I object very much to questions which put my word in doubt." In February 1913, he said, "I'm not here to amuse the newspapers. . . . I'll be damned if I will." By September he wrote a friend, "Do not believe anything you read in the newspapers. . . . Their lying is shameless and colossal!", and by January 1915 he was castigating the editors.

For its full flowering, Wilson's oratorical talent had to have the audience out front, ready to respond directly to the truth as he said it. But his purpose was always to persuade and if that required what House called "grazing the truth" he would do that. One of the best reporters of the day thought it "impossible to rely on anything he said," and there were plenty of examples to back up his opinion. Nor were Wilson's misleading statements inadvertent; he told Colonel House "he thought that lying was justified in some instances, particularly where it involved the honor of a woman. . . . He thought it was also justified where it related to matters of public policy." House disagreed. Wilson reiterated this thought in 1914, applying it to foreign policy matters. His failure to win the confidence of reporters "was doubtless very influential in setting the tides of sentiment against him at the time when he needed support most" and it also played a role in alienating such leaders as Roosevelt, Lodge, Root, and Taft.

Wilson's oratorical bent affected his whole range of behavior, including his close personal relations. He could be charming, and he was nearly always impressive, in face-to-face dealings. But he was extraordinarily prone to follow an announcement of cooperativeness and consideration with a lecture, thus communicating to his collaborators by his manner a sense that it was his prerogative to tell them what to do and be. His superb mind often made it easy for him to dominate a conversation. A friendly reporter said of Wilson,

> I have never talked with any other public man who gave me such an impression of being at every moment in complete command of his entire intellectual equipment, such an impression of alertness, awareness. . . . He gets swiftly to your point of view, passes upon the facts that you bring him, and in a few minutes time has stripped the whole situation to the bare bones and its fundamental aspects, and has rested his conclusions and decisions upon a few simple and fundamental principles—and all with an incomparable clearness of statement.

Wilson was no blundering bully; part of his persuasive power was that he put his case so well. But he could not brook opposition at close quarters. He wanted agreement, support, allegiance—not controversy. His Secretary of State thought that

> arguments, however soundly reasoned, did not appeal to him if they were opposed to his feeling of what was the right thing to do. Even the established facts were ignored if they did not fit in with his intuitive sense, this semidivine power to select the right.

His Secretary of War complained that Wilson's "overpowering self-esteem left no place for common counsel of which he talked so much and in which he did not indulge at all." As Colonel House, writing before his break with Wilson, explained, the President "finds great difficulty in conferring with men against whom, for some reason, he has a prejudice and in whom he can find nothing good." And his own physician, Dr. Grayson, thought Wilson "intolerant of advice": "If one urges Wilson to do something contrary to his own conviction, he ceases to have any liking for that person." A New Jersey associate thought that argument adversely affected Wilson's whole intellectual process: "Wilson's mind could not work under opposition, for he felt all opposition to be merely irritation."

Yet Wilson needed people, not only as political allies, but also for his own peace of mind. His letters, especially those to women, were filled with appeals for affection unsullied by their curiosity.

> Do you really want to know what the present President of the United States lacks and *must* have, if he is to serve his country as he should and give the best that is in him to his tasks? He needs *pleasure* and the unaffected human touch! He cannot live on duty. He cannot feed his heart on "great questions." He must have the constant tonic of personal friendships, old and sweet and tested, that have nothing to do with him as a politician, have no relation to his, or any, career, but touch him only as a man, ante-date his public responsibilities and will outlive them,— that *belong* to him, are part of his private and essential life!"[2]

> I, for one, need fixed points upon which to base my . . . actions from hour to hour. My friends are those fixed points. My intercourse with them helps to restore my identity from time to time, to get the confusion out of my nervous system and feel like the real Woodrow Wilson. . . .[3]

> The President of the United States is not, at any rate in this year of grace, made of steel or whipcord or leather. He is more utterly dependent on his friends, on their sympathy and belief in him, than any man he has ever known or read about. . . . He has many counselors, but few loving friends. The fire of life burns in him only as his heart is kept warm.[4]

> [I am] never so deeply content as when talking to those whom I love and respect, whom I understand and who understand me,—without explanations of any kind![5]

He told Josephus Daniels, his Secretary of the Navy, that

> You are the sort that make life and friendship worth while. It is fine to have a colleague whom one can absolutely trust; how much finer to have one whom one can love! That is a real underpinning for the soul![6]

No one understood this need of Wilson's better than Colonel House. Unfailingly complimentary, House not only flattered Wilson but also passed on compliments he heard. "My faith in you is as great as my love for you," he wrote Wilson, "more than that I cannot say." He avoided making demands on Wilson and dropped any suggestions which did not meet the President's approval. House confided to his diary that "I nearly always praise at first in order to strengthen the President's confidence in himself which, strangely enough, is often lacking." Even when he was unloading criticism on Wilson in his diary, House would write the President such things as this: "I do not put it too strongly when I say you are the one hope left to this torn and distracted world. Without your leadership God alone knows how long we will wander in the darkness." Wilson invited House to "scold" him if necessary, but House decided not to. "You are the only one in the world," Wilson once told House, "to whom I can open my mind freely and it does me good to say even foolish things and get them out of my system." And the President was quite open in explaining why he valued House: "What I like about House is that he is the most self-effacing man that ever lived."

Wilson was an orator who devoted his energies to explicating his views. He had little use for homework—"research"—and in his interpersonal relations he combined a lecturing style with rejection of opposition and a strong seeking after free affection. His was mainly a voice in the White House, an instrument for expressing great ideals. Yet even at this stylistic level, Wilson's strong inner needs peek through. For Wilson (as for Hoover and Johnson), words were weapons:

> The struggle that is on [he wrote in 1915 concerning a shipping bill] to bring about reaction and regain privilege is desperate and absolutely without scruple. It cannot be met by gentle speeches or by presidential utterances which smack of no bias of party. . . . We must not suffer ourself to forget or twist the truth as they do, or use their insincere and contemptible methods of fighting; we must hit them and hit them straight in the face, and not mind if the blood comes. It is a blunt business, and lacks a certain kind of refinement, but so does all war; and this is a war to save the country from some of the worst influences that ever debauched it. Please do not read the speeches in which I use the bludgeon. I do not like to offend your taste, but I cannot fight rottenness with rosewater.[7]

WILSON'S WORLD VIEW

Woodrow Wilson said to a supporter after his election to the Presidency, "Before we proceed, I wish it clearly understood that I owe you nothing. Remember that God ordained that I should be the next President of the United States." Despite the surprise of cynics like Clemenceau, Wilson quite openly identified his cause with God's cause. "I must do what is right!" he said. Asked once, "Do you never think yourself wrong?" Wilson tied his answer to his oratory: "Not in matters where I have qualified myself to speak." But his determined pursuit of the right once he felt he understood it also owed much to his sense that God rules the world, even if He takes his time about it. As Arthur Link summarizes Wilson's belief:

> Mankind, he felt, lived not only by the providence of God but also under His immutable decrees; and nations as well as men transgressed the divine ordinances at their peril. He shared a Calvinistic belief, held in his day mainly by Southern Presbyterians and members of the Reformed churches in Europe, in predestination—the absolute conviction that God has ordered the universe from the beginning, the faith that God used men for His own purposes. From such beliefs came a sure sense of destiny and a feeling of intimate connection with the sources of power.[8]

His life would not be worth living, Wilson said, "if it were not for the driving power of religion." And: "The way to success in America is to show you are not afraid of anybody except God and His Judgment. . . . If I did not believe that the moral judgment would be the last and final judgment in the minds of men, as well as at the tribunal of God, I could not believe in popular government."

Wilson's God was not some unearthly apparition, but One actively at work in the affairs of mankind. For Wilson, the *ultimate* outcome was not in question: God's will would triumph. But when and how and where—those questions were up to God's men on earth to discover and implement. Human sinfulness guaranteed difficulties along the way, challenged the good Christian to overcome sin in himself and to war against sin in others. But of the outcome there could be no doubt. God's men, his stewards dedicated to service, knew who they were and would know how to see the good and make it happen.

Wilson saw himself as one of those, a man destined to make the world's salvation part of his own. He joined to this religiously based world view an almost mystical faith in the democratic spirit. "The people" to Wilson were the bearers of an innate rightness, masked at times by the confusions of the world, but capable, when rightly informed and inspired, of pointing out the path. Wilson seems almost Rousseauean in his faith in the fundamental goodness of man, in the capacity of simple people to choose better than their sophisticated leaders. Undoubtedly this sentiment was reinforced by his own electoral success—but he persevered in it even after his party was defeated in 1918 and 1920. Wilson *knew*, as surely as he knew God's will, that the people were with him. (One wonders how that belief fares for Presidents in the age of public opinion polls.) "I have never had a moment's doubt," he said, "as to where the heart and purpose of this people lay." God above and the people below were joined by Woodrow Wilson.

Wilson understood, however, that institutions were necessary to make politics happen and he found in the British parliamentary tradition a model of the best way. His various proposals that Senators resign and take their case to the people, that he resign if the results were against him, reflected a British vote-of-confidence theme that runs through his writing. In *Congressional Government* he again linked this preference to oratory: representative government "is government by advocacy, by discussion, by persuasion. . . . It is natural that orators should be the leaders of a self-governing people"; in the British system that tended to be the case. Furthermore, Cabinet government unified the executive and legislative branches in a way Presidential government could not. "The very breath of such a system," Wilson wrote, is parliamentary debate. Never elevated to the level of ultimate principle, Wilson's admiration for the British system nevertheless flavored his entire political outlook—his relations with Congress, with the parties, with his advisors.

But above all this was his belief—his conviction—that God ruled the world, that "the people" expressed His will, and that he, Woodrow Wilson, whatever else he might want to be, was the bound instrument of their conjoint will. This faith held steady his vision of a world that might be better.

WILSON'S CHARACTER

The outlines of Wilson's Presidential character could hardly be clearer. He did not just work hard, he "slaved," often to the point of complete exhaustion. There were vacations and for a while he played golf every afternoon. But his nearly incessant labors place him plainly in our active category.

As for his affect toward his effort, Wilson's very frequent and intense periods of depression contrast strikingly with the fun a Franklin Roosevelt could find in the White House. Wilson's letters to his lady friends make this most evident:

> We are at the beck and call of others (how many, many others!) and almost never have a chance to order our days as we wish to order them, or to follow our own thoughts and devices. The life we lead is one of infinite distraction, confusion,—fragmentary, broken in upon and athwart in every conceivable way. . . .[9]

> How is a man to get through with days of unbroken anxiety and continuous responsibility of the heaviest kind if he does not have constant evidence that his loyal and loving friends are thinking about him,—thinking such thoughts as ought to make any man strong and confident and happy? What is to keep his spirits from sinking and the blue devils from getting him?[10]

> All day long I have been fighting against the weakness and silliness of feeling sorry for myself. I feel more than ever like a prisoner, like a sort of special slave, beguiled by the respect and deference of those about me, but in fact in durance vile and splendid.[11]

> I work hard, of course (the amount of work a president is expected to do is preposterous), but it is not that that tells on a fellow. It's the anxiety attending the handling of . . . affairs in which you seem to be touching quicksilver. . . .[12]

> I have been under a terrible strain, if the truth must be told, and am still under it. . . . I never before knew such a strain as I have undergone ever since Congress convened in April. . . .[13]

All of these complaints are from the year 1913, when Wilson was leading his Congressional party to victory in reform after reform. The bitter battles of his later Presidential years, including the League fight, were still before him and Wilson would know pains he could not even have anticipated in 1913. Everyone has his blue moments, but Wilson seemed incapable of taking pleasure even when his efforts were extraordinarily successful. After his major victory on the tariff in September 1913, Wilson responded to a friend's congratulations by saying, "I am so constituted that, for some reason or other, I never have a sense of triumph. . . ." He told House he did not feel elated at success, but moved right on to the next project. "Success does not appease him," Ray Stannard Baker wrote, "it only scourges him to harder effort. . . . His aspirations are inappeasable. He can rest upon no victory: he must press on to greater things."

Wilson enjoyed playing golf (mainly because he found it distracted him completely from official worries) and he attended the theater regularly, preferring light and easy plays. He could even joke about his appearance, as in this limerick he often recited:

> For beauty I am not a star,
> There are hundreds more handsome by far,
> But my face I don't mind it,
> For I am behind it,
> It's the people in front that I jar.[14]

But he drew a hard line between fun and officialdom; government was serious business. Once at a dinner party when some military officers put on skits lampooning administration policy and the grape-juice drinking Secretary of State, Wilson was furious and inquired about court-martial proceedings. Finally he issued a public reprimand:

> I have been told that the songs and other amusements of the evening were intended and regarded as "fun." What are we to think of officers of the army and navy of the United States who think it "fun" to bring their official superiors into ridicule and the policies of the government which they are sworn to serve with unquestioning loyalty into contempt? If that is their idea of fun, what is their ideal of duty? If they do not hold their loyalty above all silly effervescences of childish wit, what about their profession do they hold sacred?[15]

High purpose and dogged labor left no room for the light touch, no sustaining laughter in the midst of the struggle.

In his close and warm family circle, Woodrow Wilson could be a charming raconteur, a loving husband and father. Probably the "direst emotional crisis in his life," as Link calls it, came to him when his dear wife Ellen died in August 1914. Wilson was totally crushed; he wrote that he felt dead, like a machine run down, broken in spirit and wishing he would be killed. His wife had been his standby, an unending provider of encouragement and sympathy.

As Wilson groped to overcome his grief, he revealed still another facet of his political character—of what one dimension of political life meant for him. He wrote,

> You see, I am trying just now what I must believe to be the most difficult thing in the world: I am trying to live, and to live without loss of energy and zest for the daily task, on a broken heart. . . . It is possible; and I think the method is this: not to sit and look on—especially not to sit and look on at oneself,—but to project oneself as far afield as possible, into fields where one's personal feelings count for nothing, or should count for nothing, except enhanced sympathy and quickened insight.[16]

And again he wrote:

> It seems, indeed, as if my individual life were blotted out, or, rather, swallowed up. . . . I write this not to make complaint . . . but only to record a singular thing: how one in such circumstances seems to realize his submergence and to be made to feel that his individual life is suspended and cast out of the reckoning,—even in his own consciousness. . . . [H]ere I must stay for a little while; and the less I analyze my feelings the better. They are wholly irrelevant, and only mess and

> belittle matters when they intrude. Woodrow Wilson does not matter; but the United States does and all that it may accomplish for its own people and the people of the world outside of it.[17]

In the depths of personal grief, Wilson indicates in these passages that he seems to want to use his public life to blot out his private feelings. He tries to believe that he, as an individual with his own hopes and fears, his own identity, no longer exists, that he has disappeared into something larger than himself. He turns violently away from self-contemplation to the tasks Providence has allotted him.

Wilson experienced similar feelings in many other connections. The sense that his own personality simply was not involved in what he did recurred constantly in his career. The reason he pursued certain lines of policy was not that he wanted to, but that he *had* to. His letters and comments are full of such expressions: "I must push on. To linger would be fatal." He was "simply the instrument of the people" who "must insist on my own conception of my duty." "We have no choice but to obey" the mandate of the people with respect to the League, and "We cannot turn back. We can only go forward . . ." Together with all the expressions of selflessness Wilson uttered in campaigning for the League (see Chapter 2, above), these themes come down to this: "I have no liberty in the matter." He was, as he saw it, a man under compulsion, working out his destiny as involuntarily as a tree reaches for the sun.

But this way of denying himself and of projecting his feelings onto politics did not bring Wilson the serenity he sought. His strong emotional investment in policies made him rigid—"I am not the kind that considers compromises when I once take my position"—and brought upon him the outraged indignation of enemies and potential allies, as well as some success in situations where his stubbornness paid off. But over all, the personal costs were as severe as the political ones. In a 1914 speech, Wilson revealed what he often felt like inside:

> If I were to interpret myself, I would say that my constant embarrassment is to restrain the emotions that are inside of me. You may not believe it, but I sometimes feel like a fire from a far from extinct volcano, and if the lava does not seem to spill over it is because you are not high enough to see into the basin and see the caldron boil.[18]

As other passages already quoted make clear, what Wilson was restraining was rage, the impulse to lash out freely at his enemies. The sense that he was on the verge of breaking out—just about to fight—stayed with him; he appears to have devoted a good deal of energy to holding himself back. He explained this struggle a different way when he told his secretary,

> You know, Tumulty, there are two natures combined in me that every day fight for supremacy and control. On the one side, there is the Irish in me, quick, generous, impulsive, passionate, anxious always to help and to sympathize with those in distress . . . and like the Irishman at the Donnybrook Fair, always willin' to raise me shillalah and to hit any head which stands firninst me. Then, on the

other side, there is the Scotch—canny, tenacious, cold, and perhaps a little exclusive. I tell you, my dear friend, that when these two fellows get to quarreling among themselves, it is hard to act as umpire between them.[19]

Colonel House had found Wilson "strangely" lacking in self-confidence. That lack seems confirmed as we review Wilson's character. His very frequent depression and discouragement, his self-punishing working habits, his inability to laugh at himself as President, his continual defensive denial that his own preferences were involved in his decisions, and particularly the extremely high standards he set for his own performance—standards which never let him be satisfied with success—all reveal a person gripped by an extraordinary need to bolster his self-esteem. Suspended in a kind of purgatory between God and the people, Wilson everlastingly sought to justify his choices on "principle," thus adding to the force of purpose the highest of callings. He experienced in severe form the fight against the temptation to quit, to give in and leave the field to enemies who would subvert all he believed in. Instead, Wilson found a way to fight off despair and to express anger by trying to force his attention away from himself and by devoting all his talent and energy to political leadership. The instrument for that purpose was his impressive oratorical skill. Through his voice Wilson could express his bottled-up anger, could appeal for love and power, and could bring to heel the evil men who opposed him. For that to work there always had to be an issue which he could invest with moral fervor and to which he could devote his "single-track mind." In short, Wilson attempted to compensate for low self-esteem by dominating his social environment with moralistic rhetoric.

At the core of that formula was his character with its intense demands for power and perfection. The pattern revealed when we scan Wilson's character and see how that fed into—and on—his world view and style was the psychological context for his stubborn, self-defeating behavior in the League fight. That final battle brought together all these themes in one integrated package. To have given up on the League—his League—would have represented for Wilson a breakdown in his peculiar integrity, a profound disturbance of an inner arrangement which had come to mean so much to him.

HOOVER'S STYLE

Wilson in his letters and Lyndon Johnson in conversation often laid their feelings right out on the table for everyone to see. Not so with Hoover. Because so much of his Presidency centered in what he refused to do, the central fact about his rhetorical style was what he refused to say.

Hoover's rise coincided with an immense expansion of the mass media, particularly newspapers and the radio. Hoover was a genuine hero; his remarkable effectiveness in European relief activities cannot be seriously challenged. Maxim Gorky once wrote to him,

> In the past year you have saved from death three and one-half million children, five and one-half million adults, fifteen thousand students, and have now added two hundred or more Russians of the learned professions. . . . In the history of practical humanitarianism I know of no accomplishment which in terms of magnitude and generosity can be compared to the relief that you have actually accomplished.[20]

To attribute Hoover's pre-Presidential reputation to assiduous personal promotion, as some of his critical biographers did, is nonsense. He was the subject, not the instigator, of a vast public relations buildup largely owing to increasing media demands for news and to the drama and success of his works.

But Hoover in the White House "transmuted all adventure into business." He detested the office's demands for dramatization. To be sure, he believed that "The presidency is more than an executive responsibility. It is an inspiring symbol of all that is highest in American purpose and ideals." Yet he could not bring himself to practice the pretense such inspiration requires. "This is not a showman's job," he said, "I will not step out of character." "You can't make a Teddy Roosevelt out of me," he declared. On any number of occasions for political dramatics, Hoover held back, unwilling to symbolize the emotional meaning of events. The result, of course, was to convey an impression of uncaring indifference. Hoover never could acknowledge that leadership demands rhetoric, that rhetoric demands drama, and that drama demands artifice.

Hoover felt intense discomfort in his public performances. "I have never liked the clamor of crowds," he said. "I intensely dislike superficial social contacts. I made no pretensions to oratory and I was terrorized at the opening of every speech." It was the emotionalism of crowds which put him off. In *American Individualism* Hoover had written, "The crowd only feels: it has no mind of its own which can plan. The crowd is credulous, it destroys, it hates and it dreams— but it never builds." Yet Hoover's labored drafting and redrafting of speeches shows how important he thought communication with the public was; although he would not try to stir the crowd, he did make an effort to get his message across. Yet it rarely came off. As one of his staunchest defenders wrote in 1932, Hoover seemed "not to have the least appreciation of the poetry, the music, and the drama of politics." Even his most enthusiastic biographer, Eugene Lyons, thought Hoover was wrong in refusing the showman's role:

> The presidency is very much of a showman's job. Leadership from the White House must appeal to the heart no less than to the mind; it must arouse faith and fervor and courage beyond cold calculations. In insisting that it was not a showman's job Hoover was rationalizing his distaste for showmanship and his ineptitude behind the footlights.[21]

Rationalizing or not, Hoover continually displayed a front of unblinking silence before rhetorical opportunities most politicians would have jumped at.

He was no better on the receiving end of the publicity game. Public criticism hurt him, but neither did he like public praise. When Lady Astor once introduced him at a dinner as "a soft of savior of mankind," she set off a wave of applause mixed with laughter as Hoover blushed crimson. "Look at him!", the Lady said. "He is not an ideal politician. He lacks the glad hand and the perpetual smile, thank goodness." Hoover was given to sneaking into dinners after the other major celebrities had made their triumphal entries—only to be reduced to embarrassed confusion when he was recognized and applauded. "The crown of that personality is shyness," Will Irwin wrote of him.

Hoover's relations with the press deteriorated rapidly from a promising start. At his first Presidential press conference, he said he wanted to develop even more intimate relationships with reporters than his predecessors had had, and he planned to allow direct quotation of some statements, a break with precedent. He had been popular with reporters when he was Secretary of Commerce, although during the Presidential campaign he grew aloof and resentful of their probings. But on the whole, the Presidential beginning was a good one.

Soon the press grew hostile. Perhaps even before the stock market crash Hoover began to depart from his own rules, becoming more secretive and admonishing reporters for the errors of their ways. He often withdrew, without notice to the press, to his private retreat in Virginia. Several reporters were killed in the race to follow him there; those who made it were forbidden to approach the Hoover camp. He began to play favorites with reporters and to go over their heads to the editors and publishers. And particularly after the crash, many newsmen came to suspect the President of deliberate falsification. He cancelled conferences on short notice, ignored reporters' questions, and increasingly took to reading prepared statements. Eventually he turned most of the White House reporters against him. Press conferences became less and less frequent and were virtually eliminated near the end of his term.

Hoover's public addresses inspire little comment. He rarely discussed specific policies in detail, sticking mostly to vague moral principles and goals. He completely lacked Coolidge's appreciation of the uses of radio; his twenty-one radio addresses were mainly greetings to special groups rather than appeals to the nation at large.

The puzzle of Hoover's rhetoric is not *that* he failed at it but *how* he failed at it. As the account of his statements during the Depression shows, Hoover *did* have a try at the emotional uses of rhetoric: he spoke to reassure, to encourage, to calm a trembling nation. He undertook to do that by concentrating on whatever good news was available and by optimistic predictions—in other words, by a "public relations" approach to speechmaking. But he lost credibility because he distorted a reality known to a great many people by personal experience. It is almost as though Hoover had a conception of oratory as *necessarily* dishonest, which led him to disdain it, but also, when he felt forced to practice it, to speak manipulatively.

Hoover's style in personal relations was complicated and segmented. There was a loyal band of "Hoover men" who had worked with him in past ventures and called him "the Chief." The same Hoover who terrified the White House servants had very frequent guests in the White House, and his wife thought he preferred company to solitude. Yet many of these affairs were for business; Hoover in the casual company of strangers was a wet blanket. As an Englishman who had worked with him reported,

> His personality never "got across" in this country. He was always too busy to talk "sweet nothings" to society ladies; and to those who met him only occasionally he seemed preoccupied, dour, reserved. . . . Those who did not understand him even accused him of a "damping" influence in ordinary life. He was said not to be able to smile. Consequently, the people on the outside admitted his genius and his great work, and left it at that. . . . I should say that it was entirely his own fault, due to his shrinking from personal publicity.[22]

To his personal secretary Theodore Joslin and others who worked with him closely, Hoover had a certain humor and a great considerateness. Dour as he was, he was almost never unkind. But he was not out for social pleasantry. The main thrust of his social energies went into the endless round of conferences he presided over, especially after the crash. Often held in secret to avoid public panic, these meetings went on morning, afternoon, and night in the White House; many a meal was flavored with depression discussion. Hoover's purpose was "coordination" and "cooperation"—words he continually invoked to described his governmental technique. He was continually immersed in small-group decision making.

But what happened in those meetings was not "cooperation," not the give and take of people groping together toward a solution. Hoover's secretary and admirer Joslin described the process:

> Whatever the plan or the program, he always prepared it to the last detail prior to holding the conference at which he was to project it. He would give days, weeks, and on rare occasions, even months to formulating it, weighing the favorable and adverse factors, eventually deciding on the course which he believed should be pursued and sometimes reducing the contemplated action to written words. That part of the effort completed, he would list those leaders in Congress or in industry, finance or agriculture most interested whose assistance he required and summon them to the White House.
> With the assembling of the conferees, who almost invariably did not have the slightest ideas why he had asked them to come to the Executive Mansion, he would outline the situation confronting him and the country and then produce the written program he had prepared. If it were acceptable to them, he then produced a statement for publication that he had also prepared in advance, rather than leaving to discussion among the conferees the nature of the announcement that was to be made. He left nothing to chance.
> In these conferences which the depression necessitated, he always talked straight to those about him, not dictatorially but in an informative manner, conveying the pertinent information he had assembled, seeking to impress them with the conclusions he had reached.[23]

Hoover appears in this context as the man with the plan, all worked out in detail, including the press release, before he even decided who the participants should be. They arrived at his "summons"—completely unaware of the question to be discussed, were flooded with facts, and offered—"in an informative manner"—a plan to which they were expected to consent on the spot. Hoover, indeed, "left nothing to chance." His style was to use his primary political skill and immense capacity of detailed planning to dominate others, to gain their acceptance, not their counsel. Although the men and the situations were different, the similarity to Wilson's use of discussion sessions is striking.

Of course, Hoover's demeanor affected his political relations. His inability to enter into genuinely cooperative relations with others—relations involving compromise, an appreciation for the irrational in politics, a sense of the other man's position—meant that his endeavors to induce an enthusiastic response were doomed to failure. He could lead an organization of committed subordinates—as in the Belgian relief work—but he could not create that commitment among leaders with their own bases of power and their own overriding purposes.

Hoover's main weapon, though, was neither oratory nor interpersonal persuasion, but his mastery of information. He did his Presidential homework more thoroughly than any President had, albeit he was often misled by inadequate statistics. Bernard Baruch undoubtedly meant it as a compliment when he said that "To Hoover's brain facts are as water to a sponge. They are absorbed into every tiny interstice." Joslin admired his "card index" mind: "During his Presidency he retained information as he absorbed it" and he had an unusual talent for switching quickly from one subject to the next. Ray Lyman Wilbur called his "capacity not only to turn off the light on the area in which he has been working, but to turn it on full blast into the new one." Without notes or transcripts, Hoover could hold in his head the items of the most detailed conversations. He would amaze bankers with his memory of exact figures; businessmen would leave his office dazzled to discover that Hoover "knows more about my business than I do myself."

A wizard of Presidential homework, Hoover maintained in his mind a barrier he defended repeatedly: that between fact and feeling. "The most dangerous animal in the United States" he said, "is the man with an emotion and a desire to pass a new law. He is prolific with drama from the headlines. He is not on the road to fundamental advance of the liberty and progress of the American people at this time in our history. The greatest antidote for him is to set him upon a committee with a dozen people whose appetite is for facts. The greatest catastrophe that could come to our country is that administration policies or voluntary movements shall be encouraged or enacted upon the basis of emotion and not upon facts and reason." Hoover stood ready, armed with piles of information, to tame that most dangerous of animals, emotional man.

HOOVER'S WORLD VIEW

Reading Herbert Hoover's political philosophy taxes the most dedicated powers of concentration. He seemed to have a positive instinct for flat prose, a kind of thudding Latinate threnody, like balls of glue dropped from a rooftop. Explaining his purposes, Hoover put it this way:

> Our program was one of deliberate purpose to do everything possible to uphold general confidence which lies at the root of maintained initiative and enterprise; to check monetary, security, and commodity panics in our exchanges; to assure an abundance of capital at decreasing rates of interest so as to enable the resumption of business; to accelerate construction work so as to absorb as many employees as possible from industries hit by decreased demand; to hold up the level of wages by voluntary agreement and thus maintain the living standards of the vast majority who remain in employment; to avoid accelerating the depression by hardship and disarrangement of strikes and lockouts; and by upholding consuming power of the wage earners to in turn support agriculture.[24]

The substance is there. But Hoover shies away from clarifying where he places the emphasis or why he believes these moves are the right ones. No isolated passage can do justice to his thinking, but this one does catch the programmatic flavor, the penchant for lists, the emotional obscurity and the anesthetic quality of so much of Hoover's writing. He wrote a great deal, but it is hard to tell what among his phrases really engaged him.

Hoover was called the "Great Engineer"; his thinking process was essentially physical and visual, as indicated by his perpetual doodling of geometric designs as he listened, with his eyes downcast, to his conferees. When he said that the fundamental business of the country was sound he had in mind the actual factories and payrolls and delivery systems. His everlasting search for facts and his readiness to believe reports stated in concrete and statistical form—however flawed the original numbers may have been—show the focus of his attention. The world as Hoover saw it was the physically visible world. The more poetic passages in his *Memoirs* describe the fields and sky and animal life and machinery of the Iowa he remembered. Therefore, Hoover's reiteration of "principles" has a secondary quality. In his mind most of the time was an image of society—derived almost entirely from observations other than his own—as a machine in disrepair, as an interconnected system of real relationships among real people and their things.

His various pronouncements of highest values:

The first requisites of a President of the United States are intellectual honesty and sincerity.
The first duty of the President under his oath of office is to secure the enforcement of the laws.
The most potent force in society is its ideals.
The primary duty of the Government . . . is to hold expenditures within our income.
The sole function of Government is to bring about a condition of affairs favorable to the beneficial development of private enterprise.

—are probably about as meaningful in understanding Hoover's world view as is his statement (in jest?) that during the Depression "Many persons left their jobs for the more profitable one of selling apples."

Three themes gained precedence in Hoover's world view: individualism, cooperation, and confidence. He wrote a book about individualism and confessed himself "an unashamed individualist . . . an American individualist." For

Hoover, "There can be no human thought, no impulse to action, which does not arise from the individual. . . . We might as well talk of abolishing the sun's rays if we would secure our food, as to talk of abolishing individualism as a basis of successful society." Individualism did not mean equality of means, but a fair chance:

> In the American system, through free and universal education, we train the runners, we strive to give to them an equal start, our government is the umpire of its fairness. The winner is he who shows the most conscientious training, the greatest ability, the strongest character.[25]

Especially in America, Hoover thought, individualism was not so much an ideology as an instinct, something "in our very nature" and "based on conviction born of experience." The national experience had demonstrated that "Progress of the nation is the sum of the progress of its individuals." And since "The primary duty of organized society is to enlarge the lives and increase standards of all the people," government, as umpire, must protect the producer—the individual—of that enlargement and increase not only against the "deadening restraints" of government itself, but also against "the encroachments of special privileges and greed for domination by any group or class."

Such efforts require leadership; in Hoover's American system, leaders "can arise solely through the free-running mills of competition. They must be free to rise from the mass; they must be given the attraction of premiums to effort. . . . Human leadership cannot be replenished by selection like queen bees, by divine right or bureaucracies, but by the free rise of ability, character, and intelligence." The system, then, was responsible not only for preventing the suppression of individuals but also for providing them with positive opportunities.

Hoover never seems to have resolved in any very systematic way the evident problem that freedom from domination by private interests might imply, or indeed require, domination by government over individuals. Clearly the main thrust of his argument was the assertion of an individualism which "insists upon the divine in each human being" and which sees our system as designed for multiplying possibilities, openings, opportunities for "that sense of service that lies in our people."

If Hoover recognized, at least in principle, the threat to individualism from private interests, he saw the solution in cooperation, or "coordination," by which the leading elements of the community would analyze problems and agree on a course of action. The persuasiveness of the factual case would insure voluntary compliance. Unlike bureaucracy, "Cooperation appraises its methods and consequences step by step and pays its bills as it goes." It is moderate and pragmatic, not millenial and destructive. In the end, for Hoover, cooperation amounted to "self-government outside of political government," which "is the truest form of self-government." The nation's leadership did not need to be hammered into compliance; they needed to be brought together in the "cooperative spirit and responsibility in the American business world . . . such that the business of the country itself could and should assume the responsibility for the mobilization of the industrial and commercial agencies."

Hoover's government-as-umpire, then, was not to sit back and let the competitive game proceed, but actively to design and implement procedures for cooperation—voluntary cooperation—to keep the play fair. In his thought as in his action, Hoover wanted to get people to join together without being forced to, to make the system operate up to its full potential.

Hoover's continual appeals for public confidence as the Depression deepened represent a third persistent theme in his world view. Given the opportunity, a nation of free individuals would have the daring to achieve—unless they were afraid. "Fear and apprehension," he said, "whether their origins are domestic or foreign, are very real, tangible, economic forces." In the summer of 1931 he found the people "suffering today more from frozen confidence than we are from frozen securities." Cooperation required leaders with the foresight to step beyond their narrow interests. The American social system required people sure enough of their futures to take chances—reasonably but bravely. This problem, as Hoover saw it, was fundamentally psychological; confidence could be as contagious as fear, if only people would believe in themselves enough to share in it. Though he never put it this way, Hoover seemed to conceive of human nature as hopeful but vulnerable, requiring not only some realistic assessment of the odds but also the spunk to throw the dice. Leading the people amounted mainly to creating conditions for their achievement and persuading them that they were part of a trend toward better days. The last thing leadership should do was to spread defeatism, either by abandoning people or by offering them a free ride on the dole.

HOOVER'S CHARACTER

Herbert Hoover could, on occasion—rare occasion—make a joke. Gene Smith uses one of the best to lead off his book about Hoover:

> All this reminds me of the small girl who said, "Mother, you know that beautiful jug you said had been handed down to us from generation to generation?" Mother replied, "Yes, Ann, what of it?" And Ann answered solemnly, "This generation dropped it."[26]

But the evidence is overwhelming that most contemporary Hoover-watchers found him as William Allen White did, "constitutionally gloomy, a congenital pessimist who always saw the doleful side of any situation." Colonel House found him at the Paris Peace Conference "revelling in gloom"; to H. G. Wells he was "sickly, overworked, and overwhelmed," and in 1932 Raymond Moley said, "He seems to me to be close to death. He had the look of being done, but still of going on and on, driven by some damned duty." Eugene Lyons insisted that Hoover was not cold, but "a sensitive, soft-hearted person who craves affection, enjoys congenial company, and suffers under the slings of malice." But Hoover himself often confessed his displeasure in the Presidential role: "This job is nothing but a twenty-ring circus—with a whole lot of bad actors."

Also on occasion—even rarer—Hoover could cry. I have been able to find only two such times in the biographies, both when Hoover was being honored by children, once in Poland and once in Palo Alto. And at times Hoover could express anger, as when he threatened to fight the heckler during his 1932 campaign. But his demeanor as President paralleled, in the main, that of Wilson—minus Wilson's glowing rhetoric. However turbulent Hoover's soul may have been in those years, he expressed little of his feelings; he let it all hang in.

Joslin saw Hoover's motivation this way: "Figuratively, he was the father protecting his family against the troubles impending, shouldering their burdens for them, keeping the 'bad news' to himself, outwardly trying to be as smiling and cheerful as possible." But he hid the "good news" about himself as well. Over a long history, Hoover hid his goodnesses as assiduously as his troubles. He kept it quiet that he did not take the salary the government owed him as President, or that he turned down a salary of $500,000 a year to take $15,000 as Secretary of Commerce. And he was forever arranging in secret to fix up loans, trips, jobs, and the like for his friends. On May 28, 1932, three children arrived at the White House door, having hitchhiked from Detroit. Their unemployed father was in jail for stealing a car and they had come to get the President to get him out. Hoover (who ignored the Bonus Army then moving into Washington) said that "Three children resourceful enough to manage to get to Washington to see me are going to see me." He heard the full story from Bernice, the oldest at thirteen. Then he checked the facts of the case and told them not to worry. Joslin, his secretary, recalls what happened next:

> My buzzer sounded a moment after I had started the children on their way. The President was standing by a window as I entered his office. He stood back to me, looking out over the rolling south grounds. Without turning around, he said in a thick voice:
> "Get that father out of jail immediately."
> Would Mr. Hoover permit me to give the press this sidelight of him? He would not. Nothing could change his mind. Agreeing only to the barest announcement, he said:
> "Let's not argue about it. That will be enough. That is all we will say about it. Now we will get back to work."[27]

Hoover's personal depression was far older than the Great Depression, as was his habit of very hard work. Clearly he belongs among the active-negative Presidents and his behavior is consistent with their typical pattern of driven, conscience-striken, dominating, and progressively rigid characters. Perhaps the psychoanalysts could make more than I can of imagery. For instance: "In every society, however perfected, there will always be at the bottom a noxious sediment and at the top an obnoxious froth" and "the sordidness and gossip which oozes through the intellectual swamps of a great political capital," and his enthusiasm for the cleansing power of fishing as a hobby. But Hoover's taciturnity forces us into indirection. Given the pattern of his performance, it is not unreasonable to suppose that he, too, struggled against an inner sense of inadequacy, that his power-seeking reflected a strong compensatory need for power, and that his self-lacerating labor was a sacrifice before the altar of an extraordinarily demanding conscience. Even on the surface, Hoover's fight to restrain aggression is evident, as is his humorlessness. Like Wilson, he appears as a President trying to make up for something, to salvage through leadership some lost or damaged part of himself.

Eugene Lyons ends his favorable book on Hoover with the following passages, in which the images are perhaps more appropriate than the author understood:

> Herbert Hoover is a great monolithic figure. Time is rapidly washing off the mud with which he has been bespattered. The granite of integrity underneath is becoming obvious even to the less perceptive of his countrymen.[28]

JOHNSON'S STYLE

The core of Wilson's style was rhetoric, of Hoover's homework; Lyndon Johnson exemplifies, as no other President in history, an emphasis on personal relations. He was in a constant whirl of conversation, face to face and on the telephone; much of the drama and entertainment biographers find in him are evident in his perennial palaver. Johnson talking was a performer, nearly always interesting even to those who detested him. Robert Sherill's bitingly critical account, *The Accidental President*, finds Johnson "an insufferable and dangerous fellow," but at the same time looks upon "the ol' boy as a fascinatingly rousing bastard." Whatever his other sins, Johnson was rarely dull.

The famous "Johnson Treatment," his razzle-dazzle way of winning compliance, could mix verbal "supplication, accusation, cajolery, exuberance, scorn, tears, complaint, the hint of threat" with physical lapel-holding, shoulder message, elbow and knee grabbing, fingerwagging, and nose thrusting—all at a whirlwind pace. For example, Arthur Schlesinger, Jr., came for his first long conversation with Johnson armed with a long list of questions to ask him. Then:

> The Treatment began immediately: a brilliant, capsule characterization of every Democratic Senator: his strengths and failings, where he fit into the political spectrum; how far he could be pushed, how far pulled; his hates, his loves. And who (he asked Schlesinger) must oversee all these prima donnas, put them to work, knit them together, know when to tickle this one's vanity, inquire of that one's health, remember this one's five o'clock nip of Scotch, that one's nagging wife? Who must find the hidden legislative path between the South and the North, the public power men and the private power men, the farmers' men and the unions' men, the bomber-boys and the peacelovers, the eggheads and the fatheads? Nobody but Lyndon Johnson.

Imagine a football team (Johnson hurried on) and I'm the coach, and I'm also the quarterback. I have to call the signals, and I have to centre the ball, run the ball, pass the ball. I'm the blocker (he rose out of his chair and threw an imaginary block). I'm the tackler (he crouched and tackled). I'm the passer (he heaved a mighty pass). I have to catch the pass (he reached and caught the pass).

Schlesinger was sitting on the edge of his chair, both fascinated and amused.[29]

Johnson went on to his papers act, pulling out of his desk and reading off voting records. Schlesinger was, if not convinced, impressed. So was Johnson. He could crow over victories: "They talk about ca-jolery and per-suasion, but this mawning it was sheer horsepower."

Actually there were three Johnson treatments, not one, and their use depended on Johnson's relationship to the person being treated.

When Johnson dealt with a person not under his control, he was often flattering and helpful. As with the newsmen, he would try to give the other what he wanted, or at least some of it. He would promise to make the reporters "big men" by leaking stories to them. When he overwhelmed he would overwhelm with flood of argument, however fragmentary, offering the victim any number of reasons for going along. One described the experience: "Lyndon got me by the lapels and put his face on top of mine and he talked and talked and talked. I figured it was either getting drowned or joining." In this form of treatment, Johnson was "reasoning together" as he saw it, though the other person may not have been able to get a word in edgewise. His habitual strategy was to communicate dramatically how intensely he wanted compliance, and to lay before the receiver such a smorgasbord of arguments—personal, political, philosophical, or whatever—that at least a few of them would catch the listener's fancy. He would display in such circumstances an incredible concentration of attention—on the man and on himself. The effect on the listener was a sense of involvement in tense drama, rare enough in most lives, and an unwillingness to ruin it all by refusing to cooperate.

In the process of recruiting people, Johnson could sound like Little Eva crossing the ice—desperate for rescue by just the man who could do that. What must have been the effect on Schlesinger—on any intellectual—of this plea: "I need you far more than John Kennedy ever needed you. He had the knowledge, the skills, the understanding of himself. I need you to provide those things for me." Or of this appeal to Eric Goldman:

> You know how I came to be in this room. . . . I don't know how long I will be here. As long as I am the President, I have one resolve. Before I leave, I am determined to do things that will make opportunities better for ordinary Americans, and peace in the world more secure. But I badly need your help—I badly need it. And I especially need the help of the best minds in the country.[30]

Or this, as he selected Hubert Humphrey as his running mate in 1968: "Why, I've been asking everyone here in the White House and right down to the cleaning women they're for you." This was Lyndon the supplicant. "Please stay," he pleaded with the Kennedy staffers, "I don't know *anybody*."

Hubert Humphrey's response epitomizes what Johnson wanted to establish: "Yes, sir, Mr. President. You can count on me to be completely loyal, sir."

Once aboard, once clearly under Johnson's control, his people experienced the second version of the Johnson Treatment. From that point on, Johnson expected complete conformity to his will—expressed and unexpressed. His bullyragging, domineering behavior advertised itself throughout Washington. Snarling at telephone operators, threatening his Secret Service guards, Johnson behaved at times like a drunken tyrant. "It isn't that he's mean to important people," one Kennedy man said sorrowfully, "he's mean to his servants." Johnson often treated his staff as they were servants, too, as when he would regularly chew out his top aides in front of visitors. The wonder is not that turnover in Johnson's staff was unusually fast, but that his assistants stayed as long as they did. Jack Valenti's faithfulness was legendary: "If Johnson dropped the H-bomb, Valenti would call it an urban renewal project." Johnson would rage at him for petty crimes: "I thought I told you, Jack, to fix this fucking doorknob!" "Where the goddamn hell ya bin? How many times have I got to tell you not to leave your office without telling me where you're going?" "For Chrissake, do you spend all your time on the phone?" George Reedy, his Press Secretary, was once publicly addressed by Mr. Johnson as "you stupid sonofabitch." From recruitment to subordination was a regular transition for Johnson. He could take on a man after the most abject pleading—and then ignore him completely. But ignored or exploited, the Johnson man soon learned what was expected of him. Back in 1956, Johnson decided he needed James Rowe, an old friend then in a profitable Washington law practice, to run his staff outside the Senate. Rowe was reluctant. Johnson got Rowe's law partner and another close friend to put the pressure on, and finally Rowe was astonished to hear his wife chime in, urging him to give Lyndon a hand. Rowe began to melt.

> He offered to work for Johnson two days a week. Not enough. Four days? No, said Johnson, he wanted Rowe full time. In fact, he went on, Rowe should resign from his law firm. Rowe protested. Johnson, sensing victory, offered personally to call up Rowe's clients to explain. With tears now welling from his eyes, Johnson begged and cajoled. How badly he needed Rowe! Rowe finally surrendered.
>
> The mood changed abruptly. Away went the tears. "Don't forget," Johnson told Rowe, *"I'll* make the decisions."[31]

In less than a year, Rowe, who never did establish command of the Johnson staff, was back in his law firm.

Budget Bureau Director Kermit Gordon, after a rare evening out, got this greeting from Johnson the next morning: "Well, playboy, did you have a good time?" When McGeorge Bundy strode into the Oval Office to join Johnson and Lodge one day, the President snapped, "Goddammit, Bundy! I've told you that when I want you, I'll call you."

Johnson sometimes complimented his staff men, but it is interesting to see what he valued in them. Valenti, for example, is about the best fellow with me. He gets up with me every morning. He stays with me until I go to bed at night, around midnight, and he is the only one who can really take it. The rest of these fellows are sissies.[32]

Bill Moyers, one of the few subordinates Johnson did not harrass,

has a bleeding ulcer. He works for me like a dog, and is just as faithful. He never asks for anything—but for more work. He won't go home with that bleeding ulcer until nine or ten o'clock. I don't know what I'd do without him.[33]

Their virtues were unquestioning loyalty, absolute servitude; Johnson was not given to praising his men for independence of mind. Valenti was superb in this respect. In a notorious speech, he found the President "a sensitive man, a cultivated man, a warmhearted and extraordinary man. . . . like a large gray stone mountain, untouched by fear or frenzy . . ." Lyndon Johnson, Valenti continued, "thank the Good Lord, has extra glands, I am persuaded, that give him energy that ordinary men simply don't have. . . . I sleep each night a little better, a little more confidently, because Lyndon Johnson is my President." When the speech was widely ridiculed, Valenti was surprised. "What did they expect me to do, denounce the President?"

Johnson's treatment of those under his control extended, albeit in slightly more moderate form, to his highest appointees. The President would bring together a small group and get consent by polling each in turn. Senator Fulbright, Chester Cooper, and others have recalled the intimidating effect of this technique of Johnson's, standard as it is. Apparently it worked this way. In 1967 Secretary McNamara's doubts were growing about the value of more war in Vietnam. Meeting with the President and the generals, McNamara faced this situation.

"The troops that General Westmoreland needs and requests, as we feel it necessary, will be supplied," Johnson said, then asked, "Is that not true, General Westmoreland?"

"I agree, Mr. President."

"General Wheeler?"

"That is correct, Mr. President."

"Secretary McNamara?"

"Yes, sir," came a helpless reply.[34]

In *The Lost Crusade,* Chester Cooper tells how he used to feel when one of Johnson's polling sequences got underway in the National Security Council:

During the process I would frequently fall into a Walter Mitty-like fantasy: When my turn came I would rise to my feet slowly, look around the room and then directly at the President and say very quietly and emphatically, "Mr. President, gentlemen, I most definitely do *not* agree." But I was removed from my trance when I heard the President's voice saying, "Mr. Cooper, do you agree?" And out would come a "Yes, Mr. President, I agree."[35]

With subordinates, Johnson pushed: the stick replaced the carrot. Once when Johnson had been berating George Ball, McNamara, and Dean Acheson, Acheson stopped him with this: "Mr. President, you don't pay these men enough to talk to them that way—even with the federal pay raise."

The third Johnson Treatment appeared at exit time. When Bill Moyers left to become publisher of *Newsday,* Johnson let his bitterness out: "When Moyers became my Press Secretary, my popularity was at an all-time high and nobody ever heard of Bill Moyers. When he left I was at an all-time low and Bill Moyers was a world hero." Leaving Johnson was, to him, a sign of disloyalty. When Eric Goldman departed, Johnson refused even to acknowledge his resignation and let out the news that the historian had worked mainly for Mrs. Johnson. McNamara was derided when he left. But perhaps the most striking feature of phase three of the Johnson Treatment was his abandonment of life-long intimates when they got into trouble. When Johnson's man Bobby Baker, who had been his closest lieutenant for eight years in the Congress, was under investigation by the Senate for various thieveries, Johnson blandly told a television audience that a Senate committee was "conducting this investigation of an employee of theirs—no protege of anyone; he was there before I came to the Senate for ten years, doing the same job as he is doing now; he was elected by all the Senators . . . including the Republican Senators." When Walter Jenkins, the President's chief White House aide, was arrested on a morals charge, hospitalized, and retired, Johnson issued a brief statement of sympathy and said that Eisenhower had had "the same type of problem."

In conference, Hoover was a fact machine grinding out careful plans. Wilson made addresses to small audiences. But Lyndon Johnson was, in all three versions of the Treatment, out to use whatever technique would confirm his own power. Basically he took advantage of a phenomenon threaded through all of politics—pluralistic ignorance. Divisions of labor create barriers to communication across specialties; the man at the top can develop a certain amount of play in the system by varying his message as he relates to one segmented subdivision after another. He places himself at the center of the information process, interpreting reality for officials only loosely linked to one another. They learn to come to him because he is the man who knows, and he in turn fosters this dependence and works to inhibit any extraneous horizontal communication. In the Senate, for example, Johnson built his own control system out of nothing. He took over as party leader, a position which had been trivial, and made of it, through his mastery of information and persuasion, a seat of great power. He knew where the bones were buried. By assiduously cultivating individual Senators and by rearranging to his advantage the conditions under which they conferred, Johnson built his Senate empire.

He took this technique with him into the White House, but there it worked only temporarily. Unlike the Senate, the White House in its most intimate workings was under constant scrutiny. The stories got out. Johnson could not get away with high preachments in public and low bullying in private because there was nearly no really private sphere in the Presidency, no space to be "an employer somewhere between Mr. Dithers and Caligula," as Patrick Anderson puts it. Furthermore, Johnson's Senate leadership had depended on his talent for mediation, which requires as its raw material actors with real initial preferences. Senator Johnson was seldom the initiator of legislative moves; he drew together the commitments of others. President Johnson was expected to lead— that is, to stand for something well in advance of the pack. He found this role a good deal more demanding: "all you fellows must be prudent about what you encourage me to go for," he would say. Part of his difficulty, especially with respect to the war in Vietnam, was that Johnson progressively eliminated dissent among his advisors and then tried to "mediate" among a nest of hawks. Johnson "knew how to make bureaucrats hurt, but he was less practiced in making bureaucracy work."

Given a legislative program "whose time had come," given his massive majorities after 1964, and given the sense of crisis in the post-assassination months, Johnson could and did produce an impressive string of victories. In his main innovation, the transformation of Vietnam from a minor project to an all-consuming obsession, Johnson's consensus fell apart, despite all his tireless effort to suppress conflict, to muffle revolutionary changes behind a curtain of gradualism, and to develop some middle position between undefined endpoints.

But the crux of Johnson's interpersonal style was his habit of turning occasions for mutuality into occasions for domination. His rhetoric was too much an extension of his interpersonal style to be wholly effective. Clearly he never quite grasped the art of dealing with the press, never really understood the difference between a reporter and a politician. The press would be subjected to flattery and the ebullience of high table at the Johnson ranch, fed hamburgers molded to the shape of Texas—and threatened with excommunication when they misbehaved. To a reporter who asked him a trivial question, Johnson said, "Why do you come and ask me, the leader of the Western world, a chicken-shit question like that?" Another remembers an interview in which Johnson "sat with his knees pressed against mine, a hand clutching my lapel, and his nose only a few inches away from my nose. When he leaned forward, I leaned backward at an uncomfortable angle. 'Hell,' Johnson asked loudly, 'why don't you write a whole big article on just me alone?'" And with yet another reporter he entered into this exchange:

> "If you want to know what Lyndon Baines Johnson was going to do at the national convention," Johnson screamed, "why didn't you come to Lyndon Baines Johnson and ask him what Lyndon Baines Johnson was going to do?"
> "All right," said Shaffer, hiding all signs of intimidation, "what is Lyndon Baines Johnson going to do at the convention?"
> "I don't know," was the answer.[36]

The press responded by telling what happened in such encounters and by embroidering the whole affair with sarcasm; Johnson was, they said, "the first President since Roosevelt who enjoyed pulling the wings off flies"—and lifting beagles by the ears. When his control over secrecy and surprise leaked away, or when the press caught him in some obvious falsehood, Johnson responded furiously with barrages of equally incredible explanations. "Even as the credibility problem deepened," writes Hugh Sidey, "Johnson could not break himself of his habits. He persisted in staging his playlets, and almost always they backfired."

When Johnson's rhetoric seemed to go well with public audiences, he felt euphoric. He was, he said in 1964, "the most popular Presidential candidate since Franklin Roosevelt." The campaign lifted his heart: "When I get out of that car, you can just see them [the voters] light up and feel the warmth coming up at you. . . . Those Negroes go off the ground. They cling to my hands like I was Jesus Christ walking in their midst." The people, he thought, "have a baby-like faith in me." And when he was high in the Gallup poll he carried copies in his pocket and would say, "The reason I love so many polls is that over the years I've learned that they're pretty accurate."

Then when the credibility gap yawned ever wider, Johnson turned irascible. "I never used to have trouble with the press. I don't understand it." To him the problem became mainly one of technique, of mechanical projection. Photographers were forbidden to photograph him with glasses on or from the right profile. Some forty White House aides were instructed to join the Congressional audience for his State of the Union message and lead the applause; they would be watched from the balcony to see who clapped and how much. Passing up better biographies in favor of Booth Mooney's syrupily worshipful *The Lyndon Johnson Story,* the USIA distributed 250,000 copies of a book with its own little credibility gap in the first few pages:

> On the outside cover: "The complete authorized and illustrated biography by Booth Mooney."
> On the first inside page: "This is the definitive biography . . ."
> In the author's foreword: "I cannot pretend that this is an objective or definitive biography."
> In Lyndon Johnson's foreword: "This book is, then, no 'authorized biography'. . . ."[37]

But none of it worked, and Johnson's credit with the public nosedived. Even when he added his enormous energies to the task—he once gave twenty-two speeches in one day—his style undercut his message.

The problem at its base was that Johnson tried to treat crowds the way he treated individuals in the Oval Office, by dazzling them with a storm of scattered talk. "To Johnson, a crowd was to be breathed on, shouted at a bit, poked, amused, overwhelmed," and "each assemblage became like a single person seated across his desk." The result was bored amusement. Combined with the merciless intensity of television coverage and the inevitable inconsistencies as Johnson suited his messages to different audiences, his rhetoric merely complicated a life already tied in too many knots. Roaring on like "a combination of John C. Calhoun and Baron Munchausen," Johnson never got across to the generation attuned to Kennedy's cool rhetoric.

Still another aspect of his rhetoric gave Johnson trouble: his inconsistency of rhetorical mode. Not only was the message frequently full of contradiction, but he also would shift—even in the same speech—from a mode of toughness to one of conciliation, from dignity to vulgarity, from gaping vagueness to tight precision. Asked at a White House press conference what he was doing to negotiate a settlement of the war, he could go on for a long stretch of Johnson the peacemaker, in a tone of saintly pliancy. When the next question asked about military operation, he would switch to the stern Commander in Chief, in crisp control of his forces in the field. Like Wilson whose condescension belied his offers to enter a partnership with the press, like Hoover whose gloomy demeanor contradicted the optimism he wanted to convey, Johnson's shifting mode of expression undercut the believability of his claim to passionate conviction. The message could not correct what the mood communicated.

This was the insensitivity Sidey called "one of those minor tragedies in the make-up of Lyndon B. Johnson. . . . He just does not become engaged with the people he meets. He does not respond to their overtures, does not pick up opportunities to endear himself. . . . His mind is on Johnson, not Pago Pago."

Johnson's style in the management of detail—his Presidential homework—also suited his emphasis on personal relations. The details he was always most interested in concerned persons—especially their weaknesses, their vulnerabilities, their prides and fears. "On the Hill he had been a virtual encyclopedia of the fallibility of his fellow legislators." In the Dominican crisis he spent hours going over the credentials of various leaders. And as President he could draw on and deepen his incredible memory for what specific men wanted. His other subject of continuing scholarship was himself. Apparently he read one book during his Presidency, Barbara Ward's *The Rich Nations and the Poor Nations*—read it "like the Bible," he later said. But in his lifetime he admitted that since college he had not read "six books all the way through." Yet he was an avid reader, listener, and viewer of three television sets at once, when it came to commentary on Lyndon Johnson.

Eric Goldman, no great admirer of Johnson's after his bitter experience, says flatly that "I am sure I have never met a more intelligent person than Lyndon Johnson." He was an extraordinarily quick study, could pick up the gist of an argument or the details of a budget right away. Willard Wirtz thought he "had the quickest, most analytical mind I've ever seen." Certainly the image of Johnson as some drawling dimwit from the outer provinces is nowhere confirmed in the biographies. But he acquired knowledge to use it, and once used, he jettisoned it as unnecessary baggage for the next trip. An old friend of his explained:

> He told me once that when he had to know the contents of a bill or a report, he could scan it and fix it in his mind so well that if you gave him a sentence from it, he could paraphrase the whole page and everything that followed. But once they'd finished the piece of work, even if it was only a week later, he wouldn't remember the contents or even the name of the report.[38]

His mind was in the service of his purpose, which was to win through one battle at a time. Those details would soon be irrelevant. The details about men remained relevant as long as the men did, so he filed them more permanently. Similarly he mastered the rules of the game in Congress more thoroughly than any of his contemporaries, and kept them alive as he whipped the bills through. Johnson's extraordinarily quick mind made it easy for him to learn, to discard, to keep what he needed. But the focus of his labors did not lie in studies. Men were his books; knowledge was a tool to control men.

JOHNSON'S WORLD VIEW

Amidst the chaos of Johnson's verbal productions, two themes persisted, sometimes alternating in the same speech: a tough, hard, militaristic theme and a dedicated humanitarianism—Johnson mean and Johnson nice. Together they add up to a view of the world in which the strong-weak dimension is paramount. Never fully consistent in any philosophical sense, Johnson found a way to let these themes live together by separating the arenas in which they were operative. To the outer world of foreign policy, Johnson presented his hard soldierly visage. To the deprived at home, he showed his kindlier face. There were many exceptions, but these were the main themes.

It was appropriate that Johnson moved into the White House on Pearl Harbor Day, December 7, 1963. When World War II began, he had been the first member of the House of Representatives to go into uniform, and during the war he was awarded a Silver Star. Early on in Congress he had received from Roosevelt, in return for his ardent support, a seat on the Naval Affairs Committee chaired by Carl Vinson, and Johnson's schooling in the nation's military needs and wants developed further when he lost his first bid for a Senate seat in 1941 and sought an issue to cement his relations with that element in Texas which cared more for military power than for New Deal doles. Johnson got Vinson to make him chairman of a special committee on the progress of the war. That work left him disillusioned with the generals and admirals—a sentiment which never left him—but also with a vision of national military strength as the bulwark of American freedom. "We must get rid of the indecisive, stupid, selfish and incompetent among our generals, admirals and others in high military positions," he said during World War II. He was never, then, a passive follower of military persons, only an extraordinarily active advocate of more and more military power. As a member of the Postwar Military Policy Committee, and later the Senate Armed Services Committee, of the Appropriations Subcommittee for the Armed Services, and chairman of the Senate Preparedness Committee and of the Space Committee, Johnson breathed the hot breath of militant anti-Communism.

By November 1951, he was warning the Russians that "We are tired of fighting your stooges," and continued,

> The next aggression will be the last . . . We will strike back, not just at your satellites, but at you. We will strike back with all the dreaded might that is within our control and it will be a crushing blow.[39]

Three months later he was prepared to reduce Moscow to rubble to stop Communist aggression anywhere:

> We should announce, I believe, that any act of aggression, anywhere, by any Communist forces, will be regarded as an act of aggression by the Soviet Union. We should keep strength ready, the strength we are now building. If anywhere in the world—by any means, open or concealed—Communism trespasses upon the soil of the free world, we should unleash all the power at our command upon the vitals of the Soviet Union. That is the policy we should build toward. That is the policy we should maintain—for one year, for five years, for fifteen years.[40]

Interspersed among Johnson's military power statements throughout the years are occasional cautions not to go off half-cocked, not to rattle sabers and so forth, but the more persistent theme has been the tough stand against encroaching Communists. President Eisenhower contrasted his experience with House Speaker Sam Rayburn, who "was always anxious to make certain that the United States would do everything possible to negotiate," with his experience with Johnson, who "appeared to be anxious to be able to take some action, visible to the world, to indicate that we had—or the Senate had—strengthened our Armed Forces."

When the Chinese moved into Korea in 1950, Johnson, in a speech titled "The War for Survival," called the Korean conflict "a struggle without precedence in human experience."

> The American people are fed up with doubletalk in Washington. . . . We have committed ourselves to a policy of not committing ourselves. What is the result? For the common defense we have thrown up a chickenwire fence, not a wall of armed might. . . . Is this the hour of our nation's twilight, the last fading hour of light before an endless night shall envelop us and all the Western world? This is a question which we still have in our power to answer. If we delay longer, we can expect nothing but darkness and defeat and desolation. . . . We are at war not merely with Communist China, but with all the military strength and both the physical and human resources behind the Iron Curtain. Our primary and immediate goal in this war is survival.[41]

Johnson called for "immediate, full mobilization of our available manpower" and "prompt mobilization of our economy." Fourteen years later, on January 1, 1964, President Johnson sent a message to the then ruler of South Vietnam, Big Minh, saying, "Our aims are, I know, identical with yours: to enable your government to protect its people from the acts of terror prepetrated by Communist insurgents from the North. . . . Peace will return to your country just as soon as the authorities in Hanoi cease and desist from their terrorist aggression. . . . We shall maintain in Vietnam American military personnel and material as needed to assist you in achieving victory."

There is no shortage of evidence that throughout this period—and indeed throughout his escalation of the Vietnam War—Johnson could be found from time to time warning against too aggressive a foreign policy. This was plainly the case in his election campaigns in 1960 and 1964. In passages already quoted, Johnson appeared as a man determined not to widen the war, not to commit large numbers of American ground troops. But the relative consistency of his warlike stance overbalances his occasional cautions. Insofar as he had a philosophy of international relations, it was based on toughness. That was the rule; the peaceable statements were the exceptions. As Johnson moved into the Presidency in 1963, one of his Senate colleagues gave this prediction:

> Lyndon's ideas were set in thick concrete by World War II. Every big action he takes will be determined primarily on the basis of whether he thinks any other action will look like a Munich appeasement. The reasons he will give publicly for his actions will not be those he really believes, because in the Senate he said what he thought you wanted to hear. And he will not change course even when he knows he is wrong, because he has a preposterous idea he is bound to lose face if he does. The only advisors he will listen to are those who will tell him what he wants to hear, for he is not a man who tolerates listening to both sides of a problem.
>
> In addition, Lyndon sees the Cold War as permanent, the enemy unchangeable, and every anti-United States activity anywhere on the face of the earth as a deliberate act controlled by an international monolithic Communist network operating from the Kremlin in Moscow. He will pay lip-service to an East-West detente, but he doesn't believe in it. Furthermore, since his entire training has been that of a politician trying to overpower other politicians, he will rely on personal diplomacy to buy off, threaten and coerce other nations.[42]

When Johnson found in Dean Rusk an advisor who reiterated the analogy between the war in Vietnam and the Second World War over and over again, he responded warmly. The tough-guy theme seemed to suit. In the Senate Johnson's militancy may have been little more than free emotionalism from the sidelines, but in the White House, it came to count for more. "There's an old saying down in Texas," Johnson once said. "If you know you are right, just keep coming on and no gun can stop you."

The second theme in Johnson's world view, his humanitarian concern, traced back to his New Deal days and beyond, into his image of his own youth. Although he could make low cracks about Mexicans and could mount a "War on Poverty" that was not much more than a skirmish compared to what he spent on real war, Johnson stuck to his *belief* in himself as champion of the downtrodden. He was their champion, not against anyone else, but against the impersonal forces that he saw destroying their lives:

> This great, rich, restless country can offer opportunity and education and hope to all—all black and white, all North and South, sharecropper and city-dweller. These are the enemies—poverty, ignorance, disease. They are enemies, not our fellow man, not our neighbor, and these enemies, too, poverty, disease, and ignorance, we shall overcome.[43]

He saw himself as personally committed to the pursuit of their happiness. Thinking back to his students in Texas, Johnson continued:

> I never thought then in 1928 that I would be standing here in 1965. It never occurred to me in my fondest dreams that I might have the chance to help the

sons and daughters of those students and to help people like them all over the country. But now I do have the chance, and I will let you in on a secret, I mean to use it. . . .[44]

Here was a Johnson uninterested in power, dedicated to a better world:

> I do not want to be the President who built empires, or sought grandeur, or extended dominion. I want to be the President who educated young children to the wonders of their world. I want to be the President who helped to feed the hungry and to prepare them to be taxpayers instead of tax-eaters. I want to be the President who helped the poor to find their own way and who protected the right of every citizen to vote in every election. I want to be the President who helped to end hatred among his fellow men and who prompted love among the people of all races and regions and all parties. I want to be the President who helped to end war among the brothers of the earth.[45]

Thus Johnson spoke to the Congress. On the stump he could wax even more prophetic and hortatory, as he moved from his hope for bright new days coming soon into his spiritual message for the people: love one another.

> So here is the Great Society. It's the time—and its' going to be soon—when nobody in this country is poor. . . . It's the time—and there is no point in waiting—when every boy or girl . . . has the right to all the education that he can absorb. It's the time when every slum is gone from every city in America, and America is beautiful. It's the time when man gains full dominion under God over his destiny. It's the time of peace on earth and good will among men.[46]

And again:

> Let's always be nice. When your neighbor comes over to your house, and he has been living alone for a long time and he gets lonesome, even if he does kind of do all the talking you be nice to him and courteous, because everybody is entitled to associate with good company every once in a while . . .
>
> Love thy neighbor as thyself; do unto others as you would have them do unto you. No matter how long it may take, no matter how difficult it is, this above all else is the great horizon toward which we march united.
>
> Let's keep a smile on our face, let's keep faith in our heart, let's keep hope in our vision, let's move on to conquer unknown frontiers.[47]

And so on. The images stress just the kind of interpersonal kindness, harmony, and considerateness Johnson himself found it so difficult to practice. The euphoria with which Johnson spoke, his open-armed gestures, the tone of millennial promise, all portrayed a President very different from the stern Commander-in-Chief. This is Lyndon Johnson the father, caring for the weak. It is almost as if he could speak Utopia into existence, at least in his own mind, by invoking not fire and sword, but gentle Jesus meek and mild.

Johnson joined the two main themes in his world view when he offered to make available a "billion-dollar investment" for economic development and reconstruction in Southeast Asia—including North Vietnam. If only the enemy would cease molesting his neighbors, the land could bloom like the Tennessee

Valley. Here the combination of opposites reached its ultimate: the President who had in early 1965 massively escalated the war now in April called for beating the swords into plowshares. He gave no evidence that he saw a contradiction.

Max Frankel recounts an incident showing starkly Johnson's capacity to be both his major personae, almost at the same time:

> Not long ago at a White House meeting with influential publishers, Mr. Johnson was asked why he would not halt the bombing of North Vietnam. His response was no mere argument of the case. For fifteen minutes, reports a close observer of the President, "there stood Saint Francis of Assisi, bathed in light beneath his halo," pouring out a passionate confession of his yearning for peace and a vivid account of the diligence of his search. The room was rapt.
>
> Through several more questions the mood prevailed until there came the predictable inquiry: If all that is so, perhaps it is true, as some have suggested, that the President is not fully hitting the enemy as hard as he should? And suddenly, as if in full regalia, there stood the Commander-in-Chief, ticking off the target lists, the clipped statistics of damage done and the promise of the further pressures planned. Again the room was rapt.
>
> Here, as he often does, Mr. Johnson had shown his determination to be Everyman's President. But, to his critics, he seemed simply to be trying to be all things to all men.[48]

But clearly the world Johnson felt most comfortable in perceiving was neither that of bombs and troops nor that of Heavenly Valley. Eventually either would have bored him. His natural medium was the world of the deal, the world where a man at the right place and time could patch together a bundle of power, doing some good for himself and some for others at the same time. Johnson as President—the expert middleman elevated above the political marketplace—continually sought out visions of the past, present, and future, not for their accuracy but for their utility. Words were, for him, instruments of action.

As an old Johnson associate put it, "You have to ignore the President's own account of why he does things, or even what he has done." Johnson seemed to recognize this about himself when he wrote, "I know that Lyndon Johnson's view of Lyndon Johnson is not really the right one or even the desirable one," and when he complained that the President's chief problem is not doing what is right but knowing what is right. He had no political philosophy—few Presidents have, but Johnson hardly had even an ideological orientation, an approach which might have helped him steer through the roils. "I bridle at the question, what is your political philosophy?", he wrote. What he had instead was a devotion to "moderation" and a strong resistance to committing himself to any but the vaguest categories: "I am a free man, an American, a United States Senator, and a Democrat, in that order. I am also a liberal, a conservative, a Texan, a taxpayer, a rancher, a businessman, a consumer, a parent, a voter"—and "At the heart of my own beliefs is a rebellion against this very process of classifying, labeling, and filing Americans under headings." If classifying were to be done, he wanted to do it to others, as in his automatic mental card file of Senatorial predilections. For himself, he preferred to stay loose, to be one of the jugglers instead of one of the balls. Thrust into an office where that did not work, he experienced a profound disorientation and no answer to his anguished question, "What do they want? What *really* do they want?"

JOHNSON'S CHARACTER

If Lyndon Johnson's world view lacks clear definition, his Presidential character stands out like a sore thumb. He is a prime example of the active-negative type. His fantastic pace of action in the Presidency was obvious. He was also characteristically discouraged much of the time. On the wall of his Senate office he hung this quotation from Edmund Burke:

> Those who would carry on great public schemes must be proof against the worst fatiguing delays, the most mortifying disappointments, the most shocking insults, and worst of all, the presumptuous judgment of the ignorant upon their designs.[49]

Johnson in the midst of struggle—developing a secret arrangement or pumping hands in a crowd—could feel a burst of elation, but not for long. Success in gaining power gave him no pause; he felt compelled to go on. "Often at this desk I don't do what I really want to do. I do what I have to do," he said, and trying to find out what that was gave him his major frustration, turned him into "the loneliest" and "the most denounced man in the world." He would wonder aloud just what it was people liked about Jack Kennedy, and "Why don't people like me?" (To which Dean Acheson replied, "Because, Mr. President, you are not a very likable man.") He felt a stranger among his inherited advisors, extraordinarily sensitive to slurs by all the "overbred smart alecks who live in Georgetown and think in Harvard." And he wondered continually about his adequacy to be what he so desperately wanted to be, a Great President.

"Every job I've had is bigger than I am," he said, "and I have to work twice as hard as the next man to do it." Unlike some he could think of, Johnson could say "I haven't had anything given to me. Whatever I have and whatever I hope to get will be because of whatever energy and talents I have." It was all up to him. And what was he? Interspersed among his answers, which ranged from the grandiose to the pathetic, Johnson conveyed a sense of being forced, of an inner impulse he could do little to resist. "I was born the way I am. I can't do anything about it." And he was constantly questioning his own adequacy for the task. To him the Presidency was the most powerful office in the world and he was "the only President you've got," but he could not leave it at that. Sometimes he would lower his sights: "For a Johnson City boy, I've gone about as far as I can go and done a pretty good job." At other times he would try to dismiss the evaluation of others: "I don't need the salary and I don't need the job. . . . I don't particularly give a damn what they think about it." Then he could declare his independence of any need for affection: "I have to laugh at how some of these immature kids now say that I want everybody to love me. I never had everybody love me." Or for sympathy: "Don't feel sorry for me. I'm treated better than any of you." Or for respect: "We're not royal highnesses. I don't want to be king. I just want to see people. . . . All day long they call me Mr. President. I wish they'd just call me Lyndon sometimes." Or for fear: "Power? The only power I've got is nuclear—and I can't use that." But nothing he said could get him off the hook; again and again he turned back to the question:

> I know I've got a heart big enough to be President. I know I've got guts enough to be President. But I wonder whether I've got intelligence and ability enough to be President—I wonder if any man does?[50]

President Johnson's manipulative maneuvering, his penchant for secrecy, his lying, his avid interest in himself, his sense of being surrounded by hostile forces, and his immense anger all indicate, I think, a profound insecurity—not so much about his "intelligence and ability" (he knew he had those), but precisely about his "heart" and "guts." His heart symbolizes his conscience-bound need to be loving and generous, to "do unto others as you would have others do unto you." His gut symbolizes toughness, the press for power, the need to do it to the other guy before he can do it to you. Caught between those forces, Johnson thrashed about for some ground in the middle, loosing the tremendous tension he felt in a flood of talk.

Activity provided him with distraction; he found the Presidency "a hell of a whirl" with himself at the center, cool in crisis: "When the bullets start whizzing around my head, that's when I'm calmest." Especially when he was in the direst straits, those times when he felt "like a jackrabbit hunkered up in a storm," Johnson could—had to—keep his mind on the threatening situation out there, away from the nagging doubts inside. Then he could take action—"Let's go, let's go"—and pretend to himself that he would really rather be lying quietly under a tree.

In the end, Vietnam trapped him. Projecting his inner struggle onto the environment, he sought by resigning to escape from the intolerable tension. But before he reached that solution, hundreds of thousands were dead.

THE ACTIVE-NEGATIVE CHARACTER

I want to draw together now a picture of the main character themes emerging from these three cases. My thesis is that in each case highly significant policy failures were rooted in the President's character. Expressing itself through and supported by his style and world view, that character pressed him to persevere rigidly in a disastrous policy. Before undertaking to explore how that way of behaving in the Presidency might have been identified before the man became President, the behavior pattern itself needs to be stated explicitly, not in its individual detail, but in terms of the characteristic commonalities. We cannot go back and elect someone other than Wilson, Hoover, and Johnson to play out the stories in a different way. But if we can see in their cases the themes they *shared,* we will have taken a large step toward identifying the clues to watch for in future cases.

By definition, the active-negative character, compared to the characters of other Presidents, displays a high expenditure of energy on political tasks and a continual, recurrent, negative emotional reaction to that work. The category is delineated by these two variables, both of which are relatively accessible to even the casual observer. In the Wilson, Hoover, and Johnson biographies there is virtually no disagreement on these characterizations. What makes these simple dimensions interesting beyond mere description is their power in highlighting a whole range of personality qualities which emerge from the case studies and which explain *why* we find in the Presidency men who strive so mightily and enjoy it so little.

The active-negative type is, in the first place, much taken up with *self-concern.* His attention keeps returning to himself, his problems, how he is doing, as if he were forever watching himself. The character of that attention is primarily *evaluative with respect to power.* Am I winning or losing, gaining or falling behind? It is, secondarily, *evaluative with respect to virtue.* In the struggle, am I being a good person or a bad person?

The active-negative's perfectionistic conscience lends to his feelings about himself an *all-or-nothing quality.* He wavers between grandiosity and despair. Similarly there is little incorporation of a sense of the self as developing in time, progressively growing through experience; rather, there is a *now-or-never quality.* Similarly, the perfectionism imposes unclear guidelines for achievement; one is supposed to be good at everything all the time. Therefore there is a *resistance to self-definition,* a lack of clarity in the person's commitment to shared loyalties and to particular sequences of achievement building toward special goals.

The demands of conscience also impose a felt necessity for the *denial of self-gratification.* The active-negative not only behaves so as to suffer in fact—by working to exhaustion, for example—but also insists on explaining his behavior, to himself and to others, as self-sacrificing rather than self-rewarding.

The power emphasis is reflected in the active-negative's concern with *controlling his aggression.* He will tend to view himself as restrained, holding back, reining in his anger, patient despite much provocation, and so on. By building up a view of his anger as monumental, he strives for approval from conscience as a reward for the effort and suffering it costs him to hold it in.

These two themes—the denial of self-gratification and the struggle to control aggressive impulses—come together in the active-negative's perennial *temptation to fight or quit.* Images of breaking out, attacking, releasing free anger compete with fantasies of abandoning effort for quiet, relaxation, ease—even death. These are experienced as temptations in a double sense: one might get at others by striking at them or by abandoning them, and one might give in to self-gratification by removing the falling barriers to aggression or by wallowing in weakness. These tempting fantasies help the person bolster his feelings of strength and virtue as he resists them.

The active-negative lives in a *dangerous world*—a world not only threatening in definite ways but also highly uncertain, a world one can cope with only by maintaining a tense, wary readiness for danger. The prime threat is other people; he tends to *divide humanity into the weak and the grasping*, although he may also, with no feeling of inconsistency, idealize "the people" in a romantic way. In struggling to understand social causality, he restricts the explanations to *conspiracy or chaos*, fluctuating between images of tight, secret control and images of utter disorder. He strives to resolve decisional conflicts by *invoking abstract principles* in order to render manageable a too complex reality.

The active-negative's political *style is persistent and emphatic*. That is, he shows a stylistic specialization more markedly than other Presidents do (as in Wilson's oratory, Hoover's homework, Johnson's interpersonal relations), and he tends to inflexibility in shifting his stylistic repertoire. Furthermore, he is likely to *extend his primary stylistic emphasis into his total style*, to treat all occasions as if they were amenable to mastery by means of his main political habit pattern.

While the active-negative's character is taken up with his own performance, he continually seeks confirmation of his self-esteem from other people; in this sense he is highly *dependent upon positive response from the environment*. He feels confirmed in his expectations by vigorous opposition, but is disconcerted by and strongly threatened by ridicule, contempt, or personal denigration. His tendency over time is to *focus anger on a personal enemy*, usually an opponent who treats him, he feels, with condescension.

But the most pervasive feeling in the active-negative's makeup is *"I must."* He is a man under orders, required to concentrate, to produce, to follow out his destiny as he sees it. At any given moment, he feels bound by what he has already undertaken, already promised, already committed. The central conflict between virtuousness and power-seeking is never resolved, but is massively denied in the feeling that whatever one does, one has no choice. The tragic sacrifice in such a personality is the sacrifice of will. Not only others, but the man himself is reduced to an instrument. He finds it hard even to see alternatives to the course he "must" follow, much less to change that course when it proves unproductive.

From the inside, then, the active-negative type generates tremendous energies for political domination. From the outside, he seems at first extraordinarily capable and then extraordinarily rigid, becoming more and more closed to experience, including the advice of his ardent allies. Over time, he has a powerfully disillusioning effect, because so much was expected from him when he started but these expectations have been disappointed continually as the man stubbornly adheres to his course and waxes so moralistic in its defense.

This temporal process as seen from the outside is matched, I think, by a regular development in the active-negative's own character. He sees himself as having begun with a high purpose, but as being continually forced to compromise in order to achieve the end state he vaguely envisions. Battered from all sides with demands that he yield yard after yard of his territory, that he conform to ignorant and selfish demands, he begins to feel his integrity slipping away from him. In doubt about his personal strength, he experiences compromise as a steady diminution of "the most powerful man in the world" to a mere clerk, ordered about by his supposed subordinates. At the same time, he is being harrassed by critics who, unaware of the problems he faces, attribute his actions to low motives, adding insult to injury. At long last, after enduring all this for longer than any mortal should, he rebels and stands his ground. Masking his decision in whatever rhetoric is necessary, he rides the tiger to the end.

Thus in the cases of Wilson, Hoover, and Johnson, we do not have three scattered collections of attributes but a common pattern, a set of dynamically connected behavioral and psychological reactions to recurrent situations. They shared a common role—the Presidency—but they also shared an orientation toward that role. That orientation, hard to understand in terms of the realities they faced or even in terms of their own "principles," is clarified when we see how it served their inner needs. At the core of their peculiar way of approaching the Presidency was an image of the self. In each case, self-esteem was only tentatively established, continually threatened by doubt. The thrust behind their heroic efforts was the search for confirmation that they really were both strong and good. Each found within the loose boundaries of the Presidency vast opportunities to play out the drama in his own special fashion. Each failed, but in the failing found proofs that he had been right all along in seeing the world as he saw it and in acting as he had to act.

Each discovered in political life a place to make up for what had happened to him and to give scope to esteem-boosting practices he had learned long ago.

4

The Origins of Presidential Compulsion

The solution to predicting a President's character, world view, and style—before he is President—is in knowing where to look. Most commentators focus on the most recent period, but this is usually the most difficult period to untangle. How many influential observers saw in the extraordinary achievement of Woodrow Wilson as Governor of New Jersey, of Hoover as Secretary of Commerce, and of Lyndon Johnson as Vice-President or even as master of compromise in the Senate, those qualities which would, in the end, impel them to Presidential rigidity? It is not that the qualities were not there, but that they were obscured. The main reason for the obscurity is, I think, that the man on the way to the Presidency (deliberately or not) operates in a context of upward political mobility—he is on the make. When he reaches the apex of political status and power, however, he moves into an entirely different context: he has it made, or, at least, he has made it. It is the difference between climbing a mountain and standing on the top, between the race and the prize. Yet it is different from all those things, because the President stands at the very top of the heap. On the way there, men trying to cope with milieux of mobility are likely to call upon wider ranges of their political repertoires, to respond more fully to external pressures and demands, to conform more closely to the expectations of those around them. The preliminary roles are all much more restrictive than the Presidency is, much more set by institutional requirements. One need only consider the legislative performance of Senators who became Presidents to see how contradictory and misleading the signs can be.

I have argued that clearer clues are visible in the earlier life history; character is discernible in childhood, world view in adolescence, and style in the period of first independent political success. The last of these is most important for our purposes, in part because the evidence of style is usually better there than for even earlier times, and in part because style draws together in a more or less integrated package the earlier themes, making the total picture easier to see.

How then might it have been possible to discern in the early histories of these three Presidents those inner forces, structures of belief, and habits of performance that would, one day, shape their Presidencies?

For the active-negative Presidents, the central hypothesis is this: having experienced severe deprivations of self-esteem in childhood, the person develops a deep attachment to *achievement* as a way to wring from his environment a sense that he is worthy; progressively, this driving force is translated into a search for independent *power* over others, pursued with intense dedication, and justified idealistically. Whatever style brings success in domination is adopted and rigorously adhered to; but success does not produce joy—the person is frequently depressed—and therefore ever more striving is required. The shape of this character-based pattern is clear by the completion of the man's first independent political success.

Find these intense young men struggling to prove their power and virtue, working much and laughing little, and you will have found your future Wilsons, Hoovers, and Johnsons.

WILSON FINDS HIS VOICE

"How blessed I am in my home!", Wilson once wrote in his diary when he was a student at Princeton. There was much for him to be thankful for. He appeared on this earth a healthy, fat baby, with two older sisters, and a father and mother who could hardly have been more devoted to their first son. As long as they lived, his parents poured love and concern over Woodrow Wilson. And to the end of his days he never faltered in repaying their affection. In the Wilson family circle there was a good deal of laughter, games of tag and billiards between father and son, reading aloud, imitations—as in Wilson's aping of "the drunkard," an act he performed long after he was fully grown. "Are you listening to Woodrow?", his father once asked a friend as his son was speaking. "Isn't he brilliant?"

Dr. Joseph Ruggles Wilson ruled over a household well respected in the community. He was a Presbyterian minister with a large congregation, then Stated Clerk of the Southern Presbyterian church, then Professor of Theology. The family was comfortably off: Woodrow's mother inherited some money and Dr. Wilson was receiving, at the time Woodrow went to college, some $4,000 a year, a substantial income when eggs were fifteen cents a dozen. Living through the Civil War in Augusta, Georgia, the family saw much pain and hardship but experienced no real privation themselves. The Wilson home gave Woodrow a haven from the world and a tradition of excellence. He was to draw on that capital all his life.

Yet within the close family circle there were strains and demand which were to contribute heavily to Woodrow's sense of inadequacy and failure. Despite his healthy start, he was a frail, freckled, bespectacled child, not up to the rougher forms of play. Later he would have to drop out of college for fifteen months and at another time out of law school entirely when his health failed him; his mother's letters are full of concern that he not catch cold or get too tired or eat poorly. His appearance contrasted markedly with that of "my incomparable father." Dr. Wilson was a big man and extraordinarily handsome, tall, dignified, a commanding presence at home as in the pulpit. "Tommy," as Thomas Woodrow Wilson was called then, was "a delicate, silent child, shy amid a group of noisy cousins." His head was awkwardly large in back. One finger was bent out of shape. "If I had my father's face and figure," Tommy once said, "it wouldn't make any difference what I said." At Princeton he described himself as someone "You could easily distinguish . . . in a crowd by his long nose, open mouth, and consequential manner." And as a law student he asked himself, "How can a man with a weak body ever arrive anywhere?"

But far more to the point was Tommy's apparent intellectual weakness. Both the Wilsons and the Woodrows, Tommy's mother's family, were people of words. His grandfather Wilson was an editor, banker, legislator, and judge. Grandfather Woodrow held a doctorate *summa cum laude* from Heidelberg and became an editor, printer, minister, professor of theology, and college president. Tommy's father had graduated first in his class from college; to his close study of the Bible he added wide reading and a passion for clear expression. The Wilson home was a place of much talk—disciplined talk. One was expected to know what he was talking about, but even more important, to speak precisely. Files of reference books, such as *Inquire Within, or Over Thirty-Seven Hundred Facts Worth Knowing*, would be brought to the dinner table to buttress arguments. Then after dinner, Father would read aloud in his booming voice from the novels of Scott and Dickens. And as long as Tommy was home he heard Dr. Wilson preach every Sunday. In short, the boy was surrounded by the uplifting religious intellectualism that had been the family's tradition.

Tommy had a hard time with all this. He did not learn his written alphabet until he was nine years old, and he was eleven before he could read well. He had trouble learning his catechism. Kept out of school until he was almost twelve, Tommy performed poorly in class; his marks were well below average. Once his grandfather Woodrow lost patience with him and said that if he lacked the ambition to be a scholar he might at least wish to be a gentleman. Much later, his daughter recalled that he found addition problematical and stumbled over the multiplication table. Tommy, who would one day see his books translated into dozens of foreign languages, was a "retarded" child.

His father undertook to fix that. His method was severe. On Sunday afternoons he lectured Tommy on history, literature, science, and theology. On Mondays he took his son on trips to see farms and mills and factories. Of both vicarious and direct experiences, he would ask Tommy,

> "Do you thoroughly understand that?" "Oh, yes," the boy would say. "Very well then, write it out and bring it to me so I can see that you do." Tommy would take great pains to produce a composition that would pass muster. Timorously, he would submit his effort to his father. If the Doctor came upon anything that seemed in the slightest degree ambiguous, he would demand what exactly was meant. Tommy would explain. "Well, you did not say it," Dr. Wilson would snap, "so suppose you try again and see if you can say what you mean this time, and if not we'll have another talk and a third go at it."[1]

Sometimes it took four or five tries before Tommy could get by. If he used a word incorrectly in conversation he was sent to look it up in the dictionary—then, not later.

"His idea was," Dr. Wilson's granddaughter wrote, "that if a lad was of fine tempered steel, the more he was beaten the better he was."

Joseph Ruggles Wilson was well respected for his erudition and eloquent preaching, but he was also known for caustic wit at the expense of other people. "Dr. Wilson had never been one to overrate the intelligence of his parishioners or to undervalue his own worth." He was furious when his congregation voted to hire a pastor to supplement his preaching with a more personal touch in visiting and counseling—so furious that he resigned. At his next post he was again highly regarded as a preacher, but after eight years there he wrote his son that "My work here in Wilmington seems to be done, and I think I see evidences amongst the people that some of them think so, too. Yet I never preached so well. . . . The fault they find with me is as to visiting. They want a gad-about gossip."

At home, Tommy struggled to please. Dr. Wilson rode him mercilessly:

> Uncle Joseph [recalled Tommy's cousin] was a cruel tease, with a caustic wit and a sharp tongue, and I remember hearing my own family tell indignantly of how Cousin Woodrow suffered under his teasing. He was proud of WW, especially after his son began to show how unusual he was, but only a man as sweet as Cousin Woodrow could have forgotten the severity of his criticism to the value of which he so often paid tribute, in after life.[2]

Once when the clan gathered for a wedding breakfast, and Tommy was late, Dr. Wilson explained that the lad had been too excited over finding a new hair in his mustache to remember promptness. "A painful flush . . . came over the boy's face."

Tommy never found any direct way to fight back. Once he ran away to the circus. On the way home he padded his seat with cotton.

Much of his time until he was ten was spent with girls, and thereafter, when play with boys got too rough Tommy would retreat home again, where his quiet, gentle mother would comfort him. Janet Woodrow Wilson—intensely religious, proud of her family, a good musician—was Tommy's constant guardian long after he left home. Later he remembered "how I clung to her (a laughed-at 'mama's boy') till I was a great big fellow. . . . But love of the best womanhood came to me and entered my heart through those apron-strings." But she too contributed to Tommy's isolation: she had few friends outside the family and people thought her "stand-offish." Like her husband, she could get angry at anyone who attacked a family member, as when "ignorant and malicious men" disagreed with her brother and drove her to "impotent anger." But to Tommy she gave incessant love, continual care:

> My darling Boy,
>   I am so anxious about that cold of yours. How did you take it? Surely you have not laid aside your winter clothing? Another danger is in sitting without fire on these cold nights. . . .[3]

As with his father, Tommy gave his mother his complete, consistent affection.

As Tommy made his way out from the Wilson family nest, he had a difficult time of it. His brother, named Joseph for his father, was born when he was nine. Part of the difficulty was that the family moved to a new town twice in his teenage years, so he had to establish new friendships, but he was also remembered as "not like the other boys. He had a way of going off by himself" and as "an old young man." Later at Princeton he wrote one friend that "I, perhaps, am colder and more reserved than most of those who are fortunate enough to have been born in our beloved South," and to another he confessed, "When I am with anyone in whom I am especially and sincerely interested, the hardest subject for me to broach is just that which is nearest my heart. An unfortunate disposition indeed! I hope to overcome it in time!" He wrote in his diary that on one occasion he "met a good many friends who *expressed* themselves glad to see me." His mother tried to reassure him:

> You seem depressed—but that is because you are not well. You need not imagine that you are not a favorite. *Everybody* here likes and admires you. I could not begin to tell you the kind and flattering things that are said about you, by everybody that knows you. Yes, you have no lack of friends in Wilmington—of the warmest sort. . . . Why my darling, nobody could *help* loving you, if they were to try![4]

And she would urge him to "lay aside all *timidity*—and make the most of all your powers, my darling."

Tommy Wilson was no friendless freak. With his family, including his young cousins, he could be warm and playful, as he could be through life with those whose affection he felt he could trust absolutely. With regard to "his need of personal love," a discerning friend once wrote: "A person, to obtain his intimacy, had to say very definitely, 'I like you,' or 'I love you.' After that, if you were sincere, your life became his personal and unfailing concern." In his later relationships with Colonel House and especially with his woman correspondents, he developed strong affectionate ties. But he remained shy, awkward, and stilted with strangers and distant with opponents.

Once into a game, Tommy Wilson often came to dominate the play. His cousin and playmate remembered that "Tommy soon became our leader, never aggressive or noisy, but with quiet determination and firmness, he suggested and carried out some historic event. There was no discussion, he led, we followed, without question as to his ability to put through the great adventure."

"Cousin Mary," Wilson once said, "it is possible to control your thoughts, you know." Tommy grew up in a home where thought control was the order of the day. At least twice his mother wrote him the same message: "Tommy dear don't talk about knocking anybody down—no matter what they say—or, rather, don't *think* of doing such a thing." His father urged him to avoid introspection: "In short, dearest boy, do not allow yourself to dwell upon *yourself*—concentrate your thoughts upon *thoughts* and *things* and *events*. Self-consciousness is a torment: was mine at your age; has, often since then, been such. Go out from your own personality." In an essay he wrote at nineteen, Tommy warned of the need to "Overcome evil desires, those powerful and ever present enemies, by constant watchfulness and with the strong weapon of prayer, and by cultivating those heavenly desires which are sure to root out the evil one. . . . In every minor thing watch yourself and let no fiery dart enter your soul. One who thus faithfully does his duty and purifies himself in the smallest things has little to fear from the foe. . . ." As a man of fifty, Wilson could recall the cost of disciplining his mind:

> I suppose that nothing is more painful in the recollections of some of us than the efforts that were made to make us like grown-up people. The delightful follies that we had to eschew, the delicious nonsense that we had to disbelieve, the number of odious prudences that we had to learn, the knowledge that though the truth was less interesting than fiction, it was more important than fiction— the fact that what people told you could not always be relied on, and that it must be tested by the most uninteresting tests.[5]

What Tommy seems to have learned was to keep a constant check on himself, to resist temptations to act or think aggressively or selfishly, and to accomplish this systematic renunciation by controlling his attention—especially by directing it away from himself, onto "thoughts and things and events" rather than onto Tommy Wilson.

All of this left a lot of emotional energy in search of someplace to go. Later he would write a friend that "It isn't pleasant or convenient to have strong passions . . . I have the uncomfortable feeling that I am carrying a volcano about with me. My salvation is in being loved." Tommy found a way to earn love and at the same time to focus the force of those strong passions: he developed a sense of himself as someone required to engage in a titanic struggle which he could win only by the most intense effort. "I *must* be true to myself," he wrote much later, and "I must push on: to linger would be fatal." By the time he reached Princeton, he was filling his diary with regrets that he did not work hard enough and he came to "the conclusion that my friends have no doubt come to long ago and that is that my mind is a very ordinary one indeed. I am nothing as far as intellect goes. But I can plod and work." Plodding and working meant concentration, self-control: "The great mistake that I made," Tommy wrote in the summer after his first year of college, "was that I had to commence over again every time because I did not stick to what I learned." In his Princeton "Index Rerum," a commonplace book, he wrote, under the heading "Bad Habits, How to break one'self [sic] of": "Keep busy; idleness is the strength of bad habits. Do not give up the struggle when you have broken your resolution once, twice, ten times, a thousand times. That only shows how much need there is for you to strive." When he considered how "hopeless the task" of writing as well as the great authors he read, he concluded, "But one can but *try*. 'Genius is divine *perseverance*.' Genius I cannot claim nor even extra brightness but perseverance *all* can have." And in an essay on "The Ideal Statesman," Wilson at Princeton spelled out the theme:

> We can weigh the evidence of History and it is a fact of History which cannot be too often repeated that no man, whatever may have been his natural endowments of mind, has ever accomplished anything worthy of note except by untiring work and hard, though silent and, perhaps, unseen *work* . . . . [I]t is, therefore, of the greatest importance that we should discipline our minds so thoroughly that they can at once seize upon the most vital point of any subject and be so constantly on the alert that they shall always be ready to grapple thought with sinews hardened by exercise. Genius without discipline is a ship without rudder or sails—a mere inert mass. . . . And let me again remind you that it is only by working with an energy which is almost superhuman and which looks to uninterested spectators like insanity that we can accomplish anything worth the achievement. Work is the keystone of a perfect life. Work and trust in God.[6]

Thus Tommy joined the fight to control himself and the fight to achieve remarkable things through tense, determined effort. The fight was hard, but had a grim reward of its own. Much later, when Wilson was writing what he wanted to be "*the* American history of our time," he lamented, "But, oh it goes hard! . . . I pray that it may go easier or it will kill me. And yet it would be a most pleasant death. The ardour of the struggle is inspiriting. There is pleasure in the very pain, as when one bites on an aching tooth."

In Tommy's mind from an early age was an image of himself as weak-minded but, potentially at least, strong-willed. The answer was work—work to gain success, work to distract himself from dangerous thoughts, work to confirm his worthiness, and work to turn his life outward. But to provide relief for the volcanic passions inside him without violating the stern commands of conscience, work required another quality: it must be hard. He must suffer with it.

Meanwhile, Tommy's mind was moving toward a view of the world compatible with his inner needs. This world view took shape first in play—pretending with his little cousins that a bush was a castle where wicked Turks held Christian maidens to be rescued at all cost, or that Tommy as Peter the Hermit led the way to rescue the Holy Sepulchre. "Always our play was for succor," one cousin recalled, "never for revenge or ambition." Then in his early teens, Tommy began elaborating his own imaginary world, playing out in his mind adventures impossible in reality. He was the hero of the novels he read, Cooper, Marryat, Scott. But his main dream was of the sea. He was "Commander-in-Chief—Vice-Admiral Lord Thomas W. Wilson, Duke of Eagleton, vice-admiral of the red" in long, detailed memoranda which he wrote out. He described in minute detail the weight, dimensions, gunnery, rigging, shape, and speed of his mighty fleet, "Her Britannic Majesty's Squadron 'Flying Squadron,'" to which Tommy, as commander, issued the orders. For example, at seventeen Tommy described his ship *Renown:* "This graceful and beautiful vessel, now employed, as indeed she has been ever since she was built, as the flagship of Lord Wilson, Duke of Arlington, Commander-in-chief of H.M. Flying Squadron, is one of the most curious and yet one of the most beautiful in the Royal Navy. She is an excellent type of the new class of vessels that is now being introduced into the Navy and particularly worthy of notice as the fastest man-of-war ever built. Her capacity is about 4,500 tons and her original dimensions . . ."—and so on, for page after page of muzzle-loaders, bowsprits, and bower chains, and ending, "The Renown is, beyond a doubt, the fastest vessel in the Royal Navy, and it is almost certain the fastest vessel in the world. . . . Since she was built her planner and commander, Lord Wilson, has realized all his hopes as regards her performance &c.&c.&c."

Later in that seventeenth summer, Lord Wilson imagined into existence "The Royal United Kingdom Yacht Club," with thirty vessels, led by himself ("Nationality: English") as Commodore, Duke of Carlton, Admiral of the white. In what is probably the first of Wilson's many constitutions, the Commodore prescribed rules and regulations, including these:

> The Commodore shall have the same authority over the fleet of this Club as that possessed by Admirals over the fleets of the Royal Navy which they command. He shall preside over all the meetings of the Club, and no bill or resolution of any kind can pass into a law of the Club without his approval and signature. His veto makes a bill null and void, even if adopted unanimously by the Members.[7]

This was no momentary preoccupation of Wilson's; the longest and most detailed of the thirty handwritten items Arthur Link classified under "Wilson's Imaginary World" concerned his fantasies of sea command. All the mythical organizations were British, except for one naval exploit in search of pirates in which Tommy was Admiral of the United States Navy. Those interpreters confident in the explanation of symbols in fantasy might make something of this story, though it is reported only at second hand by William Bayard Hale. The government and people had been

> terrified by the mysterious disappearance of ships. . . . Vessels would set out with the precious freight, never to be heard from again, swallowed up in the bosom of an ocean on which no known war raged, no known storms swept. Admiral Wilson was ordered to investigate with his fleet. After an eventful cruise they overtook, one night, a piratical looking craft with black hull and rakish rig.

> Again and again the chase eluded the Admiral. Finally the pursuit led the fleet to the neighborhood of an island unchartered and hitherto unknown. Circumnavigation seemed to prove it bare and uninhabited, with no visible harbor. There was, however, a narrow inlet which seemed to end at an abrupt wall of rock of few fathoms inland. Something, however, finally led the Admiral to send a boat into this inlet—and it was discovered that it was the cunningly contrived entrance to a spacious bay, the island being really a sort of atoll. Here lay the ships of the outlawed enemy and the dismantled hulls of many of their victims. And it may be believed that the brave American tars, under the leadership of the redoubtable Admiral, played a truly heroic part in the destruction of the pirates and the succor of such of their victims as survived.[8]

Tommy's escape was to a world he could command and control. He built the ships in his mind, down to the last plank and mast, and he ruled over his subcommanders uncompromisingly, with the power to veto even their unanimous proposals.

Tommy's admiration for things English was not limited to ships and naval titles. At sixteen he kept a picture of his hero on the wall; as he said to his cousin, "That is Gladstone, the greatest statesman that ever lived. I intend to be a statesman, too." At nineteen he wrote in his diary on the fourth of July:

> The one hundredth anniversary of American independence. One hundred years ago America conquered England in an unequal struggle and this year she glories over it. How much happier she would be now if she had England's form of government instead of the miserable delusion of a republic. A republic too founded upon the notion of abstract liberty! I venture to say that this country will never celebrate another centennial as a republic. The English form of government is the only true one.[9]

Even in his sea-faring fantasies we can see connections with reality. Tommy's mother was born in England; some neighbors disliked her for her English ways. At least one report has her doing "her best to discourage" her boys from playing Admiral. Her own sea-going had been traumatic. She was five years old when she sailed with her family for America, only to be driven back to Ireland by a storm, the rigors of which led to her mother's death a few weeks later, leaving her father to care for eight children. So there may have been some rebelliousness in Tommy's dreams, as also in the meetings he held in the hayloft under a picture in red of His Satanic Majesty. Tommy often went off alone to the docks; once he was hurt in a fall there. And he talked of running away to sea.

About this time Tommy also undertook a project which was to consume a great deal of hard, detailed labor for several years: the learning of shorthand, or "phonography." At fifteen he was enthralled by an article on the subject in *Fran Leslie's Boys' and Girls' Weekly*, at sixteen he wrote off for a handbook on phonography, and during his stay at home after the year at Davidson he practiced religiously—copying out long passages in shorthand into notebooks. On the cover of one he wrote, "To save time is to lengthen life." He learned the "Corresponding style" and the "Reporting style" by copying on a long series of articles on "Geology," another series of forty-six articles on shorthand, and some thirty-two pages of a work *On the Study of Words,* among many other things. The work was tedious, detailed, challenging—*effortful*. And it was a form of expertise in words. Tommy's father encouraged him. The skill stayed with him and served him well as a student, teacher, and speechwriter throughout his life.

During these same years, Tommy's religious visions were developing. For him—for his family—religion was not a topic for debate, not a set of questions, but a set of answers. "So far as religion is concerned," he once wrote, "argument is adjourned." He prayed daily on his knees and sometimes he would weep in church when the hymns were especially moving. Christianity was a faith to be felt and asserted with utmost vigor in word and deed. But when at seventeen Tommy raised a philosophical question, his father wrote him, "My son, don't you worry about these doctrinal problems. Ask yourself this question: Do I love and want to serve the Lord Jesus Christ? If you can answer that in the affirmative, you need not worry." Later, remembering these adolescent days, Wilson confided in his diary, "I used to wonder vaguely why I did not have the same deep-reaching spiritual difficulties that I read of other young men having. I *saw* the intellectual difficulties, but I was not *troubled* by them; they seemed to have no connection with my faith in the essentials of the religion I have been taught." Just as he schooled himself not to think too curiously about his own feelings, Tommy learned to push away questions about his beliefs.

Much of the imagery in Tommy's religious belief stressed three themes: God judges man by standards of perfection, to which man must aspire; life is a constant struggle of good against evil; there is no room for compromise in that struggle.

In May 1874, Tommy wrote a note to himself, saying, "I am now in my seventeenth year and it is sad, when looking over my past life, to see how few of those seventeen years I have spent in the fear of God, and how much in the service of the Devil. . . . *If God will give me the grace I will try to serve Him from this time on, and will endeavor to attain nearer and nearer to perfection.*" That year he formally joined his father's church. It is not possible to tell just when he copied this quotation into his "Index Rerum," but it fits his thoughts at this period: "Leave consequences to God, but do right. Be genuine, real, sincere, true, by right, Godlike. The world's maxim is, trim your sails, and you let circumstances judge, but if you would do any good in your generation you must be made of sterner stuff, and help mold times rather than be made by them. Like the anvil, endure all blows, until the hammers break themselves." In an essay entitled "Christ's Army," published in the Wilmington *North Carolina Presbyterian* when Wilson was nineteen, he echoed the same sentiment:

> Will any one hesitate as to the part he shall take in this conflict? Will any one dare to enlist under the banners of the Prince of Lies, under whose dark folds he only marches to the darkness of hell? For there is no middle course, no neutrality. Each and every one must enlist either with the followers of Christ or those of Satan.[10]

And then Tommy spelled out his version of the doctrine of election:

How much more glorious to fight for the divine Prince of Peace, under whose glorious standards, whose shining folds are inscribed with *Love to God,* he will advance to sure victory and an everlasting reward! All professing Christians are, no doubt, more or less enthused by such thoughts as these, and hope that they can feel themselves soldiers in Christ's great army; but they do not *know* that they are such. Why should they not know? If they would be assured of the fact that their names are in the great Roll Book, let them fight for Christ. Ah! but how do this? As you would fight for any other cause. You know your enemies. They are evil thoughts, evil desires, evil associations. . . . One who thus faithfully does his duty and purifies himself in the smallest things has little to fear from the foe, and if he withal leads others by his example and precept to do likewise, and fears not to warn the enemies of the Cross to turn from the error of their ways, he may rest assured that his name is enrolled among the soldiers of the Cross.[11]

Wilson never let these principles go, even when he could not adhere to them fully in action. One's life must be guided by "a standard set for us in the heavens . . . the fixed and eternal standard by which we judge ourselves." The fight was life or death: "In the war with human passions and the war with human wrong, every man must do battle for the forces of light against the forces of ignorance and sin. . . . For a man who has lost the sense of struggle, life has ceased." There could be no deal with evil: "God save us from compromise." And no space for waverers: "He who is not with me is against me."

Before he was twenty, Thomas Woodrow Wilson had a faith too high to be questioned. The Christian life for him was a war, a perpetual striving upward toward perfection, that did not admit of degrees, ambiguities, falterings, or—worst of all—"compromise."

Tommy's first memory of the human war of politics was his hearing a shout, at the age of three: "Mr Lincoln's elected. There'll be war!" The boy found his father and asked, "What is war?" And he remembered seeing Robert E. Lee and thinking him a noble man. During the war, his father's church in Augusta, Georgia, was turned into an emergency hospital and Union prisoners were guarded in an elm grove outside. Tommy watched, "his thin pale face turned anxiously toward the groups in the grove." No one could tell "which touched him most, the stern, defiant men in their blue uniforms—prisoners in a hostile land, closely guarded night and day and marching around the enclosure while no friendly faces cheered them, or the wounded boys in gray, borne groaning into the dim recesses of the great Church." Tommy's home life was not substantially disturbed by the war, but his first perceptions of affairs of state were colored with violence and misery.

In September of his sixteenth year, he published yet another essay, on "A Christian Statesman," in which, at long last, he joined together his religious and political ideals. Like the steady Christian soldier, the statesman should never

allow party feeling to bias his opinions on any point which involves truth or falsehood, justice or injustice. He should search for truth with the full determination to find it, and in that search he should most earnestly seek aid from God, who will surely hold him responsible for the course he pursues.

When he is arrived at what he is convinced is the truth, he should uphold that truth, both by word and deed, irrespective of party. In no case should he allow expediency or policy to influence him in the least, if the support of the measures which seem expedient or politic involves a support of untruth or injustice. And let no statesman think that by silence or refraining from acting on any subject or question, he can escape responsibility. When he does not actively advocate truth, he advocates error. Those who are not for truth are against it. There is no neutrality.[12]

Four years later he reaffirmed that stand: "Tolerance is an admirable intellectual gift; but it is worth little in politics. Politics is a war of causes, a joust of principles."

In the fall of his nineteenth year—1876—Wilson was a convinced Democrat, an ardent Tilden man. When first reports showed a Tilden victory, Wilson went to a victory celebration and came home "tired out with shouting and excitement." Then when the balance of reports kept tipping between Hayes and Tilden, he was in a state of distraction for two days. But by then he was at Princeton and on his way to discovering his own political way—no longer vicariously, but directly, by experience. "A boy never gets over his boyhood," he wrote when he was a man. As Wilson found his way into action, he built on what had come before.

In the fall of 1873, sixteen-year-old Tommy Wilson entered Davidson College, a Presbyterian school near Charlotte, North Carolina. His schoolwork improved somewhat, but not much is known of his experience there. He joined a debating club, participated in some of their contests, was occasionally fined for talking in the meetings, and was thanked, in the minutes, for his assistance in copying out the Club constitution. None of his letters home survive, though he kept track of how regularly he wrote. Perhaps he had some homesickness; in November he copied out a long poem, eleven stanzas, called "The Prayer," in which the start and finish speak of Father:

> The way is dark, my Father! Cloud on cloud
> Is gathering thickly o'er my head, and loud
> The thunders roar above me. See, I stand
> Like one bewildered! Father, take my hand,
>   And through the gloom
>   Lead safely home
>   Thy child.

> The cross is heavy, child, yet there was One
> Who bore a heavier for thee—My Son
> My well beloved. For him bear thine, and stand
> With him at last, and from thy Father's hand,
>   Thy cross laid down,
>   Receive a crown,
>   My child.[13]

As late as June of his freshman year at Davidson, he intended to continue there, as shown by an "Important Memoranda" he noted to remind himself to ask his parents about going to business college "after leaving here in 1879. . . . *Beg hard.*"

But his health fell apart and he came home, where he stayed for the next fifteen months until he entered Princeton at eighteen. The Chairman of the Davidson faculty certified his success there and commended him "to those with whom he may, by any providence, be thrown."

Princeton then was a small rural college with eleven faculty members, more like a prep school than a university of today. Finding all the rooms in the dormitories taken, Tommy Wilson moved into a boarding house. He knew no one. A neighboring student got to know him and remembered Tommy as "quiet and retiring and for a time had few, if any, other friends." He was slow to strike up conversations, "a tall, slender youth of curious homeliness, detachment, and distinction." But he soon joined the American Whig Society, another debating club. He helped form the boarding house baseball team; sometimes he played twice a day. He did well above average in his studies, but failed to make the top twenty. From freshman obscurity he moved to the sophomore year and style: he was continually "coming to conclusions," such as "that very few people are bright" and that *Romeo and Juliet* was "not scholarly." By then he had a moderately wide circle of acquaintances, was an active participant in student hijinks, and was reading widely and intensively. In a short while he would be a leading figure at Princeton.

His path was through speaking. Wilson '79 was a talker; as he made friends they found him "companionable, friendly, genial, generally popular in the class," thanks in part to his fund of amusing stories, his good singing voice, and his performance as Marc Antony in a spoof called "The Sanguinary Tragedy of Julius Sneezer." But he also talked seriously, increasingly so, raising for discussion topics of the day so he could test his ideas against those of the other students.

Wilson excelled at a special type of oratory: extemporaneous debate. Though he threw himself into reading and reciting great orations, his record in formal contests, which stressed "an ornate, pompous, vapid style of declamation," was one of modest success only, and he regularly paid a fine rather than take part in essay competitions. He wanted to mean what he said and to bring others around to his point of view. "Oratory is persuasion," he wrote, "not the declamation of essays. The passion and force of oratory is spontaneous, not carefully elaborated." "What is the object of oratory?", he asked. "Its object is persuasion and conviction—the control of other minds by a strange personal influence and power." He found the example he wanted to follow in the British House of Commons, where speeches were meant to affect policy and were delivered with apparent casualness to persuade fellow members. An article describing Gladstone and others in that setting "so fired his imagination that he remembered all his life the exact place at the head of the south stairs in Chancellor Green Library where he read it." With a classmate, Tommy Wilson entered into a "solemn covenant" agreeing "that we would school our powers and passions for the work of establishing the principles we held in common; that we would acquire knowledge that we might have power; and that we would drill ourselves in all the arts of persuasion, but especially in oratory . . . that we might have facility in leading others into our ways of thinking and enlisting them in our purposes." That could hardly be accomplished in florid exercises from the podium. He much preferred to follow "the first of parliamentary orators," William Pitt, for whom, "passion is the pith of eloquence." On at least one occasion Wilson withdrew from a prize debate his father had urged him to enter, because the luck of the draw demanded that he argue against his convictions.

Lacking a forum, Wilson created one. In his sophomore year he organized the Liberal Debating Club, composed its constitution, and became its leading member. Questions for discussion were to be "political questions of the present century," proposed, in the main, by a Secretary of State, who would remain in office only so long as his opinions coincided with those of a majority of the members—that is, until he lost a vote of confidence. From then until Wilson graduated in 1879, the Club was a striking success and Wilson entered into its debates with vigor and pleasure. Once a discussion of the Civil War became so anti-Southern that he walked out and when he lost on his proposal that Congressmen serve for six years he growled to his diary: "I was overcome by opinion rather than by argument from other members present. That my arguments were sound I am convinced as I have put considerable thought on the subject." But even then, he continued, he had "an unusually pleasant time." At graduation a fellow member wrote him that he was "certain that if your talents are well directed your influence in America will not be less than Cobden's was in England."

By the fall of his junior year Wilson had enough of a reputation to fill in temporarily for the managing editor of the *Princetonian*, the campus newspaper. The following February he was elected to this post in his own right by a nearly unanimous vote of his class. Also in the fall of junior year, he was elected President of the Base Ball Association and Secretary of the Football Association, more for his leadership abilities than for athletic prowess. From then on Wilson was a man of influence, a power to be reckoned with at Princeton.

Most important was his editorship of the *Princetonian*. He ran the show. According to a fellow editor,

> He formulated policies; he was the chief. He would come around to me and say that he would like me to write on such and such. If he did not like what I wrote, it would not go in. The editors were not a cabinet and seldom met as a group. He was boss and deserved to be.[14]

Themes of power, control, leadership began to dominate the pages of the newspaper. Wilson preached against the disorder on campus, insisted on payment of subscriptions in advance, and urged that the editorial board itself—not the members of the class—select the editors. Despite criticism that he was trying to establish "the rule of an oligarchy," the latter proposal was voted in by a large majority.

He also similarly organized the sports teams. Repeatedly Wilson preached that baseball and football should be played to win, and that meant a disciplined team "controlled entirely by the will of the Captain and the President." He wrote that in baseball

> *Everything* depends upon the character of the captain and the president. With a good captain and an efficient president success is no longer a matter of doubt. . . . The president must above all things else, be a man of unbiased judgment, energy, determination, intelligence, moral courage, *conscience*.[15]

As for the football team, Wilson thundered, "The only thing worthy of serious reprehension in the playing of the team is the stubborn manner in which some of the men shut their ears to the command of the captain. Until they learn to obey they will never learn to play with effect." That year the team won all six of its games and was scored on only once.

Increasingly, Wilson's intellectual life revolved around the topic of leadership. He won a prize for his oration on "The Ideal Statesman," written in his sophomore year, in which he stressed the leader's impartiality, industry, and unselfishness: "That all the acts of a statesman should be performed without a view to self-interest needs no proof." In the fall of his junior year, Wilson wrote admiringly of Bismarck, whose harshness he was prepared to forgive:

> We can never justify the wilful disregard of justice or the wilful breaking of faith. But in a man who is conscious of great powers, whose mind is teeming with great political plans and dreaming of grand national triumphs, and who, withal, is hampered on every side by almost every circumstance of his surroundings we can at least understand an occasional breach of honor, and, in the presence of so many grand and peerless qualities and so many noble purposes, can perhaps forgive a want of integrity which so seldom exhibits itself.[16]

As Wilson's biographer Henry Wilkinson Bragdon points out, Wilson seldom went into any detail about the principles he was forever invoking, but he did discuss thoroughly his thoughts on political leadership. His essays on Bismarck and a later one on Chatham emphasized boldness, dedication to great purposes, and faith in oneself. "In neither essay," Bragdon notes, "is there any suggestion that a leader works *with* anyone."

Wilson's most important undergraduate publication was his essay on "Cabinet Government in the United States," which appeared in the *International Review* (Henry Cabot Lodge, editor) for August 1879. Leaning heavily on the works of Walter Bagehot and Gamaliel Bradford, Wilson saw the fragmentation and consequent "limping compromise" in the legislative branch as the major difficulty American government had to face. He recommended an adaptation of the English system of Cabinet responsibility to a legislature in which "full and free debates would serve to enlighten public opinion." The essential function of such a system would be to bring to the fore the most effective leaders:

> The two great national parties . . . are dying for want of unifying and vitalizing principle. Without leaders, they are also without policies, without aims. With leaders there must be followers, there must be parties. And with leaders whose leadership was earned in an open war of principle against principle, by the triumph of one opinion over all opposing opinions, parties must from the necessities of the case have definite policies. Platforms must then mean something. Broken promises then will end in broken power. . . . Eight words contain the

sum of the present degradation of our political parties: *No leaders, no principles; no principles, no parties.*[17]

Again and again, Wilson stresses success in parliamentary debate as the key to power in his reformed American system. As Bragdon concludes, "Wilson proposed such changes in the structure of the government of the United States as would provide an outlet for his special talents and a field where he might realize his high ambitions. He was in effect demanding that the entire American political system be radically altered so that he might realize his aspirations for public office and public service."

There is some evidence of a mild reaction against Wilson among Princeton undergraduates during his senior year. He was elected neither to class office nor to a place in the commencement exercises. His domination of the *Princetonian*, in organization and content, and his sharp remarks therein, made it necessary several times for him to make clear that he did not intend to give offense. At least one of his speech-giving performances in his senior year was ridiculed by the student audience. But by then he was on his way to higher platforms. He decided to train for the law in preparation for a political career. The boy who had once practiced writing first his father's signature, then his own, had at Princeton prepared his own calling cards to read THOMAS WOODROW WILSON SENATOR FROM VIRGINIA. In the fall after graduation, he left "Tommy" behind and became, at his mother's special request, "T. Woodrow Wilson."

By the end of his student days at Princeton, Woodrow Wilson had revealed his political personality. As a little boy he had felt weak, unattractive, and stupid, especially in comparison with his overwhelming father. In the family circle he was forever being told that he should do better, and he was forever failing to live up to the standards of perfection set for him. But the frustrations such a regimen inevitably engendered in Tommy could not be expressed against a father and mother who gave him so much love and protection; they were too good to fight. Therefore, with his parents' encouragement, he learned to repress anger, not to think about it, not to worry or dwell upon his feelings. Nor could he intellectualize conflict with his parents by dissenting from their strong Calvinistic beliefs: religious principles were beyond debate in the Wilson family, where faith meant the prohibition of doubt. Instead he turned against himself and developed that sense of fundamental inferiority which was to haunt and depress him throughout his life. Tommy's first decade stamped into his character the feeling that his troubles were his own fault.

Slowly he began to seek out ways to escape from the painful trap built by his upbringing. In fantasy he imagined himself a hero, a powerful dashing English Lord Commodore, magnificent orator, leader of Christ's Army. At play he dominated the action; in his imaginary world he always established himself as the man in charge. That accomplished, he focused his attention on precise detail—on exact descriptions of ships, on the loops and whirls of phonographic writing—which served to occupy a mind uncomfortable with introspection and also to enhance a sense of control over his mythical environment that he could not achieve in his real one. At the dinner table he could never seem to get his words right. Sitting in his own room, he dreamed of becoming a Gladstone.

It was of immense importance to Tommy's later life that he moved beyond fantasy to achievement, that he did not stay stuck in a passive dream world. Rather, he chose to try. If he lacked genius he would make up for that lack by perseverance, action, effort, *work*. Closing off his attention from concern with the personal origins of his endeavor or concern with the ultimate goals toward which his energies should be directed, Tommy confessed his lack of genius and his unquestioning faith, and concentrated on effort itself. He made of his life a constant struggle, not to figure out who he was and where he was going, but to get on with it. The key to achievement was tense, controlled, conscientious labor.

To satisfy his perfectionistic conscience, Tommy had to believe that his labors were for the right, for good against evil. To translate that feeling from a problem in moral philosophy to a problem solvable by effort, he adopted a stance of determined defense by invocation of "principle." That is, he concentrated on the effort involved in marching forward, fighting off temptations to quit or to compromise, grappling with the enemy. Principles and purposes were treated as given; Tommy's task was to bend all his energies toward getting them implemented just as they were, not in some partial or diluted form.

The emphasis on power in these thoughts and feelings is evident. Both the self and the external world needed to be controlled. Having found a prime motivation—and a justification for action—"principle"—Tommy Wilson at Princeton sought for a style, a set of techniques, by which he could force a reluctant environment to acknowledge his worth. He found it in the use of words, especially a particular form of oratory. Building on the intense verbal training he had had at home, he first tried out his skill in the arenas Princeton offered and then invented and organized an arena of his own. His success in extemporaneous debate brought him attention, then respect, then power. Quite consciously, he used his eloquence to establish his leadership. Tommy's first independent political success—on his own, away from his family—was his achievement of power through rhetoric. That stylistic emphasis stayed with him all his life.

Once in command of an organization, Tommy exhibited the dominating behavior which was to mark his Presidency. As editor of the *Princetonian*, he and he alone determined policy and content. And he preached what he practiced: success required that leaders lead and followers follow with strict obedience. He saw leadership not as a cooperative endeavor but as a one-man show, a matter of bold, committed, confident action by the man at the top. And especially if the leader had in his mind some grand purposes and large plans, he might be forgiven for any "harshness" in demanding assent.

Ever restless for the next battle, Tommy in his "Cabinet Government" essay drew on his understanding of and enthusiasm for things English and on his practice in constitution-making to develop a radical plan for restructuring American government. This was at least his third such effort, if we count the constitutions for The Royal United Kingdom Yacht Club and the Liberal Debating Club. In "Cabinet Government," however, Wilson dealt carefully with marking out a path to eminence for one with just his talents—the persuasive debater. The rest of his plan was, in the main, derivative from the ideas of others, but the concept of advancement through success in an advocate's war of principles was pure Wilson. His ambitions had jelled and he could imagine himself winning America as he had won Princeton.

Even before he left Princeton there were signs that his style created opposition—stubborn resistance which, if he had had no place else to go, Wilson would have fought to the finish.

This little history shows, I think, how the themes of Wilson's Presidency were foreshadowed in his early life. The pattern was there: deprivation, low self-esteem, a turning to external achievement, a confirming world view, a definitive style rigidly adhered to, a sequence from persuasion to domination, and the search for new worlds to conquer.

HOOVER DISCOVERS HIS WORK

The Wilsons were a wordy family. From an early age, Woodrow Wilson wrote letters, diaries, stories and the like, and the family's incessant talk left a great many traces in the memories and reports of relatives and friends. What a contrast to the Hoover record. There silence was part of the family religion. His people worked with their hands, not their mouths. And until he reached Stanford, Herbert Hoover was as obscure a speck on the American scene as it was possible to be. For much of the meaning of Hoover's early life we have to rely on inference from the facts rather than on direct evidence, of which there is not much. But the gist of even these sparse materials is fairly clear, and by the time Hoover left college he displayed a definite pattern of action and feeling in critical respects like that of Tommy Wilson.

Five generations of Hoovers had lived in the confining culture of Quakerism, moving about from time to time but retaining their religion and its peculiar folkways. Herbert Hoover's immediate family was particularly devout. His mother was a leader in meeting and became a full-fledged evangelist of the sect after his father died. From the time Herbert was born until he went to Stanford University, he thus experienced an atmosphere prevaded with many Quaker values: thrift, hard work, humility, a strict morality overseen by the elders, a sense of seriousness, and personal responsibility. There is no evidence that Herbert himself was "eldered"—harangued by a committee of senior churchmen for "failings of loose living"—but the example was frequently before him. Quaker gentleness forbade social aggression: "to strike a playmate was the great, almost unforgivable sin."

Hoover remembered that the children's "cries and the hushings thereof were often the only relief from the long silences of Quaker worship" and that one of the lady elders was successful in defeating a move for Sunday school singing and using the meeting house for recreation—lest the church be transformed into "a place of abomination."

Gentle and free in ideology, Quakerism was often harsh and repressive in practice. But it did offer stability and respectability, a place of belonging, a firm connection between extended families and their neighbors. As Hoover recalled,

> Those who are acquainted with the Quaker faith, and who know the primitive furnishings of the Quaker meeting-house, the solemnity of the long hours of meeting awaiting the spirit to move someone, will know the intense repression upon a ten-year-old boy who might not even count his toes.[18]

And the Quaker faith Hoover imbibed furnished a religio-social world view he was to hark back to many years later. He wrote in his *Memoirs:*

> The religious characteristics of the faith were literal belief in the Bible, great tolerance, and a conviction that spiritual inspiration sprang from the "inward light" in each individual. Thus, being extreme religious individualists, they have no paid "ministers" and no elaborate ecclesiastical organization, "the meeting" being only roughly grouped under "quarterly" or "yearly meetings" for spiritual guidance. The reflex of religious individualism is necessarily also economic individualism. The Friends have always held strongly to education, thrift, and individual enterprise. In consequence of plain living and hard work poverty has never been their lot. So far as I know, no member has ever been in jail or on public relief. This is largely because they take care of each other. Also it may be because if members evidence failings of loose living, their elders visit them in time to remedy their weaknesses or else expel them from the meeting.[19]

Herbert Clark Hoover was born on August 10, 1874, in West Branch, Iowa, two and a half years after his brother Theodore and two years before his sister May, to Jesse Clark Hoover, a 27-year-old blacksmith and farm implement salesman, and Huldah Minthorn Hoover, a seminary-educated lady of 26. One of Herbert's Quaker aunts who was there at his birth wrote to him later that "Jesse and Huldah always made much of thee because thee represented the little girl they hoped soon to have."

In his *Memoirs* Hoover devotes only a few sentences to his parents. He remembered his mother as "a sweet-faced woman" who was "in demand as a speaker at Quaker meetings" and "took a considerable part in the then vigorous prohibition campaigns." Born in Canada, she may have attended the University of Iowa for a term. In meetings, relatives recalled, "the spirit moved her beautifully." She was "an attractive and efficient woman, serious-minded even for a Quakeress." "My recollection of my father," Hoover wrote, "is of necessity dim indeed," but others knew him as a "mixer" who, one of Hoover's biographers wrote,

> loved a joke. "And once he got one on you, he'd never let up," says his younger cousin George. It tickled his sense of humor to play on the serious mind of his wife; to puzzle her with statements to palpably absurd and to observe with that chuckling laugh of his her efforts to understand.[20]

Hoover, in his *Memoirs,* follows the sentence introducing his father with accounts of two painful incidents, once when he stepped barefoot on a chip of hot iron and another time when he set fire to a barrel of tar, for which, Irwin reports, he "received a double dose of scriptural admonition and a sound whipping."

Herbert was "round and plump" as a baby, but suffered from severe attacks of croup, one of which nearly killed him in his second winter:

> At the end of a long choking-spasm, he stiffened; stopped breathing; so far as visible signs went, died. Aunt Ellen was laying out the little body when she noticed signs of life and applied strong restorative measures. He revived. His mother always believed that the Lord gave him back in answer to her prayers.[21]

The next September his sister May was born, the "little girl they hoped soon to have." Herbert had measles, mumps, diphtheria, and chickenpox in addition to his croup. And he continued to have accidents; once he almost chopped off an index finger with a hatchet. But as he grew stronger and older, Herbert became a healthy, outdoor-loving boy, happiest in the Iowa woods and fields, hunting rabbits, sledding, roaming the fields and forests with his older brother Tad.

The Hoover children spent the summer of Herbert's sixth year at the farm of one of his uncles. Suddenly called home, they found their father dying of typhoid fever. He was 34, just beginning to make a going thing of his business, just having moved into a new house. "His father's death set a period to his early childhood," Irwin writes. His mother took in sewing rather than spend the small inheritance, but she became "less and less a creature of this world" after her husband died. She spoke more often in meetings and traveled a good deal to preach in Quaker fashion at the other Iowa colonies of the sect, leaving the children under the general supervision of relatives. Herbert spent "eight or nine months" with his Uncle Laban Miles, Indian Agent to the Osage Nation, in the Indian Territory, and another summer with his Uncle Pennington Minthorn in Sioux County, Iowa. At each place the boy was worked hard but found time for country recreations. Hoover remembered his mother with affection as the one "who for two years kept the little family of four together," but it is apparent she was with the children only for short periods. Then in the winter after his eighth birthday, she died of pneumonia. "Bereavement put a sudden end to his little-boyhood, as it had to his babyhood," Irwin writes. He and the other children were left orphans in the hands of his Quaker relatives.

The children were parceled out to various uncles and aunts, Herbert to his Uncle Allan Hoover who had a farm about a mile way. "He took it hard—but with his mouth shut and grief showing only in his eyes." Farm work was hard, and "we did know of the mortgage upon Uncle Allan's farm which was a constant source of anxiety and a dreadful damper on youthful hopes for things that could not be bought." Herbert made friends with his cousin Walter and was cared for by his Aunt Millie. Probably he got together with his brother and sister from time to time. But in 1884, at age ten, he was again uprooted and sent to Oregon to live with his mother's brother, Henry John Minthorn, whose only son had just died. Various reasons are offered: Dr. Minthorn, a practicing physician, was opening an academy, so the boy would get an education. Undoubtedly his Uncle Allan's financial straits contributed to the decision. Told "thee is going to

Oregon," Herbert, "his lips closed very tight," accepted the decision. To sustain his spirits during the long train trip, little Herbert carried two motto cards in his bag, reading, "Leave me not, neither forsake me, Oh God of my salvation," and "I will never leave thee nor forsake thee." He was "at once put to school and to chores" both at home and in the academy. He spent one summer weeding onions for fifty cents a day. It was a time of "sober routine" which could not have been particularly pleasant for a boy in his early teens. His uncle was "a severe man on the surface, but like all Quakers kindly at bottom," Hoover recalled, "a silent, taciturn man, but still a natural teacher," with a tough streak in him: "Turn your other cheek," he told Herbert, "but if he smites you then punch him." Once Herbert stalked out in anger and boarded with other relatives "for a period."

He was bored with school. At last, when he was about fifteen, his uncle decided to open a "Quaker land-settlement business" in Salem and took Herbert along as office boy. Hoover recalled his teachers there with affection and writes at length about his adventures in fishing and exploring.

One day, probably in his sixteenth year, Herbert talked with a mining engineer who encouraged him to take up his profession and told of the opportunities for engineering training at the new Stanford University. Herbert "mulled it over for a year" and then, "I determined to become an engineer."

The family wanted him to go to a Quaker college, as his brother had, and secured a promise of a scholarship to Earlham College in Indiana. But Herbert argued—and this is the first indication of an opposition to his elders—that there were no engineering courses there. The family was finally persuaded when an announcement appeared that a Professor Swain, a well known Quaker mathematician, would conduct entrance examinations for the first class at Stanford University; his Quakerism gave the place a stamp of approval.

Herbert took the entrance examinations in the spring of his seventeenth year and failed, except in mathematics. Dr. Swain, because he liked the boy, because he was particularly on the lookout for young Quakers, because the new college would need as many students as it could get—or for some combination of these reasons—talked to young Hoover and encouraged him to come to Stanford for special tutoring in the summer before classes began. Herbert took this chance. He gathered his two suits of clothes, a bicycle, $160 he had saved, about $500 as his share of his father's estate, and $50 the Minthorns contributed, and was off to California.

Hoover thus left home and childhood with understandable enthusiasm. The major deprivations are clear: he lost both his parents, suddenly and unexpectedly, by the age of eight, a severe loss of affection and stability; and he had been shuffled about, against his will, from one stern relative to another; separated from his brother and sister; and powerless to shape any segment of his own life. He needed others, and he needed to get his own place in the world and hold it. All his work so far had brought him nothing but more work. Words were not yet part of his equipment; he had kept a tight-lipped sense of humiliation as person after person he relied on had agreed to abandon him to others.

There was little of politics in Hoover's family background or religious tradition. His Uncle Laban was an Indian agent and his Uncle Henry Minthorn had been one; Hoover vaguely remembered the Garfield campaign of 1880 and the lone (and drunken) Democrat in West Branch. That appears to have been the extent of his political exposure. Nor is there any record of early appearances before an audience. He did not like school: years later, asked to name his favorite subjects, he replied, "None. They were something to race through—so I could get out of doors." He remembered some of his teachers with affection, but their lessons appear to have made no substantive impression on him. At home there were no novels, "save those with Total Abstinence as hero and Rum as villain." He and his brother read—surreptitiously—*Youth's Companion,* a mild thriller of the day, and, with their cousin George acted out the parts. At first "Bertie" acted as lookout in case someone should discover this sinful behavior; then he was promoted to "super parts":

> When Tad commanded the Colonial army, Bertie was that army; he was also the white maiden bound to the stake, while George as the Indian Chief tortured her and Tad as the *Deerslayer* came to the rescue.[22]

Not even at play, then, did he take the lead.

But indoor intellectual forays never compared in Hoover's experience or memory with the outdoors and the physical. The early pages of his *Memoirs* read like a nature book, full of owls and rabbits and fish. He and his cousins played with machinery and put an old thresher back together; in Oregon he and another office boy tried to repair sewing machines for sale. The heritage was much stronger from the males of his line—the farmers and blacksmith—than from the females, with their religiousness. In the office he was efficient in detail, learned to run a typewriter, and spent as much time as he could in the hills. The focus was on things, not words. He recalls a kind teacher who got him started on *Ivanhoe,* an "opening of the door to a great imaginative world" which "led me promptly through much of Scott and Dickens, often at the cost of sleep." Nevertheless, "Oregon lives in my mind for its gleaming wheat fields, its abundant fruit, its luxuriant forest vegetation, and the fish in the mountain streams," he wrote. On Sunday evening he was allowed to read "an improving book," but one wonders how much of that there was after the Sabbath routine:

> On Sunday mornings, when work of necessity was done, came Sabbath school; then the long meeting; then dinner; then a period of sluggish rest followed by a Band of Hope meeting, where the lecturer or teacher displayed colored prints of the drunkard's dreadful interior on each stage of his downward path, with corresponding illustrations of his demeanor and conduct.[23]

Three scattered experiences in Hoover's life may have had some bearing on his later political development. In West Branch, when he was a very young boy, the Quaker congregation split over various issues of modernization, such as the abandonment of the "thee" and "thou" form of address. His mother sided with the modernists and was therefore able to continue with the main body of the group when they won the contest. She may have taken a leading part in this struggle, but in any case Herbert was exposed to a group controversy of some meaning to his family. Second, his Uncle Minthorn's business in Newberg, Oregon, was largely promotional, whipping up Eastern investors to put money into uncleared land for prune farms. Hoover's detractors among his biographers make much of this, but it is at least probable that Herbert was exposed to some exaggerated advertising in these years, put out by the man who had taken his father's place. And he recalled some evening discussions of political issues in the office:

> My chief contact with public affairs was through an elderly, retired, argumentative Democrat named Hobson and his helpers who came frequently to the office to argue matters with the Republican Quakers. The various acts of the Arthur, Cleveland and Harrison administrations, the merits of Jefferson, Lincoln, Robert E. Lee, U. S. Grant and other statesmen were argued and reargued. Free trade and protection always raised high decibels. The debate invariably ended with complete disgust of each one at the obstinacy and low intelligence of his opponent.[24]

Politics for Hoover, then, insofar as it had any important meaning, was a matter of conflicts ending in "complete disgust"; in public, words were for selling, even if that took a bit of exaggeration; and group issues were matters of principle to be won by the right side. But these were no doubt minor themes in his makeup. Unlike most men who have become President, Hoover had in his background virtually nothing of legitimating family example, identification with political figures, or practice in expressing ideas to audiences.

At seventeen Hoover entered Stanford, the youngest and, reportedly, the youngest-looking student in the first class at the new university. Will Irwin describes the effect the next four years had on Herbert Hoover:

> He had lived, so far as he was aware, a happy childhood. But after all, that sympathetic brooding which makes childhood supremely happy had been lacking to his life since he was nine [sic] years old, for the greater part of another seven years a repressed atmosphere, wherein his extraordinary intelligence had no proper soil for growth; and hard work at menial or mechanical tasks. The atmosphere of freedom, of high animal spirits, the intellectual stimulus of those original young professors who went adventuring to Stanford—these struck in. Here he knew his first joy of the intellect, here he felt the initial stirring of his higher powers, here he found his wife. Stanford became a kind of complex with Herbert Hoover. Within fifteen years his interests and his wanderings were to embrace the globe; but those golden hills above Palo Alto were always the pole to his compass.[25]

Hoover came to Stanford early in the summer of 1891 to be tutored. Still one subject short of the number required at the end of the summer, he studied a couple of physiology textbooks for two straight nights and passed an examination. He was admitted "conditioned in English"—the language came hard for him; "then and for many years he was impatient with words." He took English examinations twice a year for the next several years without success. In his senior year he failed German. The English "condition" was finally removed to allow him to graduate, when two of his engineering professors argued that his technical reports showed sufficient literary skill. In class and out of class he "said little and listened a lot; there was a wordless eagerness about him," as Lyons puts it. As a sophomore he was "shy to the point of timidity—rarely spoke unless spoken to," his classmate Lester Hinsdale recalled from their lunches together. Irwin remembers Hoover visiting him in the infirmary when Hoover was a senior.

> He did not say a word of sympathy for me—in pain and forever out of football—but I felt it nevertheless. Then, at the door he turned for an instant and jerked out: "I'm sorry." Just that; but it was as though another man had burst into maudlin tears.[26]

Hoover quietly went into action to help his friend Irwin, whose ankle was broken. He asked the nurse what he needed and how much an operation would cost; then Herbert, "in quiet and efficient control," composed a telegram to a San Francisco surgeon and had one of his student friends sent it off. When he met his future wife in a geological laboratory—he was a senior, she a freshman—he was tongue-tied and red-faced. No other girls were among his close friends at Stanford, nor were there any "frivolous flirtations." It is important to note, then, that verbal expressiveness had no part in Hoover's success at Stanford. He never found there a way to attract attention or to achieve his goals through speechmaking or even facile conversation. That mouth so tightly shut at critical moments in his childhood symbolized his verbal restraint both at Stanford and as President. Typically, Hoover talked haltingly, rarely looking his listener in the eye, with one foot thrust forward as he jingled the keys in his pocket.

Hoover's success at Stanford came from work, not words, and from a way of relating to others. He began his extracurricular career at college by hiring on as a clerk in the registration of the new class. The skill exercised was meticulous attention to detail. Later in his freshman year, Professor Branner employed him to do typing, again a matter of careful mechanical work. Then he branched out; he and two partners established a newspaper route and a laundry service for the students. These were soon sublet to other students, providing a small but regular income for Hoover. His entrepreneurial talents were beginning to emerge. Later he sold out the laundry for $40 and he and a new friend started a cooperative residence for students in Palo Also, a project he dropped soon because it kept him away from the campus.

In the summer after Hoover's freshman year, Professor Branner got him a job with the Geological Survey of Arkansas, of which Branner had been State Geologist, at $60 a month and expenses. "I did my job on foot, mostly alone, stopping at nights at the nearest cabin" in the Ozarks, making systematic notes, gathering and filing away facts and observations. The mountaineers were suspicious of traveling inquirers: "I finally gave up trying to explain." In his two subsequent Stanford summers he worked for the United States Geological Survey in California and in Nevada. Hoover was "far happier" with this work, he writes. He worked as a "cub assistant" to Dr. Waldemar Lindgren, riding a horse all day and camping out with the survey team at night. Hoover very much wanted this job. At the beginning of the summer after his sophomore year he was not yet employed, so he and a friend canvassed San Francisco for contracts for putting up billboard advertising. They signed up "a few hundred dollars" worth of contracts and went to work. Then Hoover heard of the geological survey and that there was a place for him with it. He walked 80 miles in three days to take it on.

Hoover's exact role with the United States Geological Survey should be noticed. As "the youngest member of the Geological party," he was the disbursing officer: "I had to buy supplies and keep the accounts according to an elaborate book of regulations which provided wondrous safeguards for the public treasury." Carefulness by the book was evident again, combined with outdoor energy and listening to the experts around the campfire.

Hoover returned to Stanford and extended his business enterprises. For a brief time he was a shortstop on the baseball team but soon became manager, arranging games, collecting the gate money and otherwise finding cash for equipment and uniforms. He did so well at that that he was advanced to manager of the football team. One game produced $30,018. Hoover was acquiring a reputation for management. Operating in a new and developing environment, he was in demand as the man who could—and would—take care of a wide variety of chores and enterprises for his fellows. Branner knew him for his efficiency; when other students complained that Hoover seemed to have too much pull with the famous geologist, he replied, "But I can tell Hoover to do a thing and never think of it again." These talents also gave him his start in campus politics.

Hoover was a "Barbarian" at Stanford. Fraternities developed quickly among the richer students interested in social prominence, but he was not one of them. Sam Collins, one of the oldest members of Hoover's class, had proposed a cooperative rooming house at the beginning of their sophomore year. Collins was impressed with Hoover's system and order in straightening out the finances. Under Collins' tutelage, Hoover first got involved in college politics when he was brought in with a group of "Barbarians" who organized to overthrow fraternity control of the student offices and activities. "With others who lived in dormitories and diggings," Hoover wrote, "we resented the snobbery that accompanied the fraternity system and we suspected favoritism in handling student enterprises and their loose methods for accounting for money. We declared war for reform." A zealot named "Sosh" (for "socialist") Zion declared his candidacy for student body president; "Collins swung in behind him in this campaign, and Hoover followed." He was assigned to canvass the "camp," the students who lived in rough shacks left over by the workers constructing the new college. Still he was "rather inarticulate—this repressed boy of eighteen," but he did what he could and the Barbs won, in a close vote.

The next summer Hoover worked for Dr. Lindgren, but he also thought about ways of organizing the many student activities at Stanford, some of which had been very sloppily run and one of which had involved a scandal. Hoover returned in the fall with a draft of a new constitution in which student activities would be brought together under the control of the student body. There would be a president and a football manager, but the key officer was the treasurer, bonded and double-audited, who would handle the finances. Hoover's plan was modified in some detail in bull sessions with Collins and others; they decided to put off a move for it until the following spring, when a student government sympathetic to the plan could be elected under the existing rules.

In the spring term, this group gathered again and developed a ticket, with Lester Hinsdale as candidate for president, Herbert Hicks for football manager, and Herbert Hoover for treasurer. Hoover was reluctant. He thought the treasurer, who would collect a salary, should be a graduate student.

> "But there's the salary," they said; "you can drop your work for Doc Branner and your laundry agency. The job will support you."
> "No sir!" responded Hoover, emphatically. "If I accept this nomination and get elected, there's one thing sure. I take no salary. Otherwise, they'll say I'm backing the new constitution just to get a paid job!"[27]

The "3-H" ticket won. Sosh Zion opposed the salary, but to no purpose since Hoover refused to take it anyway, even though he worked like a demon for the remaining two years at Stanford as treasurer. The new student government got the student body to pass the new constitution.

Hoover spent the following summer working again for Dr. Lindgren, who put Hoover's name with his own on the various maps and reports. "Years later, Hoover confessed to a friend that no subsequent honor had puffed him up so much as this."

The next autumn, Hoover's junior year, he was busy running a lecture series, keeping the records and accounts for athletic events, and generally making himself useful. As Will Irwin recalled,

> In the conferences over this or that problem of our bijou party in a toy state he seemed hesitant of advancing an opinion. Then, when everyone else had expressed himself, he would come in with the final wise word.... After all, ours was the world in minature. I lived to see him in councils whose decisions meant life or death for millions; yet it was always the same mind and the same method.[28]

Hoover's quiet but strict management succeeded. When he took over the job of Student Body Treasurer—a post he had invented—he inherited a debt of $2,000. In his first report a few months later, he was able to claim that "for the first time since its birth, the Associated Students is a solvent body," and the campus newspaper congratulated him on bringing order to the accounts.

Years later, the men Hoover worked with at Stanford remembered him as an effectuator, a doer, a hard-working, extraordinarily efficient manager. He found his way from being the rawest of freshmen, behind his class in scholarship, to a place of wide power, and he managed to do it, apparently, without ever once addressing a large gathering of his classmates. Hoover was the man behind the scenes, the coordinator who transformed a bookkeeping function into the pre-eminent campus leadership function. The medium was the caucus—a small conference of the top men. The message was system, order, accountability. The man who made that work was Hoover, attending carefully to every detail, caring for others in secret.

Hard work on detail also characterized his other success, his geological work during the summers. There Hoover's penchant for facts joined with his industry to bring achievement. He was often alone, and thus learned to rely on his own decisions.

That was Hoover's style: homework and his special form of personal relations, combined with a nearly complete absence of rhetoric. At Stanford he experienced what to him, given his background, was marked success with this style. It sustained and was sustained by a world view drawn mainly from his religious upbringing, stressing close restraint of emotion, responsibility for others, and an extreme individualism, and from his geological-engineering life, stressing the manipulation of things through energetic effort and attention to detail.

The motive force in Hoover's life collected itself over the years of his childhood. The child who loses his father at age six and his mother at age eight is scarred by that, no matter how many relatives try to fill the void. But besides that, Herbert had an unsettled childhood; however he may have felt about it—and there is evidence he felt badly—he was sent at critical times from one relation to another, where he was expected to perform whatever they wanted done, usually hard labor at low wages. I think he experienced a sense of powerlessness, an inability to guide his own fate, a vulnerability to sudden, externally imposed, radical changes in his life. To overcome those feelings, he strove to establish around him a world of regularity, a world he could control. At Stanford he accomplished this central purpose, establishing for himself a life-long homeplace.

JOHNSON LEARNS HIS PEOPLE

My Darling Boy:
Beyond "Congratulations Congressman," what can I say to my dear son in this hour of triumphant success? In this as in all the many letters I have written you there is the same theme: I love you; I believe in you; I expect great things of you.

To me, your election not alone gratifies my pride as a mother in a splendid and satisfying son and delights me with the realization of the joy you must feel in your success, but in a measure it compensates for the heartache and disappointment I experienced as a child when my dear father lost the race you have just won. My confidence in the good judgment of the people was sadly shattered then by their choice of another man. Today, my faith is restored.

How happy it would have made my precious noble father to know that the first-born of his first-born would achieve the position he desired. It makes me happy to have you carry on the ideals and principles so cherished by that great and good man—I gave you his name. I commend to you his example. You have always justified my expectations, my hopes, my dreams. How dear to me you are you cannot know, my darling boy, my devoted son, my strength and comfort.

Take care of yourself, darling. Write to me. Always remember that I love you and am behind you in all that comes to you. Kiss my dear children in Washington for me.

My dearest love,

Mother[29]

"I am reminded always in my work at Washington of my own origins," Johnson said, especially of his mother—"a saintly woman, I owe everything to her"—and his father—"My Daddy went broke three times during Republican administrations." All reports support the picture his mother conveys in this letter, especially the sequence, "I love you; I believe in you; I expect great things of you." She had been Rebekah Baines, eldest child of newspaper editor, lawyer, legislator, and Texas Secretary of State Joseph Baines, who had sent her off to Baylor College from a comfortable home only to see her forced, when he "suffered severe and sudden financial reverses," to take work as manager of the college bookstore. Rebekah remembered

> A well-ordered, peaceful home to which cross words and angry looks were foreign. At an incredibly early age, my father taught me to read. . . . He taught me how to study, to think and to endure. . . . He taught me obedience and self-control, saying that without them no one is worthy of responsibility or trust.[30]

Her mother had died when she was very young. Her father Joseph died in 1906 and a year later Rebekah married Sam Ealy Johnson, Jr., called "Little Sam" to distinguish him from his father, who in turn had been called "Gal Johnson" until Sam's birth, because he had joined in producing four daughters in a row before his son was born. Sam was a state legislator at the time, having recently succeeded Rebekah's father in that office. Sam was known as a doer: "he must ride faster; plow longer, straighter rows; and pick more cotton than his companions"; in the legislature he had a reputation as "a 'go-getter' [who] always succeeds in passing any legislation he introduces." He had tried school teaching, ranching, real estate, and politics but at the time of his marriage was in hard straits, having been "dealt a severe blow when the San Francisco earthquake of 1906 wiped out his cotton holdings and saddled him with a debt of several thousand dollars," as Rebekah remembered it. But he plugged away, a stubborn man who would "kick like a mule at any attempted domination."

People agreed on the character of the marriage: "The Baines have the brains and the Johnsons have the guts," as an aunt put it. Rebekah said he had to learn to live with "a completely opposite personality."

A year later the first issue of this wedlock appeared, a ten-pound boy called "Baby" for three months and then, at Rebekah's insistence, named Lyndon Baines; Sam gave his name to the second son.

Times were hard. Rebekah had been raised in town. She liked music and literature. Sam took her to a country spread where she made her own soap, hauled the water from the well, and "shuddered over the chickens." Once when he was four, Lyndon recalled, he heard her sobbing as she pumped water at midnight, and he told her not to worry, he would take care of her. The children wore homemade clothes, ate bacon fat on cornbread, turnip greens, hominy grits, and other abominations, with some boiled beef from time to time. A visitor remembered the Johnsons as "terribly poor." Sam Johnson the legislator was much ashamed when Lyndon set up as a bootblack to earn a little money. The family remained in difficult financial condition through Lyndon's childhood; when he left home at fifteen, he said, "it meant one less mouth for my poor daddy to feed."

At the time Lyndon Johnson ran for the Presidency in 1964, *Life* magazine estimated his total accumulated assets at approximately $14 million.

"Lyndon was hardly out of infancy when his mother embarked on a 'head-start' program designed to develop him into a genius," Alfred Steinberg wrily observes. She was forever telling him stories and, as she remembered, taught him the alphabet by age two, "all the Mother Goose rhymes" at three, reading by age four—at which point she marched him off to first grade. "He had to sit on my lap to recite," his teacher said. Lyndon remembered that the other children teased him unmercifully. He had to drop out with whooping cough for much of that year and start again the next. At the end of the first grade he was allowed to choose a poem to read and he took one called "I'd Rather Be Mamma's Boy." Rebekah pushed him along:

> Many times I would not catch up with the fact that Lyndon was not prepared on a lesson until breakfast time of a school day. . . . Then I would get the book and put it on the table in front of his father and devote the whole breakfast period to a discussion with my husband of what my son should have learned the night before. . . . By following him to the front gate nearly every morning and telling him tales of history and geography and algebra, I could see that he was prepared for the work of the day.[31]

With her earnings from giving "expression lessons," Rebekah paid for Lyndon's dancing lessons but he quit when he was spanked for teasing the girls. Then she got him to take up the violin. He sawed through the lessons for six months.

There were other lessons. From an early age, Lyndon Johnson heard tales of the Texas pioneers, prominently featuring his own ancestors, one of whom had signed the Texas Declaration of Independence. Lyndon's grandmother Johnson had hidden under a trap door while Comanches ransacked her cabin. His great-grandfather Baines had been a friend of Sam Houston's. But above all there was the saga of the Alamo, for which President Johnson, in a moment of excitement, once invented an ancestor. There in March 1836—Lyndon learned it by heart—stood the vicious Santa Anna with four thousand troops confronting 187 stalwarts, including Colonel Travis, Jim Bowie, Davy Crockett, and Jim Bonham inside the old Spanish church. Told that no help could get through, the Colonel calmly thanked the messenger and with his sword drew a line on the ground: "I will ask those who wish to stay with me, if any should, to cross this line. Those not wishing to make that commitment are free to leave." The silence was broken by Jim Bowie, lying sick on a litter: "Some of you boys set my bed across that line." The Colonel composed a last letter, requesting his government to "Take care of my son."

Three years before Lyndon's birth, his father co-sponsored a bill to purchase the Alamo Mission. When Lyndon was a teenager, Sam took him to see the Alamo at first hand. There the boy read Colonel Travis's last words: "Our flag still waves proudly from the walls—I shall never surrender or retreat." In 1965 President Johnson told the National Security Council:

> Hell, Vietnam is just like the Alamo. Hell, it's just like if you were down at that gate, and you were surrounded, and you damn well needed somebody. Well, by God, I'm going to go—and I thank the Lord that I've got men who want to go with me, from McNamara right on down to the littlest private who's carrying a gun.[32]

Little Lyndon, then, knew real deprivation as a child. The family may not have missed many meals, but they knew what economic insecurity looked like and what it meant to skimp on necessities. These feelings, it seems certain, were heightened by Rebekah's memories of a better life—the contrast between the way it was with her father and the way it was with Sam. She took on the project of turning her first son into an exceptional person, pushing him, driving him to learn and develop as fast as he could—or faster. Meanwhile, his head was soaking up Texism, that special mix of bathos and bravado by which scattered men deny their vulnerability. He was, he learned, descended from heroic stock. Perhaps especially because he was a "mama's boy," a lap-sitter and violin player, Lyndon took to the rough, tough Texas Ranger image hungrily, identifying with the Sam Houston tradition. From very early on, Lyndon Johnson lived with two great expectations: that he achieve beyond what any of his peers could do and that he perform like a Texas-type male.

When Sam Johnson went off to the legislature or traveled on his long trips in search of business, he would say "Lyndon, I'm putting you in charge of things while I'm gone. See that the chores get done and help your mama all you can." Lyndon as man of the house was willing to delegate a good deal of the chore responsibilities to his little brother Sam Houston Johnson and his three sisters, Rebekah, Josefa, and Lucia. When Sam was home, he would rout Lyndon out of bed—"Get up, Lyndon. Every boy in the county's got a two-hour start on you."

To the tales of Texas military heroics, Sam Johnson added news of politics. Sam himself was "ambitious . . . highly organized, sensitive and nervous; he was impatient of inefficiency and ineptitude and quick to voice displeasure," according to his wife. He had originally made it to the state legislature by means of the unwritten code of rotation by which nominations were passed around from county to county every two years. When Sam's turn came to relinquish the seat to the next man, he refused to step down. The five-dollar-a-day pay was probably helpful, but the office was also the highest a Johnson had held and could possibly be a jumping-off place for the climb to higher positions. He left the legislature when he got married and then returned in 1918 when Lyndon was eleven; in between he was continually active in political affairs and his home was a regular stop for touring politicians. Lyndon listened. He heard zany tales of Texas democracy, talk of such characters as "Pa" Ferguson who ran against high odds—"no more chance than a stump-tailed bull in fly time"—and won the governorship, vetoed the appropriation for the University of Texas, where the professors were "liars and crooks," and responded to newsmen's queries by saying, "I am governor of Texas. I don't have to give reasons." When Ferguson was impeached, Lyndon's uncle was his chief defense counsel.

Eleven-year-old Lyndon went campaigning with his father in 1918. He saw how Sam recruited support by vague intimations of patronage, handshaking forays, oratory filled with anecdote. In between engagements, Sam instructed Lyndon. "If you can't come into a roomful of people and tell right away who is for you and who is against you, you have no business in politics," he said. "When you're talkin', you ain't learnin' nothin'!" was a motto of his father's which Lyndon had printed and framed and hung on his office wall later in life—perhaps more for the benefit of visitors than for himself.

After the election victory, Sam often brought his son to Austin, where the boy would stand next to his father's desk in the legislative chamber. "He was so much like his father it was humorous to watch," a fellow member recalled. "They sort of looked alike, they walked the same, had the same nervous mannerisms, and Lyndon clutched you just like his daddy did when he talked to you. He was a little on the rough side, too." There were dramatic debates—for example, over the Ku Klux Klan—and a good deal of palaver between Sam and the wealthy lobbyists for interests from oil to beer. It is hard to believe Lyndon did not notice that a good many members lived in the Driskill Hotel where the lobbyists paid the rent, provided the girls, and kept the "drinking drys" (Prohibitionists as campaigners, but heroic imbibers in Austin) well supplied.

In 1923–24 Lyndon finished his senior year in high school and Sam once again went broke. Lyndon was class president—the class consisting of four girls, Lyndon, and another boy who "was always shy of the girls." Debating furnished the drama for the year. In a statewide contest all the participants were given the same question (whether the United States should withdraw her troops from Nicaragua) and assigned sides by the flip of a coin. Rebekah coached Lyndon but could not overcome his mumbling tone. Nevertheless, the Johnson City High team of Johnson and Casparis won the county meet. Then they lost at the district level. "I was so disappointed," Lyndon recalled later, "I went right into the bathroom and was sick." In May he graduated at age fifteen, "the youngest member of the class and . . . believed to be the youngest graduate of the school." The class prophecy was that he would become governor of Texas.

At this point comes a sharp break in the Lyndon Johnson story. Fifteen-year-old Lyndon ran away from home for nearly two years. In the summer of 1924, he worked for a while at a clerical job his father found for him in a faraway town, but he quit after a few weeks and came home. Then he and five other boys pooled their money and bought a rundown Model T Ford and left town without notice one morning in July, headed for California. Although he was the youngest, Lyndon was leader of the pack; they made the fifteen hundred miles to the coast in two weeks, living on fatback, cornbread, and molasses, camping out along the railroad tracks. They tried to make a go of it in California by picking fruit and washing dishes. Broke and out of work, the boys separated. "Nothing to eat was the principal item on my food chart," Lyndon remembered. "That was the first time I went on a diet. Up and down the coast I tramped, washing dishes, waiting on tables, doing farm work when it was available, and always growing thinner." Not until early 1926 did Lyndon, reduced to skin and bones, hitchhike dolefully back to Johnson City. "The trip back home was the longest I've ever made. And the prettiest sight I ever saw in my life was my grandmother's patchwork quilt at the foot of my bed when I got home."

Rebekah resumed her campaign to get him to go to college. Lyndon refused. Sam had fallen on hard times and was reduced to working as a road gang foreman. Lyndon and a friend went to work driving bulldozers and pickup trucks for one dollar a day. His father tried using sarcasm to push him on to better things: "It's fine to be satisfied with simple things. A man who is satisfied to be a laborer will never have much on his mind. Of course, there won't be much in it, but those who are willing to devote all their lives to a road job really don't need much." And once when Lyndon came home with a black eye after a beer hall fight, Sam berated him: "Sonny, there are a lot of ways of getting yourself noticed . . . next time you want to be noticed, try some other way."

That summer, during a revival session, Lyndon now eighteen, joined the Christian Church (Disciples of Christ)—"the business of the Disciples is unity, and it should never be forced to the periphery of our concern"—instead of his mother's Baptist church. But he continued raising hell. One time he came home with blood all over his face and his mother sat on his bed and cried, "To think that my eldest born should turn out like this." One night in February 1927, Lyndon decided he had had enough. After working in the rain all day he told Rebekah, "I'm tired of working with just my hands, and I'm ready to try working with my brain. If you and Daddy can get me into a college, I'll go as soon as I can." His mother wheeled into action and in no time at all Lyndon arrived at Southwest Texas State Teachers College in San Marcos, forty miles from Johnson City. There he was to develop the political style he later displayed as President of the United States.

Sam was broke again, so Lyndon borrowed $75 to start his higher education. When Sam said goodbye to his son he gave him yet another motivating parable: "This man I knew had a son going to college and one morning a friend stopped this man and asked him how his son was making out. 'Much better,' he said to him. 'He wrote to me that last term he was at the very top of those who failed.'"

Everything depended on Lyndon's success at San Marcos. It was a big town for that part of the country in those days, 4,000 people, including the college's 700 students. Lyndon was shocked to discover that he would have to do some extra preparatory work before he could start the regular course of study, but he leapt in with all his energy. Throughout his time at college he had few difficulties with the formal curriculum, making As in nearly everything except math: "My mother came and worked with me all night before the geometry exam, and I got a seventy, just passing." His interest soon found more exciting channels.

"Never did anyone come to town so fast as Lyndon Johnson came to Southwest Texas State Teachers College," his biographer Steinberg reports. His job history shows this. First he got work picking up trash. When he tired of that, Lyndon, no stickler for protocol, went to the president of the college and asked for something more challenging. President Evans made him an assistant to the science building janitor. After a few weeks Lyndon barged into the president's office again and said he wanted to be personally helpful to him. Evans said he already had a secretary, Tom Nichols. Lyndon insisted. Evans made him Nichols' assistant.

> According to Nichols, what next unfolded was flabbergasting. Lyndon jumped up to talk to everyone who came to the office to see Evans, and before days passed, he was asking the purpose of the visit and offering solutions to problems. The notion soon spread that it was necessary to get Lyndon's approval first in order to see Dr. Evans. At the same time, faculty members came to the conclusion that it was essential for them to be friendly to Lyndon, for they believed he could influence the president in their behalf. This erroneous idea developed because the school lacked a telephone system tying Evans' office with those of department heads, and when the president wanted to send a message to a department head or a professor, he asked his part-time aide, rather than Nichols, to run over with the note. Lyndon's tone and attitude somehow gave the impression he was far more than a messenger.[33]

Before long, Lyndon was slapping President Evans on the back and accompanying him to committee hearings in Austin, writing his reports, and answering his mail. Evans was overwhelmed. "Lyndon," he later said, "I declare you hadn't been in my office a month before I could hardly tell who was president of the school—you or me."

Lyndon also persuaded President Evans to rent him and a friend a room over his garage; lacking rent money, he got Evans to excuse payment in return for painting the garage. Evans agreed. In the spring of 1927, Johnson and his roommate painted the garage three times. Johnson got the roommate a job as "inspector of buildings." When his sister came to college, Lyndon gave her this advice: "Don't play sandlot baseball; play the big leagues. Get to know the first team." "Why, Lyndon," she said, "I wouldn't dare go up to President Evans' office." He said, "That's where you want to start."

Lyndon's career in campus politics was equally impressive. From time to time he lived in a wide variety of boarding and rooming houses, making friends and learning the system. He got to know Willard Deason, who had a special talent Lyndon wanted to imitate: the ability to memorize quickly the name, homeplace, and interests of everyone he met. Deason and Johnson would stroll around the campus, Deason greeting nearly every passerby with his name and a query about how things were back home. He also got to know a wizard of campus finance, Horace Richards, who could collect a cowboy hat full of coins by waiting outside pep rallies and yelling, "Kick in for the decorations!" when the excited students came out. Vernon Whitesides taught Lyndon innumerable stories and also took him on as star salesman of Real Silk Hose. A professor remembered, "I bought socks from him. Everybody did. Lyndon was such a salesman you couldn't resist him."

Lyndon was on his way, fast. Deason remembered that "he was always in a hurry on the campus. He never walked with leisure. It was always with long, loping strides, almost like a trot. . . . He was the only fellow I ever knew who could see around the corner."

Lyndon soon found that campus politics was run by the Black Stars, a secret society dominated by athletes. He tried to join but was blackballed by a member whose girl he had taken out. So Lyndon organized an opposition, the White Stars, and put up Deason for class president. Deason said,

> The night before the election the White Stars held a caucus and we decided that we were beaten. I said we might as well go to bed and forget it. But Lyndon wouldn't give up. He spent all night going around to the boardinghouses, calling the girls' dormitory, moving behind the scenes, giving them that old Johnson one-two-three pep talk. The next day I won by twenty votes. When ordinary men were ready to give up, that's when Lyndon Johnson was just beginning.[34]

The White Star victory made him some enemies who found his ways too dominating; it also set him up as dispenser of patronage. Shortly after the overthrow, White Stars monopolized indoor jobs on campus and Black Stars found themselves outside. In 1928, Johnson became editor of the *College Star*, the campus newspaper, at thirty dollars a month. At the same time, with his typical whirlwind energy, he took a very active part in debating, under the tutelage of Professor Howard Greene, a somewhat eccentric political scientist who stimulated Lyndon with his Socratic method of teaching in class and with his dirty stories outside. Lyndon left the substantive preparations to his debating partner. His own specialty was attack, pouncing on the opponents' weak points. The issues were not particularly compelling; following the Texas practice, Lyndon could debate from whichever side chance assigned him.

Lyndon became president of the Press Club, senior legislator of his class, student council member, secretary of the Schoolmakers club, as well as editor of the newspaper. His editorials were full of positive thinking, coming out for courtesy, "honesty of soul," and the Fourth of July. Some themes seem biographically significant:

> Personality is power; the man with a striking personality can accomplish greater deeds in life than a man of equal abilities but less personality.

The great men of the world are those who have never faltered. They had the glowing vision of a noble work to inspire them to press forward, but they also had the inflexible will, the resolute determination, the perfectly attuned spiritual forces for the execution of the work planned.

The successful man has a well-trained will. He has under absolute control his passions and desires, his habits and his deeds.

There are no tyrannies like those human passions and weaknesses exercise. No master is so cruelly exacting as an indulged appetite. To govern self is a greater feat than to control armies and forces.

Ambition is an uncomfortable companion many times. He creates a discontent with present surroundings and achievements; he is never satisfied but always pressing forward to better things in the future. Restless, energetic, purposeful, it is ambition that makes of a creature a real man.[35]

The Wilson-Hoover themes are clear in these passages, especially the strong stress on labored effort and self-control. Insofar as he needed to confirm his own pattern of action in words, beating the onward-and-upward drum would do it.

A year and a half after he had arrived at Southwest Texas, Johnson, by attending two summers, earned a teaching certificate. Sam Johnson's fortunes being at another low ebb, Lyndon got President Evans to find him a teaching job at Cotulla, Texas, paying $125 a month. He planned to return to school after one year of teaching. Cotulla, locally famous as the home of O. Henry, was a desolate, sunbaked cattle center near the Mexican border. About 2,300 of its 3,000 citizens were Mexican-Americans who spoke only Spanish. Johnson was to teach fifth, sixth, and seventh grades, but when he arrived the superintendent asked him to serve as principal as well, supervising five teachers and the janitor. Lyndon agreed. At age twenty he was in a position of authority.

At Cotulla he was remembered as "a firm administrator, a strict disciplinarian," and a man of "great energy, very aggressive, highly creative, and short-tempered," who "spanked disorderly boys and tongue-lashed the girls." He insisted that English was the only language to be spoken at school, in class, and on the playground, and he spanked those who slipped into Spanish. He piled on the homework. He gave dramatic lectures on Texas history, embarrassing his Mexican charges with diatribes against the miscreant Santa Anna. Every morning he rang the school bell and then strode into class; that was the signal for the children to rise and sing out

> How do you do, Mr. Johnson,
> How do you do?
> How do you do, Mr. Johnson,
> How are you?
>
> We'll do it if we can,
> We'll stand by you to a man,
> How do you do, Mr. Johnson,
> How are you?[36]

A student whom Johnson discovered mimicking him behind his back remembered that he "took me by the hand and led me into his office. I thought I was going to get a lecture, but that wasn't it. He turned me over his knee and whacked me a dozen times on the backside."

But none of this was enough to occupy Lyndon Johnson's immense energies. In addition to principaling, he introduced school assemblies, interschool public speaking contests, spelldowns, baseball games and track meets, and parental car pools; he coached debating and basketball at the high school, organized a literary society, and took six extension school courses (including elementary economics, race relations, and the social teachings of Jesus). He courted a girl who lived 35 miles away (and made $25 more a month than he did, which he found "very humiliating") and wrote out her weekly lesson plans for her. A girl student said that if the boys were not in the gym when he arrived to coach them, "he would coach the girls' softball team. Even then he couldn't bear to waste time." At the end of the school year he headed back to college, after he had "thanked the school board and left the exhausted educational community in Cotulla behind him," Steinberg says.

Back at San Marcos he revived the White Stars. Johnson had a way with student elections. In one contest he put up two of his men against the leading Black Star and got one of them to pretend to hate the White Stars; he won. Another time he got the rules changed so that the least important offices would be voted on first. Johnson and his allies then quickly nominated and elected the leader of the Black Stars for cheerleader, thus taking him out of the running for class president. In the midst of all this he was taking seven courses a quarter, a violation of the rules.

He graduated in 1930. The Great Depression was in full swing. Herbert Hoover believed it would soon be over.

Johnson's Presidential style, emphasizing the manipulation of persons, a focus of attention on the qualities of persons—especially their foibles—and a rather conventional idealistic rhetoric stressing will power is the same style that promoted him from a rejected road-gang bum to King of the Campus at San Marcos. It was at San Marcos that he *emerged* to public notice, that he *connected* with organized group life, and that he *succeeded*, on his own, in surpassing his expectations of himself. He was the doer, the arranger, the effectuator—the politican in a classic sense. He did it with his ears and his mouth, listening just long enough to get the gist of the system and then putting himself right in the middle of the conversation. His nickname at college was "Bull," perhaps a comment not only on his shoving persistence but also on his line of chatter.

Lyndon Johnson's world view grew, in its fundamentals, out of the tough-guy Texas tradition, the John Wayne type of hell-raking heroism, combining endurance, courage, and a sentimental idealism that dares the world to mock it. I think there were two other important themes in the way Johnson came to see the world: a picture of "niceness" conveyed to him by his mother and perhaps reflected in a man who took great care about his shoes, ties, and cufflinks; and a special respect for money, because he had had so little of it, could see how important it was, and could imagine how he could go about getting it better than his father had. But he was neither a prude nor a snob. Also in his persisting vision of life was the picture of Mexican students struggling to get along, of the vulnerability of his father's fortunes, of how hard it could be for a boy on his own to make a dollar. Later he would find those memories consistent with his political purposes, though he never had any very strong ideological commitment. Yet it was not an accident that Lyndon Johnson made himself a millionaire, with a little bit of help from his wife and his friends in the government.

As his *College Star* editorials show, and as his activities show even more clearly, Johnson placed great emphasis on self-control and determined self-discipline to achieve his goals. He, too, felt himself at the vortex of struggle, a struggle to be won by hard effort, to be savored in part for its very difficulty. The fact that Johnson's fight was to establish and exploit a kind of political credit with people makes it no less a fight; it is not something everyone succeeds at. He strove to please. In the course of that, he developed a way of transforming roles through the most energetic use of all their possibilities. The story of his movement from office boy to President Evans' chief assistant shows a pattern highly similar to what Johnson later did with the Senate party leadership; he took a little job and made it big. And as principal—man in charge, top man in his place—Johnson at Cotulla showed what he could do, what he would do, with power, constantly developing new enterprises and insisting on thoroughly dominating those under his tutelage. At college he wended his way to the top through the loosely woven fabric of the institution. Once in charge, he tightened the threads.

Behind it all was his character. And behind that was his mother. Her everlasting persistence in loving and shoving Lyndon gave him a sense of special destiny and made such extraordinary demands for achievement that as an adolescent he had to run away to escape them. But he came back, struggled some more, then gave in completely, making her ambition his own. The struggle in his character was a double battle: of the little lad on teacher's lap wanting to be Davy Crockett, and of the beer-hall brawler wanting to rise to high eminence. Those fights went on all his life; in the Presidency they came together in his image of himself as lone defender of the faith, courageously refighting the Alamo in Vietnam.

THE MAKING OF ACTIVE-NEGATIVE PRESIDENTS

The primary risk in electing an active-negative character to the Presidency is the risk of disaster, of one man's personal tragedy plunging the nation into massive social tragedy. Conceivably that risk could be worth taking, as for example when the danger of drift or inaction is even greater. But the potential for grievous harm will nearly always overshadow the positive possibilities. The fact that the nation survived in each of the cases I have reviewed is cold comfort to those individuals and families who suffered for what these Presidents did. And now that the technical instrumentalities of world destruction and domestic tyranny are developed nearly to perfection and the controls are at the hand of the President, the problem is too important to be dismissed as "soul-stuff" or left to the fictive imagination. Although we can never be certain, we have a responsibility to guess better than we have.

The picture of the active-negative President appears in layers. First there is the perseverance in following a policy despite strong evidence that it is proving counterproductive. Second, there is the fact of the President's strong emotional investment in the failing policy, a matter readily observable to staff men and reporters. Third, there is the realization that the policy line in question is not an isolated item but part of a wider pattern, that it is linked dynamically to a political personality with its own configuration of style, world view, and character.

Observers attuned to watch for these features in Presidential performances might be able to warn us—and them—fairly early that a dangerous tendency was in motion, to help head it off, and, for the longer run, to design institutional remedies, such as more inclusive consultative practices, to prevent recurrence.

But the real challenge is the challenge of prediction. If we could see before election day the character risks and opportunities in our choices, we might choose better. Today and tomorrow, that is likely to mean preferring someone else to the active-negatives on the scene.

I think the fourth layer of interpretation—an understanding of how, in the man's life sequence his character, world view, and style were put together in the first place—is the most useful to explore, especially for the active-negatives. Their Presidential problems reach most deeply into their personalities. Their character-rooted needs invade and dominate, to an unusual degree, their political habits and perceptions. A scanning of the life history from childhood through first independent political success clarifies the dynamics, because it enables us to see the construction step by step.

The Wilson, Hoover, and Johnson stories show, amid wide stylistic contrasts, certain common elements. In each case the boy was subjected to strong deprivations of self-esteem. From the child's perspective, these deprivations were imposed by parents who denigrated, abandoned, or failed to provide for the child. But the family situation was such that the anger such deprivation inevitably engenders could not be expressed directly to the parents. Wilson's were too loving, Hoover's were dead, Johnson's were too dominating. Rather, the anger was turned inward, against the self, repressed and denied for a time, except perhaps in fantasy. The child developed an extraordinarily demanding conscience which required at once rigid self-control and superior achievement.

In each case the child was able to find in his culture sources of support for his view of the world as power-ridden, dangerous, and yet amenable to control through disciplined effort. He adopted fragments of belief confirming his sense that he could and should take himself strongly in hand, that he should force his world to help him implement his version of righteousness. Closed to introspection or unable to question his need-fulfilling beliefs, he focused his mind on the problem of manipulating practical forces for change.

Eventually opportunities for political action (in the broadest sense) appeared and furnished an arena in which he could devote immense energies to projects which would gratify his need of both power and righteousness. He was able to develop there a special cluster of techniques for winning dominant positions legitimately—Wilson through words, Hoover through work, Johnson through persons. Because this stylistic pattern satisfied very strong personal needs, he fastened on it, treating it not as a flexible instrument for a particular task, but in many ways as a magic answer. Once power was achieved, the power needs emerged more clearly from behind the style; dominating behavior became more pronounced and aroused resistance.

Each of these Presidents exhibited this collection of early developments. Each moved on, in early life, to other arenas of action before the situation developed fully enough to reveal explicitly the type of rigid persistence he would display in his Presidency. But the best prediction, from the facts of these cases, at least, is that the relatively grim, intensely striving, onward-and-upward-through-thick-or-thin type is particularly liable—given ultimate political power—to play out the drama to its psychological conclusion.

5

Richard Nixon: Construction and Destruction

President Richard M. Nixon was the first one I predicted. Early in 1972, the first edition of *The Presidential Character* was published, at a time when Nixon was criticized mainly for being shifty ("Tricky Dick") rather than obsessed. He had been President since 1968. He might have been defeated by Senator George McGovern in the election of 1972, but the prediction hypothesized Nixon's victory. That happened. But far more surprising, the prediction of Nixon's danger as president came true, culminating in his unprecedented forced resignation in 1974.

The section below is printed just as it was published, well before Nixon ran for President again in 1972. The section following, The Nixon Destruction, was written and published after his Presidency blew up and he was blown out of Washington, D.C.

THE NIXON CONSTRUCTION

To get at the enduring features of Nixon's character, world view, and style, we need to look at those factors in the process of construction. Long before he was a famous man, Richard Nixon the child, the boy, and the young man put together his remarkable and elusive political personality. Well before he started his climb from hard times to the big time, the Nixon project, with himself as executive director, took on its organization.

NIXON'S MOVE ONSTAGE

Hannah Milhous's marriage to Frank Nixon had raised some eyebrows in Whittier. Hannah's family were Whittier Establishment; they had come out from Indiana in the 1890s to help settle a new Quaker community. There they built a pleasant two-story house with a picket fence and enjoyed, eventually, a bevy of children, two boys and six girls. She remembered her parents as "full of love, faith and optimism." Her father liked to sing, play the accordion, and tell tales; on his wedding day he dressed up in formal attire, top hat and all, but with light-colored moccasins. Her mother Almira—"I guess you would call her 'social'"—loved outings and gatherings at home. During Richard's youth she was an imposing matriarch, given to inspirational poetry. "I don't recall ever seeing them in despair," Hannah remembered.

Hannah came out of this family life shy and quiet. She went to the local college. Then, at 23, she married a trolley operator whose only resemblance to her jovial father was his name, Frank. Frank Nixon (the name means "he wins" or "he faileth not") had frozen his toes working at his trade in Columbus, Ohio, and had emigrated to Southern California in search of warmth. He had a sixth grade education and a fierce temper—a loud, argumentative, opinionated person. The marriage took place in 1908; five years later, when Richard was born, Frank was still struggling hard against genuine poverty, fighting to keep enough food on the table. He had tried carpentry, fruit farming, worked for the Milhous's for a while, but nothing seemed to work out. As 1912 came to an end, Frank wondered how he was going to support Hannah, their three-year-old son Harold, and yet another child soon to be born.

Richard arrived in the cold of January 1913, a very large baby of eleven pounds, with "a decided voice," a "powerful, ringing voice." There was an eclipse of the sun the next day. It is reasonable to suppose the delivery was difficult. He was given his mother's name and it was clear, as his features developed, that he shared also "the Milhous family imprint"—"the jutting jaw, thick eyebrows, tendency to jowls and upswept nose." Before Richard's second birthday, still another son appeared, this one named Francis Donald after their father. Hannah had her hands full. Once when Richard was three years old, his mother and a neighbor girl were returning with the little children in a buggy from the railroad station. Hannah was holding Donald. Richard suddenly fell out and struck his head against the wagon wheel, slicing a long, deep gash across the top of his scalp. Someone found an automobile and rushed him 25 miles to the nearest hospital, with blood pouring down all the way. A general anesthetic was administered; the sewn-together cut left an ugly scar under his hair. From at least that time on, Richard suffered from motion sickness. Hannah thought his survival was "a miracle." The following year, he nearly died of pneumonia, which left him weakened and susceptible to less severe illnesses through his childhood. As a senior in high school he would have a severe attack of undulant fever, with a temperature hovering around 104 degrees for a week; hay fever has stayed with him into adulthood.

The sudden trauma at age three was the first of a series of shocks to young Richard's system, more psychological than physical in their lasting effects. In Richard's teenage years, two of his brothers died suddenly under circumstances especially frightful. Recounting these events to a reporter in 1968, Nixon said, "I told you I had a happy childhood, but I guess I had some of the sorrows that go along in almost everybody's life." Harold was "kind of a favorite, as you can imagine, with my mother and father," Nixon said in 1968. He contracted tuberculosis.

> My mother took Harold away to Arizona and more or less stayed permanently at the nursing home for two years and kept him there and supported herself by working on the staff there, doing very humble duties, cooking and scrubbing, things like that.
> My father met the doctors' bills by selling half of the acre of land on which his grocery store stood. . . .
> When Harold came back, he was still ill, but we had hopes. One day, when he seemed to be getting better, he asked me to take him into town to buy a present for my mother. It was an electric mixer. I took him downtown, he bought the mixer, I took him home, went to school thinking how pleased he'd been with his purchase, and 15 minutes later a teacher came and told me I must go home, because Harold had just died.[1]

Harold's illness strained the family's finances close to the breaking point, took Richard's mother away and pressed her into demeaning labor for two years, and ended in startling tragedy. Richard was thrown into the oldest son role.

Meanwhile, Arthur Nixon, the fourth child, had fallen ill. Richard at 17 wrote a long, emotional essay for school, remembering little Arthur in a mothering way—his "unusually beautiful eyes . . . which seem [in his photograph] to sparkle with hidden fire and to beckon us to come on some secret journey which will carry us to the land of make-believe." When Richard was 12, Arthur caught tubercular meningitis and grew steadily weaker; Richard was called home from his aunt's in the middle of the night, and "My father met us with tears in his eyes. He did not need to tell us what we knew had happened." Two days before his death, Arthur had prayed with his mother, "If I should die before I wake, I pray Thee, Lord, my soul to take." "And so," Richard concludes, "when I am tired and worried, and am almost ready to quit trying to live as I should, I look up and see the picture of a little boy with sparkling eyes, and curly hair; I remember the childlike prayer; I pray that it may prove true for me as it did for my brother Arthur."

The youngest boy, Edward, was not born until 1930; by then Richard was in college. Through his younger years, besides Arthur and Harold, there was Donald—Francis Donald, his father's namesake, a year younger. Clearly Richard and Donald were often in conflict as children and they have not been close as adults. Donald recalls that "Dick was always reserved. He was the studious one of the bunch, always doing more reading while the rest of us were out having more fun." Donald said, "Dick always planned things out. He didn't do things accidentally. . . . He wouldn't argue much with me, for instance, but once, when he had had just about as much of me as he could take, he cut loose and kept at it for a half to three quarters of an hour. He went back a year or two listing things I had done. He didn't leave out a thing. I was only eight, and he was ten, but I've had a lot of respect ever since for the way he can keep things in his mind." It was "a real dressing down I'll never forget," Donald remembered. Much later Donald had some financial reverses a friend attributed to labor union animosity toward Richard, and Don himself complained of favor-seekers trying to reach Richard through him. "Even my little girl and my boys suffer occasionally because of their famous uncle," Don said. "More than once they have come home from school crying because their classmates, children of Democratic parents, heckled them about him." When Nixon was Vice President, Donald had no picture of him in the house.

We see two brothers dead and one distinctly cool toward him, stressing the contrast between his own playfulness and Richard's bookishness and restraint. But if Donald had no picture of Richard in the house, his mother Hannah hung on the stairwell "a huge, transparent, three-dimensional color photograph of Richard. When you press a button it lights up." From the first, she had a special relationship with her namesake son, though she was careful to give the other boys their due. In 1922, when Richard was nine, Frank and Hannah gave up on the citrus farm and scraped together enough to buy a place for a store and gasoline station in an abandoned Quaker meeting house in East Whittier. For 14 years Frank had been trying to find a way to support the family. He and Hannah considered two properties, chose one, and the following year saw oil discovered on the plot they had rejected. In the grocery and gasoline business, times were very hard in this depressed agricultural community. "The going was hard," Richard remembered. "My mother would be up before dawn, making pies to sell in the store." She put in 16-hour days, baked as many as 50 pies in a morning, and managed the entire enterprise, from bookkeeping to public relations. "Hard work had always been the keystone of her existence." Richard was her steady helper. As Donald said, "Dick had more of Mother's traits than the rest of us." Through his early teens he was her main standby in the store.

Frank Nixon was becoming more and more irascible and difficult to live with; eventually his bleeding ulcers and deafness added physical woes to his misfortunes. The family's income depended on the good will and patronage of their customers, which were threatened continually by Frank's outbursts. "He never suppressed his sentiments," argued with considerable heat about taxes, crops, and politics, became "alternately despondent and tyrannical." "Father was a bit impatient and grouchy with people," Richard said. Even Hannah admitted "It's true that he minced no words and could be very undiplomatic, but his mind was never closed." The preacher in Whittier put it more bluntly: Frank was "brusque, loud, dogmatic, strong-willed, emotional and impatient." He did the spanking when the boys needed that, but otherwise Hannah set about getting Frank out of the way. She managed the store; Frank went off each morning to Los Angeles to get the vegetables and returned to do maintenance work, meat cutting and heavy lifting. In other words, he was kept away from the customers and, one suspects, from the children, with whom he was a stern disciplinarian. Frank did teach Sunday school, "taking over an unruly class of boys and taming them." And Hannah remembered that "He liked to poke fun." But much of the time he was a mean aggressor—and unpredictably so. Frank's brother recalled him as "the more aggressive of us, slow to anger but a wild bull if things went too far. Some folks said he was quarrelsome . . . a fancy dresser . . . [who took a] keen delight in showing his former classmates that he was dressed just a little bit better and was more mannerly. He acquired a pride that became the armor of his body and soul." And "Frank believed the invitation to lean on the Lord was intended for the weak and lazy."

Frank's thorny personality put the burden of stability on Hannah, reinforcing the need for her "even temperament." He yelled and she listened. He argued and she made peace. Hardship, tragedy, grinding labor—all were part of God's plan. Her rule was "not to embarrass people," and, as Richard said, "She always tried to keep from us many unpleasant family problems, so far as budget and other things were concerned." After her interviews with Bela Kornitzer, she would often call him up to say "I'm afraid I said something yesterday which might hurt the feelings of somebody," and she told him that in a "Fund crisis," though "completely shaken," "As a Quaker I can't say I got angry, but I was terribly put out." She was, in short, the soul of repression, given to interrupting herself with "I shouldn't say this," putting her fingers to her lips.

Richard imitated Hannah. She remembered that Frank "would not hesitate using the strap or rod on the boys when they did wrong, although I don't remember that he ever spanked Richard." She thought the boy was always "very diplomatic" with Frank. Richard put it this way;

> Dad played no favorites with us. However, when you got into mischief, you had to be pretty convincing to avoid punishment. I used to tell my brothers not to argue with him because I knew that, with patience and humility, we could get along. Dad was very strict and expected to be obeyed under all circumstances. If he wanted something, he wanted it at once. He had a hot temper, and I learned early that the only way to deal with him was to abide by the rules he laid down. Otherwise, I would probably have felt the touch of a ruler or the strap as my brothers did.[2]

And his mother, asked if her son had changed, said,

> No, he has always been exactly the same. I never knew a person to change so little. From the time he was first able to understand the world around him until now, he has reacted the same way to the same situations. As you know, most boys go through a mischievous period; then they grow up and think they know all the answers. Well, none of these things happened to Richard. He was interested in things way beyond the usual grasp of a boy his age. He was thoughtful and

serious. "He always carried such a weight." That's an expression we Quakers use for a person who doesn't take his responsibilities lightly.[3]

"He was the best potato masher one could wish for," said Hannah. "Even in these days, when I am visiting Richard and Pat in Washington, or when they visit me, he will take over the potato mashing. My feeling is that he actually enjoys it."

On November 19, 1923, ten-year-old Richard wrote a "letter" his mother preserved in a drawer. That was the year he "dressed down" his brother Donald; possibly it was a time when his mother was away with Harold.

> My Dear Master:
>   The two boys that you left me with are very bad to me. Their dog, Jim, is very old and he will never talk or play with me.
>   One Saturday the boys went hunting. Jim and myself went with them. While going through the woods one of the boys triped and fell on me. I lost my temper and bit him. He kiked me in the side and we started on. While we were walking I saw a black round thing in a tree. I hit it with my paw. A swarm of black thing came out of it. I felt pain all over. I started to run and as both of my eys were swelled shut I fell into a pond. When I got home I was very sore. I wish you would come home right now.
>
>   Your good dog
>
>   RICHARD[4]

The fantasy is full of symbols. Are the boys his brothers, kicking and hurting him? Is the old and neglectful dog Jim his father, who fails to protect him? Is the final appeal a plea for his mother to come home and soothe him? And what should be made of the "black round thing" which, when touched, releases dreadful stingers? Whatever the deeper meanings, the tone, the flavor and cast of the story is plainly sad. It is a tale of hurt, panic, and depression. It fits with Richard Nixon's lifelong propensity for feeling sad about himself—with his Duke law school roommate's observation that "He never expected anything good to happen to him, or to anyone close to him, unless it was earned," and with his nickname at Duke, "Gloomy Gus," for example.

Out of his childhood Nixon brought a persistent bent toward life as painful, difficult, and—perhaps as significant—uncertain. He learned to work very hard; once in his teens he put in sixteen weeks of misery as a handyman and sweeper in a packing house, where "the whirling, churning and hammering of the packing house machinery nauseated him," and excessive labor picking beans gave him a lifelong aversion to eating them. But it was the undiscussed yet all too evident poverty, the stark terror of his near-fatal accident at three, his own illnesses, the cruel and sudden deaths of his admired older brother and his beloved younger one, his mother's prolonged absences, the constant repression and wariness his father's ragings made necessary—these were the hammer blows that drove him toward a mother who felt the very expression of strong emotions to be illegitimate. Between the traumatic events there were long stretches in which Richard felt the tension around him and learned to deal with it—especially, when, with Frank at home, the knots might suddenly tighten. Speak softly, diplomatically, carefully, and ambiguously; let sleeping dogs lie; work hard and be prepared. Those were the lessons Nixon's childhood brought home to him. Severe as the deprivations were, they were not crippling, did not leave him disabled for political life. The family hung together—at considerable psychic cost—and Richard had Hannah's unfailing support and affection. He would be able to grow, but there would always be that expectation of trouble ahead, that concentration on challenge and suffering.

THE SHAPING OF RICHARD'S WORLD

As a child, Richard "was a willing helper around the house when the chores were 'men's work.' But before submitting to tasks associated with girls, like washing the dishes, he would draw the blinds tight to shut the world out from his humiliation," his biographers Mazo and Hess report. His obvious, strong identification with his mother and his practice in playing her role left Richard with an obvious problem as he grew older: the establishment of his identity as a boy and man. His brothers teased him as a mother's boy. Richard's general reaction, especially in school, was to be anti-girl. "Oh, he used to dislike us girls so!" a classmate remembered. "He would make horrible faces at us. As a debater, his main theme in grammar school and the first years of high school was why he hated girls. One thing was strange, though. He said he didn't like us, but he didn't seem to mind arguing with us." But arguing is a form of aggression; he might have chosen to ignore the girls, but instead he was ready to fight them. Neat, clean, dignified, intellectual Richard was a "loner" in school, generally respected, but "his stock with the girls was not too high."

Through his school years, Richard was, as another female classmate put it, "too intelligent to be much fun"; in school theatricals he was "a little stiff in the romantic scenes"; at Duke he was kidded for working for a woman in the library; as a young lawyer he was annoyed at "women complainers, and naggers who had only petty grievances, but wanted to inflict punishment on their husbands." His sentimental story about his little brother Arthur refers again and again to the boy's resistance to girlishness:

> After learning that it was not a "girl doll," we finally decided that its name should be Arthur.

> There was one time when he was asked to be a ring bearer at a wedding. I remember how my mother had to work with him for hours to get him to do it, because he disliked walking with the little flower girl.

> Then I remember the grief he experienced over his hair. My parents had wanted him to be a girl in the first place; consequently, they attempted to make him one as much as possible. Each day he begged my mother for a boy's haircut, and when he finally did get it, there was not a happier boy in the state.

. . . He was doing exceptionally well in all things except drawing. He absolutely would not take interest in anything he thought common to girls.[5]

Through these passages, in the context of numerous observations about Arthur's girlish looks, 17-year-old Richard seems to be paying special attention to an issue also of importance to himself. The point for our purposes has less to do with his direct sexual identification than with what this problem implies about his struggle to grow away from being Hannah's equivalent, into a manly stance. Eventually he had to define for himself what it meant to be a man, how manliness differed from femininity.

The theme that persisted on into his political years was simple: unlike men, women are reliable. In politics, he wrote, "women basically find it much harder to lose than do men." But "this is probably a credit to them. Once they or those they admire are committed to battle, they enter into the contest with all their hearts and souls. They work harder and fight harder than men. Their commitment is greater and their loyalties more lasting. . . . [In campaigning,] the wives insisted that 'they would never give up.' And they meant it, too." A woman who disappointed his expectations of reliability was Priscilla Hiss. Questioning her in his investigation of her husband, Nixon writes, "Undoubtedly, I subconsciously reacted to the fact that she was a woman, and that the simple rules of courtesy applied. She played her part with superb skill. . . . She succeeded completely in convincing me that she was nervous and frightened, and I did not press her further. . . . I could have made a devastating case if I had also remembered that even a woman who happens to be a Quaker and then turns to Communism must be a Communist first and a Quaker second." In contrast to Priscilla Hiss, there is his long-time secretary, Rose Mary Woods, of whom he wrote, "Unlike her boss, she can never enjoy the luxury of temperament, no matter how tense the situation, how long the hours. She is the balance wheel for the whole office."

In short, women are supposed to be calm, self-controlled, steady, honest—like Hannah. Where does that leave men? In the Arthur story, Richard writes that "When he was about five years old, he showed the world that he was a man by getting some cigarettes out of our store and secretly smoking them back of the house." In Richard's own history, there are a number of more or less minor departures from his mother's rules; at Quaker Whittier College he was elected student body president on a platform advocating dancing and he confiscated a four-hole privy for the college bonfire; at Duke he did a little dancing of his own and helped some friends break into the dean's office to get an early look at some grades; he played cards seriously in the Navy, learned to cuss a bit, and at least by 1960 was taking an occasional drink. There is at least a hint in the sentence about Arthur's smoking that would connect these minor peccadillos with a sense of manliness. In 1968 he remembered what sounds like a much more serious violation. Speaking of himself in the third person, he described how "A gentle, Quaker mother, with a passionate concern for peace, quietly wept when he went to war but understood why he had to go."

In and around these scraps and hints there is, I think, a larger conflict. It is not just that Nixon is ill at ease with women close up (he is ill at ease with men, too) or that he may be stimulated by women to act impulsively (as when he proposed to Pat Ryan on their first date; "I thought he was nuts," she said), but that Richard retained in his character a special ambivalence: the unresolved conflict between his strong identification with his calm, reliable, and repressed mother, and his feeling that manliness meant being like his father—impulsive, aggressive, surprising, unpredictable. To be a man and yet remain true to Hannah—the stress generated by these contradictory demands would carry over into his political life.

Eventually, Richard would have to leave not only Hannah, but home. The tensions he experienced there reinforced his "loner" ways. Hannah's sister remembered this image of him:

> I can still see him lying on the lawn, sky-viewing and daydreaming. When he was a small boy he wanted his mother to do things for him, and he asked her rather than his father. In his teens he would sometimes grow weary of the small talk which went on in gatherings, and he would go away by himself to a secluded place, to read or just to be by himself. I always felt that he had a longing to be in educated company, where he could learn.[6]

Despite the teasing of the other boys, Richard maintained and extended his scholarship, became an excellent student, refused to give in to the temptation to "quit trying to live as I should." The conclusion of the Arthur story shows how he began to sense he had a special destiny and how he began to translate the negative morality of repression into a positive morality of achievement, one he could make his own as a way of confirming his specialness:

> I might leave the story here and let you decide why that picture means so much to me, but I shall attempt to tell you in my own words. There is a growing tendency among college students to let their childhood beliefs be forgotten. Especially we find this true when we speak of the divine creator and his plans for us. I thought that I would also become that way, but I find that it is almost impossible for me to do so. [He then tells of his brother's prayer.] And so when I am tired and worried, and am almost ready to quit trying to live as I should, I look up and see the picture of a little boy with sparkling eyes, and curly hair; I remember the childlike prayer; I pray that it may prove true for me as it did for my little brother Arthur.[7]

Adherence to the right is compelled ("it is almost impossible for me to do so") but its main message is not to quit, to keep going, keep trying. This is precisely what Richard did in school, to the pride and pleasure of both his parents. He was the family intellectual, the beginnings of a special role.

Early on, Richard began to think and dream about getting away. "My first ambition as a child was to become a railroad engineer—not because of any interest in engines (I have no mechanical ability whatever)—but because I wanted to travel and see the United States and the world." The train whistle "never failed to start me to daydreaming about the places I would visit when I grew up."

There were other connections with railroading. His father was an ex-trolley conductor, so there may have been some idea of being like—and surpassing—him. When the children were younger, they would play with an electric train in front of the fireplace, and, as Hannah recalled it, "One of the boys was the conductor, another the fireman. Richard was always the engineer"—that is, the man in charge. And there was a link with status and financial security: Richard said, "The best-off man in town was an engineer who ran the Santa Fe train from Los Angeles to Needles. Every time I saw him or heard his name I thought that being a railroad engineer was an awfully good job to have." But the reason he advances as the primary one—"because I wanted to travel"—was confirmed in Nixon's 1968 acceptance speech, as the first item in his self characterization:

> I see another child.
> He hears the train go by at night and dreams of the faraway places he would like to go.
> It seems like an impossible dream.[8]

The theme is getting away, leaving, going to undefined places different from the one he is in.

The railroad engineer idealization faded away, like so many boyhood thoughts of being a cowboy or a fireman. As a result of a fascinating confluence of influences, Richard decided instead to be a lawyer. Occasionally people who heard him debate had said the obvious, "Dick is a born lawyer." Then on his tenth birthday, in 1923, an aunt gave him a large book about American history, one he read and reread many times; in it "nonmilitary heroes"—"all of whom appeared to be lawyers"—were glorified. (This was a year of tension, the year he "dressed down" his brother Donald, the year of the "Your good dog Richard" letter, the end of the family's first hard year in Whittier.) Then came the Teapot Dome scandals; the Congressional hearings began in 1923. Frank, whose citrus farm had been edged out by oil derricks and who barely missed becoming an oil tycoon himself, railed on against the "crooked politicians" and "crooked lawyers" involved in the Harding administration oil lands scandal. Hannah remembered how this affected Richard:

> Day after day the papers headlined stories of corruption in the handling of the government's oil reserves. One day Richard was lying in front of the fireplace, with newspapers spread all over the floor. Suddenly he said: "Mother, I would like to become a lawyer—an honest lawyer, who can't be bought by crooks."[9]

Hannah had hoped he would be a musician or a preacher. He had never known, perhaps had never even seen, a lawyer. The image is indirect, vicarious, and moralistic: he will be a non-crook, joining his father's indignation with his mother's ethical principles. From that point on, the choice gave him an answer to the perennial question, "What do you want to be when you grow up?"[10]

But there was no clear implication at this point that Richard saw himself as a lawyer in politics or in government. For a long time he must have been gathering impressions of politics and politicians from Frank's indignant talk. Frank had come from a Democratic family, but was converted to Republicanism when President McKinley once visited his home town in Ohio, let Frank ride in the parade behind his carriage, and personally encouraged him to work for the Grand Old Party. "This took Frank by surprise, and, before he could think, he pledged his support. He was an active Republican ever afterward." There were no public officials "higher than . . . sheriff" in the family background as far as Richard could remember, but Frank was forever arguing about politics. He admired William Jennings Bryan, "as he believed oratory is one of the greatest talents of mankind"; a picture of Bryan was displayed on the living room wall. In 1916, Hannah remembered, she departed from the Republican faith to vote for Wilson "because of his tacit promise that America wouldn't be involved in the First World War . . . but Frank remained loyal to the Republican party." Frank himself, angry at the scandals, deviated to vote for LaFollette in 1924. But for all Frank's talk about the subject, the Nixon family was neither highly involved nor highly partisan. Richard did not register to vote until he was 25; sought as a Republican candidate in 1946, he said he guessed he must be a Republican, having voted for Dewey in 1944.

"Even in college," Richard remembered, "political battles as such never appealed to me, but I always seemed to get dragged into them to run for some office or another." His wife remembered that "there was no talk of political life at all in the beginning"; when the chance to run for Congress came along, she said, "I didn't feel strongly about it either way. . . . I felt that a man had to make up his mind what he wants to do, then after he made it up, the only thing I could do was to help him. But it would not have been a life that I would have chosen." And as for Hannah, Richard remarked, "The last thing my mother, a devout Quaker, wanted me to do was to go into the warfare of politics."

Lawyering and politics were not yet connected in his mind. Yet there was at the periphery of Richard Nixon's vision the picture of Bryan on the living room wall, and over his bed (from the age of 13) a picture of Lincoln his grandmother had given him, under which, in her own hand, were these lines from Longfellow about heroes and about leaving:

> Lives of great men oft remind us,
> We can make our lives sublime,
> And departing, leave behind us,
> Footprints in the sands of time.
>
> Footprints that perhaps another,
> Sailing o'er life's stormy main,
> A forlorn or shipwrecked brother,
> Seeing may take heart again.[11]

As yet politics for Richard was an abstraction, a matter of talk and reading. Religion was in some ways closer to home, but does not appear to have bitten very deeply into his world view. Hannah said, "We used to let the boys read a text or scripture lesson each morning after breakfast, as it was the custom in my parents' home. But Mr. Nixon had reasons not to press religion on his boys too hard." Frank had suffered through a stepmother's insistence on long morning and evening prayers. Hannah said he often told her, "I don't want to be found guilty of making the boys go through what I went through when it comes to religion," though he did insist they go to Sunday school and church. Quakerism was primarily a Milhous thing. Grandmother Milhous continued to use the plain speech, but Hannah dropped it with her children. Frank, though he converted to his wife's church, came from a long line of hell-fire-and-damnation Methodists. Perhaps there is a symbolic development in the facts that Richard grew up in a Quaker town and family, went to a Quaker college there, then departed for a Methodist law school (Duke), and married a Methodist wife; his later enthusiasm for the Reverend Billy Graham seems closer to Frank's than to Hannah's religious heritage.

Hannah's minister called her "a Quaker saint—patient, loving, quiet, unassuming, understanding. She has given everything of herself to her children and to many others as well. I have never heard her complain. I have never heard her criticize anyone. Her poise in handling difficult situations has been a wonderful lesson to me." That was the example Richard experienced, the personalized Quakerism he saw and heard at home. The theme is being quiet, accepting fate, ultimate kindness. Richard remembered that Hannah had said, at the funeral of her oldest son, "that it was difficult at times to understand the ways of the Lord but we know there is a plan, and in the end it's for the best." In a 1968 interview with the *London Observer's* Kenneth Harris, Richard went on to explain his stance toward his mother's faith:

NIXON: I do not have my parents' passivity, and I do not go along entirely with that philosophy, but the sight of their patience, courage and determination not to break down, whatever the physical and emotional strain, has been one of the finest things I have ever known. And it has certainly held me together at times when I have been under pressure. And it always will.

HARRIS: You say you do not have your parents' passivity.

NIXON: More accurately, my mother's. She bottled things up, wonderful self-control. My father was more effervescent, though he was most good-natured. Father would spank us sometimes; my mother never.
No, I do not believe in being passive under attack. Our college football coach used to say, "You must hate to lose." You must fight back in life, especially in politics, and above all when the odds are against you.[12]

Hannah's passive acceptance is invoked here as an aid in self-management, a guard against breaking down under strain, a bottling up. Richard does not reject that; he retains it for use when he is under pressure. But in fighting (that is, "fighting back" when "under attack") he asserts his father's aggressiveness. Religion is linked closely here to Richard's primary adaptive conflict; the struggle between repression and aggression. The significance of faith is fundamentally psychological. Yet the moral connection also remains—there is something wrong, something temptingly evil about fighting, even in politics.

There is another connection, less clear, perhaps less strong. Asked on another occasion to comment on his mother's view that "politics have not changed the beliefs that guided him as a boy in college," Nixon replied, as we saw before, in typically deductive style, beginning, "Obviously, any man's religion has a considerable effect on his approach to all problems," and continues:

> In my case, there isn't any question that my Quaker background, in which I was thoroughly indoctrinated in my early years, has had a very great effect on my outlook in life.
>
> One of the reasons for my intense interest in international affairs is the emphasis on peace and mutual understanding drilled into us at home, in school, and particularly in church in my early years.
>
> One of the reasons for my interest in the problems of millions of people in the less developed areas of the world is the traditional Quaker attitude of concern for less fortunate people, not only in our own country but in other lands as well.
>
> My background is primarily responsible for my strong convictions on civil rights. Our family has always been free of prejudice, whether racial or religious. All through my early years, and also at Whittier College, this whole problem of civil rights was not simply a legal issue but, above all, a great moral issue.[13]

Neither as boy or man has Richard Nixon been the prisoner of this or any other ideology; his characteristic flexibility of principle has been universally noted. What these passages show is an association: Mother's religion is linked to generally "liberal" policy trends—peaceableness in international affairs, charitable concern for the unfortunate, freedom from racial and religious prejudice. In his mind there is something good, something godly, in efforts to succor the poor, the hungry, and the war-weary. But in all that there is also something Nixon connects with Hannah, and thus with passivity, womanliness, restraint of the fighting spirit, the confinement of a home where anger had to be masked and diverted. In opposition is Frank's feeling that "leaning on the Lord" was a sop to the weak and lazy. And in Richard's gradually forming world view, politics was Frank's bailiwick; Frank was the one, Richard said, who "loved the excitement and the battles of political life."

THE START OF A STYLE

The main alternative to home was not church but school. School gave Richard chances to test and to rehearse ways of acting he would later bring together in a political style. Most obviously, he learned there that hard work could bring success. He brought home good report cards, graduated second in his class from college, third in his class from law school. He got ahead in school, he says, "not because I was smarter but because I worked longer and harder than some of my more gifted colleagues." At Duke a friend once found him working away morosely in the library. "I'm scared," Richard said, "I counted 32 Phi Beta Kappa keys in my class. I don't believe I can stay up top in that group." But he did, by sitting on his "iron butt" and studying. He attributes his "competitive drive" in those years to two factors, the first of which was simply the need to win scholarship money in the Depression years.

> The personal factor was contributed by my father. Because of illness in his family he had had to leave school after only six years of formal education. Never a day went by when he did not tell me and my four brothers how fortunate we were to be able to go to school. I was determined not to let him down. My biggest thrill in those days was to see the light in his eyes when I brought home a good report card.[14]

Success in his studies, then, was an achievement for Frank's sake, but it also left Richard with hard-labor habits. Debating was another thrust of action Frank helped along. Richard had long loved to argue, as far back as grade school. Topics were not important: "He liked to argue about anything," a classmate recalled. "No matter what was discussed, he would take the opposite side just for the sake of argument." Frank helped him prepare for his first formal debate ("It is more economical to rent a house than to own one") and Frank's brother gave him data for another ("Resolved, that insects are more beneficial than harmful"). In high school and college he became a champion debater; his team at Whittier won 27 straight contests. Richard went at it tooth and nail. A classmate said,

> Most of us remember Dick as a quiet sort of fellow until he became aroused by some discussion. Then his eyes would flash and he would unleash devastating salvos of logic. He often said: "To be a good debater, you've got to be able to get mad on your feet without losing your head."[15]

A member of his Whittier debating team recalled that "He used to pass me little notes, 'Pour it on at this point,' or 'Save your ammunition,' or 'Play to the judges, they're the ones who decide.'" The debating coach said, "He was so good it kind of disturbed me. He had this ability to kind of slide around an argument, instead of meeting it head on, and he could take any side of a debate."

The college debating style—arguing any side of any issue, not to make a substantive case but to convince judges indifferent to the merits of the case—stuck with Nixon all the way through the Kennedy-Nixon debates of 1960. It was a way to fight with the sanction of the authorities, inside an accepted system of formalities. But Richard also displayed, at least on a few occasions, a less expected verbal aggressiveness—he talked back to teachers. Once at Whittier College an elderly psychology professor propounded his theory that human motivations were primarily subconscious. Richard spoke up and challenged him, offering one of his "salvos of logic" and, the story goes, argued so effectively that the professor revised his theory. Then at Duke he repeated this performance against a law professor much like his father, one who "raised his voice, pounded his desk, put his questions bluntly with seeming lack of tact or consideration, pressed the students for detailed discussions of rape and similar cases, and in general seemed to maintain a rather low boiling point." The students felt, as one of them said, "like Christian martyrs facing the lions." But, even though he was "just as nervous as anyone else, . . . from the first time he recited in any class," Richard would "never . . . back down when he thought he was right."

Nearly always alone, Richard (named for the Lionhearted; two of his brothers were named for other kings) stood up against the powers that be and made his voice heard. Words were weapons, to be used both within the confines of debate and even, on occasion, outside the normal expectations.

At Whittier College he also became a dramatist. In his junior year he played a heartbroken old innkeeper in a play called *Bird in Hand*. The part required him to weep when his daughter ran away from home. The drama teacher said, "He tried conscientiously at rehearsals, and he'd get a pretty good lump in his throat and that was all. But on the evening of the performance tears just ran right out of his eyes. It was beautifully done, those tears." The audience turned him on, much as William Rogers and Rose Mary Woods noticed when they contrasted his shyness close up with his enthusiasm before crowds in politics. He appeared before the college trustees to argue for dancing, contending that if students were forbidden dancing on campus they would head for the evil dens of Los Angeles. He tried out for football and other teams, but, as a classmate said, "Dick had two left feet. He couldn't coordinate. But boy, was he an inspiration. He was always talking it up. That's why the chief [the coach] let him hang around, I guess. He was one of those inspirational guys." Another said, "See some underhanded act on the field, and no one could yell louder than Dick."

Too much could be made of his successes in campus politics. He was frequently elected to office, but the classes were small (his class picture shows seventeen pupils) and the faculty had a good deal to do with nominations. He became a charter member and first president of the "Orthogonians," a club of students who demonstrated their contrast to the snooty "Franklins" by wearing shirts without ties. In his junior year he lost an election to a candidate who used slogans and posters; "He had something new," Richard said. "He deserved to win. There were no hard feelings." The something new was drama, impression-making, and Richard himself learned to use these techniques.

Overall, Richard won respect in his college years, but little affection, no close friends. In a college yearbook cartoon other students are shown talking and laughing around the central figure—Richard Nixon—neat, solemn, and alone. As a senior he ran for student body president and won. Part way into the campaign, he visited a professor's mother and told her he was withdrawing from the race. His duties at the store had not given him enough time to get known, so he thought he stood no chance of winning. She persuaded him to continue; the "about to quit" pattern had its beginnings there.

At Duke his academic success continued and he tried again for football. But as his roommate for three years said, "What he lacks is the capacity of the natural athlete to react instinctively. His reactions are governed by his conscious thought processes."

Thus, by the end of Nixon's academic years, the fragments of a style were in his hands, and he had displayed the beginnings of his lifelong propensity for governing his reactions by conscious thought processes. He worked and he performed and he succeeded. The rehearsal was over. Ten years and more would go by before he emerged as a committed politician.

INTERLUDE

Those ten years were eventful for Nixon, but they add little to an understanding of his character, world view, and style. He graduated from Duke in 1937. Over the Christmas holidays of his senior year, Nixon and two classmates went to New York to seek jobs with big law firms. Nixon found the "thick, luxurious carpets and the fine oak panelling" attractive but, unlike his two friends and despite his excellent law school record, he was not given a job. He applied to the FBI but got no answer. Finally Hannah got him a job back home in Whittier, working in a law firm with an old friend of the family. He took up a routine small town practice— divorces, title searches, some trial work. He became a trustee of Whittier College. With "a group of local plungers," he organized the "Citra-Frost Company," with $10,000 capital and himself as president, to make frozen orange juice. "He worked his heart out on the thing," his law partner remembered, rushing out to the plant after office hours to squeeze orange juice into plastic bags. The enterprise folded in a year and a half. In 1938 he met and proposed to Pat; in 1940 they were married. There was about a year and a half of what sounds, in the biographies, like relatively happy times with other young marrieds. Pat was teaching school and they lived in an apartment over a garage.

Shortly after Pearl Harbor, Nixon went to Washington to work briefly in an OPA tire-rationing office, an experience which left him, he said, "greatly disillusioned with bureaucracy," with "the mediocrity of so many civil servants," and with the way "political appointees at the top feathered their nests with all kinds of overlapping and empire building." He quit in August 1942 and went into the Navy as a lieutenant junior grade. At first he had a "lost feeling"; Hannah hid whatever objections her pacifism impelled her to. As a supply officer in the South Pacific, he ran "Nixon's Hamburger Stand," took up poker very seriously, learned to cuss a little. There was not much real danger for him. He was discharged as a lieutenant commander.

NIXON VICTORIOUS

It was after the war, in 1945 and 1946, that Nixon went through the critical period which defined his style. His Navy travels were coming to an end. Back home, things were about the same. The overriding questions were where was he headed, what would he do? He had kept his eyes open during the thirties for a big-city law practice, but nothing materialized. Staying in the postwar Navy offered little chance of advancement. At a deeper level, Nixon was headed back to Hannah, back to the torpor of routine and obscurity. He had won a good deal of money playing poker, but had no clear conception what he would do with it. Certainly politics was not in his mind: "The idea that I myself might play even a minor part in practical politics never occurred to me."

He came to San Francisco and got together with Bob King, an FBI agent he knew. The Kings could not get him to go out celebrating his homecoming in nightclubs. Nixon wanted to talk quietly in their home, "not so much about his service in the Pacific, but rather about the future of America and the world. He seemed to be dreaming about some new order which would make wars impossible," the Kings remembered. Mrs. King said, "He impressed us in those days as an idealistic dreamer. Being a Quaker, he was probably anxious to redeem himself for his 'sin' of serving in the armed forces." His mood was tense, uncertain. The actor James Stewart, who was with Nixon in the Navy, recounts "Nick" Nixon's behavior at his homecoming celebration, a luncheon for more than thirty relatives and friends from Whittier and Yorba Linda:

> One of his cousins, apparently an "armchair general," knew everything and was holding forth. Nick listened with growing resentment, for he knew that the cousin probably had seen combat only on the screen of the town movie. Then all of a sudden, without realizing what he was saying, he leaned across the table and slapped down the old fellow in a language that we used only when the going was really tough. This stopped the conversation abruptly. The guests were amazed. Nick is still convinced that those who attended the luncheon remember that incident more than all that has been said about our war in the Pacific.[16]

The tension level must have been extraordinarily high for Nixon. There may have been many reasons besides Quaker guilt and concern for America's future. Surely one of them came out the following year when Nixon visited a wealthy publisher. "Well, my first impression was simply one of awe," he said. "After all, *I was nothing* at the time, *a small-time lawyer* just out of the Navy." (Italics added.)

Meanwhile, a group of disgruntled Republican conservatives in Southern California were casting about for a candidate to run against Congressman Jerry Voorhis. Voorhis looked unbeatable—he had won a fifth term in 1944 by an impressive margin and enjoyed a reputation in Washington as an effective, liberal Democrat. But the more conservative California businessmen thought he could be beaten if the Republican party would stop nominating "turkeys" and come up with an effective candidate. They turned down eight applicants and were themselves turned down by the president of Whittier College before turning to Nixon. In November 1945 one of them telephoned Nixon, then in Baltimore awaiting release from the Navy, and "asked him pointblank whether he would consider running for Congress against the popular Jerry Voorhis. Surprised, the young naval attorney said he would." He was 32 years old.

Nixon was off and running. He headed for California with a batch of photographs of himself in his lieutenant commander's uniform. Meeting with the committee, he answered questions in "short, crisp terms" and developed at greater length his opposition to New Deal controls and his conviction that returning veterans "will not be satisfied with a dole or a handout" but wanted "a respectable job in private industry" or "an opportunity to start their own business." He promised "an aggressive campaign on a platform of practical liberalism." He wrote his letter of acceptance on December 4, 1945:

> I am going to see Joe Martin and John Phillips and try to get what dope I can on Mr. Voorhis' record . . . His conservative reputation must be blasted. But my main efforts are being directed toward building up a positive, progressive group of speeches. . . . I'm really hopped up over this deal, and I believe we can win.[17]

"Why did I take it?" he asked later, and answered, "I'm a pessimist, but, if I figure I've got a chance to win, I'll fight for it."

It was a rough fight. Nixon got through the primary all right and then wrote the party chairman that "All we need is a win complex and we'll take him in November." Nixon bore in on "lip-service Americans," people "who front for unAmerican elements, wittingly or otherwise"; the public should not be "fooled" by Voorhis' conservative tone. Voorhis spent the war in Congress. Nixon swore "to preserve our sacred heritage, in the name of my buddies and your loved ones, who died that these might endure." The material issued by his campaign headquarters was a good deal worse, accusing Voorhis of "consistently voting the Moscow-PAC-Henry Wallace line in Congress."

The dramatic climax came in the first of a series of five debates Nixon and Voorhis put on. Every one of Nixon's advisors except Murray Chotiner advised against the debates, but Nixon went in anyway. "It was tough," he said. "I was the challenger, and he was the experienced incumbent. Once that debate was over, I was on my way to eventual victory." Mazo and Hess describe the climactic moment:

> There had been a small Nixon advertisement which declared, in part: "A vote for Nixon is a vote against the Communist-dominated PAC with its gigantic slush fund." Voorhis vigorously insisted that he had not sought and did not have the endorsement of the regional Political Action Committee of the CIO. At this point, Nixon leaped to his feet, drew a paper from his pocket and read a report in which the Los Angles chapter of the *national* Political Action Committee recommended that the national group endorse Voorhis. Nixon also read off the names of officers of the national organization's chapter who were also officers of the regional group. Then, dramatically, he thrust the paper at Voorhis.[18]

Nixon won by more than 15,000 votes. "Our campaign was a very honest debate on the issues," he said.

In his book, Nixon spells out his version of what the contest had meant to him:

> Up to this time in my own life, I had been through various crises which had seemed critical at the time. . . . But these crises had been primarily personal as far as their outcome was concerned. . . . Only when I ran for Congress in 1946 did the meaning of crisis take on sharply expanded dimensions. The outcome of the election would naturally have a profound effect on me. If I failed, my family and close friends would share my disappointment. But, in addition, I realized in that campaign that I must not only do the best I could because of my personal stake in the outcome but also that I must call up an even greater effort to meet

the responsibility of representing the institution which had nominated me for office, the Republican party, as well as fulfilling the hopes of literally thousands of people I would never meet, Republicans and Democrats, who were working for my election and would vote for me.[19]

A lot had happened at once. Nixon went from being "nothing" to surprise winner and Congressman from California. He emerged from obscurity to wide notice. He did it, very nearly, on his own; the critical decision to enter the debates, for example, was made against the counsel of his advisors. This was no fall-back job engineered by his mother, but an independent move based on his personal—and sudden—decision. The infusion of confidence must have been massive.

The *way* Nixon won set his style. The performance was overwhelmingly rhetorical, an exercise in impression management, innuendo, and dramatic debating. The rhetoric was backed up with very intensive homework, detailed study of Voorhis' record, the most careful calculation and memory work. What was missing in this style was interpersonal relations as a central element. Nixon mapped his own plans and executed them himself. He saw his victory as a "tremendous achievement" and "the result of three factors: intensive campaigning; doing my homework; and participating in debate with my better known opponent"—nothing there of collaboration, team effort, reliance on any other person.

The Nixon rhetoric was thoroughly aggressive. There was not much said about the "positive, progressive" program he initially intended to set forth. He arrived in Washington again with a "lost feeling" and no particular plans other than resisting labor dictation. In 1946 he had not discovered a political purpose but he had discovered in the "political warfare" his mother so disliked a way to fight his way forward with words.

In Congress the pattern soon repeated itself—the near accident of the Hiss case, the commitment and concentration, the dramatic confrontations, and especially Nixon's driving, drilling questioning of Hiss. The pattern was set; in the Presidency Nixon would return again to a style stressing intensive preparation, fighting rhetoric, and singlehanded decision-making.

PREDICTION

Nixon's Surface and Soul

Nixon's early life history shows the dynamic forces underlying his political character, world view, and style. The negative cast of his character traces back to a childhood marred by trauma and insecurity. The active solution developed out of his discovery, especially in school, that hard effort could bring success. These characteristics are not temporary, not some feature of Nixon the rising politician only, but are engrained in his personality. The vagueness of Nixon's self-image and his highly moralized concentration on managing himself go back to a home situation in which young Richard was right in the middle of an extraordinarily tense, emotionally charged family constellation. Caught between Frank and Hannah, the boy had to wend his way cautiously, alertly, ever ready for whatever sudden challenge might arise. The problem of controlling aggression was not some abstract moral conflict but a continuing, personalized experience in his home. Given that primary tension, other conflicts and identifications (regarding values for instance) took second place; Nixon's attention was focused strongly on the emotional aspects of situations, and on molding to best and safest advantage his own feelings.

The meaning of power for Nixon also takes on a clearer configuration in the light of his life history. As he grew he had to develop an identity of his own which would confirm his manliness; the available model for that was Frank. The themes of loneliness, leaving, traveling, and escaping are tied together with Frank's aggressiveness and ambition for his son. That is, Richard's need to get away from the confinement of home and his need to demonstrate his fighting strength are joined in the thrust for a special kind of power: independence. To achieve he must work and fight—but always on his own, out from under the controlling influence of anyone else. He moralized his occupational identity through the image of himself as the lone lawyer against the corruptionists, and he confirmed the choice for himself by seeing a world in which most people were weak, and lazy, and uninspired—a world in which a man with the will to win and a driving dream could, if he tried very hard, make his way out. And he found the sign of success in the experience of suffering.

Nixon's style also has deep roots in his background. The stress on impression management traces to his role in a family where the flash of drama alternates with calm. Feelings, particularly "bad" feelings, were not to be aired—at least not by him—and so one had to move by watching the signs, the nuances, the facial expressions. At school he found, in speaking, debating, play-acting, and cheering-on, ways to win and at the same time unload anger. The importance of performing just right was confirmed in his first independent political success. Independence, intense preparation, and public performing became the habits of his political life.

All of these feelings come together in Nixon's "classic crisis." There he relives each time the agony of self-definition, as he decides whether or not a crisis is "his"; the confirmation of suffering, as he wearily drives himself to get ready; the freedom of aggression, as he takes clear action; and the closure of control, as he reasserts self-restriction in the aftermath. There, in a short space of time, Nixon acts out the drama of his life—over and over again.

PREDICTION

President Nixon Predicts Himself[20]

Nixon won the Presidency in 1968. The main worry of his critics was that he would be too flexible, too unprincipled, not that he would freeze up in a pattern of rigidification. Nixon himself said he intended to anticipate and avoid crises, to disperse power in his administration, and to tone down the virulence of controversy. But his intentions contradicted his character. He needed crisis to feel alive. He would hold and concentrate power in himself. And he was bound to use his habitual scathing rhetoric to unload aggression.

These predictions were clear before he took office. So were several important Nixon strengths for the Presidency. A highly significant one was his ideological flexibility. If he lacked clear ideals and beliefs, at least he was not yet wedded to some rigid framework of principles. Furthermore, he was obviously a careful man in many respects, given to diligent preparation. It did not seem likely that he would be easily taken in by his advisors; his thirst for independence would take care of that. And his dramatic flair would insure against his becoming a clerkly President easily ignored by the public.

These predictions panned out in Nixon's first term. The old Nixon showed through in his fight to get his Supreme Court nominees approved by the Senate—and in his fury when, for the first time in forty years, the President failed in that effort. The drama of the bombing of and military "incursion" into Cambodia laid bare, as never before, Nixon wielding power alone, in secret, with enormously destructive consequences for the Cambodians and very high political costs for him, an enterprise culminating in one of the strangest speeches ever delivered from the White House. As the 1972 election approaches, Nixon's character is still intact.

This character could lead the President on to disaster, following in the path of his heroes Wilson and Hoover and his predecessor Johnson. So far his crises had been bounded dramas, each apparently curtained with the end of the last act. The danger was that crisis would be transformed into tragedy—that Nixon would go from a dramatic experiment to a moral commitment, a commitment to follow his private star, to fly off in the face of overwhelming odds. That type of reaction is to be expected when and if Nixon is confronted with a severe threat to his power and sense of virtue.

Nixon's is a special variant of the active-negative character. With his remarkable flexibility regarding issues and ideologies, Nixon can be "defeated" any number of times over specific questions of policy without feeling personally threatened. His investment is not in values, not in standing fast for some principle—although, if he were to stand fast, his doing so would certainly be rationalized in terms of principle. His investment is in himself, and Nixon's self is taken up with its management. As Margaret Mead has noted, "The President thrives on opposition. It is a form of stimulation for him." Thus he will court the strains of political resistance, finding in them yet another confirmation of his virtue.

But let the issue reach his central concern, the concern of self-management, and the fat may go into the fire. Threats to his independence in particular—the sense that he is being controlled from without because he cannot be trusted, because he is weak or stupid or unstable—will call forth a strong inner response. For Nixon, the prime form of the active-negative command "I must," is this: "*I must make my own way.*" Only when a crisis gathers around him, one he cannot escape by moving on to some alternative crisis, and he experiences a sense of entrapment, is he likely to move toward the classic form of rigidification.

The key variable here is time. "Time running out," the President wrote on his pad before Cambodia. As the clock ticks forward, Nixon confronts his future in two stages. The first is in 1972. As the election approaches, Nixon's Presidential fate will clarify itself. If the uncertainties fade in the light of the polls, and the probability of a defeat for Nixon rises sharply, this President will be sorely tempted to do what he feels he must do before it is too late. The loss of power to forces beyond his control would constitute a severe threat. That would be a time to go down, if go down one must, in flames.

Nixon victorious in 1972 would face a second clock. Then he would know exactly when his time would run out. Short of impeachment, he would be unremovable until 1976, and then would be removed for sure. No longer accountable to an electorate, the Nixon pragmatism would have to take a different focus, one not restrained by calculations of electoral popularity. Then the salience of Presidential virtue would rise in Nixon's mind, as power faded. Accountable then to God and history, Nixon would have before him the models of heroes.

Two heroes he has often expressed admiration for are Wilson and Churchill, both men who marked the world and then were rejected by their people. Their rhetorical styles and dramatic lives appeal to the theatrical in Nixon. But conceivably he could come to find an example in another man of independence, unheroic Harry Truman, who drew upon inner strengths he hardly knew he had to move beyond toughness to achievement.

THE NIXON DESTRUCTION

The section above, The Nixon Construction, was printed and sold in 1972, well before the Watergate scandal was revealed. Not an astrological prediction of details, the section gives an analytical forecast of the main themes yet to happen.

Even in truncated form, it raised the possibility of a story which came true: our nearest brush yet with a Presidential tyranny.[21]

Richard Nixon got protected by a deep political fault.

How quickly the fog of history settles over the brutal terrain of the past! Wars become romantic adventures, depressions provide material for folksy fables, the pestilence is made into an antique amusement. Thus with "Watergate." The President who came after Nixon told us it had been just a nightmare and it was all over. "The system" took care of such problems (and surely would again, if need be). There was nothing fundamental to worry about, so we should put all that nastiness behind us and move on to make a better future.

Of course, that is the Nixonian way of looking at it. He always did have a knack for diverting the public mind, whenever it began to focus too strongly on him. Like a television camera, Nixon moved from scene to scene, quickly, lest understanding set in. He knew, too, how to cooperate with the empiricism of history, by drowning the truth in the facts; today the obsessed Watergate buff can find a lifetime occupation tracing out just where, say, Ulasewicz was when he called Kalmbach on such and such an evening—much as the assassination buffs used to do. The flood of fact-packed books on the subject swells across the bookshelf.

I think Nixon was neither an accidental nightmare nor an automaton whose rise and fall were inherent in the system. He will be back, in his essentials, the next time the public elects an active-negative President. He very nearly got away with establishing a Presidential tyranny in the United States. He was caught by a mistake he could easily have avoided—whatever the system. Because it is so important to the future of the Presidency to keep it out of the hands of future Nixons, his case is worth examining in detail.

THE NIXON TYRANNY

The Nixonians at the top of the Presidency took their cues and views from the President. Under his direction, and often encouraged by personal enthusiasm, they succeeded in a wide range of tyrannous achievements:

They made secret war.

They made secret agreements to sell immense quantities of deadly weapons to nervous nations.

They supported foreign governments which ruled by terror and they helped overthrow progressive governments.

They received bribes and sold high offices.

They recruited and operated a secret White House police force and ordered them to break the law, continually and casually.

They abrogated Congress's power of the purse by impounding huge sums.

They subverted important segments of the electoral system, the judicial system, the law enforcement system, the tax system, and the free speech system.

They purposefully and systematically lied to the public, the Congress, foreign heads of state and diplomats, and the loyal leadership of their own party and administration about matters of high political significance.

There was a good deal more. The President made a practice of lying to his closest aides. He even lied to his own family again and again. Although in the end he was forced from office, he was not impeached, he was not indicted, he was not even stripped of his pension. He simply left, saying he lacked the political support necessary to govern, as if he were a gracefully retiring prime minister. Soon he was pardoned for any and all offenses he committed against the United States while he was President. His words were bought at an enormous price before they were spoken or written. At this writing, he lives in freedom and luxury in a mansion on the sunny beaches of southern California, traveling as he pleases to Peking or Paris.

The important point here is not that Nixon was a bad man (he was), or that he was mentally unbalanced (he may well have been, toward the end), or even that he was guilty of any crimes for which he could have been convicted in a court of law (we will never know). Had Nixon never been President, none of that would have mattered much. It is his *political* significance that lends immense significance to his tawdry triumph over our Constitution.

Nixon demonstrated the vulnerability of the American political system. Throughout his career, his repeated victories after disastrous defeats show with dramatic clarity how the process of evaluating potential Presidents failed miserably to predict and guard us from the machinations of an expert flimflam man. The American people had every opportunity to know what they were getting. They elected Nixon despite the most abundant evidence ever available regarding the character of any Presidential candidate.

The protection of checks and balances was similarly shown vulnerable. Nixon had no need to march on the Capitol at the head of his White House guard or to throw barbed wire around the Justice Department. He simply set up his own little government on top of the Constitutional one and dared the world to say him nay. It took four and a half years for Congress to begin to suppose that his impeachment should be suggested, and they took this move only after they had evidence hard and massive enough to choke Caligula's horse. Through nearly all his Presidency, Nixon had but to assert his authority to enhance his power, be it the power to bomb or tap, to impound or burgle, to broadcast or blackmail and bribe.

For those who take it as a sign of the system's stability that he was ultimately driven from office, it is sobering to remember that his downfall was nearly accidental. At point after point he could have been rescued by other accidents or by easy efforts of his own, as I hope to show in a few pages.

Perhaps there is some way the electoral machinery and the system of checks and balances can be readjusted, to prevent such enormous political risks. Or perhaps there is some way, without major procedural reform, to help the leaders of existing institutions acquire the vision and the will to see to it that we get quality Presidents. I see the most promising development along this line in the steady improvement of data and theory by which present-day decision-makers can predict, if not the "great" Presidents, at least the disastrous ones.

Drawing on the work of many scholars, journalists, and biographers, I was able to see some parts of Nixon's pattern before he became President. On the eve of his first inauguration on January 19, 1969, I wrote that, "The primary danger of the Nixon administration, then, will be that the President will grasp some line of policy or method of operation and pursue it in spite of its failure." I wondered that night,

> How will Nixon respond to challenges to the morality of his regime, to charges of scandal and/or corruption? First such charges strike a raw nerve, not only from the Checkers business, but also from deep within the personality in which the demands of the superego are so harsh and hard. (For every President, this kind of thing comes up.) The first defense is pleading innocent: I didn't know, it didn't affect me. The guilty party (Walter Jenkins, Bobby Baker) is not my boy, I am not involved. The ordinary processes of justice must take their course. There will not be as in Harry Truman's case a sense of loyalty to the Pendergasts no matter what the charge, or Ike's readiness as in Dixon-Yates to make all the facts public, while withdrawing a bit. The first impulse (before the above) will be to hush it up, to conceal it, bring down the blinds. If it breaks open and Nixon cannot avoid commenting on it, there is a real setup here for another crisis, a dramatic appearance in which he is vindicated.[22]

In the early spring of 1969, I followed up with a speech at Stanford asking, "Will there be a 'Tragedy of Richard Nixon?'" In this speech I suggested that Nixon was likely to follow the pattern of rigidification that had earlier been seen in Woodrow Wilson, Herbert Hoover, Andrew Johnson, and Lyndon Johnson. Other papers followed, leading up to this book in early 1972.[23] The book was filled with retrospective "predictions": we *could* have known in advance what past Presidents would do (in the main) by noticing key biographical characteristics and combining them with the main situational elements. But, with one exception, all those "predictions" concerned events that had already happened. The Nixon case was the best test so far for my theory because there it was possible to make real predictions: given certain situations, Nixon's character, style, and world view would produce certain lines of action.

Unless we are willing to lapse again into the political sleep that brought us Johnson and Nixon—that gave us a decade of disaster in the White House— we need some way to improve radically on our predictions. In that spirit, I have let stand as written the predictions in the preceding chapters, and will try in this one first to check the main Nixon characteristics against his history as it followed after the predictions, then to trace the course of his rigidification, and finally to speculate on the possible meanings, for our political future, of Nixon's peculiar obsession with appearance.

OLD RELIABLE NIXON

Strangely, no one seems to have suggested that Watergate (by which I mean the whole wash of woe that flooded forth after that gate was opened in June 1972) gave us a "new Nixon." Through so many even-numbered years in the past, the discovery of new Nixons seemed to have become a national pastime as observers hoped against hope that he was not what he had been. In the event, though, old reliable Nixon came through.

The clearest continuity was Nixon's active-negative character. As he had before 1972, he poured on energy, night and day, at home and away. His Presidential activities came to take up nearly all his waking hours and, more and more frequently as his end approached, he woke and worked at night. "As long as I am physically able," he pledged in November 1973, "I am going to continue to work sixteen to eighteen hours a day. . . ."[24] He was a man in motion, restlessly flying off to Camp David, Key Biscayne, or San Clemente, where he often plagued his Secret Service guards to "drive somewhere, anywhere." As of the end of November 1973, the President had stayed in the White House only four of the forty-four weekends of his second term; in his last six weeks in office he spent only six days there.[25]

Reliable Nixon continued also in his stance as a suffering martyr in the Presidency. Even the version of the White House tapes he himself released to the public has him in continual complaint: "This damn case!" "I've been working very hard as you can imagine with everything." "I was up so late last night."[26] He told visiting Congressmen he had been through "seven months of pure hell."[27] He refers again and again to his troubled life, in all sorts of circumstances: he wants the truth "even if it hurts me," he says, and he has "broken my ass to try to get the facts of this case." Even after his enormous victory in the 1972 election, Nixon conveyed a "joyless, brooding quality," one of his Cabinet members remembered, and talked of how all Presidents had gone downhill in their second terms.[28] Even when he sat at ease in Washington while his bombers smashed out the lives of Vietnamese peasants, his sense of proportion and comparison deserted him: the Vietnam bombing became "my terrible personal ordeal."[29]

Extensive data about Nixon's character, unavailable in 1972, appeared as the tragedy of his Presidency deepened. His intimates had cause to blacken his name, but the detail and convergence of their stories lent them plausibility. Occasional visitors from Congress and the press gave shocking and similar accounts and the President's own voice—heard on tape by members of the House Judiciary Committee and read in print by the world at large—exhibited with unusual clarity the depth and nature of his struggle.[30] Near the end, as his political defenses crumbled, so did his psychological defenses. Then Nixon revealed the fragility of his self-esteem, the fear and trembling which lay hidden behind his mask of stoic toughness. At the end he was drinking heavily, sleeping sporadically, often enraged and raging, frequently out of touch with the reality gathering around him; by one report, he was a weeping, staggering, irrational man. Theodore White saw the task of the White House staff, as of August 1974, as "the management of an unstable personality," and others, similarly averse to hyperbolic diagnoses, used similarly strong language.[31]

Nixon's own penchant for hyperbole lasted on past 1972, as he dramatized his history, seeing his life as a series of sharp discontinuities. From "the largest dinner ever held at the White House" to "the greatest year of progress since World War II," Nixon zigged and zagged through wide varieties of "toughest" decisions, "most difficult crises," and "deepest valleys."[32] As Watergate deepened, he came to think of it as a "war"—a war in which the stakes were far higher than his personal fate.[33] He told his friend Rabbi Korff that if he resigned, foreign affairs might "suffer irreparable harm."[34] As Jonathan Schell put it, Nixon "invented crises and then he made 'great decisions' to resolve them."[35] Clearly, the Nixon who saw, as he wanted and needed to see, his life as a fascinating and heroic drama was still there after 1972.

He was as insightful as ever about his own character. His speech writer William Safire, aping Gertrude Stein, noted that "to the real Nixon, the real Nixon is not the real Nixon." "Ego is something we all have," Nixon admitted, "and either you grow out of it or it takes you over. I've grown out of it. It's really a compensation for an inferiority complex. Henry [Kissinger] has that of course. . . ." As he saw himself, "I could always get along with anybody . . . no matter what I thought of them."[36] At the very time when he was refusing to obey subpoenas from the House Judiciary Committee, President Nixon issued his Law Day 1974 proclamation: "The law retains its value and force because every person knows that no man or woman is above the requirement of the law."[37] Discussing the fate of John Mitchell with John Ehrlichman, Nixon, scoutmaster for the whole troop, said, "But what the hell, I am always kind."[38] His attitude toward the press was tolerant and easy, Nixon said: "The critics don't bother me, even though I have had the most unfriendly press in history, it has never bothered me, but it deeply bothers Pat and my daughters. They see it in personal terms whereas I see the press totally in impersonal terms." Again and again, Nixon demonstrated, as Safire put it, "the uncanny ability to step outside of himself and coolly misread the man he observed."[39] As in the years up to 1972, those who looked to Nixon's own statements for guidance to his character would soon be lost.

Nixon the manager of himself, "RN" the stage director or producer of the Nixon project—that is the place, I argued in 1972, to look for Nixon's strongest emotional investment.[40] The typical compulsiveness of the active-negative person, which usually takes the form "I must," with Nixon invariably became "I must do it my way." Into his second term Nixon continued to insist on just that. The Watergate saga—particularly the cover-up—took its shape from Nixon's old sense that nothing would be right unless he controlled the way of it. His fear of being dead though living, of having no feelings, contributed heavily, I think, to his need to feel he had to do what he had to do—and in just the right way.[41] In the autumn of 1973, Nixon said, "What matters most, in this critical hour, is our ability to act—and to act in a way that enables us to control events, not to be paralyzed and overwhelmed by them."[42] His Watergate vocabulary is full of the language of compulsion: "We've just got to ride it through." "I've got to get [it] out and I've got to get it out today! . . . The White House has got to move. . . . we have to get out in front in some way."[43] The "way" was infinitely important. Safire pointed out to Nixon that his three favorite words were "in a way."[44] Nixon never seems to have judged the rightness of the "way" by any external criteria of ethics, morality, or even expediency. What mattered most was that things be done in a way that he could feel was *his* way—that is, a way that reflected his own dramatic sense of himself.

In a perceptive passage, Jonathan Schell says that on one occasion, "the President seemed to have thrown himself so wholeheartedly into his false role that in his private conversations he had begun to agonize over moral questions that were appropriate to the false role but wholly inappropriate to his real role. . . . What the President imagined to be true soon was true, as the result of his own actions."[45] The White House became a theater in which "scenarios," "scripts," "players," and "orchestration" were employed to create just the right move at the right time and place.[46] Nixon the self-manager saw to that. In what turned out to be a key comment, Nixon says, "For Christ's sake, get it. In a way that—"[47]

NIXON'S OLD STYLE AND WORLD VIEW

Nixon's political style, with its overwhelming emphasis on rhetorical manipulation, persisted strongly up to his resignation in 1974. As with the other active-negative Presidents, over time his dominant style element invaded and exploited the rest of his style. Nixon turned everything, including his intense homework and his conspirational conversations, to the task of impression management. That is not surprising, given his pre-1972 style and the habits he had developed over a lifetime in politics. What is interesting is the way Nixon's powerful rhetorical style worked, and may work again, to distort and undercut the great democratic conversation which is politics.

Nixon's rather rancid view of the world bore up well after 1972. He changed his mind on a few specific issues—but specific issues, in their substance, had never meant much to him anyhow. He told some Republican Congressmen concerned about budget deficits, "It will take you a little while to get used to fighting *for* what you've been fighting *against* all your lives."[48] If there was one thing no one could find in the Nixon Presidency, despite volume after volume, it is a serious policy direction, a program or order of priorities from the White House. To the central person in the White House, such matters were derivative, secondary to the purpose of tending to whatever came through the door of the store. As before 1972, Nixon's world view came to focus on process, not substance. That lasted till the end.

Nixon's view of human nature continued to color itself jaundiced. "Most people are good not because of love," he said, "but because of fear. You won't hear that in Sunday School, but it's true." Category after category of Americans earned his disdain. "The upper intellectual types, the soft heads" were valued less than "average people," but then Nixon didn't think much of average people either. They were the sort who "won't think it is much of a crisis unless it affects them." Education made people "brighter in the head but weaker in the spine." The "new managers" in business were pusillanimous—they "paint their tails white and run with the antelopes," Nixon thought. People were always letting you down. "These jackasses got off," Nixon told Henry Petersen. "See this Liddy is crazy and Hunt and the whole bunch conducted this (inaudible) Mitchell wasn't minding the store and Magruder is a weak fellow—and the damn thing—and then afterwards they compounded it by what happened afterwards." "Everybody wants to make a name for themselves in this (unintelligible). They'll drag it on and on and on." "Everybody's for himself." Dereliction was never basically surprising to Nixon—that's just the way people are. Virtue is the surprise. "Why did Petersen play the game so straight with us?" Nixon had to ask, as if no one had ever done that before. His old "friend" John Mitchell, along with numerous others who had staked their careers on his success, became "hors d'oeuvres" wherewith to sate the appetite of the prosecutors. "Give 'em an hors d'oeuvre and maybe they won't come back for the main course," our President told the remnant of his palace guard.[49]

In the Watergate period, Nixon's fatalism was not nearly as evident as was the part of his world view that saw chaos rampant at the very time when conspiracy was closing in. To be sure, he spoke of "history" more often than he had in the past. "The United States is once again acting with assurance and purpose on the world stage. We know where we are going. We are moving with history and moving history."[50] But in the daily life of the White House, it seemed the course of history could take most any turn. "In this matter, nothing is beyond the realm of possibility," he said, and added later, "It is breaking so fast. Everything is likely to blow around here."[51] Appointing a special prosecutor would "just put another loose cannon right there rolling around the deck."[52] The release of the Nixon tapes—edited by the President to show himself in the best possible light—conveyed to the great American public just how much like a deck full of loose cannons the Nixon White House was. At the end, the tingling fear of betrayal in the moral darkness of that place came to preoccupy its inhabitants. As the uniformity of the Communist menace faded in his mind, the *form* of Nixon's mindset found another enemy implacably stalking him in tight and evil cabal: the media.

THE POWER DISEASE

Jonathan Schell finds "the fear of impotence" a recurrent theme in Nixon's public statements, as when he worried about moves to "tie the hands of the President" or "cut off the President's legs," or when he feared that America might become "a pitiful helpless giant."[53] One need not be so psychoanalytic, for the ambiguities inherent in the concept of "impotence" could detract from the important political truth that Nixon was a President in perpetual anxiety about holding and advancing his power. In the end, he lost not only power but authority, not only sanction but office, and along the way his aides learned to discount his more ridiculous orders, such as not to serve soup because some spilled one day, or "No more landing at airports!" after a foul-up at the end of a flight.[54] Nixon's fear of losing power undoubtedly is tied to his fluctuating sense of power, which he expressed precisely when he said to his press secretary: "That's an order, Ron—no discussion. Unless, of course, you disagree.[55] Given these fears and uncertainties, it is no wonder he turned to a man of the type Charles Colson used to be, a hit man ready to obey whatever the President told him to do. "Break all the china in the White House if you have to," Nixon ordered.[56] That was the kind of man he needed. "Colson—he'll do anything. He'll walk right through doors," Nixon bragged.[57] What balm it must have been to his bruised power sense to hear his CIA Director say, "There is only one President at a time. I work only for you," or to learn that his White House general-in-residence informed a Deputy Attorney General of the United States: "Your commander-in-chief has given an order. You have no alternative."[58] At least once, Nixon in a fury undertook to rein in Kissinger. Colson reports the President's reaction to an apparent Kissinger press leak:

> He exploded, ordering me to call Kissinger at once. (It was then 6:30 A.M. in California.) "I will not tolerate insubordination," he barked into the telephone. "You tell Henry he's to talk to no one period! I mean no one. And tell him not to call me, I will accept no calls from him." With that he slammed the receiver in my ear.[59]

Of course, Nixon did tolerate insubordination—or at least he experienced plenty of it at the end, when he could not find much subordination anywhere. But he was forever railing against it at the same time as he struggled to control his own aggressive impulses. Like Lyndon Johnson, Nixon could take the pettiest ways to demonstrate his power, such as demanding, on a sudden whim, to be taken to a concert at the Kennedy Center, despite all the inconvenience and disruption an unscheduled Presidential appearance would cause.[60] This was a President who wanted to believe about himself that he was powerful—indeed, a "sovereign" who had his "subordinates" "on a short leash."[61] In a thinly disguised account of a diatribe by "President Monckton," novelist John Ehrlichman portrays his boss's power feelings:

> . . . this government is shot through with miserable little people who do not love this country. Ideologues. They would pull down our institutions if they could; they have no real concern for the well-being of America. The only thing that motivates them is their desire for the realization of their left-wing goals, in education or health or welfare or whatever their narrow little field is. And they hate me, because they know I will try to stop them. . . . Oh, I don't mind their hate. I understand it. I am the first President in this country who really threatens them, and they know it. They fear me and so they hate me. And they should fear me; I intend to root them out. I don't care that they are disloyal to me personally. . . . But the Federal bureaucracy must not be disloyal to the Presidency—or the country. I have concluded that their disloyalty has reached such a magnitude that it seriously threatens our constitutional system, and even the nation. The goddamn traitors. . . .[62]

Yet this character is a fictionalized version of the same President who had to ask his aides for permission to enter their conversation—"Can I spend a minute?"—sometimes repeatedly in the same conversational sequence, as his own version of his tapes reveals.[63]

Nixon's confused inner feelings about power would have had little political importance had not the President acted politically on them. He did, with a vengeance, and with apparent indifference to the Constitution. Almost as soon as he came into office in 1969, he had contingency plans drawn up to handle a possible national uprising. As early as that first November, in preparation for the Vietnam moratorium demonstrations, the President—who was very closely involved in the situation, despite his disclaimers—took extreme measures. The Washington police department set up a joint command with the CIA to collect "intelligence" about the demonstrators. This system was revived for the 1971 May Day demonstrations, when approximately 10,000 citizens were arrested without charges and detained. When the courts finally got around to disposing of these cases, only one defendant out of the first two thousand was found guilty.[64]

Hans Morgenthau said that Nixon tried to take "sovereign" power without risking obvious Constitutional confrontations: "the official statutory agencies of the government, subject to legal restraints, are duplicated by agencies performing parallel functions, which are organized by the ruling party and responsive only to the will of the leader.[65] From the Committee to Reelect the President to the White House secret police squads, from the Domestic Council to the Office of Management and Budget, the Nixonians paralleled regular structures with structures they could control directly. In the military, a separate, secret command system was set up to handle the secret bombing of Cambodia.[66] But the regular organizations were not neglected, for there was also paralleling from within. Nixon got the Internal Revenue Service to set up an Activist Organizations Committee, operating under "Red Seal Security" in IRS headquarters (the committee was later named the Special Services Staff or SSS) to check on the taxes of "organizations predominantly dissident or extremist in nature." As a White House memo put it, "What we cannot do in a courtroom via criminal prosecutions to curtail the activities of some of these groups, IRS could do by administrative action.[67] In September 1972, as the election approached, the full force of this machinery was turned to Nixon's power purpose: John Dean called in the IRS commissioner and demanded tax investigations on 490 staff members and contributors to McGovern's campaign. When the commissioner hesitated and his boss, Secretary of the Treasury George Shultz, told him to forget it, Nixon raged:

> I don't want George Shultz to ever raise the question because it would put me in the position of having to throw him out of the office. He didn't get secretary of the treasury because he has nice blue eyes. It was a goddamn favor to get him that job. . . . We have to do it artfully so that we don't create an issue that we are using the IRS politically. And there are ways to do it, goddammit. Sneak in one of our political appointees. . . . [After the election] the whole goddamn bunch go out and if he [Shultz] doesn't do it he is out as secretary of the treasury and that is the way it is going to be played. . . . I look forward to the time that we have the

agents in the Department of Justice and the IRS under our control after November 7.[68]

Dean told the President he was keeping notes "on a lot of people who are emerging as less than our friends." The President continued:

> They are asking for it and they are going to get it. We have not used this power in this first four years as you know. We have never used it. We have not used the bureau and we have not used the Justice Department, but things are going to change now. And they are going to do it right or go.[69]

Dean's response to this diatribe tells a good deal about the atmosphere Nixon had by then created in the house of Adams and Jefferson: "What an exciting prospect!"[70]

The Presidential subversion of the CIA, the National Security Agency, the Secret Service, the Post Office, and so on proceeded apace. The beginnings were unknown or only hinted at when *The Presidential Character* was published in 1972, but there was already some evidence of the President's power moves. His early attempts to control the bureaucracy by infiltrating it with political operatives, were in fact little more than exaggerated versions of what other Presidents had tried, but in 1970 one White House aide found an additional justification that throws more light on the mindset then operative at 1600 Pennsylvania Avenue: "It works in the Vatican. It works in the Mafia. It ought to work here."[71]

Nineteen-seventy was also the year that produced a temporary but widespread implementation of the secret "Huston Plan," dubbed for the twenty-nine-year-old White House staffer to whom the plan gave the responsibility for "domestic intelligence and internal security affairs" by means of mail-peeking, sneak-thievery, and the like. The one guideline under which Huston worked was that there were no guidelines: "All restraints which limit this coverage are to be removed."[72] The President approved this plan, then withdrew his approval only when J. Edgar Hoover, armed with his own secret files, threatened the President. Although the plan was supposedly scrapped—Huston claimed it was never formally rescinded—some of its elements were later put into effect, in such totalitarian "capers" as the Ellsberg break-in, the wiretaps on newsmen and on Nixon's own brother Donald, and the varieties of threats and acts against Americans on Nixon's steadily expanding "enemies list."[73] It was these domestic measures, in conjunction with the Presidential subversion of the armed forces, that were most significant, for they brought to bear, in illegal and harmful ways, the state's monopoly of force.

Nixon had much else to hide. One whole category of abuses—far less dangerous to liberty, but far easier for the general public to understand, and thus politically far more explosive—was bribery, by corporations seeking favors, potential ambassadors seeking posh posts, and pressure group associations seeking policy advantage. Nixon's personal attorney managed much of this market, his effectiveness enhanced by the fact that he looked honest and dignified. Another vast category of matters not for publication was the President's personal graft and advantage-taking, ranging from his massive tax cheating (his accountant said the President had gone over the returns page by page), to his luxurious estates in California and Florida, to his carefully concealed thievery of leftover campaign money to buy his wife a pair of $4562.38 diamond earrings.[74]

From the point of view of the nation's destiny, these subsidiary crimes were trivial, but from the President's point of view they were extraordinarily dangerous. Sympathetic and hostile Nixon-watchers, such as William Safire and Dan Rather, agree that Nixon had so much to hide that almost any revelation could knock down the whole house of cards. Nixon himself sighed to Ehrlichman at one point in the tapes, "What the hell does one disclose that isn't going to blow something?"[75] In other words, because Nixon had a direct and personal interest in avoiding sustained scrutiny by the press or any other skeptical observer, his sense that power depended on secrecy was mightily reinforced.

I think Nixon needed secrecy and surprise to feel powerful. Was there not in him a certain pleasure, a thrill of danger and escape, when he would look Senator Scott in the eye and say, "Hugh, I have nothing to hide. The White House has nothing to hide. I repeat we have nothing to hide, and you are authorized to make that statement in my name"? Or as he spoke with such a frank air to Elliot Richardson: "I'm innocent. You've got to believe I'm innocent"?[76] What even more transcendent gratification did he experience as he lied, again and again, to Special Prosecutor Leon Jaworski—who, *as Nixon knew*, knew he was lying? He had long made it a practice to divert attention from his misdeeds by preaching against them—damning lawbreaking as he broke the law, condemning chiselers as he chiseled away, advertising his straightforwardness while he coached his aides in perjury. Perhaps the technique worked, for the casual political audience could easily mix up the prosecution with the defense in such circumstances. But I also think (though it cannot be proved) that a Nixon hungry for crisis and fearful of the "vegetable life" might be specially needful of the kind of triumph one experiences when one has hoodwinked the enemy. This is the triumph that is especially delicious to the man filled with resentment.

From his early days, Nixon had among his inner secrets an enormous store of aggression, normally masked by his lifelong habit of self-inhibition, but occasionally breaking through the surface:

> The President's finger circled the top of his wineglass slowly. "One day we will get them—we'll get them on the ground where we want them. And we'll stick our heels in, step on them hard and twist—right, Chuck, right?"
> Then his eyes darted to Kissinger. "Henry knows what I mean—just like you do it in the negotiations, Henry—get them on the floor and step on them, crush them, show no mercy."[77]

I think lying, getting away with it, conning—these nasty, aggressive, verbally-centered initiatives—were especially meaningful to a man whose manhood had, since his early days, been connected with impropriety and harsh words. Power and aggression came together in the pleasure of control through illicit means. When Patrick Gray said, "It strains the credulity that the President of the United

States—if he had a mind to—could have done a con job on the whole American people," one can almost imagine Nixon taking it as a compliment.[78] For Nixon himself, one of Watergate's meanings was, I think, the thrill of risk on a magnificent scale and, at levels deeper yet, the shaping of a national tragic drama starring a misunderstood, unappreciated, but one day to be vindicated President.

RIGIDIFICATION ROAD

Watergate was Nixon's rigidification, his political nemesis and tragedy. The theory and data in this book, published the season before the burglary, could in no way have predicted that a certain specific event—the June 17 break-in—would trigger the tragedy of Richard Nixon. Such forecasting is the business of astrology. Rather, *The Presidential Character* predicted contingently: given certain specified conditions, and given an active-negative character like Nixon's a predictable process of rigidification was likely.

As predicted, that process was set off by "a serious threat to his power and his moral confidence."[79] Nixon moved into his crisis pattern and tried repeatedly to escape by means of his usual get-on-with-it diversion. When that didn't work, he froze up and ruined himself, along the way sapping the spirit of a political generation.

The full story of Nixon's political demise has yet to be told. There have been numerous books (and Nixon's own is yet to come), but none of them has made clear the most interesting and important biographical aspect of the story: the interplay between the private Nixon (as revealed in the tapes and the recollections of his aides) and the public Nixon (as revealed in the speeches and press conferences and summit shows). Certainly that story is too long and detailed for telling here, even if it could be done. Rather I must proceed by summary, inviting all the while the serious critic to dredge up competing evidence.

For a character like Nixon, disaster is always just around the corner, no matter how well things are going. Indeed, the better things are going the sooner you can expect disasters. In the spring of 1972, despite all sorts of good signs, Nixon was running scared. There were plenty of reasonable causes for his anxiety, for a wary fear that the election might suddenly demote him to citizen. From his perspective, he had lost, almost lost, or barely won too many times to take comfort in early poll leads. How much more distressing it must have been when the Harris poll in February had Muskie over Nixon at 43 to 40 percent, in March 44 to 39, in May 47 to 39.[80]

From Nixon's viewpoint, it was touch and go. Almost anything could tip the balance. Perhaps that was why the midnight marauders of the Committee to Reelect the President twice broke into the headquarters of the Democratic National Committee, the second break-in coming on the night of June 17, 1972. The previous year, basically the same band of sneak thieves had broken into the office of Daniel Ellsberg's psychiatrist to see if they could find material to discredit the man who released the secret Pentagon papers. Since no one had exposed the Ellsberg burglary, the Nixon campaigners had every reason to expect that they could get away with another such "caper" without excessive risk. They were hoping to pick up some useful information on campaign strategies, gossip, or whatever.

Some writers have speculated that the break-in must have had a much more serious purpose to justify the radical risk of putting five men, loaded with electronic equipment, into an office known to be guarded, into which any insomniac Democratic campaign official or worker might wander at any time. The purpose may have been to see what information, if any, Democratic National Chairman Lawrence O'Brien had in his records about contributions given to the Nixon camp by multi-billionaire Howard Hughes in 1969–70. O'Brien was in a good position to know, because at the time in question he headed a firm employed by Hughes to take care of Washington matters. J. Anthony Lukas presents evidence that Hughes, hoping to get a favorable break from the government on some anti-trust matters, slipped two bundles of $50,000 in $100 bills to Nixon's pal Bebe Rebozo. In addition, there may have been a lot more of these payments at later dates. Rebozo banked these bribes because, he recalled, "I didn't want to risk even the remotest embarrassment of Hughes's connection with Nixon," and "I was convinced that [the Hughes loan to Donald Nixon] cost the President the 1960 election and didn't help him in 1962 in California."[81]

Lukas's theory of the Watergate break-in as an attempt to discover what kind of dirt O'Brien had on Nixon is unproved. But, if later muckrakings do support this theory, they would add to the evidence that Nixon was running scared enough to take big chances, scared enough to see nearly any event as a threat to his re-election. Consistent with that thought, when Nixon learned in May of 1972 of the attempt on Governor Wallace's life, he was "deeply upset and voiced concern that the attempt . . . might have been made by someone with ties to the Republican party or the Nixon campaign. If such a tie existed . . . the President indicated it could cost him the election."[82] Far from being a President preoccupied with great and high affairs of state, Nixon regularly involved himself in the most picayune details of political calculation. Doubt must arise that this President knew nothing in advance about the Watergate break-in, down the street from the White House, when he was continually concerned, as his office neighbor Alexander Butterfield testified, with such White House matters as "whether or not the curtains were closed or open; the arrangements of state gifts; whether they should be on that side of the room or this side of the room; displayed on a weekly basis or on a monthly basis. . . . [W]hat kind of group, small band, big band, black band, white band, jazz band, whatever . . . meals and how they were served and the time of the waiters . . . the musical selections . . . whether or not salad should be served . . . the details of the walk up the driveway; whether the military should be to the right or left; which uniforms would be worn by the White House police; whether or not the Secret Service would salute during 'The Star Spangled Banner' and sing; where the photographer would be."[83] Always concerned with appearances, down to the last detail, Nixon is unlikely to have been ignorant of a move which, even in anticipation, risked the whole appearance of his campaign as a dignified exercise in the proprieties.

In his Watergate testimony, John Dean retrieved from his tape-recorder memory the fact that within a few days of the break-in he warned two chieftains at the Justice Department that "I did not know what would happen if the investigation led into the White House, but that I suspected the chances of reelecting the President would be severely damaged. . . . I did not think the White House could withstand a wide-open investigation."[84]

The way to cut this risk to the President's power was to keep the whole affair as quiet as possible until after the election. At first the prognosis did not seem bad, for the break-in was initially reported on page 30 of the *New York Times*. There were some subsequent Watergate reports, a good deal of suggestive information on campaign "dirty tricks," and opponent McGovern's eloquent warning:

> We are confronted, in short, with both a moral and a Constitutional crisis of unprecedented dimensions. Ambitious men come and go, but a free society might never recover from a sustained assault on its most basic institutions. And one can only ask, if this has happened in four years, to what lengths would the same leadership go in another four years, once freed of the restraints of facing the people for reelection?[85]

In general, though, Watergate was kept almost as far from the headlines as the White House would have wanted. A poll in October, just before the election, showed only about half the public had even heard of the Watergate break-in. Nixon was endorsed by 753 daily newspapers, compared to 56 for McGovern, and won the election by an enormous margin, 61 to 38 percent. Not until the following February would the Senate decide on an investigation.[86]

From Nixon's perspective, then, the gamble had paid off. Close attention—before the election—to the White House iceberg underlying the Watergate tip, whether by the press or Congress, constituted a very severe threat to his power because of the very real danger of his losing the election. On the other hand, the risk of covering up seemed minimal: they had done it many times before and the whole issue appeared to be fading away.

THE FEAR OF SCANDAL

The second essential reinforcement for Nixon's rigidification was the fact that Watergate threatened to reveal the President as an immoral and unvirtuous person. Indeed, the eventual revelation of the tapes elicited just the condemning reaction Nixon feared. Even in their Presidentially sanitized version, the tapes showed a Nixon he would just as soon had remained private. As Representative Mann of South Carolina put it, "The more that people know about him, it seems the more trouble he's in." Even Senator Hugh Scott, a loyalist if ever there was one, dolefully concluded that the tapes showed "a shabby, disgusting, immoral performance by all those involved." This reaction was general among Congressmen, newspapers which previously had supported Nixon, and the public as revealed in the polls. Leading churchmen were reminded of "a felon's lair" and of conversations that "reek with the stench of moral decay." Columnist Joseph Alsop reacted with "sheer fleshcrawling repulsion." The Oval Office had become "the back room of a second-rate advertising agency in a suburb of hell." To William Randolph Hearst, Jr., Nixon emerged as "a man totally immersed in the cheapest and sleaziest kind of conniving." The President not only had broken the law, his oath, and his word, but also had shattered the public's trust that their President was at least as straight as they were. Even Nixon's old standby, the Chicago *Tribune*, had to admit that the tape transcripts and the scandal about Nixon's tax returns "stripped the man to his essential character, and that character could not stand that kind of scrutiny."[87]

Rigidification is a process, a slow freeze. Nixon's rigidification developed as one piece after another of the threatening pattern fell into place. At some point in the autumn of 1973 one Republican Senator perceived a key transition: the affair had "got to the ridicule stage . . . even among serious people." Nixon himself—who kept saying he wanted to be considered "un homme sérieux" like de Gaulle—predicted, as he released his doctored tape transcripts, that "they will embarrass me . . . and . . . they will become the subject of speculation and even ridicule. . . ."[88] One of them was played at a Washington cocktail party. There was speculation that the tapes would eventually become a commercial item for disc jockeys and teenagers to chuckle over. To the active-negative mentality, ridicule is not funny. It is too close to the truth. It helps freeze a man.

CHOICE OR NECESSITY?

If Nixon's response to the Watergate accusations was simply that of a realist to reality, an inexorable ride down the slippery slope of tragedy, then his character would have little to do with it once the process was begun. One could conceive of the story that way, just as any other historical sequence can be etched retrospectively into inevitability. What happened happened. That Nixon was ridiculed or challenged or whatever could be seen as having little to do with the case, once the case became a case. The alternative is to believe, as our own personal experience teaches us, that there are indeed choices to be made, forks in the road of life, and that how and why those choices are made can have fateful consequences.

We know now that Nixon was deeply into the Watergate affair almost immediately after the break-in, if not before. The break-in occurred on June 17, 1972. Nixon aide Haldeman's notes show the President and his top team talked it over on June 20th, but the tape of that conversation was later obliterated— probably by Nixon himself, if his secretary's testimony that he ran the thing back and forth indicates anything. The June 23rd tape—the one Nixon held out to the end, the one that turned his most ardent loyalists against him—makes it abundantly clear that he was deep into what he, at least, thought of as choices about the exact way to handle the details of the cover-up. Despite all his subsequent claims that he was too busy making world peace to attend to such trivia, that all the relevant facts were out, that he and his were innocent and had nothing to hide, or that, at various points in time, he had only just recently learned what was going on, the June 23rd tape made it unmistakably clear that he had been in up to his eyeballs from the very start. In that tape Nixon told Haldeman to stop the investigation by pretending that it threatened CIA work. A haberdasher like Harry Truman, a soldier like Eisenhower, would have understood that that was not the thing to do; a lawyer like Nixon must have known that it was an "obstruction of justice." The nation's chief lawman had cut the FBI off at the pass to save his own skin. "'Don't go any further into this case, period!',", Nixon ordered Haldeman to tell the FBI.[89]

That was a choice. He could have chosen otherwise. He could have destroyed the tapes. He could have gone on television and made a clean breast of the whole affair, admitting his indirect culpability and dismissing those directly responsible. Even after the Ervin committee investigation began, he could have brought that inquiry to a quick halt by testifying—his word as President of the United States of America against that of a young lawyer assistant who admitted his own perfidy. "If the President had come to testify in the early days of the hearings, he could have bowled the legs out from under us," thought Terry Lenzner of the Ervin committee staff.[90] He could have promptly complied with the early subpoenas for tapes; it was at least possible that would have ended it. And at nearly any point before the last, he could have made a public confession of complicity, and a promise to reform, and a plea for forgiveness. In retrospect it seems that any one of these moves would have left him in the Presidency, especially considering how loath the Congress was to impeach him.

Instead, Nixon concentrated on rhetoric. In speech after speech, he urged the public to forget this Watergate nonsense and march on into the future. This was a trick that had worked so well in the past that it had become Nixon's habitual way to wind up a crisis before plunging into a new one. All the way back to the Checkers speech, Nixon had succeeded not by giving us new facts but by giving us new explanations, not by acting but by redefining the meanings of acts. I believe there were two reasons that this strategy did not work with Watergate. First, once the courts got into it, television flimflam became ineffective. A court proceeding is a social invention for focusing attention, strongly and continuously, on a set of specific experiences. It does not always work to that end, but in this case the judge, John Sirica, was one of those rare birds who will not let go until he has pulled out the whole worm. The series of judicial proceedings, culminating in the 8-0 Supreme Court decision requiring Nixon to turn over the tapes, was the least promising stage upon which Nixon could hope to play St. Richard in order to hide King Richard.

A second and, I think, stronger reason why Nixon failed in his rhetorical escape efforts was the fact that in the final analysis he did not really want to escape. Like Presidents Wilson, Hoover, and Lyndon Johnson before him, something in his character attracted him to the path of grim persistence to the long, hard, lacerating march to a tragic denouement. Of course he was ambivalent on this score; part of him wanted to escape. But another part seemed to be caught up in the same personal tragic tale, the same predestined plot arranged by the man himself for his own political destruction.

STEPS IN NIXON'S RIGIDIFICATION

Certainly all the main elements of the active-negative rigidification process, as exemplified in the stories of Wilson, Hoover, and Johnson, were present in Nixon's slow-motion fall from the heady altitudes of his 1972 election victory. Plain to see are: the sense that one must resist the temptation to "give in"; the feeling that salvation lies in effort; the perception of oneself as engaged in a lone struggle; the appeal to faith; the sense of oneself as surrounded by lurking enemies.

The Fight Against "Giving In"

Like his active-negative predecessors, Nixon moralized his preferred line in such a way as to define the alternatives as temptations. Thus resisting becomes a virtue. His "but-that-would-be-the-easy-way" habit continued: "The easiest course would be for me to blame those to whom I delegated the responsibility to run the campaign. But that would be a cowardly thing to do," he said in a television address. As soon as the cameras were off, he told the crew; "It wasn't easy." As the end approached, he said he would not resign because, "From a personal standpoint, resignation is an easy cop-out." To Senator Buckley's suggestion that he resign, Nixon replied sarcastically that, "While it might take an act of courage to run away from a job that you were elected to do, it also takes courage to stand and fight for what you believe is right, and that's what I intend to do." He told the Cabinet that he could not resign because that would change the Constitution, and so "I will go through this with my head high—right up to the end, if it comes." The temptation was always toward weakness, relaxation, collapse: "All these people have come in here crying. I ought to be the one crying. I don't want anyone crying." He wanted others to know that "I sometimes feel like I'd like to resign. Let Agnew be President for a while. He'd love it." And earlier, when discussing the cover-up with Ehrlichman, Nixon equates "being forthcoming" with "caving [in]."[91]

The point is clear: although Nixon eventually does all the things he is "tempted" to do in these passages, he does them long after they would have done him any good. Along the way, the temptations—to cry or quit or talk—must be resisted with all his moral force and fervor.

The Answer in Effort

On the other side of the temptation coin is the exhausted face of the gladiator straining upward, lost in his quest, experiencing the sufferer's confirmation that he cannot possibly be doing this from any selfish motive. We have seen the suffering-and-striving Nixon already: working to all hours, exhausted, constantly complaining and reaching for sympathy, all the while denying that he needs any of that. The tapes are full of Presidential metaphors of masochism: having to "bite the Dean bullet today," to "prick the boil and take the heat," to get beat on the head and shoulders," "to be nibbled to death by a thousand hurts," not to mention numerous variants of Nixon's "scab-flicking" simile. But far from passive acquiescence, Nixon would do unto others as he expected they would try to do unto him, by sharp, disciplined struggle, however "painful." As the "crisis" deepened in the fall of 1973, Julie Nixon wrote on her calendar, "Fight. Fight. Fight."[92]

The Lone Struggle

As far back as January 1971, Nixon realized he had an image problem regarding isolation and tried to correct it by proclaiming "Open Door Hours." Statistics were to be gathered on how many people saw the President, and aides were to "build on the theme that he's the most 'Open Door' President in history."[93] It did not work and could not last, because Nixon simply was not an Open Door person. As Watergate deepened, this famous loner of a President got loner and loner. His contacts with the press, which already had been in steep decline, became even rarer.[94] Not only did his Cabinet members have trouble seeing him; even his own lawyers were sometimes cut out. St. Clair confessed that he had not heard the crucial tapes, and Garment complained at the end, "We had no access to our client."[95] Nixon spent hours alone in the Lincoln room, which is furnished for one, the air conditioning on high, the fire ablaze at his hearth, pondering his fate to the strains of "Victory at Sea." Cynics said that when he wanted to be alone, he brought along Bebe Rebozo, and the two of them would sit together for long stretches without talking.[96] Your average politician would rather talk than eat, argue than sleep, but by Christmas 1973 Nixon "didn't want to see anyone"—a problem that would have been more severe if the converse hadn't also been true: "and no one really wants to see the President."[97]

The President's physical separation from others, dangerous as that might have been, was only part of the picture. When he *was* with others he kept them away, psychologically, by dominating the conversation or by just not listening. He jabbered on to Gerald Ford, driving him "close to distraction," according to John Osborne.[98] As part of "Operation Candor," in November 1973, Nixon went into a social blitz with Congress: in eight meetings in six days, he met with nearly all of the 234 House and Senate Republicans and with 46 Democrats.[99] Senator Barry Goldwater wasn't taken in by the sudden shift to sociability:

> I've never known a man to be so much a loner in any field. . . . The President, I think, thinks of himself as the supreme politician in this country. And being a loner, I think he sits by himself and tells himself what he's going to do. Now we went through this gesture period of having Congressmen and Senators down to see him—but it seems to have ended. . . . And as a result he's not getting advice. That's his problem, he's not getting it. And when he gets it, he won't listen to it. . . . My God, we've never had so many serious problems in the history of this nation.[100]

That propinquity may not impel communication was evident in one of these "gesture period" meetings, when Republican Senator Robert Packwood looked his President in the eye and gave him a civics lesson:

> All of us, Mr. President, whether we're in politics or not, have weaknesses. For some, it's drinking. For others, it's gambling. For still others, it's women. None of these weaknesses applies to you. Your weakness is credibility. This has always been your short suit with the news media and the general public. The problem with the public is that they no longer believe you. They no longer trust the integrity of the administration. . . .
>
> Congress has come to expect that many people who testify before it lie. It's an entirely different matter, however, when one person gives his word to another. That is a bond which those of us in politics revere highly. Those who breach that bond suffer an incalculable loss of credibility. . . .
>
> For too long, this administration has given the public the impression that its standard of conduct was not that it must be above suspicion but that it must merely be above criminal guilt. Mr. President, that is not an adequate standard of conduct for those who have been accorded the privilege of governing this country.[101]

Nixon's reply was to say, "Thank you," and move on to the next man. You can lead a President to conversation, but you can't make him listen.

The fact of Nixon's isolation is evident. What it meant to him is summed up in his comment to John Dean, on March 13, 1974: "Bullshit: Nobody is a friend of ours."[102] By April of that year, J. Anthony Lukas reports, "Nobody trusted anybody in the Nixon camp. Haldeman, Ehrlichman, and Dean were routinely taping their conversations with each other and any other potential witness." At the end of April, Nixon at last fired these brittle and prideful counselors and took on a new crew. But the new aides, as Theodore White noted, "were loyal only to the public policies of Richard Nixon, his proclaimed purposes, the record that had won for him the largest popular election margin in American history. He could trust such men to serve such public purposes, but not to protect him personally. He was alone—all alone against . . . 'the system.' "[103]

Because he was alone in his struggle, his rescue would be entirely dependent on his own efforts. Much as he felt that political leaders in the Middle East could rely "only on my words" and that agreements with the Soviet Union "were possible because of a personal relationship that was established between the General Secretary and the President of the United States," Nixon came to see Watergate as no one's but his:

Nixon went back to listen to some more tapes. He sighed again. "This is hard work. But I've got to do it. Got to do it. And it's best for *me* to do it, too."

Haig certainly didn't want to hear them himself. "Only you," he told Nixon. "Only you."[104]

"No man in public life," Nixon said in a speech, "has ever had a more loyal group of friends."[105] But in private he brooded over a biography of Napoleon, perhaps imagining his own Elba.

The Appeal to Faith

I will spare readers an extensive account of Nixon's litany of self-justifying idealisms called forth in order to protect himself from the prying eyes of reporters, courts, and special prosecutors. On the one hand, Watergate was one of those "petty, little, indecent things that seem to obsess us," one of "the murky, small, unimportant, vicious little things" that contrasted so sharply with the high task of "building a better world."[106] On the other hand, throughout his exhortations, Watergate threatened the Presidency itself, the fundamental Constitutional order, and the very peace of the world. Nothing is more familiar, to those who lived attentively through those days, than Nixon's extraordinary capacity to link his pettiest acts with his proudest purposes. The public could not be allowed to hear him plotting to fool them because "the President of the United States, under our Constitution, has a responsibility to this office to maintain the separation of power and also maintain the ability of not only this President but future Presidents to conduct the office in the interests of the people."[107] The active-negative's enormous capacity for moralistic self-justification shone brightly through the Watergate miasma.

The Emergent Enemy

"As you know, we're up against ruthless people," Nixon reminded Alexander Haig as the crisis persisted. Nixon was used to that. He lived in what he saw and felt as a *generally* dangerous world, and always had. He could sense the lurking ambushers: "I guess the Kennedy crowd is just laying in the bushes waiting to make their move," he told John Dean. His aide Safire thought he was the first political paranoid with a majority.[108]

In an interesting exhortation in February 1973, Nixon told his Cabinet what he had learned from another sovereign:

I was talking to King Hussein of Jordan. When he was sixteen years old, an assassin shot his grandfather, and he ran after the assassin and got shot himself. He made the point—if people throw rocks at you in a parade, you cannot sit down and look for protection. *The moment a leader shows timidity he encourages people to go after him.* People can sense when a leader is timid and they automatically attack. Remember, you are a member of the President's Cabinet. Try to be conciliatory when others are conciliatory toward you, but when the other side doesn't want to heal wounds, fight 'em—you get more respect.[109]

In a world of piranhas, one had better be a shark.

As the Watergate crisis failed to vanish in the wake of the grand tours, his list of enemies, so perceived, multiplied. There were the "Harvards," the Kennedys, the "upper intellectual types," the "establishment," the Jews, the Italians.[110] The famous "enemies lists" ran the gamut from James Reston to Robert Sherrill, and included such dangerous folk as Carol Channing, Steve McQueen, Barbara Streisand, Gregory Peck, Bill Cosby, Tony Randall and Joe Namath.[111] Former friends, such as Dean, Magruder, and Mitchell, and former henchmen, such as Hunt, Liddy, Barker, and the other burglars, become objects of disdain and derision, to be "stroked" or "nailed."

Elliot Richardson tried to get across to Nixon's aides that "If you're the President, there isn't any 'they'; the President has to be the first among 'us.'"[112] The lesson simply would not take. Nixon at the end was lashing out in nearly every direction at "the people who won't rest until they get me."

The other three active-negative Presidents studied in this volume—Wilson, Hoover, and Johnson—eventually fastened their ire on a single, personal enemy. Nixon did not do that. Despite many castigations of Kennedy and the Kennedys, Nixon targeted his anger not primarily on a person but on the media. There were individual targets there, too, such as Daniel Schorr and Joseph Alsop, but it was the press in general—the sum of the specifics—that got to him. Nixon was practicing his reverse-of-the-facts rhetoric when he said, "The critics don't bother me. . . . I see the press totally in impersonal terms.[113] On the contrary, Safire, who had heard Nixon fulminate that "the press is the enemy" a dozen times, explained:

> In all the world of "us against them," the press was the quintessential "them," the fount and succor of other "thems." In terms of power, the academic "them" was insignificant; the social-cultural elitist "them" was useful as a foil that would help attract working-men to a Nixon coalition; the liberal, political "them" was in the process of destroying itself by narrowing its base along severe ideological-faddist lines; but the journalistic "them" was formidable and infuriating, a force to be feared in its own right, but even more important, a magnifying glass and public address system that gave strength and attention to all the other "thems."[114]

Specifically on Watergate, Nixon said he had "never heard or seen such outrageous, vicious, distorted reporting in my twenty-seven years of public life."[115]

Surely in the long view of historical hindsight, Nixon's press will be seen as charitable in the extreme. Whether because he learned to play the press like a violin, counting on their short attention span and shallow insight, or because the press was in the main attuned to his Republican rhetoric, time and time again through Nixon's career he was forgiven by the media for sins that might have driven other politicians out of public life. But from his point of view, the press was the essential hostile threat: "they" could present his drama "in a way" different from his way, could warp his intentions away from the ideal, could pervert his most well meant initiatives, and, most important, could refuse that enthusiastic consent which, if granted, would make his way work.

VULNERABILITIES TO THE CONFIDENCE GAME

In the end, the most significant of all the many "lessons" of Nixon and Watergate was this: our political system did not protect us from an enormous and long-lasting Presidential confidence game. Nixon the rhetorician was a smashing success over the years, especially considering what he had to sell. His history demonstrates a vulnerability of the democratic system, a weakness in the nation's political fabric, through which the most loathsome deeds—disguised as bravery—can seep. He was finally pushed out of office only because of an accident. At the end of a long afternoon, some investigators for a Congressional committee stayed just a little longer, asked just one more question, and uncovered the tape system. Otherwise Nixon would have gotten off scot free and the rest of us might well be in danger of our democratic lives.

As the end neared, the Nixon rhetoric came to dominate his life. What was originally part of his style became his whole style, so that his private conversations turned into either performances or rehearsals for performances, and his homework focused on getting ready to speak. A typical rehearsal went like this:

E[HRLICHMAN]: You say to the country, "I have now had this conversation with the Judge—"

P[RESIDENT]: Yeah. Well, that's what I mean. That's what I would say.

E: The thing that I get over and over and over again from just ordinary folks—

P: Right.

E: "Why doesn't the President," so and so and so and so.

P: "Say something what's he done on it?"

E: Yeah. So symbolically you've got to do something.[116]

Or, as he put it on another occasion, "I didn't do this, I didn't do that, da da da da, da da da da, da da da da, da da da da."[117] His private performances ranged from "stroking" old friends who thought his appreciations were sincere to leading an unwitting John Dean to agree to a false version of history while the hidden tape spools turned. But it did not stop there. As we have seen, Nixon shaped, as best he could, the version of reality his own family got. And then there was the ultimate audience, himself. His aide Buzhardt thought he could always tell when Nixon was lying because the President would repeat himself over and over, "as if he were trying to convince himself."[118] His amazing reverse thinking, in which he derives his own sentiments from those he thinks the situation requires, is evident here: "You have to show you care, and of course, you must care."[119] Nixon constructs himself to fit the rhetorical exigencies. The self is swallowed by feedback. Rhetoric triumphs over preference and sentiment, instinct and conviction. "What we do" for the Nixonites came to be much less important than "what we say," which is why audiences had to be encouraged not to watch the latter too closely.

The political lesson is clear: We the people cannot count on having a

President who will try to tell us the truth. We may get one who does not even try to tell himself the truth.

If Nixon was prepared to manufacture a world for himself, he was readier yet to make one for the public, the courts, his own lawyers. Nixon told Buzhardt that both the tape and a Dictabelt summary of a crucial meeting were missing. That worried Buzhardt. What would the court say? Nixon had an idea: "Why can't we make a new Dictabelt?"[120] Short-order histories were no problem for a President for whom the distinction between art and nature had collapsed long ago. Occasionally someone stood up to Nixon's rhetorical manipulations. The poet Archibald MacLeish was invited by Nixon to write a poem commemorating the first moon landing—and instructed on how to do it: "It is important that this be viewed not only as a great adventure, but in the perspective of a search for truth and a quest for peace. Nothing man has done more significantly dramatizes the need for an understanding of the common goals of the human race."[121] MacLeish declined.

Far more often, though, Nixon met with rhetorical success. Elizabeth Drew saw that Nixon had developed "almost perfect pitch with respect to the hypocrisies that conventional people live by—the fears they don't admit, the hatred they want to express but can't, the images they would like to have themselves—and a sense of how to exploit all that.[122] Simple lying was only a minor part of it. The meanings of words were corrupted and reversed. John Doar of the House Judiciary Committee staff found himself confused, perplexed, and puzzled as he tried to grope along "down in the labyrinth of the White House in that Byzantine Empire where 'yes' meant 'no', and 'go' was 'stop' and 'maybe' was 'certainly.' . . ."[123] Nixon had long ago mastered the trick of preaching against his own continuing sins. He knew how to flit back and forth between Richard Nice (Hannah's Richard) and Richard Nasty (Frank's Richard); he even organized his speech writers on that plan of alternation. His oracular pronouncements could be taken at any number of face values, depending on which face one faced: hawk or dove, Lincoln or Churchill, Roy Ash or Roy Acuff. And he knew the art of the gesture masquerading as effort, the summit champagne toast as a try for peace, while the bombs fell or a secret grain deal went down.

Of all these effective techniques, I think Nixon's most dangerous was the misrepresenting of his intentions. Politicians *ad nauseam* break their word to the public. They often fail to carry through on their promises—as, indeed, most of us do much of the time. But at least for most of them, the promises point in the right direction: they tell the attentive public roughly what the politician would like to do, given luck and a little authority. Nixon's great success should stand in history as a warning against the Napoleon who really intends to retreat, the St. Francis with a revolver under his cassock, the robber baron in the clothes of Eugene V. Debs.

Like a mocker of his own masque, Nixon stands condemned out of his own mouth. The June 23rd tape shows him plotting one last great Checkers speech, a television performance after which he would resign—unless the cards and letters and telegrams flooded in to support him, as his new friend Rabbi

Korff suggested.[124] That never happened, but to the very end Nixon held on to his control over his image, his capacity to do it his way. Just before he left the White House for good, he made his weeping family dry their eyes and smile for the photographer; it took a lot of shots.[125] In his farewell speech he said he had been reading Theodore Roosevelt the night before and found a telling passage, when really the quotes had been dredged up by his speech writers years before.[126] And his last Presidential words told—but only in the Nixon mirror— how he felt: "And so, we leave with high hopes, in good spirits and with deep humility, and with very much gratefulness in our hearts. . . ."[127]

VOICES FROM THE PAST

In the end, the overriding question was not how Nixon fell, but how he rose. As President of the United States, empowered beyond any other human being, he had been a very high risk indeed.

For example: To give some appearance of openness, Nixon had agreed to the appointment of a Special Prosecutor, under the Attorney General. But "The Attorney General will not countermand or interfere with the Special Prosecutor's decisions or actions." Furthermore, it was agreed, "The Special Prosecutor will not be removed from his duties except for extraordinary improprieties."[128] Nixon broke those promises, fired the Special Prosecutor, and abolished his office, all on one Saturday night in October 1973. FBI agents were dispatched in the dark to take control of the offices of the Special Prosecutor and his staff, the Attorney General, and the Deputy Attorney General.[129] Washington had become like "downtown Santiago."[130] James Doyle of the Cox staff tried to take out his framed copy of a souvenir document, but an FBI agent prevented him. Doyle said, "It's the Declaration of Independence, Angie. Just stamp it 'void' and let me take it home."[131]

For example: In June of 1974 the President went to the Middle East in spite of Secret Service and CIA warnings that terrorists might try to kill him there. Pain and swelling in his leg made Nixon call in his two doctors, who saw he had a blood clot that could break loose and kill him in a moment. Both doctors demanded he cancel the trip. Nixon refused. Nor would he heed their urgent counsel that he stay off his feet. Rather, he spent hours standing up and waving in open cars and railroad carriages; he hiked around the pyramids. Unexpectedly he got out of his car and walked into a mob of Arabs, from which he was extricated with some difficulty by the Secret Service agents. He vetoed the use of bulletproof shields.[132] His doctor said: "The President has a death wish." His main Secret Service guard said: "You can't protect a President who wants to kill himself." On the way to Damascus, the President's plane was closely approached by four unidentified Russian-built MIG fighters. Nixon's pilot went through violent evasive action for several minutes before the planes were identified.[133]

For example: according to one account by a pair of Pulitzer Prize-winning reporters, a few days before he resigned President Nixon got drunk, called in Secretary Kissinger, kneeled and prayed and pounded on the carpet as he sobbed and wept about his cruel fate. The account continues:

> Kissinger touched the President, and then held him, tried to console him, to bring rest and peace to the man who was curled up on the carpet like a child. The President of the United States. Kissinger tried again to reassure him, reciting Nixon's accomplishments.
>
> Finally, the President struggled to his feet. He sat back down in his chair. The storm had passed. He had another drink.[134]

The next day, Nixon met with a group of Congressmen to tell them of his resignation. "As I am winging my way back to California," he said, "I will still have the little black box aboard the plane up to the moment of transition."[135] Nixon passed from the scene as he had entered it, winging his way.

6

The Passive-Negative Presidents

The passive Presidents pose a different danger to the peace of the world and the progress of the nation: the danger of drift. Historically they mark breathing spells, times of recovery in our frantic political life. Their contribution can be restorative. They give ear to popular needs for reassurance or legitimacy; their elections represent a public sigh of relief after a period when the apparent aggressiveness or corruption of politics has worn down the people's political energies. The psychological payoff is evident—but in an era of rapid social change the price of relaxation may be too high. The social problems do not disappear because a President neglects them. Sooner or later the accounting has to come. What passive Presidents ignore, active Presidents inherit.

The passive Presidents may be a vanishing breed. By my estimation, there has been only one passive President since Calvin Coolidge, and his case is a mixed one. Possibly the public senses that rapid change requires an active President. But insofar as the popular needs for rest and moral restoration persist and accumulate, the psychological burden on the President will increase, and eventually the people may once again call some Cincinnatus from the plow, not to get the nation moving again but to bind wounds and inspire faith.

The passive Presidents are puzzling. They hold the same place of ultimate power as Wilson, Hoover, and Johnson did, but they hold back from power's exercise. In terms of their own motives, one wonders why they take the job. In terms of political effect, one wonders how they protected the Presidency from collapse, or even significant modification, as they sidestepped positive commitments. In each case, the way they combined character, world view, and style helps make clear what it means for a man to be handed the Presidential sword only to spend much of his time trying to get it back in the scabbard.

The passive-*negative* type gives an impression of being reluctantly, unwillingly involved in his political work, in continual retreat from the demands office imposes on him. He tends to withdraw from the conflict and uncertainty of politics to an emphasis on vague principles and procedural arrangements. His presence in a political role can be explained primarily in terms of his sense of duty, which leads him to compensate for feelings of uselessness by becoming a guardian of the right and proper way, above the sordid politicking of lesser men. Calvin Coolidge was the clearest twentieth-century example. Dwight Eisenhower also showed these themes, but in a more complicated mix.

CALVIN COOLIDGE IN THE WHITE HOUSE[1]

Coolidge complained that "One of the most appalling trials which confront a President is the perpetual clamor for public utterances." But this "foster-child of silence" was anything but quiet in public. In office 67 months, he held 520 press conferences, an average of 7.8 per month, compared with Franklin Roosevelt's 6.9. He gave radio addresses about once a month. He got off to an excellent start with the reporters, cracking jokes at this first conference; their "hearty applause" on that occasion made it "one of my most pleasant memories." They were "the boys" who came along on his vacations. Clearly he enjoyed their enjoyment, particularly when he could surprise or titillate them with Yankee humor. He carefully stage-managed his "I do not choose to run for President in nineteen twenty-eight" statement, releasing the news at noon on the fourth anniversary of taking office, grinning broadly. His wife was as surprised as the reporters were. He let himself be photographed in full Indian headdress, cowboy chaps and hat, overalls, and any number of other outfits; there is a picture of him presenting a sap bucket to Henry Ford. When a friend protested that his antics made people laugh, Coolidge said, "Well, it's good for people to laugh."

His formal addresses had a completely different tone. They were sermons from the church of New England idealism. "When the President speaks," he wrote, "it ought to be an event," by which he meant a serious and dignified and uplifting event. He spoke on "Education: the Cornerstone of Self-Government," "The High Place of Labor," "Ordered Liberty and World Peace," "Authority and Religious Liberty," "Religion and the Republic," "The Genius of America," "Destiny Is in You," "Do the Day's Work," "The Things of the Spirit Come First," and "The Chief Ideal of the American People Is Idealism"—this was Coolidge in the presidential pulpit. And he was quite serious. When Will Rogers imitated his nasal twang and penchant for clichés, he was much offended and refused Rogers' apology.

Coolidge sincerely believed in hard work. He felt busy, even rushed, but his constant routine included a daily nap and often eleven hours of sleep in twenty-four. Often tired and bored, he gradually abandoned all physical exercise except for brief walks and spent much time in silent contemplation, gazing out his office window. His strength was not effort but patience. "Let well enough alone," was his motto. He was the "provincial who refuses to become excited over events for which he has no direct responsibility." He kept Harding's cabinet, let former Attorney General Daugherty, who had been tried for conspiracy to defraud the government, hang on for a long time, tried to delay his friends' efforts to boost him in 1924. Asked how he kept fit he said, "By avoiding the big problems." Most of the time Coolidge simply did not want to be bothered.

Underneath these tactics, supporting and justifying them, was a strain of mystical resignation. "I am only in the clutch of forces that are greater than I am," he wrote, despite being "the most powerful man in the world." He bore his young son's death with Roman stoicism: "The ways of Providence are beyond our understanding." The dedicated man, he wrote in his newspaper column, "finds that in the time of need some power outside himself directs his course." Coolidge could wait, storing up his meager energies with a feeling of rightness in entrusting himself to fate. "Government is growth," he said, and added: "—slow growth." He and Providence presided while the rate slowed down.

Coolidge got rid of much work by giving it to others, and he believed in doing just that. "One rule of action more important than all others consists in never doing anything that some one else can do for you." He appointed or retained "men of sufficient ability so that they can solve all the problems that arise under their jurisdiction." He rarely interfered and he resented others interfering with him. His loyal helper Frank Stearns got repeated rebuffs for his trouble. Coolidge seldom discussed political matters with his wife. He complained of Hoover as Secretary of Commerce (Coolidge called him "the wonder boy" or "the miracle worker"): "That man has offered me unsolicited advice for six years, all of it bad!"

Yet he was always surrounded by people. He and Grace entertained more than any previous family in the White House. Alone, he said, he got "a sort of naked feeling." His poker face, his long impenetrable silences at social affairs were known to all Washington and gave rise to scores of anecdotes as matron after matron tried to pry a few words from him. Occasionally he could be induced to talk about Vermont. More often, he simply sat. This was "a form of defense," his biographer says. "Can't hang you for what you don't say," said Coolidge. "In order to function at all," he warned his successors, the President "has to be surrounded by many safeguards. If these were removed for only a short time, he would be overwhelmed by the people who would surge in upon him." He learned not to smile, as smiling encouraged longer office visits. He had very little interest in women and was, his biographer says, "embarrassed when left for even a short period in the company of the other sex." Undoubtedly much of Coolidge's acerbity at dinner parties was a reaction to intensified shyness at having to cope with the matrons to his left and right. When he did speak, it was some tart, pithy puckishness, mildly aggressive, disconcerting, with a quality of surprise in a conventional conversational setting. In a rare and revealing confession, he once told Frank Stearns why:

> Do you know, I've never really grown up? It's a hard thing for me to play this game. In politics, one must meet people, and that's not easy for me. . . . When I was a little fellow, as long ago as I can remember, I would go into a panic if I heard strange voices in the kitchen. I felt I just couldn't meet the people and shake hands with them. Most of the visitors would sit with Father and Mother in the kitchen, and the hardest thing in the world was to have to go through the kitchen door and give them a greeting. I was almost ten before I realized I couldn't go on that way. And by fighting hard I used to manage to get through that door. I'm all right with old friends, but every time I meet a stranger, I've got to go through the old kitchen door, back home, and it's not easy.[2]

Coolidge "tried deliberately to suppress 'aggressive wittiness,'" but "it broke out repeatedly in quaint comments."

Even this brief account shows the main features of Coolidge's adaptation to the Presidency. Clearly he belongs in the withdrawn type. Aside from his banter with reporters, he did not particularly enjoy being President, given all the demands the role made on him, and he conserved his energies stingily. Many of his characteristics—his rural Yankee background; his persistent turning back to his past, his father, his homeplace; his avoidance of controversy and his patient faith in Providence; his penchant for reverie and retreat; his sense of strangeness in a cosmopolitan environment ("Puritan in Babylon")—agree with empirical findings on this type in a very different environment. His style within that type is also clear. Words for Coolidge were shaped heavily by his relations to different audiences. The "serious" audience was the nation, to which he addressed sermons on common virtue, purveying the illusion of specificity through epigram. In fact, his abstract pseudo-Hegelian fatalism had little clear connection with the political issues of the day. His humor at news conferences was badinage with the boys, a show with much audience participation, full of little surprises. There, as in his dinner table silences and mild insults, the focus was on Coolidge as a clown, one who could touch the heart but leave the political brain and brawn of the nation relaxed.

His philosophy helped him rationalize his leisurely pace. His method was to concentrate on matters only the President had to decide, and to define that category as narrowly as possible. Most everything could wait. And Coolidge himself could wait, with utter, unflappable calm, for longer than the last of his advisors. He also managed to rationalize his independence of others; clearly his style in close interpersonal relations cut him off effectively from much of the Washington conversational froth—but also from any effective political bargaining with administrative or legislative or party leaders. He was a loner who endured in order to serve, while the nation drifted.

COOLIDGE EMERGING

John Calvin Coolidge, Jr., was born in Plymouth, Vermont, on the Fourth of July, 1872, the first child, after four years of marriage, of John Calvin Coolidge and Victoria Josephine Coolidge. He was the nephew of Julius Caesar Coolidge, grandson of Calvin Galusha Coolidge, descendent of five generations of his family in a Vermont village. His mother was a quiet, delicately beautiful person, a chronic invalid since shortly after her marriage. Coolidge remembered "a touch of mysticism and poetry in her nature." His father was a big, stern-visaged man, a storekeeper and pillar of the community who had held many town offices and went to the state legislature. His son admired him for "qualities that were greater than any I possess," and accepted much paternal admonition without complaint.

Calvin's early hero was his grandfather "Galoosh," tall, spare, and handsome, an expert horseman and practical joker, said to have a trace of Indian blood, who raised colts and puppies and peacocks and taught the boy to ride standing up behind him. His grandmother ("the Puritan severity of her convictions was tempered by the sweetness of womanly charity") read the Bible to him and when he misbehaved shut him up in the dark, windowless attic, "dusty with cobwebs."

Calvin's younger sister Abbie, his constant playmate, was "a lively affectionate girl, with flaming red hair, who was full of energy and impressed everybody by her personality"—almost the exact opposite of her shy brother. Calvin himself was small and frail, with his mother's features; punctual and methodical, only occasionally joining in the schoolyard teasing.

So much for the cast of characters. Life began its hammer blows at this shy boy when he was six. His hero Galusha died as Calvin read him the Bible. Six years later his invalid mother, "who used what strength she had to lavish care upon me and my sister," died as a result of an accident with a runaway horse. Her passing left an indelible mark on him:

> In an hour she was gone. It was her thirty-ninth birthday. I was twelve years old. We laid her away in the blustering snows of March. The greatest grief that can come to a boy came to me. Life was never to seem the same again.[3]

Calvin was despondent too long. His family became concerned; but he kept up his school work "with no tardy marks and good deportment."

Later at the nearby Black River Academy, where his parents and grandmother had gone to school, he was unhappy and homesick, though his father brought him home nearly every weekend. In his third year Abbie joined him there; Calvin had written he hoped she could come. A year and a half later, at age fifteen, she was dead of appendicitis. Calvin came home to be with her in her last hours.

There was another unsettled time for Calvin, like that following his mother's death. He failed the entrance examinations for Amherst College. He had caught cold and stayed home "for a considerable time." In late winter he went back to Black River Academy to get "certified" for Amherst. There he worked hard, "made almost no acquaintances," and in two months was approved for Amherst. In September his father married a Plymouth neighbor, a spinster Calvin had known all his life. "For thirty years," Coolidge wrote much later, "she watched over and loved me." They corresponded regularly until her death in 1920.

Amherst was an all-male place where three-quarters or more of the students belonged to fraternities, "the most unique feature of Amherst life . . . strongly recommended by the members of the faculty," as the *Students' Handbook* said. Calvin needed no urging. He had written his father from school that he and a friend should visit the college "to see about getting me into a society there." But the scheme did not work. Calvin moved into a boardinghouse. The others there were quickly pledged. He remained an "Ouden," an outsider in a small community of clans. "I don't seem to get acquainted very fast," he wrote home in October. After Christmas he wrote that "Every time I get home I hate to go away worse than before and I don't feel so well here now as the first day I came here last fall but suppose I will be all right in a day or two." Two days later: "I feel quite reconciled to being here tonight but felt awful mean yesterday and the day before. I don't know why, I never was homesick any before." In his first two years at Amherst, Coolidge was, "to say the least, an inconspicuous member of the class." He faithfully attended class meetings, but did not join in the myriad activities, formal and informal, scholarly and athletic, religious and amorous, going on around him. He took long walks in the woods.

Nor was his social isolation balanced with scholarly achievement; his first term marks averaged 2 on a scale of 5. "The marks seem pretty low, don't they?" he wrote his father. He remembered much later that "It needed some encouragement from my father for me to continue." He had begun with the hope that he could do well in his courses with plenty of time to spare.

Thus at 21, Calvin Coolidge was an indistinct personality, inarticulate, ineffective, alone. Particularly in affection and achievement he stood on the threshold of adulthood much deprived.

In his mind he had been gathering impressions and registering experiences which would later be useful. He had known his father and grandfather as political leaders in the community. He saw how his father made decisions— "painstaking, precise, and very accurate"—and came to understand government as "restraints which the people had imposed upon themselves in order to promote the common welfare." In the summer before he entered Amherst his father took him to a gathering in Bennington to hear President Benjamin Harrison; there he heard much high oratory about the "high consecration to liberty."

As a boy he had taken a minor part in speaking "pieces," acting in amateur plays, and was even an "end man" once in a local minstrel show. Cicero's orations stuck with him from Latin classes. At graduation from Black River Academy, in a class of five boys and four girls, he delivered an address on "Oratory in History"; the newspaper called it "masterly" and his teacher said his speech was "the best one he had seen." After his freshman year at Amherst, at the Independence Day celebration in Plymouth—"Of course, the Fourth of July meant a good deal to me, because it was my birthday"—he delivered a speech on "Freedom," "burning with fervor, replete with denunciation of Proud Albion, and rich with the glorification of our Revolutionary heroes." Perhaps inspired by his freshman rhetoric teacher, this was his last experiment in the florid style of oratory.

Had Coolidge's life taken a different turn, other events, other impressions would have lasted into his autobiographical years. As it was, he had in his mind a number of important images: of small-scale Yankee democracy, of his mother reading the romantic poets, of his father succeeding by being careful, of the familial legitimacy of politics, and of himself surviving before audiences. So far he had made nothing of these resources. But they were waiting.

Of the events in his first two years at Amherst, Coolidge wrote:

> In the development of every boy who is going to amount to anything there comes a time when he emerges from his immature ways and by the greater precision of his thought and action realizes that he has begun to find himself. Such a transition finally came to me. It was not accidental but the result of hard work. If I had permitted my failure, or what seemed to me at the time a lack of success to discourage me, I cannot see any way in which I would ever have made progress. If we keep our faith in ourselves, and what is even more important, keep our faith in regular and persistent application to hard work, we need not worry about the outcome.[4]

As a matter of fact, what he calls his "transition" was triggered by events nearly "accidental"; his success did not result primarily from "hard work"; and he was, as we have seen, "discouraged" by his earlier lack of success. (Perhaps every autobiography is a mixture of real memories and new meanings, a last attempt to join together life and belief.) In any case, Coolidge began his junior year an isolated boy with no real achievements and left Amherst two years later as a young man with a distinctive style of action. In between, the whole intensity of his experience, its pace and significance, was revolutionized.

Amherst upperclassmen could wear high derbies and carry canes. Each fall the members of the junior class raced from one end of the athletic field to the other, clad in "topper" and stick. The last seven across the line had to provide dinner and entertainment for the rest. Coolidge was not last, but was one of the losers. His assignment was a speech on "Why I Got Stuck." He began in silence by turning his pockets inside out to show that he had lost all his money on the race. Then: "You wouldn't expect a plow horse to make time on the race track or a follower of the plow to be a Mercury," he said. Pitching hay didn't fit one as a sprinter. And other such comments. Then, in conclusion: "Remember, boys, the Good Book says that the first shall be last and the last shall be first." The speech was a success—the whole class laughed and gave him an ovation. It was his first such appearance and it brought him more attention and notoriety than anything he had done at Amherst so far. He began to emerge as a character, although the incident is not mentioned in his *Autobiography.*

That same year he began to attract attention as a debater. Public speaking and debating were compulsory parts of the curriculum. One of his classmates wrote: "It was in his junior year that we discovered Coolidge. In that year we began debating, and in the debates we found that he could talk. It was as if a new and gifted man had joined the class." Coolidge now became more and more adept at brief and direct statement. He won frequently in debating, perhaps every time in the junior debates. In November of that year he wrote his father proudly: "In view of the fact that yesterday I put up a debate said to be the best heard on the floor of the chapel this term . . . can you send me $25?" In January he wrote home another glowing report of a successful debate. At the end of his junior year the students in the public speaking class voted to split the prize between Coolidge and another speaker. He continued debating in his senior year. In September he was elected to present the "Grove Oration" at the graduation exercises the following June. This was meant to be a humorous speech following the ponderousness of more formal addresses. In June, after a long series of indoor sermons and addresses, the students went to the College Grove, lit up their corncob pipes and settled back on the grass. Coolidge began this way: "The mantle of truth falls upon the Grove Orator on condition he wear it wrong side out," and went on through a series of in-house jokes, continually interrupted by hecklers and shouts of laughter. "The oration was packed with what today would be called 'wisecracks,'" his biographer says, "many of them sarcastic observations on members of the faculty—remarks which, although good-natured in tone and intention, had nevertheless something of a bite." The speech was a smashing success.

In parallel with these oratorical victories, Coolidge achieved social ones. He was elected a member of Phi Gamma Delta on January 15th of his senior year. This began a lifelong, active tie, his only fraternal connection. From the start he entered into the group's affairs; a classmate recalls that

> He took a deep interest in the chapter, was most faithful in attending "goat" and committee meetings, and while he did not live at the house, he passed considerable time there. We soon began to rely upon his counsel and judgment, and he was a distinct help to us in many serious problems we had to meet at that time.[5]

He wrote his father that "being in a society" would cost a little more money. From that time on Coolidge was a faithful "Fiji," raising money, acting as the chapter's lawyer, returning to inspect the house carefully from cellar to garret, organizing (while he was President) the "Fiji Sires and Sons." His role in his brief membership as a student was that of the faithful attender and business helper; he skipped the dances and card games and "wild parties." At long last he had found a band of brothers. He was not a central figure in this group, but it is obvious that his membership meant a great deal to him after years of being left out. The moral he drew from this in the *Autobiography* is touching: "It has been my observation in life that, if one will only exercise the patience to wait, his wants are likely to be filled."

He had found a voice and developed a relationship to his audience; he had a club of friends. At the same time, Coolidge found a model, an idol with whom to identify, and a set of philosophical beliefs to guide him. This was Charles E. Garman, professor of philosophy, whose course, as Coolidge took it, ran from the spring term of junior year through senior year, moving from psychology to philosophy to ethics. "It always seemed to me that all our other studies were in the nature of a preparation for the course in philosophy," Coolidge remembered. Garman, a tall, cadaverous man with piercing black eyes, was a dramatic character, "a middle-aged Hamlet," extremely popular among the students.

Garman was in reality "a devout and rather orthodox New England Congregationalist" with a strong neo-Hegelian bent. Our interest is less in what he taught than in what Coolidge carried away from him and retained for 35 years. Garman did not carry his question-raising method to the point of not providing answers. Coolidge recalled his emphasis on rational judgment in ethical matters, the existence of a personal God and of "the complete dependence of all the universe on Him," man as set "off in a separate kingdom from all other creatures," the "spiritual appeal" of art as Divine revelation, the essential equality of men, the dignity of work and industry's right to work's rewards, "that might does not make right, that the end does not justify the means, and that expediency as a working principle is bound to fail." All of this Coolidge lays out in an unusually lengthy passage of his memoirs. Garman posted aphorisms on the walls of his classroom—"Carry all questions back to fundamental principles," "Weigh the evidence," "The question *how* answers the question *what*," "Process, not product," and so forth. But perhaps the key lesson Coolidge retained is found later in the *Autobiography* in the context of his early steps in politics, when he was elected Mayor of Northampton, Massachusetts:

> Ever since I was in Amherst College I have remembered how Garman told his class in philosophy that if they would go along with events and hold to the main stream—without being washed ashore by the immaterial cross currents, they would some day be men of power.[6]

Already the echoes of Coolidge as President are apparent.

Coolidge remembered that "We looked upon Garman as a man who walked with God," and that he was "one of the most remarkable men with whom I ever came in contact," a man who "was given a power which took his class up into a high mountain of spiritual life and left them alone with God," who had "no pride of opinion, no atom of selfishness," "a follower of the truth, a disciple of the Cross, who bore the infirmities of us all." Coolidge did not try to defend Garman's position theoretically. But

> I knew that in experience it has worked. In time of crisis my belief that people can know the truth, that when it is presented to them they must accept it, has saved me from many of the counsels of expediency.[7]

He had found a rule of life, and the words to express it with.

Coolidge had written a romantic story for the Amherst *Literary Monthly* in the summer between his junior and senior years. In his senior year he tried his hand at a very different literary task, undertaken in secret: an essay for a national contest on "The Principles Fought For in the War of the American Revolution." The Amherst History Department awarded his piece a silver medal; the following December when he was working in a law office in Northampton, Coolidge learned he was also the national winner. One of the partners asked him, "Have you told your father?" To which he replied, "No, do you think I'd better?" In his *Autobiography* Coolidge recalled that

> I had a little vanity in wishing my father to learn about it first from the press, which he did. He had questioned some whether I was really making anything of my education, in pretense I now think, not because he doubted it but because he wished to impress me with the desirability of demonstrating it.[8]

Coolidge had moved from an emotional psychology, a sentimental dramatism in his story ("Margaret's Mist") to the logic of principles, the metier of ethical philosophy which he would continue to emphasize all his life. But his "No, do you think I'd better?" also represented a change. Right after graduation he returned to the farm for a summer's work and then went to Northampton to learn law. As late as January of his senior year he had not yet decided whether the law or storekeeping would be his profession. He wrote his father then, "You will have to decide." He did know that he wanted "to live where I can be of some use to the world and not simply where I should get a few dollars together." By graduation he had decided that the law was "the highest of the professions." On his own, Coolidge sought a place, and in September 1895 he went to work in a law office in Northampton. When he joined the law office Coolidge made a break with his past. The boy whose name had been recorded in various forms now discarded the "John" and became plain Calvin Coolidge. And "during these first years he worked so hard that for three years he did not find time to go back to Plymouth." The distance was about a hundred miles.

"That I was now engaged in a serious enterprise of life I so fully realized that I went to the barber shop and divested myself of the college fashion of long hair." He who had so often written home of his successes kept the largest one a secret. He found a job without his father's help. None of the Coolidges had been lawyers. Calvin had formed his style and begun his own life. He had found a way to be; he was not entirely certain where he was going.

As we have seen, Coolidge himself attributed to his experience in the last two years at Amherst a shaping influence on his mind and heart. His biographers agree. Claude Fuess is convinced that "he was, during his first two years at Amherst, acutely conscious of his slow progress. His ambitions had been thwarted; he had failed to make a fraternity, he was unnoticed by those around him, his marks were only mediocre, and he had no compensating successes." Then "perhaps his entire political philosophy" was shaped by his junior and senior teachers as he combined a spurt of learning with social success. William Allen White goes farther: his "spirit awoke in Amherst," Garman "unlocked for him the philosophic mysteries of life," he was "baptized for life," "this reborn spirit whom Garman begot," and "Body and mind and spirit were cast into the iron mold of a fate which guided him through life."

Calvin Coolidge found at Amherst the political style that would serve him as President—an emphasis on a rhetoric of high principles, a humorous buddyhood he would later extend to reporters and advisors, and a general propensity for dodging unnecessary work. His world view—the sense of fate's inexorable march and of man's spiritual nature—fits nicely into the stylistic pattern. And Coolidge's passive-negative character infused his Presidency with an air of reluctant reaction, a readiness to pull away from problems, to wait them out, to discourage interference with his contemplations.

Other Puritans in the Babylon of Washington had drawn a different inference from the doctrine of predestination. For Wilson it meant the most energetic pursuit of goodness through government; for Coolidge it meant sit down and be quiet and let what will be be. In a strange way, that permissive spirit suited the Jazz Age, perhaps suited especially the growing throng of businessmen discovering in the stock market ways to buy something with practically nothing.

EISENHOWER IN THE WHITE HOUSE

Eisenhower as President is, I think, best approximated in the passive-negative category, though his case presents certain difficulties. He carried over into the Presidency a rigorous schedule of activity, putting in longer hours than did Coolidge, at least until illness required him to slow down. He proves an exception to the simple idea that usually holds: that the relative expenditure of energy on Presidential tasks stands as a partial symptom of one's orientation to those tasks. Furthermore, Eisenhower often displayed optimism; he was certainly no gloomy Gus in the White House, though he was often irritable and depressed. He comes as close as any President to being one who strays beyond our crude categories, enforcing the reminder that the forest can sometimes hide the trees. In the substance of his orientation, however, we can see pretty plainly themes much like those Coolidge played out more blatantly.

On a great many occasions in the biographies, Eisenhower is found asserting himself by denying himself, taking a strong stand against the suggestion that he take a strong stand. No, he would not get down in the gutter with Joseph McCarthy, not stop the Cohn and Schine hijinks. Franklin Roosevelt had usurped Congressional powers, he thought, and he would not do that: "I want to say with all the emphasis at my command that this Administration has absolutely *no* personal choice for a new Majority Leader. *We* are not going to get into *their* business." When "those damn monkeys on the Hill" acted up, he would stay out of it. Was he under attack in the press? "Listen!" Eisenhower said. "Anyone who has time to listen to commentators or read columnists obviously doesn't have enough work to do." Should he engage in personal summitry on the international front? "This idea of the President of the United States going personally abroad to negotiate—it's just damn stupid." With a new Cabinet, wouldn't it make sense to oversee them rather carefully? To George Humphrey, the President said, "I guess you know about as much about the job as I do." And his friend Arthur Larson writes that the President found patronage "nauseating" and "partisan political effect was not only at the bottom of the list—indeed, it did not exist as a motive at all." In 1958 the President said, "Frankly, I don't care too much about the congressional elections."

Pressed to appear on television, Eisenhower said, "I keep telling you fellows I don't like to do this sort of thing. I can think of nothing more boring, for the American public, than to have to sit in their living rooms for a whole half hour looking at my face on their television screens." Furthermore, he did not want to get into traditional political speechmaking: "I don't think the people *want* to be listening to a Roosevelt, sounding as if he were one of the Apostles, or the partisan yipping of a Truman." Asked to make a speech, he would respond with irritation: "What is it that needs to be said? I am not going out there just to listen to my tongue clatter!" Sometimes he would agree reluctantly: "Well, all right, but not over twenty minutes." And for all his cheerfulness in the midst of applauding crowds, he expressed a strong distaste in private for the "killing motorcades" and "another yowling mob" and the "unattractive lot" of local politicians he encountered. For whatever reasons (he had once been struck by lightning while delivering a lecture), Eisenhower "the man—and the President—was never more decisive than when he held to a steely resolve *not* to do something that he sincerely believed wrong in itself or alien to his office."

Sherman Adams explained that Eisenhower "focused his mind completely on the big and important aspects of the questions we discussed, shutting out with a strongly self-disciplined firmness the smaller and petty side issues when they crept into the conversation." In other words, he did not so much select problems upon which to concentrate as he selected an *aspect* of all problems—the aspect of principle.

When someone aggravated Eisenhower, his practice was, he said, to "write his name on a piece of paper, put it in my lower desk drawer and shut the drawer." When it came time to end his four-pack-a-day cigarette habit, "I found that the easiest way was just to put it out of your mind."

Eisenhower's tendency to move away from involvements, to avoid personal commitments, was supported by belief: "My personal convictions, no matter how strong, cannot be the final answer," he said, and the definition of democracy he liked best was "simply the opportunity for self-discipline." As a military man he had detested and avoided politics at least since, in his first command, he was pressed by a Congressman for a favor. His beliefs were carved into epigrams:

> He that conquereth his own soul is greater than he who taketh a city.
> Forget your self and personal fortunes.
> Belligerence is the hallmark of insecurity.
> Never lose your temper, except intentionally.

It is the tone, the flavor, the aura of self-denial and refusal that counts in these comments. Eisenhower is not attacking or rejecting others, he is simply turning away from them, leaving them alone, refusing to interfere with them.

His character is further illuminated in his complaints, which are concentrated around the theme of being bothered. His temper flared when he felt he was being imposed upon, interfered with on matters that he wanted others to handle. From the beginning of his Presidency he resented the heavy schedule—much of it trivial—and being constantly asked to involve himself in unnecessary detail. He "heatedly gave the Cabinet to understand that he was sick and tired of being bothered about patronage." "When does anybody get any time to think around here?" he complained to Adams. "Nothing gets him out of sorts faster," writes Robert Donovan, "than for a subordinate to come in and start to hem and haw about a decision. He wants the decision and not the thinking out loud." Leaving the White House for a ten-day Christmas vacation in 1953, he remarked, "Nothing can get me mad today. Anything that will get me away from *this* place!" His heart attack in September 1955 was triggered, Eisenhower said, when he was repeatedly interrupted on the golf links by unnecessary phone calls from the State Department. Long before that his reluctance about being bothered with politics was evident. Back in 1943 when an American Legion post suggested he run for President, Ike burst out, "Baloney! Why can't a simple soldier be left alone to follow out his orders. And I furiously object to the word 'candidate'—I ain't and won't." When he finally managed to stop the boomlet for his nomination in 1948, he said he felt "as if I've had an abscessed tooth pulled" and in 1950 he said, "I don't know why people are always nagging me to run for President. I think I've gotten too old." "Look, son," he told a persistent reporter as the 1948 speculations continued, "I cannot conceive of any circumstance that could drag out of me permission to consider me for any political post from dogcatcher to Grand High Supreme King of the Universe." Campaigning in 1952 and "told of the scheduling of yet another speech or, worse still, another motorcade, he would grate his teeth in wrath and grind out the cry: 'Those fools on the National Committee! Are they trying to perform the feat of electing a dead man?'" And, he said, "You know, once in a while I get to the point, with everybody staring at me, where I want to go back indoors and pull down the curtain."

Why then did Eisenhower bother to become President? Why did he answer those phone calls on the golf links? Because he thought he ought to. He was a sucker for duty, and he always had been. Dutiful sentiments which would sound false coming from most political leaders ring true from Eisenhower.

> My only satisfaction in life is to hope that my effort means something to the other fellow. What can I do to repay society for the wonderful opportunities it has given me?

> . . . a decision that I have never recanted or regretted. The decision was to perform every duty given me in the Army to the best of my ability and to do the best I could to make a creditable record, no matter what the nature of the duty.[9]

> . . . in trying to explain to you a situation that has been tossed in my teeth more than once (my lack of extended troop duty in recent years), all I accomplished

> was to pass up something I *wanted* to do, in favor of something I thought I *ought* to do, and then . . . find myself not even doing the latter.[10]

Eisenhower did not feel a duty to save the world or to become a great hero, but simply to contribute what he could the best he was able. Throughout his life—from the family Bible readings, from the sportsmanship of a boy who wanted nothing more than to be a first-rate athlete (and risked his life to save his leg for that), from the West Point creed—Eisenhower felt, amid questions about many things, that duty was a certainty:

> His intimates have learned that no appeal will move him more deeply than "This is a duty you owe the American people." When he was being pressed to run for the Presidency, one aide recalls that every possible argument and pressure was employed upon him, "but the only one that made any difference was that it was his duty."[11]

Another aide remembered that Eisenhower "never lost his view of himself as standing apart from politics generally and from his own party in particular"—he never saw himself as personally dominating political forces. "He has taken on a third-person attitude toward life," another observer wrote. "'The President feels—' and 'It seems to the President—' have become standard marks of his speech, supplanting the widespread and overworked 'I'. The impression he gives is of standing aside, as employer, and viewing himself as employee."

Yet Eisenhower very much wanted to make a contribution. Once while laboring over a speech he said, "You know, it is *so* difficult. You come up to face these terrible issues, and you know that what is in almost everyone's heart is a wish for peace, and you want so much to do *something*. And then you wonder . . . if there really *is* anything you can do . . . by words and promises. . . . You wonder and you wonder. . . ."

In all these respects, and also in his personal comradeship, Eisenhower fits the character of the passive-negative type. The key orientation is toward performing duty with modesty, and the political adaptation is characterized by protective retreats to principle, ritual, and personal virtue. The political strength of this character is its legitimacy. It inspires trust in the incorruptibility and the good intentions of the man. Its political weakness is its inability to produce, though it may contribute by preventing. Typically, the passive-negative character presides over drift and confusion, partially concealed by the apparent orderliness of the formalities. Sam Lubell caught the crux of this character when he saw in Eisenhower "one man's struggle between a passion for active duty and a dream of quiet retirement." And Eisenhower himself displayed the essential passiveness of his political character when he told Walter Cronkite in 1961, "The President has to be concerned with everything that happens to any human in the United States and often abroad and that is—that happens to be brought to his notice." "He once told the Cabinet," Adams reports, "that if he was able to do nothing as President except balance the budget he would feel that his time in the White House had been well spent."

Eisenhower's beliefs about the world were, in many ways, as vague as Coolidge's, with the same highly general mode of expression in epigram. He rejected extremism, radical or reactionary, and came out for the middle of the road. In policy terms, perhaps the most important Eisenhower contribution to domestic politics was his readiness, as the first Republican President since Hoover, to accept the broad dimensions of the welfare state rather than following some of his right-wing critics who wanted the New Deal repealed. Eisenhower invoked principles, but he refused to interpret them rigidly. Eisenhower had purposes, but he stopped short of pursuing them by mobilizing fully, behind his leadership, the political forces which had thrust him into office.

President Eisenhower's style centered in the organization of interpersonal relations. His remarkable rhetorical success seems to have happened without either great skill or great energy on his part. By the 1956 election voters had, by and large, forgotten all the reasons they had offered for his election in 1952 except "I like Ike." He won almost casually what so many other candidates and Presidents have sought so intensely through artifice: popular confidence in himself as man and President. Ike's very bumbling appears to have made him seem more "sincere," to use one of the favorite human qualities of the 1950s. Not above letting professional advertising men tell him what to do in his campaigns, Eisenhower as President kept editing warm words out of his speeches. In 1957, Doris Fleeson parodied his speech style with a version of the Gettysburg Address translated into Eisenhowerese, beginning:

> I haven't checked these figures, but 87 years ago, I think it was, a number of individuals organized a governmental set-up here in this country. I believe it covered certain Eastern areas, with this idea they were following up based on a sort of national independence arrangement and the program that every individual is just as good as every other individual.[12]

He much preferred—and developed an effective style in—speaking conversationally, especially about such large themes as peace and prosperity. The Washington cognoscenti might ridicule him, but he came across to the country. Walter Johnson summarizes his contribution.

> Without Eisenhower as head of the Republican party, the venom that disgraced Democratic politics in the closing years of Truman's presidency would have been rife in the nation. He purged national life of rancor. And by presenting himself continuously as standing at the moderate and reasonable center of American life, he was able to tune in on the deepest instincts of the people, who, at this stage in their history, desired pause, comfort and repose; a mood which reflected the spectacular expansion of the middle class base of American life.[13]

This man, who had little use for inspirational blather, whose speeches would not be long remembered for their eloquence, and who continually resisted demands that he lecture his fellow citizens, revitalized national confidence almost in spite of himself. He is a puzzling case. *His* political habits never stressed rhetoric, yet that is where he excelled.

Eisenhower liked to deal with problems at a high level of policy. He resisted detail, resisted involvement in the niggling issues that so often make the difference in politics. By a kind of role levitation, he could rise above any number of low-level issues, as he tried to do in the matter of Joseph McCarthy. Inevitably this sometimes left him out of touch with his responsibilities. In early 1957 Eisenhower presented his administration's budget—and promptly invited Congress, much to the amazement of his supporters there, to suggest "sensible reductions" in it. He submitted a civil rights bill and then told the press he did not himself agree with all aspects of it. *Life* magazine commented that "the fiasco of his program is in some part due to his own indecision and seeming unsureness in support of it." With painful honesty, Eisenhower would admit in press conferences that he had "never heard of" significant Administration activities. Sam Lubell found increased speculation among voters as to who was actually running the country.

Eisenhower's stylistic bent was for organizing officialdom into a smooth-running machine—a structuring version of his personal relations style. He set about this quite deliberately:

> For years I had been in frequent contact with the Executive Office of the White House and I had certain ideas about the system, or lack of system, under which it operated. With my training in problems involving organization it was inconceivable to me that the work of the White House could not be better systematized than it had been during the years I had observed it.[14]

In *The President's Men,* Patrick Anderson gives a cogent account of how Ike went about this reform. "The essence of Eisenhower's system of administration," Anderson writes, "was his belief in the delegation of authority." Retaining the basic staff offices he had inherited (Press Secretary, Congressional Relations Office, Special Counsel's Office, Appointments Secretary), the President added "The Assistant to the President" (Sherman Adams), a Special Assistant for National Security Affairs to work with a more formal National Security Council system, a Staff Secretary and a Secretary to the Cabinet (to turn that body into a regular instrument of Presidential decision-making), plus a number of Special Assistants to the President to advise him on particular policy areas. The overriding purpose of all these new elaborations was to simplify the President's task—to make sure he could save all his energies for the utmost strategic considerations, undistracted by the litter of tactics. "A President who doesn't know how to decentralize will be weighed down with details and won't have time to deal with the big issues," Eisenhower said.

When Secretary of Defense Charles E. Wilson bothered him too often with details, Ike was blunt: "Look here, Charlie, I want *you* to run Defense. We *both* can't run it, and I *won't* run it. I was elected to worry about a lot of things other than the day-to-day operations of a department."

Eisenhower's carefully charted system did save him from immersion in trivia; decisions were so thoroughly staffed that by the time they got to him a great deal of extraneous matter had been sliced away and he could say yes or no.

He was thus able, he felt, to ride herd on the immense variety and complexity of modern government. The President became the supreme coordinator, a coach of coaches, the master steersman keeping the craft moving steadily down the middle of the stream. But the system had its costs. To his natural disinclination to be "bothered" was added, as a result of extreme delegations, his staff's disinclination to "bother" him. "But the less he was bothered," as Richard Neustadt noted, "the less he knew, and the less he knew, the less confidence he felt in his own judgment. He let himself grow stale"—and thus all the more dependent on his advisors. Proposals which finally reached him were too often bland and superficial, bled white by the processes of compromise.

"The misfortune of Eisenhower's presidency," Anderson concludes,

> is that a man of such immense popularity and good will did not accomplish more. All the domestic problems which confronted the nation in the 1960s—the unrest of the Negro, the decay of the cities, the mediocrity of the schools, the permanence of poverty—were bubbling beneath the surface in the 1950s, but the President never seemed quite sure that they existed or, if they did, that they were problems with which he should not concern himself.

A character attracted by duty but repelled by politics, with a common-sensical, centrist view of the world, using a style stressing central coordination (though succeeding better on the rhetorical level), Eisenhower presided high over the nether regions of policy. Down there, much of the time, the "rich, full life" grew richer and fuller, sheltered by world peace, fed by an expanding economy. What was missing was a sensitivity at the highest level of government to the brittleness of social and political accommodations and a readiness to use power, where necessary, to stimulate creative tension.

EISENHOWER EMERGING

Like the early years of most Presidents, those of Dwight Eisenhower can be seen as placid and continuous; he was born healthy, his parents fed and loved him, he went to school, he entered a career—much as millions of other boys have done. But from the boy's own perspective, whether he is fated to be President or postman, his own particular life is far more dramatic than that. For example, Ike's earliest memory was of a startling confrontation: he was attacked by an animal about as big as he was. Ike was four years old and the animal was a barnyard gander. Looking for something to do, the boy had been gazing down into an open well. His uncle came along and "offered a long story about what would happen to me if I fell in. He spoke in such horrible terms that I soon lost any ambition to look over the fearful edge into the abyss below," and Ike sought some "less dreadful diversion." He intruded on a pair of geese and the gander came after him "with hideous hissing noises so threatening my security" that he had to "race for the back door of the house, burst into the kitchen, and tell any available elder about this awful old gander."

> Thus the war began. In the early parts of the campaign, I lost a skirmish every half hour and invariably had to flee ignominiously and weeping from the battlefield. Without support, and lacking arms of any kind, it was only by recourse to distressing retreat after retreat to the kitchen door that I kept myself from disaster.[15]

Finally Uncle Luther fixed a broom-handle weapon for the boy and showed him how to use it.

> The gander remained aggressive in his actions, and I was not at all sure that my uncle was very smart. More frightened at the moment of his possible scolding than I was of aggression, I took what was meant to be a firm, but was really a trembling, stand the next time the fowl came close. Then I let out a yell and rushed toward him, swinging the club as fast as I could. He turned and I gave him a satisfying smack right in the fanny. He let out a most satisfactory squawk and ran off. This was my signal to chase him, which I did.[16]

From then on little Ike was "the proud boss of the back yard." The incident taught him, he writes with pleasant humor, "never to negotiate with an adversary except from a position of strength."

The drama David Dwight Eisenhower (as he was christened) experienced unfolded in Abilene, Kansas, where his family moved not long after Ike was born in Texas. Even today, Abilene is a small punctuation mark in the immense, featureless Kansas plain which produces twinges of agoraphobia for touring Easterners. Under that wide blue sky, Ike grew up in a tiny house—818 square feet for a family of eight. "I don't know yet how my mother jammed us all in," he said; surely that took some adroit social coordination.

Indoors, Mother Eisenhower ruled the roost. Father was away at work most of the time; when he was at home he enjoyed contemplating a large chart of the Egyptian pyramids about which he had complex theories. His son remembered him as a "quiet and reserved" man. He was dark-complexioned; Ike was fair like his mother, so much so that he was nicknamed "Swede." Twitted for playing solitaire, she justified such unsanctified frivolity by pointing out that in that game, "The Lord deals the cards; you play them," a rule of resignation and effort symbolizing her way with life. Ike "never heard a cross word pass between" his parents, even when Father went broke because a trusted partner cheated him. Mother concurred in Father's resultant "obsession against ever owing anyone a nickel." This "warm, pleasant, mild-mannered woman never ceased to warn [her sons] against thieves, embezzlers, chiselers, and all kinds of crooks." Her views on politicians were not recorded.

Ida Stover Eisenhower may have had a natural knack for political compromise. When her boys squabbled over the sizes of their portions of cake or pie her solution was, "Now one of you is to divide it and the other to get first choice." Her counsel was peace. Father David could be rough at times. Once he beat Ike's brother so hard Ike cried and shouted and tried to hold his father's arms: "I don't think anyone ought to be whipped like that," he said, "not even a dog." Another time his father urged him to fight back at a bullying playmate. The

Halloween Ike was ten, his mother said he was too young to join his older brothers in trick-or-treating and Ike was so furious he pounded his fists bloody on a tree trunk. "My father legislated the matter with the traditional hickory switch and sent me off to bed." Then his mother came into his bedroom and sat with him.

> Hatred was a futile sort of thing, she said, because hating anyone or anything meant that there was little to be gained. The person who had incurred my displeasure didn't care, possibly even didn't know, and the only person injured was myself. This was soothing, although she added that among all her boys, I was the one who had most to learn.
>
> In the meantime, she was putting salve on my injured hands and bandaging the worst places, not failing to make the point that I had expressed resentment and only damaged myself.
>
> I have always looked back on that conversation as one of the most valuable moments of my life. To my youthful mind, it seemed to me that she talked for hours but I suppose the affair was ended in fifteen or twenty minutes. At least she got me to acknowledge that I was wrong and I felt enough ease in my mind to fall off to sleep. The incident was never mentioned again. But to this day I make it a practice to avoid hating anyone. If someone's been guilty of despicable actions, especially toward me, I try to forget him. . . . Eventually, out of my mother's talk grew my habit of not mentioning in public anybody's name with whose actions or words I took violent objection.[17]

There is the hatred soothed away, the child's resignation, the lesson learned. Ike as a boy and Eisenhower as President could, on occasion, burst forth in violent temper-storms, but thereafter he had his solution: turn your back on it, leave it behind.

Dwight Eisenhower liked to read history as a boy, especially military history; his hero was Hannibal, who retained his fame despite the enmity of generations of biographers. When he graduated from high school his classmates thought he would someday reach eminence—as professor of history at Yale. Because he read when he should have been working, his mother locked up the history books, but Ike found the key and got at this forbidden fruit whenever his mother was out. Perhaps it was her pacifism that made her dislike his reading, which tended to focus on military heroes. Much later, when he left for West Point to train for killing, Ike's mother wept for the first time in her boy's memory. Ike most admired Washington, for his "stamina and patience in adversity, first, and then his indomitable courage, daring, and capacity for self-sacrifice."

Political life rarely intruded on the Eisenhower family. When Ike was six he tumbled along after his big brothers in a torchlight parade for McKinley; at the end "there was a tiresome speech under way when my brothers and I took off for home."

He did well in school, but his interests were far stronger in athletics than in scholarship. Somewhat lazy as a boy, known for sleeping late, something of "a great bawler because I was trying to get out of doing things," at school he became a tough guy from the wrong side of the tracks. Grade school had not turned him on:

> The darkness of the classrooms on a winter day and the monotonous hum of recitations, offset only occasionally by the excitement of a spelling bee or the suppression of a disorderly boy, are my sole surviving memories. I was either a lackluster student or involved in a lackluster program.[18]

By high school he was playing a good deal of baseball and football and was a close friend of "Six" McDonald, the star pitcher. He helped organize the Abilene High School Athletic Association, wrote a constitution for it, and as a senior was elected president. "My ambitions were directed toward excellence in sports, particularly baseball and football," Eisenhower remembered of his school days. "I could not imagine an existence in which I was not playing one or both." Once he contracted blood poisoning in his leg and became delirious. The doctor came again and again, and once Ike heard him mention "amputation."

> When [brother] Ed got home, I called him and made him promise to make sure that under no circumstances would they amputate my leg. "I'd rather be dead than crippled, and not be able to play ball." The doctors . . . were frustrated by my attitude. But my parents understood. While they were against such contact sports as football, they agreed to accept my decision.[19]

Carbolic acid finally arrested the infection, but Ike missed so much school he had to repeat the year.

Eisenhower emerged from his history a believer in peace, in harmony, in cooperative endeavor. Neither of his parents pushed him toward extraordinary achievement, any more than Coolidge's had him. He was not fired up to change the world; he wanted to play baseball. His family had taught him to bear reverses stoically, to turn away from anger, and to let be what had to be. By and large, Ike's boyhood history as he recalled it much later is a picture of a child not overly energetic, trailing along behind his big brothers and responding to his mother's insistences about the chores and to her instruction, not in fighting against such evil emotions as anger, but in forgetting them. At the same time, there was a minor rebellious theme in his makeup, reflected in the stories of restraining his father, protesting against being left out of the older boys' activities, reading the forbidden history books, admiring military heroes, playing football, and occasionally raising hell in school. In response, his mother calmed and soothed him. To a neighbor lady who asked what she was going to do to stop Ike's howling, Ida Stover Eisenhower predicted, "Oh, he'll be all right as soon as he brings his kindling in." Eisenhower always had in his character that resource of tolerant resignation she gave him.

And he learned to smile. Years later Eisenhower's broad smile and upraised arms encouraged a generation. In part, that smile masked chagrin. Whistlestop campaigning in 1952, Ike wrote that "the candidate . . . steps blithely out to face the crowd, doing his best to conceal with a big grin the ache in his bones, the exhaustion in his mind." Leaving the White House for his inauguration in 1953, Ike was steaming inside at Truman for ordering Ike's son home from Korea for the ceremonies. Yet there he is in the photograph, sitting next to

Harry in the limousine, beaming widely. Politics was a botheration—at the head of his chapter on campaigning he quotes "Double, double, toil and trouble; Fire burn and cauldron bubble." But all one needed to handle its problems was strength and gentleness—"Suaviter in modo, fortiter in re," read the motto on his desk.

Ike's horizons expanded as he grew. He was always noticing the space around him. "Since I left Abilene, and whenever I've been given any choice of working quarters, my usual preference as to their size may reflect a subconscious effort to test my own capacity for the use of space against my mother's." But "I haven't always been a free agent and in the passage of years, my offices got bigger and bigger." In the Pentagon after the war, Eisenhower's office "was larger than our entire Abilene home." The President's office at Columbia University was a big, high-ceilinged place; Ike preferred a little retreat he converted into a painting room atop his residence. As head of SHAPE in Paris, he occupied another big chamber. Then came the Presidency: "In my next job, I had absolutely no choice whatsoever in the selection of my office."

Like the physical space around him, Eisenhower's life-space was continually expanding. Like his attitude toward rooms, there were a good many times when he would have preferred to trade the glory of expanded responsibility for the comfort of privacy.

After graduation from high school Ike had to look beyond Abilene for new horizons. His career plans were indefinite, but he and his mother knew he wanted an education. He worked it out with his brother Ed: Ike would work to put him through a couple of years at the University of Michigan, then, if necessary, Ed would drop out to support Ike. But then he heard about Annapolis—the Naval Academy—from a friend. One could get educated there at government expense. After hard preparation, he took the examination, but learned that he was too old for admission. Instead, he got into West Point when the top candidate failed to meet the physical requirements.

Of such fortuities is history constructed.

To recognize the tragedy that overtook Eisenhower at West Point, and to understand the way he worked himself out of it, one must suspend for the moment knowledge of his eventual success and take his contemporary values and purposes seriously. To be sure, he remembered in later years a profound feeling of patriotism as he joined the Corps. But the big thing on his mind was still sports.

> One of my reasons for going to West Point was the hope that I could continue an athletic career. It would be difficult to overemphasize the importance that I attached to participation in sports.[20]

Ike (at some stage, perhaps in the Abilene-West Point transition, David Dwight became Dwight David) was a gung-ho a football and baseball fiend as West Point had seen. He was light—152 pounds—for football and sparely built. "But the only thing to do was keep at it." Hustling to make the baseball team he agreed to practice a new hitting technique for a year. He got hurt, got up, kept at it, practiced hard at track to build up his running speed, and "set up a severe regimen of gymnastics to strengthen my arm and leg muscles." By vigorous eating he got his weight up to 174. When the football season started in 1912, "no player was more eager to prove himself" and Ike was thrilled when the coach noticed that "I showed up quite well." His "enthusiasm made up somewhat for my lack of tonnage" and he undertook to "instill the fear of Eisenhower into every opponent."

> On one occasion, I succeeded beyond my intent; an opposing player made a protest against me. He shouted to the referee, "Watch that man!" pointing at me.
>   The referee with some astonishment asked, "Why? Has he slugged you or roughed you up?"
>   The man, green and overexcited, replied, "NO! But he's *going* to."[21]

Ike played regularly on the Army varsity team; he won his football letter. He looked ahead to two more seasons.

Then he twisted his leg badly in a game, and reinjured the same leg in a riding exercise, tearing cartilages and tendons severely. From the doctors, Ike "learned to my dismay that rugged sports were denied to me from then on." No baseball, no football, no boxing, no track. "I was almost despondent and several times had to be prevented from resigning by the persuasive efforts of classmates. Life seemed to have little meaning; a need to excel was almost gone." Eisenhower's grades got worse. He began to smoke cigarettes, despite the serious penalties the regulations specified. "Things continued to run downhill." He insulted a plebe and felt "stupid and unforgivable" about it. He blew up at a professor, developing an uncharacteristic "lasting resentment" toward him. He spent almost all his vacation money on neckties rather than let a clerk know he had mistaken the prices. At a shooting gallery, Ike, in civilian clothes, was called "soldier boy" by a stranger who wanted to bet on his marksmanship. "Unaccountably, and for the first time in my life, a fit of trembling overcame me. My hands shook. Without a word, I laid down the rifle, already having paid for the shells, and left the place without a backward glance. Never before or since have I experienced the same kind of attack." Not long before graduation, he was told he might not be eligible for a commission because of his physical disability; his reaction to this stunning news was a shrug: "I said that this was all right with me." He thought he might take a trip to South America and wrote off for travel folders.

Along the way during this period of despondency, which seems to have lasted at least two years, Ike was gradually developing other ways to link up with the sports he loved. During a furlough at the end of his second West Point year he went back to Abilene for a couple of months and was asked to umpire the home games. "This chore I could perform without injury to myself." A neighboring town's club asked him to umpire a game there. He went back again to umpiring in Abilene during his graduation leave. At West Point the doctors kept trying "every experiment and exercise they could think of to get me back into condition," including "all sorts of braces," but nothing worked. Then the football coach "suggested that I could keep up my interest in football by coaching the Junior Varsity. . . . I got interested in this coaching idea and tried it." The squad did well, and Ike showed his ability to get action out of a group of men, in contrast to his supervisor whose "actions were so resisted or misinterpreted by the squad that the head coach suggested that he give me considerable leeway." Assigned after graduation to Fort Sam Houston, Texas, he coached the football team of a neighboring military school, with the encouragement of his commanding officer and the significant reward of $150 for the season, and the following year went to work coaching the St. Louis College team, greatly improving their record.

These experiences contributed to Eisenhower's style as a coordinator of action, demonstrating to a man who had been deprived of his ability to do the main thing he wanted to do that he could serve by organizing others to succeed in it. There was no sudden discovery, no dramatic shift, but, it seems probable, Eisenhower found a growing confidence and satisfaction in exercising this talent. His coaching reputation, along with his emerging capacity to manage military business under various lax commanders, may also have brought his skills in coordination to the attention of his superiors and affected his career. He wanted to go overseas to command troops and was elated when he heard that orders had been given to that effect. But then the orders were changed. His superior said "he was impressed by my 'organization ability'"—and reassigned him to take charge of setting up and commanding a training camp in Pennsylvania. Ike was much disappointed, but he built Camp Colt, for training in the new tank corps, from scratch. "Now I really began to learn about responsibility." He learned to pick men, to get them working together, to coax—and coach—ten thousand men and six hundred officers into doing their duty. When at last he was given command, at 28, of a large contingent headed overseas, Ike saw to it that every one of them made it to the embarkation point. The war was over before he could get to France.

Between West Point and the White House, Eisenhower went through many a year of military doldrums and many experiences which helped him develop his special style of leadership. He could work hard when he wanted to, and the work he did best was getting the group together. His growth paralleled an important trend in military organization. Command was becoming much less a matter of flamboyant personal leadership, much more a talent for juggling specialized, functional organizations in a chairman-of-the-board fashion. During the Second World War, Eisenhower brought that talent close to perfection as Supreme Allied Commander, coordinating a multi-national team in the most massive and complex military task ever undertaken.

As Supreme Commander, Eisenhower insisted on a team approach at the top and on definite lines of authority and responsibility extending downward. In September 1943, Lord Mountbatten, new Supreme Commander of the Southeast Asian theater, requested advice from Ike on structuring his command.

Eisenhower emphasized teamwork and effective coaching above all: *"The thing you must strive for is the utmost in mutual respect and confidence among the group of seniors making the overall command. . . .* While the setup may be somewhat artificial, and not always so clean-cut as you might desire, your personality and good sense *must* make it work. Otherwise Allied action in any theater will be impossible." Later he wrote that, "The teams and staffs through which the modern commander absorbs information and exercises his authority must be a beautifully inter-locked, smooth working mechanism. Ideally the whole should be practically a single mind." To make such a system function without confusions beyond those inherent in war, commanders were to require the strictest adherence to regular channels of communication: "All communications to the Combined Chiefs of Staff must pass through you and no one else must be allowed to send communications to the Body."

In the Presidency this style served him less well. In the invasion of Europe, Eisenhower's brand of coordination went forward in a context of definite authority; the colonels were dependent on the generals. This was hardly the case with the Executive Branch loaded with Democrats or with the temporary band of amateurs at the top, and not the case at all with Congress. In the Army, an order announced (after however much coordination) was an order to be executed; at least that was what experience taught by many a hard lesson. But in politics promulgation is just the beginning. In an Army at war, coordination takes place behind the advancing flag: the overriding purposes are not in question. In the political "order" the national purpose is continually questioned, continually redefined as part of the game.

The style was a coach's style; the Eisenhower world view, sketched in his adolescence, was further deepened by later experience. When he decided to give up a heartfelt desire to become an Army aviator, to sacrifice that in order to marry the girl he loved, he was "brought face to face with myself" and made a "decision that I have never recanted or regretted. The decision was to perform every duty given me in the Army to the best of my ability and to do the best I could to make a creditable record, no matter what the nature of the duty."

Eventually that attitude drew him into the White House. At the end of the day on January 22, 1953, he wrote a note to himself:

> My first full day at the President's Desk. Plenty of worries and difficult problems. . . . The result is that today just seems like a continuation of all I've been doing since July '41—even before that.[22]

THE APPEAL OF DUTY

What Coolidge and Eisenhower shared was a political character and, to a degree, similar views of the world. Their styles were quite different, Coolidge primarily a rhetorician, Eisenhower primarily an interpersonal coordinator. But both shared with other passive-negative people in politics a propensity for withdrawal, for moving away from conflict and detail. Their stance toward political life was one of irritated resignation. They were performing duty under duress, not crusading after some political Holy Grail. Each felt that he ought to serve, ought to contribute, ought to do what he could to make things better for America. But one senses in their attitude an assumption that merely occupying the office of President provided justification enough, and that all expenditures of energy beyond that point were extra, not required. In any case, men of this type convey a resistance to intrusion, to being bothered by demands that they perform. Beneath the surface, they seem to be saying that they should not have to initiate, that problems should come to them rather than they to the problems, and that their responsibilities were limited primarily to preserving the fundamental values by applying them to disagreements no one else in the system could resolve.

The elements in the passive-negative orientation are consistent: the man does as little as he can of what he does not like to do. Psychologically, one suspects the demands of conscience are met in part by maintaining the feeling of sacrifice—the person confirms that he is doing his duty by the fact that he does not enjoy it. Thus reluctance is a defense. Low self-esteem is counteracted by the observation that others continually turn to one for help, for useful action.

Coolidge restored confidence in the legitimacy of his office after the scandals of the Harding administration; Eisenhower did the same following Truman's "mess in Washington." Each was valued for "character" in the sense of old-fashioned personal virtue and stability, and especially for his antipolitical honesty, for his apparent disdain for the calculated ploy. Perhaps the rhetoric of politics erodes, over time, as activists press for achievement and for those vigorous verbal banners which stretch so thinly over conglomerations of compromise. Eventually the people's hunger for straight talk comes through and produces a candidate who, whatever else he may be, seems honest.

The trouble with the passive-negative type in the Presidency is that he leaves untapped the energizing, initiating, stimulating possibilities of the role. He is a responder; issues are "brought to his attention"—and there are too damned many of them. Under the flag of legitimacy, the nation unites—and drifts. Presidential dignity is restored at the cost of Presidential leadership. As long as we have no king, this type may be necessary from time to time. But while we are restoring the national spirit in this way, the body politic lapses into laxness and the social order deteriorates as neglected tensions build up. Eventually some leader ready to shove as well as to stand fast, someone who enjoys the great game of politics, will have to pick up the pieces.

7

The Passive-Positive Presidents

Politics is in many ways a loving business. Alongside the conflict and tension, politicians devote much of their attention to the caressing of egos, the embracing of the lonely, the inclusion of the left out. To suppose that all this touching, smiling, handshaking, backslapping, happiness-spreading activity is, at bottom, mere calculated hokum is to make a double mistake. The need for it is genuine beyond doubt. For those at the margins of politics, love lifts the issues above questions of morality and power to the plain of human concern; politicians continually reconstitute a sense of community, of sharing, of simple affection and mutuality as they exude the balm of political love. It is no accident that politicians learn to cram their minds with personal data so they can say, at the right moment, "Hello, Charley, how's Junior getting along at college?"

Nor does it make sense to think that all or even most of this geniality is phony in its motive. Politics attracts a lot of activists who actually like to shower people with kindness. Their conscious labor in memorizing names and faces can be a way of preparing to do what they want to do: communicate love. And among themselves, within the confining, uncertain, conflict-ridden arenas of decision-making, politicians have need of loving relationships lest the whole thing fall apart in rancor and distrust. Before the cynical observer dismisses love among the statesmen as nothing but flattery and sham, let him ask himself what friendship—real friendship—has meant in his own working life.

The passive-positive types are political lovers. Considering what politics does to some of them, they do not often wind up as lovers of politics, at least in its rougher aspects. Like the reluctant passive-negatives, they are responders, not initiators or pushers, but they go about their work with a different demeanor, an appearance of affectionate hopefulness. They accentuate the positive. They boost. They sympathize. In the Presidency they are, in many ways, nice guys who finished first, only to discover that not everyone is a nice guy.

William Howard Taft and Warren G. Harding—the two chief executives who bracketed Wilson's Presidency—illustrate this type. One was an epitome of propriety and the other his ethical opposite.

TAFT AND TR

When Taft left the Presidency, Will Rogers said, "We are parting with three hundred pounds of solid charity to everybody, and love and affection for all his fellow men." On the question of Taft's political character there is no dissent: he was from the start a genial, agreeable, friendly, compliant person, much in need of affection from wife, family, and friends. He fits the passive-positive category most closely, with his slow-moving pace and his optimistic grin. His mother often said that "the love of approval was Will's besetting fault." William Allen White noted the "easy gurgle of his laugh and the sweet insouciance of his answers," and a Senator described Taft as "a large, amiable island surrounded entirely by persons who knew exactly what they wanted." Taft could be tough and he could work hard, but both were rare exceptions. He needed a good deal of sleep: his aide Archie Butt had a regular system of coughing loudly to wake the President when he dozed off at church. At public functions, his wife took over, nudging him to consciousness as the speeches droned on. Once he lapsed into sleep as Speaker Joe Cannon "was leaning over his chair and talking most earnestly." His ponderous bulk, increasing when he overate during periods of depression, made effort specially difficult for him.

But he smiled. In his campaign, Taft supporters wore little cards that said, "Smile, Smile, Smile"—"for smiling had become synonymous with the big man who was about to become President." Both up close and at a distance, Taft displayed an apparent equanimity in cheerfulness unmatched in the Presidency. Yet curiously, as his biographer Henry F. Pringle noted, Taft had scarcely any intimate friends.

> Indeed, one of the astonishing things about Taft's four years in the White House was the almost total lack of men, related or otherwise, upon whom he could lean. He had no Cabot Lodge. He had no Colonel House. For the most part he faced his troubles alone.[1]

In this regard also, Taft fit the passive-positive type: many friends, few if any intimates. Perhaps because he found fighting so discomfiting, Taft could not develop a close team of advisors who would at the same time commit themselves loyally to him and counsel him with brutal frankness when that was required. Archie Butt thought, "I have never known a man to dislike discord as much as the President. He wants every man's approval, and a row of any kind is repugnant to him."

Taft had opinions on the big issues of his time—on the tariff, conservation, labor, and so on—but his political world view was, with one exception, amorphous and uncertain. He was a conservative progressive, but above all he was a law-lover. His mother told the press when Taft was being boomed for the Presidency, "I do not want my son to be President; he is not my candidate. His is a judicial mind, and he loves the law." Insofar as Taft had a philosophy it was this: "We have a government of limited power under the Constitution and we have got to work out our problems on the basis of law." As President he was an ardent believer in the judicial settlement of international disputes. Later, as Chief Justice, Taft felt that the Court, "next to my wife and children, is the nearest thing to my heart in life." "The truth is that in my present life I don't remember that I ever was President," he wrote. Pringle points out the depth and difficulty of Taft's legal enthusiasm:

> Taft worshipped the law; no understanding of him is possible without appreciation of that fact. The fallacy in his philosophy lies, of course, in the fact that there is no such thing as "the law." It is a mass of opinion, formulated by men throughout the centuries, and is constantly being altered. What Taft really did was to revere the law, as he understood it, himself, or as judges with whom he agreed interpreted it.[2]

Taft was attracted to Theodore Roosevelt for many reasons, one of the strongest of which was that TR stood in Taft's mind as defender of the laws—of "the guaranties of the Constitution . . . in favor of life, liberty and property"—against the "illegal ways," the "methods contrary to statute law," of profiteers who thought it "fashionable and conventional to ignore the existence of the statutes of the United States." Before he was President, Taft saw the essential quality of Roosevelt's progressivism in the proposition that "the guaranty with respect to the right of property would be undermined by a movement toward socialism," in the observation that "this movement has gained force by the use of accumulated wealth and power in illegal ways and by duress to suppress competition and center financial control in a few hands . . . contrary to statute law," and in the inference that it was necessary to enforce those laws, even if that meant taking "the great corporations by the throat" and putting "the fear of God into the hearts of their managers." In those respects, Taft claimed, "Mr. Roosevelt's views were mine long before I knew Mr. Roosevelt at all."

Arriving in the Presidency at a time when relations between the law and society were in rapid change, Taft continued to think of law as something definite, almost tangible, which, once seen, impelled belief. Much as he disliked the dissension of politics, he had a special aversion toward dissent among those responsible for interpreting the law. As Chief Justice he said, "I would not think of opposing the views of my brethren if there was a majority against my own." His own dissenting opinions were extremely rare. No, the law was not a matter of caprice or even, in the main, an instrument of social policy. It was a set of rules whose force basically depended on their continuity through the shifting tangle of events. Taft was no rigid legalistic fanatic, but once he decided what the law "was" he was not easily swayed by arguments of expediency.

The primary article in Taft's legal philosophy was his conception of Presidential power. In a lecture on "The Presidency" delivered in 1915, Taft said that "our President has no initiative in respect to legislation given him by law except that of mere recommendation, and no legal or formal method of entering into the argument and discussion of the proposed legislation while pending in Congress."

There are few expressions of aggression in Taft's recorded life, and the few that can be found are almost all directed at officials neglectful or contemptuous of the law. "I get very impatient," President Taft wrote, "at criticism by men who do not know what the law is, who have not looked it up, and yet ascribe all sorts of motives to those who live within it."

Taft's political style reflected his judicial stance toward the world and drew on his characteristic geniality. He did a great deal of campaign speaking over the years, his face wreathed in smiles, but he did not like it much; "Politics makes me sick" he wrote his wife several times. His formal addresses were like legal briefs—long, point-by-point explanations linking argument and fact, sacrificing eloquence for accuracy. Many of his private letters were vigorous and pungently put, but Taft did not have the knack for throwing forth phrases his audiences could cling to. He delivered an opinion when he might have preached revival. In reaching opinions, Taft could listen and study detail effectively, could work in bursts of energy between periods of physical and mental laxness. He seemed incredibly naive regarding the effects of his own performances politically, and much preferred to leave the wheeling and dealing to others.

In the Presidency, Taft's character, world view, and style—all formed for a different age—came together in a personal drama with profound political implications. When President McKinley was gunned down in September 1901, Taft was in Manila as his Governor of the Philippines. In a letter, Taft wondered if McKinley's successor "had the capacity for winning people to his support that McKinley had," and a few months later he noted that "Roosevelt blurts out everything and says a good deal that he ought to keep to himself." For his part, Roosevelt liked Taft. In June 1901, with typical enthusiasm, he had raised his glass in a toast to Taft and declared: "By George! I wouldn't ask any higher privilege than to be allowed to nominate Taft for President in the next national convention. What a glorious candidate and President he would make!" Taft was not interested in the job; subjected to criticism by some Senators when he returned from the Philippines, he said, "Sometimes I feel anxious to get out of the country to avoid them . . . and yet it shows my unfitness for public life for me to dislike them so and be so sensitive about them. I suppose it indicates a thin-skinned vanity." By the time Taft was inaugurated President in 1909, Roosevelt had a few doubts of his own: "He's all right. He means well and he'll do his best. But he's weak. They'll get around him. They'll lean against him."

Doubts aside, Will Taft and Theodore Roosevelt came to form a mutual admiration society of great power. Roosevelt twice offered Taft appointment to the Supreme Court; Taft twice refused on grounds that he had not completed his work in the Philippines. Then TR virtually ordered him to become Secretary of War. Taft did not want it. "It seems strange," he wrote, "that with an effort to keep out of politics and with my real dislike for it, I should thus be pitched into the middle of it." But urged on by his ambitious wife Nellie and by his brothers, Taft gave in and took the job. As his acquaintance with Roosevelt deepened, Taft came to love him; he wrote his wife that "The President seems really to take much comfort that I am in his Cabinet. He tells me so and then he tells people who tell me. He is a very sweet-natured man and a very trusting man when he believes in one. I am growing to be very fond of him." Finding that he had few specific duties as Secretary of War, Taft became a willing assistant in a wide range of Roosevelt projects. "One searches in vain," Pringle writes, "for a major issue on which Taft took a stand, even in private, against Roosevelt." Elihu Root, Taft, and Roosevelt, full of deep admiration for one another, called themselves the "Three Musketeers," with TR as D'Artagnan, Root as Athos, and Taft as Porthos; they often signed their letters with these names. Taft was very happy. People liked him. He was clearly a great help to the President. From December 1, 1905, to March 23, 1906, Taft's weight decreased from 320¾ pounds to 265¾.

Taft was a reluctant and somewhat uncertain candidate for the Presidency as early as 1905, but Roosevelt kept after him to seek the nomination, as did Mrs. Taft (who had no use for Roosevelt but the highest hopes for her Will). TR poured it on:

> Let the audience see you smile, *always*, because I feel that your nature shines out so transparently when you do smile—you big, generous, high-minded fellow. . . . Moreover, let them realize the truth, which is that for all your gentleness and kindliness and generous good nature, there never existed a man who was a better fighter when the need arose.[3]

Taft returned the compliment, as when he rose in uncharacteristic indignation at hearing a slight to Roosevelt: "When I love a chief," he said, "and when I admire him from top to toe, I cannot be silent and permit such insinuations, although they may be hidden in a jest."

Taft was nominated by an overwhelming vote on the first ballot. Through the campaign he sought TR's guidance almost every day—and of course he got it. The pugnacious President urged the gentle candidate to fight: "Do not *answer* Bryan; attack him!" "Make the fight aggressively." He told Taft to forget about "what he had said in this or that decision" and to "treat the political audience as one coming, not to see an etching, but a poster." Will was hesitant: "I am sorry," he told a friend, "but I cannot be more aggressive than my nature makes me. That is the advantage and the disadvantage of having been on the bench. I can't call names and I can't use adjectives when I don't think the case calls for them, so you will have to get along with that kind of a candidate." Nevertheless, Roosevelt continued to express his enthusiastic Taftism: "You blessed old trump," he wrote him, "I have always said you would be the greatest President, bar only Washington and Lincoln, and I feel mighty inclined to strike the exceptions." Taft in turn promised an administration "distinct from, and a progressive development of, that which has been performed by President Roosevelt. The chief function of the next administration is to complete and perfect the machinery." The image was one of a breathing spell, a time of peaceable building on the Roosevelt plan.

Taft won by 321 to 162 electoral votes over William Jennings Bryan. He pledged his reign would be "a worthy successor of that of Theodore Roosevelt." To a friend he confessed, "I pinch myself every little while to make myself realize that it is all true." He admitted to Roosevelt, "I look forward to the future with much hesitation and doubt as to what is to happen, but if we put our shoulder to the wheel and follow the course marked out by you . . . I am very hopeful that, while we may not accomplish all we have promised, we shall give evidence of an earnest and sincere attempt to do so."

Despite a bit of misunderstanding about retaining TR's Cabinet, the brotherhood of Taft and Roosevelt was firm and fine when, in the spring of 1909, Roosevelt departed for Africa. Friends of his, and Taft's family, were always fomenting discord, but the bond held. Taft said that "My coming into office was exactly as if Roosevelt had succeeded himself." In a long and affectionate letter Taft said that "When I am addressed as 'Mr. President' I turn to see whether you are not at my elbow. . . . I want you to know that I do nothing in the Executive Office without considering what you would do under the same circumstances and without having in a sense a mental talk with you over the pros and cons of the situation. . . . I can never forget that the power that I now exercise was a voluntary transfer from you to me. . . . With love and best wishes, in which Mrs. Taft joins me, believe me as ever, Affectionately yours. . . ."

But in fact, Taft was on his own. The strain hit him and his weight started to climb. He was in a difficult position. Not only was there endless speculation about antagonism between him and Roosevelt, but there were also tough issues to meet that involved the risk of decisions at variance from Roosevelt's policies. Taft tried to compromise on a tariff bill, but he alienated the insurgents and came out looking like a friend of the rich. By July, he wrote his wife (as he did every day she was away), "I am dealing with very acute and expert politicians, and I am trusting a great many of them and I may be deceived; but on the whole I have the whip hand." He was indeed deceived, as the tariff tanglers wove their fancy knots into webs of special privilege. Continually Taft turned to his wife for counsel.

After a jolly beginning, Taft's relations with reporters deteriorated. He simply did not have the TR flair for making news, and his somewhat smug judicial air made him shy away from dramatizing the issues. He sided against the raucous Joe Cannon in the contest for the Speakership, though he reserved his comments for private communication.⁴ The strain of decision began to tell on him. For a while he tried to lean on Senator Nelson Aldrich, but could not find there a substitute for TR. Taft felt rushed and depressed: "Archie, it seems to me I will never catch up with my work. . . . There is so much to be done and so little time to do it in that I feel discouraged." By June of his first White House year, he thought that "in view of the complications" he would be a one-term President. The lines in his face deepened. He often fell asleep as soon as he settled into a chair. He knew that Roosevelt would have confronted his opponents and beaten them into the ground, but "I cannot do things that way. I will let them go on, and by and by the people will see who is right and who is wrong. There is no use trying to be William Howard Taft with Roosevelt's ways."

Then came the famous Pinchot-Ballinger dispute. Rather than retain Roosevelt's man James Garfield as Secretary of Interior, Taft had appointed Richard A. Ballinger, despite a somewhat fuzzy promise to TR that his Cabinet would be kept on. A minor official, Louis R. Glavis, had accused Ballinger of letting public lands slip away to greedy business interests and intimated, again without much evidence, that Ballinger was involved in corrupt dealings. Gifford Pinchot, Chief of the United States Forest Service and a man as ardent in his championing of the conservationist cause as he was in his admiration for Roosevelt, sided with the anti-Ballinger forces as the controversy developed. President Taft thought of Pinchot as a "transcendentalist"—"a good deal of a radical and a good deal of a crank"—though as usual he kept these opinions private, and encouraged Pinchot to stay in the government and not to get involved.

Taft's stance toward the controversy was judgelike: "I am sorry about this Pinchot-Ballinger business. I think they misunderstand each other. But if they go on hitting each other I shall have to decide something between them." As the issues jelled, Taft's defense of Ballinger grew along three fronts. First, he would be loyal to his men: "If I were to turn Ballinger out, in view of his innocence and in view of the conspiracy against him, I should be a white-livered skunk. I don't care how it affects my administration." Second, Ballinger was a Cabinet member under attack by a subordinate; Taft would protect the formal lines of authority: "The truth is, the whole administration under Roosevelt was demoralized by his system of dealing directly with subordinates." Third, and most important in Taft's mind, was the law. That specified that Congress, not the Executive, had the authority to dispose of public lands. "One of the propositions that I adhere to is that it is a very dangerous method of upholding reform to violate the law in so doing; even on the ground of high moral principle, or of saving the public." Taft was a sincere conservationist, too, but the law came first.

The story of the Pinchot-Ballinger fight was spread all over the newspapers and magazines, but Taft's views were almost entirely confined to his private correspondence. "I suppose," he wrote, "the public has difficulty in getting at what it is all about." Indeed they did. In what Pringle calls "Taft's failing and his personal tragedy as a public man," Taft's "fine, brave words . . . were to lie covered with dust in locked files for decades. Only his mistakes—and his timid uncertainties—reached the headlines." After much worrying with the issue, Taft at last accepted Pinchot's resignation.

Part of his worry was what TR would think. "I get rather tired," Taft said irritably, "hearing from his friends that I am not carrying out his policies." Archie Butt said, "He is weighing Pinchot in the balance, but he is weighing also the consequences of his own act with Roosevelt. All else is nothing to him. I know it. I believe he loves Theodore Roosevelt, and a possible break with him or the possible charge of ingratitude on his part is what is writhing within him now. He can't say to his advisors, "What will Roosevelt think?"'

Meanwhile, out in the hot dark jungles of Africa, TR pursued the white rhino. Naked native runners raced up the trail to his camp to deliver missives from his anxious friends at home and from an insistent press. One message told of Pinchot's firing; Roosevelt wrote him "I cannot believe it," but held his tongue when reporters asked his views.

Another sensation at home harmed Taft's humor. He had let one of Ballinger's assistants draft a letter for Taft's signature, an exoneration of Ballinger himself. Ballinger reviewed the draft. The story leaked, Taft tried to hush it up, then called the testimony of "that damned scoundrelly stenographer . . . a lie, or to say the least a perversion of the facts." But Taft recovered: "However, I got him off my mind by ordering Ballinger to dismiss him today, and so with a clean conscience I can buckle down to this game. The beauty of golf to me is that you cannot play if you permit yourself to think of anything else." To TR's Attorney General, the whole affair was one of a series of "the most notable unbroken succession of colossal blunders known in American politics."

Roosevelt left for home. In a long letter to Henry Cabot Lodge, he first said, "I don't want you to think that I have the slightest feeling of personal chagrin about Taft," and then progressed to expressing his sorrow that Taft was working "in a totally different spirit, and with totally different results" than TR had intended when he passed Taft the torch, and ending with the hope that Taft would "retrieve himself yet." Taft had written urging him not to make up his mind about the Pinchot-Ballinger business until he had the facts directly. In private, Taft was uneasy: "He says he will keep silent for at least two months. I don't care if he keeps silent forever. Certainly the longer he remains silent, the better it will please me." Roosevelt wrote to Pinchot that "Taft has passed his nadir. He is evidently one who takes his color from his surroundings. He was an excellent man under me, and close to me."

Despite these mutual doubts, the old friends had a smiling reunion; "ROOSEVELT AND TAFT IN A WARM EMBRACE," headlined the *New York Times*. But the clouds were gathering.

The basic trouble was a characteristic Mrs. Taft put her finger on.

"Will," Mrs. Taft said irritably one August morning at the breakfast table in Beverly, "You approve everything—everything Mr. Norton brings to you, everything Captain Butt brings to you, and everything everybody brings to you."

"Well, my dear," her husband replied with a laugh, "if I approve everything, you disapprove everything, so we even up on the world at any rate."

"It is no laughing matter," Mrs. Taft said. "You don't want to fire Ballinger, and yet you approve of Senator Crane and Mr. Norton trying to get him out. I don't approve of letting people run your business for you."

"I don't either, my dear, but if you will notice, I usually have my way in the long run."

"No, you don't," Mrs. Taft retorted. "You think you do, but you don't."[5]

To Taft, aggression was taboo. To think of Roosevelt disliking him was too painful. Taft in the White House could not quite believe he had replaced TR as President. "If I only knew what the President"—that is, Roosevelt—"wanted, Archie, I would do it, but you know he has held himself so aloof that I am absolutely in the dark. I am deeply wounded and he gives me no chance to explain my attitude or learn his." Taft's despondency deepened. His wife was so worried she could not sleep.

No one should have expected TR to stay silent. Soon he was out on the hustings talking a blue streak. He received some 2,000 speaking invitations at the rate of 25 a day. He came out with such radical statements as "Labor is the superior of capital and deserves much higher consideration." Taft got edgier. Usually serene on the golf links, Taft missed a stroke and "swore a terrific oath and threw his club twenty-five yards from him in anger." TR's letters continued to characterize the President as a "kindly, well-meaning man" but one too weak for the office.

Taft invited TR to the White House in the hope they could "resume in some way our relations of yore." Hearing that Roosevelt was in a period of bleak depression, Taft said, "Archie, I don't see what I could have done to make things different. Somehow people have convinced the Colonel that I have gone back on him and he does not seem to be able to get that out of his mind. But it distresses me very deeply, more deeply than anyone can know, to think of him sitting there at Oyster Bay alone and feeling himself deserted. I know just what he feels." It is all so sad!" Taft exclaimed.

Both Taft and Roosevelt were determining whether or not to run for President in 1912; the Tafts interpreted TR's unwillingness to make an adamant denial as a sure sign of his ambition. Then came the last straw, as Taft saw it. Roosevelt made a speech advocating the right of the voters to overturn judicial decisions, excepting only those of the Supreme Court. Taft's weight rose to 332 pounds. He said, "I don't understand Roosevelt. I don't know what he is driving at except to make my way more difficult. I could not ask his advice on all questions. I could not subordinate my administration to him and retain my self-respect, but it is hard, very hard, Archie, to see a devoted friendship going to pieces like a rope of sand."

Roosevelt declared his candidacy.

Archie Butt, Taft's confidant, left for Italy; on his return trip home he was to sail on the *Titanic*. He was lost when the ship sank. Taft said, "I miss him every minute. . . . Every walk I take somehow is lacking in his presence and every door that opens seems to be his coming."

Roosevelt was attacking the Taft administration vigorously, and though "This wrenches my soul!" Taft felt he had to answer. In April 1908, Taft made a speaking tour, saying again and again, "I am here to reply to an old and true friend of mine, Theodore Roosevelt." Then he would launch into a point-by-point rebuttal of TR's charges, reaching a climax with this:

> One who so lightly regards constitutional principles and especially the independence of the judiciary, and who is so naturally impatient of legal restraints, and of due legal procedure, and who has so misunderstood what liberty regulated by law is, could not safely be entrusted with successive Presidential terms. I say this sorrowfully, but with the full conviction of truth.[6]

It was not easy for Taft to make such speeches, as the following incident indicates:

> A reporter on the campaign train found Taft slumped over with his head in his hands. Taft looked up and said, "Roosevelt was my closest friend," and then he broke into tears.[7]

TR hammered away. Taft had not only been "disloyal to our past friendship, but had been disloyal to every canon of decency and fair play," a man "useless to the American people," one who "yielded to the bosses and to the great privileged interests."

Taft went on to win the Republican nomination, Roosevelt bolted with his Bull Moose party, and the election went to Woodrow Wilson. "If I am defeated," Taft had written, "I hope that somebody, sometime, will recognize the agony of spirit that I have undergone." But he had to see it through to the end because "the whole fate of constitutional government" was at stake. The consequences for the Republican party were significant. Wilson captured the progressive banner. Not until 1928 would the progressive Republicans get a President to their liking: Herbert Hoover.

Years later Taft wrote that "I cherish no resentment against Roosevelt because such an attitude of mind is not congenial to me. It only worries the resenter and works little harm on the resentee." In May 1918, Taft, on his way from St. Louis, happened to arrive at a hotel where TR was dining alone, on his way to Des Moines. Learning TR was there, Taft walked rapidly upstairs to the dining room.

> Looking about, Taft finally located TR at a little table across the room and walked quickly toward him. Intent on his meal though TR was, the sudden stillness in the dining room caused him to look up. He immediately threw down his napkin and rose, his hand extended. They shook hands vigorously and slapped each other on the back. Those in the dining hall cheered, and it was not until then that TR and Will Taft realized that they had an audience and bowed and smiled to it. Then they sat down and chatted for a half hour.[8]

Theodore Roosevelt died on January 5, 1919. In 1921, Taft told TR's sister, "I want to say to you how glad I am that Theodore and I came together after that long painful interval. Had he died in a hostile state of mind toward me, I would have mourned the fact all my life. I loved him always and cherish his memory."

The break between Taft and Roosevelt had numerous levels and dimensions; one of those was clearly the conflict within Taft between his legalistic world view and judicial style, on the one hand, and his submissive character on the other. Taft's geniality and devotion to the law served him well—as a judge; his post-Presidential service as Chief Justice of the Supreme Court was exemplary. If he had had a different character, he might have pushed Roosevelt aside as soon as he won the Presidency, as Woodrow Wilson did the New Jersey bosses when he won his governorship. As it was, Taft nearly tore himself apart and did help tear his party apart by hanging onto his leader long after Roosevelt had, in Taft's eyes, broken with the law.

TAFT FINDS LOVE AND THE LAW

Taft's is about the best case we have for the supposition that character flows, in part, through the genes. Infant Will, his mother wrote, "spreads his hands to anyone who will take him and his face is wreathed in smiles at the slightest provocation." But whatever propensities toward geniality the baby had in his blood were generously nourished in his early environment. His mother, Louise Torrey Taft, had married a man who already had two sons by a previous marriage; she promptly began producing more family. Her first son, Sammie, died of whooping cough shortly after his first birthday. Pregnant again the next year, Louise agreed with her husband that a girl would be nice this time, but instead produced Willie, "well and hearty and a most charming baby as you would wish to see. He is a great contrast to Sammie who though good and quiet was never very playful. Willie laughs and plays constantly." She felt strongly attached to him: "I feel as if my hands and feet were tied to this baby. I suppose Mother would think it poor management but I do not understand making him take care of himself. . . ." In his early weeks she held him, at his insistence, whenever he was awake, and she nursed him until he was thirteen months old. Louise Taft wrote to her own mother of her way of rearing children:

> I do not believe we can love our children too much. I think we ought to take all the comfort we can in them while they are spared to us and if we must give them up we ought to be thankful that we were blessed by their angelic presence even for a little while.[9]

She also was concerned with "the responsibility of training children properly," if mainly by example:

> I find that Willie needs constant watching and correcting, and it requires great caution and firmness to do the right thing always. It seems to me there can be no stronger motive for improvement than the thought of the influence on our children. It is what we *are*, not what we do in reference to them, which will make its impress on their lives. They will be sure to find out our weak points whatever professions we make. . . .[10]

By all accounts she found Willie a child of the angels. When he was a year old she regretted that he was "fast growing out of the charming age of babyhood"; she cared for him through a frightening bout with dysentery; she rocked him to sleep until, in the middle of his second year, another son appeared. There would be two more children, but Father and Mother agreed that they were "prouder of him" than of the others and in Will's adolescence his father thought him "the foremost and I am inclined to think he will always be so."

Alphonso Taft, Willie's father, was seventeen years older than his wife. He worked very hard and did not have much time to spend with the children, even in the evening. In contrast to Grandfather Taft—"a pleasant, cheerful old gentleman whose whole object is to make people happy"—Alphonso was rather austere, a hardworking, competent lawyer who occasionally delivered homilies on the sterner virtues. But he could also be loving; though he preached discipline there is no evidence (in this letter-writing family) that he ever laid a hand on Willie. When Willie was three and the boys were away for the summer, Alphonso wrote, "I miss the little boys who always made so much mischief. . . . . I find that everything about the house is just as I leave it. There is no noise and no mischief . . . and on the whole it is not satisfactory to have no mischief about the house."

In his ninth year, Willie had a serious accident, a carriage wreck in which his head was so severely cut that his mother despaired of his life. She nursed him night and day and, when he recovered, wrote to his father, "I had more pride in Willie than in all the rest. He is a very nice boy still and we realize what it would have been to lose him."

Through his childhood, on into adolescence and young manhood, Will Taft bore the character of a sunny, smiling friend of all. He was not a sissy; he played his share of baseball, wrestled, and had a fight or two. Nor was his life entirely without challenge; his parents urged him to do well in school, and he did. But he was such a pleasure to have around and the Tafts treated him so comfortingly, that Will must have had an unusually easy time of it. His basic approach to life was highly person-oriented, a way of getting along by amiable optimism, nurtured in a home long on love and short on practice in overcoming obstacles by effort. He did not *need* to try very hard, or to combat oppressive parents, or to fight for his place in the crowded family constellation. His mother was right: Will learned more from her actual lovingness than from occasional preachments from the Puritan ethic. When his brothers squabbled, Will was referee.

Will was born fat; he grew tall and fatter, and got the nickname "Big Lub." He looked formidable and he acted gently, a very winning combination. If he had a fault it was procrastination. Pringle writes that "The boy was almost too perfect; he would surely have been an obnoxious youth had it not been for his placid good nature and the fact that he took few things, particularly his own gifts, very seriously." The Taft home did not ring with Wilsonian "principles" or Johnsonian tales of heroism. The Tafts went to church regularly, but Alphonso had moved from the rigors of the Baptists to the tolerant eclecticism of the Unitarian faith. Much later, when Will was offered the Presidency of Yale he refused in part because he thought his liberal religious beliefs would drive away contributions.

Two years before Will entered high school, his father, then a judge in Ohio, took part in a well publicized case which may have affected Will's view of the comparative significance of religion and the law. The Cincinnati school board was petitioned to prohibit religious instruction and Bible reading in the public schools. A group of Protestants then sued to enjoin the school board from abandoning religious instruction. Three judges, including Alphonso, were appointed to hear the case. The decision was two to one for religion in the schools—Alphonso dissenting. His argument was on technical, legal grounds, that the board had a duty and a right to keep religious controversy out of the public schools. The case hit the headlines; Judge Taft was branded as godless, and there was some uneasiness in the extended Taft family. But the judge was proud of this opinion and saw it cited many times. In the end, the Ohio Supreme Court reversed the decision and upheld the Taft opinion. If there was a lesson to Will, it was that whatever else one may believe, the law is the law. Judge Taft held firm to his legal philosophy, though it probably cost him, eventually, the governorship of Ohio.

As for young Will himself, not much can be made of his political beliefs. His views were, in general, conventional and undogmatic. If he did not change them much as he developed, that may have owed as much to their low salience in his mind as to the lack of any ideologically wrenching experiences. The truth of it seems to be that, with the exception of his devotion to the law, Taft's opinions were not very important—to him or to anyone else. To be sure, at Yale he did deliver two orations in which the theme of government restraint appeared. As a sophomore he argued that "In a Republic like ours where the powers are so nicely adjusted, because the resources of the general government are so much greater than those of any single state, there is always the danger that the former may gain preponderance. A close watch, therefore, must be kept over the encroachments of the general government." And as a senior he spoke of over-centralization of government and predicted "It is to be an age when there are no political giants because of the absence of emergencies to create them."

Taft's Yale orations represented experiments in his long, slow development of a political style. The speeches were dull; as an orator, Taft "was never fluent, facile, and ready," a contemporary recalled, even though Will had tried hard to win the speaking prizes to please his father. Also at Yale, particularly in his freshman year, Will tried the path of diligence, rising at six thirty and studying as late as ten or eleven at night. But he wrote home, "I begin to see how a fellow can work all the time and still not have perfect [marks]." "You expect great things of men," he wrote his father, "but you mustn't be disappointed if I don't come up to your expectations." Nevertheless, at graduation he stood second in a class of 132.

Taft loved Yale for its people. "Whatever credit is due of a personal character in the honor that came to me," he said as President, "I believe is due to Yale." His father had walked from Amherst to New Haven to go to Yale when the college located there. By Will's day, Yale had some distinguished faculty members, including William Graham Sumner, who "had more to do with stimulating my mental activities than anyone under whom I studied during my entire course." But it was Will's charming personality, helped along by his massive physical presence, that made him "the most admired and respected man not only in my class but in all Yale," as a fellow student recalled. He was taken into Skull and Bones. Though he neither smoked nor drank anything stronger than beer, Taft's social life reached the point where his father doubted "that such popularity is consistent with high scholarship." A big, bluff, hail-fellow-well-met, Taft became acquainted with a great many students, though he did not develop close buddyhood with any. Still, away from home, Will Taft learned that his charm worked with all sorts of people under no obligation to respond to it. He went on from Yale to study law at the University of Cincinnati; his father wrote to him there that:

> You must not feel that you have time enough to while away with every friend who comes. . . . Our anxiety for your success is very great and I know that there is but one way to attain it, & that is by self-denial and enthusiastic hard work in the profession. . . . This gratifying your fondness for society is fruitless.[11]

After Yale, Pringle reports, "for some years the particular devil assigned to William Howard Taft, the devil of lethargy, got in its work." He took his time, enjoyed his friends, studied as much as necessary but no more.

As a young man, Taft went on to try, in a calm and easy way, several occupations and in that way found the one he wanted. He was a reporter covering the law courts for a while. He did it well but did not enjoy it much. Then he became assistant prosecutor for Hamilton County, Ohio, taking the opportunity when it presented itself. He won some, lost some, but was not particularly interested in the job. Within a year he accepted a post as collector of internal revenue for the Cincinnati district; later he explained that the job came to him because, "Like every well trained Ohio man, I always had my plate the right side up when offices were falling. . . . I got my political pull, first, through father's prominence; then through the fact that I was hail-fellow-well-met with all of the political people of the city convention-going type." He stuck out the collector's job for a year, but "I did not like the office." He formed a law partnership with an associate of his father's and practiced for two years with no notable success except for an impressive speech on the losing side of a disbarment proceeding. All this time he was also moving about politically, getting to know the unpublished Who's Who of Ohio politics. Then he was appointed assistant county solicitor. And at last, at the surprisingly young age of 29, Taft was appointed to the Superior Court.

As judge, Taft found his role in the world; his enthusiasm for the judge's life never waned. "Perhaps it is the comfort and dignity and power without worry I like," he wrote. There he need not fight—he could referee. There he could use his strong intelligence to determine, on what he felt were objective grounds, the right thing to do. And there in the judicial calm he could enjoy the ease and respect of a judge's life. Thenceforward Taft's own ambitions centered on becoming a justice of the Supreme Court. He finally accomplished that—by way of service as Governor of the Philippines, Secretary of War, and President of the United States. In the last of those offices, he tried repeatedly to turn the Presidency into a kind of judicial post, a place of comfort, dignity, and power where he would take responsibility, not for innovative policy, but for applying—freely, fairly, and, if at all possible, without offending anyone along the way—the policies he inherited from his predecessor.

Taft became President nearly against his will, because his wife wanted him to. Shortly after he started practicing law, Taft began a lifelong romance with Nellie Herron. In long sentimental letters he poured out his heart to her:

> Oh Nellie . . . I believe you could be happy with me and could have a lifelong pleasure in the thought that the influence of your character and society and (I hope) love has made a good and just member of society out of one whom indifference and lassitude was [sic] likely to make only a poor stick among his fellows. . . . I ask you for everything, Nellie, and offer but little.[12]

> Oh, Nellie, do say that you will try to love me. Oh, how I will work and strive to be better and do better, how I will labor for our joint advancement if you will only let me.[13]

> I deeply regret that my manner was such as to leave the impression on your mind that I held your suggestions or arguments lightly or regarded them with contempt. I was not conscious of such feeling. . . . I beg your pardon. . . . So far from holding your opinions lightly, I know no one who attaches more weight to them or who admires your powers of reasoning than the now humbled subscriber.[14]

> I was a brute to weaken and exhaust you as I did tonight with the long walk and importuning conversation I had with you. . . . Do not coldly reason away every vestige of feeling you may have for me. . . . I have walked the streets this morning with the hope of seeing you and with little other excuse. . . . You reflected a light, the light of your pure and noble mind over my whole life. . . .[15]

At last Nellie surrendered and married Will. From then on, this brainy, ambitious—and loving—woman steered Taft away from the comforts of obscure judicial nests and toward the "bigwigs" in Washington, who eventually made him President. He turned to her again and again for guidance; again and again she persuaded him to take the path toward the White House. And once there, Nellie was never loath to express her views on Roosevelt, the tariff, or whatever. His relationship with Nellie, like his relationship with Theodore Roosevelt, rested on Taft's want—his need—for someone to devote himself to, to help, to love.

HARDING AND HIS FRIENDS

To those whose memories do not stretch back far beyond the death in office of President John F. Kennedy, it may seem incredible that the death of the "worst President," the zero point for all scales of "Presidential greatness," had just the same kind of effect on millions of Americans. Harding's death brought the eulogies of the eminent. Theodore Roosevelt, Jr., the former President's son and then Assistant Secretary of the Navy, said Harding "gave his life for the service of our country as truly as anyone in our history." To Taft it was "a great calamity," and Hiram Johnson called it "an irreparable loss." Nicholas Murray Butler, the influential President of Columbia University, felt that Harding had died "trying his best to fulfill the duties of his great office." Then the newspapers, even the hostile ones, set out their black-bordered editorial remembrances of "the beloved President" amid much funereal poetry and idealized drawings. Harding died on his way back from Alaska; a train was fixed to bring his body to Washington with no stops planned except to change engines, but from the start grieving citizens slowed its pace. In California they brought flowers, filling the coffin car, strewing them on the tracks. Groups of school children sang his favorite hymns, "Lead, Kindly Light" and "Nearer, My God, to Thee." Farmers in the fields stopped work and stood bareheaded as the train passed. At Omaha, Nebraska, 40,000 waited in the rain at two in the morning. Veterans—Civil War, Spanish-American War, World War—pulled on their uniforms and formed ranks along the tracks. The bells tolled; in the sky airplanes trailed long black streamers. At Chicago a tearful crowd of 300,000 slowed the train's progress, and across Harding's native Ohio thousands more held watch all night. In Washington the train was met by the new President and his Cabinet with a throng of the sorrowing and the curious.

Then followed the now-familiar panoply. The body was taken to the White House, where Mrs. Harding sat with the open casket into the night; "No one can hurt you now, Warren," she said, and collected from the masses of flowers a bouquet of daisies and nasturtiums to leave with her husband. Next day thousands filed past to pay their last respects. Then the coffin was taken to Union Station for the trip back to Marion, Ohio, Harding's home town. Again there were the silent crowds along the tracks; cars turned on their headlights as the train passed by. Finally the train reached Marion and the coffin was carried to the Harding home. All that hot afternoon, at the rate of 35 a minute, thousands of men, women, and children filed by the open coffin; at two in the morning the doors were closed, but by sunrise a new line had formed, and for five more hours, in the suffocating heat, Ohioans came through. When the guards finally closed the coffin, 20,000 were still waiting outside.

At the cemetery, soldiers, sailors, and marines of the honor guard carried the coffin through the ivy-grown gateway into the dark interior. They came out into the light to stand at stiff attention in a double line before the porch. A bugler with a silver cornet stepped forward to sound taps, and, as the last notes faded, a rifle detachment fired a 21-volley salute.

> The powder smoke looped in strands through the heavy air. There was the slight simultaneous click of metal as the riflemen ordered arms. The Duchess [Mrs. Harding] whispered through her veil to George Christian, then walked forward alone past the double line of servicemen and into the shadow of the vault. For several minutes she stayed there, invisible. The President of the United States,

the Chief Justice, the others waited. Then she reappeared, the indomitable matriarch, walking firmly, her veil thrown back, her chin high, and her eyes without tears.[16]

In a funeral oration before the House of Representatives, Charles Evans Hughes diagnosed the cause of Harding's death: "President Harding had no ossification of the heart. He literally wore himself out in the endeavor to be friendly." Perhaps Harding would have agreed. The previous June, setting out on his "Voyage of Understanding" to Alaska, Harding wailed to William Allen White, "My God, this is a hell of a job! I have no trouble with my enemies. I can take care of my enemies all right. But my damn friends, my God-damn friends, White, they're the ones that keep me walking the floor nights!" Throughout the trip, tired as he was, Harding could barely stay still long enough to sleep. He sat down, got up, paced, looked out the train window, sat down again. He played endless all-day bridge games. He seemed to want never to be alone and would hold others in conversation long into the night. He kept telling White he wanted to have a long talk with him, but never got to that; he repeated his remark about his friends. Obviously something was dragging at his mind, something he could not quite express. His speeches were delivered listlessly, with little of the old Harding oratorical flair. Finally, on the boat sailing toward Alaska, he asked his Secretary of Commerce, Herbert Hoover, to come to his cabin. The President asked, "If you knew of a great scandal in our administration, would you for the good of the country and the party expose it publicly or would you bury it?" Hoover replied, "Publish it, and at least get credit for integrity on your side." He asked Harding what the problem was and Harding spoke vaguely of some rumors of irregularities in the Justice Department. Hoover asked what relation Harry Daugherty, the Attorney General, had to the affair. At that point Harding abruptly cut off the conversation and never resumed it.

Later in the trip, a seaplane brought Harding a long, coded message from Washington. Harding read it and collapsed, spent the day muttering to himself and asking anyone near him what a President should do when his friends were false. On the way back, the boat stopped in Vancouver, where he seemed to brighten some, calling the Canadians "neighbors" and adding, "I like that word—neighbors. I like the sort of neighbors who borrow eggs over the back fence." Then, as his ship moved out to sea again, there was a great crash as it struck a destroyer amidships. His valet rushed to Harding's cabin amid cries of "All hands on deck!" There was Harding,

> lying on his bed, his face hidden in his hands. Without uncovering his face, the President asked what had happened, and Brooks told him there had been a slight collision. Even though everyone had been ordered on deck, it was not serious. Harding lay there, motionless. "I hope the boat sinks," he said softly, his face still hidden.[17]

Whatever else was on Harding's mind, a large part of his worry concerned the web of corruption, slowly being untangled by the press and Congress, that would eventually stand for "the Harding administration" in the public mind. Harding had set out to name a Cabinet of great men and his friends; soon he divided that formula into two parts. For example, as Secretary of State he first asked the eminent Nicholas Murray Butler. Butler refused, and Harding suggested his pal from the West, Senator Albert Fall. Butler was shocked; he told Harding Fall's reputation in Colorado was so poor he should not be named to any Cabinet post. Harding said Butler was mistaken, that Fall was a very able man, but then he turned to the impeccable Judge Charles Evans Hughes, who accepted. Harding went on to appoint Fall Secretary of the Interior, much to his later regret. Again putting talent and integrity first, he made Herbert Hoover Secretary of Commerce, despite many political objections. He was equally insistent, however, on rewarding his political mentor, Harry Daugherty, with the Attorney General's office:

> Harry Daugherty has been my best friend from the beginning of this whole thing. I have told him that he can have any place in my Cabinet he wants, outside of Secretary of State. He tells me that he wants to be Attorney General and *by God he will be Attorney General!*[18]

He felt he would be an "ingrate" not to give Daugherty what he wanted. He then decided to appoint Taft, not only ex-President but with a high reputation as a jurist and Governor of the Philippines, Chief Justice of the Supreme Court. For the Treasury, the President first asked Charles E. "Hell-and-Maria" Dawes, a colorful character who had been McKinley's Comptroller of the Currency; Dawes refused (later Harding made him the first Budget Director) and he appointed instead Andrew W. Mellon, the world's second richest man, who was, in Harding's eyes, "the ubiquitous financier of the universe." Another impressive choice was Henry C. Wallace for Agriculture, but Harding passed up Elihu Root for the mediocre John W. Weeks, recently defeated Senator and Republican contributor, as Secretary of War. As Secretary of the Navy, he appointed Edwin N. Denby, an impressive-looking veteran and millionaire auto dealer, of middling mind.

On the average it was an impressive collection, but there was a good deal of deviation around the mean. The New York *World* estimated that the Cabinet collectively owned or controlled more than six hundred million dollars. All but Hughes and Hoover became more or less regular members of the President's twice-a-week poker game.

During Warren Harding's administration, thanks in significant part to his own efforts, there were achievements and beginnings of high significance. The Bureau of the Budget was created and quickly proved its usefulness. Harding got the steel industry, and consequently others, to move from the deadly grind of the twelve-hour day to the eight-hour day, and he championed the elimination of child labor. Under his leadership an international Conference on the Limitation of Arms was held, perhaps overblown, but at least a start toward that goal. Harding spoke courageously, for his time, in the South for Negro political equality. He worked and spoke repeatedly for United States entry into the Permanent Court of International Justice. And perhaps the general confidence his Presidency inspired helped set off the galloping prosperity of the twenties.

But all this was lost in the fascinating revelations that began to emerge toward the end of his Presidency. The Harding scandals seem to have reached his attention only slowly, and perhaps only a little in advance of public awareness. Harding read virtually nothing except newspaper clippings given him daily. His grasp of policy was rudimentary and he was easily swayed by forceful argument. An old friend who once visited him in the White House heard words to this effect:

> Jud, you have a college education, haven't't you? I don't know what to do or where to turn on this taxation matter. Somewhere there must be a book that tells all about it, where I could go to straighten it out in my mind. But I don't know where the book is, and maybe I couldn't read it if I found it! There must be a man in the country somewhere who could weigh both sides and know the truth. Probably he is in some college or other. But I don't know where to find him. I don't know who he is, and I don't know how to get him. My God, this is a hell of a place for a man like me to be![19]

And he hated to turn down old political friends, "decent fellows that I have worked with thirty years," men who "have supported me through thick and thin." Yet gradually it began to dawn on Harding that all was not well in his government. In 1922, Daugherty, who saw the dread hands of "Red Agents of the Soviet Government" behind coal and railroad strikes, got an incredibly repressive injunction forbidding strikers' assembly, picketing, and propaganda—including that by "word of mouth." Hoover was furious. Young Ted Roosevelt threatened to resign. A congressman introduced a resolution to impeach the Attorney General, and the House Judiciary Committee began an investigation. The strikes were broken before the issue was resolved. But Daugherty, who believed the Reds had tried to poison him with deadly gases exuded from flowers on a speaker's stand, had raised doubts in the minds of many citizens. In 1922 Harding's Republicans were set back severely at the polls.

That same autumn, Harding began to get whiffs of headier fumes from below. The head of the Veterans Bureau, Colonel Forbes, was stealing massively and systematically from government stores, through a set of tricky processes which allowed him to drain off his share from, for example, selling 84,000 new bedsheets that had cost $1.27 a pair for 27 cents at the same time his Bureau was buying sheets for $1.03. He bought enough four-cents-a-gallon floor wax to last a century—at 98 cents a gallon. But the Colonel made far more from slices of the large funds Congress had appropriated for veterans' hospital construction. He and his assistant, Cramer, and their lady friends highballed across the country, buying and selling government land and goods at a great rate, on "inspection tours."

When Harding got his first complaint about Forbes, he ordered an investigation, was assured everything was all right, and declared the charges an "abominable libel." Then Daugherty, Forbes' enemy, got onto it and brought it to Harding again. "That can't be," the President insisted, and refused to take action. For the first time he failed to invite Daugherty home for dinner, though next day he hugged him and made up. To avoid an open scandal he had Forbes packed off to Europe to visit the disabled veterans still overseas. Forbes' assistant, Cramer, resigned. The Senate began an investigation. Forbes sent in his resignation from Paris in February 1923. Mrs. Harding said Warren "never recovered from Forbes' betrayal of himself and the administration."

The Forbes case was the only large-scale scandal to mar the Harding administration publicly while Harding was alive. But more and more stories of extortion, bribery, and general shenanigans reached Harding himself. Cramer, Forbes' assistant, killed himself, as did Jess Smith, an energetic fixer close to Daugherty. The month before he left for Alaska, Harding telephoned Nicholas Murray Butler in New York and pleaded with him to come to the White House; Butler postponed a European trip and came.

> I had a most extraordinary experience at the White House. The President came to my sitting room before I had finished breakfast and from that time, until I left at half-past eleven to return to the railway station, he hardly ever let me out of his sight for a moment. Evidently, there was something very much on his mind and he was trying to bring himself to tell me what it was. Several times during the morning, afternoon and evening he seemed to be on the point of unbosoming himself, but he never did so. He came down to the porch of the White House to say farewell, as I took the automobile back to the station, and even then seemed to be trying to tell me something which troubled him. I have never been able to guess what that something was.[20]

Just before leaving on his "Voyage of Understanding," Harding did tell a small-time reporter friend, "Someday the people will understand what some of my erstwhile friends have done for me." And he told another friend that some of his so-called friends had been "selling him all over this town, and all over the country," and that he meant to take the story of their betrayal to the people in his campaign for reelection in 1924.

What Harding would actually have done is conjectural. After his death, the whole sorry tale came out. Daugherty had the distinction of being the first Attorney General to be subjected to two congressional investigations while in office and, after his resignation, to be indicted twice for conspiring to defraud the United States. It turned out he had come into the administration $27,000 in debt, had spent at least twice his salary each year, and yet managed to deposit some $75,000 in the bank within three years. Secretary of the Interior Fall was discredited in the infamous Teapot Dome scandal. And all sorts of lurid tales of drink, drugs, sex, and grand and petty thievery bubbled to the surface. Harvard University had offered President Harding an honorary doctorate; now the Warren G. Harding College of Law changed its name. The indictments fell left and right.

Then the books began to appear. One with a tortured history argued that Harding was descended from Negroes, building a myth which had plagued him in his childhood into a fantastic structure of innuendo. F. Scott Fitzgerald's play *The Vegetable* and Samuel Hopkins Adams' novel *Revelry* painted Harding and his gang as vapidly vicious high-livers. The novel became a best seller and was made into a play and a movie. *The Strange Death of President Harding* drew on the detailed imagination of Gaston Means, an agent of the Bureau of Investigation in Harding's administration, to elaborate on the rumor that the Duchess had killed Warren in San Francisco to save him the dishonor of an impeachment trial. But the most sensational of all, *The President's Daughter*, recounted with plausible innocence Nan Britton's love affair with Senator, then President, Harding, including scenes of love-making in a White House closet. Many of the facts of Nan's account were corroborated; there is little doubt Harding had a long affair with her. But the tone, the intimate meanings, were as she remembered them rather than factual. She comes through as a worshipful girl from Ohio who fell in love with a man old enough to be her father; he appears again and again begging, pleading for her affection and the solace of love-making. It may have been that way. Clearly she was not the first; Harding had a long and intense love affair with Carrie Phillips, wife of a Marion friend. But that story was not to be confirmed until 1963, when Harding's letters to her were opened and Francis Russell wrote his thorough biography, *The Shadow of Blooming Grove*.

The President's Daughter, written in the interest of Nan's child, was an immense best-seller. Before he was in the ground for half a decade, then, the man who was buried to a 21-volley salute emerged in the public mind as a lecherous, hard-drinking, poker-playing fool, duped by his low-life friends, a weakling in the body of a hero.

Indeed, one of the reasons Harding got to be President was that he looked like one. He was the pop-art epitome of Presidential appearance; once Enrico Caruso easily fixed up a Harding photograph to look like George Washington. Those looks and his joy in "bloviating"—orating alliteratively on general Americanism—made rhetoric the center of the Harding style. He loved to make speeches. And he thought he did it very well. A large part of the reason Harding was nominated for the Presidency was the fact that he had come to the attention of his fellow Senators as a speaker who said safe things in a Chautauqua style, eloquent in a mildly uplifting fashion, without either the mind-straining logic of a Wilson or the threatening aggressiveness of an Andrew Johnson. He was a member of the Senate Foreign Relations Committee while Wilson was making his tragic tour to sell the League. Lodge and the Irreconcilables—and Harding himself—were much pleased with a speech he made then in which he told the Senate that "It will not break the heart of the world to make the Covenant right, or at least free from perils which would endanger American independence. But it were better to witness this rhetorical tragedy than destroy the soul of this great republic." The galleries cheered; Harding was so proud he had a phonograph record made with his League speech on one side and "Beautiful Ohio" on the other. Senator Penrose, boss of Pennsylvania, asked him in 1919 if he would like to be President. Harding replied that he had no money, had troubles of his own in Ohio, and just wanted to get back to the Senate. Penrose said he would look after the money and added, "You will make the McKinley type of candidate. You look the part. You can make a front-porch campaign like McKinley's and we'll do all the rest."

Harding did not always succeed as an orator. He gave the keynote address at the Republican national convention in 1916; the delegates were restless, probably hungry as his speech stretched over the lunch hour, and in any case they were more concerned with politicking than with rhetoric. They were bored and noisy; the fear in some quarters that Harding's eloquence would set fire to the convention and bring the nomination to him was unfounded, and afterwards he said, "I no longer harbor any too great self-confidence in the matter of speechmaking." But of course he did. On the Presidential platform he continued his "bloviating" way. William Allen White described Harding the orator:

> A tall, well-built man, just turning fifty, vigorous, self-contained almost to the point of self-repression, but not quite; handling himself, as to gestures, the tilt of the shoulder and the set of the head, like an actor. His clarion voice filled the hall and he was obviously putting on a parade with the calm, assured, gracious manner of the delegate from some grand lodge exemplifying the work to the local chapter. When he smiled, he knew he was smiling. When he frowned, it was with a consciousness of anger. His robust frame was encased in well-tailored clothes, creased and pressed for the high moment. . . . Harding stood there on the rostrum, the well-schooled senatorial orator, within his actor's sharply chiseled face, with his greying hair and massive black eyebrows, with his matinee-idol manner, tiptoeing eagerly into a national limelight; which—alas! he was to catch and keep from that day until he fell into tragedy.[21]

Harding was nominated in the famous "smoke-filled room" convention of 1920, adroitly managed by Daugherty as the compromise candidate to break a deadlock. Virtually unknown to many of the delegates, he went on to win the election by the widest margin in a century of Presidential politics. Like most candidates he had to feel that he himself had created a substantial portion of his success, had been more than just a rider on a wave of history. And to this feeling was added his heartfelt pleasure in appearing, performing, pleasing people, "I *love* to meet people," the President said, "It is the most pleasant thing I do; it is really the only fun I have. It does not tax me, and it seems to be a very great pleasure to them."

He spent little time on Presidential homework. Certainly he read less than almost any President and his talk was mainly social palaver. He played golf two afternoons, poker two evenings a week. He followed boxing in the sports pages. For recreation he went outside at noon every day to shake hands with the crowd of visitors, or attended the Gayety Burlesque, watching the show from a special box where he could not be seen. Faced with piles of papers, he would say such things as, "I don't think I'm big enough for the Presidency," "Oftentimes, as I sit here I don't seem to grasp that I am President," "I don't know anything about this European stuff. You and Jud get together and he can tell me later; he handles these matters for me," or "I am not fit for this office and should never have been here."

Harding's self-deprecating expressions have to be understood both as outpourings of personal doubt and as appeals for reassurance. As a man and as a President, Harding's whole being was flooded with human relations. This was related not only to Harding's character but also to his style and world view. His plea for "normalcy" reflected his perception that the nation needed an easing time, a rest from conflict and anxiety. Harding wanted to bring the people together again, after a time of troubles. "My whole job as President," he said, "will be first to get people of the United States together in better understanding, and then go get the nations of the world to a friendlier understanding of a workable world league." His image of human happiness seemed to be a kind of casual fraternity, a world in which, if everyone would just be nice and hope for the best, things would work out okay. Boosterism, optimism, letting sour grapes wither on the vine from neglect, thinking well of your fellow man and believing in America—that was about as close as Harding came to a code of life. He wanted "to put mankind on a little higher plane," he said, rather than to fight through some grand battle for principle. To Harding's way of thinking, love could make the world go round.

Harding's way to help that along was to put on a happy smile. But his spirits hit bottom when he had to choose among friends. One Christmas he had given a pardon to Eugene Debs, over the objections of the Duchess and of Daugherty. Charlie Forbes found him in black despair: "This is a hell of a Christmas!" he said, and as he walked with Forbes behind the White House, the President wept. Having chosen a good Cabinet, Harding wanted to play the role of the compromiser, the harmonizer. He spent more time on patronage than any President since Lincoln, spreading some 250,000 jobs among some 4 million aspirants; he eased civil service requirements for some 13,000 postmasterships. Yet Harding was no Lyndon Johnson. He did not pursue policy objectives through compromise so much as he tried to use compromise to escape from decision. He like politicking, and he was good at it, especially the politics of the election phase when all things seem possible, the pie infinitely expandable. But insofar as politics meant the crunch of official responsibility, Harding wanted as little to do with it as possible.

In character, Harding displays even more clearly than Taft the typical passive-positive theme: the hunger for love, the impelling need to confirm one's lovableness. Unless Nan Britton's literary imagination was far stronger than her general intelligence, her stories of Warren's desperate pleas for affection seem plausible:

> Oh, dearie, tell me it isn't hateful to you to have me kiss you! . . . I need you so. . . . Dearie, 'r y' going t' sleep with me? Look at me, Nan: goin' to sleep with me, dearie? . . . Why don't you tell me you love me, Nan darling? . . .[22]

Possibly Harding's sexuality linked in with fears of impotence; doctors at a sanitorium had once told him he was probably sterile as a result of mumps in childhood, and though he and the Duchess never had children, he said that he would "rather have a houseful of kiddies than anything else in the world." But in broader terms, Harding's desire to be, not a great President but America's "best-loved" President, opens the way to understanding him. "Really," he wrote, "I very much need to be surrounded by some of the friends whom I trust most fully." When he spoke to his old friends on the staff of the Marion *Star*, the tears ran down his cheeks as he shared bygone times with them. In the Presidency, surrounded as he was with people he thought were his friends, he sometimes felt lonely:

> I wonder if you know the feeling of a man who has been called to the greatest office in the world. There is an aloofness of one's friends, and that is one of the sad things; and in me there is a deepening sense of responsibility. I have found already that there is intrigue and untruth that must be guarded against. One must be ever on his guard. This everlasting on one's guard spoils a man.[23]

Harding had no particular interest in exercising power; in fact, he disliked it and complained about people supposing he could "take a whip and show Congress where to head in." What he wanted was real affection or, if not that, the signs of affection or, if not that, at least not disaffection. The tinsel of the Presidency pleased him, as when he was at last taken into the Masons and introduced by the Master of the Lodge as a member of the "trinity of great Masons—Solomon, George Washington, and Warren Gamaliel Harding." He was glad enough when the *New York Times*, which had considered him, at the time of his nomination, "the firm and perfect flower of the cowardice and imbecility of the senatorial cabal," came around four months later to praising him for "gradually assuming undisputed leadership." But his continual reaching out for love, and recoiling from controversy, put Harding right at the center of those who, in politics, combine passivity with a superficial optimism. Those boundaries embrace Harding the Lothario as well as the dignified Taft. In the conflict between love and the law, Taft eventually chose the law. Harding, to the last, strain as he might, could not bring himself to turn against his friends. The two shared a need, a central struggle against a depressed sense of distrust of affection. Taft's character helped split the Republican party; Harding's helped first to put the pieces back together again, then to blacken the party's name with scandal. Like Taft, Harding followed a crusader in the White House and the electorate turned to him at first for reassurance and tranquility. Not long thereafter, a fickle people began to turn against Harding—as they had against Taft—for the very qualities they had liked in the first place: gentleness became cowardice, loyalty corruption, calm laziness, laughter cynicism, loving a sign of weakness.

HARDING DEVELOPS PRESIDENTIAL FEATURES

There is a striking parallel between Louise Taft's first letter about little Will's appearance (see above) and Phoebe Harding's first letter about her baby Winnie:

I have plenty of housework, sewing, knitting to do, besides taking care of the sweetest, dearest little brother you ever saw, and you would say so if you could be with him awhile. But I tell you, Clara, they are a troublesome comfort. When I think of the great charge that is upon my shoulders, the responsibility of training him as he should be, and the care and anxiety I feel about his future. But I still would not part with him for anything in the world. I think if every child just knew the love a parent has for a child, they would never wound their feelings or do anything contrary to their wishes; but that, they will never know until they see their own offspring figuring on the stage of this life. Winnie is always walking. . . . He has a head . . . beautifully shaped. . . . It attracts a great deal of attention. Oh, we think he is all right.[24]

The baby got a lot of attention. At fourteen months he was still being carried around a good deal. Then at sixteen months came a new baby, a sister named Charity; Winnie "upset a tinful of hot water on his bosom and scalded himself so badly that when we took his clothes off his skin came too, as big as your hand on his left shoulder and breast. His hands and face were scalded too but they didn't blister." There were the "usual childhood diseases." In his fourth year, Winnie's restless father Tryon Harding quit schoolteaching after eight years—to take up doctoring, studying on his own for a couple of years and then qualifying with a year at medical college. His wife Phoebe became a practical nurse and midwife. For all the family's real financial insecurity—Tryon was an uncertain quantity, a real estate speculator, gambler, general character around small-town Marion County—Winnie probably had a fairly placid time of it, probably perceived his parents as more stable than they perceived themselves. Mother was quiet, loved flowers—a helpful neighbor with useful skills.

Not much is known about Winnie in those early days; there was a flock of other children and his parents were busy. But his reaction to a special Harding problem is revealing. The rumor persisted that the Hardings were part Negro— a damning accusation in those days at that place. The children were teased about it at school. Winnie was aware of this "flaw" at age five, and Francis Russell thinks it "left an ineradicable mark on him, first began to shape him toward the man he was to become." Instead of fighting back, "Young Warren's response was to try to placate, expressing his inner doubt in an almost mindless conformity." Much later he said to an old friend, "How do I know, Jim? One of my ancestors may have jumped the fence?" From an early age, Harding tried to solve his problems by going along, by being friendly, by sidestepping conflict and attracting affection.

He was not a particularly hard-driving boy, much preferring to hang around the village shops with a gang of friends than to work at the myriad tasks of farm life in Ohio. Once when he was twelve he got a job shucking corn for fifty cents a day, but he quit within an hour, saying the work was too hard for him. From all accounts he specialized much more heavily in friendliness than in achievement. Harding himself once told the National Press Club a little self-deprecating anecdote with its own ring of authenticity. He remembered his father telling him, "Warren, it's a good thing you wasn't born a gal." Warren asked why. Tryon answered, "Because you'd be in a family way all the time. You can't say No." And when he was editor of the local newspaper, Warren proclaimed its philosophy as one of "inoffensivism."

In other words, young Harding adapted to his early life much as young Taft had done. His oratorical bent developed early also, grew along with no very sudden escalations. At four he made his first country-school declamation, with some coaching from Mother. By the time he was eight, with McGuffey's Reader under his belt, he was a regular declaimer at weekly contests, delivering with appropriate gestures Patrick Henry's "Give Me Liberty or Give Me Death," "The Boy Stood on the Burning Deck," and "Horatius." At fourteen, Warren attended Iberia College (his father had gone there twenty years before) and under the tutelage of its three-man faculty practiced "debating, writing, and making friends," as a roommate recalled. He spoke on the question, "Has the Stage a Moral Tendency?," and other profound issues of the day, became president of the Philomathic Literary Society, and delivered the commencement address for his three-man graduating class. To his audiences, these were the standard entertainments; to Warren, they at least demonstrated to him that he could stand up and make himself heard, and that his first speech need not be his last. Thenceforward, Harding was always available to pronounce the going prejudices to local groups.

When Warren was sixteen, the family moved to Marion, the county seat, and he began wandering his way toward eminence by the most improbably indirect route. He was to become a kind of "Mr. Marion," the embodiment of an exuberant average in that town of 4,500. The boy had had enough of school, at least as a student. He tried clerking in a hardware store; that lasted a few weeks. Then he passed an examination for a schoolteacher's job and, because one of the examiners liked him, got a good appointment two miles outside Marion. He helped organize and manage the Marion People's Band, in which he played cornet; they won first prize in their class at a state band contest—his "great day of glory," Warren called it. But the rigors of teaching soon began to wear on him. "It was the hardest job I ever had," he said, and after a few months he was glad to announce that by the end of the week "forever my career as a pedagogue will close, and—oh, the joy!" Home in the spring term of his seventeenth year, Warren let his father persuade him to try the law, so he read Blackstone for a while, but gave that up, too. Then he played baseball and managed the town team. He tried selling insurance, but his first sizable deal fell through when his company discovered he had charged too little for the policy.

Nothing was working. Harding gave no sign he was particularly worried about it.

At eighteen he went off to the Republican national convention in Chicago, representing the Marion *Star,* a now-and-then newspaper some friends of his were struggling to keep afloat. He returned "a real nut on Blaine." His father got him a job on a more established newspaper, the *Mirror,* but he soon lost that post for "loafing about town and putting time on the Blaine-Logan Club instead of his job."

Warren drifted back to the *Star*. He and two friends rustled up $100 apiece and bought the paper, installing Harding as editor, two years before he would be eligible to vote. Soon Warren was writing most of the local news and selling and composing the advertising, in addition to helping set the type. He began calling himself "W. G." and grew a little mustache. He chewed tobacco. The *Star* began to prosper, in part because Marion was growing, but also because Harding had found his talent: he could sell. "As an advertising solicitor or persuader," his partner remembered, "W. G. always got on the right side of the cow. He convinced her that she ought to 'give down'." He seemed to have an instinct for it. Marionites by the dozens were startled to see their names in the paper, because editor Harding determined to publish at least annually the name of every man, woman, and child in town. He branched out, started a Republican weekly under this announcement:

> All sing the praises of the Marion Weekly Star:
> The old gent will hustle for it,
> The old lady'll rustle for it,
> The small boys will tussle for it,
> The old maids will bustle for it,
> And all united in saying 'tis THE BEST by far.[25]

Eight months later, circulation had doubled. Young W. G. offered advertising free if sales did not increase. He laughed, told jokes, bucked people up—and boosted Marion. Somehow the payroll got met. Harding gained controlling ownership when he won a partner's share in a cold hand of poker. He filled more and more speaking engagements.

The *Star*'s content under Harding's direction was a melange of gossip, needling paragraphs on the town's other papers, jokes and stories cribbed from various publications, news of local events, and even some international news. Editorially, the *Star* got aggressive when it or its officers were attacked, but generally hewed to the middle of the road and to preachments of peace. Accused of excessive partisanship, Harding wrote of a competing editor:

> The old gentleman's ideas of political differences is enmity and hate. To be a good Republican one must hate the Democrats and vice versa. . . . We are common people with common interests and the idea that political differences, so essential to our perpetuity, must make us bitter enemies is one that comes from minds warped by prejudice and schooled in hatred.[26]

On Prohibition he managed to come out more or less in the middle, noting that "Restraint people will submit to. . . . But absolute interdiction . . . always has and always will be resisted." And as for the suffragettes, "Now a woman has a perfect right to talk temperance, and the good her sex has done is indisputed, but her right to wear pants and make the night hideous on the street is questioned." When the opposition attacked Harding or the *Star*—which it did both personally and vehemently—Harding would lash back in print: "He plays the lickspittle to a class of men who like such parasites . . . he foams at the mouth . . . he rolls his eyes. . . . His sordid soul is gangrened with jealousy . . ." and so on. This appears to have been standard language for the small-town newspaper battles of the day, adding circulation-boosting dramatics to the dry goods ads, though slurs on Harding's father or on his supposed Negro ancestry would elicit special furiosities. But Warren Harding's creed, insofar as his editorials reflected that, is probably best summed up in a poem he memorized in those days and quoted on into his Presidency:

> Boys flying kites haul in their white-winged birds;
>   You can't do that way when you're flying words.
> "Careful with fire" is good advice, we know;
>   "Careful with words" is ten times doubly so.
> Thoughts unexpressed may sometimes fall back dead:
>   But God himself can't kill them when they're said.[27]

The *Star* continued to rise. Harding moved, by and large, out of the news end of it and concentrated on advertising and public relations. Increasingly he was active in politics, coming to the notice of that same Governor Foraker who had advanced Taft's career; he belonged to innumerable clubs and attended all the political conventions.

Apparently all his activity caught up with Harding. He was only twenty-two when, right after the election of 1888, he suffered a nervous breakdown and went off to a sanitarium in Michigan for several weeks, the first of five such episodes in the next twelve years. But he was soon back making his rounds—"a big, rosy-complexioned young man, handsome, enthusiastic, eager for McKinley's nomination, and evidently on the best of terms with life," as a fellow editor remembered him.

Then, at twenty-five, Warren married Florence Kling, the headstrong, dominating socially prominent lady who became Harding's "Duchess." During the early weeks of their marriage Warren was not in the best of health; he kept sending for his doctor father so often that Tryon had to move in with him. Florence was rather demanding, but she was also quite capable. When Warren went off to the sanitarium again two and a half years later, she stepped in and took over the *Star*. "I went down there intending to help out for a few days," she wrote, "and I stayed fourteen years." She ran the paper with an iron hand, brought order into the chaotic accounts, and put the enterprise on a paying basis. It was when Harding returned to Marion after Florence's takeover that he started calling her "Duchess." From then on, she managed her husband like a prize-fighter's agent, often looking the other way when he dallied in extracurricular sexual adventures, but making sure he kept on the track toward political success.

She succeeded. Harding's fame as an oratorical personage spread: "We want an up-to-date young man who can make a rattling good 30-minute speech," read a typical invitation. "From what our people saw of you at Bellefontaine two years ago we believe you are the man." "Harmonizing" Harding became a state senator. But most important, his travels took him one morning to the back-yard pump of a village hotel where, offering a chew of tobacco, he struck up conversation with another politician seeking a drink: Harry Daugherty, former Republican state chairman and recent contender for the Republican gubernatorial nomination. Daugherty eyed this distinguished looking, pleasant-talking, fine figure of a man and considered, "Gee, what a good-looking President he'd make!" Twenty-one years later Daugherty would turn that impression into a reality.

Harding's history as President was based on his history as a budding Ohio politician. Like Taft, he came to be thought of as safe and controllable by those who put him forward, as a man of no particular convictions who would do what he was told. To that virtue, Harding added his Roman emperor facade, his strong speaking voice, and his talent for expressing the most vapid thoughts in the most profound manner. Again like Taft, he was nominated in a situation where the dangers of disunity preoccupied the kingmakers. His very lack of political definition—in part a product of his character—added to his attraction: he was nominated largely because of what he was not. To the wider public, Harding's was the voice of ease. One had to frown listening to Wilson's words. One could relax and let Harding's platitudes wash over the mind like Muzak. Like Taft, Harding probably seemed to most Americans *psychologically* representative, the kind of fellow who, however lofty his position, the man on the street could get along with—enjoyably.

Advanced to the Presidency, Harding turned out to be venial only in his personal search for fraternal conviviality and sexual relief. There were thieves all around him, but he did not steal. Still, he could not face up to the spreading rot in his government—probably could not quite see it, because his attention was so heavily in the service of his need to believe his friends were really friends. He was not very interested in the Presidency as a seat of power or as a place for developing policy; his moves on issues were temporary assertions against a gathering sense of weakness and he lacked the strength to see them through to the end. So he stumbled forward, smiling and posing, deciding nothing and masking his indecision behind a cloud of words.

That is what he had learned to do, deeply as a child, more broadly as a young editor and sidewalk politico. Yet scores of eminent Republicans, clothed in Victorian dignity, could not see past the present they confronted in 1920. To them, Harding was a most presentable Senator, and whatever he may have been in the past, surely a man could grow. And the public confirmed their judgment in as massive a political landslide as the country had experienced.

THE LURE OF POLITICAL LOVE

Harding and Taft had in common the passive-positive's open, compliant—and vulnerable—character. They were very different people in many other ways: Taft the judicious exemplar of propriety, Harding the political playboy. But in character each reached out for love and sought to win it by being a winning personality. The passive-positive type lives in a marketplace of affection, trading bright hellos for smiles in return. What threatens the fragile structure of that adaptation is conflict and particularly conflict at close quarters. What Harding and Taft feared was the double-binding situation where the mass love which the Presidency provided could be sustained only by firm aggressive action against their close friends. The type's attunement to the present, the immediate—the emotional weather of this room, this day—meant that the pressure exerted by friends usually won out. The passive-positive character is built around surfaces; when the surface begins to crack, collapse is imminent.

Yet there is in this Presidential orientation a theme of great importance, resonating with strong popular needs. The loving uses of politics are, compared with true love, superficial and fleeting. But for a people in search of community, they provide a refreshing hopefulness and at least some sense of sharing and caring. That can be a motive for joining in politics, an emotional reason for staying in. The danger is its exaggeration: a President-people romance that diverts popular attention from the hard realities of politics and twists the President's own thinking from his larger purposes to his dear friends.

To the generation that came of age politically in World War I, Harding was the second of a Presidential trio that would, by the 1930s, leave them battered and disillusioned. First came Woodrow Wilson and his war "to make the world safe for democracy," leaving behind, after incredible carnage in the name of that high ideal, a world about as precariously organized as before. Then Harding who, exemplifying reassurance, went on to undercut public confidence in the nation's highest office. Finally, after a pause for Coolidge, Herbert Hoover, master of organized action to succor the helpless, presided over the casual impoverishment of millions. The real wonder is that the Presidency continued to hold out any hope at all to a generation stunned successively in the super-ego, the id, and the ego.

8

Reagan's Rise and Rule

How could there be a passive President in modern politics? Surely the demands on today's U.S. government have escalated far beyond the demands that such ancient mariners as Taft and Harding confronted. So isn't it a certainty that the President of today and tomorrow will jump up when the sun rises and strive hard all day and half the night? Doesn't it make sense that the typing of Presidents as passive might help us understand the old-time Presidents, but is hardly worthwhile for understanding Presidents we get these days?

In the 1980s, that argument turned out to be wrong. Americans got another passive-positive President, Ronald Reagan, who occupied that office for eight years.

If Reagan had acted on the public stage as he acted in his private office, Americans might have paid attention to the prediction that he would be a passive-positive President. They might have voted him down. But public Reagan came on differently, imitating the style of Franklin D. Roosevelt, one of his early heroes. Reagan the candidate seemed to be a gung-ho leader, an energetic and confident and intense and determined person who would issue his orders to his subordinates and demand that they make those orders actually happen.

To be sure, he came on as if he were a Mr. Active—looking and sounding like a leader bursting with energy, a fellow who seemed so confident and intense and determined to lead the nation in the right direction that it seemed foolish to suppose he was passive. The natural presumption is "how he looks is what he is," a thesis worth rejecting if you think hard about persons you have known, as well as Presidents you have studied. After all, Harding and Taft came on to the voters of their times as inspiring leaders. And so did Reagan, the first professional actor to step onto the stage of the White House and win in the age of television. Passive-positives are seldom what they seem to be.

An equally wrong argument is that passive-positives make love happen in politics, since affection is so meaningful to them. It is right that passive-positives typically hunger for public popularity and in-house appreciation. They want love. That does not mean that they give love. The President in office just before Reagan—one who was not a passive-positive—strongly advanced human rights in United States policy. He fought to rescue humans from abuse. Then Reagan, apparently a caring human, took over.

The new administration lavished praise and money on certain allies the Carter administration had been giving trouble to in Argentina, the Philippines, Guatemala, and El Salvador, regimes notorious throughout the world for the bloody torture and butchery to which dissenting or dubious citizens were subjected, rivaling in fury, if not in numbers, the murderous traditions of China and the Soviet Union. The techniques varied. In El Salvador, for example, government goon squads killed and kidnapped doctors, nurses, and paramedics—sometimes even during surgery—at such a rate that in July 1982, the International Red Cross threatened to leave the country.[1] On into 1983, the reports of degraded bestiality in El Salvador multiplied, not only from American Congressmen and celebrities and journalists stunned by what they had heard and seen, but also in photographs which spoke for themselves: a young man in running shoes, pants and a fresh sport shirt, lying by the side of the road with his cut-off head by his waist; a portly man propped up in a chair with his teeth and face bones dangling loose, shattered by a live charge blown up in his mouth;[2] a schoolteacher in "La Esperanza" prison (with 576 others), with livid, inch-wide scars running up his legs and across his back where acid had been poured on his bare skin; a middle-aged woman with terrified eyes, pulling up her shirt to show where her jailers had sliced her breast off;[3] whole albums of photographs of the bloodied faces of corpses displayed at a Salvadoran legal aid office.[4] Over a two-year period, the Reagan administration deported 15,800 Salvadorans who had fled to the United States, claiming that they did not need to fear persecution when they returned home.[5] The American ambassador to El Salvador estimated in 1983 that 30,000 people in that little country had been "killed illegally" since 1979; the administration in Washington, noting that the murder rate might be down to less than 5,000 per year, certified that "progress" in the protection of human rights justified American aid, and sharply increased support by millions of dollars in military and economic aid for the regime in its struggle against the

"Marxist guerrillas" who opposed it. The pattern and the effort were the same elsewhere, as the new administration paid for the military equipment and praised the fortitude of the generals in charge.

A visitor from some alien planet, discovering this pattern of cruelty and repression, might well posit a monster at the center of it, an evil Professor Moriarty or Darth Vader controlling the attack on the defenseless. Not so. At the center of the system was a fellow with a heart of gold, a kindly old grandpa, an unassuming cowboy with a twinkle in his eye who confessed that "I'm a pushover for a hardluck story."[6] Whatever else his critics had to say about him, they had to agree he was a likeable cuss, the last sort of person to want to hurt anybody. Funny fellow, too, in the style of Will Rogers, with nothing grim about him.

But Reagan won the 1984 election—in a landslide. By the end of his eight-year Presidency, the nation's troubles were even worse. The poor were in deeper trouble, while the rich escalated their profits. AIDS, drugs, homicide, and financial fraud sprawled ever wider across the nation. And the nation was in enormous debt, a burden which could strangle the future economy. The U.S. was the world's leading creditor when Reagan took over—and then became the world's leading debtor. Politics in America degenerated into playtime theatrics, put on in such a way that the people lost touch with the realities they were supposed to know. The quality of public education, essential to democracy, drifted way down, rated below a dozen other nations, including "primitive" ones. Potential democracies, uprising in the Soviet Union and Eastern Europe, were not working, were on the edge of collapse without effective aid from the United States. Reagan's military adventures—bombing, attacking, supporting secret fights, financing butchering governments, permitting massive sales of high-tech weapons—set the stage for new wars to be triggered by Presidents. After years of hidden operations, Reagan administration scandals finally came forth.

The most striking scandal was the "Iran-contra" fiasco. President Reagan had come forth loud and clear prohibiting the selling of weapons to terrorist governments in order to get them to release American hostages. But in fact his administration actually did just that—and secretly shifted the profits earned from selling arms to terrorists into the support of revolutionary forces in Nicaragua, without any Congressional approval. That revelation, expanded by lengthy Congressional hearings, gave the public a shock: the government was doing what it said it must not do, and was operating in contempt of the citizenry and their elected representatives. Reagan's popular rating dropped from 67 percent to 46 percent in one month.[7] Mrs. Reagan saw the Iran-contra crisis as "the most difficult period he ever went through."[8] President Reagan kept calling the military official who bragged about lying to Congress a "hero" and the admiral who bragged that he had kept the news from the President as "an honorable man."[9]

But not until then—far late in the game—did it come across to the public that Reagan was a passive-positive President. Subsequently, nearly all Reagan's major inside staffers wrote books which confirmed the prediction of the

Reagan character which I presented in the *Washington Post* on the day of his first inauguration, January 20, 1981.

PREDICTION

Prediction and Results

That prediction concerning Reagan stated that "As president, he will be dangerous." The five elements of my prediction were as follows:

The *climate of expectations* would be dominated by "the tide of reaction against too long and hard a time of troubles, too much worry, too much tension and anxiety" through the Carter years. Reagan came on as "a friend, a pal, a guy to reassure us that the story is going to come out all right. . . . He is supposed to make it well again. That is very likely to prove difficult, if not impossible."

Reagan's *power situation* would be fragile. His "best bet for popular support in darker months to come may well be the fury of the radical right, whose indignant disillusionment with Reagan will help him gain acceptance with moderates." He would need help winning the public, having "won in an election with the lowest turnout in 32 years." He had a modest Senate majority and conservative Democratic allies in the House. Inflation would be tough to beat and he had "no terrible social disaster going for him, such as the collapse that brought in Franklin Roosevelt, to put steam behind a burst of effective legislation in his first 100 or 200 days." After an initial romance, the media would play up "the inevitable 'performance gap' stories, featuring bobbles and corruptions on the road to Utopia."

The Reagan Presidential *style* would be dominated by rhetoric, with "little interest in homework on the issues" and little taste for "the charms of personal negotiation. . . . particularly if they involve an element of disagreement or confrontation." Further, "his rhetoric is essentially ahistorical and apolitical. He is bound to contribute to the ever-widening gap in American politics between speech and meaning."

Reagan's *world view,* despite various attributions of "ideology," would be simpler than supposed: "He is a Republican millionaire and hangs around with those folks. . . . As long as Reagan's business friends are happy with moderation, he will be, too. He is unlikely to go off the deep end with Milton Friedman. . . . His domestic economic policies may indeed turn out to be too watered down to be effective." In foreign policy, "a reasonable guess would be: distract attention by waving the fist at the Soviet Union, while quieter and more profitable arrangements are worked out 'realistically' in the Third World, unhampered by 'Utopian' human rights consideration. As president, Reagan is as likely to be 'business oriented' as ever, at home and abroad.

The Reagan *character* would be "passive-positive." That meant he would be "definitely no Nixon"—not a rigidified compulsive. Rather the danger was in "his type's tendency to drift, particularly with forces in the close-up environment. The danger is confusion, delay and then impulsiveness."

That day I thought, "The best hope is that, like Gerry Ford and Jimmy Carter, Ronald Reagan will leave the Constitution about as he found it and the nation, at peace. The worst fear is that Reagan, seeking affection, will have disaster thrust upon him."

The Iran-contra disaster did happen, as did the death of 241 American soldiers in Beirut, and numerous disasters for foreigners. Business recovered moderately, but the debt trouble soared on upward. But the main obscuration was a dazzling kaleidoscope of political fireworks. Seeing past the dazzle to the dynamics takes a calmer, theory-guided vision, rather than the day-to-day observations journalists go for.

The basic outlines are clearer now than they were then. The climate of expectations when Reagan began his rule stressed the recurrent need for reassurance, for conciliation after a time of too much combat and moralizing. As he had when he ran for Governor of California against Pat Brown in 1966, Reagan managed to get his opponent to greet the Reagan candidacy with shocked indignation and alarm. Carter, like Brown, read the Reagan verbal record and recoiled in horror, supposing he might mean it. Reagan let the fear define itself and then came on in person—in his warm and amiable person—to dispel it. As Kevin Phillips noted, "The public took comfort and relaxed."[10] Reagan thereafter appeared again and again to reassure the public that he was not as bad as they feared, not as frightening as he had been painted, not as wildly "gaga" as various columnists had made him out to be. Reagan the reassurer worked, in dramatic terms, through the Presidential honeymoon period. The public, if the polls are to be believed, suspended disbelief regarding his economic theories and opted to "give him a chance" to do his Presidential thing. As the honeymoon faded and the conflictful election of 1984 loomed ahead, Reagan the reassurer, old "Ease On Down The Road" Ron, came in for more and more concentrated criticism, especially from the press. As predicted, some of the fun started to leak out of his Presidency.

Similarly, the fundamental balance of the Reagan style persisted as predicted: the antipathy for homework, the overwhelming emphasis on rhetoric. Reagan the President not only revived the one page "mini-memo" as his favorite homework-avoider, he also eventually brought its inventor, William Clark, into the White House as his National Security Advisor—thereby underlining doubly his disdain for mastering information, since Clark, whatever else he may have been guilty of, was innocent of national security expertise. As for negotiation, Reagan held many a meeting with Congressmen and the like—and typically charmed the socks off them. But he left the dealing to his staffers. He liked to play host. Others could arrange the terms of legislation. What he spent by far the most time and energy on was speaking and getting ready to speak—honing his performance. It was there, within that rhetorical emphasis, that the essential impact of the Reagan persona was to be found. Nearly three years into his Presidency, *Time* drew a summary portrait of the Reagan Presidential style:

> Reagan is remarkably disengaged from the substance of his job. His aides no longer dismiss as glib the theory that Reagan has a movie-star approach to governing. "In Reagan's mind," says a White House advisor, "somebody does the lighting, somebody else does the set, and Reagan takes care of his role, which is the public role."
>
> White House aides, adapting to his mellow managerial style, seldom prod the President, nor he them. Instead, Reagan waits for an amiable consensus to develop among advisers, who work within the boundaries of Reagan's ideology. Except for his unbudging devotion to a military buildup and opposition to tax increases, he often accepts uncritically his advisers' recommendations. . . .

Even at the most pedestrian level, Reagan can be eerily detached, oblivious. He does not know where most of his closest advisers sit, even though some are only a few paces away from the Oval Office. . . .

Reagan's curiosity, even after three years at the epicenter of events, seems stunted. . . . He occasionally dozes off during meetings, sometimes with outsiders. . . . Even when he makes a substantial policy recommendation, he rarely follows through on it. . . . Reagan's extreme reliance on his staff leaves him badly exposed when they muff their jobs. . . .

When his staff is divided, Reagan can be caught in a crossfire. . . . "When the staff chooses up sides," says a White House adviser, "that's when the weakness of the system of delegating power is apparent. That's when it doesn't work." It does not work because Reagan lacks the temperament, and often the knowledge, to choose between the competing arguments."[11]

Reagan the passive-positive political character kept his role as he moved into the White House. His day began long after sunup and ended well before sundown. His favorite moment of the week, he said, was "climbing into that helicopter to go to Camp David,[12] where he could get into his pajamas and watch "golden oldie" movies with his wife. He also went out to his ranch in California for frequent long vacations. The passivity showed up dramatically on August 19, 1981, when two American F-14 fighter planes were attacked by Russian-built Libyan jets, which they promptly shot down. The President's advisors quickly established mutual communication—but they waited five hours and twenty minutes before they told the President. The call reached him at 4:24 a.m. He got the message—and went back to sleep.[13]

Through the first half of 1981, the President's aides grew more and more doubtful that his economic plan could work, but that did not concern Ronald Reagan, because they did not tell him.[14] "The evidence is in," the *New York Times* reported in mid-1982, "that Mr. Reagan does often serve simply as a ratifier of his advisors' decisions."[15] "For a successful man," *Time* reported, "Reagan is very passive, with little fire or curiosity. . . . Indeed, Reagan makes little effort even to learn exactly what it is that his advisors are up to."[16] One aide tried to explain the boss's languor: "He likes to lie dormant and then spring to life."[17] Compared to the schedules of a Jimmy Carter or a Lyndon Johnson, or even a Jerry Ford, President Reagan's schedule was Tahitian.

Like Cupid, Ronald Reagan kept firing away from "his never-depleted quiver of smiles," as Francis X. Clines noted.[18] If Carter had not done so much smiling, Reagan would be noted for it. He remained an egregious grinner, even when troubles loomed, even when he had, at his age, every reason to be tired and irritable, even when there was no need to be encouraging. In February 1983, Robert Kaiser tracked down and questioned nearly two dozen people who had met with the President that month: "Their accounts suggest a man who prefers fun to work, who loves to entertain and feel loved, who likes being President, but who rarely gets enthused about governing."[19] The President began his third year by reporting, "How time flies when you're having fun."[20] Reagan the booster, the eternal optimist, contrasted markedly with his negative counterparts in the Presidency.

And the main product of that combination, an emphasis on compliance, showed up and maintained itself in his White House life. He was not a hater, but he hated controversy up close. He "expected concord, and the appearance of concord, to prevail among his staff," as biographer Lou Cannon puts it.[21] Reagan's regular equanimity would collapse in the presence of real, I'm-not-kidding argument in his presence. When the unity of his top campaign aides fell apart and one of them had to be fired, Reagan agonized and suffered until Mrs. Reagan finally got him to end his suffering with a clean-cut decision. Similarly in the administration, constant friction and confrontation between his self-styled "vicar of peace," Secretary of State Alexander Haig, and nearly every other top advisor so disrupted life within his "corral of cordiality" that Reagan was at last driven to perform an unkind act in person: he fired him.[22] "Reagan likes quiet, easygoing, collegial people who can submerge themselves in a harmonic whole," Cannon notes.[23] His wife concurs: "He doesn't function well if there are tensions," she reports. "He likes everyone to like one another and get along."[24] Biographer Laurence Barrett wrote what that meant: "About one crucial fact there could be no doubt: Reagan trusted his aides not wisely but too well. He often leaned on them more often than their strength indicated."[25]

Thus, if there were those who stepped into the Reagan years expecting him to be the rigid ideologue his opponents had described him to be, or a withdrawn, philosopher-king President like his hero Calvin Coolidge, or a go-get-'em results achiever like the Roosevelts, they were wrong. They had significantly misdirected their attention to the wrong clues because they had begun with the wrong questions. Reagan was a passive-positive, linked through his extraordinary rhetorical style to a public ready, for the moment, for just such a hopeful and reassuring personality. That combination would turn out to be the simplest and the most significant thing to point out as the world rolled over towards 1984.[26]

The many books put out after 1984 by Reagan's top aides and by journalists close to him strongly confirmed the passive-positive character. Reagan on television did seem like a Roosevelt, but when the camera went off he acted like Taft and Harding—not exactly, but fundamentally. Casper Weinberger saw him as "light-hearted, serene, secure within himself, a happy man who wants to have all the people in the room that he's meeting with happy, too, and wants to have his countrymen happy and serene."[27] Lou Cannon saw him as "unbelievably passive when not on stage"[28], a President who "hugely enjoyed the spectacle of cabinet meetings, even if he did not always stay awake at them."[29] George Will, a friend of Reagan's, saw him possessed of "a talent of happiness."[30] Nancy Reagan brought out that "Of course he has his moods and his disappointment, but on the whole, Ronnie is the most upbeat man I've ever known,"[31] and "an affable and gregarious man who enjoys other people. . . ."[32]

Compared to active Presidents, Reagan was clearly a passive one. At least in his second term as President, Reagan "was often finished for the day at four o'clock, and he usually took both Wednesday and Friday afternoons off. . . . He spent about an hour almost every day lifting weights in the private gym. . ."[33] He joked about it: "I hear hard work's never killed anyone, but I figure, why take a chance?"[34] He seldom ventured out of the Oval Office to other offices, though he often took off to Camp David. In the midst of the Iran-contra crisis, Ronald Reagan took a vacation of 25 days.[35]

Ace reporter William Greider summarized the President's character well. Reagan's propagandists

> have managed to create the sense, which is known by anybody at all close to the White House not to be true, that this is an activist President. The reality, to put it mildly, is that he is a very passive man. . . . The real combat of decisions is not within Ronald Reagan so much as the people around him fighting for his mind.[36]

Reagan was highly dependent upon the people around him. As his admirer and top advisor Martin Anderson puts it, "Ronald Reagan was never called the boss by anyone," and "He would be perfectly happy and content if he did not know or hear of people's attempts to communicate with him. But when their spoken words reach his ears or he reads their written words, then he seems compelled to respond. The consequence of this unusual trait is that Reagan is very dependent upon his personal advisors."[37] Lou Cannon observed that Reagan "thought of himself as the leading man, not the producer or the director, and he usually counted on his aides and sometimes on his wife to know what was best for him."[38] He was "usually willing to say anything his advisors put in his hands."[39] While Reagan was still President, ten of his close cabinet or staff advisors produced memoirs: Martin Anderson, Terrel Bell, Anne Burford, Michael Deaver, Alexander Haig, Donald Regan, Larry Speakes, David Stockman, Helene von Damm, and James Watt, and "they offer a fairly consistent portrayal of presidential detachment and of chaotic administration led by an enigmatic monarch who reigned rather than ruled."[40] Still another aide (Jonathan Miller) put it this way: "Reagan is like a great race horse that performs well when you have a jockey that knows how to use a whip. If you don't use the whip, he'll just loaf."[41]

Thus, instead of the Presidency being directed by the President, as the voters reasonably supposed, the Reagan Presidency was directed by certain top aides who, as they shifted in and out of power, shifted policy, a move falsely attributed to the President. From the start, Nancy Reagan's friend Michael K. Deaver "became the grand producer of the Reagan presidency" and "the chief impresario of Reagan's first term as president."[42] Ed Meese, Jim Baker, and Richard Darman had strong influences early on, but Deaver's concentration on Reagan's image was predominant. Nancy Reagan "was an awesomely powerful force behind the scenes of the Reagan White House, and she was not shy about acting in her husband's interests."[43] James Baker emerged as more influential than Meese or Darman, but then Nancy Reagan, who later wrote of Baker that "I always felt that his main interest was Jim Baker"[44], focused her wrath on Baker and eventually pushed him out of the White House.[45] She and Deaver brought in Donald T. Regan to take over; the President, knowing little about it, went along. Regan explained to the President that he had something Baker, Meese, and Deaver lacked: "I've got 'fuck you' money. . . . Anytime I want, I'm gone."[46] Deaver thought "Reagan admired Reagan because, in a sense, he was exactly what Reagan wasn't: hands on." Ed Rollins concluded that "Probably eighty percent of the decisions made during his era were made by Regan."[47] By the end of two years, Regan "had eliminated virtually every official who could seriously challenge him."[48] But then, with the Iran-contra crisis, Nancy Reagan turned against him. He had made a "fatal miscalculation—underestimating the importance of Nancy Reagan",[49] which eventually did him in and led him to forced resignation. And Nancy herself then became "the de facto chief of staff."[50]

Thus the Reagan alterations, typically attributed to deep changes of his leadership mind, happened otherwise: he took on what his current chief demanded.

We may see other Reagans in the years ahead. We are bound to see other rhetoricians attuned to the modern media. We may well see future conjunctions of the man and the mood of the nation which will mightily reinforce one another. As the transition from Carter to Reagan once again demonstrated, understanding the "institution" of the Presidency tells you far less than you want to know, and provides only the shape of the stage and the arrangement of the furniture on and around which the action will take place. Theory which fails to reach the person of the President will fall short of useful prediction and that gap will prevent the speculations politicians will need as they struggle to bring power to bear on urgent problems. Therefore we ought to focus on those facets of the Reagan case that also shed light on his type and the types of conditions in which he operates.

Beyond the strong confirmation which actual experience gave to the predictions about Reagan, three questions are intriguing, regarding his character, world view and style.

1. Character is not everything. Given his passive-positive character, what explains the fact that within the first two months of its takeover, the Reagan Presidency got through Congress a startlingly novel package of economic legislation, overcoming what looked at the time like high odds against it?
2. World view is never certain. Reagan came on as a "conservative," but, as predicted, he soon had the "conservatives" furious at him and at least some of the "liberals" appreciating his "flexibility." What was it that Reagan believed in?
3. Style is significant, because it influences those it is aimed at. Reagan's rhetoric, it appears, came across. Whatever his intention, what was his actual practice and how is that likely to have affected the American people?

WINNING CONGRESS

Ronald Reagan won the election with 50.75 percent of the popular vote in a contest in which nearly half those eligible to vote did not bother.[51] In the House, Republican Reagan faced 243 Democrats and 192 Republicans. In the Senate the

Republicans had gained an edge of control, 53 to 47. A President as new to Washington as Jimmy Carter had been, Reagan might well have spent six months getting his bearings. Further, as I noted in the Inauguration Day predictions, no national disaster impelled radical action; inflation was a pain but not a tragedy. And the Republican leadership in Congress had yet to get a strong personal sense of this western maverick's political style.

A little more than six months after taking the oath, a grinning Ronald Reagan toasted his grinning staff in the White House, as they celebrated the amazing passage of his radical package of tax cuts. "His opposition lay broken before him," said *Newsweek*.[52] The Senate had voted 89 to 11, the House 238 to 195. Taxes would be cut by close to 25 percent by 1983 and, starting in 1985, the law would also cut off the big revenues inflation had been delivering to the tax collector. Critics abounded, but they had to agree that it was radical and that Reagan's win was a stark surprise.

Analysts who had reached the conclusion, based on observation over a period of years, that no modern President would be able to accomplish big changes had some explaining to do. President after President had reached for the brass ring of achievement and caught instead the broken arrow of disappointment. Reagan's victory seemed to belie that melancholy trend. Here was a President who had come in off the street and won his way.

Clearly the explanation was not that the Reagan program, in its substance and content, was the self-evident path to take. To a large number of economists and other devotees of fact and logic, the program looked bizarrely unreal. Certainly it had not attracted a clear national constituency; one could safely say most Americans did not understand it, much less back it. Rather the Reagan "revolution" owed its success to a conjunction of factors which were not likely to come together again anytime soon.

The first factor was the myth of a mandate. Congressmen went along with the President's economic plan because they thought the voters had approved it in 1980. The reasoning went this way: Reagan had gone to the country with a brand new way of engineering economic recovery and the voters went to the polls and gave it a yes. When the solid, scholarly evidence came in, that theory was shot: what had happened was that voters had said no to Carter, not yes to Reagan.[53] But the claim of a mandate, vigorously advanced from the White House, fell on empathetic Congressional ears. The Congressman—himself victorious—shares the need to believe that voters have not merely rejected his opponent but have also selected him—that they like what he has to offer. Thus the idea of a positive mandate is in itself a welcome one in Congress; to deny it would be to undermine the Congressman's own self-esteem. One White House official called the mandate business "a carefully created illusion,"[54] but it may not have taken much selling when Congressmen were so willing to accept it.

Second, there was a significant timing factor. Reagan preferred his plan right at the start, during his Presidential honeymoon. That may be one of the few times when a President stands a good chance of getting what he wants. Like Carter after 1976, Reagan continued campaigning after the election of 1980, building support beyond the electoral margin (and, incidentally, extending in that direction the "endless campaign"). Then, like Carter and his predecessors, Reagan's rating with the public began to decline, albeit gradually, almost as soon as the Bible had been shut at his oathtaking. The press, as usual, gave the new President a free shave and a haircut before they started nicking him in earnest, perhaps in part out of a sense of fairness or charity, but also because it is hard to get in the paper with stories of yet-to-happen failure. As with the mandate myth, Reagan's adroit managers vigorously played the give-him-a-chance theme. They helped him get through what may be the last remaining window of credibility in the Presidential schedule.

A third factor was the collapse of the Democrats. Congress had for years been transforming itself from a representative legislature into a specialized bureaucracy in which little committees and subcommittees concentrated on bits and pieces of policy, while a mini-platoon of Senators preened for the Presidency. The Democrats therein seemed more like a mailing list than a party. In the House, lumbering Thomas P. O'Neill occasionally got off a blast at fellow Irishman Reagan, but more often seemed of a mind to "give him a chance," as the slogan went. Especially at the start of it all, "conservative" Democrats could hope that Reagan would turn out to be one of them, as he said he was. Liberal Democrats could not seem to figure out where to hit the jazzy new "supply-side" economics idea, particularly since it promised a painless—indeed joyous—escape from economic hardship. At a key moment that spring, O'Neill took off for an extended junket to Australia.[55]

A fourth factor was charm. In Washington, Carter lacked it; Reagan had it, and he turned it on, starting with his preinaugural Washington elite dinner arranged by columnist George Will. Reagan's was not the charm of the simpering sycophant, but the man-to-man Jimmy Stewart charm, the charm of apparent sincerity, pleasure in the company of the other, the charm of the impending smile. Harding had it, as did Taft before him. Reagan in person was as hard to dislike as a laughing baby, as many a hardbitten reporter had discovered. As President, Reagan added to that personal appeal the mighty effect of the official aura, which has reduced so many critics and skeptics to worshipful helplessness as they stand in the presence of an actual President in his actual office. A democracy we may be, but these vestiges of the kingly courts of yesteryear still play their part—particularly when the President knows just how to play his part as a friendly monarch.

Yet a fifth factor was simple political bribery. Reagan's program centered on taxes. American tax laws have long stood as monuments to indirection and intrigue. Bandits who cannot directly stick up the government and carry off its treasure conspire instead to hold back from paying what they owe. The Congressman is typically dependent for campaign funds on rich people back home and in Washington, people who can also lend a hand if he should suffer defeat. He himself can usually imagine the uses to which he might put funds not paid as taxes. And the whole business is so obscure and complex that the temptation to take whatever breaks are available is nearly irresistible. Reagan and his crew, determined to get the votes they needed in Congress, set off a bidding war in

Congress, the President versus the Democratic leadership, that brought forth the less delicate Congressional appetites. "Do you realize the greed that came to the forefront," asked David Stockman, Reagan's chief dealer, of a reporter friend. "The hogs were really feeding. The greed level, the level of opportunism, just got out of control."[56] Each side broke out its display of deductions and exemptions and readjustments and depreciations to entice wavering Congressmen. In the end, by one account, the price Reagan's people paid for a dozen oil-state Congressmen reached $1.1 billion per vote in tax breaks pasted onto the bill. One White House staffer confessed that "There's a good argument that we gave away the store."[57] Late in 1981, Congress quietly voted its own members a massive deduction.[58]

A sixth factor: on March 30, 1981, a little over two months into his Presidency, Reagan was shot on the street in Washington. He was rushed to a hospital where he very nearly died, a seventy-year-old with a bullet near his heart. That kind of thing has happened frequently enough in recent years that it must be considered in the political calculus, random and accidental as it may be. John F. Kennedy was "martyred" by an assassin and his killing no doubt contributed to the subsequent passage of civil rights and other legislation. Twice Jerry Ford was shot at (but escaped injury), adding to his credit with his Congressional pals. Reagan's brush with sudden death fell in between. When he stepped before a joint session of Congress on April 28, less than a month after the attack, to sell his strange economic program, he had but to stride into the chamber to evoke an overwhelmingly sympathetic response, the flood of applause breaking over him again and again. He praised the courage of the three other men who had fallen with him that day, leaving the audience to notice his own. "We have much greatness before us," he declared, and launched into a fervent plea for his legislative package. The response of the national audience, most of whom, it is safe to suppose, do not know an investment credit from a depreciation allowance, was terrific—overwhelmingly in the President's favor, registering itself in the polls and calls to the White House and Congressional offices. That the shooting played into the shouting, and that that played into Congressional votes, there can be little doubt. Like Pisistratus in ancient Athens, rushing into the Agora covered with blood, Reagan the victim gave force to Reagan the victor.

We cannot run the history of 1981 over again, subtracting one factor at a time until we find which one or two made the essential difference. A plausible inference is that Reagan's proposal, despite its substantive obscurity, had a lot going for it in Congress. It fit the Congressman's sense that the President, like himself, owed his election to public approval of his program. It fit the time—the early, uncritical Presidential honeymoon—to a T. It got a boost from the Congressman's vulnerability to the charm of Reagan and the status of the Presidency. It was significantly helped along by tax rewards for Congressmen and their constituencies. And its principal advocate, the President himself, came on as one who had nearly given his life in the cause of advancing his program. All in all, the shape of power in Washington at that juncture of the national experience was a peculiar shape, a profile of power we may not see again for a century. If the

Reagan victory of 1981 shows that Presidents are not yet political eunuchs, it also shows that it may take an unusual configuration of forces to put into law a broad-scale Presidential program.[59]

REAGAN THE "CONSERVATIVE"?

"He is the most thoroughly ideological President since Herbert Hoover," said Theodore White of Ronald Reagan.[60] Reagan's Chief of Staff James Baker said, "President Reagan has, I think, helped to restore the good name of promises. . . . Clearly, he is following through on the basics."[61] To the best of the country's knowledge when he was elected, Reagan's ideology was "conservative" and his promises amounted to the following:

1. He would cut taxes.
2. He would cut government bureaucracy and regulation.
3. He would build a stronger national defense.
4. He would balance the federal budget.
5. He would combat the power of the Soviet Union.

And above and beyond such specifics, he would stand forth as a champion of American individualism and free enterprise, as against the New Deal welfare state which had become the major obstacle to national progress. Reagan's election was hailed by the "radical right" as a long-delayed fulfillment of their dream of 1964, when Barry Goldwater had advertised himself as Mr. Conservative. With no apparent sense of contradiction, these "conservatives" welcomed the "Reagan Revolution."

By mid-1982, not much of that talk could be heard, and by mid-1983 it had all but disappeared, despite Mr. Baker's continuing faith in his boss's intentions. The President who not only promised to cut taxes but based his whole economic strategy on massive tax cuts came out for the largest tax *increase* in the history of the United States: $98 billion. The President who not only said he would balance the federal budget but backed an amendment to the Constitution to require that balance, presented the most unbalanced budget in the history of the United States, well beyond $200 billion in the red. The President who waved his fist at the Soviet Union—that "Evil Empire" as he called it—and railed against our European allies for buying Soviet gas now let the Soviets buy enormous quantities of grain from the United States, much to their relief; by one estimate, the deal would save the Soviets roughly $32 billion in one year alone by enabling them to sell oil for grain rather than growing the grain themselves.[62] The President who promised to back a major escalation in national defense capability supported little more than a continuation of several Carter programs.[63] And the President who set out to "get the government off our backs" by cutting down bureaucracy and regulation instead left standing the major departments (Energy and Education) he had promised to destroy and put in place new executive orders to curb the first of our liberties, free speech.[64]

As James Reston of the *New York Times* put it, for Reagan "every day is a new performance. Every statement stands alone. There are no connecting rods between one light-hearted pronouncement and the other."[65] The Reagan consistency gap was matched by an ever widening coherence gap.

Others put it less diplomatically. A coldly furious Ed Crane, head of the conservative Cato Institute, wrote that "Reagonomics" had not failed—because it had been "simply a fiction" from the first. Reagan was no "ideologue"; rather, "The problem is that Reagan the politician uses ideology as a vehicle for returning to center stage. He does not—and here's where most observers go wrong—use his acting ability to advance a deeply imbued ideology."[66] As early as February 1981, conservative writer John Lofton, in an "open letter" to the President, warned him that "Your mandate for change is being subverted.[67] In January 1982, fifty-eight conservative leaders from across the nation descended on Washington and blasted Reagan for appointing "pragmatists whose political records place them on the opposite side of the Republican spectrum from the President."[68] On February 1, a delegation of conservative hard liners got in to see the President and let him know in no uncertain terms how dismayed they were by his drift to the center. By then a substantial list of conservative Reaganites had resigned. *Conservative Digest* asked on its cover, "Has Ronald Reagan's Presidency Been Captured By Wall Street-Big Business-Corporate Executive Suite-Big New York/Houston Law Firm-Eastern Liberal-And/Or Establishment-Non-Reaganite Republicans? Do You Have To Ask?"[69] Reagan's 1983 State of the Union address—full of appeals for bipartisan cooperation—sealed the case. "What a disappointment," moaned conservative columnist William Safire, who saw the speech as a "themeless pudding."[70]

As predicted, the fury from the right was not entirely unwelcome in the White House. James Wooten of ABC reported that, "Surprisingly enough, there are those inside the White House who welcome the New Right criticism. They believe it separates the President from an ideology so radical as to be politically stupid." And NBC's Ken Bode noted that, "At the White House some aides like to hear the true believers complain. They encourage it. They say it gives them more elbow room."[71] Having got himself labeled as a "conservative" and "ideologue," Reagan got points from the nation's much more numerous and powerful middlers and pragmatists every time he seemed to move in their direction.

In fact, Ronald Reagan was never in any serious or thoughtful way an ideologue of any sort. He had never made any serious study of ideologies; as for economics, he took some courses at a third-rate college half a century ago—and remembered he had to fake exams because he had not studied the material. The course of Reagan's subsequent "ideological" development is much more clearly explained by the drift of his personal development than by any philosophical pilgrimage or burst of enlightenment. To put it plainly, Reagan's conservatism has been circumstantial, not visceral. What has remained consistent in his life history is his desire to please the very rich mentors who picked him up and brought him to where he is today. The desire to please is rooted in the passive-positive's personality. That desire is focused in the course of experience, as the personality, seeking an external orientation, fastens on others to give it the guidance and direction it needs. In Reagan's case, his world view owes much more to that process of adaptation than to some intellectual or politico-religious commitment.

REAGAN'S RISE: "IDEOLOGY" AND EXPERIENCE

When he was a boy, the Reagan family went through tough times. They were inveterate hopers, these Reagans, optimists in spite of all. They never went hungry. But through the years of the First World War, his salesman father Jack bounced around Illinois looking for what he called "the big break"—from Tampico (where Ronald was born February 9, 1911) to Galesburg to Monmouth to Tampico again to Dixon, where they settled permanently when Ronald was nine. His sweet mother Nelle gave him her family name (Wilson) and her family religion (Disciples of Christ) and a lot of her attention, while his older brother Neil grew up rougher-hewn, his father's boy, baptized a Catholic like his father. Neither parent had gone to college and when Neil graduated from high school he did not even consider more education; he went to work at the local cement factory, coming home streaked with white dust. While Neil shuffled cement, his brother "Dutch" got paid for being a lifeguard, where he casually made the acquaintance of the local leisure class as he and they tanned and talked together. Dutch doubled-dated with the nephew of the owner of the factory where Neil worked, a boy whose father could let the lads drive either his Packard or his LaSalle on dates. Dutch's steady girl was the minister's daughter. Neil and his working class buddies hung out at Red Vail's pool hall; Dutch and his crowd of boys and girls got together at Fulf's Confectionary, an ice cream parlor. Thus, through those halcyon years of the 1920s, the line between the classes ran right through the Reagan living room, with younger son Ronald clearly identified with the better-off.

He went away to college, and the Depression hit. His father first lost his partnership in the newly opened "Reagan's Fashion Boot Shop" and then, on Christmas Eve 1931, got fired as a traveling salesman. Nelle went to work at a dress shop for $14 a week. Jack Reagan campaigned hard for Franklin D. Roosevelt in 1932 and, when Roosevelt won, became head of the Dixon welfare office. The family veered toward disaster but recovered. The younger son got the message. "Like many young adults of his generation," writes biographer Lou Cannon, "Reagan emerged from the period with a desire for material success and for an economic cushion that would provide security for himself and his family should another Depression strike."[72]

He also emerged with a hero: Franklin Delano Roosevelt, the man who had rescued his dad and the family fortunes from impending calamity. Reagan became an ardent Rooseveltian and voted for him all four times. He listened to Roosevelt's fireside chats on the radio and developed his own imitation, accent, cigaretteholder, and all. He memorized FDR's most telling phrases from the 1933 inaugural, especially that one about not being afraid of "fear itself." From his first vote on, Reagan was "a Democrat because my father had been."

After graduating from college, Reagan got into radio as a sportscaster—a lucky choice, as broadcasting burgeoned during the Depression. Political ideology, if any, lay dormant in his life. He wound up at WHO in Des Moines, Iowa, and did so well that the station picked him as winner of the annual WHO winter vacation in California. On the way out, he stopped to visit the Oklahoma Outlaws, WHO's barn dance band which had made it into Gene Autry's cowboy movies. In Hollywood, he looked up a pretty singer he remembered from WHO days and found her, booked and booming in the movies. He told her he wanted to get into acting, she introduced him to an agent, and his film career was off and running.

Ronald Reagan the actor looked good, moved easily, memorized his lines quickly and thoroughly, and took direction very readily indeed. He came along when routine, low budget movies were being turned out in assembly-line fashion—he made eight in one year—and so his patient, cooperative, tell-me-what-to-do attitude was a significant plus. He cooperated off the set, too. Hollywood in those days had a scandalous reputation the movie moguls thought might be hurting them at the box office, so they were glad to find a clean-cut, all-American type who would, as Reagan did, talk endlessly to the movie magazines about how normal he was. In 1940, with the untiring encouragement of gossip columnist Louella Parsons, he married the actress Jane Wyman and formed one of those Potemkin-village "Perfect Marriages" Hollywood loved to hold out as a true example against accusations of the town's orgiastic debasement; they would have two children. Reagan the handsome, moral, easy, smiling, boosting presence fitted right into late-thirties Hollywood. If he was not a major talent, he did well in regular good guy parts, culminating in "Knute Rockne—All American" and "King's Row." The few times he tried to play tough guys (for example in "The Killers," or "Nine Lives Are Not Enough"), he was far less convincing.

Politics played little part in his life then, but a seed was planted: in 1938 an actress got him to join a union, The Screen Actors Guild, which after years of effort was establishing itself as a protection against the troglodyte feudal barons who dominated the movie industry in the Depression. In 1933 they had cut the pay of contract players by fifty percent without blinking. Reagan joined, and was soon drafted to serve on the union board of directors as a representative of newer, younger actors. He was impressed; the board was "crammed with the famous men of the business," as he put it.[73] Robert Montgomery, Charles Boyer, Jimmy Cagney, Cary Grant, and other big stars treated him as an equal. The union was democratic—and also Democratic, Rooseveltian, fully in accord with the Reagan family identification. Reagan fit in and helped out.

The war came. Reagan enlisted and, too nearsighted for combat duty, spent his time making training films. When it was over he went back to Hollywood, but times and tastes had changed. Reagan had a good contract ($3500 a week) but he was no longer a young, fresh face to suit the new popular culture bursting forth in the postwar world. Nine months went by with no picture for him; he puttered around the house until everything in sight was fixed. He went on location with his wife and while she worked he spent hours, day after day, running up and down a lake in a rented speedboat. At last he got what looked like a promising part in a western, with Bacall and Bogart, but those stars dropped out and the film was demoted to black and white. Reagan went along. But from then on his film career slid down the heights of his prewar success, one disappointment after another, culminating in his role opposite a chimp in the 1951 comedy "Bedtime for Bonzo." At the same time, his wife's professional career was on the rise. This was the period in which Ronald Reagan turned to politics.

Still, as he said, "a very emotional New Dealer," he found himself in the thick of the SAG's postwar struggles and strikes. In 1947 he was elected president of the union. That same year he joined in founding California's branch of Americans for Democratic Action, the main bearer of the New Deal after Roosevelt's death in 1945. Later he served on the ADA national board. When Red-hunting Congressmen started sniffing after Communist subversives in Hollywood, Reagan testified as to his disdain for that sorry ism, which he had experienced at first hand when a Communist faction tried to take over the union. But he also said he thought they had a right to be heard, that democracy demanded the free exchange of ideas. In 1948, Reagan became head of the "Labor League of Hollywood Voters for Truman," in whose favor he made several speeches. In 1950, he backed Helen Gahagan Douglas against Richard M. Nixon for the Senate, signing on as a Douglas sponsor. At least one of her aides worried that Reagan was too radical and might hurt the campaign.

His marriage broke up. He and Jane separated in 1947, the year he took on the SAG presidency. In 1949 an unhappy Ronald Reagan went to England to make a film, complaining of the food and the taxes, returned to find he had lost out to Errol Flynn for the lead in a Western and that his studio was unloading him. He sustained a multiple fracture of his thigh playing softball, and spent eight weeks in the hospital, during which his divorce, featuring considerable payments, became final. It was not his year. At thirty-eight, he was alone and out of work, a visitor to his own children, a man who could see as well as anyone that his career was fading.

Enter Nancy Davis. Henceforth, no other person would rival her influence on Ronald Reagan. She was an attractive actress who, at the not-for-publication age of twenty-eight, felt ready for marriage. By a confusion of names, she was receiving Communist propaganda in the mail, and that scared her. Her director got Reagan, as SAG president, to agree to defend her if she got in trouble. Reagan, still on crutches, took her out. Over the next two and a half years they were an on-again, off-again item until they married in March 1952.

Nancy brought to the marriage a devotion verging on desperation. She said her life began when she met Ronnie and that the thought of living without him terrified her. No wonder. Her mother, Edith Luckett, pretty child of a poor family, had quit school for the stage before she was fifteen, and later married a handsome, blue-blooded Princeton man on his way to World War I. The marriage quickly collapsed. The father was absent when Nancy was yanked into the world by the forceps of a sweating doctor, vocally impatient to get to his golf game. One of the child's eyes was closed. "If my daughter's eye doesn't open," mother said to doctor, "I'll kill you."[74] The eye opened. Infant Nancy was carted around the theater circuit for two years before Edith finally gave up and left Nancy with her sister in a Maryland suburb. The child missed her mother dreadfully, though aunt and uncle took good care of her. She went through scarlet fever without mother and then double pneumonia. "If I had a child and she got sick," Nancy cried, "I'd be with her."[75] When mother did swoop in for a visit, in her raccoon coat, bearing gifts and glamor and chocolate candy, Nancy was thrilled—but the in-between times lasted longer. When Nancy visited her father, she could not help but notice that for all his true blood, his fortunes were waning. She was aware of the mansions across the road from her uncle's house and of the slums on the other side of her neighborhood. Nancy was sent to a private school with rich children; at Christmas they were taken to a party at the mansion of Warren Harding's pal Edward McLean. All of that was registering in her mind—but she was only seven when her mother married again and took her off to Chicago to live with a new father, Loyal Davis.

Davis was a rich and distinguished brain surgeon, whose steady, calm, dour, rock-hewn being drew Edith and Nancy like a lighthouse in a storm. Davis was also a martinet, an authoritarian terrorizer of young surgeons—and an adamant political reactionary filled with livid detestation for that apostate, Franklin Roosevelt. Nancy worshipped Dr. Davis; once she asked a judge how she could adopt him. Edith gave up acting and threw herself into the social whirl of Chicago's moneyed elite. They lived on posh Lake Shore Drive. Not long after they moved in, the Great Depression hit; Nancy could see hungry people sorting through the garbage cans in front of their apartment house. Nancy went on to private school and then Smith College, where, in between an endless round of parties and talk about parties, she did some acting. She got into the theater in New York and found her way to Hollywood and Ronald Reagan.

Nancy had push. Nancy was "social," if not downright homey. Her autobiography is a scorecard of prominent "friends." Nancy brought to marriage with Reagan a fervent attachment to the chief man in her life and to the social whirl. If she had any political ideology, it amounted to the beliefs Dr. Davis had preached. She found Ronnie when he was on the skids, and she set out to foster and cozzen him; he called her "Mommie." Lou Cannon wrote that, "Passive and pleasant, Ronald Reagan was married to a woman who was neither . . ."[76] But she did have two major human relations strengths: she stood watch over Ronnie's emotional welfare like a Roman soldier and she cultivated rich socialites like a Japanese geisha. And henceforth, whenever Reagan's political sentiments echoed those of the sainted Doctor Davis, he could count on Nancy to second the motion. The year before they were married, for example, Reagan the protector of free speech against McCarthyite repression wrote that Americans might be left free to believe Communist philosophy, but

> the so-called "Communist Party" is nothing less than a "Russian-American Bund" owing allegiance to Russia and supporting Russia in its plan to conquer the world. The very constitution behind which these cynical agents hide becomes a weapon to be used against them. They are traitors practicing treason.[77]

SHIFTING GEARS

But he was no philosopher, political or otherwise. His New Dealism was easily explainable by his family history. Now his family had a markedly different equation and Reagan began to shift accordingly.

It was a slow process. In 1952 he joined millions of other Democrats in backing Eisenhower for President and the following year he backed a Democrat for the nonpartisan mayorship of Los Angeles. None of that amounted to much compared with the drama of his own personal fortune. During the war he had put himself in hock to the federal government by deferring income tax payments, and even though he came home in the 95 percent tax bracket, the repayments were eating him up. After one bad movie too many, he dropped out of his contract, losing $150,000 worth of work. He put a second mortgage on property he owned. He and Nancy lived for a while in Nancy's apartment and then bought a small home, but Reagan could not afford to complete the furnishing of the living room. The professional pits yawned in 1954, when Reagan took a part in a Las Vegas night club act, coming on as host with a self-deprecating bit about how he had to do the introductions because he had no other talent. From competition with Errol Flynn to competition with Las Vegas waiters.

Reagan's angel then descended in the persona of a friend he had once lent a hand to, who engineered a place for him as host of television's General Electric Theater—an eight-year contract, at $125,000 per year (soon to be upped to $150,000) plus a reportedly healthy bonus from his friend's outfit. Two years later, GE even threw in a fancy new five-bedroom all-electric house on a bluff overlooking the Pacific. His primary job was to host the show, and "Ronnie fit the role of host like a lightbulb fit a socket," writes biographer Lawrence Leamer.[78] Reagan could easily do half a dozen filmed introductions in one afternoon. He would also act in the dramas from time to time (in 1960, he and Nancy starred in "A Turkey for the President"). GE President Ralph J. Cordiner added a novel feature: about three months a year, Reagan would go on a lecture tour as a GE "corporate ambassador," boosting morale at GE plants and touting the company as a good-business citizen. Reagan loved it. For some reason, he was afraid to fly, so GE sent him by train through middle America, speaking to business and service clubs as many as fourteen times a day, chatting with the local GE bosses, soaking up the mindset of men on the make in the Eisenhower years. At first he talked nothing much more than boosterism, broad-brush patriotism, and a lighthearted defense of Hollywood. But as the years rolled on, Reagan the responder responded to the environment. He hardly knew any Democrats any more. His wife, his neighbors, his business associates were "conservatives" as that word was used then. Ironically, his brother Neil, he of the working class, had registered Republican in 1931, just as Roosevelt was rescuing the Reagan family from destitution; since then he had become a big business executive himself, and he kept after Ronnie to see the light. Ronnie did. He could see what went over and he gave it to them: dramatic diatribes, full of punchy anecdotes, on how awful the New Dealers were, how important it was to get them off the backs of business, how freedom was being betrayed, etc.

The reactive (as distinct from instinctive or original) nature of Reagan's political expressions was illustrated when, trying to please, he accidentally went too far. Conservatives loved it when he started blasting the Tennessee Valley Authority, a New Deal-founded federal government electric power operation of significant proportions. Reagan apparently did not know that GE got about $50,000,000 a year by selling things to TVA. Reagan heard that company complaints had reached Cordiner, who had ruled that Reagan could say whatever he thought. Reagan phoned Cordiner:

> "I understand you have a problem and it concerns me," Ronnie said, speaking to the executive for the first time.
>
> "I'm sorry you found out about that," Cordiner said, reassuring Reagan that he could go on speaking his mind.
>
> "Mr. Cordiner, what would you say if I said I could make my speech just as effectively without mentioning TVA?" Ronnie asked.
>
> "Well, it would make my job easier."[79]

Reagan did just that, putting his anti-TVA paragraph on ice for five years, until it suited the purposes of another fellow he was working for.

That little saga of passive-positive adaptation symptomized a growing Reagan problem. He was becoming too "conservative" for GE, especially after the 1960 election (in which he was a "Democrat for Nixon"). In 1962, when his contract was up for renewal, a television cowboy show called "Bonanza" beat out the "General Electric Theater." GE let him go. "More than anything," Lou Cannon writes, "it is his GE experience that changed Reagan from an adversary of big business into one of its most ardent spokesmen."[80]

His rhetorical fervor had not gone unnoticed among the ideologues of the right. The NAM, the AMA, and even Dr. Fred Schwartz's Christian Anti-Communist Crusade got him to speak. When GE let him go, his superconservative brother Neil, then an executive in the advertising firm of McCann Erickson, took him on, as host and soap salesman for "Death Valley Days," though at first Reagan turned down the job, because, as Neil said, "I rather suppose he didn't want to work."[81] But the biggest of all conservatives on the rise was Barry Goldwater, friend of Dr. Loyal Davis. Reagan had often talked with Goldwater at the Davis's vacation home in Phoenix, and they hit it off. Now he became co-chairman of the California Goldwater campaign. That crusade reached its apex at the Republican convention and then rolled downhill all the way to the Johnson landslide of 1964. Late in October, as election day loomed, another friend of Reagan's, a millionaire named Holmes Tuttle, asked him to substitute for Goldwater when the candidate cancelled a fundraising speech in Los Angeles. Reagan came and gave them his well polished litany, rhythms, gestures and all:

> We are at war with the most dangerous enemy that has ever faced mankind in his long climb from the swamp to the stars, and it has been said if we lose that war, in so doing lose this way of freedom of ours, history will record with the greatest astonishment that those who had the most to lose did the least to prevent its happening.[82]

The opposite of Theodore Roosevelt, as Cannon noticed, "Reagan's words were radical, but his manner was reassuring."[83] The audience of last-ditch Goldwaterites lapped it up. Tuttle turned to his friend Henry Salvatori, multimillionaire finance chairman of the Goldwater campaign. "Henry," said Holmes, "That's a terrific speech. Let's run him for governor." "Oh, for Christ's sake," said Salvatori, "You can't run an actor for governor." But they thought so much of the speech that they proposed showing the tape of it on national television. Some Goldwater advisors balked: the thing looked too radical even for Goldwater, suggesting certain dangerous ideas about social security. As he had with Cordiner, Reagan called Goldwater and offered to withdraw the speech if he thought it harmful. The speech, titled "A Time for Change," winding up with "You and I have a rendezvous with destiny," flowed out into the nation's living rooms on October 27, 1964. The response was highly favorable. In a little town in Michigan, the first Reagan for President club was formed.[84]

Reagan thus emerged on the national scene as a Goldwater conservative—that is, one who would, in the name of certain "principles," tear up the federal government and start over again. Reagan's rhetoric of the early 1960s and the Goldwater connection would help many an ideological conservative see Reagan, later on, as one of them, as a true believer in a revolutionary conservative ideology. So his words seemed to announce. Far more significant for understanding Reagan's progress, though, was the link he (and his wife) made at this point with the political aspirations of their new sponsors, the super-rich of Southern California.

NANCY AND HER FRIENDS

Nancy was crucial to this link. Her Ronnie was her life and he had long since come to depend on her dependency as a mainstay of his adaptation. She could hear her father's rabid indignations. But she could see even more starkly the way things had worked out for her mother: from dangerous insecurity to the life of the Chicago socialite. Nancy gladly threw up her acting career, not for the quiet joys of family life but for "society," which, in her time and place, meant wealth. If Ronnie knew how to charm the pols, Nancy knew how to slather the idle rich with a sense that they were terribly interesting and that she was one of them. Her prep school yearbook pointed to her "social perfection" as "a constant source of amazement."[85] When she got to New York as an actress-to-be, "Her greatest performance was in maintaining the illusion of affluence and success."[86] She had a lot to make up for, a lot of need for balancing out a "very unhappy, insecure and lonely" childhood, as a close friend described it.[87] When Reagan went on to win the governorship, Nancy's coterie of rich socialites, nicknamed "The Group," was collectively delighted, though she complained that "No one in Sacramento can do hair."[88] They had little white wine lunches and lobster dinners, punctuated by afternoon trips to the fanciest dress shops, where their "vendeuses" could appreciate their standing as "professional ladies," as one clerk called them, with no apparent sense of irony.[89] They shut out the world and encouraged one another; for years, the boundaries of "The Group" held fast against any potential new applicants. They talked about each other and their parties and dresses, avoiding potentially disruptive topics like politics. The women were sprightly, if challenging to their decorators, and the men—at least in their company—were geriatrically consoling. Together they formed a cocoon, gently wrapped in money, within which they could set up their little tinkly porcelain empire, safe from the world's harsh jostling. As President and First Lady, "We visited seven countries in Europe," Nancy reports, "meeting with heads of state, foreign ministers, industrial leaders, etc. You really learn about jet lag on journeys like this!"[90] In between her accounts of yachts and palaces and dukes and queens, Nancy writes that "I think I should point out that while I'm reminiscing about these visits and dwelling on the fun times, the trips had a serious purpose. There were endless hours and days of meetings, and Ronnie spent the hours in flight poring over briefing books that had been provided by Henry Kissinger. But if you don't mind, I'm going to keep telling about the extracurricular experiences that stick in my memory. I'm a sightseer at heart. . . ."[91] Nancy loved to meet famous people, "people I never dreamed I would meet," but meeting them seemed to suffice. She found people like Marcos of the Philippines "fascinating and enlightening," and the Taiwan Chiangs gave her "truly a sense of history."[92] Nancy and her friends approached the outer world as tourists: shopping, dining, meeting the bigwigs. There was a sort of innocence about them; in their company, Nancy could find the cheery childhood she had missed.

Nancy did not think of herself as a spoiled, self-indulgent person at all. "Self-restraint marks the difference between adult and childish behavior," she told her biographical collaborator.[93] What she seems to have meant was a stylistic restraint, as in her unwillingness to join Betty Ford in dancing the boogaloo at the 1976 Republican convention.[94] "Maybe because we all tend to move in circles and choose friends who like to do what we do, we don't see the other side of life," Nancy confessed. "I know I never saw the Hollywood I often heard about—the heavy drinking, pushing starlets in pools, etc. I suppose it existed, but I never saw it."[95] Self-restraint among her friends meant mainly talking pleasantly. There were those who thought of her crowd as "absurd, just absurd," a "crazy fagotage,"[96] and there were times when a certain tackiness crept in. Nancy's best friend Betsy Bloomingdale got nabbed at the Los Angeles airport and fined $5000 for trying to smuggle in two Christian Dior dresses worth $3880 from Paris.[97] To Betsy's husband Alfred, it seems, self-restraint meant something a little different: according to Vicki Morgan, his mistress for ten years, he liked tying up nude girls and spanking them soundly. As Alfred lay dying of throat cancer, Betsy partied from coast to coast.[98] No such scandal reached Nancy herself; her stress on "self-restraint" fit well enough with the perception of many who cared little for her, a view of Nancy Reagan as a cold, highly protected person unlikely to be accused of slopping over emotionally.

What was clearest in her moral vision was that self-restraint had nothing to do with asceticism. Nancy could not bear the somewhat shabby Governor's mansion in Sacramento, so she and Ronnie moved into elegant rented digs. His inauguration as Governor was the most expensive ever, $100,000. But it was the personal luxuries that painted Nancy Reagan as the most conspicuous consumer since Thorstein Veblen thought up the phrase. By the time she reached the White House, restraint was out the window. Impatient to get the decorators into the premises she suggested the Carters need not wait around after Christmas. Wealthy admirers put up $822,641 to get the living quarters up to snuff. Someone supplied $209,508 to pay for 220 place settings of gold-rimmed china, 4,732 pieces in all.[99] On inauguration night, she festooner herself with $250,000 worth of earrings and necklace and put on one of her apparently endless supply of super-expensive, wear-them-once dresses. No pretense of plainness was left in the White House, where caterers, decorators, and other nurses of the luxury class grew fat on the Reagan richesse.

Nancy became the symbol of the new hedonism. Halfheartedly she took up a First-Lady-type cause or two, but hardly bothered to learn their basics. At one of a series of Georgetown lunches with maturing ladies, Nancy mentioned her interest in drug abuse prevention. To the dismay of her companions, her major proposal turned out to be this: "We must get marijuana out of the movies."[100] That and other experiences in the Washington social circuit, where at least some informal conversation on real-world problems is expected, pressed Nancy back toward her issue-free California pals and their hairdressers and decorators.

And she did not have far to look: when Reagan got to be President, "The Group" and their husbands moved right into the Watergate and other nearby hotels, and the regular round of parties stepped right along. There old friend Charles Wick, soon to be put in charge of the worldwide image of the United States as conveyed through the International Communication Agency, opined that just as "during the Depression, when people were selling apples . . . they loved those glamour pictures showing people driving beautiful cars and women in beautiful gowns," so now they would love a First Couple not afraid to flaunt their worldly success.[101]

Nancy's success in finding her role in life gets its significance in the Reagan story as a powerful reinforcer of his allegiance to the very wealthy. By the time he reached the White House, Reagan had long been one of them, first as a protégé, then as a multimillionaire himself. But he did not need to go any distance at all to find a person for whom wealth itself, unsullied with any significant admixture of culture or contribution, formed the central value. There she was, his bunkmate in the ranch of the rich, tutoring her instructable husband in the merits of the moneyed class.

THE RICH REAGANS IN POLITICS

But Ronald Reagan's debt to rich friends ran directly, as well as through his wife. Lou Cannon's judgment is that Reagan, "usually the reactive man, would never have sought elective office except for the insistence of those who came to him and the absence of any other untarnished Republican candidate available to run against Governor Brown. Certainly he would not have taken the initiative in seeking office."[102] Millionaire Holmes Tuttle, a friend since the time Reagan bought a car from him in 1946, took the first initiative. Tuttle could see as well as anyone that Goldwater's "extremism" just had not sold in 1964. Two months after the election debacle, Tuttle invited two big oil men, Henry Salvatori and A.C. (Cy) Rubel, and several other millionaires to his home to talk about picking somebody to run against Pat Brown. In typical Southern California style they did not need to concern themselves with party politicians, but rather pondered the candidacy as they would the hiring of a branch manager. They saw Reagan as someone they could use. Rubel said, "Reagan is the man who can enunciate our principles to the people."[103] Salvatori's attitude was equally condescending: "Reagan doesn't have great depth," he said later, "but I don't know any politician who does. He's not the most intelligent man who ever was, but I've never met a politician with great depth. I don't know of any politician who would be smart enough to run my business, but Reagan just might."[104] Next, Tuttle got the famous political campaign management firm of Spencer-Roberts to check him out; after an interview to allay doubts that he was bendable enough, the firm signed on. Then came the issues: Spencer-Roberts hired a team of behavioral psychologists, who analyzed the Reagan productions into seventeen issues, gave each a philosophical framework, and compiled eight black books of facts and sayings suitable for speechmaking.[105] Reagan was not only drafted, he was virtually reconstructed by the millionaires and their hired experts. They promptly chopped out of his speeches references to the graduated income tax as "spawned by Marx as the prime essential of the socialist state" and other rightist embarrassments. Tuttle and company, though they could easily have come up with the money themselves, thought it wise to show strength by getting forty-one rich backers to form "The Friends of Ronald Reagan" in the spring of 1965.[106] Reagan took his script and performed it again and again, dismaying the travelling reporters but delighting audiences to whom it seemed spontaneous every time. Pat Brown cooperated by damning him as a right-wing radical. Reagan won big. His manager Lyn Nofziger said that "Ronald Reagan materialized out of thin air with no political background, no political cronies, and no political machine. . . . He didn't even run his own campaign. His campaign was run by hired people who then walked away and left it. Therefore, when he was elected, the big question was, 'My God, what do we do now?'"[107]

Tuttle and his friends had answers. They set themselves up as the "Major Appointments Task Force" and instructed their boy on whom to name to what. They met monthly to develop advice and they talked to the Governor on the phone. But the millionaires did not follow his every move. They did not have to. Having put in place an administration to run the state under a Governor with an absolute passion for delegation, they could get back to piling up their assets and let the state take care of itself. Reagan relied heavily on his helpers, some of whom would be back with him in the Presidency—William French Smith, Caspar Weinberger, William Clark, and Ed Meese, for example. The Reagan administration in Sacramento lasted two terms, during which he dashed around brandishing his virtue in various high dramas (confronting the University of California, managing a homosexual scandal in his administration) and otherwise cooperating with the Democrats in welfare reform, slowing the rate of government growth, and sponsoring other moderate measures which got him credit for not being as bad as he had been thought to be. Despite his rhetoric, state spending doubled and taxes increased by the highest leaps ever. Property owners, no doubt including his rich friends, got a $4 billion bonanza of tax relief.[108] He himself paid no taxes in 1970 and perhaps other years. Through the years, with the help and counsel of his rich friends, he, too, got rich speculating in real estate.

After his governorship, virtually the same scene replayed itself—Tuttle and his friends now planned how to run him for President. Out of the Governor's office and on the road again, picking up $20,000 a speech, Reagan, reacting to his audiences, began to drift rightward, leaving behind the pragmatics of office for the thrills of the podium. In these travels, Cannon reports, Reagan's favorite reading consisted of "the *Reader's Digest*, which was full of those amazing statistics he liked to spout, and *Human Events*, which was possessed of more ideological certainty than exists in the world."[109] Out there, Reagan gathered to him the fervent ideologues, who heard how sincere he sounded, the academic systematizers, who read their various logics into his scattered arguments, and the polyester Republicans, who figured he believed his sermonettes about the Protestant ethic. They supplied his campaign with phone-talkers and door-knockers. His rich friends supplied the payroll. Then when he won, the old Tuttle gang moved in to man the government in Washington as they had the government in Sacramento. By then Reagan's "kitchen cabinet" had a definition as tight as Nancy's "Group." Most of them thought of themselves as "self-made men". All were rich and proud of it: Tuttle himself, William French Smith, Justin W. Dart (drugstore magnate), William Wilson (real estate), Salvatori the oil man, Earle M. Jorgenson (steel), Joseph P. Coors (beer), and Walter Annenberg (publishing). Meeting regularly in Washington and in William French Smith's skyscraper boardroom in Los Angeles, the old gang put together a government. Salvatori said they agreed 99 out of 100 times and Smith said Ronnie took almost all their names.[110] In Washington they set up their own offices next door to the White House in the old Executive Office Building. As Reagan's Chief of Staff Baker said, "Anytime the President's friends—members of the kitchen cabinet—want to see him we put them on the schedule."[111] The men they chose reflected their values: the top six officers of the government were multimillionaires. Ordinary millionaires constituted at least twenty-five of the top hundred.[112] In other key offices, such as the Environmental Protection Agency and the Interior Department, top officials were chosen for their obvious bent against the thrust of the laws they were appointed to enforce. In their enthusiasm, kitchen cabineteers went beyond personnel to finance: Dart and Wick dunned big corporations to pay into a "Coalition for a New Beginning" to hype Reagan's program, and old Tuttle went after big money for Nancy's White House redecoration, especially from oil executives just a month after Reagan decontrolled their prices and thus presented them with an enormous if unseasonal Christmas present. The motives of contributors were not obscure. To put on the Reagan inauguration, his friends got up "more than $8 million in interest-free loans from corporations and others. Atlantic Richfield, for an example, lent the inaugural committee $50,000 and bought half a million dollars worth of commercials to benefit the effort, and a spokesman for Arco said this reflected "'the company's interest in maintaining good relations with the incoming administration. Obviously, we are terribly interested in legislation that is coming!'"[113]

In short, Reagan's big rich senior citizen pals were not about to leave the running of the government to the ordinary three branches. Procedurally, though, they overreached themselves; some of the dunned corporations began to complain at the blatant you-gets-what-you-pays-for appeal the kitchen cabinet was putting out. Consultant Stuart Spencer let the President know the danger and the staff delicately maneuvered them out of their semi-official role (by indicating they would have to be looked at by the FBI and submit financial disclosure forms) and eventually out of the EOB (by changing the locks and phones).[114] But more than their memory lingered on. A few, like William French Smith and Charles Wick, got significant posts, but all of them had what amounted to an even higher appointment: as family friends. The Bloomingdales rented a Watergate apartment whose accompanying parking space in the garage went for $15,000; the Wicks took an $1800-a-month pad in the same building, while the Annenbergs knocked about in a suite normally renting for $750 per day, perhaps worth it to be near Justin and Jane Dart and Betty and Bill Wilson. The Reagans saw a lot of them. They all showed up for a bash for one hundred on February 6, 1981, Nancy's surprise seventieth birthday party for Ronnie. Her toast was "I know there is nothing he wants more than the continuation of your friendship."[115] These good old ties were recemented every New Years in a week-long party the Annenbergs threw for the Reagans at Palm Springs, and every July at a similar extended soiree to celebrate Nancy's birthday, hosted by the Jorgensons and Wilsons. These were but the annual benchmarks; in between came the endless round of big and little chats and feeds. Though the Reagans were refreshingly genial to Washington's rich and powerful, they were not after new friends to party with. "The glue which holds us together," said Attorney General William French Smith, "is our friendship with (Reagan) and the traditions and associations we share."[116]

Those traditions and associations were not fundamentally ideological or even tied to party politics. Reagan represented an American interest. "Reagan is comfortable," Lou Cannon observed, "with self-made, wealthy men who believe the business of America is business."[117] A one-time Reagan aide told the Wall Street Journal that "Reagan's support is populist, but he's not. All of his instincts are pro-big business."[118] Reagan's multimillionaire friends thus did not have to get to him regarding this or that bill, this or that business-bureaucracy deal. Such matters could be left to the top aides they had picked for him and to the instincts they had helped reshape over decades of nurturing the Reagan family world view.

"SUPPLY-SIDING" THE RICH

That interpretation helps make some sense of the way Reagan's apparently contradictory policies for economic recovery worked out. To believe that America's super-rich want free enterprise is to believe an absurdity. Rather, like Chrysler and Lockheed and the oil industry and agribusiness and insurance and communications and transportation and military manufacturing, the major business enterprises in the United States—lavishly financed and manned by armies of determined lawyers and lobbyists—have over a long span of years succeeded superbly in nailing into the law and practice of government an enormously complex system of sustaining privileges that they are not about to sacrifice to any old or newfangled ideology. Similarly, to believe that the United States can, all by its lonesome, shape its own economic fate by whatever novel internal measures is to add another absurdity. As Reagan's luck would have it, the unity of the major world oil-producing powers in maintaining high prices began to break down as he was waving his magic wand over the economy, so that inflation began to trend downward in the U.S. But as any consumer of plastic sandals or advanced stereo equipment can see, America's domestic flow of goods and services is tied in with the powerful tides and eddies of the international flow. And to believe in a quick and easy free-lunch fix, as advertised by "supply-side economics," in which, by a relatively minor rearrangement of taxes and spending, a languishing economy would be sparked to unprecedented vigor and achievement—that is to add the third leg to the stool of absurdity. Finally, to suppose that cutting waste and fraud in the nondefense, nonentitlement portions of the federal budget would produce the multiple billions needed to offset the tax cuts was again an immediately obvious absurdity.

Looked at from the perspective of the super-rich, however, Reaganomics did not work out too badly. Most obviously and directly, the big rich came away from the table with their plates full of legislative goodies, immediately effective in increasing their incomes. Because Social Security taxes would go up as income taxes went down, families earning less than $40,000 a year would get no tax saving in the first year.[119] But for the seriously rich, the new Reagan legislation included "a dazzling array of tax breaks on oil production, estates, charitable contributions, interest income, deposits into retirement accounts, income from new tax exempt savings certificates, and other items."[120] Great big declines in such esoterica as "marginal rates on unearned income" and "capital gains" and "stock options" meant massive quick rewards for individuals and corporations in the topmost brackets. Two features illustrate this trend. "Accelerated cost recovery"—letting businesses subtract from their tax bills the cost of equipment at a faster rate—meant in practice that companies could soon save more in taxes than they had paid for the equipment in the first place. Still another wild advantage let companies sell their tax deductions to other companies—a sort of trickle-around system.[121] Some said such provisions added up to a virtual abolition of the corporate income tax.

But taxes were only part of it. Regulatory relaxation began as soon as the new Reaganites moved into their offices and put the brakes on inspections and reports and indictments—freeing big business from onerous obstacles to profit-making without waiting for Congress to reverse itself. Proposals to jack up the defense budget promised enormous contracts unfettered by competitive bidding. From the perspective of the mega-rich, certain economic pathologies could be seen as advantages. Big government deficits and the consequent shortage of credit make credit more expensive to buy and more profitable to sell; those who have money to lend will get more for it. And troubled times put the fear of God into the lower orders. Burgeoning rates of bankruptcy make weaker enterprises readier to sell out cheap, eliminating irritating competition. Spreading fear of unemployment and of welfare cut-offs has a way of rendering the working class more cooperative and respectful of their economic betters—and readier to work harder for less money. Big money executives, with their safe nesteggs and "golden parachute" contracts protecting them against the perils of failure, have no such real worries, however much they talk about risk and sacrifice. When one adds to such tangible considerations the Reagan administration's social and symbolic advantages—money as a sign of grace—the appeal to the super-rich is clearer yet.

The rest was eyewash, as Harry Truman would have put it. The Reagan razzle-dazzle barely concealed the lack of seriousness behind his announced social policies. The overall logic of "supply-side economics" was so weak that the administration could hardly find two favorable economists to rub together. John Kenneth Galbraith thought it could only work by divine intervention and thus should be turned over to Jerry Falwell and his Moral Majority. Whatever the logic, "the calculus of Reagonomics never actually made sense," as Lou Cannon noted.[122] Perhaps because optimist Reagan found economics a depressingly dismal science, he left the calculations to his aides, none of whom was trained in that discipline. David Stockman, his Office of Management and Budget chief, trained in divinity at Harvard. Stockman discovered early in the game that the magic would not work, when he put conventional budget estimates through his computer, so he invented out of his own imagination much more optimistic estimates and got the computer to bless them on the way to the President. Obviously no serious study had been devoted to the supply-side panacea before Congress was pressed to act on it, much less before it was brought to the people in the campaign. Stockman's confession that "none of us really understands what is going on with all these numbers" leaked in a magazine article. Author William Greider reported "Stockman's account of chaotic decision-making at the top . . . a kind of natural anarchy, a helter-skelter sequence of events normally concealed from public view."[123] Angry critics were to some degree mollified when Reagan, by Stockman's report, gave him a scolding. But as late as June 1983, Stockman was still at it, then cooking numbers to show that the Reagan administration was fair, conveniently lumping figures for families with figures for individuals, conveniently ignoring the bonanza of tax loopholes the rich got in 1981, conveniently defining the wealthy as the top two tenths of one percent. The facts were that Reagan's tax policies overwhelmingly favored the already rich, and that declines in inflation had been matched by declines in wages such that the average American's standard of living had fallen since the August 1981 enactment of the Reagan plan.[124] Reagan's own income, as reported to the IRS, went up 75 percent between 1981 and 1982.[125]

Reagan's world view, shaped by his own experience, by his wife, and by his most significant friends, and made manifest in the actualities of his policies, was, I argue, a simpler matter than the ideology-hunters make it out to be. Switching policies this way and that, his "bottom line" nevertheless came through: soak the poor, feed the rich. Politically, that is an impossible line to sell in a contemporary democracy. Personally, that is an impossible conviction for a passive-positive to admit to himself. Reporter Laurence Barrett explains how Reagan dealt with the conflict when asked how his policies might have contributed to the major recession of 1981–82 or to unfairness to the poor:

> Debating these questions with him is an exercise in frustration. After a time one longs to hear Reagan declare some contemporary equivalent of "Let them eat cake." If only he would show brutal candor. If only he would argue that the system needed leeching, that the poor and the blue collars and the shopkeeper on Main Street always bleed disproportionately during such therapy. Reagan would not do that because he doesn't believe it. He will not accept the strong link between his monetary and fiscal policy, tight money and the recession. He will not buy for a moment the proposition that anyone deserving help has been victimized by his spending cuts or that the burden has been spread inequitably.[126]

Lou Cannon confirms the theme:

> Only one accusation deeply bothered Reagan. That was the charge that his programs were unfair to poor people and minorities. . . . The President, a kind man in his personal relationships, could not seem to understand that many of his critics were evaluating the results of his policies rather than his motivations.[127]

But the denial of the obvious went beyond argument to emotion. The Reagans read no challenge into the remarks Mother Teresa made when she visited them in June 1981, referring to his recent brush with death: "'You have suffered the passion of the cross and have received grace,' she said, looking directly at Reagan. 'There is a purpose to this. Because of your suffering and pain you will now understand the suffering and pain of the world. This has happened to you at this time because your country and the world need you.' "[128] Nancy wept. Ronnie was speechless.

Nancy apparently saw nothing mocking of the poor in her spoof at the 1982 Gridiron dinner, when she came on dressed in a mismatched old outfit and sang about her "Second-Hand Clothes."[129]

The Reagan world view was, in the end, an attitude—but one with strong and widespread consequences beyond their social circle. Reagan the subduer of Congress was also, in the bias his adaptation impelled, Reagan the champion of the rich. But perhaps more fateful than either of these qualities, for the nation at large and the survival of democracy, was his seemingly least important attribute: Reagan the dramatist.

THE REAGAN RHETORIC

Reagan the actor is only part—the minor part—of Reagan the political dramatist. He is miscast as a man who brings Hollywood to Washington. Long before he became a professional actor, he had trained in pretending: that he really could see the blackboard, that his father was not really a drunk, that he really could play football, that he really did belong in the rich kids' crowd. Though the Great Depression stopped Jack Reagan in his tracks, he was for years a salesman, a man who talked people into buying things, and a wonderful Irish storyteller; Ronnie experienced that presence for a long time before he met the *Reader's Digest*. His mother put on little playlets right there in the living room. His favorite reading was Tarzan, his favorite activity talking ("an incredible talker," a writer said, meaning only that there was lots of it). And when he went off by himself to play, it was to enter "a make-believe world in which heroic deeds had the capacity to transform reality," as Cannon puts it.[130] Blessed with a tall, straight body, an attractive face and a winning smile, young Ronald Reagan was a natural for high school popularity and thus for student politics and drama club.

Thus when, much later, it came time for Hollywood to make an actor of him, no lessons were necessary—they persuaded him to let his crewcut grow out and to get rid of his shoulder-padded suits. But he played himself. Of his first seven movies, four portrayed him as a radio announcer, which is what he had been for years. Keenan Wynn, who knew him a long time, said that "Ronnie was not so much an actor as a performer who played versions of himself," in Laurence Leamer's paraphrase.[131] The years in Hollywood gave him skill in technique and an actor's interest in the arts of projection, but the Reagan range, in dramatic terms, ran from A to about D, no farther. To confuse him, then, with Lawrence Olivier or even Cary Grant—that is, to suppose Reagan's success springs from the deep art of *becoming* the part and the mesmerizing effect that can have on audiences—is, I think, a mistake. He was an actor, yes, and he did moderately well when he appeared at a particular and historical junction. The

Second World War interrupted his progress; by the end of it he was already getting too old to play the "Ronald Reagan" he had epitomized: the Earnest Young Fellow Up Against Trouble.

Reagan encountered—but could not connect with—real dramatic genius in his own home. Jane Wyman, given to occasional bouts of sadness, had found him an encouragement: "He was such a sunny person. . . ."[132] But the joys of perpetual sunshine eventually palled and she could not adopt the solution her husband recommended to her: "We'll lead an ideal life if you'll just avoid doing one thing: Don't think."[133] Starting in the movies about where he did, she developed into a serious actress, first in "The Lost Weekend," then in "The Yearling," and then in "Johnny Belinda," in which she played a deaf-mute girl who is raped, nearly loses her child to the rapist, and subsequently kills the man—an extraordinarily demanding part. She threw herself into it completely. She went to a school for deaf-mutes, learned to read lips, wore earplugs to simulate deafness. The strain made her lose a lot of weight. Eventually, she could not stop herself from continuing to cry when her crying scenes were finished. At first despairing of success, she came to be possessed by the part. At home she was difficult to live with.[134] Ronnie sympathized, but he could not understand the lure and strain of that kind of acting, so different from his own. When they divorced he said he sometimes thought he should have named "Johnny Belinda" as correspondent. Jane Wyman won an Academy Award for the part. In a sense Reagan's own acting was the opposite of hers: his strength was in maintaining his persona, not, as in her case, surrendering that persona to a role: Reagan the performer shared her craft, but he was out to be engaging, not gripping. Unlike Jane Wyman, he would remain a respectable but not an exceptional actor. His act was no artifice: he played out his character. The acting was secondary—an instrument for expressing the continuing Reagan personality.

Acting was also secondary in his life history. After college, his job was sports broadcasting and, in particular, rapidly inventing baseball and football stories to go with the spare facts ("Herman grounds out.") the telegraph provided. It was essentially a literary occupation, not a thespian one. He did that so well that he progressed to a major station, made himself a regional celebrity, and won a trip to Hollywood for the excellence of his work. Again the range was narrow: the few facts set a framework and the rules of the game a boundary within which his minor variations could play—the gestures of a batter, the outfielder tossing away his cap. Reagan could handle that, much as he could master, for example, the Presidential walk to the helicopter—the stride, the pause, the smile, the upraised hand, the snappy answer to the shouted question. He became a quick study. For all his lackadaisical academic record, he had a ready intelligence and an imagination which enabled him to get his lines, imagine how they would go, and zing them out.

But as with other Presidents-to-be, predicting Reagan's style worked much better by tracing back to his first independent political success than by averaging out his various subsequent occupations. In the Reagan history, that style-shaping experience stands out starkly: appropriately, it was a single, dramatic event in which the young man, away from his family, first discovered his own special technique for winning his way with significant others.

That happened for Ronnie at an appropriately named little country college: Eureka (i.e., "I have found it"). In the autumn of his freshman year, the college trustees met to ponder the school's financial crisis and to assess their president's recommendation that a number of courses be cut and their professors fired. That plan agitated the campus, drawing together faculty members, whose livelihoods were threatened, with students who feared they would be left without the courses they needed to graduate. The trustees, perhaps hoping the students would go away, mulled the matter until midnight before Thanksgiving holidays, when they announced acceptance of the president's cutback plan. The college bell began to toll; the chapel began to fill with students and professors, an angered, tense crowd ready for action. The student committee, nine members, of whom Reagan alone represented the freshmen, huddled and set the agenda: first a basketball star senior, then the senior class president, then freshman Reagan. That meant he got to present the motion—a call to strike and bring down the president. By the time he got the floor, the pent-up fervor was straining the chapel like an overheated steam engine. He spoke, he demanded the strike, the crowd exploded in unanimous applause and standing affirmation—of the strike and, as he had to hear and see and feel it, of himself. It was a sweet victory. Just a few weeks earlier Ronnie had tried out for football with twenty-five other students; he had been the only one rejected. Now, suddenly, he was the most famous freshman on campus. The students struck for a week, the president resigned, and the faculty-firing plan was put on the shelf.

So it was political oratory that formed the experiential base for Reagan's subsequent adventures in radio and the movies and public speaking and, eventually, real politics. That crucial midnight meeting stuck with him as a mythological event he never tired of telling, in somewhat mythic form. The lesson he drew from it was this: "I discovered that night that an audience has a feel to it and, in the parlance of the theater, that audience and I were together." Read the audience, get on that wavelength and power follows: "It was heady wine. Hell, with two more lines I could have had them riding through 'every Middlesex village and farm'—without horses yet."[135] In his own life, Reagan said as he ran for President of the United States, his performance that night formed "a beginning link in a later pattern."[136] Speaking at Eureka in October 1980, he said "Everything good that has happened to me—everything—started here on this campus in those four years that still are such a part of my life."[137]

Years later, in 1984, Reagan explained how his link to the audience translated into a political career:

> I never in my wildest dreams ever aspired to public service.
> I loved that world that I was in, the entertainment world.
> So, the very fact that I'd been blessed with some success and could attract an audience, I thought that it was only right that I should use that in behalf of causes that I believed in. So, I don't know what I could have done differently.[138]

By the time Reagan reached the stage of the White House, he had more experience pleasing audiences than any American politician since William Jennings Bryan. He had mastered the arts of dramatic performance on the stage, in radio sportscasting and commentary, in the movies, in television and in specialized and general platform oratory. No other candidate in 1980 or 1984 had anything like Reagan's professional experience in the modern media. And not since Harding had a happy-talk President's character and style fit together so nicely with the public's yearning for positive thinking in politics. The President had a terrific sense of humor, which he exercised regularly in what started out to be formal prep sessions by his staff. "Being dull," he said, "is very hard for me,"[139] and he loved Nancy especially for shielding him from boredom. He and Nancy let their emotions show: for all his general geniality, the Reagans are to be found weeping sentimentally on scores of occasions from one end to the other of the biographies.

The obvious combination of public personality and media talent made it surprising that it had taken so long for the Reagan type to appear in the age of media politics. Here was a man who, at his inaugural ball, could do the apparently impossible: "Ronnie and Nancy danced intimately while thousands watched."[140] He knew how to rehearse systematically for the apparently unrehearsed, spontaneous move, such as saying "There you go again" before giving one of his memorized responses (based on leaked Carter memos) in answer to Jimmy Carter in their campaign debate. He introduced the teleprompter to the English Parliament. He could steal FDR's finest lines—"rendezvous with destiny," for example—and make them sound like his own. Painted by his opposition as a combination fool and knave, he knew how to turn those expectations to his advantage: he became one of those lucky politicians who get credit for being normal. As an entertainer/speaker at an Al Smith dinner he could surpass any Presidential candidate in sight, approximately as Rudolph Nureyev could surpass him at the polka. Reagan was specially adept at playing the injured innocent, the wounded bear, saying "I can't be angry . . ."[141] when assaulted by a critic. The minor tricks were part of his nature by then—for example, knowing how to look and move slightly but expressively when the television camera found him listening to his opponent's answer.[142] To the television audience for Presidential addresses, he spoke simple English and even used such homely but effective props as a dollar bill and 36¢ in change to make his point. His staging was superb, from his tan and tieless performance in front of the Statue of Liberty during the campaign to his inaugural on the visually correct side of the Capitol Building, where he could gesture expansively at the monumental wonders of the Mall. The television networks followed him around like trained puppies, eager to put on the news shows good happy clips from Nancy's "surprise" birthday party for him on February 4, 1983, followed a few days thereafter by the President's foray into a drugstore to buy her a Valentine.[143] Even his administration's top people seemed to have been typecast as supporting players for the Reagan performance. Surrounded by such sober types, his mildly maverick manner made him seem fresh and interesting.

THE FICTIONALIZATION OF POLITICS

That one can carry off an act like Reagan's without control and calculation—by just "being oneself" while strolling through the media minefield—is a myth beyond credibility. At least since his Hollywood days, he has been used to having his appearance managed by others. He approached playing Governor of California the same way, by following his directors. Then, when trouble came, as when a homosexual clique was found in his administration, "Ronnie was told as much, but, as he always did in emotionally difficult and complex situations, he distanced himself from the realities and went on."[144] When he finished being governor, a public relations firm, Deaver and Hannaford, took over the task of directing him. The same director/star relationship continued in his Presidential politics.

What was made to look like a Reagan move was often a performance directed by others. For instance, there was Reagan's famous performance at the 1980 "debate" in New Hampshire, in which the audience saw an indignant Reagan stride onto the stage and insist that all the other candidates, not just George Bush, should have their chance to say their piece. That broke the agreed-upon rules, so the editor of one of the sponsoring newspapers asked that Reagan's microphone be turned off. Reagan the wounded bear turned on him and spoke: "I paid for this microphone, Mr. Green!" Bush looked foolish, Reagan looked simultaneously democratic and in charge. Political reporter David Broder turned to his colleague Lou Cannon and said, "Reagan is winning this primary right now."[145] For that and other reasons, Reagan did go on to win big in New Hampshire: he got more votes than the other six candidates put together.

But the management of Reagan is all the more effective for being invisible. In this not untypical case, Reagan's manager John Sears got the idea of inviting the other candidates to the scheduled Reagan-Bush debate—and Sears went ahead and asked them without even telling Reagan, much less getting his okay, until noon of the day of the debate itself. When Bush, through his manager (and Reagan aide-to-be) James Baker refused to agree that the others should speak, here came grim-visaged Reagan, pacing up the aisle to the platform with the alphabetic four trailing behind him: Anderson, Baker, Crane, and Dole. Beside him, though, walked his aide Jim Lake, and to Lake Reagan was saying, "What am I supposed to do? What exactly am I supposed to do?" Lake said, "We're going to go up there. You're going to make this statement that these guys should be allowed to speak. If they leave, you've got to stay and debate." Reagan walked up and sat down. Lake sent a Secret Service agent up with a note: "Give 'em hell, Governor. The whole place is with you." Scowling Reagan looked up a moment and gave Lake a wink. Then stern and indignant, he played out the part.[146]

That is why thankful movie stars, receiving their Academy Awards, pay homage to their unseen but essential directors and producers.

The perfection of the Reagan act kept breaking down in the campaign because it was impossible to keep it completely under control; nosey reporters kept asking him questions, and his answers were too often downright flakey and thus newsworthy. Once in the Presidency, managing the act was much easier. Media access to the President was radically restricted. By the midterm elections of 1982, Cannon was calling him "one of the most isolated chief executives since World War II.[147] In the analogous period, Jimmy Carter had held three times as many press conferences as Reagan held, and Eisenhower, Kennedy, and Johnson had held even more than that. Increasingly his staff kept reporters away from him at staged "photo opportunities" so as not to tempt him into spontaneity. Interviews were rare and controlled. Nancy would coach him, "You wouldn't know," "We're doing the best we can," or Ed Meese would come between questions and answer with "You don't have to answer that." On the other hand, the President repeatedly addressed the nation on television and put out a regular radio program, sometimes eliciting an opposition response which was almost never as well done as the Reagan original. Reagan was not about to be shanghaied by the press if he and his attentive managers could prevent it. As always, he worked best when he could rehearse, and a major Reagan address took hour after hour of rehearsal. Preparing for the climactic television debate in 1980, Jimmy Carter studied his briefing books. Reagan and his friends did that, too, but they devoted hours to practicing the dramatics and studying videotaped playbacks of the trial runs.

Such control protects Reagan from a malady he has experienced repeatedly: getting carried away by an audience. Passive-positives are prone to that in part because they are more closely attuned to the here and now—the present, in-person audience—than others are. Nancy, his most worshipful audience, has been a steadying influence in that respect. She was away from his side when, on the spur of the moment, he told the California delegation to the 1968 Republican convention that he was a candidate for President.[148] In 1962, Nancy reports, he suddenly changed his party registration from Democrat to Republican when, in the midst of one of his speeches a woman registrar interrupted to sign him up.[149] In 1980 audiences kept inspiring him to excess. He added to a speech to the Veterans of Foreign Wars the startling idea that the war in Vietnam was a "noble cause." A group of reporters for religious publications inspired him to bubble up the thought that "creationism" ought to be taught alongside evolution in the public schools.[150] At the Michigan state fair, a woman in the audience wearing a Carter mask needled him into saying he was happy to be there while Carter "is opening his campaign down there in a city that gave birth to and is the parent body of the Ku Klux Klan," a statement wrong in every particular. "I could have bitten my tongue off," Reagan said right after the speech as he recognized the mistake. An uproar followed. Reagan had to apologize to the appropriate mayor and governor. Nancy, reading the signs, got Stuart Spencer to join the campaign and keep him from flying off; "Okay, Stu, okay," said Reagan, "I'll stick to the script."[151] In the Presidency, Reagan could much more easily be restrained from audience-inspired blurts.

Other things being equal, such dramatic calculations and controls are all for the best. The modern Presidency is of necessity a performance—a media performance—and the modern arts of President-playing are to be celebrated, not disdained. They make politics interesting and thus encourage participation. They translate complexity into simplicity, which, in real-world politics, is a prerequisite for action. At their best they enliven and expand the national classroom, where the lessons have to do with life and death. The bright side of Presidential dramatics is inspiration.

The dark side is the power of drama to overwhelm reason: the lure of illusion, the fracturing of logic, the collapse of political conversation. The dark side is the drift into the swamp of fantasy and on over the brink of disaster. Drama offers interest, but it risks political insanity. That process begins with contempt for the facts.

Reagan seemed to love facts. Unlike politicians who take their stand on the landscape of generality, Reagan was forever citing statistics and telling interestingly specific bits of history or biography. The trouble was that he very often said, with an air of resolute conviction, things that simply were not true. Reporters and opposing candidates collected the errors of Ronald Reagan by the notebookful. Far from trivial, Reagan's "counterfactuals" bore directly on major problems of public policy. If trees cause air pollution, if oil slicks help cure tuberculosis, if welfare cheats are rampant, if the Shah of Iran was a "progressive," if the Soviet economy is about to collapse "because they've already got their people on a starvation diet of sawdust,"[152] if there is more oil under Alaska than under Saudi Arabia, if billions upon billions of federal expenditures are "fat"— then follow various highly significant directions for the relevant policies. Not that his perceptions were random; they suited his rich friends far better than his poor victims. Richard Cohen reported that Reagan, at one spring 1982 press conference, "said Social Security was not 'touched' when in fact it had been cut. He said programs for pregnant women had not been reduced, but merely merged with others. They were cut—by about $200 million. He said the overall poverty budget was increased. It wasn't. The new money went for defense."[153] But the frequency of Reagan's "slips" or "gaffes" or "bobbles" was in itself amazing, especially given the heat Jerry Ford and Jimmy Carter had had to endure for far less significant blunders. More interesting, though, was Reagan's own apparent attitude toward his "mistakes": he did not seem to mind. Though he sometimes waxed indignant over accusations of inaccuracy, he typically acted like an actor who, having blown a line, has to forge right ahead without worrying over it. When a reporter quoted one of his strange statements back to him, he shrugged and said he did not remember saying that, but that he had "probably just read something from a piece of paper that had been put in front of me."[154] Or he "would just smile pleasantly or shake his head in disagreement with his critics, as if mastery of provable fact were things on which gentlemen certainly could differ in goodwill."[155] The gaffe story had developed its plot to perfection in Presidential politics, from error to expiation—but Reagan would not play. He was, it seemed, literally shameless when it came to the question of factuality. As James Reston put it, "Give Mr. Reagan a good script, a couple of invisible TV screens and a half hour on prime time and he'll convince the people they have nothing to fear but the facts."[156]

Like his dramatic skills, that attitude was rooted in his own theatrical experience. Arriving in Hollywood, he remembered being "filled with all the star-struck awe of one who had from childhood been entertained in the house of illusion—the neighborhood theatre."[157] He missed completely the GI cynicism of World War II, dwelling instead through those years in another house of illusion—making mythic films of patriotic puffery and acting in a musical comedy about the war.[158] Fantasy in Reagan's life was not, as it might be for a reporter or historian, something to guard against, but rather a point of pride. The actor is meant to be an enthusiastic fantasist, a dreamer. "So much of our profession is taken up with pretending," he wrote, "with interpretation of never-never roles, that an actor must spend at least half his waking hours in fantasy."[159] Reagan especially liked Carl Sandburg's slant on dreaming: "The Republic is a dream. Nothing happens unless first a dream."[160] David Stockman summed up the White House system at one critical era: "Every time one fantasy doesn't work they try another one."[161] Another staffer left the Reagan White House saying, "The whole administration's a fantasy that they have the power to maintain and define as normal. . . . but they have no questions. It's an administration without questions."[162] To Reagan, accusations of fantasy translated easily into praise for having the courage to dream great dreams and not to let a lot of piddling little facts get in the way. His conscience was easy—he didn't lie, he just made things up.

For years Reagan has been making up stories about himself—mythlets he seems to believe. "I'll never forget one game with Mendota," one such tale begins and goes on to describe how he lost a close football contest for Dixon High by confessing to the unseeing umpire that he deserved a penalty; though sorely tempted, "truth-telling had been whaled into me. . . . I told the truth, the penalty was ruled, and Dixon lost the game." But the fact is, as Cannon reports, that Dixon lost only one game that season—to Mendota by a score of 24-0.[163] Then he tells the one about how his brother was persuaded to go to college because an old immigrant at the cement factory said to him, "Look at me—ve'll always vork together, chust you and me, and zomeday you'll be chust like me—isn't that nize." A cute story and, according to Neil Reagan, total fiction.[164] In 1983, Reagan told Hugh Sidey of a peak experience in his life—when, at Eureka, "I played Captain Stanhope in *Journey's End*. I never was so carried away in the theater in my life. I was in the war as far as that play was concerned."[165] He added details about the cast and his role. The trouble is, he did not act in the play at all. He saw it performed when he was a freshman. Later he said that "in some strange way, I was also on stage."[166] That psychological identification had overwhelmed the facts and he had moved from his seat to the stage. "He is forever reinventing his past," as William Leuchtenburg writes, especially in juggling the history of his attitude toward Franklin Roosevelt to suit Reagan's current politics.[167] As David Broder noted, "It is apparently President Reagan's belief that words can not only cloak reality but remake it."[168] The past is raw material, to be shaped as needed for purposes of revealing dramatic truth.

Nor is Reagan's fantastic imagination devoted only to historical reconstructions. He thinks up stories he might act in in the future. After he lost to Ford in 1976, Betty Glad noted, Reagan fantasized about man-to-man confrontation with Leonid Brezhnev. As he told his son, Mike, after he lost to Ford in 1976:

> You know the real reason I'm upset? I was looking forward to sitting down with Brezhnev and negotiating the SALT II Treaty. I wanted to listen to the interpreter tell me for an hour and a half what Brezhnev wanted the President of the United States to give up in order to maintain friendship with Russia. Then, I was going to slowly get up, walk around the table and whisper in his ear, "Nyet." I really miss that. I don't think Brezhnev has ever heard that word before.[169]

In July 1982 he was still at it, telling Laurence Barrett that

> I often fantasize [about taking] Soviet leaders in a helicopter and just flying around, just kind of let them choose where we go, so it couldn't look like a planned tour, and be able to point down and say, "Yeah, those houses down there. Yeah, that house with a trailer and a boat on it in the driveway. That's a working man in America. Yes, he lives in that house. He has that boat. He drives that car to work." They could not show me comparable things in their country.[170]

Nowhere does Reagan make this attitude clearer than in his story of how segregation ended in the armed services "in World War II . . . largely under the leadership of generals like MacArthur and Eisenhower": "When the Japanese dropped the bomb on Pearl Harbor there was a Negro sailor whose total duties involved kitchen-type duties. . . . He cradled a machine gun in his arms, which is not an easy thing to do, and stood at the end of a pier blazing away at Japanese airplanes that were coming down and strafing him and that [segregation] was all changed." A reporter told him segregation lasted at least until three years after the war when Truman ordered it stopped. Reagan replied: "*I remember the scene. . . . It was very powerful.*"[171]

Reagan off-stage seemed to be engaged in creative fantasizing. Laurence Leamer notes that

> What was so extraordinary was Ronnie's apparent psychic distance from the burden of the Presidency. He sat in cabinet meetings doodling. Unless held to a rigid agenda, he would start telling Hollywood stories or talk about football in Dixon. Often in one-on-one conversations Ronnie seemed distracted or withdrawn. "He has a habit now," his brother, Neil, said. "You might be talking to him, and its like he's picking his fingernails, but he's not. And you know then that he's talking to himself."
>
> "If people knew about him living in his own reality they wouldn't believe it," said one White House aide. "There are only ten to fifteen people who know the extent, and until they leave and begin talking, no one will believe it."[172]

The uncoupling of the President from White House decision-making became a startling fact of life among his advisors. A former aide said that the President, facing a policy question, "will not go far into it because he is not really looking to make a decision. He is looking for lines to repeat when the time comes to sell. He thinks of himself not so much as the person who decides but rather as the person who markets." A current aide confessed how difficult it was to get the President to concentrate on policy specifics: "I have to prepare a script. Otherwise he will get me off the subject and turn what I have to say to mush. I have about six or seven minutes, and then he guides the conversation."[173] Similarly abroad: Joseph Kraft noted that "foreign leaders repeatedly come away from sessions with the president claiming he is a pussycat, too nice even to mention disagreeable subjects."[174]

The uncoupled quality came through also in public on those rare occasions when he spoke without a script. David Broder noted that "To hear him speak extemporaneously on domestic policy is to hold your breath in nervous anticipation of the unknown."[175] Lacking firm anchoring in the mind of the President himself, policy in the Reagan administration lurched from one accident to another. The supply-side hocus-pocus was but the most evident of a series of inventions in which the logic of politics fell apart in the presence of the logic of the theater. Theodore White saw that the Reagan budget "defied common sense—almost as much as the illusion that by sheer power alone, people can learn to slide uphill."[176] Stockman and Murray Weidenbaum slapped together figures from their "visceral computers"—their gut feeling.[177] The Reagan people had thought to propose a 5 percent rise in defense spending, but Carter proposed that figure in his final budget, so the Reaganites upped theirs to 7 percent, the President explaining that "worldwide, what we're doing in defense must be seen as different from Carter. It must be a symbol of a change in the climate as regards to defense."[178] Thus the figures had nothing much to do with actual guns and bullets, but with symbols, and so there was not much apparent need to get the figures right; the billions were tossed around with cheerful abandon. That was the dashing style in which much of the Reagan "program" got constructed, from governmental decentralization to missile development. One after another, the major new projects rolled out of the White House hangar: a new defense system, based in outer space, to turn back Soviet missiles, a new "zero option" aiming at total elimination of nuclear weapons, a new proposal for merit pay for school teachers—each enjoying its week or so in the sun before passing into the oblivion from which it had emerged. Cannon came to call the President "The Great Deflector."[179]

PLANNED DISTRACTION

It was not too long before a savvy White House aide picked up the method behind the madness and pushed planned distraction. Dick Darman proposed this list:

Hype Federalism for as long as it will play.

Develop and implement plans for minor (low cost) and symbolic actions for key constituencies—aged, Spanish-surnamed, white ethnics/blue collar, populist/rednecks, (other?).

Distract attention from economic focus until the economy is clearly turning up— via a combination of foreign and domestic actions . . .[180]

In the summer of 1983, federalism—delegating functions and their costs to the states—was virtually played out as an issue by the time the governors met to bemoan their losses of federal revenues. Step 2 of the Darman plan was in full force as the President, suddenly discovering that there were major complaints about his policies, dashed around doing his best to woo the disaffected blacks, women, Hispanics, unemployed, "etceteras" on his list with a good many "minor (low cost) and symbolic actions." With a flourish of anger at the very thought of it, he ordered his health officials to restore $500,000 cut from funds to give artificial limbs to crippled children.[181] For all the President's dash and verve, the act itself—the Reagan performance in person—was fading in effectiveness. His press conferences turned tense. A little joke he worked into his speech to the International Federation of Business and Professional Women (". . . if it wasn't for women, us men would still be walking around in skin suits and carrying clubs") went over like a stone pie. When he spoke to the American Bar Association and casually credited himself with extending the Voting Rights Act, an expert civil rights lawyer called that "The height of fraud. His Administration was at the forefront of seeking to dilute the Voting Rights Act." Joseph Lowery, head of the Southern Christian Leadership Conference, put it this way: "While the President's words are soft as a lamb, his programs bite like a wolf."[182] As the combat of 1984 loomed on the horizon the jokey old easiness of 1980 lost its appeal.

But it was item 3 of Darman's memo that posed the greatest danger. Reagan succeeded wonderfully in distracting the nation's—and the world's— attention when in 1983 he dispatched to wartorn Central America a massive fleet and thousands of American troops, supposedly for maneuvers. A Soviet ship was stopped and asked about its cargo. Added to the troops the U.S. had spread over the Middle East, these soldiers and sailors stood at risk, not only from the types of surprise missile attacks Argentina had used, only a year before, to sink British ships in the area, but also from encounters with the various right- and left-wing armed bands pursuing each other over this strange terrain. Risk was evident also in the chaos at the top—the foreign policy equivalent of the chaos in economic planning Stockman had described. Observers who had breathed a sigh of relief at the departure of Haig and Richard Allen and their replacement by George Shultz and William Clark, in what the White House liked to call a "mid-course correction," choked up again when normally placid Shultz stormed into the Oval Office and told the President he had to be in on major foreign policy moves. He had learned about the dispatch of the fleet by reading it in the newspaper. That was only a symptom of the sprawling disorder endemic in Reagan foreign policy, in which power drifted and lurched from the Secretary of Defense to the United

Nations Ambassador to the National Security Council chief to special Presidential envoys in Central America and the Mideast to the Secretary of State to, of all people, Henry Kissinger, previously Reagan's prime example of a defective part in the foreign policy machine, who was put in charge of a special commission designed to sidetrack dissent on Central American policy. The President floated along, blaming the press for the public's increasing skepticism.

The new military exercise was variously described as routine maneuvers or a massive show of force to encourage negotiations, which the Reagan administration had previously rejected. The land maneuvers were to be held in Honduras, from which a war against the Nicaraguan government was being waged with U.S. aid furnished "covertly," according to the administration, although pictures of it all appeared week after week in the news magazines. The purpose of the aid was described first as a way to stop Nicaragua from supplying arms to rebels in El Salvador and then as aiding Nicaraguan "freedom fighters" out to overthrow the government. In April 1984, it was revealed that the CIA, in violation of international law, had been laying mines in Nicaraguan harbors[183] and in October 1984 the press printed shocking excerpts from a CIA manual for revolution, recommending assassinations, blackmail, and other crimes.

But it was in Lebanon, in October 1983, that the Reagan military policies brought their first disaster, the worst since Vietnam. Two hundred and forty-one Marines died in Beirut, thanks to what a subsequent administration commission found to be a thoroughly botched mission—men virtually staked out and waiting for an accident to happen.[184] Having adamantly refused to pull them out, Reagan finally did so, but not before suggesting that advocates of withdrawal were treasonous. His own Minority Whip in the House, conservative Republican Trent Lott (R-Mississippi) complained that "You people are not in touch with reality."[185] A year later, in September 1984, another bomb in Beirut blew up at a U.S. embassy annex, killing two more Americans.

THE THREAT AHEAD

Thus the Reagan administration lurched into international military adventure, the arena where the risk of tragedy loomed largest. In the White House the President's men hid their tensions and struggled to manage his destiny by managing his image. In the short run, which is all we may have, the major danger of the Reagan administration stood out starkly: not adamance, but drift; not ideological rigidity, but accident; not obsession, but distraction. Domestically, Reagan's erratic and ill-developed dashes hurt people he never meant to hurt—by the millions. Internationally, the sudden movements of masses of armed men and weapons posed enormous risks to the tenuous stability of a changing world. At the center of it all was a President continually in search of directors to tell him what to do.

Reagan continued the Presidential posture he inherited from his parade of predecessors. That is, a President cabined with "political" advisors, promoted from among the top men of his campaign staff, innocent of experience in the high arts of statesmanship. That is, a President preoccupied with "crisis management"—reacting to one blow after another from an environment he was elected to shape, not merely respond to. That is, a President-centered government in which rational deliberation disappeared in the mystic clouds of manipulative rhetoric. On the obvious major challenges of the age—the institutionalization of peace, the establishment of the rudiments of justice in the world, and the management of world resources for the welfare of humankind—no progress whatever was evident. Instead, we continued the pattern of challengers and incumbents competing, with all the vigor and imagination at their command, to win the nation's highest authority only to realize, on the morning after, that they did not know what to do with it.

If, nevertheless, we survive for a longer run, with a chance for progress of the American democracy, we will look back on Reagan's presidency as marking a fundamental departure from the basic tradition. For democracy rests on a tacit social contract that the government will operate in the real world. As Freud understood, the alternative is enormously attractive: illusion beckons, luring not only the anxious or desperate individual, but also the distracted nation. We have seen in Naziism and in Communism how millions of people—including a good many smart ones—can be suckered into believing crazy theories as if they are factually founded. A true democratic "conservatism," unlike the brittle and frightened imitation by that name, would insist on genuine argument in politics—that is, on the systematic presentation of accurate information, to which the steady light of reason can be applied.

Judging by the forces arrayed against it, the defense of empiricism in democracy will take some doing. We exist in an era of history in which history itself is passé, an age of fictions, especially fictitious tales of the human heart, an age of feeling. Our literature is dominated by the novel, as literatures in ages past were dominated by theology or military science or the sagas of discovery. The boundaries between what really happened and what must have or might have or could have happened fade from vision. We seem less interested in testing facts than in savoring insights. Wit is popular, in political commentary as elsewhere. The anonymous and thus uncheckable source is the fashion in journalism. Our economics and, increasingly, our politics too, breathe the airs of speculation and the hope that wide agreement on an idea can somehow substitute for a demonstration of the truth of it. Our generation's contribution to communication, television, far prefers to probe for feelings than to test theories against facts. And our generation's contribution to politics, the endless campaign, still manages to throw down an iron curtain between the suppositions of running for President and the actualities of being one.

For these and other reasons, our politics is especially vulnerable to the Reagan dramatics. We do not seem to be able to pay attention very long and the attention we do pay is scant to start with. Yet that is democracy's scarcest and most valuable resource. Squander attention, or let fiction sop it up, and the democratic spirit sheds its practical incarnation and, wraithlike, sails out into the ether.

9

Franklin D. Roosevelt and Active-Positive Affection

The President is a person. For better or for worse, he and his peculiarities are with us for at least four years. He confronts whatever situation history hands him with lessons drawn from a double tradition: that of his predecessors in the White House and that of his own personal development. The former is a most variegated tradition and the one amenable to various interpretations. A close study of what subsequent Presidents have admired about Abraham Lincoln, for example, would provide an image drawn at least as much from the admirer's mind as from Lincoln's, a kind of Presidential Rorschach test. Nor has there been much certain guidance from a President's immediate predecessors; similarly diligent research would show that each new President has (*a*) rejected the route of the last President of the other party, (*b*) paid homage to the deeds of his party's last President, and (*c*) promptly set about differentiating himself from both. In this office, at least, there is no definitive rulebook, no steady instruction in how to grasp whatever torch is passed.

If the institutional tradition is clouded, so is the picture of the present. All times try men's souls, especially the times for which one happens to be significantly responsible. Presidents have to guess, as best they can, not only what actual shape the country is in but also what that shape implies for their own behavior. Thus the perception of crisis may impel one to vigorous action or calm restraint: the prescription does not follow inevitably from the diagnosis.

What real Presidents do, of course, is muddle through with the equipment they have, justifying their performances on the basis of theories they find congenial and have reason to believe the nation will find at least acceptable. Like any person facing extreme uncertainty, the President seeks within himself some ground of continuity, some identity he can recognize as his way of being. That identity is inseparable from his personal history; he senses what he is in large measure by what he was, and by what he hopes yet to be. A moment's introspection will confirm that we tend to respond to new challenges with old habits—of belief, of feeling, and of action.

The cases reviewed so far show that Presidents can get themselves into profound difficulties as they grope forward with the road maps they had found so useful on previous occasions. The difficulties are evident, the ways around them harder to see. Much as the mind doctors of today find it much easier to specify the patterns of pathology than the patterns of health, so the reasons for Presidential failure are much more readily chartable than the dimensions of success. Much of the advice scholars have to offer Presidents seems cast in this negative form: what *not* to do.

Against this background, the active-positive Presidents display virtues of omission: they avoided both obsession and lassitude. Yet they also display personal strengths specially attuned to the Presidency, strengths which enabled them to make of that office an engine of progress.

The active-positive Presidents are those who appear to have fun in the vigorous exercise of Presidential power. They seek out—even create—opportunities for action, rather than waiting for the action to come to them. Their enjoyment in Presidential initiative represents a psychological congruence of factors in which the elements reinforce one another powerfully. Fun-in-work stands for a rare integration, one in which the self need not sacrifice gratification for achievement, but rather grows outward along both fronts simultaneously. Even seen from a distance, these Presidents seem to share a sense of the self as developing. Their apparent happiness in what they do—as Presidents—stands out in contrast to the defenses other Presidents cling to. Each has shown in his own way these qualities:

A conviction of capability. *The President soon reaches the conclusion that despite weaknesses he knows about, he is fully able to meet the challenges of the job.*

Investment without immersion. *He shows a deep interest in, and strong attention to, the substance of the issues he decides to take on. He learns quickly what he needs to know and stores in memory a great deal of information he might find useful. Yet there is also a certain detachment, a distance he puts between himself and his work. He has an existence beyond his occupation. A symptom of this objectivity is laughter, at his own blunderings and those of his enemies.*

A sense of the future as possible. *In his attention, the future is more important than the past. The future is not set, not inevitable either for good or ill. It is not to be mastered by some mechanical application of "principles," but by imaginative experimentation. It will grow out of trends, possibilities, accidents, opportunities—and it can be helped along.*

A repertoire of habits. *The active-positive President uses a variety of styles, moving flexibly among a number of modes of political action. Such a President seems to base his self-definition on ground deeper than the collection of stylistic approaches he has put together over the years. His style is a bag of tools, not a way of life.*

The communication of excitement. *The President moves outward from a base of relative strength and connects with other people, stimulating their interest, invigorating their own positive imaginations. From some he may elicit a "charismatic" response; for nearly all he supplies a sense that he is at the center of fascinating events and that the center is moving.*

It is not easy to discern in the biographical accounts how these qualities developed dynamically; but that they *had* developed was in each case evident long before the man took the oath of office.

Franklin D. Roosevelt, Harry S. Truman, and John F. Kennedy were active-positive Presidents. Their characters, world views, and styles—and the character-rooted difficulties each managed to transcend—emerge best when we start at the beginning and move, as they did, toward their futures as Presidents.

FRANKLIN'S GROWTH TO JOY IN WORK

The puzzle of Franklin Roosevelt's life is this: where did the force of it come from? Roosevelt as President was obviously a mover and shaker, a man who invested immense energy and flair in the widest range of action. Yet he was one of the least self-revealing of Presidents, especially as regards the driving emotional thrust behind his effort. Similarly, as biographer after biographer has discovered to his dismay, one can excavate thoroughly among his early letters and the other memorabilia his mother saved so religiously, yet find almost no clear message of early psychological drama—no scenes of terror, no fantasies of glory, no poignant confessions of the inevitable doubts and confusions a growing boy experiences. Far more than in other cases, we are thrown back onto inference in trying to understand this most remarkable of all modern Presidents.

Roosevelt remembered the first book his mother read to him again and again, one starting

> Come Lasses and Lads, get leave of your Dads,
> And away to the May-pole hey:
> > For every he
> > Has got him a she,
> With a Minstrel standing by.[1]

But he did not remember—or at least report—what, if anything, that meant to him.

Franklin Delano Roosevelt was the only child of an unlikely union. His mother, Sara Delano, was one of nine children of a New York aristocrat who had made a fortune in the China trade and could trace his ancestry to William the Conqueror. She and her three sisters were called "the beautiful Delano girls" and her father found her too good for any of the "avalanche of young men" who courted her. Sara had dutifully sent each a little note of termination whenever her father required it—until she overrode his objections to marry one of his business associates, James Roosevelt, a widower who, at 52, was twice her age and whose son, James Roosevelt Roosevelt, was as old as she was. Though her father objected to the marriage, he gave her a legacy of one million dollars, despite the fact that James Roosevelt was himself a well heeled lord of the neighboring manor. Franklin was born into this hotbed of Victorian dignity on January 30, 1882, a "splendid large baby boy. He weighs 10 lbs., without clothes," James noted, as if the infant's nakedness were a bit of a surprise. Sara wrote that "Baby Franklin . . . crows and laughs all the time"; she was obviously delighted with him, though she recalled she almost died at his birth from a hefty dose of chloroform. By November, Baby "manages to say a semblance of Papa and Mama" and the following May "Baby walked quite alone. He is quite proud of his new accomplishment." He was by all accounts a charming child.

Three anecdotes give the flavor of Sara's way with Baby. Once when he was about two and a half, she remembered, Baby bit a large chunk of glass out of the side of a tumbler of water. Sara hustled him out of the dining room, fished the glass from his mouth, and "lectured him severely and returned him, penitent, I felt certain, to the table."

> There, if you please, he picked up the goblet with which the steward had replaced the broken glass and pretended, an impish glint in his eyes, to give it the same treatment he had accorded the first.
> "Franklin," I admonished sternly, "where is your obedience?"
> "My 'bedience," Franklin stated solemnly, "has gone upstairs for a walk."[2]

Then there was the time when Sara brought three-year-old Franklin back from Europe on the ship *Germanic*. Two days out, a heavy storm damaged a bulkhead and water poured into the Roosevelt quarters. "Mama, Mama, save my jumping jack!" Franklin howled. Sara, convinced the ship was sinking, wrapped her fur coat around her son. "Poor little boy," she told her husband, "if he must go down he is going down warm."

And one day when Franklin was five, he went into an uncharacteristic depression and could not be amused or distracted. Sara remembered,

> Finally, a little alarmed, I asked him whether he was unhappy. He did not answer at once and then said very seriously,
> "Yes, I am unhappy."
> When I asked him why, he was again silent for a moment or two. Then with a curious little gesture that combined entreaty with a suggestion of impatience, he clasped his hands in front of him and exclaimed,
> "Oh, for freedom!"
> That night, I talked it over with his father who, I confess, often told me I nagged the boy. We agreed that unconsciously we had probably regulated the child's life too closely, even though we knew he had ample time for exercise and play. Evidently he was quite satisfied with what he did with his time, but what worried him was the necessity of conforming to given hours.
> So the very next morning I told him he might do whatever he pleased that day.

He need obey no former rules nor report at any given intervals, and he was allowed to roam at will. We paid no attention to him, and, I must say, he proved his desire for freedom by completely ignoring us. That evening, however, a very dirty, tired youngster came dragging in. He was hungry and ready for bed, but we did not ask him where he had been or what he had been doing. We could only deduce that his adventures had been a little lacking in glamour, for the next day, quite of his own accord, he went contentedly back to his routine.[3]

These were his childhood crises, perhaps embellished somewhat by a mother who wanted to remember the child's independence and her own careful attention to his needs. His life was closely regulated, but lovingly so, by a mother who cared enough for him to leave him alone sometimes, and he played freely and adventuresomely with the small circle of children on the neighboring estates. She nursed him for a year and clothed him in dresses until he was five. The emotional atmosphere was protective but not repressive: "Franklin laughed a lot as a baby," Sara remembered, and he called her "Sallie" and his father "Pops" or "Popsy." He had his own pony at age four. At sixteen he had his own 21-foot sailboat. Yet through his childhood he also had to meet standards and schedules, keeping himself physically presentable and intellectually occupied much of every day. As Sara explained the system she tried to follow,

We never subjected the boy to a lot of unnecessary don'ts, and while certain rules established for his well being had to be rigidly observed, we never were strict merely for the sake of being strict. In fact, we took a secret pride in the fact that Franklin instinctively never seemed to require that kind of handling.[4]

There was structure in his life; but it was largely a structure for behavior, not thought, for performance, not feeling.

Such thought control as there was in the Roosevelt family was attempted mainly by so occupying Franklin's body and soul with healthy activities that he would forget about badness. His father "believed in keeping Franklin's mind on nice things, on a high level; yet he did it in such a way that Franklin never realized that he was following any bent but his own." His father saw to that in person. James Roosevelt presented to the outside (i.e., non-Roosevelt) world an image of stiff formality, beginning with his muttonchop whiskers and top hat and cane. He was wealthy enough to have his own railroad car, eccentric enough to keep five hundred dollars in gold always handy, established enough to refuse an invitation from the *nouveaux riches* Vanderbilts because, "Don't you see, Sallie, that if we accept their invitation, then we shall have to invite them to our house." James went into New York a few days a week to attend to business, but he was essentially the country squire. He participated faithfully, with his brains as well as his money, in numerous charitable and community enterprises. He not only "belonged," he set the criteria for belonging. He and Sara communicated to Franklin a strong sense of membership in a culture with its own givens. And there was at least this much romance in his history: once he had enlisted in Garibaldi's army for a month.

But for all his external sternness, James was Franklin's frequent companion, coach, and teacher. Franklin saw how Sara deferred to him. She ran the house, but James was in charge outdoors. Franklin followed along on his tours of the estate and by his sixth year Sara was regularly recording that "James took Franklin out ice-boating. . . . James coasted with Franklin yesterday and the day before. . . . Franklin tobogganing with James." In the summer father and son rode horses, hunted, swam, sailed boats together, and every day they walked into town to get the mail. The learning the boy experienced was full of action and specifics—how to deal with fog, trees, ice, postage stamps, fish. There was not much theory in it and not much room for standing by and watching.

Franklin, who had a great enthusiasm for sailing and for tales of the Navy, once announced he intended to go to Annapolis and become a naval officer.

> James took his son aside and with firmness told him that a nautical life was out of the question. An only child who expected to inherit an estate, James explained, could not choose the navy for it would take him too far from home. Franklin must remain on dry land—if possible, the land of Duchess County. "Study law as I did," James advised. "It prepares a man for any profession."[5]

Eventually, Franklin did study law. He also became a high naval officer. His talent for combining opposites went way back.

Throughout Franklin's childhood, the Roosevelts traveled continually, sometimes with him along, sometimes leaving him in the care of nurses and tutors at home, sometimes sending him off on his own, so that he also learned some independence. He was taken to Europe when he was two years old, left at home when he was four while his parents went to Mexico for three months. (They hurried back when he got scarlet fever.) The family kept a large apartment in New York City and a summer home at Campobello, an island off the Maine coast. They spent much time in both places. James took his son several times to the White House, where he remembered meeting an exhausted President Cleveland and later an exuberant President Roosevelt. It was in London that seven-year-old Franklin finally persuaded his mother to let him out of kilts and into sailor suits. Thus the characters circulated from time to time; the intensity of Franklin's relationship with his parents was modified, his independence strengthened, by frequent separations. At the same time, their home was always Hyde Park, waiting there, wide and familiar, for times of reunion.

"In the long shelf of the biographies of American Presidents," Karl Schriftgiesser wrote, "one searches in vain for the story of a childhood more serene and secure." Serene and secure it was, but not serene in the sense of passivity, not secure in the sense of unchallenging. Like other children, Franklin Roosevelt had to adapt to the environment he progressively discovered. His parents set a framework within which he could develop, but they were not forever urging him on to make something of himself and they did not simply coddle him into eternal babyhood. He was expected to get along; he spent much of his time with adults, met many strangers. His parent seem to have demonstrated to him that in human relations one can be caring without being anxious, and to have provided so many channels for working on things that Franklin developed little inclination to work on himself. By the time he went away to school at Groton, Franklin had a character substantial in self-esteem, reaching out in action to master things and charm people, the whole leavened with laughter. The portents were still obscure. A letter he wrote his mother when he was nearly six perhaps gave a clue:

> my dear mama
>   we coasted! yesterday nothing dangerous yet, look out for tomorrow!!
> your boy.
>
>   F.

He learned with his head, also. At home Franklin's schooling was in the hands of tutors, each of whom lasted as long as he or she could keep Sara's confidence. The boy was rather shy with the servants and teachers, had trouble "hiding the self-consciousness he felt when he spoke to anyone other than the members of the immediate family," Sara recalled. One tutor, at least, left a lasting impression on his mind: Mlle. Jeanne Sandoz. Her subjects were French and English, but she also began his discovery, in an abstract way, of people beyond Hyde Park and their troubles. Later President Roosevelt wrote, "I have often thought that it was you, more than anyone else, who laid the foundation for my education." "Franklin works well," she said in her first report, "but his obedience aside from his lessons leaves much to be desired." To a degree, Mlle. Sandoz managed to stretch Franklin's mind beyond the boundaries of a family in which, by Sara's tradition, "older members . . . carefully kept away from the children all traces of sadness or trouble or the news of anything alarming."

Mlle. Sandoz got him thinking about trouble; he appreciated it with typical Roosevelt gusto; in his composition on Egypt, based in part on *The River War* (by a young Englishman named Winston Churchill), he wrote, "The working people had nothing. . . . The Kings made them work so hard and gave them so little that by wingo! they nearly starved and by jinks! they had hardly any clothes so they died in quadrillions." For six hours a day, Mlle. Sandoz gave him lessons, so her influence with him must have been considerable. But he was not yet terribly serious about learning or anything else; his was the wit of the ten year old: "I am flourishing & have only fallen 3 times from the top story window," he wrote his mother. "With bales of love to everybody Your devoted baby NILKNARF." He read a lot, liked Mark Twain best, and later said, "If people like my choice of words and my oratorical style, it is largely due to my constant study of Twain's works which have influenced me more than any other writer." From *A Connecticut Yankee* he got the phrase "new deal."

Religion was a given in the Roosevelt family, but there is no evidence it made any great impact on him in his early years. It meant church; occasionally he would avoid attending by coming down with "what his dear Popsy calls a Sunday headache," much as he would dodge piano lessons by pleading pain from a slightly scratched finger. Tales of the sea caught his imagination more than the parables of scripture as he spent hours in the attic poring over canvas-bound log books of early nineteenth-century whaling ships.

In those years Franklin did not appear concerned about values or troubled by questions of right and wrong. He absorbed a culture so all-pervasive in his life that it needed no vigorous assertion.

At fourteen, Franklin went to Groton School. His parents had registered him there when he was two years old. Groton stressed "Christianity, character, and muscle"; the boys lived in six-by-ten cubicles, rose at seven each morning and took a cold shower, pursued a rigorous round of study and exercise all day, dressed formally for dinner, and ended the day with another study period and a handshake for the Rector and his wife. Franklin joined a class of students who had already been at Groton for two years, and he was physically and perhaps psychologically a bit behind his age in development. In general, he got on well enough with the tight knots of peerdom, though he was always somewhat apart from the rest. He tried hard in athletics, but his light build kept him from making a strong record in sports. His records in conduct and punctuality were clean as a whistle until, near the end of his first year, he realized how this could harm his reputation with the boys: "I have served off my first black-mark today, and I am very glad I got it, as I was thought to have no school spirit before." He sang soprano in the choir until his voice cracked, cheered at football victories— "Hurrah, Hurrah, Hurrah, GROTON 46, St. Marks 0, I am hoarse, deaf, and ready to stand on my cocoanut!"—and at last won an athletic event, the high kick, by hitting with his foot a pan suspended seven feet three and one-half inches above the floor. His side won in a debate: he was "not at all nervous" and his speech "came out without a hitch." All of this—plus his characteristic charm—helped him find his way to an acceptable place among his classmates during his first year at Groton, though that place was nothing like the spot he had occupied at home as the center of the universe. Nevertheless, he felt a new independence. When summer came and his parents were in Germany, Franklin accepted an invitation from a cousin to a party on the Fourth of July. Sara sent a veto. Franklin replied that she had said he could make his own plans and asked, "Please don't make any more arrangements for my future happiness." Then he wrote to her to announce he was going to spend the Fourth at Oyster Bay with Theodore Roosevelt. Sara did not like that, either, and Franklin replied:

> I am sorry you didn't want me to go to Oyster Bay for the 4th but I had already accepted Cousin Theodore's invitation & I shall enjoy it very much. . . . I am so sorry you have refused Cousin Bammie's invitation and I wish you had let me make my own plans as you said. As it is, I have accepted Theodore's invitation and I hope you will not refuse that too."[6]

Not a real rebellion, but also not the automatic conformity Sara may have expected. Most of his life Franklin Roosevelt handled pressures against his will by ignoring them, going his own way, or finding some part of the demand he could meet.

In terms of social adaptation, then, Franklin at Groton moved a notch away from his family, found he could relate to strangers—though all of his own social class—in a pleasant, casual way, and learned to persist—as in football—in group endeavors even when they seemed too difficult for him.

In terms of his developing world view, Franklin was most affected by two leading figures who became his models. One was Endicott Peabody, Headmaster of Groton. "As long as I live, the influence of Dr. and Mrs. Peabody means and will mean more to me than that of any other people next to my father and mother," Roosevelt said. Peabody was a formidable-looking, tall, handsome Yankee Christian with a golden heart; he looked after his boys as he would a family, admonishing, encouraging, inquiring. W. Averell Harriman, another young Grotonian, said of Peabody, "You know he would be an awful bully if he weren't such a terrible Christian." The headmaster was out to develop "manly Christian character," as he put it, and he meant to make the well-off Groton boys agents of social betterment. He preached service, service, service, the ministry and stewardship of the privileged as churchmen, businessmen, countrymen. In daily chapel, in innumerable talks, and in the whole atmosphere he established at Groton, Peabody rang the chimes for service. "How distressing the political outlook seems to be! One looks almost in vain for men who are willing to serve their country," he said two years before Franklin's arrival at Groton. "If some Groton boys do not enter political life and do something for our land it won't be because they have not been urged." He cared little for examining into theological puzzles; his "was the faith of a man of action, a spiritual athlete, rather than a contemplative scholar, and Roosevelt came to accept it as his own," Frank Freidel explains. The insistent lesson was: put your faith into works. Franklin joined the headmaster's confirmation class, was elected to the Missionary Society, and worked briefly in a camp for underprivileged boys Peabody had established. As President, Roosevelt recalled to Peabody that "More than forty years ago you said, in a sermon in the Old Chapel, something about not losing boyhood ideals in later life. Those were Groton ideals—taught by you—I try not to forget—and your words are still with me."

Sometimes the headmaster invited Franklin's friend and cousin, Theodore Roosevelt, to speak at chapel. Franklin was the only Democrat among Groton's one hundred and fifty students, but this did nothing to inhibit his admiration for TR, who, by the time Franklin graduated in 1900, was probably the most famous man in America. (He was also one of the most complex characters ever to reach the Presidency, given to fighting off personal depression with action: "Black care rarely sits beside the rider whose pace is fast enough," TR said.) For Franklin, Theodore Roosevelt reinforced with ties of blood and dramatic excitement the same lessons Peabody communicated more stiffly. When TR spoke at Groton, Franklin reported, "After supper tonight, cousin Theodore gave us a splendid talk on his adventures on the Police Board. He kept the whole room in an uproar for an hour telling us killing stories about policemen." The boy's attention followed Theodore's, then Assistant Secretary of the Navy, as war with Spain approached. Franklin had been reading over the works of Alfred

Thayer Mahan on sea power, and debating on the annexation of Hawaii from a Mahanian standpoint. When the battleship *Maine* was blown up in Havana harbor, Franklin wrote "We heard the news . . . & everyone is much excited. If the accident turns out to have been done by the Spaniards, I think the whole school [will] take up arms and sail to Spain!" The war excitement reached fever pitch with cousin Theodore's charge up San Juan Hill; Franklin and his roommate decided to sneak away to Boston in a pieman's cart and enlist, a plan cut short when both boys developed scarlet fever. Theodore ran for governor of New York that fall and won: "We were all wild with delight when we heard of Teddy's election," Franklin wrote, "the whole dormitory went mad."

At graduation time, Theodore Roosevelt gave a stirring speech at Groton: "If a man has courage, goodness, and brains, no limit can be placed to the greatness of the work he may accomplish—he is the man needed today in politics." From his father, from Peabody, from Theodore, the message was the same: "Serve the Lord with gladness"—and do it by undertaking some stewardship in the practical world.

"At Groton, Roosevelt learned to get along with his contemporaries," Freidel writes, "at Harvard he learned to lead them." There he did moderately well at his studies and far better, once he got onto it, at being a candidate for all conceivable offices. He began again with football, but was too light to make the team. He tried rowing and singing in the freshman glee club. At the sports and songs themselves he was not particularly distinguished, but he was elected captain of the scrub football team, captain of the third crew of the Newell Boating Club, and secretary of the freshman glee club. He was elected, among sixty-eight original candidates, one of the five editors of the Harvard *Crimson*, and soon he became president (editor-in-chief). He missed being taken into the most elite club, Porcellian; this was such a hard blow that Eleanor Roosevelt thought it gave Franklin an inferiority complex. But he went on to become head librarian of the Fly Club, was elected to the library committee of the Harvard Union, and librarian of the Hasty Pudding Club. At his graduation he was one of six nominees for Class Marshal and was elected Permanent Chairman of the Class Committee by an easy margin, winning 168 of the 253 votes.

Later he was to write that "Perhaps the most useful preparation I had in college for public service was . . . [on] the Harvard Crimson." As *Crimson* president, Roosevelt returned to Harvard for a fourth year, though he had satisfied the degree requirements in three. "Every spare moment has been taken up with the paper," he wrote. He preached the doctrine of active service: the Harvard student owed "responsibility to the University, to his class and to himself!" he exclaimed editorially. "The only way to fulfill this is to be always active. The opportunities are almost unlimited: There are athletics—a dozen kinds—and athletic managements, literary work on the University publications and the outside press, philanthropic and religious work, and the many other interests that are bound to exist"—among the last, one must suppose, he included studying.

Like Woodrow Wilson of the *Princetonian*, Roosevelt of the *Crimson* devoted a great many editorials to berating the football team, urging them on to

victory. "All that is needed is a spirit in the team of aggressive, vigorous determination"—and so on. FDR persisted along this line until a third-year law student, Henry James II, urged an end to "dealing out editorial sarcasms . . . to
amateur athletes." If Roosevelt continued his line, "The fun of the game will be
spoilt for all," James wrote. Roosevelt kept writing editorials on the subject, but
their tone became more moderate. Here as in other situations, Roosevelt listened
and responded to what he heard. He managed the *Crimson* staff effectively and
gracefully; his co-editor remembered that "in his geniality was a kind of fric-
tionless command."

Meanwhile his personal life was developing new dimensions. In December of his freshman year, Franklin's father died of heart failure. He was 72.
Sara was stunned: "I wonder how I lived when he left me." But James in his will
gave her welcome instruction: "I do hereby appoint my wife sole guardian of my
son Franklin D. Roosevelt, and I want him under the supervision of his mother."
She tried to keep busy, to take over a good deal of James's fatherly responsibility.
But she was lonely and at loose ends, wanting to be with Franklin. The summer
before he became a sophomore, he and his mother went again to Europe, where,
in Paris in September, they got the news that President McKinley had been shot.
On the way home they learned of McKinley's death and the elevation of Cousin
Theodore to the Presidency.

One effect of these experiences was to heighten Franklin's interest in
genealogy; he determined to write a term paper on the family and asked his
mother to send him copies of the entries in the front of the family Bible. After
detailing the relationships among his ancestors, Roosevelt the Harvard sophomore revealed what it all meant to him:

> Some of the famous Dutch families in New York have today nothing left but
> their name—they are few in numbers, they lack progressiveness, and a true
> democratic spirit. One reason—perhaps the chief—of the virility of the Roose-
> velts is this very democratic spirit. They have never felt that because they were
> born in a good position they could put their hands in their pockets and succeed.
> They have felt, rather, that, being born in a good position, there was no excuse
> for them if they did not do their duty by the community, and it is because this
> idea was instilled into them from birth that they have in nearly every case proved
> good citizens.[7]

That was the ideal. Franklin majored in political history and government, working hard enough to make decent grades without excessive effort, and the idea of
channeling this ideal into politics must have occurred to him more frequently as
Theodore's star rose. His distillation from the family tradition might as easily
have manifested itself in an emphasis on his father's role as country squire or on
the simplicity and gracefulness established wealth allowed, or on Dutch persistence and stubbornness. Instead, he stressed the family's "true democratic
spirit"—not democratic in the sense of identifying with the masses, not some
assertion of fundamental equality, but rather the command to do voluntarily
what others had to do of necessity—work—and to direct those energies outward

to "the community," not into mere money-making. To Endicott Peabody's preachings and Theodore Roosevelt's example was now added Franklin's own explicit internalization of what he saw of his inheritance from his father's line.

In the winter of his sophomore year, Sara decided she had had enough of sitting with her sister by the fire at Hyde Park, reading aloud from *Paradise Lost* and Dante's *Inferno;* she moved into an apartment in Boston to be near Franklin—"near enough to the University to be on hand should he want me and far enough removed not to interfere with his college life." For the rest of his sophomore and on into his junior year, she saw her son frequently, had parties for him, but tolerated separations while he tended to Harvard. She bought a town house in New York; she assumed he would be studying law there later and wanted to connect him with New York society. She seemed to be developing a vision of a life in which she could, in person, keep Franklin "under the supervision of his mother."

Then, suddenly, in the fall of his junior year in college, Franklin stunned Sara with the news that he planned to marry his cousin Eleanor Roosevelt as soon as possible. "Franklin gave me quite a startling announcement," she wrote in her diary. She reminded Franklin (who, she thought, much resembled her father, more a Delano than a Roosevelt) that her own father had not married until he was 33 and had become "a man who had made a name and a place for himself, who had something to offer a woman." Franklin at 21 was still a boy to her. He wrote a characteristic letter combining insistence with sympathy:

> Dearest Mama—
> I know what pain I must have caused you and you know I wouldn't do it if I really could have helped it . . . ! I know my mind, have known it for a long time, and know that I could never think otherwise: Result: I am the happiest man just now in the world; likewise the luckiest—And for you, dear Mummy, you know that nothing can ever change what we have always been & always will be to each other—only now you have two children to love & to love you—and Eleanor as you know will always be a daughter to you in every true way—[8]

Eleanor wrote her "Dearest Cousin Sallie" to say "I know just how you feel and how hard it must be, but I do so want you to learn to love me a little. You must know that I will always try to do what you wish for I have grown to love you very dearly during the past summer." Eleanor was eighteen years old.

Sara fought back. She counseled delay. She arranged for Franklin and his roommate to take a Caribbean cruise in February, but he returned as anxious to see Eleanor as ever. She tried to get her friend Joseph Choate, Ambassador to England, to take Franklin on as his secretary. Nothing worked. Franklin would have her. On St. Patrick's Day, 1905, 23-year-old Franklin was married. (The date was set so Theodore Roosevelt could attend; on March 4, Franklin and Eleanor went to his inauguration, where they heard the man who had campaigned as "The Happy Warrior" say, "All I ask is a Square Deal for every man.")

Once it was clear to Sara that Franklin was going to have his own way this time, she accepted defeat gracefully, wrote of "an added joy to have Eleanor now." But her way of accepting her daughter-in-law was to treat her as she wanted to treat Franklin: as her child, to be watched over and "helped." Eleanor was a prime candidate for help. She became one of those rare persons who manage to fashion, from the energies of intense early conflicts, an adult life of extraordinary creativity. Eleanor vastly understated the case when she said, "I was not a very happy little girl." Her beautiful socialite mother teased her for her ugliness, called her "Granny," berated her as a criminal for minor offenses, and made the little girl rub her mother's forehead for hours as treatment for her splitting headaches. Mother died when Eleanor was eight. Father was a handsome horseman and chronic alcoholic, increasingly away in sanitoria, who called the child "Golden Hair" and stood in her mind as a dashing prince who would come to rescue her; she would stand for hours at the front window, waiting for him to come home. He died when she was nine. Eleanor was passed on to her mother's mother, who disciplined her severely, made her wear little-girl dresses and pigtails on into her gangling adolescence, and taught her "Never cry where people are, cry by yourself." All in all, it was a hell of a childhood. One bright spot was the day her cousin Franklin had asked her to dance.

Franklin Roosevelt was not given to introspection, to serious discussion of family feelings, or to autobiographical accounts of his intimate life. Why he chose Eleanor remains an historical blank. Perhaps her shy delicacy, her quick mind, and the fact that she was Theodore Roosevelt's niece entered into his decision. He liked women, enjoyed their conversation, but at Harvard "Franklin had no serious affair with any girl, which was remarkable in view of his exuberance." Much later he did have a serious affair, with Eleanor's beautiful social secretary Lucy Mercer, but that ended when the consequences of divorce were brought home to him. At the beginning of their marriage, however, Franklin and Eleanor seemed to be thoroughly in love.

Sara took over. She virtually set the young couple up in housekeeping, tying them to her with money, directing the maids and nurses. She had two adjoining houses built in New York—one for Franklin and Eleanor, the other for herself, with one entrance, connecting doors, and matched dining and drawing rooms which could be opened together for joint entertaining. She hired the servants and saw to the decorations. When children came, she continually bypassed Eleanor to supervise their upbringing. Eleanor had to quit her settlement house work because Sara said she would bring germs home to the baby. The first two children were sickly and the third died of influenza at eight months. Eleanor was often despondent. "I was beginning to become an entirely dependent woman," she recalled. "I was completely taken care of. My mother-in-law did everything for me." She felt she was disappearing: "I was not developing any individual taste or initiative. I was simply absorbing the personalities of those around me and letting their tastes and interests dominate mine." But her training in self-repression kept her from unburdening herself to her husband.

On one occasion she did let Franklin know her feelings, and Roosevelt's response reveals an unattractive quality which would later add an important dimension to his Presidential style. He found Eleanor weeping at her dressing table and asked in bewilderment, "What on earth is the matter?" She said, "I do not like living in a house that is in no way mine, on which I have done nothing about and does not represent the way I want to live." Franklin said, "You are quite mad," told her everything would be all right, and left the room. Coldly, insensitively, he thrust aside a problem he could see no way to solve and was unwilling to sympathize with.

Not until years later, when Roosevelt got polio and Sara tried to make an invalid of him, did Eleanor win out by firing the nurses and creating an active, encouraging environment for her husband. The same man who seemed so oblivious of his wife's despair was led—largely by Eleanor—to confront suffering more directly. Once, before they were married, Franklin met her at the Rivington Street Settlement House in the heart of New York slumland. She took him along to visit a sick child, climbing up three flights of local atmosphere to a small room where the family lived. Back out on the sidewalk, Franklin looked decidedly ill. "My God!" he said, "I didn't know people lived like that!"

For five years after his graduation from Harvard, Roosevelt drifted. Freidel calls this his "dormant phase"; Erik Erikson might call it a psycho-social moratorium. In the fall of 1904 Franklin entered Columbia Law School; he got through all right, though he found it dull and was impressed with "how unimportant the law really is." He joined a conservative law firm and joked about "his unexcelled facilities for carrying on every description of legal business. Unpaid bills a specialty. Briefs on the liquor question furnished free to ladies. Race suicides cheerfully prosecuted. Small dogs chloroformed without charge. Babies raised under advice of expert grandmother etc. etc. etc." He was taking his time. "Everybody called him Franklin and regarded him as a harmless bust," a friend remembered. "He had a sanguine temperament, almost adolescent in its buoyancy." Court work brought further contact with "the poorer classes." In one case, Franklin opposed a somewhat impoverished attorney representing a decidedly impoverished woman pressing a claim against a corporation. The other lawyer in desperation asked for a settlement out of court for 300, then 150 dollars; the actual damage was eighteen dollars. When FDR got the whole story—the poverty was evident—he settled for thirty-five dollars and left a check for his personal loan of a hundred and fifty dollars.

By 1910, at Cousin Theodore's urging, Roosevelt was ready to go into politics. Tales which may represent reality have him plotting out his march to the Presidency at this point. More likely is the story that he was visited at Hyde Park by a local politician looking to recruit this rich, presentable, and well named fellow for the state assembly. The politician popped the question and Roosevelt's eyes lit up. "But," he said, "I'd like to talk to my mother about it first." "Frank," the pol replied sternly, "there are men back in Poughkeepsie waiting for your answer. They won't like to hear you had to ask your mother." Franklin said, "I'll do it."

The man he was slated to replace thought him no replacement, and angrily declared he would run again. Equally angry, Franklin told them, "I've got to run! I've told everybody I'm going to!" They shifted him to a bigger senatorial district, and he was off and running, touring the countryside in a red Maxwell car, shaking hands, beginning his speeches, "My friends . . . ," confessing "I am no orator but . . . " and "I'm not Teddy," calling most anything good "bully," coming out against the bosses and for civic virtue in the broad sense. He won by a margin of 1,140 votes of 32,000 cast, running ahead of the ticket.

Eleanor and Franklin moved to Albany. Sara came along to help with the moving and arranging, but soon returned home, leaving Eleanor to fend for herself with three nurses and three housemaids. Franklin promptly joined an insurgent faction working to upset the election of "Blue-eyed Bill" Sheehan, the Tammanyite, for the U.S. Senate. Soon the rebels made him their chairman. "There is nothing I love as much as a good fight," Roosevelt told the *New York Times*. "I never had as much fun in my life as I am having right now." He looked like a prig; Louis McHenry Howe, then a reporter but soon to join FDR and see him through his first term as President, sized him up as "a spoiled, silk-pants sort of a guy" at first, and Frances Perkins, who became his Secretary of Labor, recalled the new Senator this way:

> I have a vivid picture of him operating on the floor of the Senate: tall and slender, very active and alert, moving around the floor, going in and out of committee rooms, rarely talking with the members, who more or less avoided him, not particularly charming (that came later), artificially serious of face, rarely smiling, with an unfortunate habit—so natural that he was unaware of it—of throwing his head up. This, combined with his pince-nez and great height, gave him the appearance of looking down his nose at most people. . . .[9]

The Tammany regulars found him insufferable at the beginning, but Howe liked his spunk ("Mein Gawd, the boy's got courage"). The fight was won, in a way: Sheehan was ousted but another Tammany man was put in his place. TR wrote to say "we are all really proud of the way you handled yourself. Good luck to you!" Stubbornness won for Roosevelt that time; his fight was mainly a defensive one. But he was growing along the way. Later he remembered those times:

> Now I was in politics, now I was a politician. This moment of first success is perhaps the most dangerous crisis in the career of anyone in politics. Up to this moment, his action has been based on theory. Now he must act. . . . I found myself actively engaged with the details of government, and though I had studied these problems in the theoretical form, I found them even more absorbingly interesting because of their concreteness and their human application.[10]

To a degree his legislative experience gave Roosevelt a wider understanding of how the other half lived. But his main immediate experience of the human dimension was with the Albany politicians. "One pleasant feature is the good-fellowship of my twenty comrades in the insurgent movement," he wrote. They met at his house; so much cigar smoke seeped through the ceiling that Eleanor had to move the children's bedroom to the third floor. All along he was listening and learning from the pros:

How to avoid taking a stand on issues and becoming involved in destructive local squabbles, how to deal with local party-leaders, how to handle patronage without making an undue number of enemies, how to attract publicity, how to answer importunate letters. Above all, he learned the lesson that a democratic politician must learn: that the political battle is not a simple two-sided contest . . . but a many sided struggle that moved over broad sectors and touched many interests.[11]

And always there was the same speculation: would he turn out to be another TR?

The clerk of the state senate, speaking for a good many of his colleagues, thought not. He identified Roosevelt among "the snobs in our party . . . political accidents . . . the little fellows, fops and cads who come as near being political leaders as a green pea does a circus tent."

But shortly, when he was asked to take on Theodore's old job as Assistant Secretary of the Navy, FDR said, "How would I like it? I'd like it bully well."

Roosevelt completed his basic training for the Presidency in the seven years he served as Assistant Secretary. He began with typical enthusiasm: "I am baptized, confirmed, sworn in, vaccinated—and somewhat at sea!" He was 31 years old, so young and young looking that Senators and Navy wives mistook him for a college boy. Yet before too long he was issuing orders to admirals twice his age. Part of the attention and respect he got were paid to his name or his office, which Theodore had made a font of publicity, as FDR was not above reminding people. As Assistant Secretary TR had once bided his time until the Secretary was absent for a few days and then issued orders to Commodore Dewey to attack Manila in the event of war with Spain. FDR's boss Josephus Daniels left briefly and Roosevelt jokingly told reporters, "There's a Roosevelt on the job today. . . . You remember what happened the last time a Roosevelt occupied a similar position?"

Basically he was in charge of the business affairs of the Navy, with the help of Louis Howe, brought along from Albany. He handled personnel and budget matters primarily, but unlike other Departments the Navy had only one Assistant Secretary, so he got "my fingers into about everything and there's no law against it." The peacetime Navy was a sprawling, loose-jointed organization, not fully through the transition from sail to steam, an outfit which seemed immense at the time, with 65,000 officers and men and an annual appropriation of $143,497,000. FDR was an old sailor; he loved the panoply and seafaring talk: "I now find my vocation combined with my avocation in a delightful way." On inspection trips he would take command of whatever vessel he was aboard, often taking the wheel under the eye of a nervous captain. His ebullience, ready laughter, and obvious delight in things Navy enlivened the existence of many a sluggish command.

His transition to Washington society, greased by the TR connection and by FDR's own social assurance, came easily. Henry Adams, Louis Brandeis, Oliver Wendell Holmes, Henry Cabot Lodge, were in his social round, and he helped organize the Common Counsel Club of twenty administration and Congressional leaders who met for lunch and discussed how to win TR's disillusioned followers over to the Democratic party. The Washington elite liked him—as an easygoing, amusing, bright young man, not much more. Eleanor, that shy and delicate lady, undertook to call on some ten to thirty wives of dignitaries each day four days a week—Monday Supreme Court, Tuesday Representatives, Thursday Senators, Friday diplomats. Much of her shyness left her in this ordeal as she stepped over threshold after threshold saying, "I am Mrs. Franklin D. Roosevelt. My husband has just come as Assistant Secretary of the Navy."

Roosevelt was for a bigger Navy, but beyond that and perhaps a few themes from Mahan on sea power, he had no theory. He thrived on specifics, on the situation and what could be done with it. And he learned about situations directly. As James MacGregor Burns writes,

> It was by people—all sorts of people—that he continued to be educated in the tough, knotty ways of government. "Young Roosevelt is very promising, but I should think he'd wear himself out in the promiscuous and extended contacts he maintains with people," Secretary Newton Baker said to Frances Perkins. "But as I observe him, he seems to clarify his ideas and teach himself as he goes along by that very conversational method."[12]

Louis Howe insisted that FDR personally attend hearings on labor policy, so he would get the gist of it first hand. By that route he learned enough and got close enough to contestants on labor issues to keep in the good graces of all sides. Howe helped by taking a good deal of the heat and by modifying Roosevelt's enthusiasm for almost anyone with a bright idea for quick action. Roosevelt was never very careful about authorship; he would adopt as his own whatever good plans he heard. He preached togetherness: "Nothing to my mind promotes efficiency so much as the feeling amongst the employees that they are 'all members of the same club.'" And he invited all and sundry to come see him in Washington: "I want you all to feel that you can come to me at any time in my office, and we can talk matters over. Let's get together for I need you to teach me your business and show me what is going on."

That was his remarkable talent as an executive: to listen, to decide, to cut through bureaucratic knots, and to get some favorable action—never everything—out the other end, meanwhile placing himself at the center of decision, taking full credit for whatever worked out well. For example, FDR had to deal with the incredibly tangled system for setting wage rates in navy yards, a morass of boards, reports, appeals, and so forth, which left the workers feeling suspicious and exploited. Less than a week after he arrived in Washington, he received a delegation from the Brooklyn Navy Yard asking that he change the system for fixing their wages. FDR remembered their talk this way:

> I said, "Fine. How is it done?" "Well," they said, "do it yourself." I said, "Why, hasn't it been done by the Assistant Secretary in the past?" "No, it had been done by the officers." And then they went on to tell me how unjustly the wage scales in all of the Navy Yards on both coasts and on the Gulf of Mexico had been arranged each year by a special board of officers. After I had been there I think

three days longer, I got Joe Daniels to sign an order making it the duty of the Assistant Secretary to fix the wage scale each year.[13]

Sounds simple; in fact, despite a few minor changes, the system remained about what it was. What changed was the performance of the Assistant Secretary, who got himself into the process at several key points, got some minor raises for the employees, and established himself as the man to see on wage problems. What he did not do was worry, get lost, back away, pass the buck, pontificate, alienate opponents, reorganize everything, wait out endless studies, or come on all modest. His simplicity—infuriating to his more sophisticated and cynical critics—certainly appeared genuine to those who shared his desire to get something done.

Roosevelt experimented. That is, he did not claim that he knew the correct answer but he acted so as to find out. Nearly every large question he was involved in was a mix of policy, technique, politics, and business. Roosevelt would make a move and see what happened. When three major steel companies came in with identical high bids for armor plate contracts, Roosevelt, at Daniels' command, got a British bid, much lower, and forced the price down. He got other contracts awarded to foreign companies. But when the American manufacturers denounced this as unpatriotic and began to pick up support, Roosevelt retreated. as in May 1914 when he let an American firm have a flag contract rather than give it to a Canadian outfit with a much lower bid. Seeking a bargain on coal, he bought some of questionable quality. There was a Congressional investigation. Representative Roberts pursued him:

Now, the reports on the Vinton coal, which the Willard Bros. . . .

MR. ROOSEVELT: (interposing). That was an experimental contract which has since been stricken from the list.

MR. ROBERTS: The contract has been cancelled?

MR. ROOSEVELT: Yes, sir.

MR. ROBERTS: And are you taking any coal from Willard Bros.?

MR. ROOSEVELT: No sir; it was frankly an experimental contract to see whether the coal would turn out well. We only took a few hundred tons out of a contract for 5,000 tons, and we shall take no more.[14]

His attitude continually combined vigorous action with tentative commitment—and attention to results.

He took risks also with himself. From the start an advocate of a bigger Navy, Roosevelt progressively moved out in front of Wilson and Daniels, riding the gathering wave of preparedness sentiment as the danger of war increased. He issued a statement in support of radical expansion, though Wilson had laughed off such proposals a few days before. "Even if it gets me into trouble I am perfectly ready to stand by it," he told Eleanor. "The country needs the truth about the Army and Navy instead of a lot of the soft mush about everlasting peace which so many statesmen are handing out to a gullible public." The press picked it up. Daniels was not amused, but FDR continued to talk out, although a bit more cautiously. He took to purveying the "facts"—selected details calculated to enhance his case without committing his authority. Later he fed pro-expansion information to Daniels' most vehement political opponent, a misdemeanor the Secretary chose to overlook.

Like Theodore, he liked to put his body on the line. When he set up a calisthenics program for Navy personnel, there he was, early in the morning in his shirt sleeves, hup-two-threeing with the other bureaucrats and Congressmen under Yale coach Walter Camp's direction. When a submarine failed to surface off Pearl Harbor and all aboard were lost, FDR quickly boarded one in Los Angeles in a heavy sea and had it go through its underwater paces.

Perhaps building on his diplomatic experience with his mother, he practiced suiting his message to its target, as in this House-written note to President Wilson:

> I want to tell you simply that you have been in my thoughts during these days and that I realize to the full all that you have had to go through—I need not repeat to you my own entire loyalty and devotion—that I hope you know. But I feel most strongly that the Nation approves and sustains your course and that it is *American* in the highest sense.[15]

Wilson returned a note of warm appreciation.

FDR rarely invented policies, but he absorbed inventions from all direction, listening attentively to the most harebrained schemes and selecting from all that he heard what he wanted. "He was a great trial-and-error guy," a naval contractor said, "but he did have some good ideas." Freidel observes that

> When . . . he had an idea that was rejected, he would often take it from one man to another until he found someone who liked it. Then, armed with the approval of that one person, he would take it back and use the approval to beat down one after another of those who had disagreed. In that way, he would usually win a compromise.[16]

Sometimes he lost, but: "I have about come to the conclusion that there is an awful lot of luck in this game, anyway."

In 1914, FDR leapt into the political fray to run for Senator from New York. Overriding Daniels' advice and, most significantly, failing to consult his temporarily absent political wizard, Louis Howe, FDR plunged ahead, campaigned as vigorously as his Washington duties allowed, and went down to a two-to-one defeat. Undismayed, he said with considerable exaggeration, "On the whole, I think the primary fight was well worthwhile as I carried a majority of the counties of the State and was beaten only through the solid line-up of New York City." This and the defeat of other progressive Democrats in New York at last convinced FDR that coalition with the city machine was the only way to victory.

Through these seven fat years of adventure, Franklin Roosevelt enjoyed the ebullience, if not the arrogance, of power. "I am *running* the real work;

although Josephus is here!" he wrote Eleanor. "He is bewildered by it all, very sweet but very sad!" Sometimes his superior nettled him: "J.D. is too damned slow for words—his failure to decide the few big things holds me up all down the line." His impatience was open enough; once he began a note to the Secretary, "Do *please* get through two vital things *today*." And he could also joke with his superior, sending him copies of a requisition for eight carpet tacks. Photographs of him at this time—in Washington, inspecting the European forces, wherever— confirm what he said: "I have loved every minute of it."

When he first took on the job, Franklin wrote jubilantly to his mother. She answered "My Dearest Franklin" promptly: "Try not to write your signature too small as it gets a cramped look and is not too distinct. So many public figures have such awful signatures and so unreadable. . . . "

Roosevelt would go on to an almost accidental nomination as Vice President in 1920, his terrible bout with polio, years of unsuccessful if imaginative business enterprise, the governorship of New York, and into the White House. But by 1920 his character, world view, and style had coalesced. He had by then demonstrated to himself and to those who watched him the clear outlines of Roosevelt as President. His illness deepened his personality. Once Eleanor answered a cruel question—"Mrs. Roosevelt, do you think your husband's illness affected his mind?"—with a perceptive answer: "Yes, I think it did. I think it made him more sensitive to the feelings of people."

Roosevelt's flexible style centered in a way of relating to persons. He was not much of a speechmaker, but he slowly found out how to project his conversational manner to audiences. As Assistant Secretary, he got through best to the reporters, who saw his charm, simplicity, and enthusiasm at first hand. Similarly in campaigning, FDR was most effective in his informal words with "My Friends" the voters, even when he had little of substance to say to them. In this as in most else, he had great advantages in that the reporters and the public were curious to see what another Roosevelt in politics would say and do. FDR exploited this attention unabashedly, as he did the social connections his family passed on to him.

He also turned to people for information. In spite of all he read as a youth, Roosevelt the mature politician read little—except when he had to prepare some special case for action. The law in its research aspects never much appealed to him. He got his facts by soaking into his mind what people told him, by constantly asking questions, by listening to the substance of what he was told. Since his mind was forever on the next action, Roosevelt could hear in the midst of much palaver the essential point; if he did not hear it, he asked for it. The great advantage of face-to-face conversation as a method of learning was that he could watch the speaker, gauge his emphases, hear the tone and stress of what was being said, and see how his own ploys and responses were going over— advantages sacrificed by Presidents who rely on the telephone or on written memoranda.

Roosevelt could study hard and he could make formal speeches. His style was no frozen structure. But he was most adept in personal relations, as his

Navy work made strikingly clear. Only in his relationship as a subordinate was there some friction and impatience, but even there the normal tone between Roosevelt and Daniels was cordial good humor. People who thought him a snob made him angry. If he could get to them in person, talk a while, he usually managed to win their respect and affection. His widening acquaintance with people of different classes and backgrounds, helped along by Eleanor and Louis Howe, supplemented a natural inclination to take a fellow on his merits. But even in his earlier family life there had been little need to *assert* superiority, to mark off the Roosevelts from lower orders of humanity. By all accounts, FDR simply was not much interested in demonstrating that he was above anyone else. He was, on the other hand, quite interested in *being* at the top of the heap.

His adroitness in personal relations was evident in the way he managed to stay afloat in the swamps of New York politics and in the whirlpools of the Wilson administration, not to mention the Navy's own eddies, pools, and sink-holes. He learned the knack of communicating interest in the other, curiosity, responsiveness, and a sense of excitement in the mutual endeavor. He knew how to convey acceptance without commitment; Frances Perkins thought he had a way of saying "Yes, of course" when he meant only that he heard. Certainly he left some people baffled about his intentions. In general, the Roosevelt approach was to collect ideas the way he collected stamps, from all and sundry quarters, and then he would decide where to put them.

That was part of his vision of the world. Franklin Roosevelt rarely seems to have felt that discomfort at contradiction that pains the minds of more careful politicians. Perhaps the luxury of his upbringing contributed to that. At Hyde Park so many things were possible. Roosevelt could afford to wait, could mean-der for five years after Harvard without penalty. Time was flexible; space was, too, among the Roosevelts with their wide lands, several homes, distant travels. Franklin seemed to find in his education much less interest in where things came from—objects, ideas, people—than in what they could do, an attitude which gave his mind organization, pointed it toward an imaginable future, but left it free of chains to the past. In politics he had no set ideology. At least after his brawl with the Tammanyites, he learned to seek solutions which would not so much compromise among competing interests as transcend them, include them, give each at least something and the hope of more. He selected among alter-natives not by choosing and eliminating, but by emphasizing and ignoring.

Roosevelt believed in God. Possibly at Groton he developed, behind a bland exterior, a deep and abiding faith, as Rexford Tugwell surmises in *The Democratic Roosevelt*. FDR said little about this; once, when Eleanor brought up the topic of religious training for their children, he said he thought they ought to go to church and learn what he had learned. "I really never thought about it. I think it is just as well not to think about things like that too much," Eleanor remembered him saying. The values Roosevelt spoke of and obviously did think about concerned the obligation to serve—that old theme he picked up from his parents, Mlle. Sandoz, Peabody, Theodore, and Eleanor. The merely privileged, those who made nothing of their gifts or devoted them to amassing wealth as proof of grace, aroused Roosevelt's closest approach to contempt, later to emerge in his disdain for "economic royalists."

Yet the commandment to serve the larger community only added a fillip of principle to what Roosevelt wanted to do anyway. It was in any case a "Thou shalt" commandment, not a prohibition; FDR expected himself to act like a gentleman, but beyond that there were few negative rules at the top of his consciousness. He was not in politics to pursue some "damned duty," as Stimson said of Hoover, but in large part because he liked it. That joyfulness in what he could do stayed with him, sprung out of his character. By accident or design, James and Sara had infused a deep confidence in Franklin Roosevelt, a self-esteem so strong it could overcome the apparent end of his career when he was toppled by polio. And the quality of accretion in his early life, the stage-by-stage building and elaboration of his orientations, give evidence of a sense of the self as developing. FDR grew, sloughing off what he did not need, but mainly adding to his repertoire, deepening his confidence in his stance toward life.

THE ROOSEVELT PRESIDENCY

Franklin Roosevelt became President at a time when the public would have held its breath and supported Joe E. Brown if he seemed likely to do something about the Depression. Somewhere between 12 and 15 million men were unemployed, one family out of seven was on public or private relief, 4,600 banks had failed, half of Michigan's automobile factories were shut down, textile looms in the South were silent, farmers let their crops rot in the fields because it cost more to harvest them than they could sell them for, and in New England men and women worked for one dollar a week. The *New York Times* the day before Roosevelt's inauguration said, "No President . . . ever came to greater opportunities amid so great an outpouring of popular trust and hope." And the day after his inauguration, Will Rogers put it this way: "The whole country is with him just so he does something. If he burned down the capitol we would cheer and say 'Well, we at least got a fire started anyhow.'"

Another type of President, new to the office, might have surveyed the chaos of the country and decided to study the problem. Roosevelt acted. In the flurry of his first hundred days he could hardly send legislative recommendations to Congress fast enough or keep track of their passage amid shouts of "Vote! Vote!" On the administrative side, Harry Hopkins ("Hunger is not debatable") spent $5 million in his first two hours on the job, and later that year put 4 million men to work in just two months, telling FDR, "Well, they're all at work, but for God's sake don't ask me what they're doing." Hoover's gray government was overthrown in a burst of colorful, crusading rhetoric followed by a display of political fireworks such as the nation had not seen since Wilson's first term.

Roosevelt's approach—vigor, hope, humor—rested on his old faith in experiment. "I have no expectation of making a hit every time I come to bat," he said with the verve of a man doing nearly that. "What I seek is the highest possible batting average." Once he told Rexford Tugwell, "You'll have to learn that public life takes a lot of sweat, but it doesn't need to worry you. You won't always be right, but you mustn't suffer from being wrong. That's what kills people like us." And he counseled Frances Perkins, "One thing is sure. We have to do something. We have to do the best we know how at the moment. . . . If it doesn't turn out right, we can modify it as we go along." A lot of it did not turn out right, as Herbert Hoover and others scathingly demonstrated later on into the New Deal. But FDR's experimentalism was not in fact blind to results. Lacking scientific measurement, lacking even the crude social statistics of today, Roosevelt tried to find out how his experiments were working by opening up all sorts of lines of communication and by urging his assistants to go see what was happening where it was happening. "Pay no attention to what people are saying in Washington," he told one. "They are the last persons in the country to listen to." When he could, he went himself, cocking his head to listen to a farmer or a worker tell him what was up. Especially after his first "Fireside Chat," his mail provided an avalanche of raw intelligence which, roughly analyzed, gave him a sense of the concrete human existences out in the "field." For example:

> Dear Mr. President:
>   This is just to tell you that everything is all right now. The man you sent found our house all right, and we went down to the bank with him and the mortgage can go on for a while longer. You remember I wrote you about losing the furniture too. Well, your man got it back for us. I never heard of a President like you. . . .[17]

To Tugwell he said, "Go and see what's happening. See the end product of what we are doing. Talk to people; get the wind in your nose." By far his most relied-upon reporter was Eleanor; Franklin attended much more closely to her observations than to her views on policy. "My Missus says that they have typhoid fever in that district," he would announce to his Cabinet. "My Missus says that people are working for wages way below the minimum set by NRA in the town she visited last week." He could hear, remember, and use these data. H. G. Wells called him "a ganglion for reception, expression, transmission, combination and realization." His was no "Noble Experiment" like Prohibition, wrapped in moralistic beginnings and predetermined conclusions, but a long series of improvisations to be corrected by feedback.

This is not the place to attempt even a summary of what that method did for and to Roosevelt and the country from 1933 to 1945. He never did explain himself in any deep way. But his political personality, clear in its main outlines in 1920, persisted; those who loved him, those who hated him, and the few who were indifferent or entirely objective agreed on his special way with people, his conversational manner in public and private, his energy, his ability to shift quickly from topic to topic, his reliance on personal communication and information-gathering, his memory, and above all the inspiriting or infuriating laughter, which Winston Churchill noted when he said meeting Roosevelt was like opening a bottle of champagne.

At the beginning, however, there were those who had their doubts. Harold Laski dismissed him as "a pill to cure an earthquake" and Walter Lippmann rated him as unqualified:

> Franklin D. Roosevelt is no crusader. He is no tribune of the people. He is no enemy of entrenched privilege. He is a pleasant man, who, without any important qualifications for the office, would very much like to be President. . . . It is in spite of his attractiveness, in spite of his unquestioned personal integrity, in spite of his generous sympathies, that the judgment has formed itself among large numbers of discerning people that here is a man who has made a good governor, who might make a good cabinet officer, but who simply does not measure up to the tremendous demands of the office of President.[18]

His critics wondered if Roosevelt would be another Taft, another Harding, too soft for the job, too casual and agreeable to stand up to the pressures of the Presidency. In terms of basic political character, would Franklin Roosevelt turn out to be a passive-positive type? His continual turning to people seemed to point in that direction. Would he have the toughness to run his own government and, when necessary, fight vigorously against opponents? Then there was the related issue of his integrity, which was something Lippmann did not question but which others did. Would Franklin Roosevelt have the moral fiber to protect the national values, the Constitution, the fundamental rights and institutions? Or would he cave in to expediency?

These were questions not thoroughly answered in the first hundred days. The national climate of expectations was such that Roosevelt could act nearly as he wished without arousing immediate counter-pressures. And the power situation he enjoyed in Washington, with a Congress ready to whoop through bill after bill, posed little challenge to his character. He did hold back from some of the more radical proposals, such as nationalizing the banking system. But that was holding back, not advancing a position against resistance. The underlying question involved not what Roosevelt would do as long as the wind was blowing his way, but what he would do in a crunch.

Well beyond his first hundred days, FDR confronted two crunches that would test his mettle against his image as a political softy. First was the crunch in deciding, as the 1936 election approached, whether to move toward consolidation or toward further innovations in policy. This decision inevitably involved a choice among persons, as advisers lined up on one side or the other. The second crunch relevant to the question of FDR's political character was the fight to remove the obstacles the Supreme Court was placing before the Second New Deal. As Roosevelt quickly discovered, his decisions in that contest involved— and were seen to involve—the institutional integrity of the government.

During the campaign of 1932, Samuel I. Rosenman, who was working on speeches for FDR, proposed that he bring together some college professors to produce talk and memoranda on issues. They would not need to be big names; their expertise and judgment, not their reputations, were needed. Roosevelt said yes and the "Brain Trust" came into existence. "The first one I thought I would talk with," Rosenman told Roosevelt, "is Ray Moley. He believes in your social philosophy and objectives, and he has a clear and forceful style of writing. Being a university professor himself, he can suggest different university people in different fields." FDR said to go ahead with it. Moley became *de facto* chairman; he brought in Rexford Tugwell, Lindsay Rogers, Adolf A. Berle, Jr., and others, mainly from Columbia University. The professors rarely met as a group. But they rather quickly got beyond memo writing to more direct engagement in the policy process. Sometimes their encounters with politicians were strained. Texas Congressman Maury Maverick remembered this conversation with Tugwell:

> He used more professorial language and said something about "averting a revolution." I was going blind.
>
> Then, to prove his point, he said: "And the workers and farmers, combining their genius and (another word I couldn't get), and they shall form a nodule . . ."
>
> I blew up completely.
>
> I said, "Rex, I am sore and insulted, and do not want to hear any more."
>
> "Why?" he asked.
>
> "What in God's name is a nodule?" I said.
>
> "A nodule is . . ." began Rex.
>
> "Stop! Stop!" I shouted. "Don't tell me. Whenever you use a word that I don't understand, it makes me mad. I am an American! The word nodule is not understood by the American people, nor is it understood by me, which makes it worse. . . . Nodule my eye! Put your speech in simple language. I never heard of a nodule before. Besides, it sounds like sex perversion."[19]

Nor did the press pass up the chance for lampooning the Brain Trust, as in this adaptation: "School days, school days, Good old Golden Rule days, Moley and Tugwell and Dr. Berle, Telling us how to run the worl'." Roosevelt took them seriously; he was in considerable need of instruction, especially on economics. Tugwell probably made the most significant, long-run contribution, but at first Moley was the man at Roosevelt's ear.

Perhaps the group overestimated its influence; Roosevelt had some ideas already. But the Brain Trust helped develop and broaden his view of a policy which would return neither to laissez-faire nor trust-busting but would move on to planning, with the organized resources at hand, for rapid recovery through joint government-business-labor action. Moley was more conservative than the others and also more eloquent—he could write a clear, stirring speech. Moley became a "one-man reception committee through whom ideas had to go to reach Roosevelt," said *Newsweek* with some exaggeration. Congressmen sought him out. He worked with FDR on early drafts of his inaugural address and went along with him to see Hoover. Moley's own memory of his position was that "No one in the administration would have a more intimate relationship with the President. No one, except [Roosevelt] himself, would have more to do with making policy. . . . The time had come to begin translating policy into action. My authorization seemed to make me Roosevelt's *de facto* minister of the moment."

Moley, Tugwell, Rosenman, and Berle caucused nearly daily in the campaign, going over and over memoranda for Roosevelt, refining the ideas, simplifying the language. FDR liked what they produced: "I'm getting an awful lot of good ideas out of this group. I hope my being away in Warm Springs will not stop any of you from going right ahead. When I get back, we'll need a lot of material." Since there was no provision for White House aides in those days, Roosevelt got Moley appointed Assistant Secretary of State, under Cordell Hull. Moley had doubts about his arrangement, but Roosevelt reassured him: "Hull knows all about it. There'll be no misunderstanding with him." The new title symbolized a genuine, gradual change. Moley had started as an informal advisor. Samuel Rosenman remembered when Moley "used to stand outside my office six months ago with the hope that I would pass on some of his papers to Governor Roosevelt. This morning he acted as if he was running the government and that Roosevelt was carrying out Moley's suggestions." The transitions from producer of ideas for speeches, to discussion leader for the Brain Trust, to summarizer, then editor, then selector of themes and assigner of responsibility for speeches were subtly made. The ambiguity of Moley's relationship to Hull, initially a mere pro forma assignment for securing Moley's services as an advisor to Roosevelt, proved to be the administrative fault line along which Moley's solidarity with Roosevelt began to crack open.

As Assistant Secretary of the Navy, Roosevelt had made his way by moving, with infinite aplomb, freely about the government, paying only modest attention to the organization charts. Thus it seemed no great danger to him to set up a situation that, one could see in retrospect, inevitably would produce conflict between Moley and Hull. Roosevelt was still practicing his open-mindedness, still saying "Yes, of course" when he meant no, or blurring decisions by telling enthusiasts, "You are absolutely right. . . . It is simply a question of time."

In the summer of 1933, an International Monetary and Economic Conference was held in London. Hull headed the delegation; already this stiff-necked old Southern Senator had noticed that he and Moley did not see eye to eye on tariff questions. Moley wanted to use tariffs to protect the development of the New Deal at home. To Hull, the protective tariff was "the king of evils." The conference bogged down. FDR dispatched Moley to London as his "liaison officer." Try as he might, Moley could not keep the press—and Cordell Hull—from interpreting his presence as a takeover. The *New York Times* called him "professor *ex machina*," and the British Prime Minister joined the newsmen and officials who flocked to see him. Hull was furious, but he decided to let Moley have "all the rope he might want and see how long he would last in that London situation." Moley decided to recommend a mild statement expressing the hope that eventually the gold standard would be restored.

Much to Moley's surprise, Roosevelt not only rejected his proposal but also issued a public statement castigating the conference for "a singular lack of proportion and a failure to remember the large purposes." On his way home, a dispirited Raymond Moley sent the President a "top secret, for the President's eyes only" cable asserting that "[Senator Key] Pittman is the only member of delegation able intellectually and aggressively to present your ideas." Somehow a copy got to Hull, who went through the ceiling: "That pissant Moley! Here he curled up at my feet and let me stroke his head like a huntin' dog and then he goes and bites me in the ass!" In politer language, he let the President know it was him or Moley. Roosevelt chose, as might have been expected, to keep his highly respected Secretary of State. But he did not "fire" Moley. Rather, he had Louis Howe (it may have been Howe's idea) suggest to Moley that the state of criminal justice in Hawaii needed looking into and that Moley could take three months to do the looking. Moley turned this down. Then FDR personally asked him to move over to the Justice Department to draft anti-kidnapping legislation. Moley agreed, probably because he saw this as a graceful exit; he left in a few months to become editor of a new magazine.

Moley continued on friendly terms with Roosevelt and helped with ideas and speeches on into 1936. He did not share the view that Roosevelt was a genial jelly: "One thing is sure—that the idea people get from his charming manner—that he is soft or flabby in disposition and character—is far from true. When he wants something a lot, he can be formidable; when crossed, he is hard, stubborn, resourceful, relentless." But by late 1934, FDR's happy habit of vagueness in specifying who was what—a habit which, despite the preachments of political scientists more attuned to processes than results, served him well—nevertheless was spawning more jealous conflicts than he could smooth over. In October 1934, Donald Richberg was named head of the National Emergency Council and the *New York Times* headlined, "RICHBERG PUT OVER CABINET IN NEW EMERGENCY COUNCIL . . . NOW NO. 1 MAN." Roosevelt got angry and told his press secretary to

> Get hold of Krock and tell him . . . that this kind of thing is not only a lie but that it is a deception and a fraud on the public. It is merely a continuation of previous lies such as the headlines that Moley was running the government; next that Baruch was Acting President; next that Johnson was the man in power; next that Frankfurter had been put over the Cabinet and now that Richberg has been put over the Cabinet. . . . This whole story is made out of whole cloth and illustrates why the public is believing less and less the alleged news columns of the newspapers.[20]

On questions of policy, Roosevelt could be assertively domineering, telling Garner "You tend to your office and I'll tend to mine," telling James Rowe, "I do not have to do it your way and I will tell you the reason why. The reason is that, although they may have made a mistake, the people of the United States elected me President, not you." But when the question came to firing someone, FDR dodged; he was interested in results. If he could get rid of someone by ignoring him, sending him off to Hawaii, transferring him to some peculiar job—cooling him out—he would always do that rather than dismiss the man. He hated to have people resign. He hated to let anyone go. In 1936 he called "probably much the hardest decision I have had to make since coming to Washington" his non-reappointment of two old friends to the Federal Reserve Board. As his Presidency progressed, Roosevelt learned how to sidetrack such problems by diversion.

In 1936, though, Moley's role and fate symbolized a larger dimension of Roosevelt's character and politics. The New Deal was by then beginning to have a degree of structure; questions of its basic direction were being raised. There were a few buzzing examples of success, as in the Tennessee Valley where thousands of CCC boys were planting trees and building flood control terraces, whole new cities were being built, dams were under construction. The drama of the New Deal had caught hold. Roosevelt knew he would be renominated and could have had few doubts about the election. The question was whether to use the election to develop new directions, new thrusts forward despite rising opposition from the left and the right, or to consolidate his position by appealing for harmony. He liked Tugwell's phrase "a concert of interests" and there were early elements in his speeches stressing peace and brotherhood among business, labor, and government. In 1934 FDR told a bankers' convention:

> You will recognize, I think, that a true function of the head of the government of the United States is to find among many discordant elements that unity of purpose that is best for the Nation as a whole. Government by the necessity of things must be the leader, must be the judge of the conflicting interests of all groups in the community, including bankers. The government is the outward expression of the common life of all citizens.[21]

In the 1934 Congressional elections, Roosevelt had reached for the middle of the road—perhaps a little to the left of that—when he rejected both "the theory that business should and must be taken over into an all-embracing Government" and "the equally untenable theory that it is an interference with liberty to offer reasonable help when private enterprise is in need of help." The results had looked good: contrary to the expected midterm decline in Congressional strength, the Democrats increased their numbers in the House by nine, in the Senate by ten. Huey Long and Father Coughlin pounded away from the left, castigating "Prince Franklin" as a tool of the moneyed interests. The Liberty League hit him from the right, arguing for the repudiation of the New Deal to "combat radicalism, preserve property rights and uphold and preserve the Constitution." Roosevelt was urged to give the country a "breathing spell."

The problem came to focus in the drafting of FDR's acceptance speech for 1936. In developing programs the President had often set two or more officials to work on nearly identical or overlapping tasks, his way of maximizing his information and options and maintaining his own control. Now he tried that technique with a speech, asking Moley and FDR's political assistant Thomas G. Corcoran to prepare one draft and Rosenman and Stanley High to prepare another. Neither team was told of the existence of the other. Moley had edged over in the conservative direction; a number of his magazine articles had been criticizing the New Deal as antagonistic to business. His draft was conciliatory, calling mildly for broad generosity as the primary need of a "nation fighting the fight for freedom in a modern civilization." The Rosenman draft was a hard-driving attack on the reactionaries, calling for economic freedom to extend political freedoms won in the past.

Not surprisingly, Roosevelt asked for a draft which would weave these opposite themes together. But then there was a surprise. FDR had the four drafters in for dinner three days before the speech was to be delivered. Rosenman describes what happened:

> That night in the small family dining room for the first and only time in my life, I saw the President forget himself as a gentleman. He began twitting Moley about his new conservatism and about the influence of his "new, rich friends" on his recent writings, which had been very critical of the administration. Moley responded with what I thought was justifiable heat. The President grew angry, and the exchanges between them became very bitter. We all felt embarrassed; Missy did her best to change the subject but failed. Their words became more acrimonious. Roosevelt said that Moley's criticisms would not have received any attention but for the fact that, like Hugh Johnson's, they came from a former intimate of the administration. Moley resented this, and said something to the effect that Roosevelt's inability to take criticism was leading him down many wrong paths. While I knew how deeply Roosevelt had been stung by the unfriendly attacks on his policies by Johnson and Moley, I thought that his temper and language were particularly unjustified, not only because there were other people present, but because they were all his invited guests. It was an ordeal for all of us, and we were all relieved when dinner finally broke up. I am sure that Roosevelt felt sorry for what he had said; but I could not see how the two of them could ever resume their earlier relationship. They never did.[22]

In the acceptance speech finally decided upon, Roosevelt delivered a slashing attack on "economic royalists," whose "despotism" had been shown up in 1929 and whose only real complaint "is that we seek to take away their power." The call was not for harmony but for war. Roosevelt concluded:

> In the place of the palace of privilege we seek to build a temple out of faith and hope and charity. It is a sobering thing, my friends, to be a servant of this great cause. . . . There is a mysterious cycle in human events. To some generations much is given. Of other generations much is expected. This generation of Americans has a rendezvous with destiny. . . . Here in America we are waging a great and successful war. It is not alone a war against want and destitution and economic demoralization. It is more than that; it is a war for the survival of democracy. We are fighting to save a great and precious form of government for ourselves and for the world. . . . I join with you. I am enlisted for the duration of the war.[23]

FDR's rhetorical aggressiveness continued on into the campaign, cutting hard against the Republicans for their twelve years of "hear-nothing, see-nothing, do-nothing government" and warning that "Powerful influences strive today to restore that kind of government with its doctrine that that government is best which is most indifferent. . . . Never before in all our history have these forces been so united against one candidate as they stand today. They are unanimous in their hate for me—and I welcome their hatred."

Roosevelt won a staggering victory, defeating Alf Landon with 27,478,945 votes to Landon's 16,674,665, the largest plurality in history, and carrying the electoral vote 528 to 8.

I believe this tale of Franklin Roosevelt's personal and public relations in 1936 is highly significant for understanding his political character. Roosevelt's active-positive character, grounded in high self-esteem, strengthened by his sense of the self as developing, enabled him to overcome the conflict in his personality between peaceableness and aggression. He could fight, not simply in a calculated, strategic way, but also emotionally, personally, calling forth from his character a genuine anger long hidden behind a mask of geniality. This "softy" from the start insisted that however chaotic the structure of power beneath him, there would be no ambiguity as to who was on top; by 1936 he had made that abundantly clear to those who stood around and behind his throne. Power was where he was. Once that was established, Roosevelt's technique—neglect and diversion—for getting rid of unproductive assistants could work, could achieve the necessary economy of attention at minimum cost in political and personal strain. Moley had to go, but Moley's talents might someday be useful; Roosevelt got him out, kept him friendly initially, and was able to draw him in again later.

Thus from early in the game FDR contradicted the expectation that he would cave in to pressure. But in 1936 he moved beyond Machiavellian technique, beyond strategy, to the mobilization of his own emotional force. His blow-up at Moley showed semi-privately what his blast at the "economic royalists" showed publicly: the man was not all milk and honey, there was vitriol in him and he could reach past defenses emphasizing pleasantness to get at it. Moley's defection stung him, as did the taunts of "traitor" hurled at him by members of his own social class. In responding to such attacks this man, who kept his own attention and that of prying others turned away from self and toward external reality, revealed a psychological flexibility extending down into the self. Roosevelt's style was a bundle of arrows he could use as occasion demanded. His world view was a malleable collection of themes to be employed for the sake of results. What 1936 uncovered was a character confident enough to fight. That anger was there again on December 8, 1941, when the President's own fury glared forth as he gave the national reply to the Japanese assault on Pearl Harbor.

Roosevelt exhibited in this single illustration what I see as a major contrast between the active-positive type in politics and other types. In the examples of active-negative Presidents, Wilson, Hoover, and Johnson, we saw how each infused a particular line of policy, drawn from his special world view, with immense emotional commitment; the destructive rigidity centered on matters of opinion. In contrast, active-positive types see a much more liquid world, a world in which realities and the opinions which reflect them shift continually in no particularly consistent way. The passive-negative Presidents (and their counterparts in other political realms, I would argue), exemplified by Coolidge and Eisenhower, are less definitely committed to particular deductions from their world views than are the active-negatives. But, while they are more flexible in matters of opinion, they tend to fall back on stylistic continuities, on regularly pursued systems and habits of behavior. The active-positives, in contrast, are freer in their selections from a stylistic repertoire. Passive-positive Presidents and politicians, as Taft and Harding showed, experience their major political difficulties as a result of character rigidity and the tremendous strain of situations pressing them to alter their characteristic habit of compliance and affection-seeking. Investing less of themselves in particular styles and world views, passive-positives are in their way as rigid and restricted as the Wilsons and Coolidges. Active-positives, such as FDR and the others soon to be discussed, show how a much richer and more varied range of emotional orientations is available to the politician whose character is firmly rooted in self-recognition and self-love. The active-positive not only can *perform* lovingly or aggressively or with detachment, he can *feel* those ways. As Roosevelt's case points out, the genuineness of those feelings can come across powerfully to close associates and to the public at large.

FDR's toughness was not much in question after 1936. But soon his political legitimacy was. In 1937 Franklin Roosevelt tried to reconstruct the Supreme Court. The method he used was deception. He failed, and his actions undermined public and Congressional confidence in his Presidency. In 1938 he campaigned for the defeat of Democrats who had opposed him in this fight. He won only one such contest. In 1940, Roosevelt was reelected by a margin of less than 5 million votes of nearly 50 million cast. There were many reasons, the "court-packing" plan significant among them.

For several years, the Court had been a thorn in Roosevelt's side. In 1935 the "Nine Old Men" ruled that the oil business was beyond federal regulation, then that a pension scheme for railroad workers was unconstitutional, and in swift succession the NRA, legislation easing farm mortgage payments, and the authority of the President to remove a member of the Federal Trade Commission were struck down. It seemed every time the federal government was proposed as regulator, the Court ruled the enterprise to be regulated was not in "interstate commerce" and when state solutions were proposed they turned out to be property-taking without "due process of law." The result was stalemate. In 1936 the Court struck down a New York minimum wage law for women, and the Agricultural Adjustment Act was declared unconstitutional.

Roosevelt proceeded cautiously, but with great determination to free the New Deal's hands of their judicial chains. He played his cards close to the chest; Louis Howe had died in April 1936, and most of the conservatives had left his staff. More than ever, he was on his own. In his annual message early in 1937, he touched on the issue, saying that the founding fathers had realized new problems were bound to arise and intended "that a liberal interpretation in the years to come would give to the Congress" sufficient powers to meet them. He had been meeting with his Attorney General to devise a strategy against the Court blockade, but he told his speechwriters, "Leave the whole thing very general for now." At his second inauguration on January 20, FDR remembered later, "When the Chief Justice read me the oath and came to the words 'support the Constitution of the United States,' I felt like saying: 'Yes, but it's the Constitution as *I* understand it, flexible enough to meet any new problem of democracy—not the kind of Constitution your Court has raised up as a barrier to progress and democracy.'" In his address he emphasized that the people "will insist that *every* agency of popular government use effective instruments to carry out their will." Sitting behind him, the Chief Justice got the point—but the message was far too subtle for ninety percent of the public.

Meeting with Donald Richberg, his Solicitor General, the Attorney General, and speechwriter Samuel Rosenman (the only one not in on the plot), FDR sprung his plan. Clearly he had already made up his mind on the substance. Rosenman was asked to fix up the language. Six days later he presented the plan to Cabinet and Congressional leaders. The President said nothing of the Supreme Court attacks on the New Deal. He referred instead to inefficiency in the federal court system; buried among several reforms to improve efficiency was a blockbuster: the President would be empowered to appoint one new justice to any federal court for every incumbent justice who failed to retire at age 70. In effect, Roosevelt explained, that would mean adding six new justices to the Supreme Court.

The Congressmen were stunned. Roosevelt made it clear that he did not invite discussion. On the way back to the Capitol, the chairman of the House Judiciary Committee said, "Boys, here's where I cash in." The fakery involved was just too transparent, the tactic just too cute. The implication that justices over seventy were doddering into senility came through in this passage:

> Modern complexities call also for a constant infusion of new blood into the courts, just as it is needed in executive functions of the government and in private business. A lowered mental or physical vigor leads men to avoid an examination of complicated and changed conditions. Little by little, new facts become blurred through old glasses fitted, as it were, for the needs of another generation; older men, assuming that the scene is the same as it was in the past, cease to explore or inquire into the present or the future.[24]

It did not take long for someone to remember that FDR's most consistent backer on the Court, Louis Brandeis—whose thinking had led him to *support* the New Deal—was eighty years of age. The tired blood argument simply did not hold up. No one was fooled; many were startled into indignation. Press reaction was almost unanimously unfavorable, furious mail poured in, and the Republicans in Congress had a grand time sitting back and listening to Democrats, so soon after the Roosevelt landslide, tear into the President. Bar associations, New England town meetings, radio commentators piled on the protest. The President might as well have proposed suspending the Constitution. The public saw his senile Solomons as a kind of American cardinalate, not to be flimflammed into impotence by any President, however popular.

Quickly Roosevelt shifted gears; on March 4, he brought his argument out in the open. Using a metaphor for the branches of government, he parabled: "If three well matched horses are put to the task of ploughing up a field where the going is heavy, and the team of three pull as one, the field will be ploughed. If one horse lies down in the traces or plunges off in another direction, the field will not be ploughed." It did not work. The reaction indicated many saw one horse trampling another to death. A few days later in a Fireside Chat, FDR went at it again, tried to beat down the argument that a Constitutional amendment was the proper way to make such a change by pointing out how unlikely that was, given all the newspaper publishers and other bigwigs who would oppose it. He met head-on the charge that he was "packing the Court" but his answer was exaggerated and unconvincing: he would appoint "worthy" justices, not "spine-less puppets." The leading farm organizations and both the AFL and CIO came out against the plan.

In the meantime, Chief Justice Charles Evans Hughes, who had very nearly defeated Wilson for the Presidency, quietly began a retreat which would undercut Roosevelt's position. First Hughes let a Senator release a letter from him saying the Court was well abreast of its work. Before March was out, the Court in a five-to-four decision reversed its position of only nine months before and allowed that a state could set minimum wages for women. In April the Court upheld the National Labor Relations Act. In May the nine old men decided to let the Social Security Act stand. And on June 2, Justice Van Devanter, a staunch opponent of New Deal shenanigans, retired, leaving a place for a Roosevelt appointment and insuring a Court majority favorable to Roosevelt's policies. The battle to restructure the Court was lost.

When the President came to edit his public papers, he titled the volume for 1935 "The Court Disapproves," for 1936 "The People Approve," for 1937 "The Constitution Prevails." In 1938 the fight was still on his mind as he tried to purge Senators who had opposed him on this and other measures. He could still laugh about it, but for once he had clearly been caught out. James MacGregor Burns summarizes what had gone wrong:

> The manner of presentation—the surprise, Roosevelt's failure to pose the issue more concretely in the election, his obvious relish in the job, his unwillingness to ask his cabinet and Congressional leaders for advice—alienated some potential supporters. More important, this method of presentation prevented Roosevelt from building a broad coalition behind the bill and ironing out multifarious tactical difficulties before springing the attack—behind-the-scenes activity in which Roosevelt was highly adept.[25]

FDR had overreached himself. In part it was an error of calculation. He under-estimated the potential opposition, exaggerated the depth of his support. But it was also a failing leaders like Roosevelt, strongly oriented toward the achieve-ment of results, seem peculiarly prone to. Roosevelt did not freeze on this issue, did not turn it into an all-or-nothing crusade. But like other active-positive politicians, he showed himself, for the moment at least, too ready to bypass one of the few sacred processes of American government.

THE THRUST FOR RESULTS

The great strength of the active-positive type in politics is his hunger for and attention to results. The histories of other Presidencies are surprising in the degree to which they show President after President apparently oblivious of the effects their policies are having on people at home and abroad. Too often their attention is arrested at the level of principle or plausibility or the confirming of some personal theme. The active-positive President—and, again, his counterpart throughout politics—is far more apt to succeed in solving problems simply because he can see what he is doing. In that sense he has political vision. Usually the results he is most interested in are changes for the better in the actual conditions of life for the citizenry; he will sacrifice a good deal else, including consistency, to make that happen.

But with that focus, active-positives, trusting themselves, sometimes forget how tenuous and ambivalent public trust in politicians can be. No doubt Roosevelt really meant to appoint able justices to a restructured court; as opportunities arose, that is what he did. What he failed to see in the Court fight was that the same public that was so overwhelmingly in favor of his efforts to better their lives (at least in comparison to the Republican alternative) was also overwhelmingly unprepared to let him run the country on his own, if, as they saw it, that meant sacrificing the traditional checks and balances. The Eisenhowers and Coolidges, guardians of the proper system, may so dignify process that they neglect results. But active-positives, in their haste to make things happen, may too quickly and easily knock down the "formalities" that hold the democratic order in place.

10

Harry S Truman
and Active-Positive
Combat

The Vice Presidency has not been the focus of America's best constitutional thinking. The Founding Fathers drafted the provisions for this office over a single weekend and passed them without debate. In a startling lapse of political acumen, they seem to have seen no particular problem in providing that the runner-up for President would serve as Vice President (and preside over the Senate). Washington passed the Presidency to his Vice President Adams, then Adams to his Vice President Jefferson. But then in 1800 the system began to go awry, as Jefferson and Aaron Burr tied with 73 electoral votes each, defeating President Adams with 65 votes. The tie had to be resolved by the House of Representatives, each state's delegation casting one vote, with a majority of the states deciding the issue. After a week of voting, Jefferson won, ten to four (two states voting blank), on the thirty-sixth ballot. Perhaps foreseeing the difficulties such President/Vice President pairs as Nixon-Humphrey, Johnson-Goldwater, Kennedy-Nixon, Eisenhower-Stevenson, Truman-Dewey, and Roosevelt-Hoover might give rise to, the statesmen provided in the Twelfth Amendment for separate balloting on the two offices. To this day, however, another constitutional paradox persists in the succession of the Vice President to the Presidency when the President dies or is disabled. Hypothetically chosen for his potential Presidential qualities, the Vice Presidential nominee is in fact nearly always a man who is picked to attract votes from a faction other than the Presidential candidate's, is not so prominent that he will detract from the President's authority, and is willing to serve as a political vermiform appendix to another man. The history of this system of inheritance is not inspiring. The first accidental President, John Tyler, did manage to establish that he was really President (not "Acting President") when Harrison died in 1841, but he went on to see all but one of his Cabinet resign in a bloc when he vetoed one bill, then became the first President to have legislation passed over his veto on another matter. Subsequently the inheritance system threw up Millard Filmore, Andrew Johnson, Chester A. Arthur, Theodore Roosevelt, Calvin Coolidge, Harry S Truman, and Lyndon B. Johnson—a mixed bag slumping in the doubtful direction. Taking office, each had to bear the latent public suspicion (perhaps Oedipal in its roots), that he had something to do with his predecessor's demise.

TRUMAN SURPRISED BY GRACE

Harry Truman not only got to the Presidency this way, he was also, along with Martin Van Buren, William Howard Taft, and Warren G. Harding, among the Presidents who have had the misfortune to follow on the heels of great dramatic characters.

Truman had not wanted to be Vice President. In 1944 Roosevelt, caught between forces favoring James Byrnes and Henry Wallace, kept his counsel for a long time before finally turning to Truman, a man respected in the Senate but virtually unknown elsewhere, as a compromise. When he heard that FDR wanted him to run, Truman said, "Tell him to go to hell. I'm for Jimmy Byrnes." As his old friend Sam Rayburn remembered, Truman "was so much in love with his job as Senator from Missouri that he hated to give it up for the Vice Presidency." He stood up to the tough Democratic kingmakers—Flynn, Kelly, Hague, Pauley, Walker, Hannegan—who harangued him in a Chicago hotel room. But then the President telephoned. FDR always talked loudly on the phone and Hannegan held the receiver so the others could hear:

> "Bob," the President said, "have you got that fellow lined up yet?"
>
> "No, Mr. President," Hannegan replied. "He is the contrariest Missouri mule I've ever dealt with."
>
> "Well, you tell him that if he wants to break up the Democratic party in the middle of a war, that's his responsibility."
>
> Hannegan hung up the phone and turned to Truman. "Now what do you say?"
>
> "My God," Truman mumbled.[1]

It was a challenge an old soldier could not resist. That September, an old pal told Truman he was going to be living in the White House one day and Truman replied, "Eddie, I'm afraid I am, and it scares hell out of me." One night during the campaign he woke up in a cold sweat from a dream that the President had died and he was called to assume the office. His mind was not eased when Roosevelt, looking old and tired, addressed the Congress after his fourth inauguration sitting down, because, he told them, "It makes it a lot easier for me in not having to carry about ten pounds of steel around on the bottom of my legs, and also because of the fact that I have just completed a 14,000-mile trip." Truman was "afraid for many weeks that something might happen to this great leader," but "I did not allow myself to think about it after I became Vice President."

Truman was not given to worrying. He gave testimony to his sturdy optimism by actually enjoying being Vice President, especially presiding over the Senate and trading anecdotes with his old friends there. That was a satisfying, familiar job, one he knew how to perform effectively. As best he could, Truman put out of his mind the worries he had expressed to Henry Wallace: "Do you remember your American history well enough to recall what happened to most Vice Presidents who succeeded to the Presidency? Usually they were ridiculed in office, had their hearts broken, lost any vestige of respect they had had before. I don't want that to happen to me." As far as high Presidential policy was concerned, Truman was almost entirely out of it. "I don't think I saw Roosevelt but twice as Vice President except at Cabinet meetings," he said, and "Roosevelt never discussed anything important at his Cabinet meetings." FDR made no provision for Truman's involvement; he was too busy, perhaps too tired, and he may have had in the back of his mind the memory of a characteristic Truman *faux pas* from 1942, when Senator Truman had trustingly okayed without reading it a ghostwritten article highly critical of the administration. Roosevelt had been furious and cut off relations with Truman for months. Then during the 1944 campaign Truman had chagrined the President again by attacking a Senator whose support was urgently needed. Roosevelt was in Washington only thirty days while Truman was Vice President, so there was not in any case much chance for them to confer.

As for the big current issues, Truman knew about as much as any other careful newspaper reader. "I knew the President had a great many meetings with Churchill and Stalin. I was not familiar with any of these things."

The President's death caught Truman entirely by surprise. On April 11, 1945, Harry was his usual ebullient self. When the Senate adjourned that day the reporters flocked around him; one called him, "Mr. President," as Senators address their presiding officer. Truman flashed a smile and said, "Boys, those are fighting words out in Missouri where I come from. You'd better smile when you say that! You know right here is where I've always wanted to be, and the only place I ever wanted to be. The Senate—that's just my speed and style." The next day he whiled away the afternoon on the rostrum writing a newsy letter home, telling his folks to be sure to tune in when, tomorrow night, he would make a speech and introduce the President. At 5:10 he strolled over to Sam Rayburn's "Board of Education" hideaway in the House end of the Capitol where Rayburn's friends often gathered at the end of the day to open a bottle and "strike a blow for liberty." Rayburn gave him the message to call the White House immediately. "Please come right over," he was told, "and come in through the main Pennsylvania entrance." His face turned white. "Holy General Jackson!" he said, raced back to his office, found his chauffeur, and made it to the White House at 5:25, where he was immediately directed to Mrs. Roosevelt's study. "Harry," Eleanor said, "the President is dead." Truman was stunned into silence. Finally he choked out "Is there anything I can do for you?" Eleanor replied, "Is there anything we can do for *you*? For you are the one in trouble now."

The next day, Truman's first as President, was Friday the 13th of April. To the reporters Truman said, "Boys, if you ever pray, pray for me now. I don't know whether you fellows ever had a bale of hay fall on you, but when they told me yesterday what had happened, I felt like the moon, the stars and all the planets had fallen on me." Over the next five days, "I felt that I had lived five lifetimes," Truman recalled.

> I was beginning to realize how little the Founding Fathers had been able to anticipate the preparations necessary for a man to become President so suddenly. It is a mighty leap from the Vice-Presidency to the Presidency when one is forced to make it without warning. Under the present system a Vice-President cannot equip himself to become President merely by virtue of being second in rank.[2]

All over the country people were asking, as Admiral Leahy had asked Roosevelt a few months earlier, "Who the hell is Truman?"

TRUMAN MAKES UP HIS MIND

Harry Truman's first memory was of laughter. He was chasing a frog around the back yard; each time the frog jumped Harry slapped his knees and laughed. "It's very strange that a two-year-old has such a sense of humor," his grandmother said. Perhaps he got that from his mother, Martha Ellen Truman. She had a tart Missouri wit, a humorous skepticism, and a direct manner not easily awed by the folderol of glory that eventually settled on her boy Harry. When he was inaugurated as Vice President, he telephoned to ask her if she had heard the ceremonies on the radio. "Yes, I heard it all," she said. "Now you behave yourself up there, Harry. Now you behave yourself!" She was the one who tossed the little two-year-old Harry out an upstairs window into the arms of his Uncle below, the one who remembered how three-year-old Harry, at his grandfather's deathbed, tugged on the old man's beard to wake him up. She was the one who once advised him not to be too good; who, as an old Confederate at 92, lying bandaged and splinted in a hospital bed, snapped out at Harry Vaughn, "I don't want any smart cracks out of you, I saw your picture in the paper last week putting a wreath at the Lincoln Memorial." She was the guardian of Christian virtue in the home, but also a "Lightfoot Baptist" who liked to sing and dance despite what the hardshells said; a laughing, exuberant, outdoor little lady who, implausible as it sounds, found amusement later in life reading the *Congressional Record* from cover to cover every day.

Martha's was a frontier humor, a laughter with a streak of toughness in it, communicating at once an appreciation of shared fate and a challenge to stand up to it. Harry was her special boy, her first, after a depressing stillbirth the year before he arrived. His younger brother Vivian, born two years later, grew into the "spitting image" of his father, John A. Truman, a tough and taciturn farmer and cattle trader, given to fisticuffs on slight provocation despite the short stature which brought him the nickname "Peanuts." John was excited when Harry was born: he planted a tree and nailed up a horseshoe for good luck. He did not neglect Harry later; he took him along sometimes on mule-trading expeditions and he bought the boy his own Shetland pony. But Harry grew to prefer an occasional spanking from mother to an occasional scolding from father, so it was rugged little Vivian who became John's companion. At twelve Vivian got his own checkbook and a share in the cattle business. Harry went in for piano lessons, but Vivian would have no part of them. "Mama couldn't get a lasso big enough" to rope him into that, Harry remembered.

Harry stayed around the house, learning to cook, helping the family maid in the kitchen. He was "more like a little old woman than a sissy child," as Jonathan Daniels put it. When he was five, his sister Mary Jane was born. Harry took care of her, rocked her and sang her to sleep, braided her hair and watched over her outdoors—a little mother imitating his own mother as much as he deferred to her. Yet he also ran and played and tussled and got into mischief. From his third to his sixth year, the family lived on the 600-acre farm of Solomon Young, Martha Ellen's father, an endless place dominated by a big colonial house full of children, servants, and farmhands. "Some of my happiest and most pleasant recollections are of the years we spent on the Young farm," Harry remembered. Harry and Vivian wandered the acres looking for adventure, urging on the dogs and cats as they hunted field mice, racing around in their red wagon, plastering themselves with mud in the water hole. Grandpa drove him to the fair in his big high-wheeled cart; they would sit together in the judge's stand to watch the races—"the best time a kid ever had," Harry said. And there was a cornucopia of delicious vittles. Truman spreads them out in his *Memoirs:* "wonderful cookies . . . striped candy and peanuts . . . all kinds of candy, nuts, and fruit . . . apples and peaches . . . and were they good! . . . peach butter, apple butter, grape butter, jellies and preserves . . . sausages, souse, pickled pigs feet." It was then his father gave him his "beautiful black Shetland pony and the grandest saddle to ride him with I ever saw." Harry would ride along beside his father's big horse, helping inspect the farm.

"Those were wonderful days and great adventures," Harry remembered. They were days full of people—indulgent grandparents, aunts, and uncles, a rotating crew of cousins. Harry began to develop his antennae: "When I was growing up it occurred to me to watch the people around me to find out what they thought and what pleased them most. . . . I used to watch my father and mother closely to learn what I could do to please them, just as I did with my schoolteachers and playmates. Because of my efforts to get along with my associates I usually was able to get what I wanted. It was successful on the farm, in school, in the Army, and particularly in the Senate."

When Harry was six the family moved to Independence, his home town for the next twelve years. There Harry remembered their "big house . . . with several acres of land" and a farm his father operated nearby. This place, too, was often full of children and relatives, but here Harry stayed behind when the other children started school. His eyes were bad. He could read the big print in the family Bible before he was five, but his mother soon noticed he could not read small print. His trouble was hyperopia, flat eyeballs, and he had to get very thick glasses. "I was blind as a mole without them," he remembered. They made him chary of boyish roughhousing, reinforced his role as mediator in playground disputes, and put him into the kitchen with mother and the maid or with his baby sister Mary Jane, whom he mothered devotedly. He seems to have gone about these tasks cheerfully enough. At eight he went off to school, and liked it, but the next year he came down with a severe case of diphtheria, developing paralysis in his arms and legs so that Martha had to push him around in a baby carriage for several months. When he recovered, his friends of "the Waldo Street Gang" were swimming, skating, playing baseball, but "Harry could not play many of the games because of his glasses," Martha said, and Harry added that "The boys made me umpire"—a job in which a boy with impaired vision must have needed a good deal of decisiveness, diplomacy, and/or social credit.

Harry started playing his mother's old upright piano when he was about ten. She taught him for a while, then a neighbor lady took over, and shortly Harry started real lessons with a professional, twice a week. He got up at five in the morning to practice for two hours every day. He was serious about it; once he performed for the girls at a Kansas City boardinghouse, and he thought he might be headed for a musical career. The boys in the neighborhood teased him about his music lessons. Suddenly at fifteen he quit: "I decided it was sissy," he said later.

Harry Truman's early family life sounds warm and happy. In his *Memoirs* he keeps going back to times and people he was glad about, pleased with, had a fine time experiencing. As a little boy in Sunday school he met Bess Wallace, a pretty tomboy type, and married her when he was 35. Bess had his mother's wit, Missouri wit. Margaret Truman, Harry and Bess's daughter, remembers her father one day later in life, coming upon Bess burning some papers.

> "What are you doing, Bess?"
> "I'm burning letters to me," Mother said.
> "Bess!" said my father. "You oughtn't to do that."
> "Why not?" my mother said, "I've read them several times."
> "But think of history!" my father said.
> "I *have*," said Mother.[3]

Harry was and remained a staunch family man. "I only had one sweetheart from the time I was six," he said, and "I am always so lonesome when the family leaves." He became the extended family's common uncle:

> I was always the clearing house for all the family, even when they weren't speaking to each other. They were speaking to me. I got them all to the point

eventually where there was no ill-feeling between us. And that's a job with a Kentucky outfit. You know my four grandparents came from Kentucky.[4]

Yet for all the memories of good times and happy family ties—the main theme of Harry's early life—there was an evident tension, a sub-theme which lent a special dynamic to Harry's later emergence.

Harry, the nearsighted, piano-playing Mama's boy, wanted to be manly. In his *Memoirs* it is interesting to see how he selects and shapes his recollections.The pages covering his childhood make no mention of piano lessons, though they consumed much of his energy for years. Nor does he remember, as his biographers do, the special relation between his father and Vivian on the one side, and himself and his mother on the other. As Truman saw it when he came to write his autobiography, "My sister Mary Jane, named for his mother, was my father's favorite," and the boys shared in watching over her. And "My mother was partial to the boys," not to Harry alone. That is not the way it was according to the relatives and friends whose snippets of recall were collected over the years. Nor does he mention helping in the kitchen.

But there seems to have been nothing deeply disturbing about Harry's intimate family relationships. In fact he was a happy and active child, one who learned then that effort and pleasure were not opposites. Insofar as he felt the need to move beyond the realm of his mother, baby sister, and piano, Harry developed a special connection with his father, one different from Vivian's. That connection was politics. John Truman got into many a fistfight over politics, took a strong interest in it, at least from the time Harry was eight. "I had a white cap with a visor on it saying 'Grover Cleveland and Adlai Stevenson,'" he remembered, and "Some big Republican boys took my cap away from me and tore it up." When Cleveland won, John climbed up on the roof and tied a big American flag to the weathervane. In 1900, he took Harry to the Democratic National Convention in Kansas City and helped get him a job as a page. To Harry, William Jennings Bryan's address "was like nothing I have ever heard." Then, in 1904, he saw his first President, Theodore Roosevelt, and "was disappointed to find that he was no giant, but a little man in a long Prince Albert coat to make him look taller." Later John got in with the Pendergast machine; in 1906 that brought him a place as election judge, with Harry as his clerk, and then in 1910 John was named road overseer. Four years later, when Harry was 30 years old, his father, out on an inspection, lifted a boulder too heavy for him, fell ill, and died. "I had been sitting with him and watching a long time," Harry said. "I fell asleep for a short time and when I woke up he was dead." Harry was appointed to take over his father's post as road overseer. About that time he started attending a Democratic club in Kansas City.

To Harry Truman, then, one of the meanings of politics was the way it linked him to his father and the world of men. As a child it was a special shared enthusiasm; as an adult Harry inherited, as his first public position, the office that had killed his father, and the political connections which would eventually help him along to the Presidency. That linkage lent a cast to Harry's perception of politics. What to Franklin Roosevelt was Endicott Peabody's ideal of service by the privileged was to Truman a tough guy's territory.

Harry Truman's world view shaped itself first around the religion-of-the-deed he imbibed at home. The teachings of churches meant little to him, and his mother's "Lightfoot Baptist" faith left him conscience-free when, from about the age of sixteen to twenty, "I used to go to every vaudeville show that came to Kansas City." Doctrinal differences failed to excite him. "My Grandfather Young belonged to no church, but he supported many of them—Baptist, Methodist, Campbellite, and Presbyterian. They all met in the old church out in front of the house on the family farm on Sunday." At six he asked his Grandpa which sect was best, and was told, "All of them want to arrive at the same place, but they have to fight to see who has the inside track with the Almighty. When a man spends Saturday night and Sunday doing too much howling and praying you had better go home and lock your smokehouse." Serious Truman family discussions were infrequent and concrete. Margaret related how her father had passed on the traditional family culture:

> Even if things had been different, I don't think we would have had any long-drawn-out conversations on the subject, because we have never done that as a family. All three of us take things as they come, cope with them, dispose of them the best we can, and go on to the next thing. I have never looked far ahead or set my heart on something in the future. It has saved disappointment. . . . As a family, we had a code, which was to do the right thing, do it the best we could, never complain and never take advantage.[5]

Harry's main direct exposure to abstract verbiage orally delivered came in his late adolescence and early adulthood, when he attended political picnics outside Kansas City—"hell-roaring, rip-snorting affairs with the loudest speeches you ever heard," as one of his boyhood chums remembered them. But in general the Trumans were doers, not talkers. When Senator Truman was invited to visit Justice Brandeis, his first reaction was "I'm not used to meeting people like that." (He went, and listened, and learned a good deal.) In his early years he learned by observing the action that words provoked; loyalty as a value came home to him from his father, who beat up anybody who slurred the women in his family or jumped on his kids. Nor would John fight only for others: "If my father's honor was impugned, he'd fight like a buzzsaw," Harry said.

Harry's vision of the world came through his own eyes. By the time he was twelve he had read the Bible through for the second time and could cite chapter and verse if any questions arose. "I remember that there were a number of stories about Biblical heroes with what I thought were beautiful illustrations. . . . I also spent a lot of time on the 20th Chapter of Exodus [the Ten Commandments] and the 5th, 6th, and 7th Chapters of Matthew's Gospel [the Sermon on the Mount]." But it was history that fascinated Harry, particularly the ways individual men had shaped history. At ten his mother gave him a four-volume set of Charles Francis Horne's *Great Men and Famous Women;* he still has them. To Harry history was "true facts," not the clash of ideologies. "My debt to history is one which cannot be calculated," he wrote in his *Memoirs*, "I know of no other motivation which so accounts for my awakening interest as a young lad in the principles of leadership and government." He wanted to find out "the background of . . . events and to find out who brought them about"—an expression in capsule form of Harry Truman's vision of how things happen in the world. Men made events. "I soon learned that the really successful ones were few and far between. I wanted to know what caused the successes or the failures of all the famous leaders in history." There were two other lessons the mature Truman could discern running back into his childhood reading:

> I learned that a leader is a man who has the ability to get other people to do what they don't want to do, and like it.[6]

> I began to see that the history of the world has moved in cycles and that very often we find ourselves in the midst of political circumstances which appear to be new but which might have existed in almost identical form at various times during the past six thousand years.[7]

Leadership is persuasion. Today happened on some yesterday. Thus Truman learned one lesson he would, as President, pursue with repeated failure and one grand success; and another lesson which would help ease his mind but prove as distorting as it was instructive.

Harry read insatiably, "everything I could get my hands on—histories and encyclopedias and everything else." In school he was a good enough student, but his main education was his own exploration, behind the "paragraphs" (one for each event) in his schoolbooks. He judged for himself, and he was not given to qualifications. Once in the Senate he wrote this startling gallop of interpretations:

> In reading the lives of great men, I found that the first victory they won was over themselves and their carnal urges. Self-discipline with all of them came first. I found that most of the really great ones never thought they were great, some of them did. I admired Cincinnatus, Hannibal, Cyrus the Great, Gustavus Adolphus of Sweden, Washington and Lee, Stonewall Jackson and J. E. B. Stuart. Of all the military heroes Hannibal and Lee were to my mind the best because while they won every battle they lost the war, due to crazy politicians in both instances, but they were still Great Captains of History. I found a lot of heroes were made by being in at the death or defeat of one of the really great. Scipio, Wellington, and U. S. Grant are the most outstanding. I was not very fond of Alexander, Attila, Genghis Kahn or Napoleon because while they were great leaders of men they fought for conquest and personal glory. The others fought for what they thought was right and for their countries. They were patriots and unselfish. I could never admire a man whose only interest is himself.[8]

Machiavelli would have understood this mix of *virtu* and *fortuna*. In the crunch, though, Harry would take the virtuous failure over the devious success.

Truman's world view was shaped by three other experiences dating from his late high school years. His first paying job was janitoring in a drugstore; first thing in the morning, before school, he opened the store, mopped the floor, and swept the sidewalk, then had to dust and clean all the bottles and shelves, starting each day where he ended the day before, over and over again. He grew to detest the sight of those "interminable rows and rows of bottles"—which is perhaps why he dropped the job after a few months. Meanwhile, he had seen his Grandpa's opinion of hypocrites confirmed when, "Early in the morning, sometimes before Mr. Clinton arrived, the good church members and Anti-Saloon Leaguers would come in for their early morning drink behind the prescription case at ten cents an ounce. . . . This procedure gave a fourteen-year-old boy quite a viewpoint on the public front of leading citizens and 'amen-corner-praying' churchmen." Reputations, Harry learned, bore looking into.

The year he graduated from high school brought another revelation. Until then the Truman family, while not wealthy, was certainly well off. Harry Truman was no log-cabin President, but the heir-to-be of spacious farmlands and houses. His father at that time was worth some $30,000 in 1901 dollars, much of it amassed on the Kansas City grain futures market. Then with frightening rapidity "He lost everything at one fell swoop and went broke." Harry's hopes for college were canceled. Like Dwight Eisenhower, he tried for an appointment to West Point, but could not see the eye charts well enough. John's straits got direr and direr. He discovered some land he had bought was worthless. He sold the family home and made a small down payment on a cramped little place in Kansas City. He sold off 160 acres Martha Ellen had inherited, a farm that had been in the family for half a century. Desperately in debt, John took a job as a night watchman. Then he traded the Kansas City house for a down payment on an 80-acre farm and moved there, but a flood washed away the whole corn crop, and in 1905 John and Martha threw in the towel and moved back to the old Solomon Young place for the remaining nine years of John's life.

Harry could see before his eyes how a good and industrious man might suddenly drop through the floor of prosperity. By any objective assessment, the Trumans were on their way down and out. Harry rode it out in good humor. He picnicked with other young people, played the piano for their singing, took in the five-cent movies on his lunch hour. Part of the time he lived in a Kansas City boardinghouse with Arthur Eisenhower, Dwight's brother, who recalled that "Harry and I only had a dollar a week left over for riotous living." Harry had fun. He joined the National Guard.

The year he was 22, Harry moved out to the Young farm to help his parents. That was 1906. Over the next nine years, with much labor and careful management, and a boost from the general prosperity of an agricultural period (1909–14) which would become the standard for "parity," life got better. The farm showed substantial profits, with an income of as much as $15,000 in a good year. John paid off his debts and Harry bought a four-cylinder Stafford automobile with locomotive-size Prestolite headlights. They were not rich, but they had recovered, and out of the total experience Harry learned to keep the faith when things looked dark. The "true facts" of his own history supported hope.

When John Truman first went broke, Harry went to work at a series of instructive jobs: timekeeper for a crew of hoboes working for the Sante Fe Railroad ("If I made a mistake in favor of the hoboes, I lost the money; but if the mistake favored the contractor, he kept it"); worked in the mail room of a newspaper; bank clerk (the bank's vice president "would always remember a trivial mistake when a clerk asked for a raise"); bookkeeper. All these jobs required attention to detail, accuracy in the accounts—yet another variety of the "true facts" Harry learned to attend to.

Young Harry Truman saw the world as a place where fundamental values were given, not debated, and where individual characters shaped events. He developed a taste for information and came to think he could understand one set of details by its analogy to another past set of details, without the intervention of much in the way of theory. He learned that life was something of a gamble, and that it paid to wait out adversity with an easy mind. And he disciplined his mind to ferret out and keep track of the facts. The focus of his attention was extraordinarily empirical. History, in all its blossoming variety, was his philosophy.

Harry Truman's style took as long in jelling as that of any President. He did not seriously set his hand to the plow of a political career until he was in his late forties. But well before that, in his experience as a soldier, Harry put together the framework of a style that would serve him for well and ill in the Presidency.

The hesitancy in Truman's life reached back to his birth: "I was supposed to be named Harrison Shippe Truman, taking the middle name from my paternal grandfather. Others in the family wanted my middle name to be Solomon, taken from my maternal grandfather. But apparently no agreement could be reached and my name was recorded and stands simply as Harry S Truman." Even after he started climbing the political ladder, Truman kept getting nominated and elected to offices other than the ones he wanted. He "never really seemed to know what he wanted to do until he was nearly forty years old," Jonathan Daniels writes.

But as Alfred Steinberg, author of the best Truman biography, *The Man from Missouri*, writes: "So far as its effect on Harry Truman was concerned, World War I released the genie from the bottle." Truman saw that, too: "My whole political career is based on my war service and war associates."

Truman had quit the National Guard in 1911. When war on Germany was declared in April 1917, the Truman family fortunes were in another dip. The Young farm was mortgaged for $25,000 and Martha had also mortgaged her brother's farm to stake Harry for some oil speculations. Harry mulled over the situation, then determined to get into the fight. "It was quite a blow to my mother and sister" when they got the news. Bess Wallace wanted to get married right away, but Harry persuaded her to wait for him. He joined the old congenial bunch in a field artillery outfit and was quickly set to recruiting. Officers were chosen by vote of the enlisted men, and Harry hoped to be a section sergeant. Instead he was elected—his first electoral win—first lieutenant. In his red roadster, "He dashed about town wearing his first lieutenant's uniform," a buddy remembered. He grinned a lot. He had a lot of friends.

In September 1917 the outfit went to Fort Sill, Oklahoma; on arrival Truman was notified he was to be regimental canteen officer, with the assistance of Eddie Jacobson, an ex-salesman. Collecting $2.00 from each man, they took $2,200 into Oklahoma City and bought supplies of cigarettes, paper, and other items soldiers would want; they set up a barbershop and a tailor shop. The pair of Army entrepreneurs then sold such "bargains" as three dollar sweaters for six dollars, taking their profits but also providing what was needed. Other Fort Sill canteens went broke, but in six months the Truman-Jacobson enterprise regained the initial investment plus $15,000—a dividend of 666 percent. Truman received such a glowing recommendation from his superior that it was returned with the notation, "There isn't anybody that good."

Sent to France in March 1918, he went through five weeks of training, read in the *New York Times* that he had been promoted to Captain, and then was placed in command of a rowdy flock of Irish pranksters loosely organized as a field artillery battalion. One former officer who could not control the men had been thrown out of the Army and another had broken down with the strain. Taking command, Truman remembered, "I was the most thoroughly scared individual in that camp. Never on the front or anywhere else have I been so nervous." This was his first responsibility as top man in anything. That day the troops put on a fake stampede of the horses; after dark a fight broke out, cots were broken, and four men wound up in the infirmary.

The next morning Captain Truman called in his noncommissioned officers.

> I told them I knew they had been making trouble for the previous commanders. I said, "I didn't come over here to get along with you. You've got to get along with me. And if there are any of you who can't, speak up and I'll bust you right back." We got along.[9]

A month later, Truman's "Dizzy D" Battery began to move up to a quiet sector of the front. Suddenly, on a night in early September, they came under merciless attack by German artillery. Truman had just fallen off his horse, but as he got to his feet a sergeant yelled, "Run, boys!" and all but five took off for the woods, abandoning their guns. At that point Captain Harry discovered the voice of command: "I got up and called them everything I knew, " he said. The curses rolled out. "It took the skin off the ears of those boys," the chaplain remembered. "It turned those boys right around." From "The Battle of Who Run" on, Truman was firmly in command. The battery went on through a great deal more combat. Truman did his own reconnoitering, getting the facts for himself. He was very nearly killed so often that his men began to think he had some special protection.

The hero of one fierce, eight-day battle Captain Truman got through was Brigadier General Douglas MacArthur.

On another occasion, Truman disobeyed orders by directing fire outside his sector, thereby saving a vulnerable division from annihilation. He was threatened with court-martial for his disobedience but stood by his guns, insisting he would do the same thing again. He was not court-martialed.

One day long after the Armistice, Truman interrupted his marathon poker game to see President Woodrow Wilson's triumphant entry into Paris. Eventually he got home again. "I've always been sorry I did not get a university education in the regular way," he said later. "But I got it in the Army the hard way—and it stuck." "Captain Harry," as his Army pals would always know him, came out of the war with the respect and admiration of his men. The mama's boy afraid to join in rough-and-tumble play had demonstrated his physical courage again and again. On his own he had learned that his angry voice could turn the tide, that he was capable of swift decision in perilous circumstances, and that men would obey him if he talked to them straight from the shoulder. Above all, he had experience of a fierce loyalty in interpersonal relations; the outfit's success depended on the stick-togetherness of imperfect comrades.

Truman and Jacobson opened their famous haberdashery after the war, serving mostly old Army buddies. An Army friend who happened to be a Missouri Pendergast got him into electoral politics, not against his will. He ran for county judge and won; his performance in that office reconfirmed his faith in hard personal campaigning and in careful, honest business practice. During the campaign Truman was charged with voting for a member of the other party and he answered in a speech:

> You have heard it said that I voted for John Miles for county marshal. I'll have to plead guilty to that charge, along with five thousand ex-soldiers. I was closer to John Miles than a brother. I have seen him in places that made hell look like a playground. I have seen him stick to his guns when Frenchmen were falling back. I have seen him hold the American line when only John Miles and his three batteries were between the Germans and a successful counterattack. He was of the right stuff, and a man who wouldn't vote for his comrade under circumstances such as these would be untrue to his country. I know every soldier understands it. I have no apology to make for it.[10]

That helped make Harry Truman "Judge" Truman, with his foot on the first rung of his ladder to the Presidency. His style was formed: aggressive rhetoric, swift decision, and, among men of good political will, loyalty lasting to the final mile.

The fighting rhetoric, so clearly evident in Truman as President and campaigner, took form in the Army where Truman experienced his first independent political success—away from his family, in an activity apart from the family tradition, undertaken to the dismay of his mother and sweetheart, representing a decision that patriotic responsibilities superseded home responsibilities. Truman, the causal farmboy who wanted to be sergeant, first won election as lieutenant from his cronies, but then went on to command strangers effectively. In the Army he found his voice; he would go on to make many a dull speech, "as if attempting a phonetic rendition from a foreign language," as Steinberg puts it. But when he broke out of composition reciting to speak man to man to his audiences, the old fire and verve returned. Politics became an arena where Harry could talk the way John had acted, with phrases instead of fists.

Then such feelings of sissyhood as were left in him found their denial. The boy tied to his mother's apron strings, the nice boy in school, teased by his peers for piano playing, got back at those Republican kids who had torn up his campaign hat. But most important in Harry's psychological development toward politics, aggressive speaking gave him a way to link up with his father and to see in political warfare an extension of the bravery Harry had shown in France.

Truman's style in decision making had two large elements. One was the close attention to detail, the studious homework he drew out of his early reading, his experience in detailed jobs, and his successful canteen management and personal reconnaissance in the Army. Truman as President could and did study hard; people were often amazed at his grasp of the facts in obscure memoranda. The other element was the decisiveness—the habit of nearly impulsive assertion of definite answers—that was to bring him such difficulties as he "shot from the hip" in the Presidency. That, too, provided an important compensation. For in most of his own life career, Truman was anything but decisive. He wandered in search of a financial killing or a satisfying career until he was well into middle age. He postponed marriage, to the only girl he ever loved, until he was thirty-five. Through the sharp ups-and-downs of his fortunes runs a kind of gambling orientation, a sense of "what the hell, take a chance" as a substitute for commitment. Harry Truman as President made much of his decisiveness—too much. His continual harping on the fact that he was decisive represented, I think, a defense against its opposite, against the fear that he would lapse into vagueness, wandering, cowardice, dependence. In a world of uncertain people, Harry's style of deciding—yes or no, on the spot, right now—could be impressive, could bring him a reputation for leadership.

If Truman's rhetoric and decisiveness were, in important respects, compensatory, his personal relations style, centered in loyalty, grew more directly out of his family version of Missouri Christianity. "If Mama Truman was for you," he said "she was for you, and as long as she lived I always knew there was one person who was in my corner." Throughout his political life Truman reiterated this for-me-or-against-me theme:

> Hillman: "You know, it is said about you, that you have stood by a man to the last drop of mercy." Mr. Truman replied, "I would rather have that said about me than to be a great man."
>
> "We don't play halfway politics in Missouri. When we start out with a man, if he is any good at all, we always stay with him to the end. Sometimes people quit me but I never quit people when I start to back them up."
>
> To Admiral Leahy: "Of course, I will make the decisions, and after a decision is made, I will expect you to be loyal."
>
> Margaret, on her father's philosophy: ". . . 'the friends thou hast and their adoption tried, grapple them to thy soul with hoops of steel' . . ."
>
> "Vinson was gifted with a sense of personal and political loyalty seldom found among the top men in Washington. Too often loyalties are breached in Washington in the rivalries for political advantage."
>
> Of Tom Pendergast: "I never deserted him when he needed friends. Many for whom he'd done much more than he ever did for me ran out on him when the

going was rough. I didn't do that—and I am President of the United States in my own right!"

Senator Kilgore, on Truman's loyalty: "Any World War I officer would have done the same thing that Truman did for Dr. Graham. He was a company commander who had to be personally responsible for his men and go to bat for a guy in a jam. It got to be an inherent trait."

"Tom Pendergast has been my friend and I don't desert a sinking ship."

"If I had been willing to forget my friends, I could have had headlines in your damn paper and plenty of other papers."

"Truman never forgave anyone who cast the slightest slur on his womenfolk," Harry Vaughn declared.

Of Eisenhower's failure to stand up for General Marshall: "You don't kick the man who made you."

In his Presidency, this sense that a brave officer stuck by his men was a rule of life. "Perhaps he learned that rule too well," Patrick Anderson writes. "In later years he seemed to confuse standing by Harry Vaughn when he was under fire from Drew Pearson with standing by the men of the 35th Division when they were under fire from the Germans at Meuse-Argonne and Verdun." Truman's loyalties were hard, but also brittle: when they broke they shattered completely.

Layered above his style was a world view in which the heroes of history competed with the facts of existence. The heroic and tragic tales provided, in the beginning, an imaginary extension of his world. But later he came to dwell on the uses of analogy, seeing himself and his situation as "like" that of people in the past. He was particularly concerned to avoid their mistakes which were, as he saw it, fundamentally mistakes of character. Yet out of both the history reading and his work experience, Truman seems to have derived a highly particularistic view of the world. He saw items better than trends or themes. Like FDR, HST had no Wilsonian penchant for high logic, no Hooverian deductive chain. But unlike FDR, Truman found it hard to discern in life's discreteness the broad outlines of the big picture. His attention was, by and large, freed by a healthy character for a focus on external realities, and the very definiteness of his decisions helped clarify his experimental interventions. His difficulty was in failing to perceive that, for example, Tom Pendergast represented in American politics more than just a good man one should be loyal to.

Truman's character was clearly active-positive. He grinned his way through the most trying times. When Democratic spirits hit the bottom in the 1948 campaign, Truman said, "Everybody around here seems to be nervous but me," and he played the piano. "I never had bad luck," he thought. As President in his mid-sixties he put in sixteen- to eighteen-hour days but was "fresher at the end than I was at the beginning," his friend Charles Ross remembered. He often got angry, but rarely depressed. Once he compared the criticism he got with the "vicious slanders" leveled against Washington, Lincoln, and Andrew Johnson:

So I don't let these things bother me for the simple reason that I know that I am trying to do the right thing and eventually the facts will come out. I'll probably be holding a conference with Saint Peter when that happens. I never give much weight or attention to the brickbats that are thrown my way. The people that cause me trouble are the good men who have to take these brickbats for me.[11]

The White House staff called him "Billie Spunk."

That character grew out of a childhood full of love, security, challenge, and interest. If in his home there was not much introspection, there was frankness, a readiness to give and take corrective action. Martha Ellen does not seem to have been working out her own ambitious strivings through Harry in the way Rebekah Johnson shoved Lyndon forward. She brought him through to adolescence as a cheerful, energetic boy who liked to learn new things. But later she also took an interest in his maintaining, in the roils of politics, strong continuity with the character she and John and the others had given him. And she reinforced Harry's decisiveness.

On her deathbed in 1947, Martha Ellen asked the President, "Is Taft going to be nominated next year?"

> "He might be," Truman said.
> She trained a severe eye on him. "Harry, are you going to run?"
> "I don't know, Mama."
> Her expression was one of impatience. "Don't you think it's about time you made up your mind?"[12]

TRUMAN AS PRESIDENT

Harry S Truman entered the Presidency as a Roosevelt Democrat. For all his emphasis on the instructiveness of history, Truman could find little definite guidance from the past to determine the direction he would take. He said he had the same beliefs as he had always had, that he was a Jeffersonian Democrat, but Jefferson was really little help to him. Truman wrote that

> I apply his principles to the situation as it is today. We often hear about Jefferson's attitude toward the power of the federal government and the power of the state governments. We hear much talk about what he would have done. It seems to me that he would probably have met conditions as he found them and that he would not have departed from his fundamental beliefs. Had he lived in our day, I believe he would have adjusted himself to this industrial age without abandoning his principles.
> I had made my campaign for the Senate on the basis of a policy I have pursued all my life—that the country should be operated for the benefit of all the people.[13]

In other words, (a) no one knows what Jefferson would do now, other than meet "conditions as he found them," and (b) Truman, like Jefferson and all other Presidents, intended to act for the "benefit of all the people." Perhaps he found some comfort in the thought that Jefferson shared his American ideology. But on the stiff questions before him, Jefferson played no part.

Asked once what was the most difficult decision he had to make as President, Truman answered "Korea." Even before he was sworn in he had to make two decisions he considered as "of world-wide import"—"to carry on the war and to let the Peace Conference go on at San Francisco." On the latter, Truman recalled, "I did not hesitate a second." But historical hindsight shows us that the most critical set of decisions he had to make in his early days concerned Poland.

At the Yalta conference in February 1945, Roosevelt won acceptance of a compromise on Poland: Churchill wanted the Poles in London to take the lead in setting up a postwar government, Stalin demanded that role for the Polish government in Lublin. In typical fashion, Roosevelt proposed that both "governments" send representatives to a conference including other Polish leaders and that the conference oversee free elections in Poland. This was the toughest nut the Yalta conference tried to crack. Stalin repeatedly asserted the Soviet Union's need for friendly neighbors, a lesson he drew from the history of attacks on Russia through Poland. Only a strong, pro-Soviet Poland could "shut the door of this corridor by her own force," Stalin said, and the issue was "not only a question of honor but of life and death for the Soviet state." Churchill and Roosevelt stood by their Atlantic Charter, a joint statement from 1941 endorsing self-determination for all peoples. The debate at Yalta was sharp; finally Stalin agreed to Roosevelt's proposal, and when FDR asked how soon the free elections could be held, Stalin said within a month, unless there was a crisis on the battlefield.

The overriding fact of the situation was simple: the Soviet Army had occupied Poland. Roosevelt saw the significance of that. After the discussion he said privately that he knew the Russians could shape the agreement to their own ends, but "it's the best I can do for Poland at this time." At the end of the conference Roosevelt toasted the meeting's family atmosphere, Churchill celebrated unity against Hitler, and Stalin noted that unity was easier during than after wartime.

Hardly had the dishes been put away at Yalta than the Polish pot began to boil. Minor frictions accumulated as the Soviets made it difficult for Americans to enter Poland to evacuate prisoners, to use airfields in Budapest, to unload relief supplies at Constanta. Then Russia imposed a Communist regime in Rumania. The promises for free elections in Poland were delayed or circumvented. American Ambassador to the Soviet Union W. Averell Harriman wrote FDR that a "new relationship" of firmness was needed, and the President wrote Stalin that "a thinly disguised continuation of the present government" in Poland "would be entirely unacceptable and would cause our people to regard the Yalta agreement as a failure." Stalin's attitude rigidified progressively. He wrote in fury to Roosevelt and Churchill when he heard that the Anglo-Americans were negotiating surrender with the German troops in Italy flocking to give up to the kindlier enemy. FDR ignored Stalin's anger and replied that "It would be one of the greatest tragedies of history if at the very moment of the victory now within our grasp, such distrust, such lack of faith, should prejudice the entire undertaking after the colossal losses of life, material, and treasure involved."

FDR kept trying for cooperation. When Churchill wanted to exclude the Russians from a mission to Greece, Roosevelt wanted them in. He thought relations with the Soviet Union would "straighten out" as the United Nations got organized. In January 1945 he had told the Congress not to expect "perfectionism" after the war, and another time had guessed "The world will be mighty lucky if it gets fifty percent of what it seeks out of the war as a permanent success. That might be a high average." In his last message to Churchill, sent on the day FDR died, the President said, "I would minimize the general Soviet problem as much as possible because these problems, in one form or another, seem to arise every day, and most of them straighten out. . . . We must be firm, however, and our course thus far is correct."

Into this situation stepped Harry Truman; the "Polish question" was all Greek to him. But he was an extraordinarily quick study. Once he flabbergasted Eisenhower with his detailed knowledge of the tangled Crimean situation. On his first full day as President he read over a summary report from the State Department, which said, in part:

SOVIET UNION: Since the Yalta Conference the Soviet Government has taken a firm and uncompromising position on nearly every major question that has arisen in our relations. The most important of these are the Polish question, the application of the Crimea agreement on liberated areas, the agreement on the exchange of liberated prisoners of war and civilians, and the San Francisco Conference. In the liberated areas under Soviet control, the Soviet Government is proceeding largely on a unilateral basis and does not agree that the developments which have taken place justify application of the Crimea agreement. . . .

POLAND: The present situation relating to Poland is highly unsatisfactory with the Soviet authorities consistently sabotaging Ambassador Harriman's efforts in the Moscow Commission to hasten the implementation of the decisions at the Crimea Conference. Direct appeals to Marshal Stalin have not yet produced any worthwhile results. The Soviet Government likewise seeks to complicate the problem by initiating and supporting claims of the Warsaw Provisional Polish Government to represent and speak for Poland in international matters such as the San Francisco Conference, reparations, and territorial questions. Because of its effect on our relations with the Soviet Union and other United Nations and upon public opinion in this country, the question of the future status of Poland and its government remains one of our most complex and urgent problems both in the international and domestic field.[14]

That same day he took instruction from Director of War Mobilization James Byrnes, Secretary of State Edward Stettinius, and Charles Bohlen on the Polish situation, and delved into the secret dispatches between FDR, Churchill, and Stalin. He discovered that Churchill had already proposed speaking to the House of Commons—and thus the whole world—to expose Soviet intransigence about Poland. Truman hesitated; FDR had wanted to keep the issue under wraps, and Truman agreed. He proposed instead a joint message to Stalin—"I feel very strongly that we should have another go at him"—and outlined a draft elaborating suggestions for a composite conference of Polish elements and assuring Stalin that his Western allies were not adamant about any particular formula. There were to be three Poles from London, four from Warsaw—Truman named them—and one more Warsaw Pole the Russians would name. The Warsaw group could arrive in Moscow first, "if desired" by Stalin. The Polish leaders were "to be permitted to suggest other names, so that all major Polish groups might be represented at all discussions."

At this point Secretary of State Stettinius told Truman that Stalin had been reluctant to send his Foreign Minister Molotov rather than some lesser official to the San Francisco conference, but that Harriman had wangled Stalin's agreement to send him if the President would see Molotov. Truman approved, instructing Stettinius to draft an answer. He then turned to a long memorandum regarding instructions for the U.S. delegation to the U.N. conference.

And the morning and the evening were the first day.

From that point on, over the following several months, Harry Truman's thoughts and actions on the Polish question wavered, although in his *Memoirs* he constructs a *post hoc* image of consistent toughness. On his second Presidential day, Saturday, April 14, Harry Hopkins told him that "Stalin is a forthright, rough, tough Russian. He is a Russian partisan through and through, thinking always first of Russia. But he can be talked to frankly." Churchill kept him busy responding to his cables on a wide range of questions. No sooner had the President given a positive answer to one question that day, regarding a statement celebrating the link-up of Anglo-American and Soviet armies, than another arrived: Churchill reported that the Russian-backed Lublin government was adding new "Polish personalities," broadening its base—but that these were only people "whom they have in their power" and, while "a step in the right direction," this "would not satisfy our requirements or decisions of Crimea Conference."

On Monday he learned that Harriman thought that "Stalin's replies to President Roosevelt and Churchill in regard to the Polish question contribute little of a concrete nature toward a solution of the impasse now existing. . . . We should adhere to our interpretation of the Crimea decisions. . . . Stalin essentially is asking us to agree to the establishment of a thinly disguised version of the present Warsaw regime. . . ." But "It is possible that Stalin's only concession regarding Mikolajczyk [one of the London Poles] may lead to others which will make it possible to find a common ground for a satisfactory solution." That same morning Truman conferred with British Foreign Secretary Anthony Eden and Ambassador Lord Halifax, firmed up the message to Stalin, and fired it off. In its final version the message set out to "correct the completely erroneous impression which you apparently received" regarding American and British intentions. In fact, the message said, the Anglo-Americans did not want to ignore the Lublin Poles—they "will play, unquestionably, a prominent part." Nor was it desired to invite an "unlimited number" of Poles. But the "Crimea decision" required a broadly representative group, not one composed only of those acceptable to the

Lublin group. Then the message listed the names of representatives acceptable to Churchill and Truman.

This was Harry Truman the frank, talking straight from the shoulder to Stalin, and Harry Truman the precise, getting across the "true facts" of the situation, and Harry Truman the advance man for the Moscow conference, laying out the names and suggesting who could arrive in Moscow first. He still had no direct way of knowing what was on Stalin's mind. Not until April 24, 1945 (Truman having been in office all of eleven days), did Stalin's viewpoint come through in an extended message. *His* understanding of the Yalta agreement, he said, was that the Lublin group would be "the kernel" of a new Polish government—"i.e., the main part." A friendly Poland was vital to Soviet security, just as Belgium and Greece were vital to British security. "The Soviet government cannot agree to existence in Poland of a government hostile toward it." No one had consulted the Soviets about postwar governments in Belgium or Greece. Why should the U.S. and Great Britain "beforehand settle with the Polish question in which the Soviet Union is first of all and most of all interested and put the government of the USSR in an unbearable position trying to dictate to it their demands." "I am ready to fulfill your request and do everything possible to reach a harmonious solution," Stalin said, "but you demand too much of me. In other words, you demand that I renounce the interests of security of the Soviet Union, but I cannot turn against my country."

The crux of the situation was getting clearer to Truman. Stalin mentioned nothing about elections. In Poland and wherever else they could pull it off, the Russians were going to have Soviet-dominated governments, Yalta or no Yalta. From the Russian viewpoint, the British and Americans were going their own way in their neighborhoods while poking around to stir up trouble in Stalin's front yard.

In the midst of great uncertainties, Truman could bone up on the facts of the situation, pore over the memoranda far into the night. He read fast, digested the material, remembered the details. What he lacked was any direct experience with Stalin and Churchill, or with the vagaries of wartime summit diplomacy, which would have given him some sense of the tone and drift of those negotiations. The "agreements" he kept coming back to were not detailed, signed contracts, but tenuous and often vague understandings by which the participants strove to impose some agreed order on an unknown future. As the situations developed, each would interpret them to his own advantage. Churchill, for example, kept harping on the Soviet obligation to keep faith regarding Poland, but argued that the Allied agreement on military occupation zones was merely a tentative and alterable sketch; the American forces under Eisenhower should push on East as far as they could. Eisenhower scrupulously held back, and Truman supported that policy. An agreement was an agreement. We should keep ours, they should keep theirs. In the early days of his Presidency—when Poland had to come in among myriad other stressful events—Truman had little in the way of grand strategic common sense to draw upon. And lacking status with Churchill and Stalin, he fell back on contract.

From this point on, Truman's thinking about the Polish puzzle shows up in interesting contrasts. Like most *Memoirs*, his place the emphases where the older author wants to think the younger actor put them. The image purveyed by the elder Truman is one of growing indignation—a patient man slowly driven to intransigence by the perfidy of his antagonist. Between the time he took the oath on April 12 and the start of the U.N. conference on April 24, 1945, the Russians kept disappointing him. Harriman came through with warnings of "a barbarian invasion of Europe." Truman assured him that "I was not afraid of the Russians and that I intended to be firm. I would be fair, of course, and anyway the Russians needed us more than we needed them"—particularly for money to rebuild their country. He directed the Americans at the U.N. conference to vote in favor of seating the Ukraine and White Russia as members, a Soviet demand. On April 22, Molotov arrived for a two-day visit. The Soviets had signed a mutual assistance pact with their puppet government in Poland. Truman calmly let him know that that had not improved matters, and the next night, as Molotov bobbed and weaved, Truman slammed him hard for refusing to follow Russia's pledges on Poland. "I have never been talked to like that in my life," said Molotov. "Carry out your agreements and you won't get talked to like that," said Truman, as he remembered it.

That was how Truman, writing his *Memoirs*, and keeping in mind the scathing attacks of critics for being soft on Communism, remembered himself. But there was another side to him. In those April days of 1945 he was listening—and agreeing—when Secretary of War Stimson cautioned that "the Russians perhaps were being more realistic than we were in regard to their own security"; to General George Marshall when he noted that the U.S. needed Russian help in the war against Japan and that "the possibility of a break with Stalin was very serious"; to Stimson again when he observed that "outside the United States, with the exception of Great Britain, there were few countries that understood free elections; that the party in power always ran the elections, as he well knew from his experience in . . . Nicaragua"; to Under Secretary of State Joseph Grew when he said that "A future war with Soviet Russia is as certain as anything in this world can be certain." Truman was concerned when the cracks in the wartime alliance began to show in the press. In June 1945 he gave an off-the-record press conference for background purposes. Asked what the West could do about the way the Russians were behaving in Eastern Europe, the President replied, "Be as patient with them as you possibly can. . . . I don't blame them for wanting to have these states around them, just as we want Mexico and Canada to be friendly to us." He agreed that the Russians had made more concessions at San Francisco than had any other nation, and added, "We had damned near as many differences with the British and not so much publicity about it." Weren't the Russians excessively suspicious? "They have got a right to be suspicious. They are not a bit more suspicious of us than we are of them. . . . Half the editorials in this country are suspicious of Russia." A few days later he asked the Association of News Analysts to "Help me keep a clear and peaceable approach and understanding. . . . I really think the Russians want to get along with us. . . . They have always been our friends, and it is in their best interest." The Russians, he said, must be more or less satisfied with their government "or some twenty million of them wouldn't die for it."

The outcome of the Polish question was anticlimactic. Stalin let no fewer than twenty of the London Poles come to Moscow for the conference—and promptly had sixteen of them arrested for anti-Soviet plotting. The other four were given posts in the new Polish government, one of them as Vice Premier. In return for Soviet approval of Argentina's membership in the U.N., the Americans and the British let Poland join the family of "peace-loving states." Poland lapsed into the gray repression of police state rule, as she had been fated to do, it would seem, from the day the Russians occupied the land. On the day after Independence Day, July 5, 1945, the United States recognized the "Polish Provisional Government of National Unity."

Truman's troubles and Truman's strengths as President are illustrated in this knottiest of his early international problems. On the strong side must be counted his ability to absorb and to master the infinitely complex details of a situation. He soaked up the facts; in that he was like Hoover. Another strength was his careful, systematic listening to those who knew more than he did, whatever their opinions. And the substance of his decisions—for all his bluster—shows, in the context of his times, moderation and realism, a readiness to try hard to win but an ability to accept failure when necessary. In May of 1945, for example, the novice President blundered badly: what he thought was a routine document for his signature turned out to cut off lend-lease aid to the Soviet Union. Someone should have told him to read it first; he should have had that someone there to tell him. Ships at sea, loaded with supplies for Russia, turned about and headed home. Truman rescinded the order when he discovered the error, but he had angered the Russians.

It is difficult to judge in hindsight how Truman might have bucked the tide tearing apart the wartime alliance with the Soviet Union. It is barely plausible to suppose that he could have persuaded Congress to give Stalin some portion of the $6 billion loan the Russians wanted, or to have allowed the Soviet Union to collect massive reparations from Germany. On the other hand, it is within the realm of imagination to envision Truman shoving the Russians out of the United Nations, risking combat with Soviet troops by ordering Eisenhower to march on east, breaking off diplomatic relations, or backing the Polish army in England on some rescue mission. Those assessments have and will keep the historians busy revising one another for a good while. What does seem clear is that Truman talked a good deal worse than he acted.

In the Polish crisis as later, Harry Truman struggled to be decisive and, too often, sounded aggressive. His sense of the facts gave him a way of proposing things specifically—too specifically for the contingencies of international diplomacy. Thrust up into the Presidency and called upon to say yes, no, or maybe on questions he lacked training for or experience in, he thought he could base policy on particulars, and he was determined not to drift, not to confirm all those expectations that he would turn out to be inadequate for the job. He was Captain Harry all over again. Action was called for, and by God he would act. As he put it in a famous passage:

> Within the first few months I discovered that being a President is like riding a tiger. A man has to keep on riding or be swallowed. The fantastically crowded nine months of 1945 taught me that a President either is constantly on top of events or, if he hesitates, events will soon be on top of him. I never felt that I could let up for a moment.[15]

In world affairs, and soon in domestic affairs, Truman had boisterous tigers to ride. His simile poses sharply the alternatives as he felt them: decide or fall. Truman seems to have recognized that great decisions required time and study (which he gave them when he could), and also a largeness of vision, a kind of contextual thinking (which he gradually developed out of experience). But he saw his first duty as President to be the clear establishment of command: over himself, over events, over subordinates; and the definite assertion of his membership in the triangle with Churchill and Stalin. Men made history, and Truman gave priority to meeting that responsibility head-on.

At first—and too often later—Truman reacted to unanticipated questions with precise, yes-no answers. He shot from the hip at whatever question was thrown up to him. On April 24, 1945, Churchill called him on the telephone to report that Heinrich Himmler had opened negotiations to surrender German forces on the Western front. (This was their first telephonic conversation; Truman had it recorded.) Truman knew only that such a proposal had been put forth; otherwise "I have no other information except what I am receiving from you now." Truman asked one question: what had Himmler to surrender?

CHURCHILL: They mentioned Italy, and Yugoslavia. We mentioned everything and have included that to take in Denmark and Norway. Everything on the Western Front, but he hasn't proposed to surrender on the Eastern Front. So we thought perhaps it would be necessary to report it to Stalin; that is, of course, to say that in our view the surrender must be simultaneous to agree to our terms.

TRUMAN: I think he should be forced to surrender to all three governments, Russia, you and the United States. I don't think we ought to even consider a piecemeal surrender.

CHURCHILL: No, no, no. Not a piecemeal surrender to a man like Himmler. Himmler will be speaking for the German state as much as anybody can. And therefore we thought that his negotiations must be carried on with the three governments.

TRUMAN: That's right, that's the way I feel exactly.

CHURCHILL: I see, of course, that's local surrender on the front, Himmler's allied front. And then Eisenhower is still authorized to take the surrender, well, then he will wish to surrender.

TRUMAN: Yes, of course.[16]

It was this type of oral context in which Truman was again and again to respond with insufficiently considered answers. Lacking information, he was nevertheless all too ready to reply definitively. That happened repeatedly to him in press conferences, where a reporter can quote as the President's own some phrase the reporter invents if the President agrees to it. At least two of the phrases Truman was identified with and castigated for—the characterization of anti-Communist investigations as a "red herring" and the description of the war in Korea as a "police action"—emerged in this fashion. When the Korean war was deepening in 1950, Truman told reporters that "we will take whatever steps are necessary to met the military situation, just as we always have." One of them followed up with, "Does that mean that there is active consideration of the use of the atomic bomb?" Truman shot back: "There has *always* been active consideration of its use." Most newspapers left out the "always" and the news created a sensation. In England one hundred Members of Parliament signed a letter of protest, there was a long and intense debate on America's intention to A-bomb Korea, and the Prime Minister was cheered when he announced that he would go to Washington to discuss this crisis with the President. In 1952, after Truman took over the steel mills, a reporter asked, "Mr. President, if it is proper to seize the steel mills, can you, in your opinion, seize the newspapers and radio stations?" Truman did not hesitate: "Under similar circumstances, the President has to act for whatever is for the best interests of the country"—which the press translated into "Yes." "Dictator" Truman was raked over the coals. And by the time he could say, at his next news conference, "That was a lot of hooey," the damage had been done.

Similarly, his offhanded remark after Potsdam, "I like Joe Stalin," was heard, reported, and distorted into a representation of national policy. Truman was a spontaneous man, ready to say what he felt and thought rather than hold it back. And he never mastered the politician's rhetorical talent for dissembling.

By 1947 he was aware of the problem: "The President of the United States has to be very careful not to be emotional or to forget that he is working for one hundred and forty-five million people primarily, and for peace in the world as his next objective."

The way Truman's soldierly rhetoric served him badly and the way his fact-orientation and determination to command reinforced that propensity to ill effect come through in the Henry Wallace affair. Truman the politician had helped dispense two pieces of high patronage he ultimately came to regret. Having defeated Wallace for the Vice Presidency in 1944, Truman as presiding officer of the Senate cast a tie-breaking vote for Wallace's confirmation when FDR named him Secretary of Commerce. Then, after assuming the Presidency, Truman named his other chief rival for the Vice Presidency, James F. Byrnes, Secretary of State. Before 1946 was over Truman fired both of them in acrimonious controversies.

Wallace had a high, broad vision of the "Century of the Common Man," a belief in human potentiality, a general hope for the future, and a rhetorical bent for inspiring progressives of similar mind. As he would show in 1948, this taste for the philosophical could leave him vulnerable to practical error. Certainly his whole style of thought contrasted markedly with that of earth-bound Harry Truman. As the cold war began to take shape, Wallace stood back and looked at the general situation and concluded that the nation, darting from crisis to crisis, was lurching toward disaster. The direction was wrong; the solution was redirection in the light of a fresh analysis. In March 1946 he wrote Truman suggesting "a new approach along economic lines" to the Soviet Union:

> We know that much of the recent Soviet behavior which has caused us concern has been the result of their dire economic needs and of their disturbed sense of security. The events of the past few months have thrown the Soviets back to their pre-1939 fears of "capitalist encirclement" and to their erroneous belief that the Western World, including the U.S.A., is invariably and unanimously hostile.
>
> I think we can disabuse the Soviet mind and strengthen the faith of the Soviets in our sincere devotion to the cause of peace by proving to them that we want to trade with them and to cement our economic relations with them. To do this, it is necessary to talk with them in an understanding way, with full realization of their difficulties and yet with emphasis on the lack of realism in many of their assumptions and conclusions which stand in the way of peaceful world cooperation.[17]

Wallace went on to suggest a new conference of men "capable of speaking in terms of the general problems involved" as well as the specific ones.

Truman, deep in tangled complexities, ignored Wallace's letter. Wallace thought for four months, then produced another, much longer letter which reached the press and argued for a peaceable reorientation. The massive build-up of American military power must, he thought, "make it look to the rest of the world as if we were only paying lip service to peace at the conference table. . . . We are telling the Russians that if they are 'good boys' we may eventually turn over our knowledge of atomic energy to them and to all other nations." A new policy should "allay any reasonable Russian grounds for fear, suspicion, and distrust."

Truman, riding the tiger, noted that Wallace "had no specific proposals how this might be accomplished without surrendering to them on every count." He thanked Wallace for his effort.

In September 1946, while Secretary Byrnes was grappling in Paris with the Russians and British over Poland and the other satellites, Wallace came to the White House for a conversation with Truman. He told the President he planned to make a speech two days later at a New York rally for Soviet-American friendship. Some part of their conversation—thirty minutes, fifteen minutes, thirty seconds, depending on whose *post hoc* account is right—was spent in discussing the content of Wallace's speech. Wallace was to speak the evening of September 12. At 4 o'clock that afternoon, Truman held his regular press conference. Many of the reporters had advance copies of the Wallace speech, and they questioned him about it:

> Q: In the middle of the speech are these words: "When President Truman read these words, he said they represented the policy of this administration."

THE PRESIDENT: That is correct.

Q: My question is, does that apply just for that paragraph or to the whole speech?

THE PRESIDENT: I approved the whole speech.

Q: Mr. President, do you regard Wallace's speech as a departure from Byrnes' policy?

THE PRESIDENT: I do not. They are exactly in line.18

Then the fur began to fly. Wallace said, "The real peace treaty we now need is between the United States and Russia" and "On our part we should recognize that we have no more business in the *political* affairs of Eastern Europe than Russia has in the *political* affairs of Latin America, Western Europe, and the United States." Then came the clincher: "To make Britain the key to our foreign policy would, in my judgment, be the height of folly. Make no mistake about it: the British imperialist policy in the Near East alone, combined with Russian retaliation, would lead the United States straight to war. . . I am neither anti-British nor pro-British; neither anti-Russian nor pro-Russian. And just two days ago, when President Truman read these words, he said they represented the policy of his administration."

The press blazed forth with headlines about this new direction for American foreign policy. Byrnes got the news from a British correspondent and hit the ceiling; he sent Truman his resignation to take effect if Wallace's outbursts were allowed to continue. Senator Arthur Vandenberg, in Paris to demonstrate Republican support for Truman's foreign policy, said "I can cooperate with only one Secretary of State at a time." At the White House and the State Department chaos reigned.

Truman waited a day, then called the press in to tell them his previous answer had been given "extemporaneously and my answer did not convey the thought I intended it to convey. It was my intention to express the thought that I approved the right of the Secretary of Commerce to deliver the speech. I did not intend to indicate that I approved the speech as indicating a statement of the foreign policy of this country. There has been no change in the established foreign policy of our government." Not many believed him. *Time* magazine called the President's explanation "a clumsy lie."

Wallace let a day pass, then announced "I stand upon my New York speech. . . . I shall within the near future speak on this subject again." At the end of the week Truman fired Wallace: first he wrote a scathing note to him, then withdrew and destroyed it at Wallace's request, then phoned Wallace and asked for his resignation ("He was so nice about it I almost backed out!" wrote Harry to Mama and Mary). At a press conference that day Truman joined the reporters in laughter as the usher asked them to seat themselves "a little to the left, gentlemen, a little to the left," and read his brief announcement. His *Memoirs* give a long account of all this, but make no mention of a letter to Wallace. In his letter home, Truman said, "Well, now he's out, and the crackpots are having conniption fits. I'm glad they are. It convinces me I'm right. . . ."

Truman's own attitude toward the Russians was not rigidified at this point; it was ambivalent. Early in 1946 he told Byrnes that "unless Russia is faced with an iron fist and strong language, another war is in the making." But in March, after ex-Prime Minister Churchill delivered his "iron curtain" speech in Missouri, Truman said U.S. relations with Russia were "as cordial as they always have been. When two horse traders get to bargaining, they sometimes get pretty rough with each other, but they hardly ever wind up in a fistfight. They usually make a trade. That is what we propose to do with Russia. I have no feeling but of the friendliest sort for Russia."

Harry Truman was not, as the cold war got colder, frozen into an ideological position. The Wallace affair was, purely and simply, an accident, a blunder created by his stylistic propensity for quick, plain answers to whatever was asked him. In this case as in others, the substance of the issue got lost because his quick-draw rhetoric transformed the matter into a crisis of personalities. Wallace the philosopher passed him in the night: "I do not understand a 'dreamer' like that," Truman said. But once Truman's impulsiveness disclosed Wallace the insubordinate, the President felt he had to act in order to affirm his leadership, as he had once done with a rowdy bunch of Irish noncoms. "Some of the generals and the admirals and the career men in government," he wrote in an unmailed letter, "look upon the occupant of the White House as only a temporary nuisance who will soon be succeeded by another temporary occupant who won't find out what it is all about for a long time and then it will be too late to do anything about it." That was not going to be true of Truman, he determined.

Truman's hair-trigger tongue spoke from a mind—a character—which had found a way to make peace with itself by a mental policy of "no regrets." He reached out for action from a position of inner strength; that made him capable of and motivated for a positive life, one in which he would make marks on his environment. He took himself seriously, recognizing himself as a person with special strengths as well as acknowledged limitations, trusting himself enough to believe that he could figure out what to do if he could get the facts and that he had the courage to live with the results. He had learned to live with adversity, to wait it out with good humor. Most important for his continued self-acceptance was his way of structuring his experience temporally. Truman called the first volume of his memoirs *Year of Decisions*, and he went at "Presidenting" as an experience divided into discrete decisional events. This approach meant framing the flow of history so as to create choice-points, sharply defined in a binary fashion, around which to organize his energies. That required discovering amidst complexity the critical issue, learning the data bearing most directly on that issue, posing the alternatives in either-or terms, deciding, expressing the decision, and then putting the matter aside. In his performance as President, that technique insured that Truman's associates would learn to see (a) the President as the one who would decide, and (b) their own inputs as most effective if posed in this style. In that way Truman banged his way to the top of the power process, shedding rivalrous advisors and those who could not or would not adapt to his way of working. The advantages were sharpness, debate, clarity; the disadvantages, narrowness, disruption, error. Truman himself put it this way in 1958:

> All my life whenever it comes time to make a decision, I make it and forget about it, and go to work on something else; and when these things came before me, as President of the United States, I made the decision on them, and went into the next thing. You never have time to stop. You've got to keep going because there's always a decision just ahead of you that you've got to make, and you don't want to look back. If you make a mistake in one of those decisions, correct it by another decision, and go ahead.[19]

For Truman himself the decision-centered style meant that he was constantly stimulating feedback which could provide the opportunity for learning. From the start of his Presidency, Truman began accumulating experience, noticing what happened as an obvious result of what he did. Such learning was extremely difficult for a Harding or a Coolidge because they could not see clearly enough what it was that they did. Much of the feedback Truman got was negative—"To err is Truman" became a popular slogan. He was able to grow in office (and in himself) because he found a way to separate the moral castigations from the substance of the arguments he received. He could learn the substance quickly, and his motive-centered morality left him free of guilt and anxiety once he had chosen to the best of his ability: "Once a decision was made, I did not worry about it afterward." The certainty that he was doing his best let him sleep soundly, eat heartily, and laugh exuberantly through the most trying of times. Six months into his Presidency he told a Masonic audience that the office "is an all-day and nearly all-night job. Just between you and me and the gatepost, I like it." At Potsdam that year, Winston Churchill found Truman—the same Truman who was surrounded on all sides with problems of terrifying significance—behaving with a

> gay, precise, sparkling manner and obvious power of decision. . . . He invited personal friendship and comradeship. . . . I felt here was a man of exceptional character and ability, with . . . simple and direct methods of speech, and a great deal of self-confidence and resolution.[20]

Near the end of his Presidency Truman wrote his daughter that "Your dad will never be reckoned among the great. But you can be sure he did his level best and gave all he had to his country. There is an epitaph in Boothill Cemetery in Tombstone, Arizona, which reads, 'Here lies Jack Williams; he done his damndest.' What more can a person do?"

Truman's main difficulties as President arose when he had to—or felt he had to—react swiftly to an external demand for decision, such as at his press conferences. The decision to drop the first atomic bomb and the decision to intervene militarily in Korea were of this type. In both cases he leapt over the first phases of his decision-making process and quickly reached a choice which involved, as it turned out, the direst consequences. But as he developed wider experience the great initiatives of his administration also emerged—the Truman Doctrine, the Marshall Plan, NATO, Point Four. Under his leadership, the policy of containing Communism by preventive military and economic shoring up of regions threatened by Soviet expansionism developed its positive thrust, particularly in Europe. This is not the place to go into what that eventually came to or how it all might have been different. From the perspective of the Presidency, Truman took massive initiatives at a time when such initiatives seemed unlikely, given the circumstances of his accession to the office, his own qualifications, and the condition of the country.

Harry Truman liked to say that "When you're at the bottom you've got no place to go but up." In 1946, his fortunes dipped close to the wrong end of the barrel. After Roosevelt's death the country had rallied around him, as Americans do in a Presidential crisis. Then the Gallup poll gave him 87 percent approval—three percent higher than FDR's top rating. A year and half later, as the Congressional elections approached, Truman was down to 32 percent. The nation was in a surly mood. The war was over and people wanted to get on with the rich full life. Roosevelt was dead, Churchill turned out of office, the great crusade which had united the country—and suppressed all its ordinary conflicts—was done with. Yet what the people found was sky-rocketing inflation, black markets, continual strikes, meat shortages, quarrels among the armed services, firings at the top of the government, the housing shortage, fears about the new atomic bomb, partisan battles in Congress, and growing rifts among the wartime allies. The climate of expectations called for a time of reassurance and recovery, after all the sacrifice and moral uplift of the war. A large part of the public did not find Truman reassuring. He got it from all sides: both the Communists and the unions were against him, while the Republicans berated him for being soft on Communism and unions. Whatever was wrong with the Presidency, the Republicans, out of power since 1933, could claim it was none of their doing, and urge throwing the rascals out. As usual, these emotions focused on the man in the White House. The slogan "Had enough?" got a strong play. Pundits such as Walter Lippmann pronounced their solemn judgments:

> It is not, I think, an exaggeration to say that the condition of the Truman administration is a grave problem for the nation. How are the affairs of the country to be conducted by a President who not only has lost the support of his party but is not in control of his own administration? . . . Mr. Truman is not performing, and gives no evidence of his ability to perform, the functions of the Commander-in-Chief. At the very center of the Truman administration . . . there is a vacuum of responsibility and authority.[21]

Democratic candidates for Congress left Truman's name unspoken, using recordings of FDR's voice instead. The electorate trooped to the polls and let Truman have it: the Republicans captured both houses of Congress for the first time in 18 years, winning firm control with a margin of 57 in the House and 6 in the Senate. Senator J. William Fulbright, Democrat, suggested Truman appoint

Vandenberg Secretary of State and then resign to make him President. The Republican Eightieth Congress, led by men with an old itch to lay waste to the New Deal, opened its deliberations. The smell of retrenchment was in the air.

On the home front not a great deal of retrenchment happened, but neither did Truman get far with his Fair Deal. Congress passed the Taft-Hartley Act over his veto, outlawing the closed shop but allowing the union shop and otherwise regulating collective bargaining. It did not turn out to be a "slave labor act" or to have a great deal of practical effect. The same Eightieth Congress blocked Truman proposals for public housing, Social Security extension, anti-lynching law, anti-poll tax law, a Fair Employment Practices Commission, aid to education, and his anti-inflation program. It passed a tax bill favoring the rich, over yet another Truman veto. Although it was not his intention, Truman was planting the seeds of progressive legislation for the future, a garden of ideas whose time would eventually come. But in terms of implementation, the Fair Deal was a general failure.

Nevertheless, this repudiated President, the year after the election debacle of 1946, engineered the most massive international peacetime aid program in history, and in 1948 got it accepted by Congress. Still thoroughly lacking his own electoral mandate, Truman built outward from piecemeal response to Soviet moves toward a new concept of reconstruction for Europe. Luck played its part. So did Truman's own growing Presidential imagination and his skill in Presidential maneuver.

Early in 1947 the British said they could no longer afford to pay for bolstering the security of the Greek and Turkish governments. Truman had known of their difficulties as early as 1945. Now the United States would have to take over to prevent the success of Soviet pressure against those countries. The President proceeded with utmost care, moving toward a decision the way he had always wanted to. The studies were extensive, the reports of investigating teams detailed, the consultations widespread through the administration and the foreign governments involved. Putting aside what Republicans had so recently been saying about him, Truman held repeated conferences with the Congressional leaders, many of whom had strong isolationist leanings. In March 1947 he set forth to the Congress the essence of the "Truman Doctrine" in three brief sentences:

> I believe that it must be the policy of the United States to support free peoples who are resisting attempted subjugation by armed minorities or by outside pressures.
> I believe that we must assist free peoples to work out their destinies in their own ways.
> I believe that our help should be primarily through economic and financial aid which is essential to economic stability and orderly political processes.[22]

In typical Truman either-or fashion, he went on to contrast "our way of life" with that of "totalitarian regimes" and to pose economic security as the best defense against subversion. In May, Congress passed the measure. Truman signed it in

Kansas City's Muehlebach Hotel; he had rushed there to be with Martha Ellen when, at 94, she died on May 22.

The Marshall Plan was an immense escalation and a large conceptual step beyond aid to Greece and Turkey. Presidents themselves rarely think up such things. This one developed out of Walter Lippmann's deliberations on the condition of Western Europe, which had been described in that spring of 1947 by Churchill as "a rubble-heap, a charnel house, a breeding ground of pestilence and hate." On April 5, Lippmann, drawing on what he knew of schemes already afoot in the State Department, wrote, "The truth is that political and economic measures on a scale which no responsible statesman has yet ventured to hint at will be needed in the next year or so. . . . The measures will have to be very large—in Europe no less than an economic union, and over here no less than the equivalent to a revival of Lend-Lease." To make the aid effective, Lippmann said, Europe should be considered as a unit, the countries conferring on their needs and developing definite joint requirements and plans for their recovery.

Truman planned to use the Lippmann idea for a speech, but he was tied up in Washington and sent Acheson to pinch hit for him. Acheson also stressed a unified Europe approach, but his talk got little notice in the United States, though considerable attention from the European press. Then General George C. Marshall, Truman's new Secretary of State whom the President considered "the greatest living American," developed the plan in his Harvard commencement address on June 5. "The initiative, I think, must come from Europe," Marshall said. "The role of this country should consist of friendly aid in the drafting of a European program and of later support of such a program so far as it may be practical for us to do so." With some adroit public relations help from Acheson, the Marshall speech created a sensation. British Foreign Secretary Ernest Bevin grabbed the ball and ran with it; he did not check with Washington at first for fear the plan would turn out not to be official. By September, sixteen European nations had cooperated in a reconstruction plan and requested $22.4 billion over four years.

President Truman proceeded carefully. Three special committees explored the practicalities: one, under Secretary of Commerce Harriman, looked into what the United States could afford in fiscal, economic, and political terms; the second, under the Secretary of the Interior, examined the drain that plan would mean on American natural resources; and the third, under the Chairman of the Council of Economic Advisors, assessed the impact on the national economy. Thus Truman had his facts, and they came from sure and eminent sources.

Next the President again swallowed his partisanship and persuaded 18 members of the House of Representatives, led by Republican Christian Herter of Massachusetts, to go to Europe and see for themselves. They stayed a month and a half. They were, in the main, persuaded by what they saw. Even isolationist Everett McKinley Dirksen came back converted and became an active advocate.

There was opposition; Senator Taft, William's son, warned against an "international WPA," and there were others. Truman released the three reports recommending the Marshall Plan and showing how it could be done. Then in

November 1947 came another major step down the road to Congressional approval: Truman called a special session of Congress and asked for a relatively small ($597 million) appropriation as an emergency measure to help Europeans get through the winter. The ice was broken. In December the President presented the whole immense program, asking $17 billion from the pockets of U.S. taxpayers. "We must decide whether or not we will complete the job of helping the free nations of Europe recover from the devastation of war." With few exceptions, Congress and the press reacted favorably. The Soviet Union helped things along in February by taking over Czechoslovakia and in March by initiating their program of restrictions on access to Berlin. The Marshall Plan, with some amendments, was approved by a vote of 318 to 75 in the House and by an overwhelming voice vote in the Senate, on April 2, 1948. Decades later, the Marshall Plan countries had grown prosperous and remained democratic.

Truman had moved flexibly, systematically, and with a profound sense of political forgiveness. Most significant for our argument, Truman had grown, had stretched his mind and deepened his understanding beyond the narrowly empirical reactionism with which he had begun. His sources of information were widespread and various. He brought the doubtful Republicans right into the center of the policy. And his large view and purpose caught the imagination of a public which, only a few months before, had seemed to have little use for him.

Truman went on to win the election of 1948 in a smashing upset victory, despite the supreme confidence of his opponent and the emergence of two minority parties composed largely of ex-Democrats.

On the afternoon of Saturday, June 24, 1950, the North Korean army invaded South Korea. On Sunday afternoon the Security Council of the United Nations (minus the Russians, who had walked out) voted 9–0 to label the invasion a breach of the peace and to call for an immediate cease-fire and withdrawal. That night Truman met in Washington with the whole top layer of his military and diplomatic advisors, all of whom counseled action. Truman ordered General Douglas MacArthur to evacuate Americans from Korea, protect them by air, and get all the supplies and ammunition he could to the South Korean army. The 7th Fleet was ordered into the Formosa straits. The next morning Truman pointed to Korea on the map and said, "This is the Greece of the Far East. If we are tough enough now, there won't have to be any next step." That night, again meeting with his "war cabinet," Truman ordered MacArthur to give direct air and naval support to the Republic of Korea (ROK) forces. As the meeting concluded, the President said, "Everything I have done in the past five years has been to try to avoid making a decision such as I had to make tonight." The next morning Truman met with Congressional leaders and his full Cabinet: no one opposed what he had done. That night the U. N. Security Council called on U.S. members to help South Korea repel the attack.

Before the week was out, President Truman authorized MacArthur to dispatch American ground combat troops to Korea. The war was under way. Before it was over, scores of thousands of Americans would become its casualties.

What happened from that point on is well known. President Truman placed his confidence in MacArthur, who soon found need for many more American troops. Truman, backed by the U.N. resolution, poured them in, and eventually MacArthur, by a brilliant surprise landing at Inchon, pushed the enemy back to the 38th parallel, the line dividing North and South Korea. Truman hesitated about permitting that line to be crossed; the Chinese had warned that they would consider such a crossing as an act of aggression against North Korea. But in order to obtain a defensible battle line Truman authorized the crossing, and to insure against further aggression from the North he instructed MacArthur to undertake "the destruction of the North Korean Armed Forces." MacArthur made two cease-fire appeals to the enemy. When these were ignored, he ordered his forces "to destroy the North Korean Army and unify the entire nation." In October, Truman went to Wake Island in the Pacific for a conference with MacArthur, at which the general gave his intelligence estimate that the Chinese would not enter the war. But in November large numbers of Chinese troops poured into Korea. MacArthur was authorized to bomb bridges over the Yalu River separating China and North Korea. But soon MacArthur's forces were also under heavy air attack and he requested permission for American planes to pursue the attackers back across the borders and to bomb their airfields. Truman refused this request for fear of spreading the war into China.

Later in November, some 200,000 new Chinese troops crossed the border and hurled back the Americans. It was more a rout than a retreat. MacArthur reported that "This small command is facing the entire Chinese Nation in an undeclared war. Unless some positive and immediate action is taken, hope for success cannot be justified, and steady attrition leading to final destruction can reasonably be contemplated. . . . The general evaluation of the situation here must be viewed on the basis of an entirely new war against an entirely new power of great military strength and under entirely new conditions. . . ." By mid December the situation was worse; *Time* called the defeat a military disaster, "the worst the United States has ever suffered."

By this time an exhausted and embittered Harry Truman was meeting almost every day with his "war cabinet." Captain Harry was on the spot; no one could decide but him. From history he remembered Dunkirk and wondered whether he would see a Korean version. His commander in the field was calling desperately for an end to the inhibitions he thought responsible for his desperate situation. Truman recalled MacArthur's bravery when they had served in France; his feelings of loyalty, of backing up the man in the field, welled up. MacArthur was reporting an entirely new war, one in which the Chinese had committed hundreds of thousands in a clear attempt to defeat and humiliate the United States and the United Nations. Only a few years after World War II, boys were being pounded to pieces in a war whose purpose they did not, could not, understand completely.

Most deeply, the President felt a bitter moral exhaustion. For years he had been struggling against just such an eventuality. The Communists had pushed and pushed, apparently insatiable in their greed for expansion. He had been extraordinarily patient with them. Now it seemed the end of the time for trying to persuade, cajole, bluff, buy, or threaten. If he did not act decisively now, the policy of containment would result in one dash after another putting out fires around the globe, at the cost of untold American casualties. Words had not won the day, nor had limited warfare.

Still another memory was in Truman's mind. One of his early decisions as President was to give the go-ahead for dropping the first atomic bombs on Japan. Within a few days, the Japanese surrendered, ending that bloody and vicious contest once and for all. The first American President to lose a war would have to be someone other than Harry Truman.

On February 1, after a sleepless night, President Truman met with his war cabinet to announce his decision. Requiring utmost secrecy, he told his advisors he had issued the necessary messages to order the immediate employment of atomic bombs against Chinese military installations in Manchuria. The 7th Fleet had been simultaneously ordered out of the Formosa straits and commanded to facilitate in every way practical the landing of forces under Generalissimo Chiang Kai-shek on the Chinese mainland. These actions, he explained, were taken in response to the military situation reported by General MacArthur, which he summarized in detail. That afternoon the President would appear before a joint session of the Congress to ask for a declaration of war against the People's Republic of China.

That, of course, is what did not happen. The tale told here in italics is fiction. But it could have been fact. The process it describes fits, I think, what might have happened in the mind of an active-*negative* Harry Truman. The real Harry Truman, in contrast, did not fasten onto that track and ride it to the end. He finally managed to get peace talks going with the North Koreans; but he would not agree to the repatriation, clearly against their will, of thousands of North Koreans captured in the South who refused to go home. The cost of that decision was some 80,000 American casualties before the enemy finally relented and gave up the demand for forced repatriation. The armistice was signed July 27, 1953, six months after Truman left office.

The critical difference between the active-positive and active-negative pattern in such circumstances is in the former's ability to accumulate experience without accumulating anxiety, frustration, and guilt. Both sides of the equation seem significant. Truman did not become embittered and morally exhausted. His characteristic grin is there, in photograph after photograph, as added testimony to the verbal reports. He did not experience that sense of progressive diminution that develops in the active-negative mind as it moves through compromise after compromise. Decisiveness meant for him a way of making up his mind how he felt about a matter, a way of confronting it directly and choosing what he wanted; this enabled him to move on with a free will and a whole heart. The active-negative type, on the other hand, is never quite ready to give of himself, risk himself in the same way. He moves on, but he carries with him a residue of resentment and reluctance, of unresolved conflicts which continue to pile up in his mind until he feels tremendous internal pressure to express it. The result has often been a rigid insistence on his own special solution, one clearly at odds with the assumptions of his critics, one which allows him to see himself as a lonely, virtuous, suffering fighter against essentially evil opponents.

Truman never fell for that. Korea trapped him, once the decision to introduce large numbers of ground troops was made and once he accepted MacArthur's judgment that the Chinese would not intervene. His values trapped him when he would not agree to forced repatriation. Certainly it can be argued that these were terrible mistakes, that Truman bought relatively small advantage at an immense cost in lives, money, and political credit. Even if that is true, Truman's character cannot be said to have made it happen. The war did not become his personal crusade, did not engage his pride system in a contest of courage between himself and the Chinese. His problem, unlike that of Wilson, Hoover, and Johnson, was first impulsiveness and then excessive trust in the information he received. With the initial invasion, he acted too quickly, in an atmosphere of galloping consensus among his advisors, before an opposition viewpoint had a chance to develop. Perhaps he relied too heavily on the debate that had gone into the formulation of a United States strategic posture, as expressed for instance in NSC-68, a National Security Council paper which recommended "meeting each fresh challenge promptly and unequivocally."

But he did not freeze. Five days before the Chinese invasion was verified, Truman was napping in his underwear in a second-floor bedroom in Blair House, his temporary residence while the White House was being repaired. At 2:20 P.M., a pair of Puerto Rican revolutionaries approached the house and suddenly fired 31 rounds at the door and the front of the house. Truman jumped up and ran to the window. One of the attackers got up two of the front steps before he was gunned down. A guard looked up and saw Truman and yelled "Damn it! Get back! Get back!" A White House guard and one of the Puerto Ricans were killed. In the panic a supposed witness told a breathless reporter "They've broken into Blair House. They've killed the President and seven Secret Service men!"

At a few minutes before 3:00, Truman calmly left to make a speech at Arlington Cemetery. "A President has to expect those things," he said. "The only thing you have to worry about is bad luck. I never had bad luck." Over Secret Service objections, he continued his daily morning walks.

Five days later, Truman replied to MacArthur's emergency request cautiously: "You are authorized to go ahead with your planned bombing in Korea near the frontier including targets at Sinuilu and Korean end of Yalu bridges. . . .The above does not authorize the bombing of any dams or power plants on the Yalu River. . . . Because it is vital in the national interests of the U.S. to localize the fighting in Korea it is important that extreme care be taken to avoid violation of Manchurian territory and airspace."

Truman eventually fired General MacArthur for exceeding his authority. MacArthur had taken to issuing statements and letters in which he extended his views beyond strategy to policy, continually urging an expansion of the war. MacArthur was the hero of World War II in Asia, had gone on to be virtual king of Japan; he had been in the Far East for nearly 14 years. Truman kept the general on long after his complaints began to appear in the U.S. press. There was never a good time to get rid of him. When MacArthur's forces were succeeding in the field, Truman would have sacrificed a great deal of political capital in firing him. When the tide turned against MacArthur, Truman felt he had to stand by him. "I should have fired MacArthur then and there," Truman said later of one of the general's statements in an American magazine complaining of the "extraordinary inhibitions" under which he had to fight. But he waited and waited, congratulating MacArthur on his wins and warning him again and again not to flow forth in public with global visions. Finally in March and April 1951, the crunch came. Truman and his top advisors had decided to move toward a cease-fire and negotiations through the U.N. On March 20, a draft statement was circulated to 14 allies—and to General MacArthur. MacArthur's copy had a cover letter: "State planning Presidential announcement shortly that, with clearing of bulk of South Korea on aggression, U.N. now prepared to discuss conditions of settlement in Korea." Truman had prepared a careful statement concentrating on Korea itself and stressing the restoration of peace and security. Four days later, MacArthur suddenly disrupted all these plans with his own large interpretation of things. Red China had been whipped on the battlefield, he said:

> The enemy, therefore, must by now be painfully aware that a decision of the United Nations to depart from its tolerant effort to contain the war to the area of Korea, through an expansion of our military operations to its coastal areas and interior bases, would doom Red China to the risk of imminent military collapse. These basic facts being established, there should be no insuperable difficulty in arriving at decisions on the Korean problem if the issues are resolved on their own merits, without being burdened by extraneous matters not directly related to Korea, such as Formosa or China's seat in the United Nations.[23]

Having rattled his saber, MacArthur went on to set the scene for peacemaking:

> I stand ready at any time to confer in the field with the commander-in-chief of the enemy forces in the earnest effort to find any military means whereby realization of the political objectives of the United Nations in Korea, to which no nation may justly take exceptions, might be accomplished without further bloodshed.[24]

Truman was furious. To Senator Kilgore he said, "I'll show that son of a bitch who's boss. Who does he think he is—God?" His senior advisors shared his anger, but Truman held his fire for two weeks, sending only a reminder to MacArthur that he was supposed to clear statements with Washington. Truman tried to think it through calmly: "I tried to place myself in his position . . . and tried to figure out why he was challenging the traditional civilian authority in our government."

But he waited. Then on April 5, 1951, Representative Joseph Martin rose in the House to read a letter MacArthur had sent him, including this:

> It seems strangely difficult for some to realize that here in Asia is where the Communist conspirators have elected to make their play for global conquest, and that we have joined the issue thus raised on the battlefield; that here we fight Europe's war with arms while the diplomats there still fight it with words; that if we lose this war to Communism in Asia the fall of Europe is inevitable, win it and Europe most probably would avoid war and yet preserve freedom. As you point out, we must win. There is no substitute for victory.[25]

Thus, by this point, MacArthur had threatened China, undercut the President's peace initiative, disobeyed the order to clear statements with Washington, insulted the Europeans, sneered at diplomacy, and, in effect, invited the Congress to correct Truman's mistaken, pusillanimous policy. Still Truman waited. Five days went by before he fired the General.

The MacArthur affair, extending over several years, illustrates the problem Truman had with questions of loyalty. His family upbringing, his Army experience, and his political beginnings had all driven into his skull the importance of standing by your own. But that kind of loyalty involves a dependence dangerous in the Presidency. Truman's attitude toward loyalty distorted his Presidency along three dimensions.

The first concerned his top advisors and subordinates. The idea was to have a great man of frank mind ready to serve anonymously, like Marshall and Acheson. But Truman also inherited or appointed eminences like MacArthur who were unwilling to play that role. Truman drew a sharp distinction, in his behavior, between those who had signed on to serve under him and others outside his team. The outsiders could denounce him scathingly, as did Taft, and yet retain his respect and cooperation. During the 1946 campaign Truman had called Al Whitney of the Brotherhood of Railroad Trainmen "un-American" and "an enemy of the people"; Whitney came back with, "You can't make a President out of a ribbon clerk." After Truman vetoed the Taft-Hartley Act, Whitney made an appointment to see him. To work up his nerve he walked twice around the White House before going in. Then:

TRUMAN: "It's good to see you, Al. You look wonderful. Let's not waste time discussing the past. Let's just agree we both received bad advice."

WHITNEY: "Mr. President, I'm a third-generation Irishman who's part Scotch and you know they are kind of hotheaded sometimes."

TRUMAN: "I'm made up on the same plan."[26]

But Truman was puzzled and confused when some high subordinate of his turned out to be a "prima donna." For all his public aggressiveness, Truman in close relations very rarely expressed anger. "He cannot bear to hurt a friend," Margaret wrote. On his desk was the slogan, "THE BUCK STOPS HERE"; he would have to be firm sometimes. But he was extraordinarily chary of close combat. That feeling shows up in a long series of "misunderstandings" between Truman and the people he eventually fired. Again and again, Truman's memory of what happened in tense personal conversations varies markedly from what the other man remembered.

For example: Francis Biddle, the Attorney General Truman inherited, had opposed him on a patronage matter. Perhaps also for other reasons, Truman determined to get rid of him, but instead of doing it in person he had his press secretary call Biddle and tell him his resignation was accepted the "day after tomorrow." Biddle asked for and got a personal interview. Biddle's version was that he inquired who his successor was to be and Truman told him Tom

Clark. Biddle said, "Unhappily, Mr. President, I do not approve of your choice. And I most urgently suggest that you study this matter further before making up your mind." Truman's version was that "Francis Biddle had been a good Attorney General, and there was no ill feeling between us. I did not ask him to quit. He quit voluntarily. . . . I asked Biddle whom he would recommend to take his place, and he suggested Tom Clark. . . ."

For example: Secretary of State Byrnes returned to Washington in December 1945 for a talk with Truman. Truman recalls that "I read him the riot act." "A Secretary of State should never have the illusion that he is President of the United States." Byrnes' memory said, "The fact is the President did not on that occasion nor at any other time express to me disapproval of any position I took at the meeting of Foreign Ministers . . . nor of any statements I made on our foreign policy."

For example: Wallace and Truman agree that they did in fact have a conversation in the White House before Wallace delivered his New York speech. According to Wallace, Truman took one copy and Wallace another and they spent thirty minutes going over it together, after which Truman said "it was okay." Truman's recollection was that his talk with Wallace lasted only fifteen minutes, was taken up mostly with other matters, and that Wallace brought up his speech just before he left. "There was, of course, no time for me to read the speech, even in part."

For example: when Truman met with MacArthur on Wake Island, Truman retained the unlikely memory that MacArthur was apologetic about his embarrassing public statements and that he and the general "talked fully about Formosa." MacArthur, in his later testimony before a Senate committee, said the subject of Formosa had never come up at Wake Island.

At the very least, Truman seems to have experienced tension and ambiguity in these and similar encounters. His early determination to establish his authority and his later determination to see his policies properly executed made it seem necessary for him to take a hard line from time to time in personal confrontations. But it was very difficult for him to do this. People familiar with his tough-guy reputation, based largely on public performances, were often surprised at his mildness in person. The mixture of responsibility and loyalty in this sense was never fully resolved.

Loyalty in a second sense made possible what both the Republican and the Democratic Presidential candidates in 1952 called "the mess in Washington"—the sorry tale of graft and corruption and nincompoop behavior that tarred Truman's Presidential dignity. Far from all Truman's appointees were of the George Marshall stripe. His personal physician played the commodities market, then lied about it to Congress; his Appointments Secretary went to jail for fixing a tax case; one of his secretaries accepted an $8,500 mink coat; his military aide saw nothing wrong with accepting the gift of not one, but seven deep-freezers. It was a ragtag crew, a buzzing clot of "five-percenters" and "influence peddlers" flitting around Washington making arrangements for a price.

Early in his political career, Truman had decided to have nothing to do with the money side of political campaigns. Furthermore, his mind was taken up with problems larger than those of John Maragon and his ilk. Still, he could not have been oblivious to the news stories and investigations that revealed official after official on the take. But his sense of what Patrick Anderson calls "loyalty down" made him stick to good Missouri pals long after they had betrayed his trust. Some of them had helped him in the past and he would not turn his back on them. Tom Pendergast had been straight with him, Truman remembered, and "When Tom Pendergast was down and out, a convicted man, people wanted me to denounce him. I refused. I wouldn't kick a friend."

The epitome of this type of relationship was Harry Vaughn, the White House buffoon who liked to tell reporters they should be nice to him so he could help them with the President. Back in World War I, Vaughn had—by accident—saved Truman from a superior's wrath. When the Congressional investigation into graft and corruption began to get close to him, he went in to offer the President his resignation. As Vaughn remembered, Truman "got up and walked over and put his arm around my shoulder. He said, 'Harry, they're just trying to use you to embarrass me. You go up there and tell 'em to go to hell. We came in here together and, God damn it, we're going out together!'

In a rather different third way, Truman's feelings about loyalty showed up as the great Joe McCarthy witch hunt to root out Communists in government got underway. Well before McCarthy got into the act, Truman had to deal with the problem. In 1946 the newly victorious Republicans were determined to "clean the Communists and fellow travelers out of the government." There were some startling revelations in FBI reports Truman read that indicated at least a strong possibility that some Communist spies had in fact penetrated the government, a plausible supposition in any case. But the response of the Red hunters was so exaggerated, and in the end so ineffective, that the whole affair has come to stand as a prime example of the madness that occasionally sweeps through American politics. Once the paranoid image of Communism as a communicable disease caught hold, there could be no stopping the speedy logic by which those who inhaled the germs were as guilty as those who spread them. The spy stories fascinated and frightened people, and then offered a convenient explanation for every ill from Russian intransigence to high meat prices.

In 1949, Senator Pat McCarran, a might power in the Senate appropriations process, inserted a provision in the State and Defense appropriations bills giving those departments the power to fire any employee as a security risk with no appeal. News began to reach Truman that people were being fired right and left (especially left). In 1950, Truman sent a message to Congress asking legislation to provide at least a modicum of protection to the accused. McCarran came back with an Internal Security bill which would require all Communists and Communist front organizations to register with the Justice Department (thus making themselves automatically indictable under the Smith Act), the denial of defense plant employment and passports to Communists and Communist "dupes," the deportation of any alien who had ever been a Communist, and, in wartime, the detention "of any person as to whom there is reason to believe he might engage in acts of espionage or sabotage." This fruitcake bill passed the Senate by a vote of 70 to 7 and the House by 354 to 20. Truman vetoed it and sent a hard-hitting message. The House voted to override, 286 to 48; the Senate delayed, and Truman pushed hard, with the help of a brave and cheerful first-termer, Hubert H. Humphrey, to stop passage. But the Internal Security Act of 1950 became law when the Senate overrode the veto by a vote of 57 to 10.

Such was the temper of the time. Truman's response was uneven: he defended stoutly the likes of Acheson and Marshall against the ludicrous charges that they were soft on Communism, but he did not take a direct case to the public against the McCarrans and McCarthys. Truman's emphasis from the start was on procedures—establishing machinery capable of identifying any real security risks without damaging the rights of accused. The program failed on both counts. By the middle of 1952 some 4 million Americans had been screened, tentative charges were brought against 9,077, formal hearings were held regarding 2,961, of whom 378 were denied employment or dismissed: .002 percent of the total. And the cost in terms of chilling effect on debate, organizational participation, employment in private industry, and breakdown of social trust was immense. The Russian-style dossier, full of shady clues and casual opinions, became a reality for large numbers of Americans.

That was not what Truman meant by loyalty. His mind was not attuned to the wiles of paranoia, and it is doubtful that he was much concerned with the theoretical issues beyond a devotion to the Bill of Rights. In his *Memoirs* he introduces the chapter discussing the loyalty question with his views on prejudice against races and religions. For Truman, the whole spirit of the thing was wrong. His answer was to admit, largely on political grounds, that some program was necessary, and to try to make it as fair as possible. Loyalty to him was not some abstract emotion. It was personal. He meant to stand by his own—and he stood by—not to coerce the political baptism of anybody.

WHAT TRUMAN WAS NOT

Harry Truman as President displays a number of features important to our argument. Clearly he was an active-positive type, displaying high self-esteem and continual enjoyment in the exercise of power. His style was flexible and balanced: an aggressive, informal rhetoric; a penchant for soaking up facts through study, and deciding, without much theory, between alternatives posed in either-or terms; a personal relations style based on a strong sense of personal loyalty. His world view was emphatically nonphilosophical—values were simple for him, not a matter of great concern. He saw men as the makers of history, character as the wellspring of behavior. From his inner confidence and self-recognition he drew the strength to grow in office, to develop through learning without anxiety, as a person and as a President.

Truman is most interesting in the final analysis for what he might have been. If Franklin Roosevelt's character made it plausible to think of him, at first, as leaning in the passive-positive direction, toward a compliant emphasis, Truman's aggressiveness places him near the active-negative end of his category. Had he grown up less sanguine, less full of laughter, more discouraged by the troubles he encountered, Truman might have made use of politics to palliate some inner bitterness. He might have fastened upon some line of policy and made it his personal crusade, pursuing a narrow course to disaster. Often his words made him sound that way and the public often took him at his word. But based on the facts of Truman policies, he did not freeze around some obsession. During a period of immense complexity, uncertainty, and strife, Truman felt his way along. The outcome was far from ideally satisfactory. It might have been tragic.

11

John F. Kennedy
and Active-Positive
Commitment

DOUBTS ABOUT KENNEDY

John F. Kennedy barely made it into the Presidency. He was elected in 1960 by the narrowest margin ever—120,000 votes in a total of 69 million cast, so that nearly any category of Americans could claim to have put him over the top. His win in the electoral college, 303–219, concealed the fact that he beat Richard Nixon by less than one tenth of one percent of the popular vote; votes for minor parties meant that he received less than half the votes for President. Most of the states had voted against him, as had majorities of whites, college graduates, high-income people, women, Protestants, farmers, old people, small-town folk, and business and professional people. Defying all the rules of "availability" so confidently taught in the textbooks, this young, 43-year-old Catholic from a small state took over the world's most powerful office with history's shakiest public mandate.

The party balance in Congress—262 Democrats to 174 Republicans in the House, 65 Democrats to 35 Republicans in the Senate—was deceptive. Most Democratic members were generally progressive and pro-Kennedy, but conservative Democrats and Republicans together numbered more than the Kennedy supporters. In the committees the picture was worse, particularly in the House Rules Committee—gatekeeper for legislation from all the others—where two mossback Democrats, Howard Smith and William Colmer, regularly joined their conservative Republican colleagues to tie up legislation in a 6–6 stalemate. And in the hard calculus of politics, many a Democratic Congressman had run better than Kennedy had.

Eventually, fate would have it that John Kennedy would be President for only a few more than a thousand days, compared to Franklin Roosevelt's twelve years and Harry Truman's nearly seven years. Whatever he would be remembered for, the record would have to be established quickly.

Nor did he have another advantage Roosevelt and Truman had enjoyed—a clear contrast with his defeated opponent in terms of political principles. During the campaign, Arthur Schlesinger, responding to the uncertainty many voters felt, wrote a book called *Kennedy or Nixon: Does It Make Any Difference?* Audiences watching the famous Kennedy-Nixon debates on television, the first of which (like nearly anything else) seemed to have tipped the scale in Kennedy's favor, got a clearer impression of the candidates as persons than of their policy differences. Kennedy the campaigner set a mood, a tone, an attitude different from Nixon's; but at the time he assumed office not many citizens had a picture clearer than that of the woman who said she would vote against Nixon because she "didn't like the look in his eyes, especially the left one."

The professional President-watchers also had their doubts, of which three were uppermost.

Maturity: The aging seers of the Democratic party in particular wondered whether this youngster had enough experience-hardened fiber to stand up to the heat in the White House. This was especially true of those members of Congress who could remember Jack as a 29-year-old Congressman who looked nineteen and appeared for House debates in khaki pants with his shirt-tail out. Harry Truman, apparently confusing Kennedy with his father, wrote a letter to "Senator Joseph Kennedy" asking whether he honestly thought he was ready to be President. Eleanor Roosevelt, referring indirectly to Kennedy's *Profiles in Courage* and to the influence of his reactionary millionaire father, said, "I feel that I would hesitate to place the difficult decisions that the next President will have to make with someone who understands what courage is and admires it, but has not quite the independence to have it." Only one President, Theodore Roosevelt, had been younger when he assumed office.

Commitment: Was Kennedy a liberal, a conservative, or what? His energy was apparent, its direction obscure. He seemed detached, cool, reluctant to commit himself ideologically. James MacGregor Burns, looking ahead to the Kennedy Presidency, noted that Roosevelt had said the office "is preeminently a place of moral leadership" and that "All our great Presidents were leaders of thought at times when certain historic ideas in the life of the nation had to be clarified." "It is precisely in this respect," Burns noted, "that Kennedy's critics, especially in the liberal wing, have trouble imagining him in the White House. What great idea does Kennedy personify? In what way is he a leader of thought? How could he supply moral leadership at a time when new paths before the nation need discovering?" Kennedy's priorities—the causes he would be willing to go to the wall for—were unclear; some liberals wondered if they were in for a continuation of the Eisenhower era of middle-of-the-road compromise on key issues.

Competitiveness: Robert Kennedy's management of his brother's campaign had left painful wounds. The Kennedy steamroller, tough, efficient, ruthless, seemed to some nothing more than a machine for winning, for whatever the purpose, whatever the cost. Kennedy's bruising drive to win, his thirst for combat, brought him respect from politicians of like attitude, as could be seen in 1956 when Lyndon Johnson had announced "Texas proudly casts its vote for the fighting sailor who wears the scars of battle." But others saw the Kennedys in politics as *merely* competitors, playing the game—as a game—for all it was worth.

Somehow John (a saint) Fitzgerald (a politician) Kennedy (a multi-millionaire) would have to deal with the expectations that he would turn out to be too naive, too facile, or too ruthless for the Presidency.

KENNEDY'S GROWING PAINS

John Kennedy was born May 29, 1917, the second son of Rose Fitzgerald Kennedy, daughter of the Mayor of Boston, and Joseph Patrick Kennedy, one-time peanut vendor and bank clerk, at that time employed as assistant general manager of a shipyard at $20,000 a year. This was a role which brought him into frequent negotiations with the then Assistant Secretary of the Navy, Franklin Delano Roosevelt.

John was not an easy child: he had trouble eating, caught scarlet fever, then diphtheria. Through his youth he was ill much of the time and always seemed to be having trouble with his back. John's frailty was the first of many contrasts with his older brother Joseph Patrick, Jr., the sturdy first son and inheritor of his father's name. "When we were growing up together," Robert Kennedy said, "we used to laugh about the great risk a mosquito took in biting Jack Kennedy—with some of his blood the mosquito was almost sure to die."

Soon the basic pattern of the family was set: Father Joseph devoted sixteen hours a day to business; before long he was traveling extensively, piling up the fortune that would make him a millionaire well before he was 35. Joseph's jobs and headquarters changed with such dizzying speed that Rose lost track of them. In any case, she decided to stay put and bear children; she produced nine in seventeen years: Joe, John, Rosemary, Kathleen, Eunice, Patricia, Jean, Robert, and Edward. Joseph's influence was strong. But Rose ran the show day by day as the family grew. Every morning she went to mass, every evening she read the children stories—Bible tales, *King Arthur and His Knights*, and so on. In between, Rose often got out of the house for bridge or tea, from which she was often called away to tend to some home matter, though there were various Irish maids in the house.

Rose Kennedy's way with her children sounds exceptionally purposeful, not in the sense of pressing them to suffer now to fulfill ambitions later, but more in the Sara Roosevelt style: a concern with present character and manners.

Obviously she was no casual mother. "When I held my newborn baby in my arms," she said, "I used to think that what I said and did to him could have an influence not only on him but on all whom he met, not only for a day or a month or a year, but for all eternity—a very, very challenging and exciting thought for a mother."[1] She wanted her children to be "stimulated by their parents to see, and touch, and know, and understand, and appreciate"; so stimulated, they should find their own way. Not given to preaching at her children, she nevertheless tried to "tend to the roots as well as the stems, and slowly and carefully plant ideas and concepts of right and wrong, religion and social implications and applications." Her religious instruction centered on faith, not theology. For the children she wanted

> a sense of responsibility and a sense of security. They knew exactly what they were expected to do and tried to do it for the most part, and the confidence, I think, of stability, which some children do not have and which older people do not always have, and I always told them that if they were given faith when they were young, they should try to nurture it and guard it because it's really a gift that older people valued so much when sorrow came or difficulty came.

In matters large and small, "You always take the time to explain why you take a certain action." She always tried to be home by five—"that's the time that coughs start and the time the maids are apt to be tired"—and she would whack a child with a ruler when necessary.

Sensible, attentive, fair, interested more in setting the conditions for growth than in channeling its direction, Rose believed in her children's individuality even though, with so many of them, each often had to fend for himself. There is strangely little in her biography of the specialness of her relationship with any of the children as individuals. She encouraged the children's curiosity. After hearing her tell of Jesus entering Bethlehem, Jack asked, "Mother, we know what happened to Jesus Christ, but what happened to the donkey?" And the children gave her affection. When Rose told Jack that President McKinley had once said her sister was the prettiest girl who had ever visited the White House, Jack asked, "Why didn't he say it to you, Mother?" But there is no indication she made concessions for his sickliness, much less coddled him. Her focus was on the children, each and all, but she did not, it appears, favor any one of them, as her husband most decidedly did.

Rose Kennedy's descriptions of her mothering have an abstract air about them. She describes a system (possibly because that is what she was asked about) more than this or that individual, this or that incident. "We were computerized at an early age," daughter Eunice said, "but fortunately by a very compassionate computer." Certainly system was needed in such a large family. The daily schedule was precise: lunch at 1:15, dinner at 7:30, latecomers required to start with whatever course was on the table. Their rooms (in the family's new twelve-room house) were divided by folding partitions so the children couldn't as easily "knock each other down or gouge each other in the eyes with toys." She was forever thinking up projects for them. She created a hierarchy, trying to bring up the "older children so they do things in a good way, and give them lots of attention," because the younger children were "great imitators and will follow the older ones' example." On index cards she kept close track of their sizes, diseases, weight, dentistry, and the like.

All of this may sound a good deal more severe than it was. The Kennedy home was a place of much action and laughter, a lively, brawling mob of children overseen by a mother who knew when to look the other way. Father Joseph's burgeoning affluence helped: each child had his own bedroom, plenty of toys, and since "Members of any big family know that a single bathroom will cause disputes," she said, "we always had at least three." Nurses, governesses, cooks, and servants diluted the parental strain. Rose's compassion for her brood was manifested as attention and encouragement. But she was tough, and stories of her comforting a tearful child or commiserating with the wounded or sharing the confusions of adolescence are notably absent.

Once John Kennedy said of his mother, "She was terribly religious. She was a little removed, and still is, which I think is the only way to survive when you have nine children. I thought she was a very model mother for a big family."

Father Joseph did not have to be continually present to make his presence felt. "I can feel Pappy's eyes on the back of my neck," Jack said in 1945 to a Navy pal. Rose shared Joseph's insistence on challenging the children to achieve and she carried through with that in his absence. At the dinner table there was always discussion about current political matters—mostly personalities—and no trivial topics were allowed. Sometimes the argument go so hot a family member would stalk out in anger or burst into tears. When Joseph was there his opinions were dominant in all debates. Jack remembered the family talks as "mostly monologues by my father . . . well, not exactly monologues. But we didn't have opinions in those days. Later, the discussions included us more, but mostly about personalities, not debates on issues and things. I never had any particular interest in political subjects in those days." (One subject was taboo: money.) What comes through as important in the later dinner debates was the struggle of wits and emotional force—not the truth of the matter. It was not a Wilsonian home. Once after feelings ran high in a talk-fight with Jack and Joe on one side and Father Joseph on the other, Rose expressed concern. "I can take care of myself," Joseph said. "The important thing is that they fight together."

Joe Kennedy, Sr., pressed his children hard to compete, never to be satisfied with anything but first place. The point was not just to try; the point was to win. One time he sent two of his children away from the dinner table because they had goofed off in a sailing race that day. It was always go, move, fight, win—at talk, sailing, touch football, or whatever. When Jack was a student at Harvard he tried desperately to make the swimming team so he could help whip Yale. Then he fell ill with flu and a high fever and was taken to the infirmary and commanded to rest. Instead, each night a friend would help smuggle him out of his sickroom to the gym, where he would swim lap after lap before sneaking back in time to have his temperature taken. Later the mad excitement of competition at Hyannis Port weekends would become famous.

The fighting spirit persisted in the children, but there was something else in the father's tutelage: a strong sense that he cared. President Kennedy recalled,

> My father wasn't around as much as some fathers when I was young; but, whether he was there or not, he made his children feel that they were the most important things in the world to him. He was so terribly interested in everything we were doing. He held up standards for us, and he was very tough when we failed to meet those standards.[2]

That memory proves out in the letters between father and son when Jack was a student at Choate. He wrote his father that he had "definitely decided to stop fooling around. I really do realize how important it is that I get a good job done this year, if I want to go to England. I really feel, now that I think it over, that I have been bluffing myself about how much real work I have been doing." Father answered with "great satisfaction" in Jack's "forthrightness and directness that you are usually lacking," and continued:

> Now, Jack, I don't want to give the impression that I am a nagger, for goodness knows I think that is the worst thing any parent can be. After long experience in sizing up people I definitely know you have the goods and you can go a long way. Now aren't you foolish not to get all there is out of what God has given you. . . . After all, I would be lacking even as a friend if I did not urge you to take advantage of the qualities you have. It is very difficult to make up fundamentals that you have neglected when you were very young and that is why I am always urging you to do the best you can. I am not expecting too much and I will not be disappointed if you don't turn out to be a real genius, but I think you can be a really worthwhile citizen with good judgment and good understanding. . . .[3]

Such letters came about as a result of Jack's difficulties at Choate, where he lived under the shadow of his older brother, and where his housefather found him— as he wrote the parents—"casual and disorderly in almost all of his organization projects. Jack studies at the last minute, keeps appointments late, has little sense of material values, and can seldom locate his possessions." Jack dodged. "Maybe Dad thinks I am alibiing but I am not," he wrote his mother. "I have also been doing a little worrying about my studies because what he said about me starting of[f] great and then going down sunk in."

As a child, Jack tried to please his parents, to live up to their standards, and they repaid him with support, encouragement, and attention. He did not become a little Lord Fauntleroy; there was a great deal of fun in his life, and at least until he was a Harvard sophomore he played a good deal more than he worked. Like the other Kennedy children, he grew up optimistic, aggressive, humorous, and outgoing. But within the family, Jack had a special problem of adjustment that set him off from the other children and gave his character a special twist. This was his relationship with his brother Joe.

"Joe was the star of our family," Jack said. "He did everything better than the rest of us." Joe was the first-born, his father's namesake, and a healthy, strong child in contrast to Jack, who was continually ill with one thing or another. His father made no bones about it: Joe was his favorite, far more like him than Jack was. Rose's system for concentrating on the older child as an example for the rest reinforced Joe's special position. Joe Sr., agreed: "I think a lot depends on the oldest one, and how he turns out. The younger ones follow his example." And as Joe grew, he became an extraordinarily handsome, gregarious, athletic young man. Joe Sr. was convinced this lad would be President some day. The father-son relationship was deep and intense. In 1944, Joe Jr., a 29-year-old pilot, was killed when his plane exploded over England shortly after takeoff on a mission against German rocket sites. Joe Sr. was shattered. For months this normally ebullient go-getter spent hours each day sitting alone and listening to symphony records. Old friends found him "in wretched shape; he could not reconcile himself to the loss." Thirteen years later, reporter Bob Considine interviewed the elder Kennedy as they sat at lunch in the Palm Beach sunshine. Considine asked him about the children, and Kennedy happily ran down the list, relating this one's achievements, that one's qualities. Considine noticed that he left out Joe, and asked him to comment on his eldest. Joe Sr.'s reaction, Considine relates,

> was a terrible thing to see. He sat there at the table weeping, unable to speak or to control himself, for almost five minutes. It seemed to the rest of us like an hour. Finally, he pulled himself together and wiped his eyes but still he couldn't talk. He gestured toward his wife and said, "She can tell you about him I can't."[4]

Jack and the others prepared a memorial volume, *As We Remember Joe*—"I think that if the Kennedy children amount to anything now or ever amount to anything, it will be due more to Joe's behavior and his constant example than to any other factor"—but Joe Sr. could never bring himself to read the book. In those pages Jack Kennedy described the qualities Joe stood for in his mind:

> Things did not come easy to him. I think his accomplishments were due chiefly to the amazing intensity with which he applied himself to the job at hand. I do not think I can ever remember seeing him sit back in a chair and relax. Even when he was still, there was always a sense of motion forcibly restrained about him. And yet this continuous motion did not have its roots in restlessness or nervousness but rather it came from his intense enthusiasm for everything he did and from his exceptional stamina.[5]

Restrained intensity: that would become a Jack Kennedy trademark.

What counts for our purposes in understanding the relationship between Joe and Jack is the effect it had in shaping Jack's character. The primary family influence on both boys was to inculcate through experience an active-positive orientation toward life. Like their brothers and sisters, the two older sons learned—from the behavioral example of their parents as well as from their own experiments—to adapt by focusing energy and attention on doing interesting things joyfully, with an expectation of growth, in a framework of discipline. To that broad picture, the Joe-Jack relationship adds differentiating dimensions.

These two boys stood at the top of the childhood hierarchy; after them came five girls (one of them, Rosemary, turned out to be retarded) before Robert and, at last, Edward. In such a competitive family it would be incredible to suppose that Joe and Jack would not joust for preeminence. Joe had a hot Irish temper. Once at Harvard a friend made some casual wisecrack about his grandfather, "Honey Fitz"; Joe jumped up and took a swing at him. Another time he threw his little brother Teddy overboard for failing to handle a sail properly. But especially for Jack, as he recalled later, Joe's temper was "a problem in my childhood." Frequently Joe had to act as substitute father. With the younger children he was gentle and patient, but he bullied Jack unmercifully. The two fought so furiously that the other children would run upstairs and hide in fright, while the muscular Joe pounded away at his slender brother. The fight usually ended with Jack exhausted and humiliated, pinned to the floor. Joe Sr. would not intervene. Jack would have to learn to fend for himself. Playing football, Joe liked to fire a bullet pass at Jack and grin as the younger boy collapsed with the force of it. Once on their bicycles the two boys tore straight into one another because neither would turn aside; Joe was not hurt, Jack required 28 stitches.

At Harvard together, Joe and Jack shared dinner almost every night; they were not enemies. But the conflict continued within the brotherhood. Joe advised Jack he was too light for football. Jack went out for football and injured his back so severely it would plague him the rest of his life. Joe was forever stealing Jack's girls—"Get lost, Baby Brother. I'll take over." He usually did. When Jack lined up a date with Gertrude Niesen, a beautiful young singer, Joe horned in and set Gertrude aflutter. Miss Niesen recalled, "I was very young and it was very exciting, very flattering, very wonderful. Joe was a *terribly* good-looking guy. He was much better looking than Jack at that particular time. If I'd been a little older and really understood what was going on—."[6] Jack was furious.

In retrospect, Jack seems to have noticed aspects of Joe's personality few others saw; possibly they represent some combination of what Joe was and what Jack wanted to remember of him. He saw in his brother

> A slight detachment from things around him—a wall of reserve which few people ever succeeded in penetrating. I suppose I knew Joe as well as anyone and yet I sometimes wonder if I really knew him. He was very human and most certainly had his faults: a hot temper, intolerance for the slower pace of lesser men, and a way of looking—with a somewhat sardonic half smile—which could cut and prod more sharply than words. But these defects—if defects they were—were becoming smoothed with the passage of time.

Jack Kennedy's identification with his brother as a tough, impatient but restrained winner was part of the equation. Another part was the differentiation between the two by which Jack established a separate identity. Physically Jack resembled his mother, Joe his father; Jack was quiet, Joe boisterous; Jack liked to read, Joe liked to talk. As their father put it, Joe "was altogether different from Jack, more dynamic, more sociable and easy going. Jack in those days back there when he was getting out of college was rather shy, withdrawn and quiet." Joe's way of handling people, his parents included, was an overwhelming charm—his father's magic smile. Jack made more use of guile, was more protected. Up until Joe's death there was a larger contrast: Joe won, Jack came in second. Afterwards, Jack Kennedy had to handle comradeship and combat with a ghost. Joe and his father had often talked about how Joe might be President some day.

The Kennedy way of looking at the world, in its broad outlines, grew from the same family soil. There was first the fact of being Irish in a town with an Irish mayor but a community and, to a large degree, a business world dominated by the Boston Protestants. Irish-ism to old Joe Kennedy meant fierce resentment at discrimination, carried in his memory from tales of his immigrant grandfather and his saloon-keeper father who struggled to give his son a better chance. Joe Sr., left Boston for New York and Hollywood to make money—but also to get away from the firm prejudices Massachusetts kept demonstrating to him. He bought a summer place in Cohasset, a favorite watering place for Old Boston families, but was blackballed when he tried to join the country club. "It was petty and cruel," a friend said. "The women in Cohasset looked down on the daughter of 'Honey Fitz'; and who was Joe Kennedy but the son of Pat, the barkeeper?" When Jack was at Harvard, Rose once asked an upper-crust friend of his, "Tell me, when are the nice people of Boston going to accept us?" Everywhere Joe went—including Harvard—he seemed to run into prejudice against the Irish. "I was born here. My children were born here. What the hell do I have to do to be an American?" he demanded to know. In his own life he gave the answer: win. By the time his children grew up, prejudice against them for their heritage was on the wane, but Jack ran hard up against it in 1960 when he reached for the top.

Through Rose, "Irish" had a different, if complementary, connotation. Her father "Honey Fitz" was a charming old fellow, cleverer than he seemed, who often visited with the young Kennedys. John Fitzgerald had started off better than Patrick Kennedy—he was "lace-curtain Irish," indicated by "fruit in the house and nobody sick"—and had worked himself up through politics to being the first native-born son of Irish parents to be elected Mayor of Boston. On all occasions he was prepared to offer his melodic rendition of "Sweet Adeline," to josh with opponents in the Boss Curley style: "And where were you last year, Freddy, when Al Smith ran for President? You were home, with your little red slippers on, reading the *Ladies Home Journal*." For Jack and his brothers and sisters, Honey Fitz brought home the romantic side of being Irish, the eye-twinkling leprechaun gaiety; a man could be like that and at the same time be a tough-minded political boss.

Then there was the fact, the increasingly evident fact, that the Kennedys were richer than your average American. Some of Endicott Peabody's preachments about the duties of the privileged got through to them, reinforcing their search for ways to be active and productive. Riches also meant, as they had for Franklin Roosevelt, freedom from niggling details. Thus Joe Jr. could telegraph one of his father's minions to get him theater tickets, and a hundred other doors opened at a slight shove. However, the children were not given lavish amounts of spending money; as a boy Jack addressed this petition to his father:

My recent allowance is 40c. This I used for aeroplanes and other playthings of childhood but now I am a scout and I put away my childish things. Before I would spend 20c of my 40c allowance and in five minutes I would have empty pockets and nothing to gain and 20c to lose. When I am a scout I have to buy canteens, haversacks, blankets, searchlicgs [sic], poncho things that will last for years and I can always use it while I can't use chocolate marshmallow Sunday ice cream and so I put in my plea for a raise of thirty cents for me to buy schut [sic] things and pay my own way around. . . .[7]

The family taboo on talk about money at the dinner table and the evident unconcern with want in the family—despite pleas for allowances—left Jack with a lifelong carelessness in personal finance, to the irritation of friends who were forever having to pay for his meals and cabs because he had no cash. It also seems to have prevented snobbishness, at least regarding wealth. Jack could say later, with considerable disdain, that Richard Nixon had no class, but that it had nothing to do with money.

The Irish immigrant heritage, the easy escape from distinctions of wealth, and especially the way Rose and Joe handled democracy in the household gave the Kennedy children, including Jack, a way of approaching others directly, openly, and with a presumption of equality. They were a tightly knit unit against the world; if they condescended it was as a meritocracy looking down on the lazy, incompetent, and unimaginative.

Behind and beneath those themes was Catholicism, which was, as Rose explained, a thing to *do*. The details of theology meant little; faithful performance meant much. The doing was in church and in life, every day. But there is little evidence that Jack was seized by any religious fervor. From his childhood, Catholicism was right because it was there.

Jack's own ideas may have received some coloration from the heroic tales his mother read to him, but he does not appear to have done a great deal of serious thinking about his own ideas until late in his Harvard years. He went off to Catholic boarding school at thirteen; he was a bit homesick at first. Here he began to show a lifelong contrast between personal absentmindedness and an excellent memory of what he read: "Though I may not be able to remember material things such as tickets, gloves and so on I can remember things like Ivanhoe and the last time we had an exam on it I got ninety-eight." Politics barely touched him. That fall of 1930, as the world was coming unstuck for millions of Americans, Jack wrote home, "Please send me the Literary Digest, because I did not know about the Market Slump until a long time after, or a paper. Please send me some golf balls. . . ." At Easter he had to drop out for the rest of the year after an attack of appendicitis.

The next year he went to Choate, where Joe was doing well and where he got to know rich boys who were not Catholic. He continued to go out for sports, wrote home for chocolate pie, graduated 64th in a class of 112, and was voted "most likely to succeed."

"The star of the family" had gone on to Harvard, his father's school. Jack decided to go to Princeton, but first had a summer at the London School of

Economics, studying under the famous socialist Harold J. Laski, who remembered later that "his mind was only just beginning to discover the enchantment of thought." Jack got sick with jaundice and had to come home early; the same disease struck again at Christmas; he dropped out of Princeton for the rest of the year, then decided to go to Harvard after all.

Harvard in the fall of 1936 was alive with political controversy. As James MacGregor Burns puts it, "The Harvard campus, like other college campuses, was boiling with ideas, fads, stunts—a ferment of protest against parents, deans, and, more in the 1930's than ever before, politics and the world situation. . . . But Jack Kennedy had no part of this." In junior year (Joe had graduated), his interest began to pick up. He majored in political science, stressing international relations. That spring Harvard let him travel in Europe; Joe Sr., now Ambassador to England, gave his permission but required written reports from each capital—"Probably the strongest impression I have goten [sic] is that rightly or wrongly the Poles *will fight over* the question of Danzig—" and so on.

Then, in his senior year, Jack Kennedy's mind came alive; he buckled down to a project that, as he wrote his father when he finished, "represents more work than I've ever done in my life." This was his senior thesis, later published as *Why England Slept.* In typical fashion, Joe Sr. claimed he gave Jack the idea, but that was not Jack's memory: "I wouldn't say my father got me interested in it. They were things that I saw for myself." On the thesis Jack won *magna cum laude* (like Joe, he graduated *cum laude*); the book would sell 80,000 copies and start Jack on a career as a journalist. His father approved for a characteristic reason: "You would be surprised how a book that really makes the grade with high-class people stands you in good stead for years to come." The book earned about $40,000 for Jack. He bought a Buick and donated the English royalties to the bomb-devastated town of Plymouth.

Assessing *Why England Slept,* both Burns and Schlesinger are struck by the "emotional detachment" that makes it "so aloof and so clinical." The world was falling apart again, and there was Jack Kennedy coolly surveying the dynamics thereof. The *Blitzkrieg* had rolled out over Europe, and Kennedy wrote:

> As Hitler pointed out with some truth, in his cleverly worded letter to Daladier in August, 1939, shortly before the outbreak of the war, much of what he had done in Europe rectified wrongs that had been done at Versailles, and which should have been righted long before.
>
> However, as Hitler pointed out, no post-war statesman had been powerful enough or sure enough of his own domestic position to make any great concession to Germany. Thus at first, many people objected to Hitler because of his method of doing things, rather than what he actually did. And this sort of indignation does not result in the state of mind that calls for huge armaments.

There is little to show that *Why England Slept* was written during an academic year which began in September with the German invasion of Poland and ended in June with Dunkirk. As Burns writes of Jack in those days, "Alert, inquisitive, receptive, but somewhat remote, he looked at the world with quizzical gray eyes."

One of the general arguments of the book was that the British people were more to blame than their leaders for the country's unpreparedness. Joe Sr. picked him up on that: he wrote Jack not to go so easy on the leaders, who are "supposed to look after the national welfare, and to attempt to educate the people." Jack replied: "Will stop white washing Baldwin" and explained in his concluding chapter that "My reason for trying to ascertain in what measure each group was responsible was because I believed that to dismiss the matter purely as a question of poor leadership would mean that America would lose the benefit of the experience England has been going through.

But neither the author's coolness nor his handling of the question of blame catches the fundamental implication the book has for Kennedy as President. The first sentence of Chapter I is, "Before beginning any discussion of British rearmament, it is important to know what the psychology of the nation was at the commencement." This psychological emphasis pervades the entire book. The statistics on armaments, the quotations from documents are there, but the reiterated theme is the analysis of the mind of the British public. *Why England Slept* can be opened at random to find such observations as these:

> Because of the inertia of human thought, nations, like individuals, change their ideas slowly.[8]

> No discussion of Britain's psychology would be complete unless some mention were made of the natural feeling of confidence, even of superiority, that every Englishman feels and to which many Americans object. This feeling, while it is an invaluable asset in bearing up under disaster, has had a great effect on the need Britain felt for rearming. The idea that Britain loses every battle except the last has proved correct so many times in the past that the average Englishman is unwilling to make great personal sacrifice until the danger is overwhelming.[9]

> It takes shocks—hard shocks—to change a nation's psychology.[10]

> These factors all combined to produce a feeling of complacency, a luxury England could not afford.[11]

> The slow change from a psychology of disarmament to one of rearmament has been traced.[12]

> People in America, filled with the myth of Britain's invincibility through the centuries, could not understand Chamberlain's desperate efforts to avert a war. They felt, and many still do feel, that Hitler in 1938 was merely bluffing.[13]

The book's title asks a causative question; Kennedy's answer is that England slept because her people, thanks to numerous myths and misperceptions, were incapable of arousing themselves to the necessary actions fast enough. But what would it take to arouse them? In his first italics on page four, Kennedy shows the answer: "*For the Englishman had to be taught the need for armaments; his natural instincts were strongly against them.*" And at the end of the book the theme is repeated with application to America:

I say therefore that we cannot afford to let England's experience pass unnoticed. Now that the world is ablaze, America has awakened to the problems facing it. . . . We can't escape the fact that democracy in America, like democracy in England, has been asleep at the switch. . . . To say that democracy has been awakened by the events of the last few weeks is not enough. Any person will awaken when the house is burning down. What we need is an armed guard that will wake up when the fire starts or, better yet, one that will not permit a fire to start at all.

We should profit by the lesson of England and make our democracy work. We must make it work right now. Any system of government will work when everything is going well. It's the system that functions in the pinches that survives.[14]

Thus the Harvard senior anticipated his Presidential campaign a score of years later. To both Jack Kennedy, B. A., and President John F. Kennedy, the fundamental problem of governing a democracy was psychological: how to overcome the inertia inherent in man's nature. The answer was political, in the large sense of informing the nation of its true condition and arousing it from its slumbers. That would not happen without men to broadcast the facts and ring the alarm.

In his later book, *Profiles in Courage,* Kennedy noted again that

the voting public frequently suffers from what ex-Congressman T. V. Smith called the lag "between our way of thought and our way of life." Smith compared it to the subject of the anonymous poem:

There was a dachshund, once so long
He hadn't any notion
How long it took to notify
His tail of his emotion;
And so it happened, while his eyes
Were filled with woe and sadness,
His little tail went wagging on
Because of previous gladness.[15]

As the war deepened, Jack Kennedy first tried to get into the Army but was rejected because of his back, then wangled his way into the Navy, got his father to pull strings for a sea duty assignment, and wound up as commanding officer of a patrol torpedo boat in the Pacific. One night in August 1943, a Japanese destroyer suddenly appeared and slammed into his PT-109, slicing the little ship clean in half. Two men were killed at once. The rest fell into a sea aflame with burning gasoline. Kennedy was thrown across the deck on his back. "This is how it feels to be killed," went through his mind. He pulled himself together and started rounding up the survivors. When one badly hurt man said he could not make it back to the boat, Kennedy yelled, "For a guy from Boston, you're certainly putting up a great exhibition out here." The remains of the battered crew gathered on the part of the boat still above the surface. Kennedy asked whether they wanted to fight or surrender, if the Japanese came for them. "There's nothing in the book about a situation like this," he said. "A lot of you men have families and some of you have children. What do you want to do? I have nothing to lose." They decided to swim for a small island three and a half miles away. This took four hours; Jack Kennedy, his back zinging pain through him with every stroke, pulled the most seriously hurt man through the water by gripping his life jacket strap in his teeth. They crawled ashore exhausted and vomiting.

For four days Kennedy and the ten others seached through the coral shallows, lived on cocoanut milk, and tended their severe cuts and burns. Jack was the cool commander, though his back was severely injured; when a rescuing native brought him a message headed "On His Majesty's Service," Jack laughed. "You've got to hand it to the British," he said. When a PT boat finally came, he yelled "Where the hell have you been?" "We've got some food for you," was the reply. "Thanks, I've just had a cocoanut," Kennedy said.

It had all happened quickly. Jack's mother answered the phone in Hyannis Port to hear an excited friend say "Jack's been saved!" "Saved from what?" she asked. Joe Sr. had known for a few days, but could not tell her. Joe Jr. got the news and was delighted that his brother had been saved; once he took that in, the old competitive feeling returned. Jack had already beaten him to an officer's commission; now he had beaten him to the heroic action Joe had been pleading for. Returning briefly to Hyannis Port from England, Joe Jr. in his bright uniform was welcomed home at dinner with the family, and a guest, a prominent judge, offered his toast: "To Ambassador Joe Kennedy, father of our hero, our *own* hero, Lieutenant John F. Kennedy of the United States Navy." There was a pause, but that was the end of the toast. Joe Jr. reddened, grinned determinedly, and raised his glass.

Far from home and on his own, Jack Kennedy had shown extraordinary physical courage and the capacity to keep his head in a crisis. In later campaigns he made no objection to mention of the fact that he had served in the Navy, but he disliked talking with strangers about his heroic deeds. On an Edward R. Murrow "Person to Person" program, he passed it off as "an interesting experience" and he wondered why anyone would want to write a book or make a movie about it. His re-injured back would continue to plague him; finally in 1954 he risked a dangerous operation—"I don't care, I can't go on like this"—and barely recovered from a subsequent infection. Last rites were pronounced. On through his Presidency, Kennedy experienced hard pain nearly every day. He hid it well.

Jack Kennedy's admiration for courage—Hemingway's "grace under pressure"—had its roots in personal experience. The meaning of courage burned into his mind when Joe Jr. died a year after Jack's PT boat rescue, and his sister's husband was killed in France a year later. In 1945, he filled a notebook with clippings and letters about those two and included the following quotation from Churchill on Raymond Asquith's death:

> The War which found the measure of so many men never got to the bottom of him, and, when the Grenadiers strode into the crash and thunder of the Somme, he went to his fate, cool, poised, resolute, matter-of-fact, debonair.[16]

His wife said later that "The poignancy of men dying young haunted him."

Out of the Navy in 1945, Jack pondered what to do. He thought of college teaching, but he lacked an advanced degree. *Why England Slept* had done well and he had done some writing for the Harvard *Crimson;* he decided to try journalism. Friends of his father got him a job with International News Service. He covered the San Francisco conference of the United Nations, "from a GI viewpoint." He was not impressed; to a friend he wrote:

> When I think of how much this war has cost us, of the deaths of Cy and Peter and Orv and Gil and Demi and Joe and Billy and all of those thousands and millions who have died with them—when I think of all those gallant acts that I have seen or anyone has seen who has been to the war—it would be a very easy thing to feel disappointed and somewhat betrayed.[17]

He talked to Cord Meyer, another young veteran, who was trying to start the World Federalists, and wrote in his notebook an explanation echoing *Why England Slept:*

> Admittedly world organization with common obedience to law would be a solution. . . . Not that easy. If there is not the feeling that war is the ultimate evil, a feeling strong enough to drive them together, then you can't work out this internationalist plan.

And he summarized pessimistically:

> *Danger of too great a build-up.*
> Mustn't expect too much.
> A truly just solution will leave every nation somewhat disappointed.
> There is no cure all.[18]

He went on to cover Truman's Potsdam conference and various events in Europe. His style was a mite too stilted for readers of the Hearst press, who must have puzzled over such erudite quotations as "A quarrel is a very pretty quarrel as it stands. We only spoil it by trying to explain it." In any case he was finding journalism less and less to his liking. "I felt it was too passive," he said later. "Instead of doing things, you were writing about people who did things."

Impatient for action, Kennedy at 28 was still uncertain where he was headed. He returned to Boston, where he found an opportunity staring him in the face. In the fall elections, James Michael Curley, "The Purple Shamrock," gave up his seat in Congress and got himself elected Mayor of Boston. The vacancy was there; a man who could get through what was sure to be a free-for-all Democratic primary could win the election.

Later Father Joe liked to remember that he had put Jack into politics. "I told him Joe was dead and that it was therefore his responsibility to run for Congress. He didn't want to. He felt he didn't have the ability and he still feels that way. But I told him he had to." Jack would go along with this: "It was like being drafted. My father wanted his eldest son in politics. 'Wanted' isn't the right word. He demanded it. You know my father." And on numerous occasions Jack would say "I went into politics because Joe died," "I'm just filling Joe's shoes. If he were alive, I'd never be in this," "If he'd lived I would have gone on being a writer." It is not necessary to see Jack as his father's passive pawn or his brother's stand-in to explain his entry into politics. There were many reasons, including the sudden opportunity and the restricted alternatives, as well as Jack's own interests and predilections. "Everything seemed to point to it in 1946," he said in 1960. Yet obviously the connection was there. In 1960, Walter Cronkite asked him about the Joe-to-Jack torch-passing and in answering Jack made a slip revealing that influence: "And then he was killed in the war and I came back from the war and I was in the hospital for a while and *his seat* became vacant." (Italics added.)

Jack Kennedy would never break away from his family. But in his race for Congress in 1946 and in his early days in the House, Kennedy's political style took on its main outlines. (Richard Nixon's was developing simultaneously.) From that point on, politics was his calling.

Now the whole family focused its effort behind him, and yet he had to win it himself. The core of his style was rhetoric, but a markedly different kind from the "Honey Fitz" Irish romanticism the district was used to. The district was a fantastically gerrymandered melange of slums plus Harvard, Irish plus Italians, dock-workers plus Unitarians. There were ten candidates for the nomination, including a WAC major and two men named Joseph Russo. As news of his candidacy got around he was called a "carpetbagger," a "poor little rich kid" with no roots in the district. Others like James Michael Curley thought of him as nothing but the son of his parents. "Kennedy!" Curley said. "How can he lose? He's got a double-barreled name. . . . He doesn't even need to campaign." Joe Sr. spent hours on the telephone and many thousands of dollars to see that Jack won. But Jack set out to win for himself.

He put together a "junior brain trust" consisting of men of his generation, friends from Choate and Harvard and the Navy— "all veterans, all weary of Boston's noisy and corrupt politicos, all hardheaded and businesslike, all looking for new faces in politics," as Burns describes them. The campaign slogan was "The New Generation Offers a Leader." There were also some old pals around, but one day when Honey Fitz wandered into a strategy meeting, the manager said "Get that son-of-a-bitch out of here!" Jack said, "Who? *Grampa?*" And out Grampa went. Jack himself stalked through the district, house to house, swallowing his shyness and walking up to sullen groups of strangers on the sidewalk. Watching one such incident from across the street, Father Joe said, "I never thought Jack had it in him." His assistant Dave Powers remembered that Jack "went into alleyways and climbed the stairs of tenement houses where politicians had never been seen before. . . . Nobody else had ever taken the trouble to come to them."

His manner was quiet, factual, direct, and increasingly confident as he quickly became an old hand at approaching people. His speechmaking, halting at first, gained power: "He slowly developed a style of direct, informal, simple speaking, without high-blown rhetoric or bombastic exaggeration, that to some of his listeners was in happy contrast to the oratory of the old-fashioned politicians," Burns says. Yet he found he could also call occasionally on the Fitzgerald in him. Once, at a rally, when he was making a strong speech for veteran's housing, an old Irishman named Jackie Toomey queried, "What about the *non*-veteran?" Jack snapped back with "Yes, sir, the *non*-veteran too." After the meeting a smiling Jackie Toomey circulated among the crowd saying, "You see—he's for the non-veteran too." Kennedy also learned to speak toughly. At another rally the WAC major, in her white uniform, gave him a public raking-over and then whispered to him, "Don't pay any attention—it's just politics." When Kennedy's turn came he gave a harsh counterattack.

The whole thing was organized down to the last detail. The Kennedy sisters scheduled the candidate for five or six house parties an evening, supplying flowers and silverware for those in the slum neighborhoods. Joe Sr. saw to a saturation advertising campaign. The climax came in a formal reception at a Boston hotel; every registered Democrat received a hand-addressed engraved invitation; fifteen hundred sweating Bostonians, mostly ladies in fancy dress, showed up to shake hands with Jack and with the former Ambassador to the Court of St. James, resplendent in white tie and tails. (That was Joe Sr.'s first and only campaign appearance. Asked to make a speech he said, "No more speeches for me. Jack's going into politics.")

There was not a great deal of talk about "style" in politics before the Kennedys. The campaign had an elan, a dash and flair, flowing outward from the brave-young-candidate to his audiences. People saw in him what they wanted to: the Irish lad made good, the crisp Harvard mind, the battle-scarred veteran, the scion of unfathomable wealth, the handsome, humble fellow destined for mysterious greatness. Whatever it was, it added up to charisma, a pawed-over concept Kennedy brought back to clarity. For all his apparent modesty—perhaps in part *because* of that—Jack left people feeling they could do better and enjoy it. Even then, Kennedy and the Kennedys went around enspiriting people, calling forth their hope.

Kennedy won with 22,183 votes, almost double the vote of his nearest contender. He had discovered he could win, not by relying on the battered and strife-torn regulars, but by building his own organization. The Kennedy machine, then as in 1960, used whatever fragments it could gather together but counted only on commitments to the man himself. And as the hopeful soon found out, the commitment was a one-way street. A fellow Congressman noted that "The thing about Kennedy that sets him apart from all other Boston Irish politicians, and, for that matter, from most politicians everywhere, is that he seldom feels obligated to anybody." People were expected to work for Kennedy because they thought he was right, not for jobs and contracts. When the Boston pols saw that he meant that, they were puzzled. In Washington one of his first decisions was not to sign a petition to pardon Curley, then serving concurrent terms as Mayor of Boston and federal prison inmate convicted of fraud.

Kennedy talked programs for his constituents; he was for them but not of them. Similarly in Congress he kept his distance. A few days after he took office a friend met him on the Capitol steps and gave him some advice. "I told him 'Jack, if I were you starting in down there, I'd *marry* [House Speaker] John McCormack. I'd hang around with him in the House, eat dinner with him a couple of nights a week, listen to everything he had to say and ask for advice.' You know what Jack did when I told him that? He backed away from me in horror as if I had pointed a gun at him." Later Kennedy explained his independence by the fact that he was not beholden to the big politicians: "I came in sort of sideways," he said, not through the party ranks.

As a first-term Congressman Kennedy was not accorded excessive attention. He generally supported New Deal legislation, worked hard and spoke forcefully for public, low-cost housing, against the Taft-Hartley bill regulating labor; he replied vigorously to the charge that Catholics had divided loyalties. In foreign policy he blasted the Truman administration for losing China. With time the issues would change, as would his positions on them. But his political character was established, the broad outlines of his world view sketched in, and the style which brought him success firmed in his behavior. Later he would explain some of his early stands as due to the fact that "I'd just come out of my father's house at the time, and these were the things I knew." But he had indeed left his father's house, and "Once I came into politics and political life, then, of course, you are on your own, and your judgments are your own."

In his notebook of 1945–46, he wrote:

> To be a positive force for the public good in politics one must have three things; a solid moral code governing his public actions, a broad knowledge of our institutions and traditions and a specific background in the technical problems of government, and lastly he must have political appeal—the gift of winning public confidence and support.[19]

John Kennedy, then, brought from his childhood an orientation toward life, a combination of "vigor" and laughter, a way of approaching experience with an expectation of success. He could see how he had grown from sickliness to heroism, from second place to first, from casualness to commitment. In the family he learned love without sentimentality, acquired the capacity to act forcefully and yet with detachment. His parents did not raise him, they tended him, let him grow, fostering and stimulating such urges to excel as he had. In his relationship with his older brother, Jack developed a sustained rivalry and identification, one he was never allowed to escape by surrendering to passivity. The tension lasted, but at a critical turning point in Jack's own life, Joe was suddenly gone and Jack was in his place. That helped bring out and strengthen the gregarious, aggressive, and movie-star qualities in him—opened his character more and sharpened his thirst for action.

John Kennedy's world view drew first on the meanings of being Irish—secondhand memories of Mother's sensitivity and Father's ire at discrimination. The world was not necessarily fair. Beside that was the Honey Fitz spirit—gaiety in the face of injustice, laughter and a kind of innocence amidst the weeds of politics. The world was not necessarily hopeless. And as Father's stark example demonstrated, one who kept the faith and let the devil take the hindmost could find power. At last, in writing *Why England Slept,* John Kennedy turned his cool analytic eyes on man in modern democracy and began to see images of slumber and arousal that would recur to him again and again. There he started to reach beyond analysis to preach the gospel of awareness, decision, action. In the war he put his body on that line, showed himself how daring could stare down death. And in his brief fling at reporting after the war, Kennedy confirmed his view that meaning inhered in the substance of social behavior, not in the forms of institutions. The substance was harder.

Entering politics, Kennedy found his style. The step was crucial: from his father's house to the House of Representatives, from watching to doing, from notetaker to notable. The success of it confirmed a rhetoric of calm, straightforward, direct expression without condescension or sycophancy, combined with the natural projection of mystery, sex appeal, to-the-manner-born confidence. Kennedy had already shown he could study hard when he wanted to; in the campaign he practiced cranking into his brain the names and predilections of the heretofore anonymous, and in Congress he showed a selective attention by which he could bypass much of the fog on the way to the harbor. The grinding work of the campaign was his to do, too, not from the isolation of headquarters, but up the stairwells of tenements. Through it all, he insisted on perfection and then some.

As for personal relations, the Kennedy style in politics meant a crew of young, sharp colleagues undismayed by their lack of experience and undaunted before their elders. It was a GI operation, short on sham, long on sarcastic wit, a crew of hell-bent regulars all about the same age, letting their performance say for them how they felt about their leader. Competence counted. That established, the Kennedy team jelled—but not too closely—around the candidate.

But it was in "the gift of winning public confidence and support" that Kennedy knew he would find his main thrust and challenge. Fourteen years later, as he moved on the Presidency, he reached back into his past to find a way beyond the critics' doubts.

KENNEDY AS PRESIDENT

There was a gap of fourteen years. Kennedy had his ups and downs, and it would be wrong to say he did not continue to grow as Congressman, Senator, contender for the Vice Presidential nomination in 1956. But Kennedy as Presidential candidate and as President of the United States could have been anticipated; his style, world view, and character had their roots in his earlier years.

The Kennedy rhetoric—only partly a matter of speechmaking—was much the same as it had been from the start, though the Presidential candidate showed a confidence in delivery well beyond his 1946 performance. But the directness, the projection of restrained rage, the intellectuality, the humor and statistics, candor and vagueness were his trademarks. He urged without preaching, inspired without condescending. And the effect on his partisans was electric. Theodore White remembers not so much the size of the crowds as their "frenzied quality." The response to Kennedy was symbolized in "the jumpers":

> The jumpers made their appearance shortly after the first TV debate when from a politician Kennedy had become, in the mind of the bobby-sox platoons, a "thing" combining, as one Southern Senator said, "The best qualities of Elvis Presley and Franklin D. Roosevelt." The jumpers were, in the beginning, teenage girls who would bounce, jounce and jump as the cavalcade passed, squealing, "I seen him, I seen him." Gradually over the days their jumping seemed to grow more rhythmic, giving a jack-in-the-box effect of ups and down in a thoroughly sexy oscillation. Then, as the press began to comment on the phenomenon, thus stimulating more artistic jumping, the middle-aged ladies began to jump up and down too. . . .[20]

The "star quality," the Kennedy "mystique" was there again. Apparently Kennedy's personal cool, his critical stance toward self-satisfaction, his call for a higher standard of performance, and his thirst for action—or some part or symbiosis of those—fit the mood of the young, and, increasingly in a culture where the young are thought to show the way, the not so young. After the television debates with Nixon, Kennedy was remembered not so much for what he said as for the impression of expertise, precision, and judgment he conveyed.

The Kennedy name had acquired such magic in some quarters that, for example, another John F. Kennedy, a stockroom foreman at a razor factory, got himself elected twice as Treasurer of the State of Massachusetts, simply by putting his name on the ballot; his campaign expenses were $100 in 1958, most of it for an election night victory party. He rode around in a chauffeur-driven limousine, and appointed his relatives to substantial positions.

As the vote in 1960 showed, not everyone shared this enthusiasm for Kennedy, and the regular tides of party and class—plus a significant backlash against Kennedy as a Catholic—shaped the outcome in familiar ways. But Kennedy as rhetorician, in the campaign and later, did manage to express for the nation something a great many felt: that we had become too easy, too soft, had drifted long enough, and that it was time to get moving again. The Peace Corps was the most dramatic example of this release of practical idealism; the applications streamed in and Congress authorized 500, then 5,000, then 10,000 in 1964. Volunteers worked in 46 countries, and even Barry Goldwater gave his support. The enthusiasm spread beyond the Peace Corps to service through politics and government. The Civil Service Commission reported a sharp upswing in college graduates seeking government careers, and many fresh faces suddenly began to appear in the ranks of candidates for local, state, and national office. On the campuses, the "Silent Generation" stirred itself to interest and action along many fronts. Kennedy had announced a new standard of excellence, a new approach stressing realism and rationality. This new activism may have been burdensome for the worn warriors of the New Deal, for the ideologues of left and right, and for many to whom life seemed excellent enough, but the young ate it up.

As for President Kennedy's personal relations style, that, too, reflected his way with people close up when he experienced his first independent political success. In the campaign and in the White House, Kennedy was surrounded by men of his own generation and orientation. Most of his White House staff had gone through college in the thirties, a fair number to Harvard; there were at least a dozen Rhodes scholars circulating at the top of the Executive Branch. Of his first 200 top appointees, half had government or political experience, 18 percent were university or foundation people, and 6 percent were businessmen. (In the Eisenhower administration, 42 percent were from business, 6 percent from universities and foundations.) Most were veterans, some like Kennedy and George McGovern were war heroes. Serving a President who inspired idealism, the Kennedy men in the White House were doers, not dreamers. "There was not a reformer among them, as far as anyone could tell," Richard Rovere wrote. "Pragmatism—often of the grubbiest kind—was rampant." Yet their pragmatism did not breed overcaution; "They would try anything," Arthur Schlesinger remembered. The war had given this "New Frontier generation its casual and laconic tone, its grim, puncturing humor and its mistrust of evangelism," Schlesinger wrote.

All was not roses among them. Kennedy liked to call them, perhaps with a trace of irony, his "band of brothers," and in some ways the White House atmosphere did resemble that of a fraternity house. The tensions were there, as they had to be in such a collection of ambitions and energies. Publicly team players, privately they were not, as Theodore Sorensen put it, "wholly free from competitive feelings or from scornful references to each other's political or intellectual backgrounds." What held them together was Kennedy; when he was gone their brotherhood faded. He treated them, by and large, with respect and a direct, informal manner, concentrating their talk on the matter at hand. His work life and his social life were two different things. Sorensen, the President's "alter ego" at work, was not, and apparently never cared to be, part of the partying Kennedy circle. The thing at work was work. Kennedy showed continual concern for the feelings of his men, possibly remembering how "the star of the family" had treated him and reacting against that, but he was extraordinarily demanding, occasionally angry, and given to sloppily demarcated delegation of tasks that inevitably multiplied frictions.

Yet he drew them together around an overriding task, his own success, and he demonstrated every day his detailed attention to and appreciation for what they did. He knew his advisors would disagree and he wanted to be in on the nittiest of the facts and arguments. Later when the flood of issues and details got beyond him, Kennedy had to organize more tightly, had to learn the art of creative neglect. But his penchant for fact, for crisp proposals in place of vague analyses, kept the strings in his hands. He read faster than anyone around, got through the newspapers before most had finished the comics, and digested—and remembered—endless reams of fact, opinion, and surmise in memoranda.

Especially with his brother Robert, John Kennedy talked in shorthand, often interrupting the other halfway through his sentence as he caught the thought.

Kennedy's general slant on the world maintained itself in the White House. He found Earth an exciting place to live, and said so. His emphasis on arousing democracy to action is obvious, from "Ask not . . ." on. The toughness theme was also there, perhaps exacerbating a tendency to see the Communists in the role of Hitler in World War II. William G. Carleton felt that Kennedy "needlessly fanned the flames of the Cold War" at first, and that his inaugural address was "already historically off-key, more suited to the Stalinist era than 1961." Kennedy the rationalist, Kennedy the systems man, Kennedy the calculating seemed to relax the restraints against aggressiveness in occasional rattlings of the saber. He had come along into politics immediately after a war in which the good guys and the bad guys were sharply distinguishable. Some of that climbed up into his brain again.

Kennedy had to keep his picture of the world steady despite the jarring criticism he received, particularly on the "Catholic issue," but also in blasts of invective against his person, his family, his staff. Equally disturbing might have been the flood of favorable goo that began to flow long before Kennedy's death. Richard West asked, with tongue in cheek, in 1966,

> Which Kennedy to you most enjoy reading about? Life-enhancing, life-affirming, wry, funny, coolly committed, amazingly young, tough-minded Jack? Caustic, cutting, thrusting, restless, aggressive, astonishingly mature, tough-minded, fun-loving, loyal, compulsively hard-working, ruthless Bobby? Or quiet, wry, life-affirming, life-enhancing, amazingly young, loyal, coolly ambitious, funny, surprisingly tough-minded Ted? There is much to be said for quiet, wry, astonishingly mature, seven-year-old John. He has not yet been gushed about by driveling Madison Avenue hacks and adoring professors.[21]

Kennedy is known to have been embarrassed at maudlin praise and angered by prejudiced criticism (especially when it bit too close to the truth), but neither managed to depress him. He kept his balance by laughter—or, perhaps better, his humor was a symptom of balance. Unlike Calvin Coolidge in every other way, Kennedy used wit as a sea anchor.

Had he delivered the greatest inaugural address ever given? Kennedy himself lampooned it in a speech to the faithful:

> We observe tonight not a celebration of freedom but a victory of party, for we have sworn to pay off the same party debt our forebears ran up nearly a year and three months ago. Our deficit will not be paid off in the next hundred days, nor will it be paid off in the first one thousand days, nor in the life of this Administration. Nor, perhaps, even in our lifetime on this planet. But let us begin. . . .[22]

Did he live by Hemingway's code of courage, "grace under pressure"? He said it reminded him of a girl he knew by that name. Was he the tool of an amoral, foreign religion? In the midst of the 1960 campaign he joined Nixon in addressing the annual dinner in Al Smith's memory:

Mr. Nixon, like the rest of us, has had his troubles in this campaign. At one point even the *Wall Street Journal* was criticizing his tactics. That is like *Osservatore Romano* criticizing the Pope.

One of the inspiring notes that was struck in the last debate was struck by the Vice-President in his very moving warning to the candidates against the use of profanity by Presidents and ex-Presidents when they are on the stump. And I know after fourteen years in the Congress with the Vice-President, that he was very sincere in his views about the use of profanity. But I am told that a prominent Republican said to him yesterday in Jacksonville, Florida, "Mr. Vice-President, that was a damn fine speech." And the Vice-President said, "I appreciate the compliment but not the language." And the Republican went on, "Yes, sir, I liked it so much that I contributed a thousand dollars to your campaign." And Mr. Nixon replied, "The hell you say."[23]

Was he the world's most lovable man? Once when Red Fay's four-year-old daughter shied away from him, Kennedy said, "I don't think she quite caught that strong quality of love of children so much a part of the candidate's make-up which has made him so dear to the hearts of mothers."[24] Was he the smartest, best-informed man ever to seek the Presidency? In September 1960 we get the following exchange:

QUESTION: Senator, you were promised military intelligence briefing from the President. Have you received that?

MR. KENNEDY: Yes. I talked on Thursday morning to General Wheeler from the Defense Department.

QUESTION: What was his first name?

MR. KENNEDY: He didn't brief me on that.[25]

Did Kennedy aspire to the power and glory of the Presidency? In Charleston, West Virginia, September 19, 1960:

QUESTION: I am for Mr. Kennedy. And may I visit you when you are the President of the United States in the White House? I have tried three times and cannot get in.

MR. KENNEDY: Let's meet outside and we will get it all set.[26]

Was he a man whose courage in battle steeled his soul for the Presidency?

QUESTION: Mr. President, how did you become a war hero?

MR. KENNEDY: It was absolutely involuntary. They sank my boat.[27]

Did he see his role as a "splendid misery," a grim drama against overwhelming odds? "I have a nice home," he said, "the office is close by and the pay is good."

Much unlike Lyndon Johnson's, Kennedy's humor was often directed at himself. He could laugh at his supposed swank, his relation to his father, his wife's elegance, his authority, his decisiveness, his looks, clothes, and accent. He could laugh—at least chuckle—at the troubles he had. He liked old Everett McKinley Dirksen's comment that a Kennedy legislative recommendation would have "all the impact of a snowflake on the bosom of the Potomac"; and when he heard that McGeorge Bundy was being considered for another job, Kennedy moaned in deadpan, "I wish somebody would offer *me* the presidency of Yale." Sorensen was with him continually and remembers only one occasion when he spoke with any bitterness about the burdens of the office—just after a conference with Senators and a few minutes before he was to go on television to tell the world about the missiles in Cuba. We have Sorensen's testimony that "John F. Kennedy was a happy President," in the Aristotelian sense of the full use of one's powers along lines of excellence; Sorensen has collected snippits of proof from scattered Kennedy press conferences and interviews:

> The job is interesting. . . . It represents a chance to exercise your judgment on matters of importance. . . . I find the work rewarding . . . the Presidency provides some happiness (under Aristotle's definition). . . . There are a lot of satisfactions in the Presidency. . . . You have an opportunity to do something about all problems . . . and if what you do is useful and successful . . . that is a great satisfaction. . . . This is a damned good job.[28]

Like Harry Truman and Franklin D. Roosevelt, John Kennedy was an active-positive President. The central adaptive strength of that character is the sense of the self as developing, demonstrated externally in evidence of openness, experiment, flexibility, and growth.

To those professional President-watchers who raised doubts about John Kennedy's capacities, his humor and happiness may have seemed irrelevant. Early in his term, those who were skeptical of his maturity—judgment seasoned by experience—suddenly found their doubts massively confirmed. The Bay of Pigs invasion was straight out of *Alice in Wonderland*.

In the dawn's early light on April 17, 1961, about 1,400 Cuban exiles invaded Cuba to overthrow the Castro regime and its army of more than 200,000 soldiers and militiamen. These seem like bad odds, but the American Central Intelligence Agency, which had been training and encouraging the exile band, gave assurances that there were 2,500 organized resisters to Castro in Cuba, that 20,000 more Cubans sympathized with the resisters, and that when the attack came a quarter of the Cuban population would actively support the invaders. This was not based on any evidence, because the CIA had not been asked to get evidence on the question, and the Cuba experts in the State Department had not been asked about it either. Otherwise, they would have known that a poll showing Castro with overwhelming support among the Cuban people already had been widely circulated in the U.S. government. This poll only confirmed the opinion of a respected reporter who told the President the same thing well before the invasion, a view reinforced the morning of the attack when Castro's police arrested 200,000 people in Havana without difficulty and without mass uprisings. The President as Commander in Chief had ordered that no Americans take part in the little band's attack but someone had to stake out the landing areas; American frogmen were the first troops ashore, were immediately discovered, and the alarm sounded. The attack was supposed to be secret but

Castro had reason to think something was afoot when his air force of 55 planes was attacked on the ground two days before. Five of them were actually put out of action by a force of old World War II B-26 bombers, unmarked and flown on such small gas supply from far-away Nicaragua (rather than from Puerto Rico or Florida) that they could spend only a short time over their targets. But that was before the actual invasion by the exile troops.

In order that the United States not be seen as overly involved, the only air action was supposed to be by Cuban exiles in B-26s, and these planes did drop great loads of supplies. But the wind blew the loaded parachutes into the sea and jungle where the exile troops could not get them. The 1,400 invaders, whose average age was 29 and who numbered among them 135 soldiers, 240 students, and a various mixture of businessmen, professionals, peasants, and fishermen were soon faced with 20,000 of Castro's troops equipped with modern weapons as well as by fast Castro armed jet trainer planes which the CIA had dismissed as not very good. As the exiles hit the beaches, they watched for an expected air attack from their side, but that had been canceled because it would look too much like the United States was attacking a tiny neighbor. As a result, Castro's planes destroyed much of the exiles' ammunition before it could be brought ashore, including one ship in which was loaded the entire ammunition reserve for ten days and most of the communications equipment. Many quickly ran out of ammunition; then the canceled air strike was uncanceled and set for that night, only to be canceled again because the weather turned cloudy. On the way in to the beach, numerous exile boats had been wrecked on coral reefs which had not been mentioned in the CIA briefing three days before. But even though they were in great difficulty, the invaders knew (because the CIA had told them at the briefing) that 500 guerrillas were nearby to help them, that paratroops were dropping inland, and that another, larger exile force would soon join them on the beach. Also, they knew that two other attack forces were landing in other parts of Cuba and that, if need be, after 72 hours the United States Air Force and the United States Marines would come in and fight for them. But, however encouraging, none of those things was true; the 1,400 were in fact on their own. Their orders specified that if they got into too much trouble they should either fall back to the beaches, which they had not yet got past, or escape to the mountains where they would take up guerrilla warfare against Castro. This would be a new experience for almost all of them because they had had no training in guerrilla warfare; but this did not matter anyway because the escape-to-the-mountains idea was actually planned only for the original strategy of invasion at Trinidad near the foothills of the mountains. When the landing site was changed to the Bay of Pigs some weeks before, it was forgotten that the mountains were eighty miles away across impenetrable swamps and jungles. So the war went ahead on the beach.

The members of the provisional government the 1,400 invaders were going to install in Cuba had not been in Nicaragua where the force had begun, but had held sway in New York City; the night before the invasion, acting on an agreement they had worked out with the CIA, this Cuban Revolutionary Council moved with great secrecy to Florida so that they would be ready to go to Cuba and establish their rule. Next morning they tuned in their radio to hear that they had announced the start of the invasion, which was news to them. This, in fact, had come from a CIA man dictating press releases over the telephone in the name of the Cuban Revolutionary Council to a New York friend of his in public relations who passed the news along to the mass media. This made up for the silence imposed on the Council by the CIA. This enforced silence served to prevent the exile leaders from pressing for employment of the thirty exile combat fliers who were kept back in Miami while their fellow pilots were dropping from exhaustion in the fight; it also prevented them from continuing to demand explosives to blow up the Havana electric power plant, under which their agents had had a tunnel ready for more than a month. They did get word that the invasion was not going well, but they were encouraged when, on the third day, the radio broadcast another bulletin in their name announcing that most of the invaders had escaped to the mountains.

There was no truth to this announcement. The invading men and boys fired off their ammunition too fast (according to the subsequent investigative report by U.S. General Maxwell Taylor) and after the main ammunition reserve ship was sunk and another large freighter full of supplies went down, the remaining two exile-manned ammunition freighters took off for the south. The U.S. Navy chased the fleeing ships and turned them back, but by then Wednesday morning daylight was coming and the crews threatened to mutiny if the Americans did not protect them on the way in. The CIA in Washington vetoed this idea, but during the same night CIA pilots did help out the exhausted exile pilots by replacing some of them in B-26s and also by flying (contrary to the President's command) Navy jets in support of the B-26s. Unfortunately, the Navy jets timed their action by Cuban time, which is an hour later than Nicaragua; the B-26s used Nicaraguan time, getting to the beachhead an hour early to find no fighter support. Four Americans were killed when the B-26s they were flying got shot down. That same night in Washington, the President attended for two hours a white-tie reception for Congressmen and their wives in order to prevent undue speculation about the situation in Cuba being a disaster, then came back to the White House to meet with the CIA deputy director for operations. The latter recommended that U.S. planes be ordered to attack from a carrier, and the President responded that on Wednesday morning six unmarked U.S. planes could cover the B-26s, but not attack. But by then it was almost over. Castro's forces captured 1,113 of the exiles, holding them for 20 months until Christmas Eve, 1962, when they were freed in exchange for $53 million worth of medicine, baby food, and other items.

This whole sorry business took place before Kennedy had been in office a hundred days. From first to last it appears to have infected everyone it touched with one form or another of mental lapse. In his book *Six Crises*, for example, Richard Nixon recounts an incredible tale about his position on Cuba in the 1960 campaign against Kennedy. Nixon said he had long been urging an exile invasion and was pleased when the CIA was ordered, early in 1960, to supply arms, ammunition, and training for the mission. Then, in the campaign, Kennedy was reported as advocating this Nixon plan. Nixon was enraged; he felt that revealing his backing for the project would blow its cover. So, in "what was probably the most difficult decision of the campaign," Nixon reasoned this way:

> There was only one thing I could do. The covert operation had to be protected at all costs. I must not even suggest by implication that the United States was rendering aid to rebel forces in and out of Cuba. In fact, I must go to the other extreme: I must attack the Kennedy proposal to provide such aid as wrong and irresponsible because it would violate our treaty commitments.[29]

So Nixon came out strongly against Nixon's plan.

How had Kennedy fallen into this disaster? Combing through the complex history, Sorensen notes five erroneous assumptions the President had made:

1. That the landing could be kept quiet and unspectacular.
2. That the invaders could escape to the mountains if necessary.
3. That the exiles understood U.S. forces would not enter the fight.
4. That the attack would trigger mass uprisings in Cuba.
5. That Castro's forces were weak and disorganized.[30]

The "blame" for these mistaken assumptions had to rest with the military and intelligence chiefs who had propounded them. But in a larger sense, as Kennedy realized and readily admitted afterward, the blame was his for not requiring them to prove their case. He was not alone in that error. As Irving Janis points out in his brilliant study of "fiascoes" in Presidential foreign policy decision-making, the Bay of Pigs episode provides many illustrations of "groupthink"—a social-psychological process which seduced such hardy and capable souls as Dean Rusk, Robert McNamara, Douglas Dillon, McGeorge Bundy and Robert Kennedy to go along with the plan and weakened the resolve of others to express their doubts. Yet not only doubts, but stern opposition had been expressed to the President well before the action.

The Chairman of the Senate Committee on Foreign Relations, J. William Fulbright, gave the President on March 30, 1961, a memorandum strongly opposing the plan. Even a successful overthrow, he argued, would "be denounced from the Rio Grande to Patagonia as an example of imperialism" and as a direct violation of treaties and legislation. A failing operation would tempt us to use American forces, in which case "even under the paper cover of legitimacy, we would have undone the work of thirty years in trying to live down earlier interventions." Fulbright continued,

> To give this activity even covert support is of a piece with the hypocrisy and cynicism for which the United States is constantly denouncing the Soviet Union in the United Nations and elsewhere. The point will not be lost on the rest of the world—nor on our own consciences.[31]

In a meeting with Kennedy and the military and other chiefs on April 4, Fulbright emphatically denounced the plan as grossly out of proportion to the threat from Castro and directly contradictory to the country's moral position in the world. After that meeting, Arthur Schlesinger told the President that he, too, opposed the plan and next morning Schlesinger delivered an opposition memorandum to Kennedy, following that with another two days later. Schlesinger said that "If we could achieve this [overthrow] by a swift, surgical strike, I would be for it," but he found utterly implausible two assumptions of the plan:

No matter how "Cuban" the equipment and personnel, the U.S. will be held accountable for the operation, and our prestige will be committed to its success.

And

Since the Castro regime is presumably too strong to be toppled by a single landing, the operation will turn into a protracted civil conflict.[32]

Schlesinger went on to argue that "if the rebellion appears to be failing, the rebels will call for U.S. armed help; that members of Congress will take up the cry; and that pressures will build up which will make it politically hard to resist the demand to send in the Marines." The operation would jeopardize the "reawakening world faith in America."

Between them, then, Schlesinger and Fulbright raised several explicit challenges to the plan being so confidently and vigorously advanced by the Secretary of Defense, the Joint Chiefs of Staff, and the Director of the Central Intelligence Agency. The President was not without questions in his head. What appears to have distorted his thinking were at last these dimensions of the problem:

—He had an almost personal animosity toward Castro and had taken a tough anti-Castro line in the campaign.
—New to the Presidency, he placed his trust in military professionals and discounted advice he got from amateur quarters.
—He continued to think he could call the whole thing off at the last moment, and never resolved clearly the choice between a quiet infiltration and a highly publicized invasion.

When it was all over, Kennedy in public shouldered all the blame; his Gallup poll rating leaped up to 82 percent, but his professional reputation suffered enormously. In private he would fume against the CIA and the Joint Chiefs: "My God, what a bunch of advisers we inherited. . . . Can you imagine being President and leaving behind someone like all those people there?" After a decent interval he replaced the CIA Director. But the Bay of Pigs had confirmed a view of Kennedy as too wet behind the ears to control his government, too naively bellicose to look beyond the "game" of international cold war, and/or too "detached"—à la Eisenhower—to reach beyond a presiding-officer role and assume responsible command.

The prime question was whether he could or would grow beyond this early disaster. I think he did, in stages of experience, from his meeting with Khrushchev in Vienna of June 1961, through the steel price conflict in early 1962, and culminating in the Cuban missile crisis later that year. But first there was yet another indication—in the "Great Space Race"—that his thinking was still affected by the competitive drive to win whatever there was to win.

Back in the campaign when Kennedy was making much of the "prestige gap" between the United States and the Soviet Union, he had held up the competition to explore and control outer space as a prime example. In Pocatello, Idaho, he said that other nations "have seen the Soviet Union first in space. They have seen it first around the moon, and first around the sun. . . . They come to the conclusion that the Soviet tide is rising and ours is ebbing. I think it is up to us to reverse that point." Again and again he pounded at this theme, connecting it by juxtaposition with the race for superiority in delivery systems for nuclear weapons. In his inaugural address and first State of the Union addresses he called for East-West cooperation—"Together let us explore the stars"—but when the Soviets rejected that, Kennedy set out to beat them. When on April 12, 1961, five days before the Bay of Pigs landing, Soviet cosmonaut Yuri Gagarin zipped around the globe in less than two hours, Kennedy's resolve set.

The fundamental reason for Kennedy's interest in space programs is clear as a bell. Sorensen wrote that to Kennedy the space gap "symbolized the nation's lack of initiative, ingenuity and vitality under Republican rule. He was convinced that Americans did not yet fully grasp the world-wide political and psychological impact of the space race." Here was a theme drawn straight from *Why England Slept*. The utility of the space programs was "political," "psychological," symbolic—those things, far more than the practical utilities of the space program, weighed on Kennedy's mind. He hammered away at his space advisors:

> Now let's look at this. Is there any place where we can catch them? What can we do? Can we go around the moon before them? Can we put a man on the moon before them? What about Nova and Rover? When will Saturn be ready? Can we leapfrog?[33]

The spacemen told him it would be an immense task to overtake the Russians, could be done only with a crash program similar to the Manhattan Project which had developed the atomic bomb, would cost something on the order of $40 billion, and, as Jerome Wiesner quietly said, "Now is not the time to make mistakes." But Kennedy was impatient:

> When we know more, I can decide if its worth it or not. If somebody can just tell me how to catch up. Let's find somebody—anybody. I don't care if it's the janitor over there, if he knows how. . . . There's nothing more important. . . . I'm determined to get an answer.[34]

The answer he fastened on was to put a man on the moon. "No single space project in this period," he told Congress, "will be more impressive to mankind or

more important . . . so difficult or expensive to accomplish." But it was all worthwhile because,

> In a very real sense, it will not be one man going to the moon . . . it will be an
> entire nation. For all of us must work to put him there. This is not merely a race.
> Space is open to us now; and our eagerness to share its meaning is not governed
> by the efforts of others. We go into space because whatever mankind must
> undertake, free men must fully share.[35]

There was a great deal more of such rhetoric; whether the immense
treasure and energy and risk involved in the moon program would produce
significant new discoveries or techniques was obscure (it is still obscure). But
none of that was of great significance to a Kennedy, out to win first place.
America must "set sail on this new sea" and become "the world's leading space-
faring nation." At bottom it was a sporting proposition:

> But why, some say, the moon? . . . And they may well ask, why climb the highest
> mountain? Why, thirty-five years ago, fly the Atlantic? Why does Rice play
> Texas? . . .
> We choose to go to the moon in this decade, and do the other things, not
> because they are easy but because they are hard; because that goal will serve to
> organize and measure the best of our energies and skills. . . .
> Many years ago, the great British explorer George Mallory, who was to die on
> Mount Everest, was asked why did he want to climb it, and he said, "Because it is
> there."
> Well, space is there, and . . . the moon and the planets are there, and new
> hopes for knowledge and peace are there.[36]

In the end the United States beat the Soviet Union to the moon.

But Kennedy was right, at least at first, about the psychological impact.
The space shots culminating in the 1962 flight of Colonel John Glenn captured
the national imagination as football games do the local imagination. For a while,
at least, this very expensive show played to a highly appreciative audience. When
the Russians went ahead, we offered our congratulations and set out to forge on
to first place again. The space program was, as President Kennedy said, symbolic, which, in political terms, can mean real. It left unsolved all the messy
problems on earth, but when those soured one could look heavenward.

Kennedy's more serious political maturation developed in two other
stages on the way to its most severe challenge. He met with Nikita S. Khrushchev
in Vienna on June 3 and 4, 1961. He came back saying that "somber" would be
the best word to describe their interchange. Actually there was a fair amount of
humorous joshing, but he was keenly impressed with Khrushchev's toughness,
persistence, and unbending assertiveness. He had prepared for the meeting by
studying all Khrushchev's available speeches, his background, even his psyche.
The meeting was "invaluable, it was invaluable," he said. At dinner, Mrs. Kennedy had fallen into conversation with the Soviet Premier and suggested he send
her a puppy from a space dog's litter; two months later the dog was delivered in
Washington by two nervous Russians. But Kennedy himself noted Khrushchev's

"internal rage." If he had thought of Castro as a paper tiger, he was unlikely to make that error with respect to Khrushchev.

The critical issue was Berlin. Khrushchev said he would sign a peace treaty with East Germany. Kennedy asked if that would block access to Berlin. Khrushchev said yes. Kennedy said the United States would not give up its access rights. Khrushchev said his decision was firm. "If that is true," said the President, "it will be a cold winter."

Kennedy returned to the United States by way of England, where he found a soul brother in Harold Macmillan. "It was the gay things that linked us together," Macmillan said, "and made it possible for us to talk about terrible things." When he got back to Washington the debate on Berlin got underway in the administration. The Bay of Pigs was scarcely a month old. Kennedy decided with little hesitation that Berlin was not to be surrendered. He would risk nuclear war for that. But his second decision was equally important, from the perspective of his Presidency: he himself would take complete charge of the situation. He studied with extraordinary thoroughness every feature of it: German, Soviet, Allied, Congressional, Executive. The response to Khrushchev would be orchestrated step by step—for example, seeking authorization to call up reserves but not calling them up. Khrushchev gave a tough speech. Kennedy waited.

The details of the Berlin crisis are less important here than their upshot for Kennedy's development. There was a good deal of posturing on both sides: eventually Khrushchev built the Berlin wall, blocking the way of the growing tide of emigrants from East Germany, and dropped the deadline for a treaty with East Germany. In the decision-making process, Kennedy moved far more deliberately and forcefully than he had in the Bay of Pigs crisis. Particularly important was the fresh attention he gave to the non-experts, especially the non-military non-experts. The saber-rattling suggestions came in, in the form of phrases suggested for his speech:

GENERAL TAYLOR:	"I hear it said that West Berlin is militarily untenable. And so was Bastogne. And so, in fact, was Stalingrad. Any dangerous spot is tenable if men—brave men—will make it so."
ED MURROW:	"We cannot negotiate with those who say, 'What's mine is mine and what's yours is negotiable.'"
THE STATE DEPARTMENT:	"The solemn vow each of us gave to West Berlin in time of peace will not be broken in time of danger. If we do not meet our commitments to Berlin, where will we later stand?"[37]

The foremost exponent of toughness was Dean Acheson, Truman's Secretary of State, so often accused of being a striped-pants sissy and so often called upon by Presidents for the clarity of his mind. Acheson was prompt with a long memorandum in which he argued that the particulars of the Soviet arguments about Berlin were strategically trivial: they were testing our will. Therefore to move to negotiations would be a sign of weakness, one to be avoided. The American response should be primarily military. The U.S. should build up its nuclear and conventional forces, let Khrushchev sign whatever papers he chose, but move rapidly with American forces if access to Berlin was in fact disrupted or denied. Kennedy listened. Arthur Schlesinger, who, as he says, was on the outer fringe of the discussions, wrote a counterpiece which illustrates what one perceptive participant-observer thought he could say in the atmosphere developing around Kennedy: the Bay of Pigs muckup, he suggested, had stemmed in large part from "excessive concentration on military and operational problems and the wholly inadequate consideration of political issues. This error seems likely to be repeated here." Khrushchev might sign the treaty and then do nothing to interrupt Berlin-bound traffic. The danger was in repeating the Bay-of-Pigs style of defining the issue:

> To put it crudely, as: Are you chicken or not? When someone proposes something which seems tough, hard, put-up-or-shut-up, it is difficult to oppose it without seeming soft, idealistic, mushy, etc. Yet . . . nothing would clarify more the discussion of policy toward the Soviet Union than the elimination of the words "hard" and "soft" from the language. People who had doubts about Cuba suppressed those doubts lest they seem "soft." It is obviously important that such fears not constrain free discussion of Berlin.[38]

Kennedy pondered. "Winston Churchill said it is better to jaw, jaw than war, war, and we shall continue to jaw, jaw and see if we can produce a useful result." At the same time he called up 160,000 men and proposed substantial increases in the defense budget. His stance was tough but wary. He listened to the divided allies—his elders De Gaulle and Adenauer in particular—but noted that nations "who speak with [such] vigor now" should not forget who carried the major military burdens. "All of them have different ideas of how it ought to be done, and we have to . . . present a position which has some hope of working out. . . . There is daily consultation . . . but . . . it takes a long time. . . ." Partly in response to Schlesinger's thinking, Kennedy tried an old FDR ploy: he got Acheson to work on a "political program" for Berlin, and asked Rusk to turn his attention from arms to negotiations. The papers were due in ten days, at teacher's office.

In the end, Kennedy said, "I think [the Communists] realize that West Berlin is a vital interest to us . . . and that we are going to stay there." Or, in a less public version referring to Khrushchev, "That son of a bitch won't pay any attention to words. He has to see you move." Kennedy moved, but he also talked. In sharp contrast to the Bay of Pigs deliberations, Kennedy had taken charge. He knew his antagonist, appreciated his toughness, calculated what would move him. In the "Berlin Task Force" which met for a critical four days in August, Kennedy probed and challenged the "experts" as he had never done before. Uniforms and battle ribbons did not unbalance his decisions.

In that short time since the Cuban fiasco, I think, Kennedy the naive and Kennedy the excessively detached were disposed of in reality, if not entirely in the minds of the President-watchers.

Kennedy the competitor was aroused again in April 1962, when, one day, Roger Blough, president of U.S. Steel, dropped by the President's office to let him know that steel prices were that day raised $6 per ton, an increase which would cover four times the cost of the new labor contract Kennedy had managed, with some sweat, to get labor to accept four days before. The President had no advance notice; Blough's mimeographed release was being given out while he talked to the President. The news was a stunning blow and the President was furious, though he kept his temper. Blough had just recently been perfectly content to have the President's help in holding the line against an inflationary labor settlement. Now he was suddenly—casually—undercutting the President's credibility with labor. "I think you're making a mistake," said Kennedy cooly. In private (but soon in all the newspapers), the President said, "My father always told me that all businessmen were sons-of-bitches, but I never believed it till now." He had been duped, taken, put upon. The anger flashed up. Secretary of Labor Arthur Goldberg joined Blough and Kennedy; soon Goldberg was raging at Blough, who departed. The staff gathered and read more in the President's grim look than in his understated words: "This is a setback." The question was what to do? But that had to be postponed temporarily as the President attended his second white-tie reception for Congressmen and their wives.

Kennedy wheeled out his arsenal of threats, investigations, persuasions, and connections, but concentrated mainly on public opinion. At his press conference he laced into the steel men, using his ice-cold-fury voice:

> . . . a wholly unjustifiable and irresponsible defiance of the public interest. . . . In this serious hour in our nation's history, when we are confronted with grave crises in Berlin and Southeast Asia . . . a tiny handful of steel executives whose pursuit of private power and profit exceeds their sense of public responsibility can show such utter contempt for the interests of 185 million Americans. . . . Some time ago I asked each American to consider what he could do for his country and I asked the steel companies. In the last twenty-four hours we had their answer.[39]

Within 72 hours of Blough's visit, after furious exertion by all concerned, U.S. Steel capitulated as several smaller competitors agreed to go along with the President. Blough visited the White House again. Asked that evening how the talk with Blough had gone this time, Kennedy replied, "I told him that his men could keep their horses for the spring plowing."

What is of interest for understanding Kennedy the competitor, how he grew, is what happened next. It was April of an election year. Kennedy had few votes to gain from steel executives, who had contributed twenty-five times as much money to Nixon in 1960 as to Kennedy. Perhaps he could have drawn and quartered them publicly from April to November, for political reasons. Add the fact that Kennedy felt he had been assaulted in his dignity by a high-class liar and the aggression seems even more likely. What Kennedy did, however, was to issue orders against any gloating statements, any talk of retribution. He told his staff it was "important that we not take any action that could be interpreted as vindictive." He spoke softly to the U.S. Chamber of Commerce and kept his peace while the Chamber president referred ominously to "dictators . . . [who] usually come to power under accepted constitutional procedures." Business protests kept pouring in; Kennedy said, "It is hard as hell to be friendly with people who keep trying to cut your legs off." But he did. He was not anti-business, he told Hugh Sidey, "They're our partners—unwilling partners. But we're in this together. . . . I want to help them if I can." The President congratulated Blough when he was honored by a law school, invited him back to the White House, and appointed him head of an advisory committee.

This small contest and its aftermath gave some glimmer of further growth in Kennedy. He did not accept Blough's behavior. He did not, it seems likely, come to think of Blough as a friend. But he did attain a perspective of the situation from Blough's position, and acted to make that tolerable to him. A humiliated, resentful president of U.S. Steel would be little use to him. Kennedy's ability to see how things look to the eyes of one's enemy was strengthened.

A quality close to the center of the active-positive character is the capacity to incorporate experience. That means more than "learning" the "lessons" of experience. From a review of what he did and what happened to him, a person may be able to abstract propositions, principles, rules of conduct, and so forth, with the intention of applying them to future situations. In that process, the person treats himself as an object of observation and derives from what he sees descriptive and normative generalizations. The result can be useful, producing maxims which, when later problems arise, clarify the analogy of the new problem to past ones and make it possible to draw an inference for behavior. The capacity to incorporate experience also includes, but is again more than, the accumulation of accurate and useful information about external reality; this process requires a mind free enough of distorting influences to see the facts clearly and to organize them productively. Finally, the capacity to incorporate experience is, and is more than, continuity; a person uses his past experience as a point of departure, moving outward from that and thus saving himself from endless calculations regarding the totality of life's novelties.

The evils connected with these virtues are obvious. The self-spectator may, in effect, dispose of experience by posing it abstractly, as in the defense mechanism called intellectualization. The information-hound may make a life of compilation. The continuity buff may close his mind to new alternatives. Examples close enough to the mark would be, in order, Richard Nixon, Herbert Hoover, and Dean Rusk.

The active-positive shows a different kind of involvement and commitment to his own experience that enables him to incorporate its meaning more directly into his behavior. Roosevelt, Truman, and Kennedy all invested themselves seriously in what they were doing at any given time, putting themselves as well as their policies on the line. Their humor and detachment also gave evidence of an inner confidence, an expectation of winning but a readiness to endure failure without defeat. As each moved from decision to decision, he accumulated not just abstractions or information but also judgment, savvy, a feel for the interplay of self and situation. A great deal of such learning is unconscious; the learner may be hard put to tell how he went about it. The active-positive person seems to treat his life as a connected series of experiments in commitment. As each experiment passes into the past, he shakes off regret and holds onto memory. But it is a memory of the whole self, not just of the mind; the experience is a trial or test of a way of being, not just of a way of acting or thinking.

For John Kennedy, experience in crisis decision-making culminated in the Cuban missile crisis of October 1962. He had some lessons in his head, such as the axiom he had learned at the Bay of Pigs: "Never trust the experts!" He knew a good bit more about his government and world problems than before. And he had begun to elaborate an approach moving out from a combination of firmness and the search for negotiations. Perhaps most important, Kennedy had experienced Khrushchev.

The missile crisis was essentially a highly risky race against the clock, in a game without rules played against an opponent whose intentions were obscure. It was a play in three acts with the denouement right at the end.

Act One opened on the night of Monday, October 15, 1962, when photo-intelligence analysts notified McGeorge Bundy that Soviet medium-range missiles were being installed near San Cristóbal in Cuba. Letting the President, tired from a long campaign weekend, sleep on, Bundy checked further and informed Kennedy about the situation the next morning while he was reading the newspapers in bed. Sorensen reports the President took the news "calmly but with an expression of surprise"—a complex emotion which also included anger. On at least three recent occasions Khrushchev had assured Kennedy that no such thing was afoot, and on at least as many occasions the President had told Khrushchev it had better not be. Kennedy ordered Bundy to arrange two data presentations that morning, first for Kennedy alone, then for a meeting of advisors—a selective list of trusted top officials and advisors including Sorensen and Robert Kennedy—to be held at 11:45 A.M. At the briefing for the President the evidence removed all doubt: Soviet missiles capable of striking targets in the United States with nuclear warheads were in an advanced state of preparation. The President said they looked "like little footballs on a football field." There were 16 to 24 of them. They would be operational within two weeks. With a range of 1,100 miles, they could hit Washington, Dallas, Cape Canaveral, St. Louis, and/or anything in between.

The President's first directive called for more photographs. As the week went on the intelligence revealed new dimensions of the danger. On Wednesday other installations were discovered and assessed as ready for firing within one week. On Thursday the intelligence chiefs estimated the Cuban missile capacity as approximately half that of the entire Soviet Union. The missiles were being aimed at specific American cities. With atomic warheads, they could in a few minutes kill 80 million Americans.

From the start Kennedy insisted on increasing the amount of critical evidence and making it directly available to him before reaching any decision. There was quick agreement at the meeting that something must be done, although, as the options were articulated, "Do nothing" was included among them.

The main possibilities were arrayed at that time, including an air strike, a block-ade, an international inspection team, and a direct approach to Castro. But the President made another critical decision at this point: not to make a decision immediately, but to continue meeting with the same group, augmented from time to time, to explore the possibilities. The group, later formalized as the Executive Committee of the National Security Council, met nearly continuously for the next twelve days. There was not much time, but in Kennedy's judgment it was time enough to get the picture straight before acting. The "Ex Comm" was sworn to the strictest secrecy and the President conveyed to them a strong sense of colleagueship. When General Shoup, commandant of the Marines, said, "You are in a pretty bad fix, Mr. President," Kennedy replied, "You are in it with me."

Thus act One set the wheels in motion. The group's assignment could hardly have been more precise: get those missiles eliminated. But the President made it clear that he wanted a full survey of the possible methods. He withheld his own initial opinion that some quick military action against the missiles was necessary.

Act Two was the Ex Comm deliberations. Between meetings, members were deep into their own special responsibilities. Secretary of Defense McNamara, for example, favored a blockade, but he quickly instigated steps to prepare armed forces for more direct action. (Others prepared evacuation plans for the President and a skeleton government. From a room off a back hall of the White House a voice was heard saying, "The area is beneath several hundred feet of rock, there is plenty of room and a cafeteria. . . .") But in the meetings them-selves an atmosphere of equal interchange developed. Sorensen writes,

> Indeed, one of the remarkable aspects of those meetings was a sense of complete equality. Protocol mattered little when the nation's life was at stake. Experience mattered little in a crisis which had no precedent. Even rank mattered little when secrecy prevented staff support. We were fifteen individuals on our own, repre-senting the President and not different departments. Assistant Secretaries dif-fered vigorously with their Secretaries; I participated much more freely than I ever had in an NSC meeting. . . .[40]

There was no chairman. The President was often absent, which lifted the sense of helpership that can inhibit frankness. The exchanges were often heated, and people changed their minds from day to day as the debate swung back and forth. Throughout there was an extraordinary absence of deference to rank or exper-tise, as Sorensen noted. Particularly the military men found themselves pep-pered with questions. One air-strike advocate went through this questioning:

"What will the Soviets do in response?"
"I know the Soviets pretty well. I think they'll knock out our missile bases in Turkey."
"What do we do then?"
"Under our NATO Treaty, we'd be obligated to knock out a base inside the Soviet Union."

"What will they do then?"

"Why, then we hope everyone will cool down and want to talk."[41]

Sorensen remarks that "It seemed rather cool in the conference room as he spoke." Kennedy disagreed: "They, no more than we, can let these things go by without doing something. They can't, after all their statements, permit us to take out their missiles, kill a lot of Russians, and then do nothing. If they don't take action in Cuba, they certainly will in Berlin."[42]

In sharp contrast to his performance in the Bay of Pigs decision, Kennedy pressed and pushed and interrogated. What were the facts? What would be the consequences—positive and negative—for a hypothesized course of action? Dean Acheson's eloquence, Curtis LeMay's forcefulness, McNamara's knowledgeability failed to sway him as he dug into the foundation for each opinion. When a majority for a blockade emerged on Thursday and the group presented this as their recommendation to the President, he quizzed them again, found their reasoning unsatisfactory, and sent them back to work.

On Saturday morning Robert Kennedy called the President in Chicago where he was campaigning and told him the group was ready to meet with him again, having split into subgroups, exchanged and commented on each other's memoranda, and concluded that a blockade was the answer. The President had met with Soviet Foreign Minister Gromyko on Thursday, remaining impassive while Gromyko discussed various moves and finally got around to yet another reaffirmation that no offensive weapons would be brought into Cuba. "It all seemed to fit a pattern," Kennedy said later, "everything coming to a head at once—the completion of the missile bases, Khrushchev coming to New York, a new drive on West Berlin. If that move is coming anyway, I'm not going to feel that a Cuban blockade provoked it." He carefully read to Gromyko his earlier warning against missiles in Cuba, but kept quiet about their discovery.

As the President flew back to Washington on Saturday, U.S. armed forces around the world were mobilizing. Missile crews were put on maximum alert; the B-52 bomber force was sent into the air with atomic bombs. More than 100,000 troops were gathering in Florida. Meanwhile, the 22,000 Russians in Cuba worked frantically to get the missiles ready to fire. Kennedy delved into phase after phase of the U.S. preparation. Told Castro's planes were easy targets parked in lines on his airfields, Kennedy ordered air photos of American airfields and found the same condition.

That afternoon the President decided on a blockade, or "quarantine" as he would call it to avoid unnecessary implications regarding Berlin. The next morning, Sunday, the last chink was put into the decision: Kennedy was told that an air strike against the missile positions might not knock out all of them. At least a few might be able to fire. The blockade plan was firm.

All day Monday, October 22, 1962, the President worked to line up support among allies, the two ex-Presidents, the Cabinet, and others; he put the finishing touches on his speech to the nation for that evening at 7:00. At 5:00 P.M. he met with twenty leaders of Congress who had been called back from their campaigns to Washington; this was by far the most difficult consultation of the series. The secret had been so well kept that the Congressmen and Senators were completely in the dark. Some sharply resented being kept out of the picture, but the most forceful reaction, from Senators Russell, Fulbright, and others, was the charge that the blockade response was far too weak—the United States should bomb the hell out of the missile sites and invade Cuba. Later the President said, "My feeling is that if they had gone through the five-day period we had gone through—in looking at the various alternatives, advantages and disadvantages . . . —they would have come out the same way that we did." Not having brought them in, he would never know.

In his address that night, Kennedy told the world what was going on in Cuba, described step by step the blockade procedure, and got to the crux of it in this sentence:

> It shall be the policy of this nation to regard any nuclear missile launched from Cuba against any nation in the Western Hemisphere as an attack by the Soviet Union on the United States, requiring a full retaliatory response upon the Soviet Union.[43]

The fat was in the fire.

Act Three would feature many dramatic events as Kennedy carefully supervised the blockade and felt around for Khrushchev's response: one American U-2 plane was shot down over Cuba, another wandered by mistake into Soviet air space; Adlai Stevenson confronted Soviet Ambassador Zorin at the United Nations; Russian ships steamed toward Cuba, and Russian submarines appeared; the first ship boarded—sighted from the destroyer *Joseph P. Kennedy, Jr.*—turned out to be made in America, owned by Panamanians, registered in Lebanon, and sailing for Cuba under a Soviet charter. But the theme of the third act would have to be Khrushchev's response and Kennedy's careful determination to help him out of the box *he* was in. One reason Kennedy liked the blockade alternative was that it provided time for Khrushchev to think and ways for him to respond to the first steps moderately; if he took this opportunity, perhaps no other steps would be necessary. "I am concerned that we both show prudence," he wrote to Khrushchev, "and do nothing to allow events to make the situation more difficult to control than it is." Kennedy had recently read Barbara Tuchman's *The Guns of August;* he talked about how national leaders had stumbled into World War I. "The great danger and risk in all of this is a miscalculation—a mistake in judgment." His was the highly delicate task of (a) making sure Khrushchev knew what the United States intended and planned, without (b) pushing the Soviet Union into a corner from which the only escape would be aggression.

Kennedy proceeded with extraordinary caution. The interception line for the quarantine was pulled back 300 miles (from 800) to give Khrushchev more time. A Russian tanker, *probably* full of oil rather than missiles, was allowed to pass. Despite the nearly unanimous urging of his advisors, he refused to permit retaliation against the anti-aircraft missiles which shot down the American U-2 pilot. To guard against accident he ordered U.S. atomic missiles disarmed, to be rearmed only on his specific order.

Most adroit was his response to Khrushchev's confusing responses. There were two letters. The first, obviously written by Khrushchev himself, said, "You can be calm in this regard, that we are of sound mind and understand perfectly well that if we attack you, you will respond in the same way. But you too will receive the same that you hurl against us." Then he offered a trade: the U.S. to promise not to invade Cuba and to lift the blockade, the Soviet Union to stop supplying weapons to Cuba and to destroy or remove the ones already there.

Before this message could be answered, another letter from Khrushchev, obviously drafted by the Soviet Foreign Office, suggested a different deal: "We will remove our missiles from Cuba, you will remove yours from Turkey. . . . The Soviet Union will pledge not to invade or interfere with the internal affairs of Turkey; the U.S. to make the same pledge regarding Cuba." The Turkish business was not unexpected. Much to his surprise and chagrin, Kennedy discovered during the Cuban missile crisis that his orders of eighteen months ago to the State Department to negotiate those (obsolete) U.S. missiles out of Turkey had never been fulfilled, falling repeatedly into the gumbo of bureaucratic diplomacy. While these Turkey missiles would be no great loss, Kennedy did not want to appear to be responding to a threat.

Robert Kennedy invented the answer: ignore Khrushchev's second letter, respond positively to the first. The President agreed. As Robert Kennedy reported,

> During the crisis, President Kennedy spent more time trying to determine the effect of a particular course of action on Khrushchev or the Russians than on any other phase of what he was doing. What guided all his deliberations was an effort not to disgrace Khrushchev, not to humiliate the Soviet Union, not to have them feel they would have to escalate their response because their national security or national interests so committed them.[44]

The "final lesson," brother Robert wrote, was "the importance of placing ourselves in the other country's shoes." The deal was on. On Sunday morning, October 28, 1962, Khrushchev threw in the towel. An exhilarated Ex Comm gathered to await the President. Bundy reported that Kennedy had received the news with "tremendous satisfaction," but now he walked in casually, "without a trace of excitement or exultation," and began to deal with subsequent problems. "He laid down the line we were all to follow," Sorensen wrote: "—no boasting, no gloating, not even a claim of victory."

Kennedy's growth from the Bay of Pigs to the Cuban missile crisis seems evident. In between, other crises helped to shape his approach. In command, in the assessment of information, in the technique of consultation, and in empathy with his opponent, clearly John Kennedy had grown. He was, at that point, a professional President.

Had Kennedy survived and won re-election in 1964, he would have come hard up against the crisis of Vietnam. What he would actually have decided cannot be known, but as of the spring of 1963 he had the intention of withdrawing all American forces after the 1964 election. He told Mike Mansfield at that time that his arguments had persuaded him that such as the only possible course—"But I can't do it until 1965—after I'm reelected." He explained that

> In 1965, I'll be damned everywhere as a Communist appeaser. But I don't care. If I tried to pull out completely now, we would have another Joe McCarthy red scare on our hands, but I can do it after I'm reelected. So we had better be damned sure that I *am* reelected.

That fall before he went to Texas, Kennedy issued an order for the withdrawal of 1,000 American troops from South Vietnam by the end of the year, despite hard objections by some of his advisors. On October 2, 1963, the President gathered the National Security Council to hear the report of Secretary of Defense McNamara and General Maxwell Taylor, just returned from Saigon. Kennedy asked McNamara to make a public announcement after the meeting that 1,000 men were being withdrawn immediately and that the U.S. would probably withdraw all American forces by the end of 1965. "And tell them that means all of the helicopter pilots, too," Kennedy said. One day in November, Kenneth O'Donnell and Dave Powers asked him how he could withdraw and still maintain American prestige in Southeast Asia. "Easy," Kennedy responded. "Put a government in there that will ask us to leave."[45]

Once re-elected, perhaps by a massive margin such as the Democrats won in 1964, would Kennedy have carried through on this intention or would he have found yet another reason for postponement? We will never know.

There remained the question of commitment, James MacGregor Burns' question: "What great idea does Kennedy personify? In what way is he a great leader of thought? How could he supply moral leadership at a time when new paths before the nation need discovering?" Kennedy faced up to the question of commitment in civil rights.

A man's inner commitment—especially a politician's—is much harder to discover than his external behavior. Sorensen says that

> In 1953 John Kennedy was mildly and quietly in favor of civil rights legislation as a political necessity consistent with his moral instincts.
> In 1963 he was deeply and fervently committed to the cause of human rights as a moral necessity inconsistent with his political instincts.[46]

Schlesinger reports that civil rights leaders in the late fifties considered Kennedy "sympathetic" but "detached"; as Martin Luther King, Jr., put it, Kennedy showed "a definite concern" but not a "'depthed' understanding." In between that time and late 1963, the Negro revolution ran forward. Kennedy ran, not too fast, with it; along the way he discovered what he believed.

During the 1960 campaign Kennedy talked tough. "Only a President willing to use all the resources of his office can provide the leadership, the determination and the direction . . . to eliminate racial and religious discrimination from American society." Again and again he charged that the Eisenhower administration had failed to eliminate discrimination in federally financed housing, an act the President could (and, he implied, this President would) end with the "stroke of a pen." Early that year the sit-ins had started; in the ex-Confederate South, six years after *Brown vs. Board of Education*, .06 percent of Negro students were in desegregated schools. Learning that King had been arrested and jailed in Georgia and sentenced on a technicality to four months' hard labor, Kennedy telephoned Mrs. King to express his sympathy and Robert Kennedy called the Georgia judge who had passed the sentence. The next day King was released. The news spread rapidly, an event in October that helped bring Kennedy the overwhelming support of Negro voters in November.

Yet when the election was over, there was not much Kennedy action. Kennedy did not appoint a task force on civil rights among those he set up for the transition. In his inauguration day parade he noticed there were no Negro Coast Guardsmen; he phoned the Secretary of the Treasury that night, and by 1962 the Coast Guard Academy got one. He asked his Cabinet members to explore possibilities in their departments, and he appointed an unprecedented number of Negroes in high federal jobs—the precedents not being hard to beat. A President's Committee on Equal Employment Opportunity was put under Vice President Lyndon Johnson. There were meaningful efforts on poll taxes and employment and voting rights. Kennedy proposed the first Negro Cabinet member. His brother the Attorney General increased the number of Negro attorneys in the Justice Department from ten to fifty.

But out there in the country, black Americans found life about the same. Among their leaders there was a growing sense of disillusionment with the President. Where was that "stroke of the pen"? More important, where was the moral leadership for racial equality?

Kennedy's answer was simple—too simple. He said he did not have the votes. Civil rights legislation had been killed in the last Congress, and the one he now faced was worse. In the House he lacked the votes to get through or around the Rules Committee; in the Senate he did not have enough to cut off a filibuster. Talking with the Negro leaders Kennedy said, "Nobody has to convince me any longer that we have to solve the problem, not let it drift on gradualism. But how do you go about it? If we go into a long fight in Congress, it will bottleneck everything else and still get no bill." He encouraged the ADA to exert pressure for economic legislation, but when the ADA's Joseph Rauh suggested some civil rights pressure would also be useful, Kennedy banged on the table and said, "No, there's a real difference. You have to understand the problems I have here." He was not for gradualism, he said, but "a lot of talk and no results will only make them madder." At a press conference he said pointedly, "When I feel that there is a necessity for Congressional action, *with a chance of getting that Congressional action*, then I will recommend it." In long memoranda, Roy Wilkins and Martin Luther King detailed a "Second Emancipation Proclamation." Kennedy held back, though there were any number of smaller actions, such as getting administration officers to refuse to make speeches to segregated audiences. Through 1961 no new Kennedy legislation in this field was sought or enacted, the stroke of the pen was repeatedly postponed, and support for the 1961 freedom riders was limited to an assertion of their right to travel freely. It was all so cautious, so strategic, for the man who had run "flat out, all out" for the Presidency.

Then in the fall of 1962 the forces for the "Battle of Oxford" began to gather. It was mostly Robert Kennedy's show, but step by step John was brought into it. James Meredith, a black man, applied for admission to the University of Mississippi at Oxford, was turned down, went to court, and after a year and a half of dogged persistence, got a ruling from the Fifth Circuit Court that his rejection was "solely because he was a Negro." Justice Black of the Supreme Court upheld that. The Governor of Mississippi, Ross Barnett, forthwith announced: "We will not surrender to the evil and illegal forces of tyranny." Robert Kennedy telephoned to suggest the Governor should not defy a court order and couldn't they work something out? Barnett would not cooperate. On September 20, 1962, along came Meredith to register for school, accompanied by federal marshals and by Ole Miss students singing "Glory, Glory, Segregation." The Governor himself turned Meredith back. Robert Kennedy cited the top three officers of the University for contempt and got a restraining order enjoining Barnett from interfering with Meredith's registration. Barnett was furious. Amidst much other rhetoric he said to the Attorney General, "It's best for him not to go to Ole Miss." Robert Kennedy replied softly, "But he *likes* Ole Miss."

Then the full-scale circus began. The Governor said he could give in gracefully if a force of federal marshals would approach him standing guard at Ole Miss and draw their guns on him. Ugly crowds began to gather. Meredith and the marshals (eventually there would be 550 of them) made another approach, but drew back when the mob seemed close to breaking out of control. Barnett was found guilty of civil contempt and ordered to purge himself by the next Tuesday or face fine and arrest. Finally on September 28, 1962, Robert Kennedy and General Maxwell Taylor met to plan for the deployment of federal troops. Barnett came up with another idea: the people of Mississippi would raise however much money it cost to send Meredith to any University outside Mississippi.

Increasingly, President Kennedy was drawn into the situation. On September 29, with the Attorney General by his side, he telephoned Barnett and pressed him to cooperate. Hanging up, he puzzled, "You know what that fellow said? He said, 'I want to thank you for your help on the poultry program.'"

Police, national guardsmen, marshalls, thousands of non-students, and some students ganged into Oxford and the melee got underway, with bricks, bombs, bottles, and guns. Two were killed; two hundred marshalls and guardsmen were injured. There was little humor in John Kennedy's voice when he now took the telephone from his brother's hand and said, "Listen, Governor, somebody's been shot down there already and it's going to get worse. Most of it's happened since those [Mississippi] police left and I want them back. Goodbye"—and the President slammed the phone down.

The rioting continued. "The President looked drawn and bleak," Sorensen remembered. "He refused to accept our suggestion that he had done everything he could. Through the long night of waiting and telephoning, he cursed himself for ever believing Barnett and for not ordering the troops in sooner. At least one of the two deaths, he believed at the time, might have been prevented had the Army arrived when he had thought it would." The President went on television with a plea for lawful behavior.

Barnett capitulated. Meredith was registered. Goons shot up his father's house and fellow students harrassed him constantly. Mainly by sheer will, and some help from a lone professor, James W. Silver, Meredith stuck it out and graduated in August 1963. Less than two months after the Battle of Oxford, John Kennedy stroked with his pen and signed the executive order on housing.

In February 1963, the President sent an eloquent message to Congress condemning racial inequality because "Above all, it is wrong." But the legislative proposals were minor. Roy Wilkins had pointed out that in 1962 the federal government had put some $650 million into Mississippi and, along with the Civil Rights Commission, urged the President to figure out how to keep those monies from being used to reinforce segregation. Kennedy hesitated on the question of cutting off funds. "I am not sure. . . . I can't do it alone. . . . The Commission report would be better directed at the Congress. . . . It would not be understood." He would prefer that the Commission not publish its report. "It will make a lot of people mad up there and may make my own efforts more difficult."

Then in April 1963 came the protests in Birmingham, the town King called "the most thoroughly segregated big city in the U.S." The police there turned fire hoses on marching children, released dogs to attack women. The President said it made him sick—but for the moment he was stymied. Federal troops were sent in. A wave of national indignation, led largely by churchmen, began to gather. On May 21, George Wallace, Governor of Alabama, succeeded in barring a Negro student from that state's university until he was forced to give in to federal troops. Kennedy went on television. He did not hold back: in a strident voice he said that if the Negro was barred from the good life, "then who among us would be content to have the color of his skin changed and stand in his place? Who among us would then be content with the counsels of patience and delay?" Did the country mean to say "that we have no second-class citizens except Negroes; that we have no class or caste system, no ghettos, no master race except with respect [to] the Negroes?" It was "a moral issue." He would ask Congress for a commitment "that race has no place in American life or law."

His own commitment was crystalizing. The night of Kennedy's television speech Medgar Evers, director of the Mississippi NAACP, was murdered in front of his house. Kennedy invited Evers' family, including the children, to the White House. Afterward Schlesinger said to him, "What a terrible business," and Kennedy replied, "Yes, I don't understand the South. I'm coming to believe that Thaddeus Stevens was right. I had always been taught to regard him as a man of vicious bias. But, when I see this sort of thing, I begin to wonder how else you can treat them."

On June 19, 1963, Kennedy sent his new civil rights bill to Congress. In addition to what was previously proposed, he added to the package authorization to cut off federal funds from any project that practiced race discrimination, a ban on discrimination in public accommodations, and authority for the Attorney General to take the initiative in suits to desegregate public schools. It was strong stuff for the times. He told Congress he was not for violent demonstrations, but the moment for action had arrived. And:

> I ask you to look into your hearts—not in search of charity, for the Negro neither wants nor needs condescension—but for the one plain, proud and priceless quality that unites us all as Americans: a sense of justice.[47]

Over the following weeks the President pushed, shoved, mobilized, met, talked, cajoled, and threatened to get the bill moving. His stand was costing him heavily: the Harris poll reported that his actions in civil rights had turned 4.5 million white voters against him. National approval of his administration fell from 60 to 47 percent. "This is a very serious fight," he said. "We're in this up to the neck." Kennedy's commitment was complete.

There were compromises along the way. He pressed particularly hard in the House to get the Judiciary Committee to send its report to the Rules Committee. That report came through on November 21, 1963, as the President was leaving Washington to make some speeches in Texas.

Some called this legislation, which finally passed in 1964, "the Second Emancipation Proclamation." Celebrating the centennial of the first one, Kennedy said, "The Proclamation was only a first step—a step which its author unhappily did not live to follow up."

KENNEDY'S COMMITMENT

Kennedy's ultimate commitment on civil rights revealed, I think, the most significant feature of his political character. Somewhere along that road he lost his cool. His drive, his humor, his rousing spirit, and his remarkable political style were not invented by biographers after he was gunned down in Dallas. The inner confidence he had acquired as a youth freed him to grow as President, through one crisis after another to a grasp of the full potentialities of the office. But there was in the minds of many who watched him that continuing doubt, whether in the last analysis he cared for anything enough to lose for it. Not that he anticipated losing office, despite the 1963 polls and votes. With high good humor he was looking forward to the 1964 election—which he hoped would be a straight fight against Barry Goldwater and a landslide for himself and his party in Congress. He told at least one friend that with that in hand he could bring off the withdrawal from Vietnam of the modest force he had sent there, among other progressive moves. Those were hopes amidst uncertainty; he might wind up impeached, as he speculated during the Cuban missile crisis. But in the civil rights struggle, Kennedy took a stand on what he himself had come to believe. His detachment did not make him wander off in the Coolidge manner, retreating and waiting for unavoidable issues. That, I suspect, was a temptation for him stronger than the temptations of compliance or tragic defeat. The minor theme of separation from action is there in his history—in the long childhood illnesses, the quietness and thoughtfulness which marked him off from his brother Joe, the initial move toward "passive" journalism or teaching. But he beat that, overcame it, showed in the end a caring he had long kept to himself.

Then it was all over and Lyndon Johnson was President.

12

The Crucial
Ford Transition

Gerald R. Ford came on too fast for confident prediction. A reluctant Nixon took him, in October 1973, as his Vice President, to replace the disgraced, accused, and resigned Spiro Agnew. In stark contrast, Ford was just what Diogenes had been looking for—Mr. Clean himself—as became clear when hundreds of FBI agents fanned out across the country on a failing mission: to search out Ford peccadilloes. There was no real trouble about his nomination: it seemed everybody loved him. The American Political Science Association had named him a "Congressman's Congressman." "I feel that I am among friends," he said as the hearings began, and when he came to the House chamber to take the oath he promised, with refreshingly credible sincerity, to "do the very best I can for America." The stock market went up twenty-six points.[1]

It was nice to have a non-crooked Vice President, but few thought Ford would rise above that post. He did not think so himself, and even said he did not intend to be a Presidential candidate in 1976, as Coolidge had said of 1928. After laying his hand on the Bible in front of all his old Congressional friends, he turned to the President and said, "You have my support and loyalty." But whatever Ford's intentions, most thought with David Broder, one of the country's best-informed political reporters, that Ford as a potential Presidential candidate for 1976 could "probably be safely ignored."[2]

There were Congressmen with doubts about Ford, but as one of them put it, Ford votes "wrong most of the time, but he's decently wrong."[3] Given the national climate of expectations, his decency was an enormous advantage—and a distraction from hard questions about his beliefs and skills. Besides, since he was only Vice President, it did not seem to matter much.

PREDICTION

The following June, I wrote that "Until and unless Mr. Ford moves beyond disclaiming any intention to run in 1976 and refuses outright, the hypothesis has to be that he will be no lame-duck President," and went on to suggest some questions to ask about him. By September 1974, with Ford President, I thought the odds of his candidacy had escalated to a probable "yes," despite his non-declarations. Still, the important question was what kind of President he would be for his remaining term and perhaps beyond. On the basis of not very much data, I told interviewers in September 1974, "I hope he'll be 'active-positive,'" but I also worried "whether Mr. Ford is going to be in the long run too genial to be President." I saw him as "obviously an open and candid person" who was unlikely to turn into "a compulsive, hard-driving ideologue who's going to dig his own political grave" or one given to "trying to escape from politics . . . rising above the political turmoil of his time." But all his talk about "communication, conciliation, compromise, and cooperation" gave me pause, wondering whether he might have an overdose of Harding in his composure.[4]

I should have known better, and the mistake is instructive: I had slid over into the concomitants of the character distinctions, forgetting the definers. "Active," in my scheme, was not an attitude but a behavior—day-to-day output of energy—and Ford had been hyperactive all his political life.

Strands of the Ford style and world view were gaining clarity even as he assumed office. He would exemplify "simplicity, directness"; had "been a person who's helped to arrange compromises and co-ordinate things"; was one who "may not push so easily"; would "continue the Kissinger policies" and not "be involved in a lot of dramatic summitry." Ford had "been a strong defender of patriotism and national defense," I said, and "I think the whole symbolism of America means a lot to him. That comes across as genuine—seeing America as a nation with a progressive mission to perform in the world." The Ford "view of human nature is a highly positive one. He wants to believe the best about the people he deals with in politics, about other world leaders and also about the American people. He will appeal to the straight-out patriotism that most Americans still feel."

I tried to sum it up this way, on the basis of evidence available in September 1974:

> He has never indicated that he thought of himself as an intellectual, so I don't think he's going to be a sophisticated President in the sense that, say, Kennedy was. And I'm sure that he's going to say some things that some of your more skeptical colleagues in the press are going to think are sort of dumb from time to time. But I think that Ford is going to be pragmatic, and he is unlikely to adopt terribly rigid stances. He's going to try to make the policies he adopts work, but I don't think you're going to find him hanging on to something after it's proved that it's not useful. I'm hopeful that he will be ready to admit it when he makes a mistake.[5]

In December 1974, Jerald F. terHorst's excellent biography, *Gerald Ford and the Future of the Presidency*, came out and furnished a richer store of background material for interpretation. And eight months of Ford as President gave President-watchers plenty of events to think about. By April 1975, I had seen enough to take more definite stands. "The good news," I said, "is that we have a President whose troubles are not rooted in his character. He has demonstrated the characteristics I talked about in our first interview last September—openness, flexibility, personal growth in the office, a readiness to consider alternatives to his plans. . . . I see him as an 'active-positive' President, along with Franklin Roosevelt, Harry Truman and John Kennedy." The concern about Ford's "compliant streak, a certain geniality . . . that might lead us into a period of drift" had been dispelled, in my mind, by Ford's decisive and vigorous actions.[6] Much of what he did was wrong, by my politics, and his batting average with the Democratic Congress was not impressive. But he was no Presidential patsy. He defied public opinion when, a mere month after Nixon resigned, Ford granted him an unconditional pardon for any federal crimes Nixon "committed or may have committed or taken part in" as President.[7] Ford gambled that he could weather the storm of angry reaction that was touched off by the pardon. He pressed on Congress a comprehensive energy and economic package, vetoed bills right and left. But on the other (active-negative) hand, he did not compose any "enemies list" and he met in frequent, friendly, genuine consultation with the Congressional barons. And he could laugh at himself, kidding his own rhetorical stumbles—"I told my wife I knew this speech backwards and now I'm proving it."[8]

Ford's main troubles were not character troubles. The "fundamental tension" in him, I thought then, was between "the inheritance from his whole natural way of thinking"— orthodox conservative Congressional Republican incrementalism—and "the national vision that's Republican, Democratic, conservative, liberal, radical, reactionary, that takes the whole scene into account."[9]

When, a year and a half later, Ford was narrowly defeated in the Presidential election, what his Presidency had meant was clearer. The Johnson-Nixon nightmare need not be the Presidential norm, did not spring from some dark necessity in the contemporary political system and culture.

FORD REVS UP

An hour into his Presidency, Gerald Ford said, "I can't change my nature after sixty-one years."[10] That nature was born on Bastille Day, 1913, in that pause before the curtain went down on Victorian optimism and hypocrisy. He was christened Leslie Lynch King, Jr., but his parents' marriage broke up when he was two, so his mother, Dorothy, moved to Grand Rapids, Michigan, to take refuge with her parents. She met Gerald R. Ford at a church supper; not long after, they were married, and the baby's name was changed to Gerald R. Ford, Jr., when his new father adopted him.

The labels probably meant nothing to the child at that age; indeed, he did not learn that his biological father was someone other than the real and present one until he was seventeen years old. What the changes meant to him when he was one and two—the different smells and sounds and faces, his mother's tears—is obscure. Dorothy was the continuity.

"Junie" (for "Junior"), as he was called in boyhood, was a large, strong, active youngster with a will of his own. For his first five years he was only-child cock of the walk; then Tom was born, followed by Richard when Junie was eleven, and James when he was fourteen.[11] Mother Dorothy was sometimes sick but was remembered as "vivacious, effervescent, fun to be with"—a church-working, garden-digging, antique-collecting, neighborhood homemaker who specialized in caramel candy.[12] People liked to come by at Christmas to see her living room, piled high with products of her cooking and stitchery.

Father Ford had been a high school dropout (typical enough in those days), but as his boys were growing up, he was increasingly successful in the paint business. To Junie, as Jerry remembers, Dad "said what he meant and meant what he said." And "when Dad told us to do something, we did it. There was never any question about that. He was the final authority; all of us really looked up to him. But he could be your friend as well as your father. Mother was great, too, lots of fun and very soft-hearted and always doing things for us boys and Dad, the neighbors and, heck, for everybody. But I guess Dad was the strongest influence on my life. I've often thought, even nowadays: now how would he have done this?"[13] Many a time later, son would call father for advice.

Junie had his chores, from coal shoveling in the morning to dishwashing in the evening, but it was not all work. Mother organized Sunday adventures, picnics, trips to the beach or the woods or the zoo. Dad played ball with the boys and got them used to golfing, hiking, swimming, and fishing. The Fords were gregarious people. Mother got into all sorts of church and charity projects. Dad was a veritable entrepreneur of love—organizing programs for poor kids, directing a recreation house in the high-crime district, putting together a summer camp, helping run the Boy Scout troop. Mother teased Dad about that: if he had put those energies into the business, the Fords would have been rich.[14]

It was a suburban life, games on the ball field and the ice pond, crack-the-whip and something called "pom-pom-pullaway." Junie had the usual gang of pals, including the son of a black chauffeur who lived in the neighborhood; much later this friend tried to put himself back into "what it was like in those days" and recalled "Jerry was a rich boy—but a regular guy. . . . We were always going at it, going to be the best in games. I was pretty fast in those days and he was kind of clumsy. But with that blond hair . . . the girls were always shooting at him. It didn't seem to buzz him though. He was kind of shy."[15]

So much for child Ford as the biographers knew him in 1974—which is not notably more or less than what was known about the childhood of Harry Truman in 1945. Sketchy as it is, the memories point in the active-positive direction: the boy had love aplenty and challenges to meet. He learned to try, and to enjoy it. His childhood was no cramped box of intense ambiguities, but a wide field for personal and social experiment. No wonder he could say, as various soul-plumbers delved for his Presidential personality, "I'm disgustingly sane."[16]

JERRY'S WORLD

Nineteen days into his Presidency, Ford prophesied that "The code of ethics that will be followed will be the example that I set."[47] His other ethic—and the world view that supported it—took shape in those years of high school and beyond when "Junie" became "Jerry," connecting with wider identities. Part of it was Dad and Mother; he could hear their judg-e-ments (as he pronounced it) on the choices they faced in myriad connections: tell the truth, keep your word, make it work. Part of it was the peer code of the late 1920s, the "roaring" quality of which, in Grand Rapids, probably diminished to not much more than an occasional car cruise through the red-light district. For all his "shyness," Jerry got the top prize in a movie-house contest to choose the most popular high school senior in town—a trip to Washington, D.C. Something of a high school quality would stick with him all his life, a sort of knowing sincerity. "Jerry never lorded it over anyone," his best friend remembered. "He was well-liked."[18]

There were at least three more distinctive themes weaving themselves into his world view in those years. Mother took him regularly, sometimes accompanied by Dad, to Grace Episcopal Church, an upper middle class congregation in a middle class community. What was significant for Jerry here is the fact that at Grace Episcopal the message deviated markedly from the dominant Dutch Calvinism of the Grand Rapids community. Founded by an immigrant Hollander who came over in 1847 because the state church had gone loose, the Dutch denominations concentrated on sin and law, repeating Sunday after Sunday the Ten Commandments. That spirit pervaded the community; for example, one newspaper would not publish on Sunday lest the Fourth Commandment be violated, and to learn who was drinking cocktails with whom, the newspaper reader had to look for accounts of "canape" parties.[19]

Like the Dutch churches, Grace Episcopal was a repetitious church, where sin and law were not neglected, but where prayers were continually offered to a "Father of all mercies." Each communion time, June-becoming-Jerry heard the same words, as the service reached its climax:

> Almighty God, our heavenly Father, who of his great mercy hath promised forgiveness of sins to all those who with hearty repentence and true faith turn unto him; Have mercy upon you; pardon and deliver you from all your sins; confirm and strengthen you in all goodness; and bring you to everlasting life; through Jesus Christ our Lord. *Amen.*[20]

On a Sunday many years later, President Ford listened to that and the rest, returned to the White House, and issued a secular pardon for Richard Nixon. But back in his early days, his church life had this meaning: he was rescued from his community's predominant religious concern with avoiding the darkness of evil and trained instead to focus on the light at the end of life's tunnels.

Still more affecting, because it connected with his own questing initiative, was Jerry's experience as a Boy Scout. Scouting was, in those times before cynicism replaced sincerity as a key to youthful popularity, an all-right activity, but Jerry went way beyond the normal, becoming an Eagle Scout, the highest rank, attainable only at the end of a very long maze of merit badges. There, too, he heard himself saying one of those endlessly repeated incantations, which, stored in the mind of a young fellow, come back to the mind of a man. It went: "On my honor, I will do my best to do my duty to God and my country, and to obey the Scout Law; to help other people at all times; to keep myself physically strong, mentally awake, and morally straight."

But church was Sunday and scouting spare time. Jerry's passion for school work was moderate; his grades clustered around B, which in those days was "above average." For Jerry Ford, the big thing at school was sports, and his sport was football. He was a natural athlete. Bone, muscle, and nerve cooperated to boost him ahead of his gangly peers, so that at sixteen (which happened to be 1929) he started on a track to great success just as his father's fortunes, along with the nation's, first leapt up, then sagged precipitously down. Football was a *serious* game; to succeed you had to *commit* yourself. A tough, gifted coach slotted Jerry into the center spot, which, as Ford always had to point out later, took talent. None of this sliding the ball to a thigh-nudging quarterback and then falling under the pile. President Ford explained: "Every center snap truly had to be a pass between the legs, often leading the tailback who was in motion and in full stride when he took the ball. I don't mean to be critical, but I think that is why you see so many bad passes from center on punts and field goals nowadays—they don't have to do it enough. I must have centered the ball 500,000 times in high school and college."[21] And it took stamina: you stayed in until you got hurt. The same players handled offense and defense, and on defense Jerry ranged as a roving linebacker. He excelled; for three straight years he made the "All-City" roster and after graduation, Michigan State, Northwestern, Harvard, and the University of Michigan invited him to visit. He chose the Wolverines. His high school coach saw to it that he got a scholarship, and Jerry was off to Ann Arbor, where he lived in "the cheapest rooming house I could find" and worked his way through college. But he had to wait three years, sitting on the bench most of every game, until Michigan's all-America center, Chuck Bernard, got out of the way. Finally he had the chance to start regularly in his senior year and was named most valuable player—but the team lost seven of eight games. Jerry later got a job as assistant coach at Yale, wangled his way into the law school, and made it creditably through in a class including ninety-eight Phi Beta Kappas among its 125 members.[22] Still later in the Navy, he served as a physical training officer, and in after years he kept up his golf and swimming. His political rhetoric was full of sports images.

What did his mind bring away from all that body motion? "Thanks to my football experience," he said, "I know the value of team play. . . . It is, I believe, one of the most important lessons to be learned and practiced in our lives. You learn to accept discipline. My experience in games like that with Minnesota helped me many times to face a tough situation in World War II or, in the rough-and-tumble of politics, to take action and make every effort possible despite adverse odds."[23]

Team play, discipline, waiting out your chances. A football incident illustrates the Ford orientation. Michigan was to play Georgia Tech—but not if one of Jerry's friends and teammates, who happened to be black, came on the field. The truckling university administration gave in to the threat. Jerry pondered. Should he protest by refusing to play? He called his Dad, but Dad said it was his decision. He played, but when a Georgia Tech lineman laughed about the "nigger," Jerry and a teammate waited a few plays, then blocked the miscreant so hard he had to be carried away.[24]

Thus the impulse was: do the right thing. The decision was: play with the team. The opportunity was: smash them when you have a chance.

Ford was nowhere near politics in those years, but his political world view was forming. It was a simple one. Sustained effort—and *patience*—could yield success, the key ingredients of which were luck and trying. Team play makes it work, not the razzle-dazzle of any individual. You do what you are told you have to do, wait your turn, then play your damnedest. People are basically good: show them your goodness—in demeanor and behavior—and they will like you. Morality meant allegiance, to God and country, and to Dad's rule and example of directness, honesty, persistence. And over it all—history, human nature, questions of "ethics"—rules a Father of mercy, a Forgiver, whose promise is unfailing love.

Yet something was missing. Those years of rah-rah and hit-'em-again were desperate times for millions of Americans, including many a citizen of Grand Rapids. Dad Ford weathered it and recovered handsomely. Jerry was a "rich boy," good-looking and popular; he was one of the few who wore a coat and tie to school.[25] His family was from English stock, not "Hollanders" or "Polacks,"—a background that hadn't turned him into a snob, but on the other hand hadn't taught him a clear concern for the social disaster around him. However, he—and Dad—knew what slim times were like: Jerry worked for two dollars a week in high school.[26] And he had before him his father's lifelong effort to lend a helping hand to society's losers. It was a pattern he might have picked up on intellectually, but instead he seems to have relegated *caritas* to a restricted, personal ethic. His political beliefs were shaped around an ethic appropriate to his sociological status in life. Thus an aide to President Ford saw him as "the kind of guy who would take his shirt off his back and give it to a poor kid he saw on the street and then walk in and veto the day care program."[27]

Speaking at a football dinner in Chicago in 1974, the President said, "I'd like to take the whole United States into the locker room between halves," to talk up "what's right with America."[28]

THE FORD STYLE

One night in the 1940s when Ford was serving on an aircraft carrier, a terrific typhoon came up. The ocean went mad. Three destroyers sank with most of their crews. Ford's carrier caught fire. He was in bed below when the alarm sounded; he dashed up to the reeling flight deck, slipped and "slid across the deck like a toboggan," he remembered. "I put my feet out, and fortunately, my heels hit the little rim that surrounds the flight deck—I was heading straight for the ocean. I spun over on my stomach and luckily dropped over the edge onto the catwalk just below. We lost five seamen or officers during that storm—sliding over the side and into the sea—so I guess I was one of the lucky ones."[29]

Thus, one type of experience Jerry Ford shared with such Presidents as Franklin Roosevelt, Harry Truman, Dwight Eisenhower, John Kennedy, and a President-to-be, Jimmy Carter, was a handshake with death, up close. Like them, Ford came away with a strong reinforcement of something that was there before—the sense that "I was one of the lucky ones." And like a whole generation of young men who, in their innocence, had gone off to fight, he came home with questions larger than those about his own fate. "A change happened within me during the war," he said. "In college I had been a real isolationist. But the war and being overseas changed my mind about the role that American should play in the world."[30]

Up to that point, politics had played no important part in his life, although he had done some dabbling before the war. In the spring of 1940, Jerry was caught up in the campus excitement as Hitler's *Wehrmacht* lashed across Europe, threatening Britain itself. Like other safely positioned golden youths, Jerry felt the urge to "do something." The best prospect immediately available, from Ford's viewpoint, was Wendell Willkie, a big, shaggy, outspoken businessman who had mastered the art of seeming not a politician and who set out to challenge Roosevelt's shocking bid for an unprecedented *third* term. Jerry went down to New York weekends to work for Willkie (whose motto was "*Win* With Willkie"), and in the summer he worked full time in Grand Rapids in the Willkie campaign. Dad was skeptical, partly because his son might get dirtied by politics and partly because the family could use some Jerry-generated summer income. But, when Dad saw how determined Jerry was, he characteristically shelved his objections and offered the boy some helpful advice about how to do it.[31]

Dad said to go see Frank McKay, a bigtime Republican boss who seemed to collect at least one cherry from every pie baked in political Michigan. McKay kept Jerry waiting four hours, then dismissed him with hello-goodbye.

After the election—Willkie lost but carried Michigan—Jerry happened into a conversation with McKay's arch-enemy, a determined dentist who called his organization "The Home Front" after the English farmers who were preparing to wield their pitchforks against Nazi paratroopers. The dentist was trying to launch a reform movement within the party that would oust McKay and clean up Michigan Republican politics. He invited Jerry to join. "Oh boy," Jerry answered enthusiastically, "You can count me in on that."[32] But first there was a war to be fought.

The dentist wrote to Jerry in the Navy, and Jerry wrote to Dad, "If the Home Front ever asks you to do something, don't turn them down. I'm going to get into this thing when I get back from service and I'll take your place. So don't turn them down." Dad listened, and against his better judgment agreed to serve on the County Committee.

Jerry came home, joined a well known law firm, and played golf. He was single, thirty-three, and apolitical. The budding interest in politics that appeared before the war was to all intents and purposes among the casualties. But he was a veteran, and he soon found himself in league with other ex-GIs who were trying to build their little houses and ran into the McKay-linked banking, zoning, and real estate interests of Grand Rapids. Jerry organized an association that bucked the interests and won—not everything, but some land and some key law changes. For the first time, he had stepped over into politics and scored. But he was not yet carrying his own ball.

He caught it in 1948. Michigan's Senator Arthur Vandenberg, who had made one of those rare changes of mature political opinion—from isolationism to fervent, practical internationalism—was being bedeviled by the Congressman from Jerry's district, a man nearly twice Jerry's age with the Dutch name Jonkman. Like Richard Nixon, Bartel Jonkman had quickly picked up the social vibrations that were soon to explode into McCarthyism. To Jonkman, the Vandenberg-backed Marshall Plan for reconstructing postwar Europe was anathema, and Jonkman said so at every opportunity. Thus Vandenberg was looking for someone to unseat this bothersome critic. He found his man in handsome young veteran Jerry Ford. Later Ford remembered, "I thought about it and thought about it and finally I decided that although I probably couldn't win, he ought to be challenged. I told them I would go."[33] He figured the odds at three to one against him, especially since Vandenberg felt obliged to stand above the fray and made no public move for Ford. Jerry seemed so much the sacrificial lamb that Jonkman disdained to campaign against him.

So it was not the hope of victory but the spur of conscience that pressed Ford to compete. His senior law partner gave him time off with pay, and Ford hit the trail like a whirling dervish. "I worked like hell. I really covered those counties," he recalled.[34]

He got a quick briefing from Jerald terHorst, a local reporter who would later become President Ford's first press secretary but whose duties at this time consisted of filling the candidate in on which cows were which colors. Ford visited seven farms before eight A.M. one day in the pouring rain. Patiently he waited while each farmer got his words together. He made notes of their complaints and, when he shook hands as he was leaving, he asked them to "Remember the name—Ford. If I get to Congress I'll remember what you've told me." At one farm, Jerry got carried away: he promised a dairyman that if he won he would work for two weeks in his barn—a seemingly safe bet, given his chances. After the election, "There I was, every morning, from four-thirty until about nine-thirty, helping with the cows, cleaning up the barn, you name it. . . ."[35]

Everywhere he went, Ford challenged Jonkman to debate. Jerry's issue was Vandenberg's: "I believe in aid to Europe, with emphasis on making certain the common man in the countries we aid gets the maximum benefits. That is the way to build democracy." He was no great shakes as a public speaker; sophisticates thought him ignorant. But he candidly confessed his ignorance when necessary, and said, "but I'll find out for you." His ideas may have seemed consequential to him, but not much so to the voters, to whom the price of milk meant more than a European renaissance, or to the band of Home Front Republicans on his team, who were bent on knocking off the McKay-Jonkman axis. It was personal contact politics, flat-out, every day and night, the "technique" by which many a supposedly secure incumbent has been toppled. Jerry swept the district—23,632 to Jonkman's 14,341. They figured the campaign had cost $7,200. Shortly thereafter, Elizabeth Bloomer Warren became Mrs. Gerald R. Ford.[36]

The Fords went off to Washington, where Jerry took his place in the last row on the House Republican side. He was lucky to find a first-rate aide, John Milanowski, a former speech teacher and link to the Grand Rapids Polish community. When this connection infuriated certain local elements who warned Ford to get rid of "the Polack pope-lover," Ford put his arm around his friend's shoulder and said, "John, don't worry. We'll kill 'em with love."[37] John spent hours coaching Ford in oratory, with no great success. He progressed to believable but fell short of inspiring.

Ford's leader was Arthur Vandenberg: "I really admired him. He was my mentor." Vandenberg passed on the wisdom which suited so well the needs of the senior Congressional sages—concentrate on committee work, cultivate the constituency, let the bigwigs make speeches on the floor. The rookie Congressman took this advice to heart and soon became a committee man *par excellence,* particularly adept at mastering the tangled details of defense budgets. He and Milanowski established what terHorst calls "one of the smoothest 'district-serving' systems on Capitol Hill."[38] Every last letter was answered. He spoke rarely and kept to the point. The Congressional barons, unsurprisingly, came to like him, and Ford, ever the loyalist, built into his style their delicate ways, into his thought their assumptions. He began to think he would like to be Speaker some day. He felt he could count on a lot of chums—like young Representative John Kennedy in the office next door, young Representative Richard Nixon upstairs. He spent more than a quarter-century in the House of Representatives. Not until that game was over and Jerry Ford was suddenly thrust onto a much wider field would anyone—himself included—see the Presidency as his goal.

FORD MODEL PRESIDENCY

The style and world view and character Jerry bolted together in those early years were there to draw on when Ford suddenly had to shift gears for an uphill Presidency. His big advantage was the obvious contrast to his predecessor; if he had sat down and kept quiet, Ford might well have been able to glide through to re-election. But his country was in trouble—the worst recession since World War II—so he moved. He feared that the national attention might squander itself on Nixon-Nixon-Nixon for months, or even years. So, preparing the way with proposals for amnesty for Vietnam war resisters and draft refusers, he issued his famous pardon, suddenly destroying his political honeymoon and sending a message to every prisoner in jail that "equal justice under law" was a farce. Just as all the props were collapsing in Vietnam, he unrealistically called for hundreds of millions more in military aid. He turned foreign policy over to a wizard of dramatic negotiation whose *ad hoc* successes obscured deepening world chaos. And he stood as firm and fast as he could against all sorts of "wild" schemes to spend the country out of recession, countering them with some tame schemes of his own.

But if he was often mistaken (and history will have to judge that), Jerry Ford the President neither froze nor faded. In his sixties, he showed that he wasn't too old to grow, and grow fast. When the seemingly inevitable military crunch came and an American ship was captured, he kept cool: "We've got a little crisis," he said, "I don't know what it is, but these crises always seem to occur on Monday."[39] He did some adroit zigging and zagging among the political factions, with the result that the challenge to his renomination came from his party's *right* wing even though he had always been considered a conservative Republican. He slept easy, kept in shape, and took the day's enjoyments for his own, laughing with his wife over her report that he had wakened her by muttering, in some dreamed receiving line, "Thank you, thank you, thank you." Even in defeat, in 1976, he had an upbeat heart: "In the long run the American people have an awful lot more good in them than they have bad. . . . I am an optimist today. I always have been," he said a few days before leaving office.[40]

To those who see no Presidential virtue in anything less than large leaps forward, Ford was a Presidential failure. He was—is, has always been—a step-by-step thinker of the Republican persuasion (the only such among the active-positives at least since Theodore Roosevelt). So it is hardly surprising that he did not leap over the wall of his "principles" to trumpet grand themes. He was not intellectual enough, not literary enough, for our increasingly wordy political culture, hip to a symbolic politics of gesture. Nor did he understand why that culture can afford to romanticize the Harry Trumans of this world only in retrospect. But he knocked into a cocked hat, once and for all, the idea that the Presidency *had* to turn a man into a majesty.

In the end, Ford's weighty legacy was as simple as this: he revived his country's hope for faith in government. When he first took over the shambles his predecessor had left behind, President Ford put it this way:

> I believe that truth is the glue that holds government together, not only our government but civilization itself. That bond, though strained, is unbroken at home and abroad. In all my public and private acts as your President, I expect to follow my instincts of openness and candor with full confidence that honesty is always the best policy in the end. My fellow Americans, our long national nightmare is over. Our Constitution works; our great Republic is a government of laws and not of men. . . . I now solemnly reaffirm my promise I made to you last December 6: to uphold the Constitution, to do what is right as God gives me to see the right, and to do the very best I can for America. God helping me, I will not let you down.[41]

In that sense, the most important sense, he did not let us down.

Beyond Character

Presidential character is the core but not the whole. Readers and writers who are concentrators on personality can make a heavy mistake: supposing that the qualifications of a potential President come down to nothing much except the candidate's basic inside psychology. Given the complexity of politics, there is always a popular temptation to reduce the focus of judgment to morals (Has he behaved badly?) or appearance (Does he seem Presidential?) or combativeness (Is he running ahead?) But we academics are probably the ones even more likely to be tempted to suppose that once you carefully discern the character, you've got it, and that the rest of the factors—world view, style, power situation, and climate of expectations—are neglectable peripheries.

For politics, that is wrong. The key correction is this: a person with a healthy personality can carry that strength into political harm. A person 'well-adjusted', 'mentally healthy', 'psychologically strong', etc., may still wind up making mistakes. Even a politically defined personality, such as Presidential character, may not be an adequate predicter for choosing the right candidate. Beside character, style and world view are highly significant. Specific skills are needed for the presidency and they are not at all determined by character. Neither is world view, what the person believes in politically, in real relation to what he or she does. That, too, is not a product of character; persons with the same character types may have very different beliefs.

The following cases focus on this differentiation between character and the other factors. Two modern Presidents illustrate the two main distinctions. Both were active-positives. But one suffered a major setback as President because of the absence of a single skill, as predicted, which a President needs in Washington, D.C. The other prediction was also correct: again, a President with an active-positive character, and with highly professional Presidential skills, had a very major problem in the realm of world view, resulting in catastrophic disasters. During a Presidential campaign, the voters need to know each candidate's record—including the real style and world view his life so far has demonstrated.

13

Jimmy Carter: Predicted and Reviewed

This section was written, exactly as printed below, *before* Jimmy Carter swore by the Bible that he would take the office of President. The next section, "Jimmy Carter Reviewed," was written *after* he left the office. The two together illustrate how prediction operates and how character is to be seen as one, but not the only one, of the main factors we need to discover.

JIMMY CARTER PREDICTED

Jimmy Carter was barely a blip on the national political horizon when, in September 1974, *U.S. News and World Report* surveyed the 1976 Presidential scene. The man for President Ford to beat, they thought, was some part of Kennedy-Wallace-Jackson-Muskie-Mondale-Bentsen-McGovern-Stevenson-Bayh-Church-Udall-Bumpers-Wendell Ford-Askew-Byrne-Gilligan. And seven months later, the editors were hypothesizing Senator Edward Kennedy as the choice of a deadlocked Democratic convention, because "With a host of contenders and more presidential primaries than ever before, it now seems certain that none will emerge with enough delegates to win a first-ballot nomination, or even an early-ballot victory."[1] By then, Carter had been stepping along the road to the convention for thirty-three months. In another year and a half, America would elect a new President called "Jimmy," not only (as with James Madison) by his intimates, but by every Tom, Dick, and Harry in the land.

Since childhood, Jimmy Carter had been a reader. As an adult, he took a speed-reading course and found he could consume three books a week. Among many books, he read this one—twice he recalls—and in early 1974 he wrote me an encouraging note that included an invitation to come over for a visit. My wife and I had a February speaking date at Georgia Southern College in Statesboro; we were glad that gave us the opportunity to spend the night with the Governor and Mrs. Carter and the family on the way home. After an elegant and entertaining dinner, there was a classical guitar concert downtown, and then a nice long conversation about politics, the governor barefooted in a blue jeans outfit. I was impressed by his quickness and graciousness, fascinated by the ways he was trying to beat through the barriers between him and the voters. We went home thinking he certainly was an interesting governor. I have not seen him since, except as all of us have seen him. Two and a half years later, I was surprised to discover he remembered the book.

In July 1976, two days before he was nominated, Carter had a relaxed chat with David Broder and two other *Washington Post* reporters. Asked whether he would find the Presidency a rewarding and fulfilling challenge or the frustrating and embittering experience some men had found it, Carter said, "I think I have been heavily influenced by James David Barber's writings and I think a lot of my ideas come from there." Did he think of himself as "an active positive"?

Carter laughed. "That's a subjective analysis," he answered. "That's what I would like to be. That's what I hope to prove to be. . . . I think there were some who felt at ease with the job and looked forward to every day with anticipation, who were not uncertain of their own status and felt compatibility with the American people, and were not fearful of the Eastern liberal establishment, and did not see the Vice President or the Congress as a challenge to them, and recognized the strength of the office itself is enough guarantee of their status. I hope I would have that sense of being secure. I think I will if I'm elected. . . . I think probably that is my best answer that I can give you. I think I would enjoy it."[2]

I mention these little episodes, eminently neglectable in Carter's life, to set aside two distractions: first, that my book might have so shaped Carter's presentation of himself, in his *Why Not the Best? Why One Man Is Optimistic About America's Third Century* and in his performances, that the evidence therein is precooked to my various recipes; second, that I might have been charmed out of objectivity by the élan and ease of the Carter hospitality. Plausibility is against the first proposition. Character persists. It cannot be tailor-made for campaign purposes. Carter could no more have made himself into an active-positive after reading my book than I could have become a Presidential candidate after reading his.

Besides, no one has to be content with plausibilities on this point. The proof is in evidence, not speculation, and there is much evidence beyond what Mr. Carter has supplied, thanks to the enterprise of some enlightened reporters.

Against the second point, which concerns my own biases, I can make no defense except denial, which may be no more plausible than assertions to the contrary. Again the evidence is what counts. And as for the predictions, written as we approach inauguration day, 1977, the evidence of a history yet to be will decide.

ARCHERY: 1924

Jimmy Carter arrived in Wise Sanitorium on October 1, 1924, as President Calvin Coolidge was trying to rouse himself to stave off the challenge of John W. Davis. His family lived in Archery, Georgia, a place left out of laws and maps, incorporated only in the minds of its inhabitants, known, if at all, as "near Plains." Named with all his father's names, James Earl Carter, Junior, was a sickly baby, in and out of the hospital with severe colitis for two years, scaring his parents with diarrhea and blood to the point where they wondered whether their first-born would make it. By luck, his mother, Lillian Gordy Carter, had been through scary times before with other people's babies in her work as a registered nurse. She found a country doctor who prescribed a saturated solution of corn starch that brought little Jimmy through his first terror and into good health. Before long, he was digging into fried chicken, chicken pie, chicken salad, and various bean and beef supplements to a fowl diet. He even came to savor catfish, provided it was soaked long enough in steak sauce. Following the medical wisdom of that period, Lillian fed him on a strict schedule—"exactly on time," she said.[3]

Just as Jimmy was recovering, Mother had to concern herself with another life, new baby Gloria, a feisty bundle of energy who, before long, could and did beat up her older, smaller brother. "Up till now," Gloria said in 1976, "I've been the happiest member of our family," despite some radical downs over the years.[4] A mere three years after Gloria's birth, Jimmy had another baby sister to share things with, Ruth, who was later to stand with him when his world spun out from under his feet. Ruth was Daddy's darling; "Gloria was much more rebellious against Daddy than Ruth was. Ruth was just her father's little girl," Jimmy remembers, and adds, "I can't explain it psychologically . . . it was kind of an accepted thing. I didn't feel any jealousy over it. Gloria and I were almost of equal age and we were competitors with each other."[5]

Gloria became "more or less the leader of my children," Lillian said. Jimmy would tease the girls and pull their hair, "but they usually got along just fine. . . . Once she [Gloria] hit him with a monkey wrench and he shot her in the behind with a BB gun," setting off squalls that persisted till Daddy drove into the yard, judged the situation, got out his peach tree switch, and "whipped" Jimmy's behind. Indeed, most of the six paternal "whippings" Carter remembers so vividly (after the one he got at age four or five for taking a penny from the Sunday School collection) were for "arguments" with Gloria.[6]

If the child's first focus of attention is his own digestion, his second is Mother, and then the other humans he comes to recognize and contend with and, if lucky, love. Jimmy's mother, pressed in 1976 for childhood anecdotes, said he had "the dumbest boyhood of anybody I've ever seen," meaning most ordinary and normal, like a million other childhoods.[7] She resisted the relentless demand for the romantic and dramatic tales mothers have a way of recreating from the material of the years before their child became a historical personage, years in which her thoughts were on nurture, not the recording of it. When her first son first told her he was going to run for President, her question was "President of what?"

Yet neither Carter nor his mother was or is ordinary. Novelist Reynolds Price, a writer not given to soapy sentimentality, sized up Lillian Carter in person, starting with

> . . . her strong rich face, lit with joy and the certainty of power around the great eyes. All her story is there. She has stamped all her children with the Gordy good looks—a still, grave radiance that slowly melts into broad delight at the life before them . . . her lock-jawed passion for decency, justice, and her life's conviction that the only honorable surrenders are surrenders to laughter and mercy. If she's mostly given over now to laughter, pride and sass, she has earned her fun; and within the fun, one can sense rock—a broad standing-shaft of rock which one could reach and stand on if one were in need. . . . Like all family women, she has lived for others' needs; and the story of her children is spun on those poles— their need, her provision, now their various repayments.[8]

She was seventy-eight then; half a century before, at Jimmy's recovery, she had the same basic composition: a big-boned, warm, vocal, intellectually inclined, independent farm woman, practiced in hard-headed, whole-hearted compassion through many a ten-hour day of nursing, extraordinary in her discovery of the safety and pleasure of spontaneity. People should call her "Miss Lillian" she said in 1976; "Mrs. Carter" was for Jimmy's wife. Was she for helping the elderly? "Sure . . . I'm going to be old myself someday."[9] In a televised interview at the height of the 1976 Democratic convention, she had Walter Cronkite blushing with delight at her generous insouciance.

She had her vulnerabilities. Her father was a postmaster, who may have been the first to think up rural free delivery and from whom, she said, she got the "liberalism" which set her apart from the local ideology. But: "I never cared much about my kin. I'll tell you why. We were the poor side of the family, and they didn't know me till Jimmy was Governor." She liked where she lived, but said, "I never had close friends, I was never one to be running in and out of people's homes." Her mind-speaking manner was a wonder to some, like the ninety-eight-year-old black neighbor who said, "Miss Lillian is afraid of no man. She says what's bothering her, and shoot, if you don't like it, she ain't about to stop and ask you why." But another neighbor said, "Lillian Carter always felt she was better than us. . . . She thinks she is so smart and we're so dumb." Long after she became a rich lady, she could quip, "Everybody in Plains either loves me or owes me," masking whatever pain was in the division.[10]

Family—her own family—was her solace and mainstay. She herself had grown up in a family of thirteen, including her grandmother and two adopted children. Her father, called "Jim Jack," was a laugher and a singer back then, and a man with a claim on a source of solace beyond the family circle; he and the local black bishop would vibrate the Gordy living-room with certain old songs:

> The King of love my Shepherd is,
> Whose goodness faileth never;
> I nothing lack if I am His
> And He is mine for ever.

Lillian felt lucky in her marriage, at twenty-five, to Earl, who was then thirty and coming along with his grocery, dry cleaning, and farm enterprises—"a fine catch, you know." She disagreed with his "conservative" viewpoint, but would stand ground with him, and he with her: "Earl was of his time. Of his time. He was not like me, certainly, but he did not stop me from doing what I wanted to do. . . . He was simply a Southern man who lived at a certain time." Jimmy arrived a year after their marriage and when he was old enough to play outdoors, she saw to it that he did not get too much midday sun, being so fairskinned. "The children had an easy life," she remembered. "We wanted them to be happy. They went to the movies every Saturday." Much later Jimmy said, "I'm much more like my mother than I am my father." He says he wishes he had ten children.[11]

Earl Carter is not alive to let us see in what he is, what he was. His last child, Billy, following his first by thirteen years (and thus not part of that early constellation of mother, father, Jimmy, and the girls), has much of his father's spirit and image according to his big brother. "That's because we look alike," Billy explains, "and I'm more outgoing than Jimmy. I enjoy a party, too."[12] Earl gave Billy his own father's name. A joke-loving, beer-sipping, church-avoiding gas station operator, Billy ran for mayor of Plains in 1976 and lost. His favorite mock-redneck litany gives some hint of his father's humor:

> I got a mamma who joined the Peace Corps and went to India when she was sixty-eight. I got one sister who's a holy roller preacher. I got another sister who wears a helmet and rides a motorcycle. And I got a brother who thinks he's going to be President. So that makes me the only sane person in the family.[13]

But Billy, like Earl, has a hard nose for business. While Jimmy was off being Governor, Billy managed the complicated family warehouse and farming operation, building its worth to between two and three million dollars.

Jimmy remembered that "Daddy loved to have a good time and enjoyed parties much more than did my mother" and that "My father was my friend"— "friend," not "pal"; Jimmy called him "sir."[14] He was also the man who wielded the peach switch over Jimmy's bottom exactly six times, possibly inflicting pain, surely shame. He was known publicly in the territory as a hard man, typical of a clan who would "do like they wanted to do. They'd set a stake and then go after it," his brother Alton said. His family had lived there since the century before last, Irish-rooted people. Earl's father bought up land, got the timber cut, and made good money selling railroad ties, right up until he was gunned down in a street fight when Earl was twelve, leaving the boy in the care of his brother, Alton, whose rule was "Make him mind, in the first place, and keep him busy." "Everything Earl laid his hand down on," Alton said, "when he picked it up, there was three or four dollars." He grew up busy and lucky. Not that he got rich: young Jimmy Carter and his sisters found the bathroom was in the back yard, the water faucet was an outdoor hand pump, warmth in the winter cold came from fireplaces and from hot bricks and down comforters that served to cut the bed chill, light was the yellow glow of kerosene lamps. But Jimmy writes that "All in all it seemed a comfortable and enjoyable place to live." There is no evidence that Earl and Lillian fretted over their lot in life or made their children feel they were hard up. A little defensively, Miss Lillian says, "We didn't feel poor and we always had a car. We had the first radio in Plains. We had the first TV set."[15]

But the parents did make the children work. As early as his fourth or fifth year, Jimmy had jobs to get done—he was water boy for the field hands. He also had his own commercial enterprise. He would toddle down the tracks into Plains and sell little bags of peanuts on his own, saving his profits so that, at age nine, he had enough to buy five bales of cotton. He stored them a few years and then sold them for enough to buy five houses, which he rented at a good rate.[16] From an early age he had to get up with the rest of the workers when the big bell clanged in the dark of 4:00 A.M. during harvest time, and he took his part in field plowing, cotton mopping, peanut stacking, fence fixing, mule catching, wood chopping, syrup boiling, guano spreading, and the day-after-day cozening of chickens, as the seasons rolled. It was hard work, often monotonous work, but obviously, as any little boy could tell, people survived it, even enjoyed it at times, and no one worked harder than the man who demanded it, Mr. Earl. The son could see with his own eyes what the father did, taste with his own mouth the fruits of labor. Work was concrete, continuous in time and space, immediate, shared, indisputably productive, and culturally normal—everybody worked, and ought to. Sometimes work did not work: places where the invading Bermuda grass survived every torment were surrendered and the fight transferred to more yielding ground.

Earl called the boy "Hot," short for "Hot Shot." Earl would say, "Hot, would you like to turn the potato vines this afternoon?" Hot had alternative recreations in mind, but, he recalled, "I always said, 'Yes, sir, Daddy, I would.' And I would do it. But he didn't have to give me any direct orders. But I never did disobey a direct order my father gave me." What was expected of him was made clear enough without precise command. Jimmy was a "good boy," obedient, but "it wasn't a namby-pamby sort of thing." As he got older he could face up to Earl a bit. He took him on in tennis and, though he never could beat him, sometimes he scored. The celebrated six switchings Jimmy received show some edges of rebellion. Once, when he got mad at the sleep-destroying noise from his partying parents and their friends, Jimmy took his blanket out to the treehouse and would not answer when his father called him in. The "whipping" followed, as the day the night. In mildly masked aggression, Jimmy recalls (right after recalling that "whipping") that he "felt desperately sorry" for Earl when Earl tried on his first new tailor-made suit and it bagged grossly oversized around him. "I remember that no one in the family laughed," he writes. The son could feel the sting of embarrassment when, as a high school boy, he had to wear a pair of the high-button ladies' shoes Earl had stocked too many of, and again when Earl cut his hair too short. All in all, though, it sounds like a relationship of mutual respect, layered over love and the resistance that signals separate identities. Earl was no Frank Nixon, angrily and unpredictably berating his boy, no Reverend Wilson, teasing his son into retardation. Jimmy's father taught him how to do things and, by example, what a man could be.[17]

But if life got too tight between oldest son and father, Jimmy had lots of other people to relate to. The area was teeming with children; outdoors it did not mean much that all of them were dark-skinned—at least in the early years. The throng had spare time to play; they "rode mules and horses through the woods, jumped out of the barn loft into huge piles of oat straw, wrestled and fought, fished and swam."[18] Jimmy and his best friend A. D. Davis (who moved in with the Carters when he and Jimmy were thirteen, to help with baby Billy) stole rides on Earl's prize calf, "Gene Talmadge." The boys liked the rainy season—too wet for much work—when the water rising in the creeks elevated the catfish to their dangling hooks. A good tree climber, Jimmy got to go out at night with the grown-up hunters to climb up and shake down the treed raccoon or possum.

And there were the other, blood-connected, relations. Stolid Uncle Alton, Earl's brother; "Sissy," Lillian's youngest sister; Cousin Hugh, who became a worm- and cricket-grower and state senator; Earl's mother, Nina, a pretty, old lady of Plains, kept company by a different grandchild each night of the week, Jimmy's being Friday. And so on. In circles widening out from Archery were scads more relations, visiting and being visited, and back in time were four generations on the same land, on back to Wiley Carter, born in 1798.

Talking to Bill Moyers in 1976, Carter put it this way:

> I had a stability there, you know. When things started going wrong in my life, my father and mother were there, and my sisters and brother were there. And my church was there. And my community was there—that never did change. Never has changed yet. [Laughs.] But there was something there around which I built my life.[19]

Forty years before, when he was twelve, he had summed up the aspirations of character learned from all those folks, in a school report on "Healthy Mental Habits":

> There are certain habits of thinking which have a good effect upon health. If you think in the right way, you'll develop:
>
> 1. The habit of expecting to accomplish what you attempt.
> 2. The habit of expecting to like other people and to have them like you.
> 3. The habit of deciding quickly what you want to do, and doing it.
> 4. The habit of "sticking to it."

5. The habit of welcoming fearlessly all wholesome ideas and experiences.
6. A person who wants to build good mental habits should avoid the idle daydream; should give up worry and anger, hatred and envy, should neither fear nor be ashamed of anything that is honest or purposeful.[20]

One night the next year, Jimmy borrowed the family pickup truck and drove into Plains for his first date.[21]

Thus a life that started with sickness almost unto death was moving toward confidence and adventure. If he had hurt a lot as a baby, he could trust in Mother's competent caring. Father's governing solidity, their "thereness" in times of terror and joy. They were a striving family, proud of their past, making their own future, capable of looking life full in the face. Effort was a given, pleasure a gift. Lillian and Earl showed Jimmy that people he loved could be different—not only in their "liberalism" and "conservatism," but in personal style—and still love one another, perhaps the more so for their differences. The boy found out there were standards he was expected to meet, such as obedience and not fighting with his sister, but that when he broke the rules and took his punishment, the rule-makers took him back again, fully and freely. He should try hard and do better, but in the stories he tells so easily now, including stories of his wrongness and weakness, there is missing that lowering guilt that settled over some pre-Presidential childhoods, like fog on a windless sea, leaving the child stranded in hopelessness.

In the Carter household, action was not only permitted, it was required. There was space around Archery and time for play, for all kinds of physical and social experiments in the flexing and testing of potentialities. His twelve-year-old's list was a list of *habits*, for out of the casual flux of childish experience, it seems he was trying to pull together some continuities, some endurances, some attitudes worth "sticking to"—though, of course, one could make too much of a homework assignment. Yet in this little list are clues, I think, to his present and future. The first five of six commandments are positive—things to do, ways to cultivate. Rule six disposes of the negative residue. The list begins with analogues, as I see them, to the "two basic questions" candidate Carter said Americans ought to ask themselves. "Expecting to accomplish what you attempt" gets translated into "Can our government be competent?" and "expecting to like other people and to have them like you" into "Can our government be honest, decent, open, fair, and compassionate?" I think these themes, in their tension and complementarity, took hold of Jimmy quite early, grew out of the working and likings of the Archery years. And down the road was waiting for him yet another meaning to the ideas of striving upward toward perfection and outward toward a world of neighbors.

There were strains in the fabric, a too-big younger sister, another Daddy's darling, "whippings" and embarrassments, and no doubt Lillian and Earl felt strained sometimes over their own first experiment in child-rearing. Lillian's restricted social life, Earl's necessary struggle with farming through the Great Depression—such worries get through to an attentive youngster. But the leaven of laughter worked its way; Jimmy's parents laughed so much they woke him up. In that family of characters, said by some cynic to have been created by Central Casting, there was a surplus of rescuing ribaldry. Jimmy grew up quieter than most of them, but he smiled a lot.

And one more thing, setting off on his first date, young Hot Shot knew not only where babies come from—farm boys acquire that privileged knowledge early—but also what it could be like to be a man or a woman. His models were rich in their variety. Lillian was warm, but also a tough worker and talker, not to be tread upon. Earl was hard, even mean sometimes; in Jimmy's early years that is probably what came through predominantly. But he took care of his own and partied the while. A man who can say, easily, as Jimmy Carter did, that he is much more like his mother than like his father, was not set up for a life of proving what needed no proof, his manliness.

ANNAPOLIS: 1943

Many a time Jimmy had hiked or ridden from Archery into Plains, to visit, and then come out home again. Plains was different: "During my childhood," he wrote, "I never considered myself a part of the Plains society"—neither did Miss Lillian—"but always thought of myself as a visitor when I entered that 'metropolitan' community."[22] Later Atlanta and Washington would replace Plains as places for an outsider to break in and prove himself. Plains was where they had medicine shows and the traveling circus, log-cutting contests put on by the axe salesmen, Halloween carnivals, and marble games. It was the metropolis where, as a high school student, Jimmy's mind took an expanding leap.

Jimmy's interest in getting himself educated went back to his fifth year— the same time he started selling peanuts, if the tales are true, a time of expanding horizons. Lillian's brother Tom Gordy, a world-traveling Navy man whom Jimmy described as "my distant hero," sent the boy postcards and pictures, stimulating in his nephew a desire to go to the Naval Academy at Annapolis. Earl agreed. He had served in the Army in World War I; the academies gave a free education; none of Earl's family had even graduated from high school. Jimmy wrote for the catalogue, pored over its every paragraph, and pondered whether such sins as "malocclusion of teeth" or "retention of urine" would bar his admission. Earl set quietly to work cultivating the Congressman who would make the decision. As the crucial moment approached, Jimmy gorged on bananas to meet the weight requirement and rolled his feet over Coca-Cola bottles to fix his flat feet. It was quite an ambition for an Archery boy. The family must have thought he had something special.[23]

In school, he demonstrated strong talent, building on strong preparation. His mother was forever reading books and books became his favorite Christmas present. At age four he got from his godmother, who must have had either unusual prescience or an overstocked library, a set of all the works of Guy de Maupassant. Earl's outdoor eyes were not much for reading, though he would leaf through *U.S. News and World Report,* but his lessons in practical technology linked up with school science. In class, Jimmy found he could get through his lessons quickly and read whatever he wanted, tucked behind the textbook. Mostly he wanted cowboy and Indian stories, and was pleased—momentarily—when his teacher prescribed something called *War and Peace.*

That teacher, Miss Julia Coleman, was one of that remarkable breed who sense in the mixed minds of adolescents, for all their surface cynicism and ingratitude, the excitement of excellence. This bent little near-sighted woman served her student family a whole cafeteria of intellectual wonders: dramatically read great poems, colorful great paintings, and some approximation of great music in her requirement that each play an instrument, be it only the ukelele. She jostled their minds with a program of contests—debating, essays, recitations, spelling, playacting, Bible memory, reading contests for gold and silver stars. Jimmy ate it up. As he had tried to beat the farm's champion cotton-picker (he lost), in school he took on the Plains brains, and won. He would have been class valedictorian, they say, if he hadn't skipped school to go to the movies. (Teeny Ratliff got it.) Miss Julia ran a tight ship, by the book. But he graduated from high school at sixteen, spent a year in a nearby junior college and another year at Georgia Tech, and was off to Annapolis in 1943. He weighed 121 pounds, age 19.

The academy's academic program, all required courses except the choice of a foreign language (his being Spanish), stressed engineering: the way things work, a link to Earl's mechanical instruction. Classes were small and run competitively. There was "constant pressure for speed and accuracy," the homework was impossible to complete, and was supplemented with endless practical exercises such as summer cruises through submarine-endangered waters in creaking ships sparable from war duty. Discipline was harsh and quick and inevitable—"There was no way to escape, not even for the best behaved of midshipmen," Jimmy recalls. Public speaking and dancing exercises were required of the young gentlemen. Carter did well enough, finishing fifty-ninth in a class of 820, without excessive grinding. He sought out extra burdens, memorizing hundreds of aircraft silhouettes while on guard duty, learning to fly seaplanes, listening with rapt and scientific attention to classical records. It was a busy life, with a significant possibility of death to follow, for the nation was at war, and Carter and his classmates expected to graduate to combat assignments. He recalls it as "a time of challenge, excitement, and learning."[24]

Then during his second summer cruise, in 1945, the whole picture changed. Harry Truman made the Japanese surrender. The was was over; who needed the Navy?

The overriding challenge fell away, the purpose of the enterprise gone. Carter graduated with his class and started a two-year hitch of sea duty. He got some technically interesting assignments, some travel, but it was a downbeat time, hacking around in left-over ships: "I became most disillusioned with the Navy, and the military in general, and probably would have resigned had not I and all Annapolis graduates been serving 'at the pleasure of the President.' "[25] Then his own pleasurable anticipations picked up when he heard about submarines—"tough, dangerous, and demanding" duty, sophisticated machinery, requiring meticulous attention, the Navy's new thing, run by an alert elite, the commandos of the sea. He applied, got in, trained six months in 1948, and emerged as a full-fledged submariner. Down under the water he found challenge aplenty. Men went mad there, and Carter saw it happen once. Even without any enemy looking for them, submariners had their own war, a war against the elements, against fear, against mechanical failure. You had to keep thinking all the time and an officer had to see to the delicate dovetailing of specialized teams. Carter was so often seasick that he carried his vomit bucket with him to the bridge.[26] One night, surfaced in a roaring Pacific Ocean, a wave swept him off into the cold sea—normally a killing experience—but by luck another wave dropped him back on the deck, thirty feet aft.

His commanding officer reported him as one "who no matter what he does ends up being the boss."[27]

By 1950, Carter had applied for assignment to the program that was developing the Navy's first atomic submarines. The three-and-a-half-hour selection interview brought him up against a demanding Moses named Hyman Rickover, whose steely stare and unsmiling countenance soon had the applicant in a cold sweat. He recovered a bit when he was asked his class standing at Annapolis. (Rickover had stood first.) The dialogue went something like this:

CARTER: Sir, I stood fifty-ninth in a class of 820!
RICKOVER: Did you do your best?
CARTER: (pauses, gulps) No, sir, I didn't *always* do my best.
RICKOVER: (long pause) Why not?
CARTER, shaken, exits in silence.

Rickover became Carter's hero. He was a maverick outsider, an engineering genius shuttled aside by the Navy bureaucracy until he was finally found and empowered by President Harry Truman. It is not hard to tell why, from Carter's own account about:

probably the greatest engineer this nation ever produced . . . a scientist . . . completely dedicated . . . works very, very hard.

He has absolutely no tact—doesn't care for anything. As a matter of fact, all the time I worked for him he never said a decent word to me. However, he did change my life because he had one characteristic, and still has it, which has always been unique. He would never accept mediocrity or low average achievement in relation to anything he did or anyone under him did.

I helped him and a few others develop the first two atomic submarines . . . and whenever the Admiral would come around to inspect my work, if I had done a perfect job—which wasn't too often, but every now and then I did—he never said a word, never once did he say, "good job, Jimmy" or "well done, Carter." If he found no fault, he simply looked, turned around and walked away.

However, if I made the slightest mistake, in one of the loudest and most obnoxious voices I ever heard, he would turn around and tell the other people in the area what a horrible disgrace I was to the Navy and that I ought to be back in the oldest and slowest and smallest submarine from which I had come.[28]

Carter's reaction sounds profound: Rickover "demanded from me a standard of performance and a depth of commitment that I had never realized before that I could achieve. And I think second to my own father, Admiral Rickover had more effect on my life than any other man." As a candidate for President in 1976, Jimmy Carter said, "I want to be tested in the most severe way."[29]

Life is a continual knotting and loosening of strands. The total fabric of it, in any life-period, is a mixed weave. To highlight a certain continuing strand in Carter's development, I have pulled it out of context. That strand—the drive for excellence—comprises, I think, about a third of the Carter world view and illustrates an important outgrowth of his character.

The character part is evident. Carter was excited, again and again, when he was shown some vista of high being and some path of becoming by which he might excel. He wanted to grow, to move out to meet life, felt restless and bored with the routines of each new plateau. Perhaps Tom Gordy, certainly his father, Miss Julia Coleman, and the Navy duties given identity-focus in the person of Hyman Rickover—were angels of ambition calling him to stretch his talents beyond what could be merely expected of him. In other words, he showed a sense of the self as developing, a pleasure in the adventure of achievement. He had no answer to Rickover's "Why not?" Part of his purpose was to render the question unnecessary. Furthermore, it was not just a matter of doing his best— the best effort he could make. Rickover (Miss Julia, Earl) wanted *results*: the proof was in the pudding, not the stirring. Carter would carry away that orientation. Living it took stubborn tenacity and the courage to bounce back from failure.

Perhaps as important, he had been, and felt, lucky.

PLAINS: 1953

There were other strong strands, pulling in different directions, in those Navy years. Annapolis was not all work and no play. Jimmy kept a diary the first year, with "My Stretch in the Service" embossed on the cover. From the first night, he was a member of a gang of plebe victims, the diary says:

> Of course all of the plebes were rather apprehensive about what was to come. We later found out that our fears were well-grounded. The first night after supper the halls were lined with youngsters who were anxious to try out their new authority. . . . We had to tell our names and home state to every youngster we saw. . . . My main trouble was that I smiled too much. I soon learned to concentrate on a serious subject when passing a group of the yapping 3/C. I also learned to "wipe it off."[30]

He could wax collegiately sarcastic, about an orating knot-teacher ("Some philosopher"), about the Navy keeping the boys in heavy uniforms in 90 degree heat ("The Navy really uses judgment about everything. Never just blindly follows regulations—always quick to make a change for the better.")

There was gossip about girls, fun in minor crimes: "During the last few days I have really been 'getting away with it.' I've been caught at five different reportable offenses and haven't been fried yet."[31] In a Halloween skit he played Fearless Fosdick in a skirt, an experience he found so hilarious he wrote out the plot and dialogue. He got homesick, and however hard the hazing, there were loyalties he would not violate—they never could make him sing "Marching Through Georgia"—but the graduation yearbook summed him up this way:

> During plebe year Jimmy spent a large part of his time learning songs for the first classmen, but the only time he raised his voice after that was to shout, "Brace up!" or "Square that cap!" Studies never bothered Jimmy. In fact, the only times he opened his books were when his classmates desired help on problems. This lack of study did not, however, prevent him from standing in the upper part of his class. Jimmy's many friends will remember him for his cheerful disposition and his ability to see the humorous side of any situation.[32]

A classmate remembers him as "a private kind of guy" but he had his friends, and his humor belies the image of constant earnestness. Later, the submarine life was tough, but they were all down there in the same small boat. Carter liked it because it was "embryonic." The closeness imposed respect for privacy, but "It was for me, a time of unreserved masculine behavior," a "liberation from the restraints of civilized life," with a "degeneration of behavior, a closeness just among men which I liked."[33]

Nor was he, despite long absences, cut off from Plains. He wrote home a lot. "Dear Gloria, Please do not call me 'Hot' and please do not write to me on lined notebook paper with pencil."[34] Earl came up to see him his first Thanksgiving at Annapolis, and he went home for Christmas. Visiting home again just before his last Annapolis year, he got started with an even better intimacy: cruising around in a rumble-seated Ford with a friend, they came upon sister Ruth and her pretty friend Rosalynn Smith, made a double date for the movies.

Rosalynn held Jimmy at bay for months, but they were married at last in the heat of July 1946. Rosalynn was a nineteen-year-old graduate in interior decorating. Her father had died (despite Miss Lillian's nursing) when she was thirteen, so her mother had to eke out a living as a seamstress. Rosalynn rose to the occasion, as she was to do right into the White House. After her marriage, she moved to Norfolk and, during her husband's long absences, managed on seventy-one dollars per month beyond the rent. At first she looked up to him— "I guess I always idolized him. He was older and so good looking"—but before long she was looking across at him. In 1976, Carter remembered that "I was by far the dominant person in the marriage at the beginning, but not any more. She's just as strong, if not stronger than I am. She's fully equal to me in every way." They named their first son, born in 1947, John William after her grandfather; James Earl ("Chip," perhaps as in "off the old block") followed three years later; then Jeffrey in 1952—all while their father, in his twenties, was sailing away all over the place.[35]

Baby Jeff was still baby Jeff when, in 1953, the Carters quit the Navy and went back to Plains to live. At the peak of his Navy career, thinking he might one day be its topmost officer, enjoying good money and Rickover's stimulations, Jimmy chucked it all. Earl—"I remember my father often walking back and forth in the yard looking up at the sky, praying that the weather would be clear enough to plow the crop before it rained again"—that Earl of Plains, lay dying, long before his time, and Jimmy rushed home for a chance to have a last talk "about old times together" before the end.[36]

Earl's death revealed what that "hard" man had done and meant. As he passed, hundreds came to give him words, flowers, favorite foods. The state legislators, among whom he had won membership for his last year, marked his ending. Jimmy and Ruth, Daddy's darling, carried the news to the farm's black workers the night he died, and saw, to Jimmy's surprise, their tears spring and flow. It turned out Mr. Earl had been a veritable closet foundation—cast at need, debts forgiven, scholarships, dresses for the little neighbor girls. In contrast, sister Gloria remembered Jimmy musing, "If I died, nobody would really care. Not really care."[37]

When Carter's leave was up, he went back north to Rosalynn and the children. He had "some torturous days" thinking, feeling what to do. He talked it over with a fellow officer, who recalls, "He was really torn by the situation. It was agony. His father was the mainstay of that town—the banker and the landowner. He was a baron in a feudal situation. Jimmy had a strong sense that nobody in his family could hold it all together but him. He felt that if he didn't go back and take the burden, the *town* would die." Miss Lillian recalls that "Jimmy didn't want to come back to Plains. He hated to give up his career." Perhaps the center was falling apart: not long thereafter, young Billy joined the Marines (he said, to show he was a "badass") and Lillian took a place as a fraternity housemother at Auburn University and started a nursing home in Blakely, Georgia. Most important, Rosalynn most definitely *did not* want to go back to Plains, back between those mothers and all those kin, with her three boys. She and Jimmy wrangled hard over it, "the first really serious argument in our marriage."[38]

The terms of that argument are unrecounted. In the end, though, Carter concluded the best thing to do was to go home, and the reason, he wrote as he ran for President, was, "I had only one life to live, and I wanted to live it as a civilian, with a potentially fuller opportunity for varied public service." He called up his mother in the middle of the night and said, "Mother, I have no alternative. I'm going to come home." They made the trip and settled into Plains's public housing project, rent $30 a month.[39] The family business was in trouble, for Earl had some $90,000 out in shakily secured loans.

In a sense, intimacy had won out over excellence. Jimmy Carter's need for high achievement, his excitement when exposed to possibilities of excellence, was very real and stayed real for him. Yet as his Annapolis diary shows, he never had been an isolated, mechanical man. I think he was figuring out what to take seriously—and how seriously. He was trying to discern what his particular life really meant. One might call it an identity crisis, building over the years. He could make a game of life's little harassments, could see how externally determined breaks and blocks made all his choices conditional, but he had also seen what his own initiatives could make of the available materials. When push came to shove, family loyalty won out over personal ambition. He saw it as a broadening, from a restricted striving upward to a wider community life. Rosalynn, perhaps, saw it as a narrowing, from the cosmopolitan to the parochial. Together, though, they chose to meet their responsibilities—his to his homefolks, hers to him.

Mr. Earl's secret life, exposed to his son too late for the expression of filial gratitude, shifted the ground of Jimmy's identity, reinforced his sense that one can be hard *and* kind, competent *and* compassionate. Not that the choice to come home was simply a matter of sentiment or philosophy, for economic realities were pressing. But his reasoning about it (in the brain, in the viscera) refocused his vision of his world.

Carter had to learn farming over again and catch up with the new methods. Rosalynn's business talent had vast new complexities to deal with. Their first year home saw "one of the worst drought years in the history of Georgia."[40] Net income was $254. Then, in long years of work far easier to write about than to perform, the Carters built a fortune, valued today at about $5 million. Some of Earl's celebrated money-luck came their way, but the prime ingredients were main force and determination.

That same first year home brought news from Washington. The Supreme Court said it was against the law to sort children into different public schools according to the melanin content of their epidermal pigmentation, a physical feature around which certain cultural perceptions had been organized.

Those on the paler side of the spectrum called themselves "whites"; those whose skins were darker—dark at all—were named by the whites: respectfully "Negroes," contemptuously "niggers," but day by day, in Jimmy's world, an easier phrase, "colored people." Only after an attitudinal revolution would they baptize themselves with their own name, "black," once a word for slaves, now a proud exaggeration matching that of "white." Some of the whites were mean, some of the blacks were lazy; when times got hard or tempers flared, the side feeling hurt would translate "some" to "all" and paste a lot of pejoratives on the other, "race." It was not an equal contest, for whites decided which abstractions were real and thus consequential to experience.

The words were at once registers of and instigators of life-shaping deeds. Mankind changes its mind mysteriously, groping for ways to link life and meaning, to wring from new combinations enhancement and defense. Jimmy landed back in Plains just at a time when an explosion of new meanings was being ignited, a process which, in time, would shake loose many a bond, fuse others, and clear the way for a new conception of what was "natural," what had "always" been right. When at last the society decided that justice for blacks was "an idea whose time has come," most people could forgive their yesterdays and get busy shaping tomorrow.

Miss Lillian heard the difference the words made: "When my husband was alive and the children were growing up, there was no such thing as segregation and integration. There were things for the blacks and things for the whites. That's all." She knew what she believed, whatever they called it, but she was never one to take the traditional advice of the social smoothers: think what you want, do what you want, but talk like the rest of us. No one would be called "nigger" in her house, and no child of hers was allowed to address an adult black by his or her first name without the respectful preface "aunt" or "uncle." Her professional work went on too busily to bother with diagnostically useless distinctions. A black who worked for her said, "Miss Lillian's house was just like a colored person's house, far as colored people. She was about as good a white lady as I've ever seen." Yet she was a "white lady" and her home was not the same.[41]

She did what she could, but in those days it was like swimming against the tide. The front door was a boundary. When black Bishop Johnson's son came home from his college up north, Lillian let him in the front door and served him coffee—which sent Mr. Earl out the back door. When the bishop himself wanted to talk to Earl, he sent his driver around to the back door and Earl met the bishop in the yard. Even outdoors there were required separations: the black workers were allowed to join the Carters when they set the radio on the window sill to listen to black Joe Louis box white Max Schmeling. But when Louis smashed Schmeling into unconsciousness in the first round, the blacks went silent, said "Thank you, Mr. Earl," walked across the tracks into one of their houses, closed the door, and *then* broke forth in pandemonious celebration. Jimmy's pal, black A. D. Davis, could, as a child, have the run of the Carter house, but when Lillian took him to the movies with her flock and sat them together downstairs, A. D. watched awhile and then snuck off to the balcony. Later he explained, "I didn't see anybody in there colored but me, and I decided I'd go up there where colored people sit."[42]

Miss Lillian was a "lady" and thus had leave to expect certain "natural" courtesies from males. But once in the 1950s Jimmy tried to let a black woman get her wagonload of peanuts ahead of a line of white men—"You fellows don't mind if the lady goes first." They minded: that was no "lady," that was a "nigger." At least one white customer left in disgust at this affront to the common understandings.[43]

Such understandings went way back, had been learned at many a mother's knee. They were not invented in some burst of evil creativity, they were inherited—that is, each Jimmy and each A. D. found them already there, in all their apparently unalterable ubiquity. Their force was their conventionality. Thus, "Mr. Earl, he was sort of a hateful man," a black remembers, but adds: "People in those days were *all* kind of mean, and I guess he had to go along with the rest of them." One could go along a long time hardly noticing, certainly not feeling guilty, at least until certain rites of passage called attention to the understandings. The train that could be made to stop at Archery had one passenger car, but when Jimmy took his first ride on it he and his black companions had to separate and sit apart. They could stand together, but had to divide to sit down, as he could have noticed the first time he went to the movies or the first time blacks were let into his church for a funeral. The first day of school, the bus came for the white children and left the black children behind to walk to their school nearer by. A subtler transition came when, somewhere along the way, A. D. was supposed to start calling Jimmy "Mister Jimmy." Lillian's influence can be seen in what happened: A. D. said, "I don't know whether I'm ever going to say 'mister' to you at all"; Jimmy said, "I don't blame you. I wouldn't either." They kept their names. But when Jimmy, at school, heard the black accents in his own speech, he worked at talking "white," and insisted Gloria do the same.[44]

Gunnar Myrdal, in his famous study, *An American Dilemma*, found hope in the fact that racist practice conflicted with the predominant American beliefs. There was a "cognitive dissonance," as we would call it now, in which the egalitarian beliefs might win out over the repressive customs. But there were so many ways to mute the psychological conflict. For instance, not noticing, Carter writes, "It seems hard to believe now, but I was actually a member of the county school board for several months before it dawned on me that white children rode buses to their schools and black children still walked to theirs!" Then there was silence. Home on Navy leave, Jimmy proudly told Earl how his whole crew refused to attend a fancy party because their one black member was excluded. Earl could not see what there was to be proud of in that. So "he and I agreed to avoid racial subjects on my rare and brief visits home."[45] And there were a thousand other ways. The human brain seems to have an enormously rich store of tonics against the pains of contradiction, including all the ambiguities in the language.

Thus it is all the more impressive—and meaningful for Jimmy's world view—that Miss Lillian kept pushing. Where did Jimmy's "liberalism" on race come from? "Yes, he got that from me," she said, "I've always been like that. My father was never a racist, and I grew up trying to be compassionate and kind to everyone. . . . I've stood alone in Plains, Jimmy and I have stood alone." That is, her son got it from her, and she got it from her father. The transportations of belief are often personal and particular, especially where people grow up closely and visibly interdependent. Perhaps that was a long-range advantage, something his community had over places where life had been more rationally and abstractly divided into distinct components. In 1976, speaking in Boston, Carter said, "When civil rights legislation was passed, I didn't have to walk across the street and say, 'Hi, I'm Jimmy Carter. I've been your neighbor for the last 41 years.' I've known black people and they know me." And if he had trained the blackness out of his accent, he hadn't lost the trace of it that still can be discerned in the rhythm of his speech. One can hear the congregation's interpolated encouragements at each period in his sermon to a black church in Indianapolis: "They care for me and I care for them. We have a lot in common, a belief in one another. We share a common faith in Christ. We speak the same language. We sing the same hymns. We've seen the same poverty and the same disease. We've seen the same struggles in the South and the same growth. We've overcome the same obstacles. It has found us together in the spirit of brotherhood and love."[46]

In the early post-Navy years in Plains, though, Jimmy Carter was no civil rights militant. Racial issues confronted him and he tried to meet them with the integrity appropriate to Lillian Carter's son. He was of his time, but he also knew his place—out front if necessary. Sometimes that took stubborn resistance, as when the White Citizens' Council came calling three times to recruit him—first two, then eight or ten, then thirty or thirty-five neighbors, escalating their threats from displeasure to boycott of the business. And he told them to go hang, the only man in Plains not to join. Sometimes it took a reactive initiative. He missed a deacon's meeting and discovered later that the deacons had voted, eleven to zero, to keep blacks out of the worship services. At the next congregation meeting, Jimmy stood up and reminded them where they were—"This is not my house; this is not your house"—and urged a change of mind. Out of the two hundred people there, fifty-odd voted and Jimmy garnered six votes: his, Rosalynn's, his son Jack's, his son Chip's, Lillian's, and one other. He got on the school board and worked to fix up the black schools, but at the same time he went along with white parents who wanted a black school located farther away from *their* school. He backed an integrationist school consolidation plan (Cousin Hugh was on the other side), but made no discernible protest against the extra pay and privileges white teachers got.[47]

He gave up when some white businessmen got a black school bus stop moved to a back street, telling his black housekeeper, "Lexie, there's nothing I can do." When his friend Warren Fortson, the county attorney, was being driven out of town for proposing a biracial committee, Jimmy collected two hundred signatures on his behalf. "Jimmy got boycotted again because he spoke up for me," Fortson said. "He sure and hell did. They tried to fry him for it. In my book, that's pure courage." On the other hand, when guns were fired at the home of blacks who worked in a little biracial religious commune, he kept his sympathy private. "It's a shame and a disgrace on Sumter County that something like this is going on. I with there were some way it could be stopped."[48]

The time was the *1950s,* the place was *Georgia.* Decades later, retrospective moralists unfamiliar with the situation saw with their usual clarity how Carter should have been a Rap Brown, a Stokely Carmichael. Moralism collapses history; people forget that it was 1955 when Rosa Parks refused to move to the back of the bus in Montgomery, and set Dr. Martin Luther King, Jr., off toward the limited objective of integration of local bus seating, that the Selma march came more than a decade after that. In the perspective of infinity, Jimmy Carter shared his neighbors' sinfulness. But maybe the Sumter County school superintendent was closer to the mark, using labels well understood at the time, when he testified, "I would say he was more of a conservative than a liberal in most respects, but he was a lot more liberal than his neighbors." And though he did not explode his world, he was a person who, in the words of another neighbor, "never did try to hide what he was."[49]

So in those days, Jimmy Carter did not hide his beliefs, did wish there could be some way to stop the injustices, did speak out courageously when hard decisions split the neighborhood. He may have been afraid, but he did not hesitate to stand against nearly everyone—friends, relations, customers, neighbors, deacons—if that had to be. But he stood, he did not lead. He was not a "civil rights activist." Later, when possibilities of power came his way, he showed more clearly what he would do to get it and what he would do with it in hand. What was significant in these years between childhood and politics was the package of politically relevant beliefs he was putting together—his gathering world view. He was an active person, but also an attentive one, maintaining "a posture of learning" through these experiences, absorbing relevant images and drawing conclusions important for *his* life.

How did history work? He could see that his history had worked when he reached out for opportunity. People like Rickover made their marks on the world by holding in mind impossible superlatives, demanding of themselves and others nothing but the best. The demands were never met, never could be—in a sense were not meant to be met. Rather they were counsels of perfection that could lend daily life a certain gallantry, could make meaningful—and enjoyable—the chosen endurances. Perfection was to be held in *mind* (in one's being) as a goal. But in the realm of action (becoming), where results counted, one always had to settle for less. History was thus neither fixed nor randomly fluctuating. The rhythm of life's seasons could break in unpredictable ways. One could not foresee when a war would end, a wave wash you overboard, a father die, a drought come. But the mule could be guided: leaders who had the imagination to discipline themselves might beat the odds of historical chance and personal stagnation.

Carter's knack and training in engineering also affected his mind. William Greider of the *Washington Post* perceived that "He has the faith of a technocrat, believing in the mechanics of objects and situations, confident he can figure out how they work." Carter developed, I think, a sense of a real world usefully discernible through metaphors of mechanism—a sort of hydraulic world view. A stalled submarine engine could be fixed because it was a machine: its parts made up an ordered whole, designed for motion. To fix it you had to get out the blueprint and understand it. That sense would carry over in Carter's penchant for political blueprints, long-range strategy memos, big pictures. In his list of self-identifications, he included "planner."[50]

Along the way he was picking up impressions of people. There were at least three varieties. "The People" was a romance, an idealized appreciation of the heroism of the everyday life. His interpretation of Tolstoy was that leaders come and go, but "common, ordinary people" make history—"Their hopes and dreams, their doubts and fears, their courage and tenacity, their quiet commitments determine the destiny of the world."[51] Bob Dylan, he said, was a friend of his, his "favorite book of all time" was James Agee's *Let Us Now Praise Famous Men*, his favorite poet was Dylan Thomas—all singers of Rousseau's refrain. Then there were his people, his folks, some so close they seemed a part of his self, some a little farther out but still within the circle of intimacy and all-forgiving loyalty. His mind could widen that circle, probably did when he, having left Archery, came home to Plains. And last there were people he knew, friends like Dylan, and his Annapolis roommate, acquaintances, neighbors, co-workers—merging out into a real-world counterpart of The People, a corrective, in part, to the sentimentality of the ideal. But it is interesting that he came to know and like a lot of *different* people—different from him, different from one another. He decided to speak white, but he liked blacks. He would get good grades, but he expressed no contempt for his idle classmates; he helped them with their studies. His racist neighbors were still his neighbors. He was quiet and nearly puritanical personally, but he liked to get to know other talented types, like Greg Allman and Hunter Thompson. When Norman Mailer came to Plains, Carter was nice to him.

In all three visions of people, Carter saw them positively, as sources of good motives and morals. Not necessarily wisdom.

What were his visions of the central moral-political conflicts? In his time and place, the issue was race; he was not taken up with such other big issues of the 1950s as witch-hunting for Communists or the war in Korea. But as out of the chrysalis of "colored people," "blacks" were born, Carter saw with two sets of eyes. One saw—up close—the face of evil behind the bland conventionality of the system. If he had no clear vision of the way things ought to be, no comprehensive social utopia, he could see that the way things were was wrong, and he said so. He stood with Lillian and came to believe that Earl would have come around, given time. He has had, from some quarters, an historical bum rap on this point. Just *talking* as he did was dangerous and wearying.

But his other set of eyes saw his neighbor behind the racist's sneer. One had a responsibility to be practical, to work on the specifics without sacrificing all chance of leadership in a quixotic crusade. That was a hard line for a moralist to draw, for there were ready excuses for cowardice and indifference lurking there. Carter took it one step at a time, believing, as Jim Jack Gordy's grandson, that time was on his side.

ATLANTA: 1962

Grandfather Gordy had spent some time living in Archery, so Jimmy had a chance to hear his stories. He was a politician, as is evidenced by his survival as postmaster, an attractive spoil, through four different Presidencies. He was such a political buff that long after he was comfortably pensioned, he took a job as doorkeeper at the state capitol to keep in the know. His great friend and champion was Tom Watson, roaring advocate of the small farmer against the titans of the Eastern establishment, who first reached out toward, then turned rabidly against, the Southern black. Watson was Congressman, then Senator. Gordy kept after him for years before he got Watson to push through the bill that established the rural free delivery system.[52]

Jimmy drank all that in. He and the family went to every kind of political rally—he remembered one where a speechmaking Senate candidate was upstaged by a bread-slicing machine. In 1936, the Carters were so enthralled as they listened to the Republican national convention on their battery-operated radio that, when the radio went dead, they took it out in the yard and hooked it up to the car battery to hear Alf Landon get nominated.[53] In the Navy, Jimmy got to Washington now and then, stopping to visit the Senate chambers, talking with Senator Richard Russell. He followed Rickover's political fortunes. It was all at the edges of his mind, but available for memory when his time came.

When Earl died, Lillian was offered his seat in the state legislature, and when she declined they gave it to a friend of Earl's. It crossed Jimmy's mind to ask for it himself, but he let it pass. He thought about the state senate, but he found out a senate seat was not much of a prize: as in some other states, it was rotated among three counties, for two-year terms, so no one could get much of a handle on the job. Busy as he was farming, Jimmy tried the organizations route instead. He became president of the state Certified Seed Organization, district governor of the Lions Club, president of the Georgia Planning Association, chairman of the Sumter County school board, and member of the local library board and hospital authority.[54] His first serious campaign—though not as a candidate—was to get the school merger plan passed. He failed, but got in some practice speech making and handshaking.

The candidacy bug was nibbling at him. The state was reforming the legislature, putting an end to the rotation system. The new senate seat would represent seven counties. He talked the idea over with a visiting pastor who bunked with the Carters for a week, and the pastor was appalled that such a fine young man would consider such a lowdown life: "If you want to be of service to other people, why don't you go into the ministry of some other honorable social service work?" he asked. Jimmy's thoughts were jelling. He said, "How would you like to be a pastor of a church with 80,000 members?"[55]

So when, in 1962—the year John Kennedy met the Cuban missile crisis and Richard Nixon lost the California governor's race—Jimmy Carter ran for the state senate in Georgia, that was no strange departure, given his progenitors and cogitations. It was an uphill race from the start. His opponent for the Democratic nomination, who was a friend, had been elected from one county, but when the system was changed, and they had to run a new seven-county election, the politicians gathered around the man chosen in the now invalid race. Undaunted, Carter's folk took off in all directions, running what he remembers as an "amateurish, whirlwind campaign."[56]

The only issue was "fair play," which, as it turned out, Carter could put to his advantage. He was the outsider, butting in. His opponent cried for "sportsmanship": the Sumter County electorate "should think of the future good will in the new district and not try to throw its weight just because it has the largest number of voters," he said in a newspaper ad. Carter ad-ed back: his opponent "had every opportunity not to qualify if he objected to competition."[57]

Jimmy dashed around and in one courthouse came upon a scene right out of the eighteenth century, before the secret ballot. There sat Joe Hurst, the local boss, who was also a moonshiner and a state representative, at a table on which the campaign cards of his favorites were spread. As each voter came in, he showed them whom to vote for, and watched the ballot marking. Even so, he was not taking chances with this persuasive practice. The box was stuffed with more than a hundred "votes" cast by the dead and departed, their ballots neatly stacked in alphabetical order. The ghosts were all for Carter's opponent.

Carter said he didn't think that was the right way to do. The boss allowed he would do it his way, as he always had. Carter raised a mighty fuss, then called up his friend John Pope, a burial vault salesman, and got him to come over and watch. Carter went off campaigning. Pope stayed after the polls closed, for a wild argument before a crowd of locals. Carter went home to tally the returns with the family. Miss Lillian was apprehensive. "He's so naive," she said, "Just so naive."[58] Soon the trend was clear: defeat. The normal thing to do was be a good sport, try again another day. He had carried his own county handsomely.

Instead, Jimmy gave Gloria that big grin and took off to join John Pope. Pope remembers a transformation: "I saw the real burning desire to win that I had not really seen before. It really meant everything to him." Another old friend recalled that Carter "was terribly indignant and he got on his boxing gloves and hired him a lawyer and he made a fight." The lawyer was Warren Fortson. Together they started collecting affidavits from citizens whose votes had been cast unbeknownst to them or who had seen violations happening. It was scary work. Pope raged at Hurst: "Joe, don't you know there's going to be a hereafter? Don't you know you're not going to get away with it this time?" Hurst told the foreign upstart to go home and added, with *his* grin, "By the way, you may be interested to know, I've put three men in that river out there for doing less than you're doing here today." As Pope and Carter went around importuning frightened folks to contribute affidavits, a Hurst spy or two was always at their elbows, taking notes.[59]

While the fraud was still in process, Carter had gone over to a café and called in the media—the nearby Columbus paper promised to send a reporter. Some hours later he returned to the courthouse and there was the reporter with Joe Hurst, chatting like old school chums on the steps. The resultant story made Carter out a sorehead. Hurst's confidence had basis: among other things, he was an official of the state department of agriculture, was said to control eighty-seven jobs in a community of two thousand less-than-well-off inhabitants.[60]

Pope and Carter made a quick study of the election law. It was hard to find a paragraph Hurst had not violated. They took off for Macon, where the Georgia Democratic party was celebrating the victory of their new young progressive candidate for governor, a lawyer named Carl Sanders. Sanders gave them no more than the time of day. Another possible helper, they were told, had been sent home drunk in a private plane. Pope said, "We couldn't talk with anyone there who had any hope for Jimmy at all, that would even bother to be interested." Carter said, "We could hardly believe it!"[61]

Back home, Jimmy's cousin Don helped him get hold of John Pennington, a reporter for the big-time *Atlanta Journal*. Pennington came down and investigated in person and, as William Greider puts it, his "stories turned Carter's lonely little squabble over a senate seat into a statewide embarrassment."[62] They decided to go to court and hired a slow-talking, quick-thinking Atlanta lawyer, Charles Kirbo, to plead the case. Judge Crowe presided, an aging tobacco chewer who had often said the courts ought to stay out of politics. Kirbo drawled at him about chicken thieves dragging a bush behind them to erase their footprints; afterwards, outside, Kirbo told the judge, an old friend, that if he couldn't see his way clear to a decision, he ought to ask Miss Clara (Mrs. Crowe) to take a look at the case. Next day, the judge ruled for Carter.

But, by a quirk of law, the loser in court was allowed to appeal to the local Democratic party committee, a body controlled by Joe Hurst. A hearing was held, the committee retired a second, the door opened, and Joe announced that Carter had lost again.

This time the ad hoc firm of Carter, Kirbo, Fortson, and Pope set out to appeal to the state Democratic executive committee in Atlanta, through the party secretary. But it turned out the party secretary had gone off on a vacation trip with Carter's opponent's campaign manager. The state party chairman was gone, too. The Saturday before the Tuesday general election, Kirbo tracked the chairman down hunting pheasant near the Canadian border. He explained the situation, convinced the chairman to have the party executive committee declare Carter the nominee, and had the secretary of state order the ballots changed. The Carter team spent Sunday finding the appropriate officials in each of the seven counties, getting the ballots, and hand-stamping each one with his name.

But on Monday the opposition went to court once more. At midnight—seven hours to poll-opening time—the Carterites got a Superior Court judge to order that all the names be struck from the ballots so the voters could write in whom they wanted. Still, in two of the counties, the election officials refused to obey the order since it did not come from the secretary of state. On election day, both candidates blanketed the district with handbills and dinned out radio ads, to try to tell voters how to vote.

Jimmy Carter won by 1,500 votes. Then, sick and tired, he went to bed.[63] In January he went to Atlanta as a state senator. One of the bills he helped get passed in that session was a new election code. Hurst was later convicted of vote fraud in an earlier election and then went to jail for selling moonshine.

At some exuberant moment of the campaign, probably responding to a typical, ignorant question, Carter had promised to read every bill. In Atlanta, he ran into 2,500 bills, surely excuse enough for modifying his intentions. Instead, he took a speedreading course and read them all, which taught him a great deal about the mechanics of government and about the risk of making promises. One of his early speeches was against the notorious "thirty questions"—clever constitutional conundrums composed to confound black citizens who had the temerity to try registering to vote. But he also voted for some segregationist amendments to the state constitution. And he had the gall to oppose a constitutional amendment calling for the worship of God, a move which earned for him, in some quarters, a reputation as an atheist.[64]

But his main reputation in the senate was as a hot shot legislative professional. He got there early and stayed late, five days a week instead of the usual four. He prowled the bureaucratic hallways quizzing startled officials at length about just what they did there. He soaked up facts. Other senators began to turn to him for advice, to accord him a certain authority. After a while, his colleagues voted him one of the five best senators, no doubt a gratifying experience if not quite up to Admiral Rickover's standard. He was put on the appropriations committee and on a special education commission; he served two terms.

That is about what we know, in factual terms, of Jimmy Carter's first independent political success.[65] For the meanings, we must rely on reasonable inference and Carter's own memory of what it meant to him, a memory no doubt shaped by the autobiographical requirements of his campaign for the Presidency. Yet, even if there are distortions, what Carter wanted to make of that experience nevertheless has its importance, because it represents his own marriage of wish and history. And the history, if not yet verified with certainty, can be Carter did not get some secret faker to write his autobiography. (No one I know of has yet suggested that *Why Not the Best?* was written, grammatical errors and all, by anyone other than Jimmy Carter.)

He says he "really learned a lot from this first experience with politics." The unbelievably tangled campaign, he recalls, left this impression:

> I began to realize how vulnerable our political system was to an accumulation of unchallenged power. Honest and courageous people could be quieted when they came to realize that outspoken opposition was fruitless. Those who were timid and insecure could be intimidated. The dishonest could band together to produce and divide the spoils, and they could easily elect officials who most often seemed respectable but who would cooperate in order to gain a title or an office. Jury lists and voter lists could be controlled. Welfare recipients and other dependent people could be aided or deprived. Political favors could be delivered to high officials. And the local news media sometimes looked the other way.
>
> But there were other lessons I learned, too. The most vital was that people intimidated by corrupt public officials don't necessarily like it; if given some leadership and a chance, they are willing to stand up and be counted on the side of decency and of honest politics and government.[66]

That first style-stamping experience extended on into his senate service, from which he wants to remember that he learned:

> The confusion and complications of state government were almost unbelievable. There were many niches in which special interests could hide. . . . Once a program had been in operation for a year, there was little likelihood that it would ever be closely examined again. It would just grow inexorably like a fungus, slowly absorbing for itself larger and larger responsibilities and budgets. . . . It is difficult for the common good to prevail against the intense concentration of those who have a special interest, especially if the decisions are made behind locked doors. What occurred was not illegal, but it was wrong. The 259 members of the legislature were almost all good and honest men and women. A tiny proportion were not good and honest. In the absence of clear and comprehensive issues, it is simply not possible to marshal the interest of the general public. . . . Those who make decisions in our government are most often relatively isolated from the citizens most affected by the decisions. . . . Even the most compassionate business or political leader is often prevented by his natural experience from understanding the particular problems of those most needy for whom he is concerned.

The effectiveness of a government bureau responsible for social programs has dramatically different import for public officials and the recipients of services. . . . It is obvious that almost inherently the weak, poor, inarticulate, and illiterate citizens feel most severely the consequences of society's ills, and thus contribute to the perpetuation and even aggravation of the problems faced by us all. . . . Secrecy is an increasingly pervasive aspect of our governmental process, and with only one or two exceptions is unnecessary and counterproductive. Leaders who deliberately hide their actions from the people rarely do so with benevolent motives. . . . *There is nothing illegal or immoral about all of this. But it must be recognized for what it is.* . . . Our own basic law, as expressed in historic documents and in court decisions, does represent a striving for justice and fairness, but the practical result often falls far short of our hopes and expectations.[67]

In addition to the political conclusions he drew from that early experience, from the campaign and from his senate service, there were also, I infer, some lessons about himself, and their sticking power was all the stronger because what he did succeeded. As with other Presidents-to-be, his history showed a pattern: he had emerged from the relative obscurity of Plains to the relative prominence of Atlanta. His family helped him, not only by energetic campaigning but also by providing a familiarity with political doings and a family-sanctioned activity. But *he* had taken the initiative—he was not drafted—and he had insisted on seeing the fight through to the end. Once in the senate, he made his own way. He had demonstrated a side of his character not that clear before: he could be "stubborn as a South Georgia turtle," as an old politician said of him.[68]

Carter had won with a rhetoric of indignation, an appeal to the better and braver civic mind, friends-and-neighbors politicking, and the display of a character bent on excellence (as in the promise to read every bill). Issues, in the sense of concrete, detailed proposals for government action, appear to have played little part. But once in office, he spoke of programs which included comprehensive plans for reform in education, taxation, mental health, election law, and budgeting. There are no tales of spellbinding speeches, dramatic revelations, high-powered public relations techniques, witty epigrams, or philosophic peregrinations. But the way the people's government cheated the vulnerable made him mad—the madder because he himself had almost been cheated out of legitimate victory—and he said so. He wrote his own material.

He excelled at his political and governmental homework, as he had at Miss Julia's. He proved a quick study, not only learning such facts as happened to come his way, but actively searching out needed information, old and new. In the process, he "became an expert on many unimportant matters," but, in the campaign and in the senate, he learned to link his empiricism to realistic and goal-directed uses—he got facts for a purpose.[69] There is no evidence that he was overly affected by the social sciences.

In these early stories, it is hard to tell how good Carter was at negotiation. In the Plains years he seems to have been something of a loner (setting aside family ties), though he and Rosalynn had a few young married friends. The business was a family affair, though it must have involved business dealings with suppliers and customers. In the campaign crisis, he quickly recruited an effective team. Kirbo is still with him, Pope came back to see him in the governor's office with an appeal for a break in insurance policy (which Carter, gently, turned down), and Fortson, from a distance, still follows his career. But even in his own account of the senate years, there is very little "we," very little sense of the collaborative, and almost no mention of the many names a team politician would have relished recalling. Indeed, there are only two names in Carter's chapter on his senate years, neither a colleague: Horace Tate, executive director of the black teachers' organization, who, the author notes, "became one of my early supporters when I ran for state office"; and Reinhold Niebuhr, known to Carter through his books, the man who "observes the sad duty of politics is to establish justice in a sinful world."[70] He dwells—though unrancorously—on the sins of the legislative world, but what is missing is pleasure and practice in the give and take, even the friendships, many a member has found rewarding. His colleagues admired him as a brain, but one misses any claims of the heart. He made himself a leader, but the ordinary playful palling around, which facilitates both corruption and fruitful compromise, was not part of his style.

IN AND OUT OF THE SLOUGH OF DESPOND: 1966

He was riding high again. A fellow legislator said he ought to run for lieutenant governor. Carter grinned and said, "Why *lieutenant* governor?"[71]

Georgia Democrats, meanwhile, had been riding low. In the year of Lyndon Johnson's landslide, 1964, Barry Goldwater swept Georgia, the first Republican Presidential candidate to win there since Reconstruction. Miss Lillian ran the county Democratic headquarters for that election. Repeatedly, her car was soaped and the aerial knotted. Son Chip, aged fourteen, got beat up at school for wearing a Democratic button. Worse, in the larger scheme, Republican Howard "Bo" Callaway (later Nixon's Secretary of the Army and Ford's campaign manager) carried Carter's home district and became their Congressman. Callaway's ideology had been plastic enough for him to switch parties, and by 1966 he was dangling off the right Republican wing; his bumper sticker said, "I fight poverty—I work."[72] He was very popular, unopposed for his party's nomination.

In 1966 Carter decided to go after Callaway. He announced his candidacy for Congress right after the senate adjourned that spring, and took off campaigning. Suddenly he got a lucky break: the leading Democratic candidate for governor dropped out and Callaway shifted his ambition to the governorship. Carter could sail into the Congressional seat. But here and there, people began that mysterious "mentioning" process which has produced many a candidacy. Who could possibly beat Callaway for governor? Maybe Jimmy Carter. And Carter, in classic response, began to think, "Why not?" He and his friends studied the statistics and developed the usual bloated estimates of potential money support. Carter gave up safety and reached for danger. There were personal dimensions to this decision, for Callaway was a West Point graduate, a "wealthy textile heir," leader of the "Young Republicans" arrayed against Carter's "Young Democrats," the man who had tried to thwart Carter's crusade to get a four-year college in southwest Georgia. "When we were around each other," Carter remembered, "both of us were somewhat tense."[73]

To take on Callaway, Carter had first to get the Democratic nomination. Lots of candidates besides Carter had heard the call, but the race winnowed down to former Governor Ellis Arnall, a liberal, Lester Maddox, a downspout demagogic populist race-baiter, and Jimmy Carter, an unknown—"Jimmy Who?" the newspapers dubbed him. Carter put on another whirlwind campaign, though less amateurish this time. He wore off twenty-two pounds and wore out his vocal cords. One of his orations was: "If I ever let you down in my actions, I want you to let me know about it and I'll correct it. I promise never to betray your confidence in me."[74] All he needed to do was finish second to qualify for the runoff. Near the end, the Carters thought it looked good.

He finished third. Maddox won the runoff. Callaway got the most votes in the general election, but another crazy quirk in the Georgia constitution let the Democratically controlled legislature pick the governor from the two top vote-getters, and they chose Maddox. With perhaps a little maternal dramatization, Miss Lillian's memory is that her Jimmy "cried like a baby."[75]

But memories vary, Gloria says he rested a few days, then took his family to the beach and "came home talking about the shrimp boats, went down to the office and started talking about the next campaign." Kirbo set up a November fundraising dinner at which Carter, who was toasted by all factions, intimated, in the glow of appreciation, that "There may yet be another day."[76]

Ruth remembers, from that same time, a broken Jimmy who called her home to share "the personal, big secret" of his despair, and "that moment of sitting out in that woods under the tree when Jimmy's whole life went before him, as he held his face up, the tears were just falling, and he said, 'Ruth, I don't know how I hesitated. I'll give up everything. I would rather have what you have than to even be President of the United States.' "[77]

"Jimmy did talk to Ruth," Rosalynn remembers, "and she did have an impact on him—but there was none of this going out under the pine trees and having some sort of religious experience."[78]

Jimmy Carter remembers—well, all and none of the above. He did walk in the woods with Ruth and she did ask him if he would be willing to give up politics, but—as he recalls—"I thought for a long time and had to admit that I would not." In *Why Not the Best?* he sails right by—"My church life became far more meaningful to me"—and on into the peanut business. But it was no jolly time: "I was going through a stage in my life then that was a very difficult one. I had run for governor and lost. Everything I did was not gratifying. When I succeeded in something, it was a horrible experience for me."[79]

Such is the nature of biography. When life is happening, no one feels any great need to make a narrative of mixed experience, and when that is later demanded, art shapes memory.

What was to trouble, inspire, and confuse different multitudes in times to come was that Jimmy Carter became a Christian. In 1976, article after article would plumb his soul and many a reporter would have to cram fast on this strange religion, as if it were some ethnological eccentricity brought back from Pago Pago by Margaret Mead. It would scare nervous pragmatists, who don't mind Christians as long as they don't really mean it. And it would conjure up burning crosses, rabid literalists, Wilsonian rigidity, Nixon's prayer breakfasts, and many another ghost of "Christians" past.

The Carters had always been Christians in the relaxed sense of the American vocabulary. Each evening, Earl had the children come down in their pajamas and bend against him to say their prayers. He taxied them to church on Sunday, though as often as not he would leave them there while he strolled downtown for some unsanctified conversation. Miss Lillian attended services, but she was no "churchophile": "I'm a Christian, the way I see it. But I do a lot of things the ladies of the church think I shouldn't do. . . . I think there's a difference between religion and Christianity. . . . I think I'm on the right side of God. I think He likes what I do."[80]

In his own religious (in Miss Lillian's sense) life, Jimmy Carter had exceeded the requirements, like a First Class Scout bucking for Eagle. He was baptized at the regular time and taught Sunday school at eighteen. When he got homesick as an Annapolis freshman, he went to the chapel and prayed. He volunteered to teach a Sunday school class of ten-year-old girls (including the admiral's daughter), and he brought some religious arguments to bear in student discussions "about why we are here, who made us, where we should go, what's our purpose." On shipboard, he taught Sunday-school some more and led the submariners in an Easter service. Back in Plains, he took over Earl's place as a deacon, again taught Sunday school, went with the pastor on recruiting visits for the annual week-long, revival service, and spoke in neighboring communities on such topics as "Christian Witnessing."[81] A friend gave him a copy of *Reinhold Niebuhr on Politics*[82] and they had some talks about it; indeed, the friend remembers it became "a political Bible" for Carter, and that the two of them concluded that "love and kindness meant a great deal in one-to-one relationships but not in dealings with structures and corporate groups."[83]

All these things were going through Carter's mind before the fall of 1966, in a Georgia Eden, before the fruit of the tree of knowledge had been eaten: "I never knew anything except going to church. My wife and I were born and raised in innocent times. The normal thing to do was to go to church."[84]

Politics delivers its verdicts harshly. In 1966 Carter could not, like a business executive denied a promotion, keep it in the family, say he had been "reassigned": he had been *defeated*, despite all his competence and energy and élan. Nor, he found, could he fall back at ease among "the normal things." Something was gnawing at him. Sitting in his pew in the Plains Baptist Church, he heard the preacher demand to know, "If you were arrested for being a Christian, would there be enough evidence to convict you?" The thought crossed his mind, "I could probably talk my way out of it!" and the thought came back when, preparing a speech, he methodically added up all the "visits I had made for God"—an impressive 140. Suddenly he remembered the campaign and the enormous energies he had poured into that—"300,000 visits for myself in three months, and 140 visits for God in fourteen years!" He read the Book of Luke, "to understand more clearly the admonitions about pride and self-satisfaction." Big deal Jimmy Carter. He was no Christian; he was "the Pharisee," loudly advertising how wonderful he was.[85]

His reaction was to try hard and do better. "I began to expand my personal service in the church"; he made more speeches, to as many as 5,000, traveling to Pennsylvania and Massachusetts for week-long missionary stints. In the midst of his hot campaign for governor in 1970—this time to win *for sure*— he excused himself for a week to work at a mission in an Atlanta slum.[86]

Underneath all the action, though, something was going on; examples were sinking in. Ruth had been with him when Earl died and his hidden ways of loving were revealed. In the late 1950s, approaching her thirtieth year, Ruth, drowning in a suburban swamp of children, chauffeuring, tennis lessons—that I-can't-do-it-all feeling so many mothers of the 1950s shared, not knowing they shared it, feeling it was "Their Fault they could not find Happiness"—Ruth said the hell with it and broke down. Somehow she got to a place called Camp Fartherest Out, a religious retreat from which she painfully, then exuberantly, advanced to newness of life. Healed, she took up healing. Like Earl, she hid that from the Carters of Plains at first. But as she campaigned with brother Jimmy in the summer of 1966, he could tell she had a secret, some deep tide unaffected by the surface winds and waves. That is what she got across to Jimmy, that time in the woods.

Other strands began to draw together. In those business years before he got hot for politics, he often sat alone in the warehouse office, whittling, thinking, reading poetry. Miss Julia's kind tyranny had left him with a taste for literature; he and Rosalynn used to listen to records of Dylan Thomas reading aloud. They pondered the stanzas. Carter puzzled particularly over the last line of Thomas's "A Refusal to Mourn the Death, by Fire, of a Child in London," which goes, at the last, like this:

> Deep with the first dead lies London's daughter,
> Robed in the long friends,
> The grains beyond age, the dark veins of her mother,
> Secret by the unmourning water
> Of the riding Thames.
> After the first death, there is no other.[87]

Something was working on Lillian Carter that same year of 1966. She saw on television an ad for the Peace Corps that noted "Age is no barrier" so she applied, was accepted, went to the University of Chicago to learn two dialects, and was gone for two years of nursing duty with sick and dying people in India. She left in her sixty-eighth year and came back in a wheelchair, thirty pounds lighter.

Over there, despite all her sturdy strength, Miss Lillian became intimately acquainted with death and discouragement. "India was killing me," she said. "I just couldn't bear it. I couldn't touch the dirt, the blood, the lice, the leprosy. I hadn't the strength to bear the horrible cruelty and indifference." She got off by herself and closed her eyes and asked for something. "And Christ let something come into me, and I knew I could do anything. I could wipe up blood . . . and blood had always appalled me, and I could touch leprosy without running to scrub my hands raw. I could stay in India."[88]

Earl was dead, Lillian away, when Jimmy, their defeated first-born son, took off on the first of those missionary ventures, to Lock Haven, Pennsylvania. He and an aging Texan (who, as it happened, was also a peanut farmer) had a hundred families to call upon. Carter went along as number two man, listening while the Texan, who had trouble with words, haltingly had his say. "Oh, I could do much better," Carter thought, but the old man got across somehow and Carter began to stick his oar into these unfamiliar waters. "I soon realized," he said, "that when I thought I had failed, that was the very time when the people were convinced . . . and I realized that it wasn't me or my brilliance or my fervor that made the difference. It was something else." He called up Rosalynn to tell her about it. She said, "Jimmy, you don't sound like the same person. You sound almost like you're intoxicated." He said, "Well, in a way I am."[89]

The other time he took off for Springfield, Massachusetts, rehearsing his Spanish for work in the Puerto Rican ghetto there. The former aspirant for Chief of Naval Operations bunked in the YMCA with a team led by a husky Cuban named Eloy Cruz. Mornings, afternoons, and evenings they knocked on door after door, often meeting anger at the disturbance. Once they found an old couple with an infant. The child's mother had been killed in a freak accident and the young father had gone berserk, tried to kill himself and the baby. They pressed money on the old people. Making their last visit on a later day, in a cold rain, by accident they found the father, barricaded behind his door. "We know your baby," Cruz said. The door opened and they talked with him, urged him not to kill himself. Carter's memory suddenly found some words to say to him: "Behold, I stand at the door and knock: if any man hear my voice, and open the door, I will come to him, and will sup with him." Somehow, the young man chose life.[90]

Carter was puzzled by Cruz. How did it work? Cruz said, "You only need to have two loves: one for God, and one for the person who happens to be standing in front of you at any given moment." And when they said good-bye to one another, Carter asked his friend how a rugged guy like him could be so gentle. Cruz's embarrassment drew him back to his mother tongue: "Senor Jaime, Nuestro Salvador tiene los manos que son muy suaves, y El no puede hacer mucho con un hombre que es duro."[91]

In his campaign for the Presidency, Carter was at first reticent about the faith he had found, and then, as questions kept focusing on it, he tried to explain:

In 1967 . . . I formed a very close, intimate relationship with God, through Christ, that has given me a great deal of peace. . . . It was not a profound stroke of miracle. It wasn't a voice of God from heaven. It wasn't anything of that kind.

It wasn't mysterious. It might have been the same kind of experience as millions of people have who do become Christians in a deeply personal way. . . . I don't think God is going to make me President by any means. But whatever I have as a responsibility for the rest of my life, it will be with that intimate personal continuing relationship.[92]

God created us in his own image, hoping that we'd be perfect, and we turned out to be not perfect but very sinful. And then when Christ was asked what are the two Great Commandments from God which should direct our lives, he said, "To love God with all your heart and soul and mind, and love your neighbor as yourself." So I try to take that condensation of Christian theology and let it be something through which I search for a meaningful existence. I don't worry about it too much any more.[93]

Still, what was that "something" that kept showing up in the most amazing places? In the end it was not an argument, but a story. And its meaning was in an old song, Jimmy's favorite from childhood on, written the year after his earliest Plains-buried ancestor was born, by an Englishman who had "servant of slaves" carved on his tombstone.[94] Grown-up Carter could hear how it sounded, after the voices found themselves in the first verse:

'Twas grace that taught my heart to fear,
And grace my fears relieved;
How precious did that grace appear,
The hour I first believed.[95]

THE ROAD TO WASHINGTON: 1976

Against lots of wise advice, Jimmy Carter went on to run for governor once again, in 1970, and this time he won. He continued to grow—inside and in the office—but the basics of his character, world view, and style, developed in those early years, were there to build on. The nomination race, against "a topsy-turvy grab bag of candidates," was another supercharged, all-out effort. The most considerable of the candidates was Carl Sanders, the former governor who, when Carter was being flim-flammed out of his senate nomination, had had no helping hand. Carter beat Sanders in a rough campaign, lit into him as a fancy-pants, do-nothing establishmentarian. Carter raised some themes the symbolic analysts could link to George Wallace ("Isn't it time somebody spoke up for *you?*"), and some of his staffers went too far in their enthusiastic inventiveness, as when they encouraged racism in depicting Sanders as an integrationist. And when Carter's running mate turned out to be none other than Lester Maddox, Carter said more than he probably meant: Maddox was "the essence of the Democratic party . . . he has compassion for the ordinary man. I'm proud to be on the ticket with him." But he also consistently called for fairness to blacks and whites and promised that qualifications, not race, would rule in making appointments. "Blacks should be treated the same as whites, have the same privileges and responsibilities as whites," he said. And in his inaugural address he reached back to the theme of the early Tom Watson: "Our *people* are our most precious possession" and "The time for racial discrimination is over." As governor, he increased the number of black state employees by 50 percent (to about 11,000 of 50,000); on state boards and commissions he found only two blacks, and appointed 53 more; he organized effective biracial disorder units, had the Reverend Martin Luther King, Jr.'s portrait hung in the state capitol, and started 136 day care centers run by welfare mothers. Julian Bond, civil rights leader and state senator, found him rigid and unreasonable, but it was hard to find any evidence that he was a racist.[96]

His report on his years as governor is organized under specific headings ("Sickle Cell Anemia," "Cash Management") with sections under each on "Unmet Needs," "Action," and "Results." The results of his reforms were exaggerated in his 1976 campaign, making it easy for critics to obscure the fact that they had been substantial. Government reorganization, for example, did not really reduce three hundred agencies to twenty-two, because in fact there had only been sixty-five *budgeted* agencies when he began; the rest were on paper. So were 2,100 jobs his campaign claimed he eliminated. Actually, state employment rose substantially, and unlike some previous governors, he let compassion rule over efficiency by waiting out retirements and resignations rather than firing people.[97] What is clear above the details is a comprehensive approach, based on close study and a long view, resulting in more than incremental gains, over a wide variety of policy fields. He also involved himself personally in several engineering-type problems, such as how to mow the grass along the highways, and how to put handicapped people to work typing forms.

Carter's legislative relations were often stormy. He would not play the customary patronage and special privilege games, and many felt this traced to a personal failing. Hamilton Jordan, then his executive secretary, said that "Jimmy is not easy to get close to. He doesn't have enough time in his life to let people get close. He doesn't understand the personal element in politics, though nobody is better at campaigning." Not that he was withdrawn: he was constantly dealing with members, showering them with facts, and he once spent a whole day on the House floor speaking for his cherished reorganization plan. But he was late to compromise, hard to convince. Again, though, the proof was in the pudding. When he came in, he had only about fifteen supporters against some 250 opponents and indifferents. Yet he got the legislation through, most of the most important of it, even though his reorganization plan passed by only one vote. By that time, he and Lester Maddox were no longer even political friends, and when Maddox tried to block the bill, from his position as presiding officer of the senate, he found that he didn't have clout enough to beat the governor. Some called Carter "Jungle Jimmy."[98]

He made extraordinary efforts to connect with the citizenry. Support for the reorganization plan was mustered in fifty-one meetings throughout the state, for example, and he set a day a month aside for ordinary Georgians to come in and talk. There was a governor's phone line, a rotating crew of mansion guides recruited from all over, ready reception for citizen's groups, and, when the legislature faltered, dramatic appeals to "the people."

Through all these roils, Carter kept a certain humor, especially about the supposed grandeur of his high office. In a 1973 speech he told this tale on himself:

> Early one morning, immediately following my campaign, when I made my first foray into the rest of Georgia after becoming Governor, I went into a restaurant in southwest Georgia and I asked for an order of hotcakes and the girl in there brought me one little piece of butter. After I had finished about half the hotcakes, I called her over and I told her that if she didn't mind I'd like to have some more butter. She turned around and walked away and said, "No." I figured she didn't understand what I meant so, the next time she came around, which was quite a while later, I said, "Young lady, would you come over here a minute please; I'd like to have another pat of butter." And she said, "No," and she left again. Finally, I asked the security man who was with me to go get her and bring her back. When she walked over, I said, "Listen, I don't want to make an issue of this, but I want some more butter." She said, "You're not going to have it." And, I said, "Do you know who I am?" She said, "Who?" And I said, "I'm the Governor of Georgia." She said, "Do you know who I am?" I said, "No." She said, "I'm the keeper of the butter."[99]

Already his mind's eye was turning to even greater glories. He and Rosalynn got a jigsaw puzzle map of the United States of America, to master where the states were. And after much thought and planning and hustling, a little event in Iowa brought the Carter blip onto the national radar screen. A straw poll at a dinner (carefully packed by the Carter team) showed him first choice, and a front page story in the *New York Times* said, "Carter Appears to Hold a Solid Lead in Iowa as the Campaign's First Test Approaches."[100]

PREDICTION

Predicting President Carter

Carter was not averse to categorizing himself: "I am a Southerner and an American. I am a farmer, an engineer, a father and a husband, a Christian, a politician and a former governor, a planner, a businessman, a nuclear physicist, a naval officer, a canoeist, and, among other things, a lover of Bob Dylan's songs and Dylan Thomas' poetry." Yet, he felt, people too often got him wrong. "I'm a human being," he said, "I'm not a packaged article that you can put in a little box and say, 'Here's a Southern Baptist, an ignorant peanut farmer who doesn't have the right to enjoy music, who has no flexibility in his mind, who can't understand the sensitivities of an interpersonal relationship. He's got to be predictable.'"[101]

Much as Carter might wish otherwise, the people had to predict about him, had to guess from what he had been what he would be as President. As they puzzled with that problem in 1976, Carter said, "Sometimes I think people look too hard. They're looking for something that isn't there. I don't think I'm that complex. I'm pretty much what I seem to be."[102] But like every human being, he contained multitudes. The problem was to pick, from those crowds of identities, the ones which would shape his Presidency, and thus our lives.

Shakespeare taught us that one can smile and smile and be a villain; Eisenhower taught us that a smile can conceal a sense of botheration. Even Nixon could smile while his insides ground, and old Bill Taft, with his "Smile, Smile, Smile" motto, had a largely dismal time trying to be President. So it is not to the now-famous Carter grin we must look for signs of political happiness, but to the self, discernible, however dimly and indirectly, in his life experiences and his reactions to that experience.

No one questions his activity. He is, has been, and will be an extraordinarily energetic person and politician, up-and-at-'em, day after day, often right past the lunch hour and into that afternoon period when your average politician wants a drink. His friend Charles Kirbo calls him a "workaholic and a playaholic." The roots of that active orientation toward life go all the way back, to a childhood in which energetic performance was mightily reinforced, and the child discovered that exertion brought better rewards than withdrawal or passivity.

I believe he will also turn out to be a pleasured President, finding, as did FDR and HST and JFK, that life in the Oval Office can be fun—is, on the average. He has taken the unusual step of writing his own autobiography, a precedent, one hopes, for all future Presidential aspirants. In it he recounts remembered reactions of normal joy, punctuated to be sure with crises of the spirit. But he dwells on the pleasures, the positive possibilities, as he did in his boyhood list of "Healthy Mental Habits." He will be an active-positive President.

Confidence in that prediction is strengthened by the confidence his upbringing gave him. The trauma of his first two years was surmounted and he became a healthy, happy child, thanks to his mother's luck and determination. Jimmy's self-esteem drew on hers: he could feel her steady presence, hear her laughter, see her own confident independence. He grew up in the bosom of a family of "characters," all of whom, for all their differences, loved him—even Gloria, even Earl with his peach tree switch. Life in all its buzzing variety was there to be enjoyed, and that he did. His being was not smothered in spoiling concentration—Lillian and Earl had their own lives to lead. But they were *there* and he could count on them, not only for sustenance but also for nurture and encouragement. Life for Jimmy Carter, from near the start, was no dismal duty. It was an adventure.

Home base was a place to hit home runs from. He quested way out beyond what anyone could reasonably expect of a child of Plains: to college, to high naval affairs, to the political top of his state and nation. But he kept coming back—for good, he thought once. Even when Plains became a kind of headquarters for Presidential kitsch, he could remember and draw upon its genuineness. He is a rooted man who knows where home is. That, too, should contribute to a sense that he can grow beyond his roots.

Like the other active-positive Presidents, his character-based troubles are going to spring from an excess of an active-positive virtue: the thirst for results. The temptation to go ahead and get some high thing done by some temporary low route may swing him off course, as with Roosevelt and the Court, Kennedy and the Castro problem. But like them, he is unlikely to persevere in an obviously losing line of action. Carter has been stubborn as a south Georgia turtle, but his stubbornness has not extended to self-defeat. That is because, like his favorite President Harry Truman, he has his eyes open. Like Truman, he leans in the active-negative direction but is unlikely to let his strain of compulsiveness push him over the brink.

Carter's world view, politically speaking, was there before he found amazing grace. This is important for his Presidency in two senses. First, his beliefs about people and history and political morality connect with the broadest streams of American tradition, which, while profoundly affected by Christianity, wash on wider shores. Jefferson's cool deism could take in the Carter conception of a fundamentally virtuous citizenry, who, given the chance, could impart to a government of their own a yeomanly rectitude. Harry Truman, a very Lightfoot Baptist, could go along with Carter's sense that leadership vigorously and visibly exercised can rally social energy by enspiriting people, reminding them of strengths they had forgotten. And Hannah Arendt could have conversed easily with Carter about the "banality of evil" and the easy ways the great pervert the law. Carter has not hidden his belief in Jesus Christ— his faith forbids that—but his politics do not derive, in the order of his experience, from texts and languages foreign to the secular American vocabulary.

To put that in predictive form: Carter the President will try to call to the American spirit as, say, Theodore Roosevelt did, not as Billy Sunday did.

Second, but first in terms of the personal meaning of his politics, Carter's trust in Christ is a democratic resource. Christianity is one root of democracy. The idea of equal justice under law, for example, did not spring full blown from the brows of the Founding Fathers. Carter the Christian *person* sees a world lit by a transforming Presence, layered over a darker world where justice needs establishing, where mercy, reached for, may be missed. Historically, what politicians have done in the name of Christianity gives pause, for that has included both the Inquisition and the Emancipation Proclamation and all sorts of other enslavements and liberations. In Carter's experience, however, faith extends the democratic impulse, and presses him outward toward a loving relationship with "the person who happens to be standing in front of you." It reminds him on the one hand, of the dignity of the individual, however short he may fall of "competence," and, on the other, of the natural tendency earthly powers have to see that their own bread is buttered first

But it reaches far deeper than that, into his character, demonstrating that significant character change after the early years of life, though improbable, can happen. And in that dimension, Carter's convictions will, I think, prove even more important to his politics. The experience of conversion from casual to serious Christianity was, for him, a letting go, an inner surrender of pride, which freed him from resting the case for his self-esteem wholly on the shaky argument of secular "success." He recognizes in himself a tendency toward pontification and too harsh a judgment of his fellow humans, but his religion is a religion of forgiveness and renewal. Politically, I think this helps him stay open to "ideas whose time has come"—a wonderful concept which allows a polity to forgive itself for yesterday and move on out into tomorrow. Thus I think people who worry that Carter will try to impose some Baptist conformity—which cannot even be imposed on Baptists—or that he, like Wilson, will come to confuse some line of policy with the will of God, are wrong. Carter's religion is not a conclusion; it is a search.

The Carter style will prove most clearly strong in the homework element. To exceptional intelligence he adds exceptional curiosity, memory, and the logical capacity to link large ideas to deep data bases. I doubt he will often be caught with his facts down—for example, in press conferences. But when he is shown to be mistaken, he will admit it and correct it—perhaps not right away, but in time. If the past is any guide, he will organize his intellectual life around comprehensive, long-range goals, and show impatience with incremental thinking.

Carter's rhetoric will take getting used to. As his managers realized, he has that magic television appearance and conversational mode of discourse they used to call "Kennedy cool." Once in office, his rhetoric may take on a more practical and programmatic flavor. But he is likely to carry over from campaigning a penchant for idealistic expression, for grand appeals to the best in people. Nor is he likely to lose that edge of indignation which is, in his performances, all the more powerful for being rare. The press will, as ever, switch back and forth between their images of Christian Carter and Jungle Jimmy, but they will find him hard to report in the traditional ways because he was given to pronouncing absolutes as if they were about to happen and then, of all things, apologizing when they don't. Like every President he will be misunderstood and will himself contribute to the misunderstanding. As in the past, he will try to reach past his media translators, going directly to the people, and he will pick and choose among reporters when it comes to access. A frequent charge against him will be excessive optimism, and he will find it frustrating when his high purposes are no longer news but his fumbles in pursuing them are. Yet it is obvious that he has found rhetorical themes which resonate strongly with intense public needs. That will be his strong point.

His stylistic weak point is negotiation. It is a mistake to suppose that good negotiation consists of instant collapse and agreement with all other sides. A good negotiator presses hard and then knows when to yield something to gain something better. Carter has brought that off in the past, but in a different context, by remaining adamant nearly to the end. But Washington is not Atlanta: his Congressional and bureaucratic negotiating partners have much stronger bases of their own than had their Georgia counterparts. If he runs true to form, he will try to envelop the whole negotiating process in transcendent purposes, will invoke the goal to aid the deal. But particularly because he would feel contagiously uncomfortable in old Sam Rayburn's "Board of Education" gatherings, and because he will be strongly tempted to go public when his opponents are verging on success, Carter will have a rough time selling legislators on the idea that it is incumbent on *them* to follow the maxim: "To get along, go along."

What he has going for him in the power structure is formidable. His party controls Congress, and thus Congressional Democrats have a stake in his success. They recognize how low the public has come to rate them: it took an impeachment drama to display their virtuous aspect. Most Congressmen would just as soon keep living in Washington—but, year by year, more and more of them seem less and less dependent on party and President to keep their seats. And for all its party disarray, Congress is organizationally and administratively stronger now, by a long shot, than it was only a few years ago. So the point is not that they will fall into line behind President Carter as their forebears fell in behind Franklin Roosevelt or that Carter will try or succeed in "purging" them if they do not. Rather, their stake is in an achieving government, in which their contribution is clear, lest the electorate lapse into a blind, throw-the-rascals-out surliness. Therefore, I think, Congress and Carter will fight, and out of their wrangling will come substantial, visible new thrusts toward real progress.

Similarly, the bureaucracy has a stake in the Carter administration. Fearful of being shuffled out, they are also hopeful of being brought back into decision-making and achievement by a President who knows a lot about what they do. On both fronts, then, Carter is likely to find hard fights and important successes.

The Court is inscrutable, stocked with aging liberals and relatively young conservatives. They may lean to oppose this Democrat, but how and on what is unpredictable. And the world scene is too chaotic to characterize intelligibly.

But in the end, it is the developing national mood, the climate of expectations, which will be most fateful for President Carter. We have become a nation of uneasy skeptics, suspicious of all the powers that be, listening in the political cacophony for some reliable theme. Carter has an enormous advantage in following Nixon, who was thought to be unprincipled, and Ford, who was thought to be incompetent. But uneasy eyes are on him. The politics of gestures will not sustain hope long, and political faith is fragile. It will take achievement—real progress—to convince a nervous nation that this President named Jimmy is The People's man.

JIMMY CARTER REVIEWED

The preceding prediction, written and published before Carter became President, turned out—as we should always expect—to be imperfect. But the basics anticipated did happen. What the review of Carter's Presidency brings out best, I think, is that the voter's assessment needs to reach beyond character to style, beyond the personality to the person's methods of operation.

Carter was not the first President to face that problem.

By the time George Washington had decided he simply could not escape the duty to be President, he put his mind to the question of how being President should be done. On May 10, 1789, he wrote at length to John Adams, Alexander

Hamilton, and John Jay, seeking advice on managing Presidential vicinity. How much time should he set aside for "receiving visits of Compliment"? Would it "tend to prompt impertinent applications and involve disagreeable consequences" to announce his availability for business callers every morning at eight? Could he rotate dinner invitations among "official characters," including Congressmen, "without exciting clamours in the rest of the Community"? And "in what light would his appearance *rarely at Tea* parties be considered"? Washington explained why he asked:

> Many things which appear of little importance in themselves and at the beginning, may have great and durable consequences from their having been established at the commencement of a new general government. It will be much easier to commence the administration, upon a well adjusted system built on tenable grounds, than to correct errors or alter inconveniencies after they shall have been confirmed by habit. The President in all matters of business and etiquette, can have no object but to demean himself in his public character, in such a manner as to maintain the dignity of Office, without subjecting himself to the imputation of superciliousness or unnecessary reserve. Under these impressions, he asks for your candid and undisguised Opinions.[103]

Like the first President, though a good deal later in his term, the thirty-ninth President confronted the human relations question and sought out "completely frank" advice. In July, 1979, Carter asked not three, but several platoons of advisors, official and civilian, to join him at Camp David for an exercise in critical analysis. They gave it to him straight. Carter sat on the floor and took notes. "It's not easy for me to accept criticism and to reassess my ways of doing things," he confessed to his diary.[104] On May 30, 1979, President Carter had a dinner at the White House for some nongovernment people. I was invited, but could not attend because that was the evening my daughter Sara graduated from nursing school in Chicago. In attendance were Daniel Bell, John Gardner, Bill Moyers, Christopher Lasch, Haynes Johnson, Jesse Jackson, and Charles Peters, along with Patrick Caddell, Jody Powell, and Rosalynn Carter. Several participants agree it was an awkward evening. The President seemed to be seeking confirmation that his problems could be traced to some malady of the public. The guests thought he had himself to blame.[105] I was not invited to the Camp David meetings in July 1979. Far from unanimous in counselling what he ought to do, Carter's critics almost all agreed that his Presidency was foundering, with its inadequacies already "confirmed in habit" nearly three years after his election. The following year, 1980, the voters tossed him out, preferring as President none other than Ronald Reagan. The Washington consensus, apparently concurred in by many west of the Potomac, had Carter as a dud—some would say a disaster, a Presidential catastrophe. Can the relatively optimistic predictions sketched out in the last chapter, written before his inauguration, square with this downbeat outcome? More precisely, how do the specific anticipations of Carter-the-President's character, world view, and style fit or depart from the subsequent reality?

PROMISES, NOT PROGRAM

Like Eisenhower in 1952, Carter in 1976 had run against Washington, indignantly charging the national powers with evil as well as error. Both came upon the Presidential scene—not by accident—just when a public worn out with stories of calculating politicians on the make hungered for a time of moral revitalization, of simpler and straighter virtues, a time to bring back George Washington's spirit to Washington, D.C. When such a prophet at last arrives in the Babylon he has been castigating, he should not be surprised to encounter resistance. There were those in town who did not identify themselves as bad people. Indeed the town was loaded with Very Important Democrats, in and out of Congress, who stood ready to contribute their guiding wisdom to this brash and unlikely outsider—provided he approached them with the appropriate deference. Given some luck and a lot of diplomacy, Carter might have been able to mobilize a considerable governmental force. In the House, big, bluff Thomas P. O'Neill, Jr., "Tip" to his friends, presided as Speaker over a more than two-to-one majority of Democrats, 118 of them elected for the first time in either 1974 or 1976 and thus perhaps ready to share Carter's new directions. In the Senate, majority leader Robert C. Byrd, a stern and steady West Virginian, enjoyed a comfortable margin of votes and the confidence of such Senatorial barons as Muskie, Church, Humphrey, and Long and a relationship of mutual respect with his Republican counterpart, Howard H. Baker. And for all their wariness of welcome, the so-called Washington establishment, including the main media leaders, were prepared to tag along for at least an initial sprint with yet another new President.

As he later recognized, part of Carter's problem was that he came to office without clear priorities for action. He arrived with a rather scattered collection of programmatic ideas which had sprouted in the campaign. But to Carter himself, with his strong moral bent, these fragments were "promises" and he meant to keep them all. What he had was a list. What he lacked, according to his closest aide, Hamilton Jordan, was "a unifying political philosophy that had been affirmed through his election."[106] He came to office with large principles and an eye for detail, but in between, where a coherent program might have been, was a lot of air. His speech writer James Fallows felt the frustration: "You can't inspire people with a jigsaw puzzle."[107] Carter could see he had this problem: he wrote in his diary before his first month in office was over that "Everybody has warned me not to take on too many projects so early in the administration, but it's almost impossible for me to delay something that I see needs to be done."[108] Between his election and inauguration he had undertaken nothing less than "inventorying the country's problems and determining what should be done about as many of them as possible. At least for me, it was natural to move on many fronts at once."[109] He would "have to depend upon, of course, the congressional leaders to decide in which order they will address these major efforts," he said.[110] This scattering of priorities had a predictable outcome.

Carter's first hundred days saw "a jumble of programs and deadlines, forced marches and sudden retreats, which blurred the thrust of his Presidency," as Robert Shogan noted.[111] Near the end of 1978, Carter told Bill Moyers "I feel my life now is one massive multiple-choice examination, where things are put in front of me and I have to make the difficult choice."[112] Out of office, writing his memoirs, Carter thought, "It now seems that it would have been advisable to have introduced our legislation in much more careful phases—not in such a rush."[113]

No clear national emergency (as in 1933) spurred Carter's eclectic program. No one else, in or out of government, appeared to have a strong and clear idea of Democratic priorities for the next four years. Nor has it been typical for other new Presidents to arrive in Washington with a well organized list of priorities in their pockets. But if Carter was going to succeed in negotiating results in Washington, he was at least going to have to say what he wanted most. Eventually, he saw that. He learned, but he learned late, and at least in hindsight he appears as a politician who, time after time, arrives at some nearly self-evident conclusion long after the lesson would have done him any good. There are many examples, culminating in his finding, after the 1980 election, that "my power as a defeated President was not equal to that of one who is expected to remain in office."[114] Surely trying to get Congress to go for everything at once has to rank as a prime mistake, a lapse in the basics of negotiation that Carter and those who helped him might have seen and acted on.

NEGOTIATING WASHINGTON

But the problem went beyond the ordering of priorities. Carter and the Carterites came to town and proceeded to alienate, as if by plan, one after another of the leaders whose cooperation would be essential to their purposes. Whatever these potential allies might have agreed to when they got down to bargaining over the *content* of policy, they quickly took offense when White House manners insulted them.

Carter had little taste for dealing—"not much of a trader," he called himself—and he too often found Congressional delays and machinations not merely hampering, but also "disgusting." After being well battered in Congress, he claimed to have learned a lesson: "We had an overly optimistic impression," he told the *New York Times,* "that I could present a bill to Congress that seemed patently in the best interests of the country and the Congress would take it and pretty well pass it. I have been disabused of that expectation."[115] Later, too, he saw his Washington problem more clearly: that "having run deliberately and profitably as one who had never been part of the Washington scene, I was not particularly eager to change my attitude after becoming President. This proved to be a mistake."[116] How he had supposed one might accomplish a reformation of government without participation in or persuasion of Washington remains a mystery. He did not always agree with Hamilton Jordan, but Jordan's view may not have been far from his own: returning to Washington after the election of 1980, Jordan reports, "For almost four years, the Washington establishment had been like a pack of jackals, lurking near a wounded animal, smelling its blood, but hiding in the bushes and peering out only from time to time. Now that their prey was dead, they descended on the carcass with a vengeance."[117]

But Carter did not have to like Congressmen. What he did have to do was win them, and there was no chance of achieving that without, as preliminary step number one, telling them what he was up to. If there is any one way to destroy the cooperation good government depends upon, it is to surprise your friends.

Speaker O'Neill's surprise began when he showed up for the inaugural gala at the John F. Kennedy Center, his $300 tickets in hand, and discovered he had been given seats in the last two rows of the gallery. Next day he phoned Jordan with a prediction: "Some damned day your boss is going to be looking for something, and he'll be asking you where the hell it is. And then I'll teach you the lesson of your life, because what he wants will be in the Speaker's pocket, and it will be all locked up."[118] O'Neill's gorge rose another cubit when he learned—but not from Carter—that the President had nominated two Massachusetts Republicans for significant posts, one of whom, Elliot Richardson, was thought to want to be Bay State governor, as did O'Neill's son. This time old Tip let young Jordan have it: "I don't think you understand, son. The next time you do this, I'm going to ream your ass."[119]

Before he had been in office a week, Carter asked certain Senators to the White House for an energy briefing—without telling Senator Byrd. Senator Byrd gently suggested that it might be best "to let the leadership know about these meetings so that we can suggest which senators should be involved."[120] Later Carter decided to call in three Republican Senators to advise him—unbeknownst to their party leader, Senator Baker. Senator Baker quipped, "Don't do that again, Mr. President, or I'll bust your balloon."[121] Much against their collective grain, Senator Edmund Muskie, chairman of the Senate Budget Committee, Secretary of the Treasury Michael Blumenthal, and Representative Al Ullman, chairman of the House Ways and Means Committee, had gone along with a Carter tax rebate scheme; in Washington fashion, they argued vehemently against it in private as they loyally defended it in public. Carter changed his mind and withdrew the plan. But he neglected to tell his allies, leaving them hanging out there defending the flag he had abandoned: Blumenthal spoke his supportive piece the next day to the National Press Club. All three learned of the switch by reading the newspapers. All three—important powers Carter would need—expressed their not-so-private fury.[122]

President Carter's least popular move, early on, was a measure to cut back pork barrel water projects, the "dam nonsense" Congressmen loved to win and sell back home as demonstrations that they could milk the federal cow for all she was worth. The total money spent for these follies was a relative pittance, given the defense budget, but the projects were dear to the hearts of the relevant politicians, who had labored long and hard to get them into the budget. Lacking priorities but reflecting a promise, Carter went at them with his axe. Congressional indignation mounted; Carter invited the furious to the White House and one of them, steaming with ire at the numerous lucrative projects to be denied his home state, rose to announce with exquisite sarcasm, "My name is Russell Long, and I am the chairman of the Senate Finance Committee." Senator Gary Hart felt betrayed: "I was lied to, and I don't like being lied to." Meanwhile Hamilton Jordan, approaching his mid-thirties, pronounced that "the dams are nonnegotiable."

Thus the Carter approach to cooperative relations in Washington managed at one time or another to infuriate—*not* by policy differences, but by the merest lapses of the easiest thing a President has to do: cluing in your allies—at least the following: the Speaker of the House of Representatives, the chairmen of the House Ways and Means Committee and the House Interior Committee, the majority leader of the House of Representatives, the Senate majority leader and minority leader, the chairmen of the Senate Armed Services and Finance Committees, and the oldest Congressman around, 79-year-old Milton Young. Those were the notables directly affected; they talked, of course, to a good many others.

The Carter assaults on the manners of Washington concerned big and little matters. At the latter end, for example, was food. Down in Plains some time past, the Carters had provided Hubert Humphrey what he remembered as "Coca-Cola and a damned old sandwich with stringy roast beef wrapped in cellophane."[123] Both Byrd and O'Neill groused that Carter the President gave them nothing but rolls and coffee at White House breakfasts, not the full breakfast they were used to.[124] The President's number one Congressional relations man, Frank Moore, delivered his judgment: "I don't think the President is going to change on that, and I don't want to change. You can't serve a full breakfast in the cabinet room. And I don't want to have to go back over to the family quarters to eat."[125] Carter himself said he found it "interesting and exciting for me to talk politics and government with . . . congressional leaders and to see them gamely eating a delicious Southern lunch—cheese grits and country ham."[126] Such stories showed the "mean" Jimmy of the 1980 campaign, the petty aggressor. The effect was to create needless irritation instead of the ease which smoothes the way for agreement.

Far more serious was the kind of behavior Carter's ardent backers kept slamming into as they tried to work his will. Esther Peterson, veteran of half a century of effective work getting legislation to protect labor, women, and consumers, had worked with Congress for Truman, Kennedy, and Johnson. At seventy, she looked like a grandmother and operated like a pro. Carter made her his consumer affairs advisor and set out to get a new, independent agency to protect consumers. This effort was kicked off on June 1, 1977, at a pep rally meeting where Ralph Nader, Bert Lance, Frank Moore, Esther Peterson, and President Carter himself led the cheers. Then the business lobbies swung into action. Peterson began to encounter serious resistance as she moved around the country making speeches. Worse than that, the Carter White House, in the person of Frank Moore, began edging away from the fight. She could hardly get to Moore, much less to the President. Moore finally told her he did not give a damn about the bill and that she was wrong to entangle the President in such controversy. Puzzled, Peterson turned to Speaker O'Neill, who helped her work up a compromise bill he thought could be passed at the end of October, despite the business lobby efforts.

On November 1, the administration suddenly withdrew the bill which would create the agency Esther Peterson had been scrapping for all this time—withdrew it and *then* let her know it had been withdrawn. She could not believe it. To cool off, she flew home to Utah, but then called the President, who said he shared her sorrow. "Mr. President," she replied, "I'm not only sorry, I'm mad." Carter said he was surprised she had not been consulted. She told him the bill had been jerked before they even got a good head count. Carter went into his calm-down-and-tell-me-all-about-it routine, but Peterson blew up: "Mr. President, *I cannot do this.* Your people don't know how to get a bill through Congress. They don't know the basic tools of how to operate there, of using the powers we have there as a party. Maybe my techniques aren't right, but at least we used to pass some legislation." Carter told her to come talk to him when she got to Washington. She did more: she laid it all out in writing—not only why consumer protection was a natural issue for him but how his people could win in Congress, step by step, an early step being one the White House had not achieved in nearly a year in office: getting the home telephone numbers of the members of Congress. Carter met with her, persuaded her not to resign, put the bill back in and supported it with encouraging notes and calls to Congressmen, though he never made a direct appeal to the public, which, polls showed, was overwhelmingly in favor of the new agency. But business put the screws on and found more and more they could win over Congressmen, not because they were against consumer protection, but because they would not stand for the way they were being treated—manhandled or neglected—by the Carter White House. The bill lost, 227 to 189, a dismal start for 1978. The *New York Times* railed against the President's ineptness. A *Washington Post* editorial said, "The most tiresome cliché of the political season is the hearty comment that President Carter learns quickly. It's like saying that a pitcher going into the third game of the World Series is showing a knack for picking up the rules of the game."[127]

Perhaps, then, I was not too far off the mark in arguing that Jimmy Carter's "stylistic weak point is negotiation" and to predict that he would "have a rough time selling legislators on the idea that it is incumbent on *them* to follow the maxim: 'To get along, go along.' "[128] Throughout his term, Carter again and again returned to his bad negotiating habits, his long-time resistance to playing cooperative politics among interdependent power brokers. Significant to his negotiating problem was an intellectual component; for all his reading of books about the Presidency, Carter came into office with some fairly strange ideas of how to make it work, such as acting as his own chief of staff; using the Cabinet, in meetings open to the press, as a collegial body to make the big decisions; giving the Secretaries independent authority to run their departments, while requiring them to sign off on each and every regulation issued; holding his band of youthful campaign advisors tight around him, fending off disruptive intruders; putting his relationships with the press on an entirely different—much more open—basis than ever in the past. Part of the problem seems to have been a sense that good motives can make up for botched operations. Thus Carter had hardly found his seat in the Oval Office before he placed a cheery call to Tip O'Neill: "I just want you to know that I will be able to work with you and the members of the Congress, and we'll get along great together."[129] But what followed, followed. Good motives were also supposed to be demonstrated by his frequent confessions of error, a Carter innovation which did not always succeed in disarming his critics, any more than did his identification of himself as among those "deeply committed to establishing government as moralistic and decent."[130] But the main root of Carter's negotiating style problem was, I think, traceable to his first independent political success, when, as a Georgia politician, he succeeded largely on his own, not by dealing, but by knowing more than anybody else, bulldozing those he could not convince, and taking his case to the public when close-up consent slipped away from him.

Slow he may have been, but President Carter learned. Not so much from the preachments of the wise as by his own experience. Throughout his Presidency he had a political hearing problem, the one John Gardner described: "Jimmy Carter listens but he doesn't always hear."[131] Late in the game, Carter, like Ford, shocked the shockable (especially in Washington) by an unnecessarily clanky Cabinet shuffle, giving rise to gallows humor: "If you see the President coming and he's got a pin in his hand, run like hell, because he's got a grenade in his mouth."[132] But for all that, Carter recognized his problem and set out to fix it. He brought Congressmen into the White House at a faster rate than had Johnson or Kennedy, in large groups, small groups, social and business groups, and all by themselves. He brought in old hands like Clark Clifford and younger hands like Anne Wexler. His appointments generally could be criticized more for representing standard Washington types than for putting in amateurs, and he went far beyond his predecessors in affirmative action—appointing blacks, women, and members of other neglected groups to significant jobs. The youth brigade in the White House itself (where Ham gave Zbig the name "Woody Woodpecker" and Zbig retaliated by calling Ham "Porky Pig") supplemented stodgier types at State and Justice. And time and again in the Carter Presidential story, Carter, learning that someone was angry or alienated, got that someone in for a face-to-face chat.

By 1978, some of the lessons of failure had taken. In April the President took his staff up to Camp David and faced the Congressional problems head on. By then Carter himself was hard at work lobbying for his Panama Canal treaties, which would give up United States control of these obsolete facilities; the President personally took the issue to every Senator and he got Frank Moore to work more effectively with Vice President Mondale, Senators Byrd and Church, and others, so that the treaties went through that spring, 68 to 32.[133] His batting average with Congress, in terms of bills passed, went up to respectable numbers, though the most important tax and energy bills that passed were mangled versions of what he had asked for. Like other learning Presidents, Carter might not have been able to wash away his political faults, but he could at least recognize them and take steps to control the damage they might cause.

NEGOTIATING PEACE

Carter the inept negotiator hit bottom in the public opinion polls in the summer of 1978. Then within weeks, he emerged as a negotiating genius. Joseph Kraft (in his own words) said so, and the *Wall Street Journal* wrote of President Carter's "brilliant success" and "inspired leadership." Henry Kissinger said he deserved the "gratitude of the American People and the whole world." *Time* and *Newsweek* had him "Born Again!" and his rating in the Gallup poll went from 38 percent approval in August to 56 percent in September. A Republican Senator tried to get the Senate to put him up for the Nobel peace prize.[134]

Carter's newfound glory resulted from his achievement in getting President Anwar Sadat of Egypt and Prime Minister Menachim Begin of Israel to agree on the rough outlines of a peace both could live with. Carter proved that while he may not have been much of a trading partner with Congress, he could be extraordinarily effective as a trade arranger operating between these chieftains, whose nations had a long history of mutual detestation.

He took on the task against unanimous advice from his foreign policy team. What he suggested to them was simple: get the two leaders to Camp David and Carter would get them to agree on a peace plan. Cuckoo, they said. That would do nothing but set the stage for another Carter-the-clown story when yet another puffed-up hope popped and fizzled. Recognizing that "the prospects for complete success were very remote," he said he would try it anyway.[135] In terms of his professional reputation as President, he did not have a great deal to lose.

Carter had met Sadat in April, 1977, an experience he describes in his memoirs with all-out Biblical fervor: "A shining light burst in the Middle East scene for me."[136] They got along. That spring day in Washington they talked for hours, trying on one another the signs of trust a Southerner would look for: family stories, tales of village life, childhood memories, and, tentatively, the outlines of ambition, so that Carter came to see Sadat as "my close, personal friend." Even more exciting was Sadat's apparent readiness, as Carter's probes revealed, to consider bending a bit from Egypt's hard-line stance toward Israel's presence in the Sinai desert. Sadat left. That night Carter told his wife it had been "my best day as President."

In the midst of much else, Carter undertook extensive study of and occasional palaver with various Arab leaders, slowly building the details of possible areas of agreement. Back in Washington he had long talks with Hubert Humphrey and Arthur Goldberg on Mideast problems and prospects. In July 1977, Begin made his visit to Washington and, having succeeded in establishing the expectation that he would be a rigid, right-wing troglodyte, had only to act moderately nicely to impress Carter as "quite congenial, dedicated, sincere, deeply religious . . . a very good man." That November Sadat, to general amazement, visited Jerusalem. But negotiations slid downhill from there, until, by the following summer, stalemate set in. Carter then decided to make his move: in August 1978 he dispatched the invitation via Secretary of State Cyrus Vance and, lo and behold, Sadat and Begin said yes at once.

The President set the conditions. No media—the press set up in a nearby Maryland town and spent day after day reporting that they knew nothing. No traffic with the outer world—when the Israelis invited some Washington friends to dine with them, Carter quickly had them uninvited. And no pre-meeting expressions of negative or inflexible positions. The three leaders, Jew, Christian, and Moslem, opened the deliberations with a common prayer. It soon became evident that Begin and Sadat had to be dealt with separately until the shape of a settlement emerged, so Carter took to walking fifty yards north to Sadat's cabin (Dogwood) then fifty yards west to Begin's cabin (Birch), for seemingly endless talk. Carter told Begin how fine Sadat was, told Sadat what a very good man Begin was. But there was a great deal more to it than flattery. Jimmy Carter diligently studied every technical, legal, and geographic aspect of the matter; he talked not only with the leaders but with aides and ambassadors, often until two and three o'clock in the morning, after which he was up again at six or seven. One meeting lasted eleven hours. He took the main part in preparing twenty-three successive drafts of an agreement, many in his own hand. He listened and listened. Once he jumped up to block the door when Begin and Sadat were about to walk out on the talks. At least once, he read Begin the riot act in private, loudly demanding that he stop niggling and start acting like a statesman. He took them to the Gettysburg battlefield so they could meditate about neighborly slaughter. On the eleventh day, the Secretary of State, ashen-faced, broke in on a Carter meeting to tell him Sadat had packed his bags and ordered a helicopter. The President stalked over to Dogwood Lodge and made it icily clear that friendship or no friendship, he would view Sadat's departure as a violation of his personal promise; on the other hand, if Sadat would stick with it, Carter would insist that there be no subsequent diplomatic hanky-panky with the terms of an agreement.

Sadat stayed. Then, at the last moment, the Israelis developed objections. Carter's secretary, Susan Clough, suggested that this might not be a bad time to deliver to Begin the autographed photographs she had of Begin, Sadat, and Carter, including one for each Begin grandchild. Carter walked over with them; there was Begin, sitting on the porch looking dismal. Carter remembers what happened:

> I handed him the photographs. He took them and thanked me. Then he happened to look down and saw that his granddaughter's name was on the top one. He spoke it aloud, and then looked at each photograph individually, repeating the name of the grandchild I had written on it. His lips trembled, and tears welled up in his eyes. He told me a little about each child, and especially about the one who seemed to be his favorite. We were both emotional as we talked quietly for a few minutes about grandchildren and about war.[137]

Begin took him into the cabin, asked everyone else to leave, and quietly reviewed the situation. Carter returned in gloom to his cabin. Then Begin telephoned. "I will accept the letter you have drafted on Jerusalem," he said. After thirteen days, they had a deal. In the months ahead, much more remained to be worked out. Carter himself labored long and hard to get the detailed bricks and mortar into the foundation of the Camp David accords.

But it was Carter the triumphant who was greeted by a joint session of the Congress that September with cheer after cheer—as if he were a hero home from the wars. "Blessed are the peacemakers," he quoted, as the cameras found Sadat and Begin and Rosalynn Carter.[138] It must have been a gratifying moment. It must have made him wonder whether this could be the same Congress he had been getting to know since inauguration day.

By Jimmy Carter's own estimate, he spent more time on Middle East peace than on any other international problem during his Presidency, and when you add his work on the Panama Canal treaties, straightening out relations with China, economic summitry, and a try at negotiation with the Soviets, the total must have come to a large proportion of his effort. Hamilton Jordan reports that Carter met with more than forty heads of state in his first year—many more than Kennedy, Johnson, or Nixon.[139] Like other modern Presidents, Carter experienced the exquisite appeal of high diplomacy, especially as compared with the detail and tangle of domestic affairs. For all their sighs about the rigors of ceremony, Presidents love it; it sets them up. Carter expressed this precisely when he wrote of the end of his summitry with the Chinese: "The enjoyable ceremonies were over. Now we had the difficult job of getting legislation through Congress to implement the agreement."[140] Tippling with Brezhnev (though Carter got the waiter to give him "a tiny glass" and he "shifted to a somewhat milder drink") amounted to "really a very pleasant evening."[141] Arriving in Cairo for more talk with Sadat, he and Rosalynn "felt a glow of welcome, warmth, and friendship which remained throughout the visit," but which must have faded as he headed home again.[142] From Japan to Arabia, Jimmy Carter kept running into leaders he liked doing business with, statesmen who knew how to put a menu together. And somehow things seemed to move along so much better internationally: "Under our Constitution, the President has much more authority in foreign affairs—and therefore decisions can be made more quickly, more incisively, and usually with more immediate results."[143] Carter's whole last year in office would be dogged by an international horror. But until that happened, he, like others, discovered that after all there could be something to graduate to after being elected President: from President of the United States to "Leader of the Whole Free World." Within the Carter White House, the only subject to rival it in spontaneous interest and emotional investment was campaign politics.

Negotiation, then, was a Carter disaster in Washington and a Carter triumph at Camp David. In the former, he was meant to be a partner; in the latter, he acted as a kind of supervising go-between, a third party, though a very hard-working one. The balance was against him, though: one diplomatic victory versus months of stumbling through the Washington hen house.

HOMEWORK

If negotiation was Carter's stylistic weakness, homework was his stylistic strength. Unlike the Presidents just before and just after him, Jimmy Carter was a rabid empiricist, a data-hound, an information freak in the White House just as he had been in the Georgia senate. Considering how many of Jordan's Washington "jackals" were on his trail, in Congress and the media, it is surprising how rarely Carter was caught with his facts down. He was and remained a speed-reader and map-scanner, a list-making blueprint planner and memorandum annotator. One of his weirder ideas when he first came in was that he would clean out his in box every day, leaving the desk clear each night. For too long, his own queries generated so much paper flow that even his speediest reading could not keep up and his quick attention had far too many little lights to watch. He personally assigned the White House tennis courts. The reporter Robert Shogan happened by when this Leader of the Whole Free World was on his way to a meeting about aircraft engine noise. Like a student trying to take every course at once, Carter soaked up the material but it was not until well into his term that he got it organized into useable categories. When he did, though, he knew his stuff and could make it work for him. "I just study all the time," he said.[144]

RHETORIC

The Carter rhetoric was meant to be different: he said he'd never lie to us. Indeed he meant the whole range and demeanor of his relations with the public to be different. The whole thing would be open and aboveboard, with reporters welcome to high-level meetings and to the President's frequent press conferences. He would reach out to "average Americans" directly, as he did in his flying visits to various stunned citizens on their humble porches, and in his call-the-President phone-in, a one-time experiment assisted by Walter Cronkite. And his regime would symbolize the opposite of the dreaded "Imperial Presidency," as witness his decision to walk home from his inaugural, to get his aides into Chevrolets and tourist class plane seats, his initial ban on the playing of "Ruffles and Flourishes" to mark his appearance, and his resolution of the staff debate over what he should wear for his first fireside chat (denim jacket versus suit coat) by picking a button-up sweater. As the world leader business picked up, the symbols shifted and the "irresponsible" press found access harder than they had hoped.

The press conferences fell off in frequency, but the incidence of intimate White House dinners with various revered journalists picked up. It has to be said that not many journalists thought highly of Carter as his term progressed, perhaps in the main because he and his team never quite got the knack of feeding the press what they needed in order to excel at their work. White House defensiveness showed: when a silly story had Hamilton Jordan spitting ice cubes at a lady in a bar, the White House chugged out thirty-three pages of defense, including depositions from the bartender and observant patrons, thus making the matter front-page news throughout the nation. Joshing with Deng Xiaoping, Chinese Communist Party Vice Chairman, Carter offered to trade him 10,000 journalists for 10,000,000 Chinese, to their mutual agreement. After his Cabinet shake-up in the summer of 1979, the President, angry at the coverage, dropped his commitment to twice-a-month press conferences and challenged reporters "to look at the substance of what I have done" rather than just the Washington elite reaction.[145]

Carter might have been better advised to keep up the press conferences, in which he often excelled, and drop some formal addresses, in which, increasingly, his rhetoric faltered. From the first, his best—in stylistic terms—performances were the informal give-and-take sessions in which he responded directly to the audience, especially a small audience. His success in the 1976 Iowa caucuses, essentially won in living rooms, drew on that skill. But the substance of his 1976 general orations also rang a bell: the time was right for his moral message of civic virtue, in the backwash and aftermath of a sullied Presidential history. Then, people were up for a sermon; by the approach of 1980, sermons were wearing thin. Eugene McCarthy's quip that Carter's was the "eloquence of a mortician" gained currency; more and more Carter seemed "like a man who's come down from a slightly higher level of church administration to give a talk to your congregation on good sound business reasons why you ought to tithe," wrote Roy Blount.[146]

By the 1980 national convention, the President himself had recognized the preacher problem and shifted gears, designing his speeches in good engineering fashion, arguing his case, touching on various listed categories of supporters. More and more, his preparation time went into the pieces of the argument rather than the effectiveness of the delivery. At Bonn, in the summer of 1978, Carter's writers, recalling John F. Kennedy's famous "Ich bin ein Berliner" line, gave Carter a bit of Schiller to say, "Alle Menschen werden Brüder wo dein sanfter Flügel weilt."[147] It had taken Kennedy an hour, it is said, to get his little line down right. Carter tried his harder quotation a few times and listened to a German speaker say it, but it came out Georgia and the audience missed it. Carter the explainer and justifier was not igniting audiences at home, either, so he looked around for a way to change. At the convention, Edward Kennedy delivered a rollicking attack on Ronald Reagan, quoting Reagan's more idiotic statements to the delegates and getting back gleeful roars of "No, no, no!"[148] The next night, Walter Mondale lashed Reagan all over again, and got his own supportive refrain going: "but not Ronald Reagan!"[149] By contrast, the President gave a sober and systematic speech generally experienced as anticlimactic, which he noticed. In the campaign, noticing he was getting nowhere with preaching or lecturing. Carter came out fighting like Mondale and Kennedy. Reinforced in the hothouse of the Democratic convention, this would turn out to be the worst possible rhetorical style for 1980, a year in which the public's need was not for conflict but for reassurance—that soothing product Ronald Reagan sold them so effectively. Deaf to that theme, Jimmy Carter reverted to his

"Jungle Jimmy" style and, despite repeated warnings and urgings from his staff, stuck with it. The media buzzword for rhetorical Carter that season was "mean."

CARTER'S PRESIDENTIAL CHARACTER

Carter's earlier critics spotted, even in his campaign, his various stylistic lapses and tended to put them down to inexperience or indifference. Carter was seen by some as just one more master of the non-performing arts, one of those modern hustlers adept at claiming titles, cashing checks, and delegating work. When he emerged as "mean," some said they had known all along he had deeper troubles, that his smiling exterior masked a burdened soul and that he was leaking hate stored up long ago. Carter's character came into question.

By my simple scheme, his place on the active-passive dimension stayed clear all through his Presidency. He was usually up and about an hour before the Secret Service woke him at 6:00 a.m., got to the office by 7:00, and stayed there until dinner twelve hours later. At first he put in two or three additional hours in the evening. Six weeks into his Presidency his appointments secretary figured he was averaging a seventy-one hour week. Then he and his top aides took a speedreading course which enabled the President, he reports, to read four times as fast as he had been, so he could knock off the after-dinner labors most evenings and relax. He and his family came to love Camp David; they spent nearly the equivalent of a year up there, more than any other First Family, according to Hamilton Jordan. But those, too, were working times. On the active-passive dimension, Carter comes off clearly as predicted: one of the active ones.[150]

The positive-negative placement is not as clear-cut. My predictive phrasing, that Carter would "turn out to be a pleasured President"[151] rings too hopeful in history's light, for the fact is that Carter had a lot of down days. He told Hamilton Jordan that "1980 was pure hell—the Kennedy challenge, Afghanistan, having to put the SALT treaty on the shelf, the recession, Ronald Reagan, and the hostages . . . always the hostages! It was one crisis after another."[152] When other memoirs appear, such as Jody Powell's and Walter Mondale's, we will have a better picture of Carter's average affect toward the job, of the day-to-day impression of happiness or sadness he conveyed to those around him. For now we must make do mainly with his own memories and summaries—always suspect, though it is unlikely a President would risk blatant contradiction of the shared opinion of intimates yet to write their own histories.

Carter's own reports range from that of his inauguration—"It's been just about a perfect day"—to "the worst day of my life," when the attempt to rescue the hostages in Iran failed. Sometimes his comments are mixed, as when he writes that the Panama effort left him "exhausted, exhilarated, and thankful." His battles with Congress brought "big disappointments," but then "all the strain, frustration, and hard feelings of the year were quickly forgotten in the glow of adjournment." Similarly the Mideast negotiations were fraught with "some of the most unpleasant experiences of my life" but ushered in "one of the most gratifying achievements." When the Carters first moved into the Presidential digs, Rosalynn said, "I believe we're going to be happy in the White House" and her husband comments that "Rosalynn's prediction proved to be correct." And he sums it all up like this: "For me, Rosalynn, our children, and my mother, the four years I spent as President were for the most part an exciting and rewarding time." Tentatively, pending intimate revelations yet to come, I judge the balance positive; if not entirely a "pleasured President," Jimmy Carter was "for the most part" pleased with the experience.[153]

Other, less direct evidence, weighs in the same direction. James Fallows, Carter's chief speechwriter for the first two years of his Presidency, writes incisive criticism of the Carter style, but finds Carter the character "a stable, personally confident man, whose quirks are few."

> Carter is unusually patient, less vindictive than the political norm, blessed with a sense of perspective about the chanciness of life and the transience of its glories and pursuits. I left his service feeling that when moral choices faced him, he would resolve them fairly; that when questions of life and death, of nuclear war and human destruction were laid upon his desk, he would act on them calmly, with self-knowledge, free of interior demons that might tempt him to act rashly or to prove at terrible cost that he was a man.... (I)f I had to choose one politician to sit at the Pearly Gates and pass judgment on my soul, Jimmy Carter would be the one.[154]

Then there were those traces of healing laughter, not only at evil others but also at homely self. He said he was glorying in the inaugural adulation— "Look, look, look!"—until he heard "There goes Billy's brother!" His purpose, to "put on the image of a common man" instead of "a strong and able leader," had "succeeded very well."[155] On his inauguration day he wrote in his diary about the time, earlier on, when one of his staffers asked the White House cooks if they could do Southern cooking. "Yes, Ma'am," said the cook, "we've been fixing that kind of food for the servants for a long time!"[156] Even in the "pure hell" of 1980, he could kid around with Jordan and Powell on occasion. Through all that, he writes, he "simply took one day at a time." Further, "Rosalynn and I had a kind of blind faith that we would be successful in overcoming great political odds, as we had done so many times before."[157] Carter says he set out to be, like Harry Truman, "a good President," but "I did not wish to go down in the history books as a 'great' leader of America who finally won a war I myself had started."[158] To that end, Jimmy Carter prayed without ceasing, "more than ever before in my life," asking wisdom, getting at least "a great help" which "removed any possibility of timidity or despair as I faced my daily responsibilities."[159]

But the proof of the Carter character, as he, like Truman, stepped along the brink of compulsion, would be evident in a harder test, a long, harrowing ordeal during which Satan would dangle before him the deadliest of temptations.

CHARACTER TEST

The easier task of political and military intelligence is to report the past and present the facts of a situation. By far the harder task is to figure out what will happen next. Prediction, even when stated in terms of contingencies, requires weighing the significance of facts in their historical context and then moving out from the certainties of yesterday into the probabilities of tomorrow. It is hard, but it has to be done. Choices to guide action are otherwise impossible. On October 20, 1979, Jimmy Carter decided, on the basis of the intelligence then available to him, to let the Shah of Iran fly from Mexico to New York City for treatment of his advanced cancer. That choice ruined the rest of his Presidency and very likely sank his chances for reelection. But from another perspective, that decision set for Jimmy Carter the test of character in its severest form.

The Shah of Iran was one of those exotic dictators beloved of the "tough" school of American diplomacy: to be sure, his prisons echoed night and day with the screams of tortured men, women, and children, but at least he had his country under control and could fight off even more despicable opponents, if only we furnished him sufficient weaponry. That estimate fell apart in January, 1979, when a revolution sparked by a mesmerizing Moslem named Khomeini forced the Shah to run for his life to Egypt, then Morocco, then the Bahamas, and then Mexico. Carter was urged to let the Shah come to the United States, notably by ex-Secretary of State Henry Kissinger and New York banker David Rockefeller, and by his national security advisor Zbigniew Brzezinski, who argued this would be the decent thing to do for America's old friend. Carter demurred. The situation in Iran was chaotic and there were many vulnerable Americans there.

One day in February, 1979, a mob of Khomeini fanatics seized the American embassy in Tehran, killing one Iranian and taking hostage the Ambassador and 100 other Americans. The assault lasted three and a half hours before Iranian authorities managed to get the demonstrators to go home. Anti-Shah rhetoric was mounting in Iran; the demand was to send him back to Iran to receive appropriate vengeance. Carter had held out a long time against the let-the-Shah-in idea, but at last, when his friend Cy Vance advised it, medical diagnosis and treatment requirements urged it, and a direct check with the Iranian Prime Minister and Foreign Minister assured him the American embassy would not be violated, Carter gave in. At one staff meeting he had asked, "When the Iranians take our people in Tehran hostage, what will you advise me then?"[160]

And that is just what happened on Sunday, November 4, 1979, when, triggered by Carter's fateful hospitality to the Shah, the Khomeini mob descended again, this time to stay. Carter immediately went over the situation with Vance. "We were deeply disturbed," Carter remembers, "but reasonably confident that the Iranians would soon remove the attackers from the embassy compound and release our people."[161] The President sat tight, as the hours ticked by. The official government in Iran could do nothing, it turned out. Khomeini was in the saddle and he blessed the takeover. The mob became a collective national hero. The worry shifted from how soon the Americans would get out to whether they would get out at all.

Carter's immediate reaction was anger at "those bastards holding our people,"[162] but his immediate action was to think and talk. "I spent most of the day, every spare moment, trying to decide what to do," he wrote in his diary on November 6.[163] Easiest was the decision not to trade the Shah for our people, as demanded; that would be craven. But then what? Planning for a possible rescue mission was started. Companies with Americans in Iran were asked to get them out. The Algerians, Syrians, Turks, Pakistanis, Libyans, the PLO and others were asked to intercede with their fellow Moslems. Former Attorney General Ramsey Clark, who had some acquaintance with Khomeini, was dispatched to meet with him, bearing a handwritten letter from the President of the United States; the Iranians would not let Clark in. Carter gathered his advisors for long discussions, and he had them look up what the government had done in similar crises, such as the *Pueblo* seizure. He set in motion action to expel Iranian students residing illegally in the United States. On November 9, he met with the hostages' families and reviewed with Cyrus Vance criteria for a punitive military action against Iran. He refused permission for Iranians to demonstrate across from the White House. On November 12, he ordered a cut-off of United States oil imports from Iran. On November 14, he impounded some $12,000,000,000 worth of Iranian assets in the United States, arguing that it would be "a good way to get their attention."[164] There was deliberation; there was action; there was no panic. "We'll have to try a lot of different things," said the President.

As the crisis developed from acute to chronic, stretching out over the days and weary months, a lot of different things indeed did come to Carter's mind and the minds of the American millions. At any time, Carter could have found massive domestic support for bombing Iran. The nation's sense of outrage would have found glorious expression in a burst of aggression. Or he could have found reason, perhaps in the law, to reluctantly deliver the foreign Shah back to his people, in exchange for our people. Or he could have launched a rescue mission right away—to *do something!*—however ill prepared. Or he could have agreed to let the hostages be put on "trial" in Iran, in exchange for possible steps toward their release. Or he could have done nothing, let it sit and stew, while he got going on his campaign for reelection. Down any one of these more or less plausible paths lay the probability of disaster. Carter tried a range of other moves, shunting aside the urge to relieve the tension in some blazing denouement. It is probably correct to say he was obsessed with the problem. As he put it later, "I would walk in the White House gardens early in the morning and lie awake at night, trying to think of additional steps I could take to gain their freedom without sacrificing the honor and security of our nation."[165] But he was not obsessed with a particular solution. Having succeeded the year before in a process of negotiation at Camp David, he chose to try to find the basis for a deal, treating Khomeini, a "crazy man" to Carter, as if he were "a rational person," supposing that somewhere in the Khomeini vision of Islam there might be a reflection of Anwar Sadat.[166]

On December 4, the President announced his candidacy for reelection the following year, saying "At the height of the Civil War, Abraham Lincoln said, 'I have but one task and that is to save the Union.' Now I must devote my considered efforts to resolving the Iranian crisis."[167] He wanted another term, but he stepped out of the campaign.

There are many ifs one could raise about the negotiations to release the hostages, a prime one being why Mr. Hamilton Jordan, with his relatively restricted experience of the theory, practice, or language of diplomacy, especially diplomacy with the subtle Persians, found himself jetting back and forth to Europe and Panama, in and out of disguise, to parlay for the hostages' release. But the decisions came back to Carter, and Carter had the advantage of two informed and experienced advisors of opposite dispositions on the matter: aggressive Brzezinski in the White House and cautious Vance at State. Logically that arrangement made little sense—who was in charge of foreign policy? But the conflict served the President precisely as he needed to be served, by sharpening his vision of the real alternatives.

Christmas came. Carter kept the national Christmas tree dark; he would light it when the hostages got home. Suddenly, two days later, Soviet troops poured into Afghanistan and he had another international emergency to cope with. Word came back that the hostages in Iran were forced to lie on hard floors with their hands tied, deprived of sleep by constant noise and light, refused conversation or exercise. Carter was "sickened," but kept on probing, now through the United Nations, now through the Swiss embassy in Tehran, now through a French lawyer and an Argentine businessman and the President of Panama. Nothing worked. Then on January 31, a piece of good news: six Americans had been spirited out of Iran by the Canadian diplomats there; big signs saying "THANK YOU CANADA!" went up in Washington, and it registered with Carter that "our first rescue mission had been successful."[168] An unrelated but welcome boost came in February when the United States hockey team beat the far-better-rated Soviets at the Olympic games; Carter welcomed our boys to the White House with a big grin.

But week after week of diplomacy proved fruitless. On April 10, 1980, Carter noted in his diary that Iranian terrorists were threatening to kill the hostages if Iraq—in their eyes an American puppet—attacked Iran. Carter conferred the next day with his National Security Council (minus Cyrus Vance, vacationing in Florida) and decided to move ahead with a rescue mission. When Vance returned, he let the President know he opposed that operation primarily because it would endanger the hostages. The President listened, but decided to go ahead, and the military planning began to gather an inexorable momentum.

The preparations were phenomenally detailed. The strategy was to land in the Iranian desert, go into Tehran in old Iranian trucks, get the hostages out of the embassy and out of the country by air. Available to Colonel Charles Beckwith's crack "Delta" rescue team were the blueprints of the embassy, up-to-date intelligence on the identity, location, and schedule of every hostage and guard, and satellite pictures identifying every car and truck in and around the compound. A mock-up of the embassy was built somewhere in the American west and the Delta team, after much preparatory training, went through eight full-scale dress rehearsals. The 97-man team learned to sleep by day and work by night. Their "uniform" for the attack would be Levi pants, black-dyed Army field jackets (with an American flag covered with tape, to be ripped off as they went over the wall into the embassy), unpolished boots, a dark Navy watch cap and a dark flannel shirt of the soldier's own choosing; beards and long hair were OK. Day after day they practiced embassy breaking and entering: blow up the door, jump into the room and fire at the Iranian-dressed—not the American-dressed—dummies seated therein. Did they ever hit the wrong one, asked Jordan. "Sir," replied Beckwith, "Delta played in the Rosebowl, not the shitbowl. Any man that ever hit an 'American' dummy was not a Bear Bryant-type player." To make sure the attackers got it right, the dummies were rearranged in the darkened rooms for each practice. Just to double-check, Colonel Beckwith and the other Delta officers took turns sitting in for the "American" dummies, no doubt breathing regularly as the soldiers crashed in and shot off live ammunition.[169]

On April 17, 1980, Cyrus Vance explained his lonely opposition to the rescue mission to Hamilton Jordan: "Generals will rarely tell you they can't do something."[170] On April 23, Vance gave the President his letter of resignation. On April 24, the rescue mission went in. Two of the eight helicopters failed to reach the rendezvous; a third broke down after landing. Beckwith cancelled the mission. But a fourth helicopter, maneuvering to take off, crashed into a transport plane, killing eight young men. Three others were badly burned. The rest were brought out safely, as the world learned of the attempt and the result.

Carter was stunned. Later he called that day "one of the worst of my life." He asked Jody Powell to find a copy of John F. Kennedy's speech following the Bay of Pigs disaster. Vance expressed his sympathy and Carter, wryly acknowledging his friend's foresight, wondered if Vance might draft an explanation of what happened. At the memorial service at Arlington cemetery on May 9, Carter met the families of the dead, the suddenly manless wives and children and old folks; he "feared that some of them might rebuff me," but they crowded up and hugged and comforted him.

In the silence after the speeches, a squadron of jets flew low overhead, and as they passed, one plane peeled off and slowly fell away, leaving a gap in the formation as the rest flew on.

TEST RESULTS

Khomeini and company crowed over their defeat of the invading Americans, but they did not cut off negotiations. Carter and company went back to the seemingly endless round of indirect talks and hints and messages, through the spring, the summer, on past the November election, month after month of failed initiatives and collapsed deals. Not until January 20, 1981—inauguration day for the new President—did the hostages at last head home. That afternoon, Jimmy Carter, having made it through the morning's ceremonies, flew back to Plains; his helicopter landed on the downtown baseball field in a Georgia drizzle and he and Rosalynn walked through the cheering crowd to a bunting-draped platform while the high school bands belted out their brassy oom-pah-pahs. Carter spoke: "Just a few moments ago . . . I received word officially for the first time that the aircraft carrying the fifty-two American hostages has cleared Iranian airspace." It was over. "Every one of the fifty-two hostages is alive, well, and free." The crowd let rip a tremendous Rebel yell, the bluegrass band sounded a reel, and Jimmy took hold of Rosalynn and danced her around the stage.[171] Thus January's joy completed April's mourning, too late to help Carter's power, but in time to lift his spirit.

The Carter character was, I think, severely tested by the Iranian hostage crisis and not found wanting. He left behind some positive achievements in foreign affairs, notably the Panama Canal treaties, the Camp David accords, and a steadier link to China—not major, permanent breakthroughs perhaps, but props against the collapse of fragile peace in an age of chaos. The Iranian situation came down to this: unlike Wilson, Hoover, Johnson, and Nixon, this President did not freeze onto some disastrous line of policy and ride it to the end. Rather he kept his head, and kept his mind open, flexibly and energetically pursuing some way out of an apparently hopeless situation. If Carter was also slow to learn how to operate in Washington, he was also slow to commit the nation to deadly adventures. Philip Geyelin, editorial page editor of the *Washington Post*, made these comparisons on June 10, 1979:

> By about this time in his presidency, Dwight Eisenhower had approved CIA-supported coups in Iran and Guatemala. John Kennedy had bungled the Bay of Pigs and so misrepresented his will and resolve to Nikita Khrushchev that we had, in quick and frightening succession, a Berlin crisis and Soviet missiles in Cuba. Lyndon Johnson had dispatched combat troops to South Vietnam and the Dominican Republic, dealt inconclusively with riots in Panama, intervened in the Chilean elections by not-so-covert CIA activity, begun bombing North Vietnam. Richard Nixon had widened the Vietnam war to Cambodia and Laos. Gerald Ford had suffered 40 U.S. Marine casualties, directly or indirectly, in order to rescue about an equal number of crewmen from the *Mayaguez*. Saigon had fallen; the frantic American evacuation was a humiliation.[172]

Perhaps Carter was lucky that the rescue mission failed in the desert; for all its planned precision and practice, the operation had a Rube Goldberg quality to it, a vulnerability to "Murphy's Law" that whatever can go wrong will go wrong. But when it did fail, that would have been just the moment for an active-negative Jimmy Carter to buckle on the armor of bitterness and call for a crusade. Near the end of his time in office, he wrote in his diary that he had "instructed my people this weekend to prepare for a breakdown in negotiations and possible hostage trials. I will declare a state of belligerency or ask Congress to declare war against Iran." But he went on to outline intermediate steps to be taken in trade and diplomacy prior to "military action like a blockade or mining," and he noted

"I hope these actions won't be necessary."[173] So it might have come to war. That it never did owes much to the reserves of confidence and balance Carter could draw on when his crisis found him.

Carter bears the blame for the compassionate folly of letting the Shah come into the country; despite the uncertainties, he might have predicted the Iranian reaction. Then, one could argue, once it became clear that his leverage over Khomeini had disappeared and that there was nothing left to do until the Iranians decided to free the hostages, Carter should have put the issue aside and moved on to more productive topics. In other words, he may not have done as well as he might have done. But it is clear he could have done a great deal worse.

POWER SITUATION

Writing about the power situation Carter would face, I too glancingly saw the world scene as "too chaotic to characterize intelligibly."[174] By the end of the Carter years, it was possible to see more clearly how vulnerable the United States had become to international developments beyond our control. Japanese industry could lay waste Detroit's automotive capability and throw thousands out of work. An international oil cartel could set prices we had to pay, mocking domestic attempts to control inflation. International bankers, responsible to no government, could generate enormous suffering and insecurity through their foolish mismanagement of debt and investment. Our arms race was linked to the Soviet arms race. And most spectacularly, a piratical regime in a third-rate country like Iran could suddenly demand a very large proportion of the President's attention, his scarcest and most valuable commodity. This deepening pattern of dependency continually frustrated planning, reduced American diplomacy to crisis management or, at best, patched-up, knock-on-wood agreements between pairs of powers. We practiced "shuttle diplomacy," whether that meant Henry Kissinger jetted back and forth between Cairo and Jerusalem or Jimmy Carter jogged back and forth between Birch Lodge and Dogwood Lodge at Camp David. Virtually nothing was done, or had been done for years, to build the stable, responsible, continuing international institutions necessary to control international chaos and check the drift to disaster. The configuration of power (interdependent anarchy) and the patterns of response typical of contemporary governments set the broad framework in which Carter the diplomatist had to operate.

CLIMATE OF EXPECTATIONS

The climate of expectations—and Carter's try at changing that—defined even deeper layers of constraint and possibility. Carter got to be President in significant part because he expressed the moral theme people wanted to hear in 1976. He tried to call on that sentiment regarding energy policy, with his "Moral Equivalent of War" appeal, and regarding nuclear weapons control, with his earnest insistence on strategic arms limitation talks with the Soviet Union. Neither appeal took hold, for a variety of reasons; one was that moralism ages quickly in our politics, and thus the tone of Carter's rhetoric seemed discordant as 1980 approached. But another reason, more relevant to future leaders, is that Carter was trying to get people excited about crises they had yet to experience. To be sure, there were some scattered and temporary gas and fuel oil shortages, and long ago there had been Hiroshima. Nevertheless, Carter's problem was analogous to FDR's in the period before Pearl Harbor: how do you reorient the nation's attention and energy to take strong action, at considerable cost, to meet challenges which have not yet hit home? On the energy front, failure to act in advance might well signal very real hard times for our children. On the nuclear front, failure to think ahead will mean the end of the world.

Carter called, but the sea of indifference lapped on as usual. The problem of discerning crises yet to be would haunt his successors, too—if they were lucky enough to avoid actual tragedies.

CARTER'S WORLD VIEW

Jimmy Carter's proudest memory remained his work for human rights; he felt he had "printed that commitment on worldwide consciousness," he told Theodore White.[175] The Carter world view, as predicted,[176] did not express a narrow or literal Christian orthodoxy, but rather the invocation of the purposes the government was meant to pursue. When he first announced his candidacy, in December 1974, Carter harked back to political values Tom Paine and Jefferson and Theodore Roosevelt could endorse: "That this country set a standard within the community of nations of courage, compassion, integrity, and dedication to basic human rights and freedoms." Later he wrote that "I was familiar with the widely accepted arguments that we had to choose between idealism and realism, or between morality and the exertion of power; but I rejected those claims. To me, the demonstration of American idealism was a practical and realistic approach to foreign affairs, and moral principles were the best foundation for the exertion of American power and influence."[177] In a world whose "realists" had had their day, the time had come for recognizing that American power, at least, would be exercised for certain fundamental values beyond its own survival and existence, namely the values our Declaration of Independence asserted to justify our birth as a nation. From the start of his Presidency, Carter raised the human rights issue, not only with the torturing satrapies of the third world, but also with the Soviet Union and China. His intention was to put every national leader up against the question, "What do my own people and the outside world think about the protection of human rights in my country?"[178] Criticism rolled in from the realists—but political prisoners, fearing most the world's neglect, got out the word to keep it up. In practical terms, Carter set in motion policies which led to prisoner releases in the short run and in the longer run to marked improvement in human rights in such countries as Argentina and the Philippines. But at its base the change was spiritual.

Championing human rights cut across the grain of tidy arrangements of convenience by which all parties tacitly agreed not to worry too much about the misfits and minorities who kept speaking out of turn. It flew in the face of a fashionable cultural relativity which, in the name of tolerance, would let intolerance rule, justifying tyranny as but one among an array of fascinating customs. Carter would not buy that. The rights were human—not American—or even Western. This view of the world, strange to realists and relativists alike, challenged, for a time in the Carter administration, the widespread view that the United States stood for nothing but itself. Instead, "the world was reminded by salvaged lives that America cares about freedom and justice." That, the President thought, was "a sufficient accomplishment to justify all our efforts."[179]

14

George Bush: The World View Dilemma

Given the real American Presidency, where power focuses on one individual, the voters need to know the candidates' characters in advance of casting their votes, so that, in the worst of times, they can choose the less dangerous one, and in the best of times, they can choose the one who will advance the probabilities of life, liberty and the pursuit of happiness. So Presidential character is no extraneous, marginal matter of concern; history shows it has made great differences in this country and abroad.

But among the factors, character is one, not all. As with style—the skills for being President—we need to know the candidate's world view, because that is what he believes in and therefore is likely to try to implement. World view has become much more important than it used to be. True, every President's world view has been significant, but usually in the past there was also a shared world view: the party platform. If you wanted to know what a party—including the President—was likely to do with power, you would read the platform to get its priorities, directions, and set of practical interpretations of American principles. But then, in recent years, the parties fell apart. The platforms (created by some national party committee and published in a tome inches deep) became irrelevant. Many voters do not even know which candidates are with which parties, much less what the parties stand for, if anything. So the focus on the President's world view is a sorry but necessary consideration. As it turns out, predicting it is not easy, but worth the work.

456

UNFOLDING THE BUSH MYSTERY

Predicting George Bush's performance in the White House was a challenge. Nearly a year before he was elected, Bush was one candidate among many. Bush's critics called him a "wimp"—that is, a passive-positive like William Howard Taft, Warren G. Harding, or Ronald Reagan. In *Newsday*, the year before the 1988 election, my question focused on his supposed wimpishness: "Is that Bush? Apparently not. The evidence is that Bush is an energetic person, even a striver, and that he is forever conveying an upbeat humor and optimism. Those who know him like but also respect him, think of him as a person of integrity. Tentatively, I would say Bush is an active-positive. . ."[1]

By the summer of that election year, asked "What about George Bush?," I was puzzled that "The basic question about Bush, I think, is not character, but world view. What is his vision? What is his direction?" And

People who have known him say he is happy in his work. He does a lot for people, and things of that sort.

Still, we have a very obscure picture of how he operated in these great titles in his resume. I think, how can it be that that question has been on the table for months and months and I haven't read any stories that say, George Bush came forward with this or that and really carried the flag and stuff like that. What I've heard is that people who worked with him liked him because he was fair-minded and he brought them together and they would compromise on things and work out a relationship, and they had respect for one another and so forth. But there wasn't some kind of direction.

That appeared to be significant.

The issue is that vision is crucial. The challenge of the presidency, the tricky international situation, is just tremendously important for the next president—the need for the government of the United States to take a strong initiative to institutionalize peace, to stabilize economic and other relationships internationally. We need a president who is not only mentally healthy, but who has the strength to move forward—somebody who not only doesn't have a fever, but has the strength to run a marathon.

I wouldn't be surprised to see that Bush's media managers recognize the problem and have him, at the convention in New Orleans, make a stunning speech that is full of vision. But what you have to ask is, has this guy kept with his visions in the past? Has there really been a connection between his supposed vision and his actions?[2]

But the mystery of Bush's world view hung on. We should have solved it in advance of November 1988. At least before he took office, George Bush's world view uncertainty came out—the perception that what he happened to say was not going to be reliable guidance to what he would do. I also predicted that in spite of the obscurity of his direction, he was indeed likely to take on missions, as he had done in the past. But what missions? The mystery remained.

Then by the end of his first Presidential year, a rough but major thrust of his veiled world view began to emerge. Bush's rhetoric never damned the poor, but his actions fed the rich.

And then, not until another year had passed did it come forth that President George Bush was instead primarily Son George Bush, a person whose world view missions related much more to distinguishing himself, a task he took on in his teenage years. That connection poisoned humanity, here and abroad.

January 19, 1989: The New York Times

PREDICTION

George Bush: In Search of a Mission

By James David Barber
Durham, N.C.

Candidate Bush turned out to be a surprise. President Bush may be a bigger one.

Those who think he will be simply a steady, middle-of-the-road chairman of the White House team might well be wrong. There are signs that this Presidency could be far more innovative—for better or for worse—than the last one.

Candidate Bush started with the "wimp" image, which made most observers think he could not win since he would do most anything to escape confrontation. That supposition was reasonable enough, given his loyal lap-dog service to Ronald Reagan. Wimpism seemed confirmed by his career and childhood, in which he and his brothers feared their father and followed their mother's adamant insistence that they come on humble.

But in the 1988 campaign, he attacked Michael S. Dukakis with scathing and insulting assaults on his patriotism, integrity, philosophy, record and appearance. And he came across in his convention speech as a man of emotion, a person of passion—not a wimp. He chose the Vice Presidential candidate *he* wanted. He hit at reporters, even Dan Rather, and moved them around like checkers as they tried to get near him.

He trashed his glasses, rolled up his sleeves, zipped around in his motorboat and jogged like some recovering Olympic. The news about Mr. Bush—at the time the votes were gelling—was that he was a tougher fellow than many had supposed, or even that he had suddenly become so.

Reporters, required to get news, thought they saw other surprises. Mr. Bush claimed he cared for the poor and wanted to be kind to them. Contrasting himself with President Reagan, he said "I like what's real." In imitation of Gary Hart, he issued a dare to reporters, "Read my lips." Mr. Bush said, "No new taxes." He said he wanted to be known as a champion of education and of environmental reform. Above all, Mr. Bush, artfully coached by his theatrical directors, got journalists thinking it plausible that his campaign image represented his reality—a myth if ever there was one.

But then the election ended and the national amnesia process began. In tune with the climate of .expectations, cycling on after the combative election, Bush the conciliator emerged, wrapping his arms around those he had just been stabbing in the back. The season of political despair, disillusionment and degradation was passed away and faith, hope and charity came on. A new era.

Mr. Bush's Presidential style was defined in his first independent political success in Texas in 1962, when as local party chairman he defused a conflict between the John Birch Society and establishment Republicans. Bush the negotiator took that on as his main talent, and so it remains.

His rhetoric is coachable as the '88 campaign brought out. He speaks about as well as Gerry Ford. His homework falls short of B-plus, as demonstrated by his lack of knowledge about such heavy issues as abortion and defense. When it comes to curiosity about reality, George Bush is no Jack Kennedy, no Harry Truman. He inherits from Mr. Reagan a practical prejudice for the rich masked by "conservatism," and a readiness to manipulate the media.

Why expect from President Bush anything other than a continuation of the Reagan mythological politics?

A close look at Mr. Bush's world view and character in the context of the situation he confronts makes plausible a different pattern. Although Mr. Bush, sounding like Herbert Hoover, urges us to believe that all is going well, the truth is that it is not. The evidence is at last coming through that there is trouble in River City—big, deep, harsh trouble that seems about to drop upon us.

One need only speak aloud certain words to recall what is happening: drugs, deficit, nuclear weapons, disease, economic domination, foreign ownership, weakened education, dollar decline, third world debt, terrorism, slipping technology, children in poverty, refugees, environmental deterioration, guns for sale, human rights violations, civil wars.

The worst political danger is interdependence plus anarchy. To suppose that these global cancers will simply waft away if we just dream on is folly, and folly competes with conspiracy as the worst of political solutions.

We need to get peace and justice organized—institutionalized—internationally. Not just a flaky summit meeting now and then, or some little bilateral agreements. Turning around our international decline is going to take major new initiatives, large-scale and long-term, backed by the public. How might a President Bush make that happen? How might he destroy the chance?

Mr. Bush wants a mission. It is important that he likes normal, ordinary politics and that he invests much energy in that work. His character is active-positive, a pattern that means he is ready to learn, to change, to develop in office, as distinct from the fixated types, such as Richard Nixon or Lyndon Johnson.

In his convention acceptance speech he declared that "I am a man who sees life in terms of missions . . . missions defined and missions completed." Could George Bush not take on a mission to build a system of peace and justice in this world?

That could happen. Mr. Bush's life has been dramatized time and again from his viewpoint by his taking on major missions. Going off on his 18th birthday in 1942 to be the youngest Navy pilot in World War II—which he now cites as his first mission—was a thrill. He put himself up for duty, as his father kept preaching and practicing, and for devotion to others as his mother kept demanding. He got far away from the fear of father and interference by mother. We won the war. He won the Distinguished Flying Cross. Mission Accomplished.

After Yale and marriage, he took on a second big mission in 1948, changing his life by moving to Texas. To be sure, the suggestion came from a family friend and he did not have to provide his own finances. But from George Bush's viewpoint, moving to West Texas was a move to another world. There, from Mr. Bush's perspective, they developed a life of their own, demonstrating that he could shape his own existence far from Greenwich, Conn.

Years later, in 1975, President Ford asked Republican National Committee Chairman Bush to come over and "discuss the future." Mr. Ford mentioned that the Ambassadorships to Britain and France were open. To Mr. Ford's surprise, Mr. Bush asked to be envoy to China, having "come to a decision much like the one we made in 1948. Back then we had decided not to do the traditional thing, but to head for the West."

The pattern strongly suggests that George Bush sees himself as enlivened and inspired by a mission into a new, different, distant, unknown land. Could he move out into the real world and take on the challenge of forging peace and justice, not in the failed Reagan manner but in a new and different way? Given Mr. Bush's past, that is conceivable. He is not stuck with consistency.

On the other hand, Mr. Bush's hunger for mission could carry us all over the brink of disaster. To whom will he look for the mission? Some spin doctors like those who drove his campaign? His right-wing Chief-of-Staff, John H. Sununu? His managerial Secretary of State-designate, James A. Baker 3rd? Sir Lancelot has become King Arthur. Who knows to whom he will look for guidance?

The ultimate danger is war. That was Mr. Bush's first big mission. The inevitable frustration Mr. Reagan's left-over debt imposes on any new domestic program could make him angry. So could the natural desire of the press to avoid being spun as it was before, and thus to criticize him as weak. Congressional Democrats may well stand tall against his administration's recommendations.

Economic realities, even beyond the deficit, pose a most difficult obstacle to any major political mission. One of Mr. Nixon's in-house conspirers, H. R. Haldeman, noted that Mr. Bush would "do anything for the cause." Turning to a military cause, even beyond the dimension of the Grenada invasion that Mr. Bush helped to orchestrate, is always going to be a temptation for this President. That could confirm his recent reaction to the story that Mr. Baker would use him as a puppet: "I am not a damned piece of meat."

The Bush potential is there, as it turned out to be for Harry S. Truman, who fostered the Marshall Plan. Or as it turned out to be for Lyndon Baines Johnson, who fostered the Vietnam disaster. We cannot assume he will just sit still and shut up. If he does believe in what he says he does—including reality—the better turn could happen.

The crux of the matter was that Bush was quite likely to take on missions. But what they would be, no one could guess in advance. Bush had emerged as an active-positive character. His experience proved he had the skills needed for a Presidential style. But why was his world view so blank? And was it really likely that he would not just drift through his term of office, but would take on missions after all? Bush's past—oddly different from Carter's or Reagan's—began to obscure the answer, a bit at a time.

THE BUSH BEGINNINGS

This fellow George got his character in his childhood. Activity and happiness happened nearly all the time. He was born on June 12, 1924, less than two years after his brother Prescott, Jr., and not long before three other children: Nancy, Jonathan, and William. They lived in a big house with a nice yard in Greenwich, Connecticut, one of New England's most trouble-free villages, owned and occupied by rich people. Their mother was sweet to the Bush flock, but she also got them active, pressing duty on them at home and then at school. Their father was often away, but when he was at home he acted dignified and mildly humorous. The children had food to eat, time to sleep, places to play. They were healthy. They liked one another. George especially liked his big brother, so much so that when Pres, Jr., started to go to school, George sadly missed him, so the parents got permission to send little George to school with his brother a year early. Later on, George and Pres, Jr., were given a gift: separate rooms, their old common one divided by a wall. But then they were lonely. They got the wall taken down so they could room together.

No dying siblings, no poverty, no fear of going broke, no parents madly different or long gone or drunk or miserable or demeaning, such as some other Presidents grew up with.

Most of the action revolved around sports—baseball, tennis, golf, and all kinds of enjoyable games to be played with vigor while sticking to the rules. There were prayers every morning and church on Sunday, and their mother had them learn to care for one another. Summertime was jolly time; they took off to stay at Kennebunkport, Maine, by the ocean, where their mother's father had ten acres and a ten-bedroom house, and had built a smaller summer house for the Bushes. The grandfather took the kids boating out onto the sea when they were small and when they got big enough he let them go boating alone and have picnics on the shore.

In short, George Bush had a happy, active childhood which registered on his personality as pleasure in exercising energy. His parents did not reward him for passivity or respond to negative behavior. Nor did his brothers and sister or grandparents or numerous cousins and guests deviate, on the average, from rewarding his active-positive character. The result was a personality ready to seek life as an adventure.

But from the very start, certain factors begin to suggest why Bush's world view emerged as a puzzle rather than a committed focus. World view in this Presidential context means what the person comes to believe in—not simply abstractly or intellectually or theologically, but in terms of real guidance toward action by one's actual self. Character does not necessarily forge the shape of world view. The health of personality does not define the direction the person seeks, the belief the person links—or tries to link—to what he or she actually does.

Bush dedicated his autobiography "To my mother and father, whose values lit the way."[3] But in fact the parents did not focus their light on the children much or often. As a child and youth, George was more often with his mother than with his father. George's younger brother William Henry said, "There wasn't a lot of interface with Dad as very young kids," so "If you had a problem, you went to Mother."[4] George's older brother was labeled with their father's name, Prescott; George got all three names of his mother's father, George Herbert Walker, and took on the nickname "Poppy" because his mother called her father "Pop." In the summer, they stayed at the Walker place in Maine. George's father came up there only for parts of Saturday and Sunday each week, and typically joined his wife Dorothy in stretching out on the lounge to listen to the weekend symphony on the radio. Weekdays mother left the children to have dinner together while she went off every evening to eat with Grandfather Walker; she spent much more time with the children in the summer than their father did, though leaving them for dinner "afforded the five youngsters welcome freedom from parental discipline for at least part of every day."[5]

Back in Greenwich, George's father "was home only a few nights a week"[6] and he arrived late from his office in New York, had dinner, and took off for a Greenwich function, such as chairing the town meeting. In the morning, the family had breakfast together—but with the *New York Times* and the *Herald Tribune* sprawled on the table for reading. Their hired driver drove father to the train station and returned to the house to take the children to school, so there was little time for talk in the morning or the evening.

What did George learn from his mother? George wrote that she "taught us about dealing with life on a personal basis, relating to other people."[7] But the main lesson, repeatedly described, was "Don't brag!" George recalled that "I spent my whole life learning not to talk about myself from my mother."[8] She got them used to not bragging about anything, not even when they won a ball game! What else it was that she planted in the mind of her son is unknown. Indeed, one of her main teachings, George remembered, was not thought-sharing but sports:

> She wasn't big, but she was a match for anyone in tennis, golf, basketball, baseball—for that matter I don't recall a footrace Mother was ever in that she didn't come in first. Even when her teenage sons outgrew her, she could bring us down to size whenever we'd get too full of ourselves.[9]

But she also had a special, close relationship with the son named after her father, George. Walt Harrington explains:

> In personality, . . . George took after his ebullient and empathetic mother. He liked pleasing people, and it was often said that he'd someday become a minister. "He was the easiest child to bring up, very obedient," said Mrs. Bush. She and George were great friends, sometimes even getting under the skin of the stiff-necked Prescott. George and his mother often broke into giggles at Sunday service, earning Father's glare. She also told the children that when Prescott, Sr., joined the Elks, he sat naked on a huge cake of ice as his initiation. The idea of father naked on a cake of ice had them in stitches—if Father wasn't around. Says Jonathan, "Dad was no laughing matter."[10]

As for father, George Bush himself writes that he "had a powerful impact on the way we came to look at the world," though he thinks "Our mother's influence and example were equally strong."[11] Bush's biographer Nicholas King puts it more strongly: "Prescott Bush was the single greatest influence in young George's life."[12] Biographer Fitzhugh Green even has Prescott shape the book: "The boy is father to the man, and George Bush is no exception. But the father of the boy was such a paramount figure in George's life that Prescott Bush's story comes first."[13] Others agree: "Bush came by his view of the world through inheritance—that is, through his father. . . . George Bush's life has been a struggle to live up to his father's example without destroying—or even questioning—the great man's myth."[14] And "According to friends and family, the presence of Prescott Bush has always loomed over George Bush's life."[15] Long after George's childhood and even after his father's death, observers thought "The fire in Bush's belly is fueled by his father's legacy."[16]

In a number of important respects, George did what his father had done. George went to a private prep school as had his father, entered the same college his father had attended, played baseball (first base) at Yale as his father had, and joined the same fraternity. Like his father, George left school for war, came back and married, produced a flock of children, went into business, joined the Republican party, and ran for Congress—all of which his father had done. That imitation is clear.

But it is little wonder that the *content* of a world view remained obscure and frazzled in the mind of George Bush—thanks to his father. Here is a sense of Prescott Bush's relationship to his children:

> He made a deep and lasting mark on his children. "We were all a little afraid of Dad," remembered Jonathan Bush. The senior Bush was not one for long, heart-to-heart talks. Instead, after some particular achievement he would drop an approving note that might be signed "devotedly, Dad." Sparing with his praise, Prescott Bush seldom intervened with his offspring, but instead made clear his own set of high values. Within the family, remembers Dorothy Bush, there was little introspection or heavy analysis. After a hard week on Wall Street, Prescott Bush spent most weekends swinging a golf club at the nearby Round Hill links. His wife sometimes urged him to take the boys along. "Oh, Dottie," he would answer, "if they want to learn, they'll pick it up." Instead the father much preferred to gather his family around their shiny Steinway piano, his rich voice leading the way, and pound out songs by ear. Regularly he brought home a group of fellow crooners, nicknamed the Silver Dollar Quartet, or the better known Merry Macs. On occasion the celebrated bandleader Fred Waring would drop by.[17]

There was little talk together; rare sports together; few meals together. The children, of course, saw their father (at six feet, four inches, he was hard to miss), and occasionally heard him say something, but there is not one account I can find—including in George Bush's own autobiography—of the father seriously and overtly concentrating on a child or offering to share his thinking. Nor did the children create problems for their father. George's mother remembers the child George as "a peacemaker," one who "never instigated an argument that I remember."[18] George himself recalled that "My father was very strong. He was so strong and so big and kind of overpowering—loving but overpowering." He did not lecture to the children, being too busy for that. George recalled that "I just watched him with admiration."[19] But at the same time, "Dad was really scary."[20] Was it hard for him to differ with his father? "It never occurred to me to differ. I mean, he was up here [lifts right hand as far as he can] and I was this little guy down here."[21]

Occasionally, Father Bush watched George, too—playing baseball.[22] On the rare occasion, when George could play golf with him, Prescott won: "George Bush never could beat his father at golf, even when the old man was in his seventies."[23] Father Bush spent many an hour singing with his children—but not with George. George was left out of that activity because he was the only one who did not have a good voice.[24] So for hours upon hours, Prescott Bush related to his children in one sharing activity, with only the one son George completely excluded from it. Biographer Green notes that "while the rest of his family was singing, George would always find something else to do. Perhaps this was an early step in distancing himself from his father."[25] And yet, as the quotes above indicate, George thought of his father then and thinks of him now as a very major factor in his world view.

For a son to see his father as a major influence on him is not surprising.

But two puzzles cloud George Bush's orientation to his father: their separation, being apart nearly all the time, and the fact that neither George nor any other biographer comes up with an account of what it actually was that Father Prescott represented to son George, what he meant to him.

The possible alternative shapers of George's world view might have been school and church. But neither really were sources for the Bush vision. Bush's autobiography as well as the available biographies do not include one single account of his learning anything in any school other than sports. Not in the Greenwich school, Phillips Academy, or Yale was there a experience in which his vision was affected by his learning. Not that George Bush himself was an exotic exception in those days in this regard. At both the academy and Yale, the style was to be intellectually cool, not to come on as a scholar but rather as a gentleman satisfied with a C grade. Leaving home at age 13 to follow his big brother to Phillips Academy outside of Boston, George got into sports and did well enough in his school classes. But in his junior year, he suddenly contracted a lung infection which put him in the hospital and made it necessary for him to spend an extra year at the school. This was a piece of luck, as it turned out, because he grew taller than most and was older than most, which helped him win the presidency of his senior class and a flock of student and sports offices.[26]

He then went off to the war and became the youngest pilot in the U.S. Navy. He flew 58 combat missions in the Pacific; on one he was shot down and rescued from the sea by a submarine in which he spent a month. He got home at age 20, as an experienced veteran having earned three Air Medals and the Distinguished Flying Cross.[27] As soon as he got back, at Christmas 1945, George married Barbara. Then he entered Yale encountering an unusual situation. Some 8000 veterans were admitted as freshmen the same year, so that classes were typically jammed with hundreds of students listening to lectures. Instead of the regular four years, the bachelor's degree would be awarded after two and one half years, so that Yale at Bush's time was a speedy, crowded educational novelty which he experienced while living off campus with his wife and a large group of other young couples. George himself did better than many, winning honors and graduating as captain of the baseball team.

There is not a bit of evidence that any moment of those many years of school had any effect on his mind, much less his world view. Similarly, George Bush spent many years at home and at schools bowing his head in prayer, and worshipping in church, but there is not a bit of evidence that his religious experience in any way shaped or transformed his vision. Rather it meant, as did much of his family talk, that he was supposed to be virtuous—honest, merciful, fair, and the rest.

The clearest observation about George Bush is the obscurity of his political intentions. Running for President, he himself confessed that "I have opinions of my own—strong opinions—but I don't always agree with them."[28] As Jack Germond and Jules Witcover pointed out,

> When George Bush took the oath of the presidency at the Capitol on January 20, 1989, and repeated his vision, first expressed in his acceptance speech in New

Orleans, of a "kinder, gentler nation," he was in effect asking for the American electorate to understand that getting elected required one George Bush, and governing the country effectively required another. He was telling the voters that the campaign could be discounted as a dependable guide to what his behavior would be in the White House.

But if the campaign for the presidency is supposed to provide the voters with the material with which to make an informed decision on the individual they want to lead their country, they should see the same one on the campaign trail as the one who eventually is sworn in and addresses them on Inauguration Day. That did not happen. . . .[29]

Bush's admirer Harry Hunt, III, confirms the puzzle from Bush himself:

> After twenty years in politics, Bush is still far easier to place by his class than by his beliefs. He firmly maintains that he could give it all up if the breaks go his way. "As far as I know now, if I don't stay on this current path, I will get out of politics and stay out of politics," he says. "Just as I've shifted gears in my life before, I'll shift them again. I don't want to leave the impression that I'm lacking interest in what I'm doing. But I just don't want always to be plotting a political future."[30]

His admiring biographer, Fitzhugh Green, concludes that "George Bush tries for vision as he talks about a thousand points of light where all Americans can work together to help the unfortunate. . . . So far he has offered no specific vision of what he wants the country to do and be under his presidency. . . . Bush would be well-served to promulgate a 'vision" or two' "[31]—this was Green's recommendation *after* Bush was elected President.

The editors of Time magazine sum up the puzzle:

> Often he seemed out of control, too eager to please, a figure not certain of where he was going or even who he was. What did George Bush really believe in? Whatever his convictions, would he stand behind them? The questions themselves were almost insulting. But there was about Bush the lingering perception that he was too weak and unsure to lead. More than most other politicians, he was a paradox. A brave war hero, he was mocked as a wimp. Modest and ingratiating, he was at times downright nasty. A Phi Beta Kappa student at Yale, he could sound incoherent and sometimes even goofy. What was one to make of George Bush? Did he possess the personal force and imagination for leadership, or was he just a sycophantic smoothy? . . . . White House aides who had attended hundreds of small sessions with the Vice President said they had no idea what he really thought.[32]

Active-positive character? Yes. Presidential style? Yes. World view? Despite decades of Bush politics, still unknown.

BUSH THE ARISTOCRAT

But the study of politics offers yet another way to discern a President's world view: by what he does rather than what he says. After a year of his energetic but inconclusive work in the White House, Bush began to pattern his actions as an aristocrat—a person who says all kinds of things but takes action in one economic direction. A rough answer began to emerge: Bush and his advertisers kept broadcasting razzle-dazzle images and sounds to make politics complex and puzzle the citizenry. That kind of rhetoric is historically typical of aristocrats, who often pursue their fortunes behind the tangled muddle of their popular assertions.

January 27, 1990: The New York Times

PREDICTION

The Silver Spoon in Bush's Mouth, and Policies

The threat of a Bush disaster comes not from his character or style but from his beliefs. That could change. Let's hope it does. . .

But what beliefs really guide his actions?

He believes in aristocracy. He acts to advance the rich and the powerful. Historically, aristocrats like George Bush have managed to ward off the challenge of real democracy, not by damning the people (at least in public) but by confusing them. Mr. Bush used that distractive power in his 1988 campaign, by flashing the flag and damning prison furloughs. He came across as a strong advocate for uplifting education and the environment and the homeless.

As it turns out, George Bush did none of the above. What he had said—as if he believed in democracy—turned out not to be a promise of action but a substitute for it. He misled the inattentive public by projecting a plausible image. That is a classic method aristocrats use for diverting government from consent of the governed. Mr. Bush's motto should have been: "Read my lips, but don't count on me."

In fact, he has been working for the welfare of the rich. He damns taxation and shunts off responsibility for the sick, poor, abused, illiterate, aged and jobless onto private charity, echoing the appeals of Herbert Hoover during the Great Depression. Like other aristocrats, Mr. Bush says he cares, but postpones the project.

He simplifies his emotions, but complexifies his behavior. He sweeps aside history and planning in favor of immediate wheeling and dealing. He surrounds himself, not with a Rooseveltian "Brain Trust" to gain perspective, but with assistant managers to grab the present. He claims credit for any good that happens, such as the rise of democracy in the world as if his applauding was an exercise of power. He advocates values that his actions undercut such as "a kinder and gentler America".

An aristocrat much prefers a secret Star Chamber to a public parliament. Mr. Bush's vision makes democracy domestic only, while international relations are to be secret and thus not subject to democratic revelation. Secrecy serves the insiders. It also obscures acts that the public would find shockingly wrong, such as their tax money being funneled overseas to vicious mass murderers and torturers and thieves in power in Central America, Turkey and China.

That Mr. Bush hustles for the rich and the powerful should have been no surprise. Not only is he related to Queen Elizabeth I, but he has spent his life cooperating with such people. His grandfather was a big businessman, his father a big businessman and he himself became one in Texas—a millionaire. His uncle supplied the investment that produced his fortune. He belonged to three exclusive country clubs in Houston.

In the House, his father got him assigned to the Ways and Means Committee. He ran for the Senate with big money supplied by Richard Nixon, whose leadership he later devoted himself to as head of the C.I.A. and the Republican Party. As Vice President, Mr. Bush focused on enhancing the power of the President he had opposed. To get his own Presidential power, he did whatever his media advisors thought advantageous.

In other words, the world view of this President can be taken not as some ideology or religion, or as a political mission like Jimmy Carter's fight for human rights. Rather, it is simply the readily predictable aristocratic orientation of a man trained throughout his life by experiences that run counter to democracy.

But he need not follow that line, and one day he may not. An active-positive person is not obsessed. Aristocrats in the Presidency have included the Roosevelts, for example, and many a political leader has departed from his rich friends and devoted himself to the people.

Given the major crises and opportunities now confronting the U.S., we need a President who will advance real democracy—not class greed and the lust for power—at home and abroad.

Three times in his past, Mr. Bush has left behind the aristocrats and gone into what he saw as a new world: into the Navy at age 18 against his father's guidance, away from Connecticut and off to Texas to start a business and on to China despite President Gerald Ford's offer of the ambassador's post in Britain or France.

Despite his aristocratic leanings, then, President Bush could become the modern Mr. Democracy. For those of us who would like to see a President who works for genuine democracy, that is the best hope we have—until 1993, at least.

The potential for change was there—given the fact that Bush the active-positive had a character different from those driven by a fixed obsession. But his past had supported his aristocracy. Such elitism he inherited from his family and saw confirmed in his brothers and sister and even in his own children. His own economic and political successes fit the bill. Money came from his relatives and their friends. He worked hard to make more. Power came from his fellow power-holders whose benefits he promoted and advanced when he became a Congressman, Ambassador to the United Nations, chairman of the Republican National Party, director of the CIA, and Vice President of the United States. In each case he served the Republicans who wielded national power. As President, far from acting on his previously sworn concern for public education, public health, and public welfare, Bush postponed any such deeds in favor of protecting the rich against taxes and providing big money opportunities for the military hardware producers and international dealers.

Thus George Bush's world view appeared to be emerging with a certain congruity, a possible regularity, despite the confusing statements concerning his intentions. His was the view of aristocracy, related to the culture from which he had emerged rather than from any pecularities of his own particular experience. The lesson appeared to be that his inconsistent appearance had hidden his consistent behaviors. George's father had calmly kept working in business and politics for the well to do, steadily and quietly helping them out. Aristocracy confirmed what? Would George take on the same?

AT HOME: LOVE THEM AND LEAVE THEM

At the time of the Japanese attack on Pearl Harbor, December 7, 1941, George Bush was a 17-year-old student at Phillips Andover Academy prep school in Massachusetts. Shocked by the attack, he thought he should enlist. His mother tried to talk him out of it; his father, also against his enlisting, nevertheless said nothing.[33] That Christmas, George met and fell in love with a lovely girl, a good cotillion dancer named Barbara, only 16 years old. Then early in June, at his graduation day, Secretary of State Henry L. Stimson gave the commencement address, urging the students to go on to college, not to enter the service right away. Walking out of the chapel, George's mother asked him, "Has this changed your idea?" He said, "Not a bit!"[34] His father was there; he asked George if he would take Stimson's recommendation and go to college. George said no. He enlisted in the U.S. Navy air service on the day of his 18th birthday, June 12, 1942.

Such were the facts. But the crucial revelation is what that decision meant to George himself. By his own memory, his father at that time was "an imposing presence, six feet four, with deep-set blue-gray eyes and a resonant voice."[35] George recalled that

> I had wanted to go right into the Navy when the war broke out. But *my parents and relatives were upset; they felt that the thing for me to do was go on to college*. Yet I was shaken by what had happened at Pearl Harbor, and I was patriotic and wanted to do something about it. *So I dug in my heels and pulled it off*. I won my wings and commission at the age of 18, at the time the youngest pilot in the United States Navy. I was determined to see combat and then after the war get into college, so I did. I've always been one to concentrate on what's at hand.[36]

Asked about it another time, George gave a stumbling answer: "I had a very powerful father. . . . Very much of a leader and admired by everybody, and I didn't want to do something on his, I had a kind of a, not a competitive thing with him, but *I wanted to go out and do something on my own*."[37] On the day of George's birthday, his father shook his hand and put him on the train. George remembered that *"It was the first time I had ever seen my Dad cry."*[38] Biographer Fitzhugh Green asks "whether the young man wasn't trying already to step free of his father's sway as much as to fight for his country."[39] Biographer Nicholas King notes that

> Nearly all his classmates went on to college, but George wanted to achieve something right away. He wanted to achieve it in his name and not in the name of his father or his family. He wanted to *"get out from under."* This desire for achievement was to be the motor, as well as the fuel, of much that he did later on.[40]

Intensity was there. Asked "Was it a shock to go off to war from your background?", George answered, "It was *the* shock."[41]

OFF TO TEXAS

George went through combat and at the end of the war entered Yale and got his degree. His father set out to get him a job, having already used his own membership on the board of Pan American Airways to arrange a job for Pres Jr., his oldest son. Green reports that George's "father wanted to contribute ideas and opportunities."[42] A partner of Brown Brothers, Harriman, his father got them to break the company's rule against nepotism and offer George a position. "I had a soft job on Wall Street all set," he said, "But *I wanted to do something on my own.*"[43]

George did not take that job—and did not even mention it in his autobiography. He noted that he could not go on to graduate school or take a Rhodes scholarship in England "without outside financial help"[44]—which his father might have provided. As George put it, "I began my job search."[45] He sought a job with Proctor and Gamble and was turned down. "I'll never forget it," George Bush recalled. *I've had an I'll-show-those-guys attitude ever since.*"[46] Neil Mallon, president of Dresser Industries, an oil company in Texas, in which Prescott Bush had long been a senior director and to which Brown Brothers, Harriman, had supplied big money, offered to take George on as its only trainee; he accepted, but he does not mention in his autobiography his father's relation to that business.

Neil "might have added," George wrote, "that if I really wanted to find *something different in life than what I'd known*, the place to find it was west Texas."[47] Elsewhere George Bush puts it this way: "If I were a psychoanalyzer, I might conclude that *I was trying to, not compete with my father, but do something on my own.*"[48] His wife Barbara said about the move to Texas that "I think we'd have probably not grown up as quickly. I think it was very good for our marriage. . . . When you are a couple all grown up, nobody's son or daughter, nobody's shadow, you are you."[49]

Biographers confirm that view. Howard Hurt thought the move to Texas

> was a break with tradition, a departure from the preordained path through life, and it carried the risks of failure and social ostracism and also the possibility of triumph. Although going into the oil business instead of investment banking did not connote oedipal violence, leaving the East was a sign of leaving the nest, of an escape from the shadow of his father. But it wasn't a breaking off of relations. After all, his father had gotten him the job."[50]

Green thought Bush's "interest was piqued by the idea of physically, at least, cutting loose from his blood and school ties in the East."[51] And "Now, somewhat like a prisoner freed from others' disciplines and expectations, he faced an uncharted future." It was "truly the first day of the rest of his life," a time when "He was, at last, commander of his fate and master of his soul."[52] King saw that the decision was "in keeping with his resolve to break away from home and family"; he supposes that George "did not want success in life to be handed to him, and much as he loved and revered his father, he wanted to move out of the paternal shadow, strike out on his own, to face a challenge of his own finding, just as he would seek it in later years."[53] The Time magazine editors saw that George made "another important decision on his own, rejecting his father's advice to follow him into the investment-banking business and instead taking off for Texas. Such unexpected moves, friends figured, were George's way of asserting independence from his father and making up for a life of privilege."[54]

The thesis that George saw the move to Texas as a move away from his father explains why George Bush's autobiography portrays his adventures in the Texas oil business as if he were winging it on his own, risking failure and then achieving a million dollars. Working hard in Texas, he saw a new lesson of life: "Do your best and don't look back."[55] But what his autobiography brushes aside is the fact that his father helped get him the job in the first place, and that two and a half years later he started a new enterprise with money from his mother's brother, Uncle Herbie, who had watched him play ball at Yale, had played golf with him, and had stayed sometimes at Kennebunkport. He also got $50,000— big money in those days—from his father for the new company. George mentions that his Uncle Herbie "had helped us with funds and his expertise as an investment banker when we started the company," and then says: "But in business as in politics, you can only go so far relying on the backing of relatives and friends. Along with other *independents*, we stayed busy working up leads and contacts . . ."[56] Harry Hurt 3rd points out that "One of the few embellishments Bush has allowed in his life story is the notion that he built himself a business from scratch. In fact, he did it with family money—including money from his father."[57]

In 1953, three major events hit George Bush. His daughter Robin, born while he was living in Texas, died at age four of leukemia—a horrible blow for her father and mother; in the years following, they gave birth to three sons and a daughter, who, with George Jr., duplicated exactly the number and gender combination as George Sr. grew up with. The same year, Bush and a couple of friends set up a new company, Zapata Petroleum, with money from family connections in New York. And it was in 1953 that Prescott Bush entered the Senate of the United States. Politics as a possible occupation entered the mind of George Bush via his father: "Politics entered into my thinking in other ways in the years that followed, *especially after Dad went to the Senate* in 1953."[58]

OFF TO WASHINGTON

Prescott Bush had tried for a Senate seat in 1950 and again in 1952, without success. But then a Senator died and Prescott was dragged into yet another run, despite his aristocratic resistance: "I've had it. . . . I'm not going around that state with my hat in my hand." But he won, and in the Senate, he "began the career that today nobody remembers very distinctly," though he played frequent golf with President Eisenhower, having served as president of the United States Golf Association.[59]

A Texas friend of George's remembers a conversation back then when Bush raised the question, "What do you think you'd like to do with your life?" George answered his own question, saying, "I really feel that some day I want to go into public service. I think I'd like to get into the government. . . . I don't know if I want to be a politician, but *I'd like to hold office like my father*. That's what I'd like to do with my life."[60] But George held back for years. "My opinion . . . differed from my father's" opposition to gas deregulation. Texas corporate types phoned George to say, as he recalled, that "I'd damn well better get my father turned around." They threatened his business: "Unless my father 'got right' on deregulation, 'that's all she wrote for you, Bush, because we're gonna run your ass out of the offshore drilling business.'" George "tried to keep my emotions under control . . ."[61] He did express his opinion to his father, who, however, did not change his position on the bill, but told his son, "Don't you worry about it. . . If there's any aftereffects from it, just tell me about them, and we'll take care of that."[62] The bill George hoped would pass was vetoed by President Eisenhower, Prescott's golf buddy. Having concentrated in his autobiography on this difference with his father, Bush concludes: "But the incident didn't dampen my growing interest in going into politics. *I'd achieved everything I'd hoped for when we moved to Texas.*"[63]

But in fact years went by before George took on politics. And his inaction "concerned" his father. In 1961, Prescott, at a fund-raising event in Washington, asked the chairman of the Republican Party for George's county, "Jimmy, when are you going to get George involved?" The county chairman said, "Senator, I'm trying. We're all trying." The chairman went home and offered his own position to George, who turned it down. But they kept pressing him. Then in 1962, Prescott finished his second Senate term and retired because of poor health. Only then did George accept the local party chairmanship.[64] As biographer King points out, "Now was the time to think of his long-cherished ambition to enter public service as his father had done before him. Prescott Bush was only two years retired from the Senate, and it was therefore natural for his son to shoot for the same electoral goal."[65]

So in 1964 George Bush won the Republican primary and ran for the Senate as a far right, Barry Goldwater-type Republican: against civil rights bills, against the nuclear test ban, and against Red China's entry to the United Nations. Bush lost, but got more Republican votes than anyone had gotten in Texas. He took on politics as a career, being, as he wrote, "young enough to look for new challenges."[66] He sold his holdings in the oil company in 1966, and ran for Congress as a more moderate Republican, though supporting the Vietnam war, and won. Being just a freshman Congressman, it was a surprise that he was put on the House Ways and Means Committee—a surprise event which happened because his father pressed the Democratic chairman to make it happen.[67] His campaign and experience in the House of Representatives defined and confirmed his style of politics, affecting the homework, negotiations, and rhetoric he would eventually carry on to the Presidency.

His strongest memory following his 1966 victory was that of a vote which surprised his constituents. In Congress, he supported the successful Civil Rights Act for open housing. He came home and spoke to angry Texans at a Ramada Club session, some of whom booed at him when he was introduced. A speaker came before him, saying that the Civil Rights Act "will lead to government control of private property, the Communists' number one goal."[68] Bush stood up and spoke, giving his argument. A friend remembered that he said, "I did what I thought was right. We agree on most issues. This one we don't agree on. I hope I still have your support. But if I don't have your support, I hope I still have your friendship. If I don't have your friendship, I'm sorry, but I have to vote with my conscience."[69] The audience quieted down—and then, to his surprise, when he finished, they stood up and gave him a standing ovation. In his autobiography, he notes that "More than twenty years later I can truthfully say that nothing I've experienced in public life, before or since, has measured up to the feeling I had when I went home that night."[70] He took a chance, and won.

The next election came up in 1968. Bush won it, without opposition. Then in 1970, President Richard Nixon encouraged him to run for the Senate, offering to get him a cozy job in Washington if he lost. George's father advised him to stay in the House, to carry on with that secure office. But George decided instead to run for the Senate. Biographer Gail Sheehy saw that as "the first time he stood up to his father."[71] Through the campaign, George's "father's strong conviction that American involvement in Vietnam was a terrible mistake"[72] clashed with George's appeal to hawks by being in favor of America's war in Vietnam.

George lost the race. Early the next year, President Nixon appointed him ambassador to the United Nations. Being in New York, George saw his father more often; when Prescott came by, his son would greet him with a kiss and hug. "Like a little boy," says biographer Hurt.[73] A staffer said that "I never saw a man show so much affection for his father."[74] The next year, Prescott developed lung cancer. On October 8, 1972, he died, in the same New York hospital where little Robin had died nineteen years before. George wrote in his autobiography that "It was a real blow for me, for all his children. We had lost a best friend."[75] George remembered that "When my dad died, somebody wrote me a letter and said, 'When your dad dies you lose your best friend.' It made a tremendous impact on me."[76] Biographer Green concludes that "Perhaps the greatest giant George Bush had ever known exited Bush's life."[77]

Early the next year, Nixon got Bush to take on a job which Barbara Bush saw as the worst: chairman of the Republican National Committee. *"I'm really glad Dad is not alive,"* George said. *"It would have killed him to see this happen. He thought we were the party of virtue and all bosses were Democrats."*[78] Not until August 6, 1974, a few days before Nixon, about to be impeached, quit the Presidency did George Bush recommend that he resign.

Vice President Gerald Ford took over Nixon's Presidency. Bush's hope was that Ford would choose him as his Vice President, but instead Ford chose Nelson Rockefeller. To Bush, Ford offered two exciting possibilities: ambassador to Great Britain or to France. To Ford's surprise, Bush asked to be envoy to China. His own autobiographical memory was that "As far as Barbara and I were concerned, *the best 'future' we could imagine was one that took us as far as possible from the immediate past. . . . We'd come to a decision much like the one we made in 1948. Back then we decided not to do the traditional thing,* but to head for the West."[79] A year later, President Ford got him to come back and take over the Central Intelligence Agency.

In a book of interviews given by George Bush, he spelled out a lifetime analogy:

> You can make decisions that people don't like without incurring their wrath. Often *how* you do something is more meaningful than *what* you do.
>
> To achieve something in this world, you've got to be willing to take risks. That's where my critics end up confused about me. I don't fit neatly into their mold.
>
> I should have gone to college at 18, but I joined the Navy; I should have stayed back East and worked my father's prosperous business, but I went West and started out on my own. I'm convinced that you can't just sit around waiting for things to happen. You've got to take the chance, go after it, take the tough assignment.
>
> President Ford offered me an ambassadorship to England or France—pretty glamorous duty. I opted for China. Advisors warned me against going to the CIA; it was supposed to be a political dead end. It was the worst time to go over to the agency, but I grew from the experience.[80]

Time passed. George Bush sought the Presidency. A friend explained, "He has the fire in his belly." Biographer Hurt said, "The fire in Bush's belly is fueled by his father's legacy."[81]

In 1979, Bush fought for the Republican Presidential nomination, out on the road campaigning 328 days during the next twelve months.[82] He lost; Reagan then got him elected as Vice President. He served obscurely in that job for seven years before he set forth for the Presidency again. At that point he said that "This week I begin a new challenge—running for the biggest job in America. Now it's time to define my own agenda."[83] To the surprise of the country—and hot news for the journalists—candidate Bush chose as his Vice Presidential running mate Dan Quayle, virtually unknown to the public and extremely implausible as a potential President to those who did know of him. Garry Wills thought that "Bush saw the vice-presidential selection process as a way of showing he was his own man."[84] The campaign held another surprise when Bush, the supposed "wimp," attacked his Democratic opponent Dukakis in rough and tough style. In November 1988, Bush was elected President of the United States. At that moment he "underwent a remarkable transformation," brushing aside his campaign attacks as, at his subsequent inauguration, he brushed aside the major priorities his campaign had emphasized. Bush the President embarked repeatedly in new directions.

THE PATTERN FROM HIS BOYHOOD

The development of Bush's world view is obscure. There may be, one of these years, a biography which radically clarifies the story. But even the hints now available point at a possibility: that the Bush is the George, that his beliefs relate strongly to his boyhood, not just to his contemporary perceptions.

Bush the boy had a problem. On the one hand, his parents took care of him with remarkable responsibility, meeting his welfare needs generously. But on the other hand, he himself was an item to his parents. They taught him, they fed him, they provided recreation, they financed his projects. They liked him as a lad who was cheery and a good student. But the main lesson he got from his mother was that he should not focus on himself. And the main thing his father gave him was benign neglect, liking him and dominating him from a distance, but very rarely having anything personal to do with him. Like most teenagers, George Bush reached that time of life in which one feels the necessity of recognizing oneself as a person. Identity is needed. Part of it comes from recognizing beliefs for oneself which are identical with the beliefs of parents. But revolution is usually added in the form of beliefs distinct from others, including the dominant others, such as parents. That double tension normally gets resolved over a period of years on the way into adulthood, by the youth moving past the conflict of self versus parents to a self-growing concord of beliefs, fusing the past in the light of a hoped-for future.

Reviewing the available Bush history reinforces a simple explanation for his world view problem: he never resolved the conflict. Instead he acted unpredictably, due to the continuing ambivalence between pro-parent and anti-parent beliefs, so that what he actually did was to go with them for a while and then against them for a while, registering in the reality of his life a need to do a pair of opposites rather than the need to concord them into a guiding unity. Even after he got to the White House, over age sixty, Bush still had that lingering, personal heritage of him and/versus them, a view up close, as distinct from a view of the world as it now is and soon may be. Bush's world view is not representative of his nation's forbearers or of the people, but of intimate others.

George Herbert Walker Bush remembered what came into his mind at the moment of his Presidential victory: "I wondered what my old man would say if he could see his little boy now."[85]

OFF TO WAR

George Bush as President expressed philosophical principles:

> I will never apologize for the United States of America. I don't care what the facts are.

> I'm a practical man. I like what works.[86]

> I want to offer the hope of freedom to countries around the world because that's the basis of our very being in this country, our own freedom.[87]

> As President, I mean to work toward a new harmony, a greater tolerance, an understanding that this country is a partnership.[88]

In the crisis of the coming of war in 1990–1991, he advocated "a New World Order." But just as the specific intentions he expressed in campaigning had but wobbly relations to his actual policies as President, so his principles bore no clear connection to his White House actualities. George Bush's world view was not based either on deduction or continuity, though his empirical curiosity existed. What turned out to be a major danger resulting from his election to the Presidency was that he did indeed take on missions, but he selected them on the basis of his internal world view perspective, strongly related to his adolescent life, especially in terms of the need to surprise others. The war with Iraq, a human disaster, illustrated strongly the overpowering influence of Bush's need to shock his father and mother rather than simply "take care that the laws be faithfully executed." Like plenty of other Presidents, George Bush gladly turned away from domestic politics, given all its troubling complexity, to international politics, where the President could act like King of America.

Early in his Presidency, as Commander in Chief, Bush had sent military forces off to make killing attacks in Panama and then in El Salvador. After the Panama attack, he got strong criticism from Congress for acting suddenly and without real deliberation by a crisis management team in the White House. Then in November 1989, rebels in El Salvador took over a hotel where American military advisors were staying. Bush sent commandos; the threat they posed to the rebels helped rescue the Americans. Bush said, "We moved very rapidly" and "We had a very good, orderly process that resulted in our being able to do that."[89] His process was to meet with some of his top advisors. The Pentagon was angered that he went public, since commandos were supposed to operate in secret. Bush noted that he did not clear the action in advance with the President of El Salvador, but rather "I told him what we were going to do and he acquiesced."[90] In short, from Bush's own perspective, a sudden, secret, fast military action by the White House got potential American hostages out of El Salvador.

The year passed. Then 1990 saw the Iraq crisis.

Iraq had been at war with Iran virtually throughout the Reagan administration, 1980–1988. Iraq initiated the attack. About one million soldiers and civilians were killed, more butchered to death than in any other war anywhere since World War II. Reagan's administration backed Iraq against Iran, basically because Iran might otherwise take over the Middle East. Reagan's foreign policy required that we have relations with Iraq after 17 years of separation, giving the Iraqis not only secret intelligence but also big money: agricultural credit guarantees and Export-Import Bank financing. Iraq became the world's biggest purchaser of U.S. rice and one of the biggest buyers of U.S. corn, wheat, and other grains. As the New York Times' Leslie H. Gelb surmised, "No one did more than the Reagan and Bush Administrations to build up Saddam's legitimacy and power."[91]

In August, 1988, Iran ended the war, thrilling the Iraqis, but despite U.S. aid, Iraq was heavily in debt to the tune of some $80 billion. This amount was more than its whole gross national product, much of it due to be paid back fast. In 1989, the new Bush administration provided greater aid for Iraq, pronouncing Saddam Hussein's Iraq as one of the "key friendly states" in the Mideast, being "vital to U.S. national security."[92]

Money and "friendly" support for Iraq by the United States moved forward—in spite of serious challenges. The Iraq military was developing biological and chemical weapons, as well as nuclear weapons; the nuclear development was so dangerous it triggered a bomb attack by the Israelis. Amnesty International had verified repeatedly, by hard evidence, that Iraq's government was a major, systematic violator of human rights, torturing prisoners by burning them as they hung from the ceiling and killing many of their own people. In that regard, Iraq was no exception to dictatorships in the Middle East, such as Syria, Turkey, Saudi Arabia, Kuwait, and others. But in early 1990, the U.S. State Department's annual Human Rights Report called Iraq's human rights performance "abysmal." Tens of thousands of their Kurdish minority—men, women, and children—had been killed with poison gas by the Iraq government.

That February, an editor of the Voice of America, who said he was "reflecting the views of the U.S. Government,"[93] broadcast that "The rulers of these countries hold power by force, and fear, not by the consent of the governed. . . . the tide of history is against such rulers. The 1990s should belong not to the dictators and secret police, but to the people."[94] Saddam Hussein was enraged by that—so Bush's ambassador to Iraq issued a statement of "regret" and pronounced that "It is absolutely not United States policy to question the legitimacy of the government of Iraq or interfere in any way with the domestic concerns of the Iraqi people and government."[95] Back in the State Department, Secretary of State James Baker held a meeting in which they ruled that henceforth all Voice of America editorials about Iraq would have to be cleared before they could be broadcast.

Saddam Hussein repeatedly damned Israel, so some Congressmen pushed to cut off his money from the U.S. But Bush's State Department pushed that proposal aside, in part because "all we would be doing is hurting U.S. rice producers and U.S. firms looking for business."[96] A Congressman from California, Tom Lantos, said it "boggles my mind" that the administration hoped that "Iraq under Saddam Hussein will turn in the direction of being a responsible and civilized and peace-loving and constructive member of the international community."[97]

On July 20, 1990, the talking gave way to military action. Intelligence brought out that thousands of trucks full of Iraqi troops were rolling toward the Kuwaiti border. The Kuwaiti dictatorship was Iraq's rich neighbor, with average individual incomes about ten times more than Iraq's. Invasion looked likely. A few U.S. concerns were expressed and a few small military exercises were implemented, but basically the Bush administration issued a clear message of noninvolvement. "We do not have any defense treaties with Kuwait and there are no special defense or security commitments to Kuwait," said a State Department official, and the U.S. ambassador told Saddam Hussein that the U.S. had "no opinion" about his potential clash with Kuwait. Iraqis and other Arab chiefs kept hinting that no invasion would happen.[98] That very summer, Iraq kept getting, more than any other nation, the profit of U.S.-subsidized grain sales.[99] The Senate voted to cut off agricultural credits and military technologies to Iraq, but that did not happen.[100] The very day before the Iraqis rolled into Kuwait, Bush's administration approved a sale of $695,000 worth of data devices to the Iraqi government.[101]

That fall of 1990, the Bush administration, much like the Lyndon Baines Johnson administration in the fall of 1964, "began planning an offensive campaign to dislodge Iraqi forces from Kuwait . . . even as Administration officials insisted in public that the only mission of United States forces was to defend Saudi Arabia and enforce United Nations sanctions."[102]

THE PRESIDENT'S SURPRISE

George Bush the aristocrat was obviously supporting the international money-hustlers even in this crisis and he was obviously operating foreign policy close-in with his mini-team. As Donald Oberdorfer observed, "More so than most of their predecessors, Bush and Baker operate U.S. foreign policy in an intensely personal and informal fashion, interacting freely in person or by telephone with foreign leaders and paying much less heed to career professionals."[103] But after August 2, 1990, when 80,000 Iraqi soldiers rammed across the border into Kuwait, Bush began to emerge as a virtual monarch, an individual making his own decisions to direct the nation's most high and wide actions. The president felt no responsibility to tell the people the truth of his directions.

On August 3, President Bush got together with his top advisors and a reporter asked him whether the United States was prepared to intervene militarily. He said, "We're not discussing intervention."[104] But he telephoned the king of Saudi Arabia and told him the United States would stand by the Saudis. That same day, the Congress of the United States adjourned for a month-long holiday, as usual, leaving behind a committee to confer with the President, and authorizing the House and Senate leaders to call a special session if necessary. But Secretary of State Baker made his view clear to both the House and the Senate: that the President himself could decide to launch an attack against Iraq without consulting them at all.

George Bush went on television the following week, when thousands of American troops were on their way to Saudi Arabia, and he defined a clear restriction:

> I want to be clear about what we are doing and why. *America does not seek conflict,* nor do we seek to chart the destiny of other nations. But America will stand by her friends. *The mission of our troops is wholly defensive.* Hopefully, they will not be needed long. *They will not initiate hostilities, but they will defend* themselves, the kingdom of Saudi Arabia, and other friends in the Persian Gulf.[105]

Soon the commitment to defense, not offense, was trashed—but the President held back from telling that fact to the public or even to its representatives. As two New York Times writers noted, "The dimensions of the planned military buildup were closely held by Mr. Bush and his inner circle."[106] At the end of

October, he ordered that the plan for attacking be kept secret until after the coming November election.[107] Congress again recessed, but Bush refused their proposal that he consult with a formal group they had left behind or call an emergency session if war was to be initiated. So Congress declared that its own leadership could call their own emergency session if necessary.[108] But that they did not do.

Some members of Congress did sign up against the war, declared that the President had no right to start war by his own individual decision, and insisted that the President could not, on his own, shift from defense to offense, given the War Powers Resolution that allowed only an emergency defense to be instigated by the President. Fifty-three members of the House of Representatives and one Senator joined in taking the case to court against the President-only war decision; the court ruled "that the Constitution clearly requires Congressional authority prior to an offensive military action by the President." The judge was ready to issue an injunction to enforce that rule if a majority in Congress supported it.[109] By then the troop "dimensions had become enormous—doubling the 200,000 American forces, calling up thousands of reserves, and setting forth a huge bombing campaign in mid-January, to be followed by a huge ground-campaign in late February."[110]

In one two-hour meeting, it was President Bush himself who decided to start the offense war and to get support from the United Nations, dispatching Secretary Baker to make that happen. George Bush kept that business secret until November 8, 1990, two days after that year's national Congressional elections, because, as a White House official explained, "Nov. 8 was a very important date because it was after Nov. 6."[111] Senator Sam Nunn, chairman of the Senate's defense committee, got the news—one hour before the public got it.[112] That announcement of a great big turn-around, from defense to offense, from the risk of war to the certainty of war, "got a sharp reaction from Capitol Hill, and the press was saying that nobody knows why we are there, and it looked like we had a big domestic problem."[113] Hearings held by Congress brought forth major experts, such as former Secretaries of Defense, arguing strongly for economic sanctions against Hussein rather than war. But an article George Bush published, "Why We Are in the Gulf," did not even bother to mention the Congress.[114] And when Senator Edward Kennedy asked Bush's Defense Secretary Dick Cheney whether Bush needed the approval of Congress to go to war, his answer was, "I do not believe the President requires any additional authorization from Congress before committing U.S. forces to achieve our objectives in the Gulf."[115]

Still, Bush's personal visions shifted. On December 16, in a television interview, he said the U.S. action had Saddam Hussein "still unconvinced." Then two days later, he said, "My gut says he will get out of there." Such shifting "reflected the President's mood swings in the weeks leading right up to the January 16 decision to launch the air war." On January 2, 1991, he said he would decide for or against the war no matter what Congress or the people had to say.[116] He came on television nearly tearful and infuriated over the current report of Amnesty International about Saddam Hussein's disgusting torture and murder of Kuwaiti citizens, but he did not mention his former support of that villain or his Mideast allies with the same kind of practice.

Meanwhile, Secretary Baker, with no formal authorization from the Congress, flew from country to country to build a Bush-supporting coalition in the United Nations. No one was asked to remember that the Reagan administration had derided the United Nations and refused to pay them America's dues or that the UN had blasted the United States for invading Panama—a blast brushed aside with contempt by this country's government. When Israel had invaded Lebanon, killing some 20,000 people, the UN Security Council voted to denounce the aggression—but the United States vetoed the measure.[117] Baker did manage to recruit support from UN leaders, including a number of hungry dictatorships in need of money. Representative Henry B. Gonzalez of Texas, who proposed that Bush be impeached for violating the Constitution, asserted that the President had been

> bribing, intimidating and threatening others, including the members of the UN Security Council, to support belligerent acts against Iraq. The debt of Egypt was forgiven; a $140 million loan to China was agreed to; the Soviet Union was promised $7 billion in aid; Colombia was promised assistance to its armed forces; Zaire was promised military assistance and partial forgiveness of its debt; Saudi Arabia was promised $12 billion in arms; Yemen was threatened with the termination of support and the United States finally paid off $187 million of its debt to the UN after the vote President Bush sought was made. The vote was bought. . .[118]

The United Nations Security Council voted in favor of the U.S. war against Iraq. Several other nations promised troops and loans. Such events strengthened Bush's purpose. But there were Congressmen who did not see that as an adequate authorization.

President Bush did meet with some Congressmen on January 9, 1991. Secretary Baker was in Geneva talking with the Iraqi Foreign Minister Aziz. The Secretary phoned the President with a downside report. Here is the kind of conversation the President had with the Congressmen:

> "The President excused himself to take the call and was gone for about eight minutes," said Representative Mel Levine, Democrat of California. "When he came back, our conversation stopped. The President's whole demeanor had changed. He was somber and grim. You could see it all over his face. He looked at us and said two words: 'No progress.' I felt it was a defining moment. He was a different man. When we asked why the meeting had lasted so long, he simply said: 'History.'"[119]

And from then on—Wednesday, January 9—"all the President's advisers agreed that war was now inevitable."[120] The next day, Thursday, Congress did at last take up a formal session on the question of war. But by that time, the President's actions had nearly decided it all. Bush had sent nearly half a million American troops to Saudi Arabia, had committed the U.S. to a United Nations coalition, and had set up a deadline—the next week—for war unless the Iraqis pulled out of Kuwait.

Years ago, President Eisenhower had declared that "I will never be guilty of any kind of action that can be interpreted as war until Congress, which has the Constitutional authority, says so."[121] Germond and Witcover on January 12, 1991, said that "Only now, at the 11th hour, has Bush gone to Capitol Hill, when the situation has advanced so far that voices raised in caution inevitably will be painted by some as unpatriotic or worse."[122] As a result, no real debate happened even in the Senate; speaker after speaker came on television saying what he thought rather than deliberating directly with the other elected leaders, very few of whom were even present in the chamber of the Congress.[123] Despite the reality of the situation, Bush simply asserted the opposite: "As a democracy, we've debated this issue openly and in good faith, and as president I have held extensive consultation with the Congress."[124]

In fact, the democracy established by the framers of the Constitution was set aside by Bush. "The Framers did not confer authority on the President to initiate war or military hostilities, to transform defensive actions into aggressive wars, or to defend U.S. allies against attack. From the Framers' eighteenth-century perspective, only Congress could change the nation's conditions from peace to war." But from a long series of twentieth-century war blunders, a new perspective emerged: "the modern view of the President as a king-general who exercises prerogative or discretionary power to make foreign policy, initiate war, and conclude peace treaties."[125] Despite Bush's monarchical military assertions, Congress, very late in the game, did pass a resolution to authorize the President to initiate military action against Iraq, providing that he would inform the House and Senate leaders that he had "used all appropriate diplomatic and peaceful means" to get Iraq to comply with the UN resolutions and that such efforts had failed. The vote was close: 52-47 in the Senate, 250-183 in the House.[126] That was Saturday, January 12, 1991. The United States went to war against Iraq on Tuesday, January 15, 1991.

Technically speaking, Congress had declared war. But in terms of the reality of democracy, the government of the United States had shifted its major policy priority to a nearly total focus on the Middle East; had mobilized and assigned nearly 500,000 troops to one major military mission; had committed itself to obey certain major, significant demands passed by the United Nations and a coalition of allies; and had set up a schedule of precise dates for war action—all done *before* Congress acted. This mission of the United States was not a decision by the people's representatives. It was a decision by the President. Whatever the details of complex legal procedure, the Bush administration had established a precedent for future Presidents, authorizing a President to take on the nation's most extensive military deployments and military treaty-making on his own, and then, having set forth an enormous train rolling fast toward war, to force a quick vote through Congress.

CONSENT OF THE GOVERNED?

Similarly, that fundamental basis of democracy called government by consent of the governed—public discourse and then public support—did not happen.

Publicly as well as Congressionally, George Bush's fuzzy world view regarding war confused the country. AP noted that "Speculation about Bush's state of mind has been growing. . . ."[127] A. M. Rosenthal of the *New York Times* tried to speculate what Bush was thinking, "But exactly what the President believes about that or plans to do, nobody knows—perhaps including himself."[128] Columnist Garry Wills saw that "Mr. Bush has given us a whole series of justifications for our presence in the gulf—oil, jobs, protection of Saudi Arabia, 'liberation' of Kuwait (perhaps by destroying it), the return of the 'legitimate' (autocratic) rulers to Kuwait, the removal of Saddam Hussein's power or weaponry or existence. It is clear that these rationales shift so often because it is hard or impossible to stand solidly on a single one."[129] As the time of our attack came near, Bush was "revealing as little as possible about his plans to the American people and to Congress" and he demonstrated "his willingness to commit the world's most powerful nation to a course that he alone determines."[130]

National Security Advisor Brent Scowcroft, up tight with Bush in the White House, defined well the crucial question: "Can the U.S. use force—even go to war—for carefully defined national interests, or do we have to have a moral crusade or a galvanizing event like Pearl Harbor?"[131] But not only was that question not answered; it was not brought forth by Bush or his administrators to the American people.

Instead, pro-war propaganda flowed out of Washington. The Republican National Committee did a mailing to 500,000 of their regular party funders, urging them to write letters to their local newspapers in support of the war and against the peace protesters.[132] President Bush sent a letter to more than 450 college newspapers the week before he started the war, suddenly coming forth as a champion of human rights against Iraq.[133] Although hundreds of thousands of anti-war Americans demonstrated time and again in cities throughout the country, soon virtually no reporters covered such events or revealed such items as that between 900 and 1000 anti-war protesters were arrested on January 15, 1991 and that the next day, called "Bomb Them Day," 371 protesters were arrested. From January 17 to 30, of the 878 sources in the published war reports, only *one* was a leader of a peace group—though lots of Super Bowl athletes were reported as pro-war.[134] Of the 25 largest U.S. newspapers, only one, *Rocky Mountain News*, came out mainly against the war.[135] The Kuwaiti government had sent to Washington, D.C., more than $5 million, paid to a professional American public relations organization to generate pro-Kuwait war news. In the same Washington, D.C., some 45 national organizations, including organized families of the military, rushed together for anti-war effort, but virtually nothing got reported. As Sam Donaldson put it, even back in August 1990, "It's difficult to play devil's advocate, especially against such a popular president as Bush."[136]

The war started with tremendous air attacks against the Iraqis. The air attack war lasted only 43 days, with the ground war halted after only about 100 hours. In the "good" news, "only" 323 Americans were killed, although, of course, many more were wounded.[137]

Once the war had started, reports from the Middle East were very strictly censored by the military, allowing for nearly no disappointing news. The television news was virtually all composed of stunningly fascinating air attack scenes, including the fireworks of new weapons, fast-flying planes, bomb drops, and the like. Hardly any television showed scenes of what happened on the ground when the bombs fell. In fact, thousands of civilians were killed and wounded, in Baghdad and elsewhere, and some 80,000 to 100,000 Iraqi soldiers were killed—in effect, a statistical abstraction, since the killing was not shown. When one videotape showing such horror did come to New York, it was aired by WNET and many copies were sent around privately, but NBC and CBS top officials refused to show any of it.[138]

Instead, there was much television coverage of jolly American soldiers saying they wanted to fight soon, then hundreds of Iraqis surrendering with happy greetings to their enemies. When the war against Saddam Hussein succeeded in forcing him out of Kuwait, news focused on the happiness of our troops coming home—obviously making their families glad they survived, but with that gladness being translated into pro-war emotion, expressed by flying flags. Only when new disaster began to be revealed in Iraq, with scenes of thousands of starving and murdered Kurds who had rebelled against Saddam Hussein at the instigation of the Bush administration, did anti-Bush columns and editorials begin to emerge in major papers at home. As late as April 25, 1991, approximately 500 Kurds were dying each day.[139] But Bush's pleasures were repeatedly celebrated: planes landing full of homecoming soldiers welcomed by their folks and paraded through the town.

Bush the Episcopalian declared that the prayers he offered had won the war, thanks to God. There was little news coverage of the fact that the nation's Episcopal church leaders were working vigorously against the war, or even that the World Council of Churches had, on February 20, 1991, "called for an immediate and unconditional ceasefire on the Persian Gulf war."[140] For months, advocates against the war were denigrated as traitors and unpatriotic Americans, their message suppressed. Television blared forth time and again its own ads and news bites boasting the wonderful happiness of the war and the flag and the President. Bush did what he could to sustain such events, though the typical wartime Presidential popularity began its typical slide downward.

HE HIMSELF

This President took on "a 6½ month crisis that he has personally shaped and directed."[141] And "The personalizing of the matter as support for the president, as if that were support for the nation, is indicative of the loss we have undergone of our original ideals. We are being asked to do the king's will."[142]

Time and again, the President appeared as an individual whose emotions of the moment decided national action:

> I want peace.
> I will continue to be patient.
> I will not say exactly what I will do.
> Consider me provoked.
> I'm not all that hopeful.
> I want Congress on board.
> I want 'em all home, as soon as possible.
> I don't feel we are closer to a peaceful solution.
> I've had it.
> My gut says he [Saddam Hussein] will get out of there.
> I do not have that much of a feel.
> I do not want to see one kid lose his life.

The mind of Bush shaped the fate of thousands of humans. He had said that "The only alternative to human tyranny is the rule of law," but now he did not act like a real believer of that creed.[143] What he did believe in—his world view—remained obscure. Having decided something, he would say, "Well, I've done the best I could and that's all I can do." George remembered that the doctor who treated him in Texas for a bleeding ulcer "told me I should work to the fullest on things I could handle, but I should put out of my mind things I couldn't do anything about. I've done it ever since and my ulcer was cured."[144]

Acting without worrying can drift into acting without thinking. But perhaps the new Bush personal assertions, his new standing as "King of America," might have reminded him of another realm of his life: when his mother used to demand that "I don't want to hear any more about the Great I Am." As late as 1987, Bush said of that experience, "It stuck." Even when Mother Bush was 86 years old and George was running for President, she called him up and said, "You're talking about yourself too much, George." By 1991, President Bush was forever talking about himself: how he felt, at the moment, about what he would do himself with his royal power.[145]

But then he wept on an occasion. At a dinner for governors, at the White House, singer Gary Morris sang "Bring Him Home," a song "about a father praying for his son to be brought home from combat" and "the President stood up with tears in his eyes, thanked Morris, and declared, "We will bring them home."[146]

15

Adding It Up

This strange book, written in chunks over a period of twenty-five years, is addressed to the future. It is both less and more than history: less in that it makes no claim to be the whole story of the Presidential past; more in that it dares to draw from what has been a picture of what yet may be. It is meant to help the thoughtful and sensible citizen sort out the significant particulars involved in the next Presidential choice, but also to help us hear, despite the cackle of daily events, the fundamental cultural themes that echo through the White House time and time again. With luck and determination, we can use what we know to build the conditions for survival—even progress.

CHARACTER AND CULTURE

Before a President is elected, debate centers on his stands on particular issues, his regional and group connections, his place in the left-right array of ideologies. *After* a President has left office and there has been time to see his rulership in perspective, the connection between his character and his Presidential actions emerges as paramount. Then it becomes clear that the kind of man he was stamped out the shape of his performance. Recognizing this, we ought to be able to find a way to a better pre-figuring, a way to see in potential Presidents the factors which have turned out to be critical for actual Presidents.

484

Look to character first. At least by the time the man emerges as an adult, he has displayed a stance toward his experience, a proto-political orientation. The first clues are simple: by and large, does he actively make his environment, or is he passively made by it? And how does he feel about his experience—is his effort in life a burden to be endured or an opportunity for personal enjoyment? From those two starting points, we can move to a richer, more dynamic understanding of the four types. The lives of Presidents past and of the one still with us show, I think, how a start from character makes possible a realistic estimate of what will endure into a man's White House years. Character is the force, the motive power, around which the person gathers his view of the world and from which his style receives its impetus. The issues will change, the character of the President will last.

The swirl of emotions which will surround the next President—and the one after that and the one after that—cannot be wished away. For better or for worse, the Presidency remains the prime focus for our political sentiments and the prime source of guidance and inspiration for national politics. The next and future Presidents will each inherit a climate of expectations not of their making. If one or more is lucky and effective, he can call forth from that climate new energies, a new vision, a new way of working to suit a perennially new age. Or he can help us drift into lassitude or tragedy. Much of what he is remembered for will depend on the fit between the dominant forces in his character and the dominant feelings in his constituency.

Deep in the political culture with which the President must deal are four themes, old in the American spirit, new in contemporary content. A President to suit the age must find in these themes a resonance with his own political being. The dangers of discord in that resonance are severe.

POLITICS AND THE DRIVE FOR POWER

Americans vastly overrate the President's power—and they are likely to continue to do so. The logic of that feeling is clear enough: the President is at the top and therefore he must be able to dominate those below him. The psychology is more complicated. The whole popular ethic of struggle, the onward-and-upward, fight-today-to-win-tomorrow spirit gets played out vicariously as people watch their President. The President should be working, trying, striving forward—living out in his life what makes life meaningful for the average citizen at work. Life is tough, life is earnest. A tough, earnest President symbolizes and represents that theme, shows by the thrust of his deeds that the fight is worth it after all. Will he stand up to his—and our—enemies, or will he collapse? Has he the guts to endure the heat in the kitchen? Will he (will he please) play out for us the drama that leads through suffering to salvation?

To a character attuned to power, this popular theme can convey a heady message. It comes through loudest to the active-negative type, whose inner struggle between aggression and control resonates with the popular plea for toughness. For Wilson, Hoover, Johnson, and Nixon, and for active-negative Presidents in the future, the temptation to stand and fight receives wide support from the culture. The most dangerous confusion in that connection is the equating of political power—essentially the power to persuade—with force. Such a President, frustrated in efforts at persuasion, may turn to those aspects of his role least constrained by the chains of compromise—from domestic to foreign policy, from foreign policy to military policy, for instance, where the tradition of obedience holds. Then we may see a President, doubtful within but seemingly certain without, huffing and puffing with *machismo* as he bravely orders other men to die.

Short of that, the active-negative character may show his colors not in some aggressive crusade but in a defensive refusal—as Hoover did in his adamant stand against direct relief. Although such a stand may undermine his immediate popularity, it, too, resonates with the culture's piety of effort. Paradoxically, the same public which may turn against a President's policy may respect him for resisting their demands. The President shares with them the awareness of a historical tradition of the lone hero bucking the tide of his times in favor of some eternal purpose. Particularly now that the President is restricted to two terms, in that second term the temptation to clean up one's integrity and long-term reputation with some unpopular heroism may be very strong indeed. This may not require an active-negative President to feel he must follow the martial model. What he may well feel impelled to do is to rigidly defend some position previously stated, to translate some experiment into a commitment.

For a long time, potential Presidents attuned to the ethic of struggle will continue to appear on the candidate lists. For the child is father to the man, and they received their basic cast of mind a long time ago—as did many of their constituents.

POLITICS AND THE SEARCH FOR AFFECTION

Sometimes the people want a hero, sometimes they want a friend. The people's desire for community in an age of fragmentation, their need to sense themselves as members sharing in the national doings, strike a chord within the passive-positive President. From his youth he has personified the politician as giver and taker of affection. There he found reward for his air of hopefulness in the many friends he attracted and the smiles he helped bring to their faces. Raised in a highly indulgent setting, he came to expect that almost everyone would like him and that those who did not could be placated by considerateness and compromise. He needed that. For behind the surface of his smile he sensed how fragile his supply of love could be, how much in need of protection was his impression that he was lovable.

The affectionate side of politics (much neglected in research) appeals to a people broken apart less by conflict and rivalry than by isolation and anxiety. Most men and women lead lives of *quiet* desperation; the scattering of families, the anonymity of work life, the sudden shifts between generations and neighborhoods, the accidents caused by a wavering economy, all contribute to the lonesome vulnerability people feel and hide, supposing they are exceptions to the general rule of serenity. Politics offers some opportunities for expressing that directly, as when brokenhearted people line up to tell their Congressman whatever it is they have to tell. But for many who never tell anybody, politics offers a scene for reassurance, a medium for the vicarious experience of fellowship.

This can affect a President or Presidential candidate. He can come to symbolize in his manner the friendliness people miss. Whatever he is to himself, his look-on-the-bright-side optimism conveys a sense that things cannot be all that bad—and a sense of "God knows he has more to worry about than I do." So there can develop between a President's cheerfulness and his people's need for reassurance a mutually reinforcing, symbiotic ding-dong.

Every President is somewhat passive-positive (and partly each of the other types); all have drawn a sustenance of sorts from the cheering crowds and flattering mail. At the extreme, this sentiment can lapse over into sentimentality or hysteria, as with the "jumpers" for Kennedy screaming "I seen him, I seen him." Then the show business dimension of politics comes to the fore. The President as star brings his audience together in their admiration of him, lets their glamorization of him flow freely around the hall, where, for a moment at least, all experience simultaneously the common joy of his presence. The transformation of a middle-aged politician into a glamorous star is a mysterious process, one perhaps understood best by the managers of rock groups. A most unlikely case would be the political beatification of Eugene McCarthy. Somehow the man catches on, becomes an "in" thing; he ceases to be a curiosity and becomes a charismatic figure. What is important in that, besides the gratifications it supplies the public, is what it can do to the star himself. For a Lyndon Johnson it meant a confirmation of power. But for a passive-positive type, a modern-day inheritor of the Taft-Harding-Reagan character, such adulation touches deeper. The resonance is with his inner sense that such fleeting expressions of allegiance are the reality of affection.

These themes reinforce the obsession with technique that affects so much of contemporary political rhetoric. Political cosmetology becomes a fine art, despite the lack of evidence that it changes votes or polls. The money floods into the hands of those who know how to make a silk purse statesman out of a sow's ear politico. Politics is sexualized; the glance and the stance are carefully coached; the cruciality of just the right rhetorical flair is vastly exaggerated; the political club becomes a fan club. Ultimately the technique itself becomes an object of evaluation: people admire the man who does the most artful job of conning them. There are present-day equivalents aplenty of whom Harry Daugherty could say, as he said of Harding, "Gee, what a great-looking President he'd make!"

All of this can make an incompetent like Harding think he is not only qualified for high office but also personally attractive. That is the dividing line for the individual, comparable to the transition to charismatic follower in the audience. The personal need for such pseudo-love is fundamentally insatiable—the applause pours into a bottomless pit. The larger political danger is that such a man will convince himself and others that he has untapped talents, only to discover later that he does not, and to reveal that to all who inquire.

The affection problem for realistic politicians is to help us love one another without lapsing into sentimentality or hero-worship. The passive-positive character feels the problem, but is too easily diverted by the sham and sentimentality of politics to do much about it.

POLITICS AND THE QUEST FOR LEGITIMACY

The President exists solely in the minds of men. The White House is not the Presidency any more than the flag is the nation. This "institution" is nothing more than images, habits, and intentions shared by the humans who make them up and by those who react to them. There is not even, as in a church, a clearly sanctified place for it; the Oval Office is no altar—it is an office. The reverence people pay the President, the awe his visitors experience in his presence—all that is in their heads—and his. A fragile base for Presidential stability? Only to those who see in the tangible appurtenances of life a foundation more secure than man's sense of life's continuities.

In our culture the religious-monarchical focus of the Presidency—the tendency to see the office as a sort of divine-right kingship—gets emphasized less in dynastic, evangelical, or even ecumenical ways than in a quest for legitimacy. The essential legitimating quality is trust. The problem is not in the succession—the transfer of power from one rightful ruler to the next; even after assassinations Americans do not hesitate to accord authority to the new President. Rather, it resides in a fear that the men entrusted to rule are proving all too human, are politicking away the high dignity and ancient honor of the Republic for hidden reasons of their own.

The dangers people seem to fear are two, pride and perfidy. Mechanically these come down to too little and too much compromise, but it is not a mechanical matter. Pride is feared when a President seems to be pushing harder and faster than the issues call for—and doing that more and more on his own, without proper consultation. FDR's attack on the Supreme Court is an example. The primal version is the fear of tyranny growing out of hubris. The response is to wish for a return to the Constitutional restraints, a reassertion of the basic system Americans have elevated to an article of political faith.

Perfidy stands for betrayal due to character flaw, subtler than the constitutional form. Legitimacy is threatened not so much by one who would break the rules as by one who seems to break trust in the image of the President as dignified, episcopal, plain, and clean in character. Part of the public mind always realizes that the President is only a man, with all man's vulnerability to moral error; part wants to deny that, to foist on the President a priestliness setting him above the congregation. There is a real ambivalence here, one that makes it all the more necessary to reassert legitimacy in the Presidency when the pendulum swings too far. Presidents realize this. They try to be careful not to "demean the office." But especially after a time when the feeling has been growing that the Presidency is getting too "political" and that evil persons (Communists, grafters) are crawling too close to the throne, the call for a man of unquestionable honor will go out.

The appeal for a moral cleansing of the Presidency resonates with the passive-negative character in its emphasis on *not doing* certain things. It also reinforces the character attuned to moral appeals to duty. A man who cares little for the roils of politics or the purposes of policy may respond much more strongly to the appeal to save the nation, keep the faith, bring back the oldtime way of our forefathers. Such a man is eminently draftable. In the end he has no answer to the question, if not you, who? So he serves. In serving, the moral themes push his mind upward, stimulate whatever pontifical propensities he has. Especially if he is basically an apolitical man, unused to the issues and the informal processes of negotiation, he will find ways to rise above all that. For Coolidge the tendency was toward a proverbial, increasingly abstract rhetoric, for Eisenhower the drift was toward a Mosaic role—final arbiter of otherwise unresolvable conflicts. The effect is to unbuckle the President from politics, leaving the forces at hand free to charge off in their own directions.

CREATIVE POLITICS

But in the culture also is an awareness of these ills and dangers. The sham of the typical Presidential campaign has not gone unnoticed. The militant tough guys, the technocrats who counsel so coolly about kill-ratios and free-fire zones, the puffed-up claims for low-budget programs, the violations of Constitutional rights rationalized as protections of Constitutional order, the substitution of abstract moralisms for substance—I am not the first to point out these pathologies. Amidst much confusion, the public, especially in an election year when attention is paid, sees with a slow but stubborn vision the very distortions its own needs have helped to create. The press and television help with that; a President or candidate who knows how to say simply what many feel deeply can make an even greater contribution to cutting away the underbrush of lies and bluster.

Nor does the people's disillusionment easily sour into despair. Kennedy's call for vigor stopped short with his murder; Johnson's initial politico-religiosity fell apart; Nixon pleaded for national reconciliation and then polarized opinion; Carter called for competence and seemed to practice its opposite. Yet aside from a few pathetic Weathermen and their Birchite counterparts, most Americans want to make the system work and are capable of doing so. The generation which went through the Wilson-Harding-Hoover disillusionments did recover. The cultural memory of that recovery has not disappeared, even in this age of the momentary. Beyond the candid confession of failure, the task of Presidential leadership these days is to remind the people that their past was not without achievement and that their future is not yet spoiled.

That is in the active-positive spirit. Those themes resonate with a character confident enough to see its weaknesses and the potentialities it might yet grow into. The active-positive Presidents did not invent the sentiments they called forth. They gave expression in a believable way to convictions momentarily buried in fear and mistrust. From their perception of a basically capable public they drew strength for their own sense of capability. For like everyone else, active-positive Presidents feed on reinforcements from the environment. What is different about them is their ability to see the strengths hidden in public confusion and to connect with those strengths.

A goodly part of the contemporary disillusionment is the gap between what people see governments doing and what they hear politicians telling them. The rule is policy-making by-guess-and-by-God, always in a hurry. The odds of success—that is, actual, significant improvements in the lives of citizens—are reduced by the general lack of attention to the real results of policy. When people see the contrast between headline Washington "victories" and how it is to get to work in the morning, they wonder.

The active-positive Presidents help get past that gap by focusing on results beyond Washington. FDR's insistent curiosity about how life was going for people, Truman's hunger for "the facts," Kennedy's probing questions in the Cuban missile crisis illustrate how a character in concord with itself can reach for reality. Active-positive Presidents are more open to evidence because they have less need to deny and distort their perceptions for protective purposes. Their approach is experimental rather than deductive, which allows them to try something else when an experiment fails to pan out, rather than escalate the rhetoric or pursue the villains responsible. Flexibility in style and a world view containing a variety of probabilities are congruent with a character ready for trial and error, and furnish the imagination with a wide range of alternatives. A people doubtful about government programs as the final answer to anything might well respond to a candid admission of uncertainty, a determination to try anyway, and a demonstration of attention to results. The need for energetic, optimistic realism in the Presidency will be with us as long as the office endures. If we but pay attention to the characters who can offer that, we may yet move on to the future our children deserve.

LOOKING FORWARD

Our attention to persons running for the Presidency is nearly completely dependent on journalism. From the start of the United States, newspapers have been an important medium for the citizenry, few of whom had any chance to see and hear the candidate in person. Magazines in the nineteenth century began to add deeper understandings, and in the twentieth century broadcasting spread information wider, though with less depth. Freedom of the press has been an essential piece of democracy, because what voters know is primarily what journalism teaches.

But journalism today is in need of political improvement. Candidates' characters can best be ascertained from their biographies rather than from their stagey, momentary appearances. And biography is one of the nation's most interesting forms of learning, as is evident in the sales of books of biography, and the public's interest in such television programs as "60 Minutes." World view can be elicited by real debates in a Presidential campaign—not the "debates" in recent years, which are nothing but mini-press conferences on television. Instead, a debate should be concentrated on one question for a significant period of time, so that logic and evidence may be brought forth for citizens to evaluate the thinking of a candidate regarding one major challenge. Investigative reporting can dig out how a candidate has actually operated in the past, especially at the beginning of his or her independent political endeavor. Odd as it seems, that is a better predicter of style than what the candidate had just been doing in politics. Planning coverage, journalists should take special notice of the current climate of expectations in order to avoid the recurrent temptation to oversimplify judgment about the candidates, such as how purely moral they are, how conciliatory, how much ahead and behind in the polls, etc. And the power situation needs reporting; a potential President is too often thought of as an infinitely potent power, but that is never true. As in any sport or war or dating, the situation makes a difference. Journalism can—and it may yet—greatly advance the public reasoning needed to get Presidents who will do the right things.

It may be that someday down through the years the United States will develop a political system in which the Presidency is but one of several major forces. Certainly it seems likely that the Congress will eventually reconvert itself from a fragmented collection of little specialized hierarchies into a single deliberative body in which equal representatives debate and decide the major political questions of the day. It is at least possible that the steady preachment of one scholar after another urging the revitalization of political parties will take hold and come to pass. No other political mechanism ever invented has approximated the party's success in building a common front linking the leaders and the led in a common purpose. It is even conceivable that the Supreme Court, and the whole legal structure it stands on, will learn how to break through the toils of complexity that now threaten the very legitimacy of the idea of law itself, and stand as the trusted ultimate guardians of American justice.

If any of that ever happens, I am willing to predict that a President will be in the middle of the fight. But the era before that renaissance is and will be a Presidential era. It will be up to the Presidency, more than any other force of government, to grapple with the terrors and the possibilities of a new age, a new world, a new generation of both vicious and worthy Americans.

That age will throw at Presidents-to-be two overarching challenges. Will we find ways to harness the enormous new powers of technology and organization to the ancient task of building a humane and life-sustaining polity? Will we find ways, in time, to turn aside from the escalating probability that our world and all that is in it will pass into oblivion because humans could not control their explosives? We need Presidents who know how the world works and how Washington works in it, Presidents who have mastered the skills it takes to make the White House an efficient machine for social progress, Presidents who can call up from their own characters the steady, hopeful, insistent reasoning to shape a good life from a mixed society. We yet may find the best Presidents before the great American adventure stops.

Notes

CHAPTER 1

The book's central concepts have grown on me through a series of previous studies. See: *The Lawmakers: Recruitment and Adaptation to Legislative Life* (New Haven: Yale University Press, 1965); "Peer Group Discussion and Recovery from the Kennedy Assassination," in *The Kennedy Assassination and the American Public*, Bradley A. Greenberg and Edwin B. Parker, eds., (Stanford: Stanford University Press, 1965); *Power in Committees: An Experiment in the Governmental Process* (Chicago: Rand-McNally, 1966); "Leadership Strategies for Legislative Party Cohesion," *Journal of Politics*, Vol. 28, 1966; "Adult Identity and Presidential Style: The Rhetorical Emphasis," *Daedalus*, Summer 1968; "Classifying and Predicting Presidential Styles: Two 'Weak' Presidents," *Journal of Social Issues*, Vol. 24, 1968; *Citizen Politics* (Chicago: Markham, 1969); "The Interplay of Presidential Character and Style: A Paradigm and Five Illustrations," in *A Source Book for the Study of Personality and Politics*, Fred I. Greenstein and

Michael Lerner, eds. (Chicago: Markham, 1979); "The Presidency: What Americans Want," *The Center Magazine*, Vol. 4, 1971.

CHAPTER 2

[1]Arthur S. Link, "The Case for Woodrow Wilson," *Harpers Magazine*, April 1967, p. 93.

[2]Woodrow Wilson, *Constitutional Government in the United States* (New York: Columbia University Press, 1917), pp. 139–40.

[3]Alexander L. and Juliette L. George, *Woodrow Wilson and Colonel House* (New York: John Day, 1956), p. 273.

[4]*Ibid.*

[5]*Ibid.*, p. 314.

[6]Gene Smith, *The Shattered Dream* (New York: William Morrow, 1970), p. 5.

[7]Eugene Lyons, *Our Unknown Ex-President: A Portrait of Herbert Hoover* (Garden City, N.Y.: Doubleday, 1948), p. 267.

[8]Harris Gaylord Warren, *Herbert Hoover and the Great Depression* (New York: Norton, 1959), pp. 182–183.

[9]*Ibid.*, p. 193.

[10]*Ibid.*, p. 208.

[11]Eric F. Goldman, *The Tragedy of Lyndon Johnson* (New York: Knopf, 1969), p. 518.

[12] Alfred Steinberg, *Sam Johnson's Boy* (New York: Macmillan, 1968), p. 767.

[13]Goldman, *op. cit.*, p. 412.

[14]Rowland Evans and Robert Novak, *Lyndon B. Johnson: The Exercise of Power* (New York: New American Library, 1966), p. 541.

[15]U.S. Foreign Relations Committee, Senate, *Vietnam: Policy and Prospects 1970,* Hearings, 90th Congress, 2nd Session, 1970.

[16]Franz Schurmann, Peter Dale Scott and Reginald Zelnick, *The Politics of Escalation in Vietnam* (Boston: Beacon Press, 1966), p. 37.

[17]David Kraslow and Stuart H. Loory, *The Secret Search for Peace in Vietnam* (New York: Random House, 1968), p. 102.

[18]*New York Times*, March 6, 1969, p. 14.

[19]New Haven *Register,* June 30, 1971, p. 1, quoting from "Pentagon Papers."

[20]George and George, *op. cit.*, p. 230.

[21]Gene Smith, *When the Cheering Stopped* (New York: Morrow, 1964), p. 52.

[22]George and George, *op. cit.*, p. 295.

[23]Arthur Walworth, *Woodrow Wilson* (Boston: Houghton Mifflin, 1965), p. 370.

[24]Leon H. Canfield, *The Presidency of Woodrow Wilson* (Rutherford, N.J.: Fairleigh Dickinson University Press, 1947), p. 233.

[25]*Ibid.*

[26]George and George, *op. cit.*, pp. 279–80.

[27]Smith, *When the Cheering Stopped,* p. 120.

[28]Smith, *The Shattered Dream,* p. 68.

[29]*Ibid.*, p. 211.

[30]Lyons, *op. cit.*, pp. 253–54.

[31]Arthur M. Schlesinger, Jr., *The Crisis of the Old Order, 1919–1933* (Boston: Houghton Mifflin, 1957), p. 247.

[32]Lyons, *op. cit.*, p. 235.

[33]Hugh Sidey, *A Very Personal Presidency* (New York: Atheneum, 1968), p. 167.

[34]*Ibid.*, p. 236.

[35]Goldman, *op. cit.*, p. 330.

CHAPTER 3

[1]Alexander L. and Juliette L. George, *Woodrow Wilson and Colonel House* (New York: John Day, 1965), p. 23.

[2]Arthur S. Link, *Wilson: The New Freedom* (Princeton: Princeton University Press, 1956), p. 86.

[3]*Ibid.*

[4]*Ibid.*, p. 87.

[5]*Ibid.*, p. 89.

[6]*Ibid.*, p. 122.

[7]*Ibid.*, p. 151.

[8]*Ibid.*, p. 64.

[9]*Ibid.*, p. 86.

[10]*Ibid.*, p. 87.

[11]*Ibid.*, p. 88.

[12]*Ibid.*

[13]*Ibid.*, p. 90.

[14]*Ibid.*, p. 61.

[15]*Ibid.*, p. 79.

[16]*Ibid.*, p. 465.

[17]*Ibid.*

[18]*Ibid.*, p. 68.

[19]Joseph P. Tumulty, *Woodrow Wilson as I Know Him* (New York: AMS Press, Inc., 1921), p. 457.

[20]David Hinshaw, *Herbert Hoover: American Quaker* (New York: Farrar, Straus, and Giroux, 1950), p. 404.

[21]Eugene Lyons, *Our Unknown Ex-President: A Portrait of Herbert Hoover* (Garden City, N.Y.: Doubleday, 1948), p. 29.

[22]*Ibid.*, p. 34.

[23]Theodore G. Joslin, *Hoover Off the Record* (Garden City, N.Y.: Doubleday, 1934), p. 21.

[24]Harris Gaylord Warren, *Herbert Hoover and the Great Depression* (New York: Norton, 1959), p. 295.

[25]Herbert Hoover, *American Individualism* (Garden City, N.Y.: Doubleday, 1922), p. 40.

[26]Gene Smith, *The Shattered Dream* (New York: William Morrow, 1970), frontispiece.

[27]Joslin, *op. cit.*, p. 11.

[28]Lyons, *op. cit.*, p. 337.

[29]Rowland Evans and Robert Novak, *Lyndon B. Johnson: The Exercise of Power* (New York: New American Library, 1966), p. 105.

[30]Eric F. Goldman, *The Tragedy of Lyndon Johnson* (New York: Knopf, 1969), p. 9.

[31]Evans and Novak, *op. cit.*, p. 110.

[32]Alfred Steinberg, *Sam Johnson's Boy* (New York: Macmillan, 1968), p. 632.

[33]*Ibid.*, p. 633.

[34]*Ibid.*, p. 820.

[35]Chester L. Cooper, *The Lost Crusade* (New York: Dodd, Mead, 1970), p. 223.

[36]Steinberg, *op. cit.*, p. 436.

[37]Booth Mooney, *The Lyndon Johnson Story* (New York: Avon, 1964).

[38]Steinberg, *op. cit.*, p. 500.

[39]Robert Sherrill, *The Accidental President* (New York: Pyramid Books, 1968), pp. 184–85.

[40]*Ibid.*, p. 185.

[41]Steinberg, *op. cit.*, p. 312.

[42]*Ibid.*, p. 724.

[43]Evans and Novak, *op. cit.*, p. 496.

[44]*Ibid.*

[45]*Ibid.*, p. 497.

[46]Goldman, *op. cit.*, p. 253.

[47]*Ibid.*

[48]Max Frankel, "Why the Gap between L.B.J. and the Nation?" *New York Times Magazine,* January 7, 1968, p. 41.

[49]Steinberg, *op. cit.*, p. 407.

[50]Hugh Sidey, *A Very Personal Presidency* (New York: Atheneum, 1968), p. 283.

CHAPTER 4

[1]Alexander L. and Juliette L. George, *Woodrow Wilson and Colonel House* (New York: John Day, 1956), p. 7.

[2]*Ibid.*, p. 8.

[3]Doris Faber, *The Mothers of American Presidents* (New York: New American Library, 1968), p. 86.

[4]Arthur S. Link, ed., *The Papers of Woodrow Wilson* (Princeton: Princeton University Press, 1966), Vol. I, p. 50.

[5]Henry Wilkinson Bragdon, *Woodrow Wilson: The Academic Years* (Cambridge, Mass.: Belknap Press, 1967), pp. 7–8.

[6]Link, ed., *op. cit.*, pp. 241, 244–45.

[7]*Ibid.*, p. 55.

[8]*Ibid.*, pp. 21–22.

[9]*Ibid.*, p. 149.

[10]*Ibid.*, p. 181.

[11]*Ibid.*

[12]*Ibid.*, p. 188.

[13]*Ibid.*, pp. 33, 35.

[14]Bragdon, *op. cit.*, p. 35.

[15]*Ibid.*, p. 38.

[16]Link, ed., *op. cit.*, p. 313.

[17]Bragdon, *op. cit.*, p. 62.

[18]Herbert Hoover, *The Memoirs of Herbert Hoover* (New York: Macmillan, 1963), p. 7.

[19]*Ibid.*, p. 8.

[20]Will Irwin, *Herbert Hoover: A Reminiscent Biography* (New York: Century Press, 1928), p. 7.

[21]*Ibid.*, pp. 7–8.

[22]*Ibid.*, p. 15.

[23]*Ibid.*, p. 30.

[24]Hoover, *op. cit.*, p. 17.

[25]Irwin, *op. cit.*, pp. 33–34.

[26]*Ibid.*, p. 60.

[27]*Ibid.*, p. 54.

[28]*Ibid.*, p. 62.

[29]*New York Times,* January 2, 1967, p. 17.

[30]W. C. Pool, E. Craddock, D. E. Conrad, *Lyndon Baines Johnson: The Formative Years* (San Marcos, Tex.: Southwest Texas State College Press, 1965), p. 32.

[31]Alfred Steinberg, *Sam Johnson's Boy* (New York: Macmillan, 1968), p. 15.

[32]*Ibid.*, p. 20.

[33]*Ibid.*, p. 37.

[34]*Ibid.*, p. 41.

[35]Pool *et al., op cit.*, pp. 119, 123, 126, 132.

[36]Steinberg, *op. cit.*, p. 47.

CHAPTER 5

Note: A chapter titled "The Demand for Self-Management," concentrating on Nixon as Vice President and his first term as President, 1968–72, is omitted. It is available in editions 1 through 3 of *The Presidential Character.*

[1]San Francisco *Chronicle,* Friday, January 3, 1969.

[2]Bela Kornitzer, *The Real Nixon: An Intimate Biography* (Chicago: Rand McNally, 1960), p. 79.

[3]*Ibid.*, pp. 45–46.

[4]*Ibid.*, p. 57.

[5]*Ibid.*, pp. 62, 65.

[6]*Ibid.*, p. 46.

[7]*Ibid.*, pp. 65–66.

[8]Richard M. Nixon, *Six Crises* (New York: Pyramid Books, 1968), p. xv.

[9]Kornitzer, *op. cit.*, p. 19.

[10]"Oil" as a symbol had a recurrent appearance in Nixon's career. One of his first law cases was a fraud case involving oil well equipment; in 1950 Drew Pearson charged that Senator Nixon's early political backers were big oil men; and when the Fund story broke, Hannah saw the headlines reading

"A NEW TEAPOT DOME." Kornitzer, *op. cit.*, pp. 128, 157, 191.

[11]*Ibid.*, p. 41.

[12]San Francisco *Chronicle*, *loc. cit.*

[13]Kornitzer, *op. cit.*, p. 239.

[14]Nixon, *op. cit.*, p. 318.

[15]Kornitzer, *op. cit.*, p. 112.

[16]*Ibid.*, p. 147.

[17]Earl Mazo and Stephen Hess, *Nixon: A Political Portrait* (New York: Popular Library, 1968), p. 37.

[18]*Ibid.*, p. 39.

[19]Nixon, *op. cit.*, p. 13.

[20]This section summarizes Chapter 12, "Nixon Now and Then," as it appeared in the first edition—published in the spring of 1972, before the Watergate crisis—and the second edition (1977). The paragraph beginning "These predictions were clear . . . "and the section from "This character could lead the President . . ." to the end, ". . . beyond toughness to achievement" are verbatim from the 1972 edition.

[21]At the end of the Nixon regime there was a coup: the Presidency was run by a general who, by the luck of the draw, had a passion for reason, if also a certain lack of moral imagination. The general, who more than a year previously had ripped out Nixon's taping systems without permission, in the summer of 1974 entered into negotiation with the Vice President regarding the conditions under which he could come to power—the general again acting on his own. Another military leader, the Secretary of Defense, established a system by which he could veto the Commander in Chief's orders to the armed forces. A Presidential order conveyed to the Secretary of State elicited the reply, "Tell the President to fuck himself." (Bob Woodward and Carl Bernstein, The Final Days [New York: Simon and Schuster, 1976], p. 199). No tanks in the streets. No bearded madman gesticulating from a balcony. Just some quiet little rearrangements to keep things going—without the interference of the "People's Choice." Fortunately it was one of the Nixon administration's few Horatios, rather than one of its many Iagos, who grabbed power. A system that has to depend on that kind of fortune is dangerous.

[22]James David Barber, "A Summary of Predictions of Richard M. Nixon as President," a paper distributed to colleagues at the Center for Advanced Study in the Behavioral Sciences, Stanford, Calif., January 19, 1969, pp. 6, 18.

[23]See also "Some Strategies for Understanding Politicians," *American Journal of Political Science*, Spring 1974.

[24]Elizabeth Drew, *Washington Journal: The Events of 1973–1974* (New York: Vintage Books, 1976), p. 108.

[25]Theodore H. White, *Breach of Faith: The Fall of Richard Nixon* (New York: Atheneum Publishers, Reader's Digest Press, 1975), p. 292; Drew, *Washington Journal*, p. 138; White, *Breach of Faith*, p. 306.

[26]*Submission of Recorded Presidential Conversations to the Committee on the Judiciary of the House of Representatives by President Richard Nixon* (Washington, D.C.: Government Printing Office, 1974), pp. 580, 696, 836.

[27]J. Anthony Lukas, *Nightmare: The Underside of the Nixon Years* (New York: Viking Press, 1976), p. 450.

[28]White, *op. cit.*, pp. 218, 171.

[29]*Submission of Recorded Presidential Conversations . . . by President Richard Nixon, op. cit.*, p. 1304.

[30]Another source of data may eventually be available and important: the recordings Nixon made for himself alone. His attorney J. Fred Buzhardt heard some of them; Woodward and Bernstein report he found them "a dark, almost Dostoevskian journey into Nixon's fears, obsessions, hostilities, passions, and inadequacies." Woodward and Bernstein, *The Final Days*, p. 405.

[31]White, *op. cit.*, p. 13.

[32]Drew, *op. cit.*, p. 199; Jonathan Schell, *The Time of Illusion* (New York: Alfred A. Knopf, 1976), p. 306.

[33]White, *op. cit.*, p. 168.

[34]Woodward and Bernstein, *op. cit.*, p. 297, pp. 352–53.

[35]Schell, *op. cit.*, p. 333.

[36]William Safire, *Before the Fall: An Inside View of the Pre-Watergate White House* (Garden City, N.Y.: Doubleday & Company, Inc., 1975), pp. 600 (italics omitted), 406.

[37]Lukas, *op. cit.*, p. 493.

[38]*Nixon, op. cit.*, p. 380.

[39]Safire, *op. cit.*, pp. 607, 603.

[40]*Ibid.*, pp. 360ff.

[41]Safire, *op. cit.*, p. 534.

[42]Drew, *op. cit.*, p. 49.

[43]*Nixon, op. cit.*, p. 711; Lukas, *op. cit.*, p. 326.

[44]Safire, *op. cit.*, p. 482.

[45]Schell, *op. cit.*, pp. 329, 332.

[46]*Ibid.*

[47]Drew, *op. cit.*, p. 251.

[48]Safire, *op. cit.*, p. 276.

[49]*Ibid.*, p. 588; Drew, *op. cit.*, p. 252; Safire, *op. cit.*, pp. 588, 589; *Nixon, op. cit.*, pp. 1095, 378, 462; Lukas, *op. cit.*, pp. 321, 324.

[50]Schell, *op. cit.*, p. 208.

[51]White, *op. cit.*, p. 217; Lukas, *op. cit.*, p. 326.

[52]*Ibid.*, p. 416.

[53]Schell, *op. cit.*, p. 372.

[54]Safire, *op. cit.*, p. 287.

[55]*Ibid.*, p. 286.

[56]*Ibid.*, p. 559.

[57]Charles W. Colson, *Born Again* (Old Tappan, N.J.: Chosen Books, 1976), p. 72.

[58]Lukas, *op. cit.*, pp. 85, 438.

[59]Colson, *op. cit.*, p. 79.

[60]*Ibid.*, Chapter Four, "The President's Night Out."

[61]*Nixon, op. cit.*, p. 641.

[62]John Ehrlichman, *The Company: A Novel*, p. 275, ©1976 by Simon & Schuster. Reprinted by permission.

[63]*Nixon, op. cit.*, pp. 476, 349.

[64]Schell, *op. cit.*, pp. 30, 71, 150–51.

[65]Hans J. Morgenthau, "The Aborted Nixon Revolutions," in David C. Saffell, ed., *Watergate: Its Effects on the American Political System* (Cambridge, Mass.: Winthrop Publishers, Inc., 1974), p. 308.

[66]Schell, *op. cit.*, p. 212.

[67]Lukas, *op. cit.*, p. 22.

[68]*Ibid.*, p. 26.

[69]*Ibid.*

[70]*Ibid.*

[71]Drew, *op. cit.*, p. 168.

[72]White, *op. cit.*, p. 135.

[73]Staff of the New York Times, *The End of a Presidency* (New York: Bantam Books, 1974), p. 218.

[74]Lukas, *op. cit.*, p. 367.

[75]See Safire, *op. cit.*, pp. 656–57; Dan Rather and Gary Paul Gates, *The Palace Guard* (New York: Harper & Row, 1974), p. 308; *Nixon, op. cit.*, p. 269.

[76]Schell, *op. cit.*, p. 320; Woodward and Bernstein, *op. cit.*, p. 61.

[77]Colson, *op. cit.*, p. 45.

[78]Schell, *op. cit.*, p. 288.

[79]*Ibid.*

[80]Lukas, *op. cit.*, p. 8.

[81]J. Anthony Lukas, "The Hughes Connection," *New York Times Magazine*, January 4, 1976, pp. 8ff. Donald Nixon, it will be recalled, enjoyed in 1957 the largesse of Mr. Hughes in the amount of $250,000, "loaned" on the security of a $13,000 plot in Whittier, to rescue Donald's spoiling "Nixonburger" business—in straight financial terms hardly the kind of investment by which one gets to be a multibillionaire. On at least three previous occasions, the White House had tried to dig up dirt on O'Brien; the last time, John Ehrlichman confessed, "I wanted them [the IRS] to turn up something and send him [O'Brien] to jail before the elections."

[82]Drew, *op. cit.*, p. 28.

[83]Schell, *op. cit.*, p. 285.

[84]Lukas, *Nightmare, op. cit.*, p. 246.

[85]Frank Mankiewicz, *Perfectly Clear: Nixon from Whittier to Watergate* (New York: Popular Library, 1973), p. 262.

[86]Schell, *op. cit.*, pp. 220, 291; Lukas, *Nightmare, op. cit.*, p. 277.

[87]Drew, *op. cit.*, pp. 256, 262, 271.

[88]*Ibid.*, p. 133; Safire, *op. cit.*, p. 689; Drew, *op. cit.*, p. 247.

[89]Woodward and Bernstein, *op. cit.*, p. 271.

[90]White, *op. cit.*, p. 232.

[91]Lukas, *Nightmare*, p. 338; Drew, *op. cit.*, p. 198; White, *op. cit.*, p. 294; Woodward and Bernstein, *op. cit.*, pp. 386–87, 435; *Nixon, op. cit.*, p. 1270, pp. 468–470.

[92]*Ibid.*, pp. 457, 509, 611, 1161; Safire, *op. cit.*, p. 370; Drew, *op. cit.*, p. 99.

[93]Jeb Stuart Magruder, *An American Life* (New York: Atheneum, 1974), p. 140.

[94]Safire, *op. cit.*, p. 349.

[95]White, *op. cit.*, p. 271.

[96]Rebozo's 1973 Christmas card bore a startlingly cynical Yuletide greeting: "Neither material wealth, fame, power, nor admiration necessarily brings happiness." Drew, *op. cit.*, p. 151.

[97]Lukas, *Nightmare, op. cit.*, p. 467.

[98]Drew, *op. cit.*, p. 240.

[99]Lukas, *Nightmare, op. cit.*, p. 450.

[100]Drew, *op. cit.*, p. 151.

[101]Lukas, *Nightmare, op. cit.*, p. 452–53.

[102]*Ibid.*, p. 307.

[103]*Ibid.*; White, *op. cit.*, p. 221.

[104]Woodward and Bernstein, *op. cit.*, p. 202; Drew, *op. cit.*, p. 298; Woodward and Bernstein, *op. cit.*, p. 45.

[105]Lukas, *Nightmare*, p. 537.

[106]*Ibid.*, p. 398.

[107]Congressional Quarterly, *Watergate: Chronology of a Crisis*, Vol. 2 (Washington, D.C.: Congressional Quarterly, 1974), p. 170A.

[108]Woodward and Bernstein, *op. cit.*, p. 45; Safire, *op. cit.*, p. 275.

[109]*Ibid.*, p. 685.

[110]White, *op. cit.*, p. 254; Nixon, *op. cit.*, p. 101; Woodward and Bernstein, *op. cit.*, p. 169; *Time*, May 12, 1975, p. 74.

[111]Marvin Miller, compiler, *The Breaking of a President*, Vol. I (Therapy Productions, 1974), p. 85.

[112]White, *op. cit.*, p. 180.

[113]Safire, *op. cit.*, p. 607.

[114]*Ibid.*, p. 341.

[115]Drew, *op. cit.*, p. 75.

[116]*Nixon, op. cit.*, p. 373.

[117]Lukas, *Nightmare, op. cit.*, p. 297.

[118]Woodward and Bernstein, *The Final Days, op. cit.*, p. 84.

[119]Safire, *op. cit.*, p. 324.

[120]Woodward and Bernstein, *The Final Days, op. cit.*, p. 27.

[121]Safire, *op. cit.*, p. 147.

[122]Drew, *op. cit.*, p. 407.

[123]White, *op. cit.*, p. 310.

[124]Drew, *op. cit.*, p. 404. Cf. Lukas, *Nightmare, op. cit.*, p. 550.

[125]Woodward and Bernstein, *The Final Days, op. cit.*, p. 421.

[126]Safire, *op. cit.*, p. 631.

[127]Woodward and Bernstein, *The Final Days, op. cit.*, p. 455.

[128]Drew, *op. cit.*, p. 49.

[129]Lukas, *Nightmare, op. cit.*, p. 268.

[130]Drew, *op. cit.*, p. 52.

[131]Lukas, *Nightmare, op. cit.*, p. 441.

[132]*Newsweek*, June 24, 1974, p. 23.

[133]Woodward and Bernstein, *The Final Days, op. cit.*, pp. 216–20.

[134]*Ibid.*, p. 423.

[135]*Ibid.*, p. 443.

CHAPTER 6

[1]Most of the following material on Coolidge appeared previously in my "Classifying and Predicting Presidential Styles: Two 'Weak' Presidents," *Journal of Social Issues*, Vol. 24, No. 3, 1968, and is reprinted here by the kind permission of the Society for the Psychological Study of Social Issues.

[2]Claude M. Fuess, *Calvin Coolidge: The Man from Vermont* (Hamden, Conn.: Archon Books, 1965), p. 25.

[3]Calvin Coolidge, *The Autobiography of Calvin Coolidge* (New York: Cosmopolitan, 1929), p. 13.

[4]*Ibid.*, p. 60.

[5]Fuess, *op. cit.*, p. 54.

[6]Coolidge, *op. cit.*, pp. 99–100.

[7]*Ibid.*, p. 67.

[8]*Ibid.*, p. 74.

[9]Dwight D. Eisenhower, *At Ease* (New York: Avon, 1968), p. 120.

[10]*Ibid.*, p. 232.

[11]Samuel Lubell, "Ye Compleat Political Angler," in Dean Albertson, ed., *Eisenhower as President* (New York: Hill and Wang, 1963), p. 18.

[12]Quoted in Walter Johnson, *1600 Pennsylvania Avenue* (Boston: Little Brown, 1960), p. 319.

[13]*Ibid.*, pp. 317–18.

[14]Patrick Anderson, *The President's Men* (Garden City, N.Y.: Doubleday, 1968), p. 133.

[15]Eisenhower, *op. cit.*, p. 37.

[16]*Ibid.*, p. 38.

[17]*Ibid.*, p. 58.

[18]*Ibid.*, pp. 98–99.

[19]*Ibid.*, p. 102.

[20]*Ibid.*, p. 16.

[21]*Ibid.*, pp. 23–24.

[22]Dwight D. Eisenhower, *Mandate for Change, 1953–56* (New York: New American Library, 1963), p. 151.

CHAPTER 7

[1]Henry F. Pringle, *The Life and Times of William Howard Taft* (Hamden, Conn.: Archon Books, 1964), Vol. I, p. 385.

[2]*Ibid.*, p. 129.

[3]*Ibid.*, p. 335.

[4]For example, see *ibid.*, p. 410.

[5]William Manners, *TR and Will* (New York: Harcourt, Brace, Jovanovich, 1969), p. 175.

[6]*Ibid.*, p. 226.

[7]*Ibid.*, p. 227.

[8]*Ibid.*, p. 305.

[9]Doris Faber, *The Mothers of American Presidents* (New York: New American Library, 1968), p. 100.

[10]*Ibid.*

[11]Isabel Ross, *An American Family* (New York: World, 1964), p. 67.

[12]Pringle, *op. cit.*, p. 69.
[13]*Ibid.*
[14]*Ibid.*, p. 77.
[15]*Ibid.*, p. 78.
[16]Francis Russell, *The Shadow of Blooming Grove* (New York: McGraw-Hill, 1968), p. 603.
[17]*Ibid.*, p. 588.
[18]*Ibid.*, p. 427.
[19]*Ibid.*, p. 559.
[20]*Ibid.*, p. 567.
[21]*Ibid.*, p. 272.
[22]*Ibid.*, p. 532.
[23]*Ibid.*, p. 430.
[24]*Ibid.*, p. 34.
[25]*Ibid.*, p. 65.
[26]*Ibid.*, p. 66.
[27]*Ibid.*, p. 76.

CHAPTER 8

Cf. James David Barber, "Lessons from Candidate Reagan," Chapter 17, *Politics by Humans: Research on American Leadership* (Durham, N.C.: Duke University Press, 1988); "Presidential Politics and the Myth of Conciliation: The Case of 1980," Chapter 11, Alexander Heard and Michael Nelson, eds., *Presidential Selection* (Durham, N.C.: Duke University Press, 1987); "The Politics of Conciliation," Part III, *The Pulse of Politics: Electing Presidents in the Media Age* (New York: W. W. Norton & Company, 1980); "Congress, Press and Public Must Share Blame for Crisis," Boston Globe, November 30, 1986, A 21; "A Government in Disarray Drifting Toward Accidents," Los Angeles Times, December 7, 1986, Part V, p. 1; "A Critic's View of Reagan's Tussles With the Truth," People's Magazine, March 9, 1987, pp. 40ff; "How Irangate Differs from Watergate," New York Times, August 9, 1987; "President Still Hasn't Explained," Miami Herald, August 16, 1987, C-1; "Candidate Reagan and the sucker generation," Columbia Journalism Review, November/December 1987, pp. 33–36.
[1]David S. Broder, "When Doctors Disappear," *Washington Post*, June 26, 1983.
[2]Patt Derian, "El Salvador: This is Progress?," *Washington Post*, February 6, 1983, p. B7.
[3]Adam Hochschild, "Inside the Slaughterhouse," *Mother Jones*, June 1983, pp. 18ff.

[4]Richard J. Meislin, "El Salvador: The State of Siege Continues," *New York Times Magazine*, February 20, 1983, pp. 34ff.
[5]*Newsweek*, July 4, 1982, p. 15.
[6]Ronnie Dugger, *On Reagan: The Man & His Presidency* (New York: McGraw-Hill, 1983), p. 340.
[7]Jane Mayer and Doyle McManus, *Landslide: the Unmaking of the President 1984–1988* (Boston: Houghton Mifflin, 1988), p. 368.
[8]Nancy Reagan with William Novak, *My Turn: The Memoirs of Nancy Reagan* (New York: Random House, 1989), p. 109.
[9]Mayer and McManus, *op. cit.*, p. 389.
[10]*Washington Post*, July 25, 1982.
[11]*Time*, February 6, 1984, p. 23.
[12]Laurence Leamer, *Make-Believe: The Story of Nancy & Ronald Reagan* (New York: Harper & Row, 1983), p. 376.
[13]Lou Cannon, *Reagan* (New York: Putnam's, 1982), p. 398.
[14]Steven R. Weisman, "Reaganomics and the President's Men," *New York Times Magazine*, October 24, 1982.
[15]Howell Raines, "With Haig Leaving, Reagan Closes a Compatible Inner Circle," *New York Times*, July 4, 1982.
[16]*Time*, December 13, 1982.
[17]Steven Weisman, "Reagan Term at Midpoint," *New York Times*, January 21, 1983.
[18]*New York Times*, September 16, 1980.
[19]*Washington Post*, February 17, 1983, p. B1.
[20]*New York Times*, January 21, 1982, p. A8.
[21]Cannon, *Reagan*, p. 376.
[22]"The Phrase is Howell Raines," *New York Times*, July 4, 1982.
[23]Cannon, p. 394.
[24]*Time*, December 13, 1982, p. 16.
[25]Barrett, *Gambling*, p. 33.
[26]In 1982, biographer Laurence Barrett asked Reagan to respond to my characterization of him as passive-positive, explaining the term with a collection of associated adjectives rather than the key definers, namely "How much energy does the man invest in his Presidency?" and "Does he seem to experience his political life as happy or sad?" Predictably, Reagan let "positive" pass and questioned "passive" and, missing the personal focus of the character factor, argued that his administration had done all sorts of things. He telephoned Barrett the next day to continue the argument, along the same lines. As

Barrett notes, "He missed the point. His personal involvement and awareness were at issue, not his interest in fighting crime or, much more importantly, his desire to change the face of government." While Barrett does not think Reagan could be "squeezed into any schema as neat as Professor Barber's," he sees the Reagan character as "opposite" to that of active-negatives Johnson and Nixon—which would make Reagan passive-positive. See Barrett, *Gambling*, pp. 22–24.

27Lou Cannon, *President Reagan: The Role of a Lifetime* (New York: Simon & Schuster, 1991), p. 180.

28*Ibid.*, p. 181.

29*Ibid.*, p. 183.

30*Ibid.*, p. 795.

31Reagan and Novak, *op. cit.*, p. 104.

32*Ibid.*, p. 106.

33Mayer and McManus, *op. cit.*, p. 26.

34*Ibid.*

35James David Barber, "President Still Hasn't Explained," Miami Herald, August 16, 1987, p. C-1.

36Mark Hertsgaard, *On Bended Knee: The Press and the Reagan Presidency* (New York: Farrar Straus Giroux, 1988), p. 26.

37Martin Anderson, *Revolution* (New York: Harcourt Brace Jovanovich, 1988), p. 291.

38Cannon, *op. cit.*, p. 53.

39*Ibid.*, p. 63.

40*Ibid.*, pp. 175–6.

41Mayer and McManus, *op. cit.*, p. 32.

42Cannon, *op. cit.*, p. 53.

43Hertsgaard, *op. cit.*, p. 24.

44Reagan and Novak, *op. cit.*, p. 241.

45Mayer and McManus, *op. cit.*, p. 22.

46*Ibid.*, p. 36.

47*Ibid.*, p. 42.

48*Ibid.*, p. 364.

49*Ibid.*, p. 379.

50*Ibid.*, p. 380.

51Theodore H. White, *America in Search of Itself: The Making of the President 1956–1980* (New York: Harper & Row, 1982), p. 412.

52*Newsweek*, August 10, 1981, p. 16.

53Arthur H. Miller, "What Mandate? What Realignment?," *Washington Post*, June 28, 1981.

54Quoted in C. T. Hanson, "Gunsmoke and Sleeping Dogs," *Columbia Journalism Review*, May/June 1983.

55Barrett, *Gambling*, pp. 146ff.

56William Greider, *The Education of David Stockman and Other Americans*, (New York: Dutton, 1982), p. 58.

57*Newsweek*, August 10, 1981, p. 17.

58Ralph Nader, Introduction to Ronald Brownstein and Nina Easton, *Reagan's Ruling Class*, (Washington, D.C.: The Presidential Accountability Group, 1982), ix.

59This line of reasoning owes a good deal to Richard Neustadt's *Presidential Power* (New York: John Wiley, 1963).

60White, *op. cit.*, p. 419.

61James A. Baker, III, "Managing the White House," *Princeton Alumni Weekly*, March 23, 1983, p. 15.

62*Washington Post*, October 10, 1982.

63Walter Pincus, "Behind Reagan's Tough Talk, A Unilateral Arms Reduction," *Washington Post*, January 10, 1982.

64See above, p. 535.

65*New York Times*, October 10, 1982, p. E 19.

66"Reagan Never Meant What He Said," *Washington Post*, August 19, 1982.

67Quoted in Cannon, *Reagan*, p. 316–317.

68*Conservative Digest*, February 1982, p. 33.

69*Conservative Digest*, February 1982.

70*New York Times*, January 27, 1983, p. 23.

71Both quoted in *Conservative Digest*, February 1982, p. 11.

72*Ibid.*, Reagan, p. 17.

73Cannon, *op. cit.*, p. 73.

74Leamer, *op. cit.*, p. 22.

75*Ibid.*, p. 26.

76Cannon, *op. cit.*, p. 146.

77Quoted in Cannon, *Reagan*, p. 87.

78Leamer, *op. cit.*, p. 176.

79*Ibid.*, p. 188.

80Cannon, *op. cit.*, p. 94.

81Leamer, *op. cit.*, p. 193.

82*Ibid.*

83Cannon, *op. cit.*, p. 98.

84Reagan's political history is tellingly described in William E. Leuchtenburg, "Ronald Reagan's Liberal Past," *New Republic*, May 23, 1983.

85Leamer, *op. cit.*, p. 39.

86*Ibid.*, p. 57.

87Cannon, *op. cit.*, p. 141.

88Leamer, *op. cit.*, p. 211.

89*Ibid.*, p. 260.

90Nancy Reagan, and Bill Libby, *Nancy* (New York: Morrow, 1980), p. 207.

91*Ibid.*, pp. 208–9.

92*Ibid.*, p. 203.

[93]*Ibid.*, p. 140.

[94]Leamer, *op. cit.*, p. 257.

[95]Reagan and Libby, *op. cit.*, p. 102.

[96]Leamer, *op. cit.*, p. 233.

[97]*Ibid.*, p. 259.

[98]*Ibid.*, p. 373.

[99]Cannon, *op. cit.*, pp. 340; Leamer, *op. cit.*, p. 345.

[100]Leamer, *op. cit.*, p. 334.

[101]*Ibid.*, p. 357.

[102]Cannon, *op. cit.*, p. 102.

[103]*Ibid.*, p. 103.

[104]Leamer, *op. cit.*, p. 195–96.

[105]Cannon, *op. cit.*, p. 108.

[106]Leamer, *op. cit.*, p. 196.

[107]Cannon, *op. cit.*, p. 119.

[108]Leamer, *op. cit.*, p. 234.

[109]Cannon, *op. cit.*, p. 197.

[110]Leamer, *op. cit.*, p. 285.

[111]Nader, See footnote # 58, viii.

[112]Nader, See footnote # 58, vii.

[113]Dugger, *op. cit.*, p. 216.

[114]Barrett, *op. cit.*, p. 79.

[115]Leamer, *op. cit.*, pp. 293–94.

[116]Nader, see footnote # 58, xiii.

[117]Cannon, *op. cit.*, p. 309.

[118]Dugger, *op. cit.*, p. 119.

[119]Barrett, *op. cit.*, p. 409.

[120]Steven R. Weisman, "Reaganomics and the President's Men," *New York Times Magazine*, October 24, 1982, p. 84.

[121]Barrett, *op. cit.*, pp. 409–10.

[122]Cannon, *op. cit.*, p. 337.

[123]William Greider, *op. cit.*, p. 122.

[124]Robert Greenstein, "Stockman is Still Cooking the Numbers," *Washington Post*, June 19, 1983, p. B1.

[125]Jack Anderson, "The Taxes the Candidates Pay," *Washington Post*, July 10, 1983, p. B7.

[126]Barrett, *op. cit.*, p. 413.

[127]Cannon, *op. cit.*, p. 415. *cf.* Reagan aide Michael Deaver: "I'm sure the stories that bother him most are the ones that say he lacks compassion. Because he is a compassionate man, a caring person. Those do trouble him." *Washington Journalism Review*, April 1984, p. 25.

[128]Quoted in Barrett, *op. cit.*, p. 124.

[129]Leamer, *op. cit.*, p. 359.

[130]Cannon, *op. cit.*, p. 19.

[131]Leamer, *op. cit.*, p. 98.

[132]Cannon, *op. cit.*, p. 62.

[133]Leamer, *op. cit.*, p. 115.

[134]*Ibid.*, p. 143.

[135]Cannon, *op. cit.*, p. 36, quoting from Reagan's autobiography.

[136]Quoted in T. R. Reid, "Reagan: A Life Built on Performance," *Washington Post*, October 22, 1980.

[137]Cannon, *op. cit.*, p. 34.

[138]*Time*, February 6, 1984, p. 22.

[139]Barrett, *op. cit.*, p. 25.

[140]Leamer, *op. cit.*, p. 18.

[141]Jack W. Germond and Jules Witcover, *Blue Smoke and Mirrors: How Reagan Won and Why Carter Lost the Election of 1980* (New York: Viking, 1981), p. 257.

[142]*Ibid.*, p. 278.

[143]C. T. Hanson, "Gunsmoke and Sleeping Dogs: The President's Press at Midterm," *Columbia Journalism Review*, May/June 1983, pp. 27ff.

[144]Leamer, *op. cit.*, p. 213.

[145]Cannon, *op. cit.*, p. 253.

[146]Leamer, *op. cit.*, pp. 267–68; Cannon, *op. cit.*, pp. 253–54.

[147]Lou Cannon, *Washington Post*, November 7, 1982, p. 1.

[148]Leamer, *op. cit.*, p. 215.

[149]Reagan and Libby, *op. cit.*, p. 155.

[150]Leamer, *op. cit.*, p. 277.

[151]Germond and Witcover, *op. cit.*, pp. 210–220.

[152]*World Press Review*, January 1982.

[153]*Washington Post*, April 11, 1982.

[154]Dom Bonafede, "The Press and the Hollywood Presidency," *Washington Journalism Review*, January/February 1981.

[155]Germond and Witcover, *op. cit.*, p. 224.

[156]*New York Times*, January 29, 1984, p. E19.

[157]Leamer, *op. cit.*, p. 97.

[158]*Ibid.*, p. 123.

[159]*Where's the Rest of Me?* Ronald Reagan & Richard G. Hubler (New York: Dell Pub. Co., Inc., 1965), p. 10.

[160]Quoted in Leamer, *op. cit.*, p. 328.

[161]Cannon, *Reagan*, *op. cit.*, p. 332.

[162]Leamer, *op. cit.*, p. 331.

[163]Cannon, *Reagan*, *op cit.*, p. 36.

[164]Leamer, *op. cit.*, p. 81.

[165]*Time*, July 11, 1983, p. 16.

[166]Cannon, *Reagan*, *op. cit.*, p. 36.

[167]William E. Leuchtenburg, "Ronald Reagan's Liberal Past," *The New Republic*, May 23, 1983, pp. 18ff.

[168]*Washington Post*, February 12, 1984.

[169]Quoting *Newsweek*, July 21, 1980, p. 53. Betty Glad, "Black-and-White Thinking: Ronald

Reagan's Approach to Foreign Policy," *Political Psychology*, Vol. 4, No. 1, 1983, p. 63.

170Barrett, *op. cit.*, p. 30.

171Cannon, *Reagan*, 20. Emphasis added.

172Leamer, *op. cit.*, p. 344.

173*"How Reagan Decides," Time*, December 13, 1982, p. 15.

174*Washington Post*, January 10, 1982, p. B 7.

175Quoted in Leamer, *op. cit.*, p. 352.

176White, *op. cit.*, p. 422.

177Barrett, *op. cit.*, p. 142.

178*Ibid.*, p. 178.

179Subsequent works have illustrated much more Reagan's fictionalizing of politics. For example, in a 1988 speech at the Republican National Convention, he pronounced that "The facts are stupid"—a slip when the text said "The facts are stubborn." His aide David Gergen pronounced that "This President speaks in parables." Reporter David Broder said, "It is apparently President Reagan's belief that words can not only cloak reality but remake it.", [p. 299, "The Myth of Conciliation," in *Presidential Selection* (Durham, N.C.: Duke University Press, 1987), edited by Alexander Heard and Michael Nelson]. His aide Larry Speakes said, "If you tell the same story five times, it's true.", (p. 60). Lou Cannon notes that "the aides had adopted Reagan's own standard of judging stories by their impact rather than their accuracy.", (ibid.). Martin Anderson said, "Whenever somebody told him something, he assumed they were telling the truth.", (p. 180). James Baker said, "The world of illusion suited Reagan.", [p. 837, Lou Cannon, *President Reagan: The Role of a Lifetime* (New York: Simon and Schuster, 1991)]. One of his children said, "He makes things up and believes them.", (p. 30). John Sears said, "Now everyone knows that Ronald Reagan doesn't know what he's doing.", [p. 371, Jane Mayer and Doyle McManus, *Landslide: The Unmaking of the President 1984–1988* (Boston: Houghton Mifflin, 1988)].

180Quoted in Barrett, *op. cit.*, p. 391.

181*Newsweek*, August 15, 1983.

182*Time*, August 15, 1983, p. 11.

183*New York Times*, April 10, 1984, p. 1.

184Robert Kaiser, *Washington Post*, January 15, 1984, p. D 1.

185*Washington Post*, February 12, 1984, p. A 17.

CHAPTER 9

1R. Caldecott, *Come Lasses and Lads* (London, Routledge, 18??), unpaged.

2Gerald D. Nash, ed., *Franklin Delano Roosevelt* (Englewood Cliffs, N.J.: Prentice-Hall, 1967), p. 73.

3*Ibid.*, p. 73.

4Frank Freidel, *Franklin D. Roosevelt: The Apprenticeship* (Boston: Little Brown, 1952), p. 23.

5Allen Churchill, *The Roosevelts* (New York: Harper & Row, 1965), p. 180.

6Freidel, *op. cit.*, p. 46n.

7Churchill, *op. cit.*, p. 219.

8Freidel, *op. cit.*, p. 66.

9Nash, *op. cit.*, p. 80.

10Emil Ludwig, *Roosevelt: A Study in Fortune and Power* (New York: Garden City Books, 1941), p. 53.

11James MacGregor Burns, *Roosevelt: The Lion and the Fox* (New York: Harcourt, Brace, 1956), p. 43.

12*Ibid.*, p. 53.

13Freidel, *op. cit.*, p. 201.

14*Ibid.*, p. 214.

15*Ibid.*, p. 250.

16*Ibid.*, p. 310.

17Richard Harrity and Ralph G. Martin, *The Human Side of F.D.R.* (New York: Duell, Sloan and Pearce, 1960), unpaged.

18Gene Smith, *The Shattered Dream* (New York: William Morrow, 1970), p. 90.

19Patrick Anderson, *The President's Men* (Garden City, N.Y.: Doubleday, 1968), p. 33.

20Arthur M. Schlesinger, Jr., *The Coming of the New Deal* (Boston: Houghton Mifflin, 1959), p. 547.

21Walter Johnson, *1600 Pennsylvania Avenue* (Boston: Little Brown, 1960), p. 84.

22Samuel I. Rosenman, *Working with Roosevelt* (New York: Harper & Row, 1952), p. 105.

23Johnson, *op. cit.*, p. 89.

24Rexford G. Tugwell, *The Democratic Roosevelt* (Garden City, N.Y.: Doubleday, 1957), p. 398.

25Burns, *op. cit.*, p. 314.

CHAPTER 10

1Dwight Durough, *Mr. Sam* (New York: Random House, 1962), p. 47.

[2]Cabell Phillips, *The Truman Presidency* (New York: Macmillan, 1966), p. 54.

[3]Margaret Truman, *Souvenir* (New York: McGraw-Hill, 1956), p. 356.

[4]William Hillman, *Mr. President* (New York: Farrar, Straus, and Young, 1952), p. 35.

[5]Margaret Truman, *op. cit.*, p. 96.

[6]Harry S Truman, *Year of Decisions, 1945* (New York: New American Library, 1955), p. 139.

[7]*Ibid.*, pp. 139–40.

[8]Hillman, *op. cit.*, p. 190.

[9]Phillips, *op. cit.*, p. 13.

[10]Alfred Steinberg, *The Man from Missouri* (New York: G. P. Putnam's Sons, 1962), p. 63.

[11]Hillman, *op. cit.*, pp. 90–91.

[12]Steinberg, *op. cit.*, p. 294.

[13]Harry S Truman, *op. cit.*, p. 22.

[14]*Ibid.*, p. 26.

[15]Harry S Truman, *Years of Trial and Hope, 1946–1952* (New York: New American Library, 1956), p. 13.

[16]Truman, *Year of Decisions, op. cit.*, p. 107.

[17]*Ibid.*, p. 610.

[18]Phillips, *op. cit.*, pp. 130–31.

[19]Columbia Broadcasting System, "Three Presidents on the Presidency," 1958.

[20]Phillips, *op. cit.*, p. 88.

[21]*Ibid.*, pp. 160–61.

[22]Truman, *Years of Trial and Hope, op. cit.*, p. 129.

[23]*Ibid.*, p. 500.

[24]*Ibid.*, p. 501.

[25]*Ibid.*, p. 505.

[26]From Steinberg, *op. cit.*, p. 298.

CHAPTER 11

[1]Gail Cameron, *Rose* (New York: Putnam, 1971), p. 85.

[2]Arthur M. Schlesinger, Jr., *A Thousand Days* (Boston: Houghton Mifflin, 1965), p. 79.

[3]Richard J. Whalen, *The Founding Father: The Story of Joseph P. Kennedy* (New York: New American Library, 1964), p. 170.

[4]Joe McCarthy, *The Remarkable Kennedys* (New York: Dial Press, 1960), p. 103.

[5]*Ibid.*, p. 104.

[6]Hank Searls, *The Lost Prince* (New York: World, 1969), p. 97.

[7]James MacGregor Burns, *John Kennedy* (New York: Avon, 1960), p. 24.

[8]John F. Kennedy, *Why England Slept* (New York: Funk, 1961), p. 3.

[9]*Ibid.*, pp. 22–23.

[10]*Ibid.*, p. 57.

[11]*Ibid.*, p. 109.

[12]*Ibid.*, p. 182.

[13]*Ibid.*, p. 185.

[14]*Ibid.*, pp. 230–31.

[15]John F. Kennedy, *Profiles in Courage* (New York: Pocket Books, 1960), p. 15.

[16]Schlesinger, *op. cit.*, p. 87.

[17]*Ibid.*, p. 88.

[18]*Ibid.*

[19]*Ibid.*, p. 106.

[20]Theodore H. White, *The Making of the President 1960* (New York: Atheneum, 1961), p. 331.

[21]Quoted in James Tracy Crown, *The Kennedy Literature* (New York: New York University Press, 1968), pp. 21–22.

[22]Tom Wicker, *Kennedy Without Tears* (New York: Morrow, 1964), p. 20.

[23]Bill Adler, ed., *The Complete Kennedy Wit* (New York: Citadel Press, 1967), pp. 36–37.

[24]*Ibid.*, p. 43.

[25]*Ibid.*, p. 55.

[26]*Ibid.*, p. 70.

[27]*Ibid.*, p. 91.

[28]Theodore C. Sorenson, *Kennedy* (New York: Harper & Row, 1965), p. 367.

[29]Richard M. Nixon, *Six Crises* (New York: Pyramid Books, 1968), p. 382.

[30]From Sorenson, *op. cit.*, pp. 302–3.

[31]Schlesinger, *op. cit.*, p. 251.

[32]*Ibid.*, p. 254.

[33]Hugh Sidey, *John F. Kennedy, President* (Greenwich, Conn.: Fawcett Publications, 1963), p. 119.

[34]*Ibid.*, p. 120.

[35]Sorenson, *op. cit.*, p. 526.

[36]*Ibid.*, p. 528.

[37]*Ibid.*, p. 591.

[38]Schlesinger, *op. cit.*, p. 386.

[39]Sorenson, *op. cit.*, pp. 450–51.

[40]*Ibid.*, p. 679.

[41]*Ibid.*, p. 685.

[42]Robert F. Kennedy, *Thirteen Days* (New York: Signet Books, 1969), p. 14.

[43]Sorenson, *op. cit.*, p. 700.

[44]Robert F. Kennedy, *op. cit.*, p. 102.

[45]Kenneth O'Donnell, "LBJ and the Kennedys," *Look*, August 7, 1970, pp. 51–52.

[46]Sorenson, *op. cit.*, p. 470.

[47]*Ibid.*, p. 499.

CHAPTER 12

[1] Elizabeth Drew, *Washington Journal: The Events of 1973–1974* (New York: Vintage Books, 1976), pp. 92, 143.

[2] *Ibid.*, p. 142; James David Barber, *New York Times,* June 22, 1974, p. 29.

[3] Drew, *op. cit.*, p. 143.

[4] *New York Times,* June 22, 1974, p. 29; *U.S. News and World Report,* September 2, 1974, p. 23.

[5] *Ibid.*, pp. 23–25.

[6] *U.S. News and World Report,* April 28, 1975.

[7] *New York Times,* September 9, 1974, p. 1.

[8] *U.S. News and World Report,* April 28, 1975, p. 28.

[9] *Ibid.*

[10] James David Barber review of terHorst's *Gerald Ford and the Future of the Presidency, Washington Post,* December 1, 1974.

[11] Jerald F. terHorst, *Gerald Ford and the Future of the Presidency,* (New York: The Third Press, 1974), pp. 27–28.

[12] Bud Vestal, *Jerry Ford Up Close: An Investigative Biography* (New York: Coward, McCann and Geoghegan, 1974), p. 49.

[13] terHorst, *op. cit.*, p. 34.

[14] *Ibid.*, p. 35.

[15] *Ibid.*, p. 29.

[16] Barber, *New York Times,* June 22, 1974, p. 29.

[17] Barber, *Washington Post* review of terHorst, December 1, 1974.

[18] terHorst, *op. cit.*, p. 37.

[19] *Ibid.*, p. 25.

[20] *The Book of Common Prayer* (New York: Seabury Press, 1953).

[21] terHorst, *op. cit.*, pp. 36–37.

[22] *Ibid.*, pp. 41, 43.

[23] Vestal, *op. cit.*, p. 61.

[24] terHorst, *op. cit.*, p. 42.

[25] Vestal, *op. cit.*, p. 58.

[26] terHorst, *op. cit.*, p. 39.

[27] *Time,* October 4, 1976, p. 23.

[28] Vestal, *op. cit.*, p. 28.

[29] terHorst, *op. cit.*, p. 48.

[30] *Ibid.*, p. 12.

[31] *Ibid.*, Chap. 1.

[32] *Ibid.*, p. 11.

[33] *Ibid.*, p. 16.

[34] *Ibid.*, p. 20.

[35] *Ibid.*, pp. 3, 25.

[36] *Ibid.*, pp. 4, 22, 23.

[37] *Ibid.*, p. 54n.

[38] *Ibid.*, pp. 55, 60.

[39] *Time,* October 4, 1976, p. 23.

[40] *Time,* January 10, 1977, pp. 15–16.

[41] terHorst, *op. cit.*, p. 188.

CHAPTER 13

[1] *U.S. News and World Report,* April 28, 1975, p. 25.

[2] *Washington Post,* July 16, 1976, p. A 12.

[3] *U.S. News and World Report,* April 28, 1975, p. 25.

[4] *Washington Post,* July 16, 1976, p. A 12.

[5] Bruce Mazlish and Edwin Diamond, "Thrice-born: A Psychohistory of Jimmy Carter's 'Rebirth,'" *New York,* August 30, 1976.

[6] Martin Schram, *Running for President: A Journal of the Carter Campaign* (New York: Pocket Books, 1976).

[7] *Ibid.*, p. 47.

[8] Reynolds Price, "Family Stories: The Carters in Plains," *Time,* January 3, 1977, pp. 26–29.

[9] *New York,* June 14, 1976, p. 40.

[10] *Time,* January 3, 1977, p. 29; Schram, *op. cit.*, p. 51; *Newsweek,* September 13, 1976, p. 25; *New York,* June 14, 1976, pp. 40, 41.

[11] Schram, *op. cit.*, p. 51; *New York,* June 14, 1976, p. 42; Leslie Wheeler, *Jimmy Who? An Examination of Presidential Candidate Jimmy Carter: The Man, His Career, His Stands on the Issues* (Woodbury, N.Y.: Barron's Educational Series, 1976).

[12] Transcript of Bill Moyers interview with Jimmy Carter, May 6, 1976, on *USA: People and Politics,* produced for PBS by Wallace Westfeldt, p. 6.

[13] Schram, *op. cit.*, p. 135.

[14] *Ibid.*, p. 137; Jimmy Carter, *Why Not the Best?* (Nashville, Tenn.: Broadman Press, 1975), p. 14.

[15] Moyers interview transcript, p. 8; Peter Goldman, "Sizing Up Carter," *Newsweek,* September 13, 1976, pp. 22ff; Reynolds Price, "Family Stories," p. 26; Carter, *op. cit.*, p. 14.

[16] *Ibid.*, p. 25.

[17] Wheeler, *op. cit.*, p. 2; Moyers interview transcript, p. 8; Carter, *op. cit.*, p. 15.

[18] Goldman, "Sizing Up Carter."

[19] Moyers interview transcript, pp. 36–37.

[20] William Greider, "A Carter Album," *Washington Post,* October 24, 1976, p. A16.

[21] Wheeler, *Jimmy Who?*, p. 8.

[22]Carter, *op. cit.*, p. 19. Excerpts reprinted by permission.

[23]*Ibid.*, p. 41; Schram, *op. cit.*, p. 52; Wheeler, *op. cit.*, p. 14.

[24]Carter, *op. cit.*, pp. 44, 43, 47.

[25]*Ibid.*, p. 48.

[26]Wheeler, *op. cit.*, p. 18.

[27]Carter, *op. cit.*, p. 50; Wheeler, *op. cit.*, p. 19.

[28]Robert W. Turner, *"I'll Never Lie to You": Jimmy Carter in His Own Words* (New York: Ballantine Books, 1976), pp. 88–89.

[29]Moyers interview transcript, p. 4; Greider, "A Carter Album," p. A17.

[30]Greider, *loc. cit.*

[31]Greider, *loc. cit.*

[32]Greider, *loc. cit.*

[33]Schram, *op. cit.*, p. 53; Wheeler, *op. cit.*, p. 18.

[34]Price, "Family Stories," p. 29.

[35]Carter, *op. cit.*, p. 63; Wheeler, *op. cit.*, p. 17; *Playboy*, November 1976, p. 84.

[36]Carter, *op. cit.*, p. 60. Carter had been away from home a long time and had visited infrequently, separated from the Plains family by sea distances and then by responsibilities to his and Rosalynn's family.

[37]Howard Norton and Bob Slosser, *The Miracle of Jimmy Carter* (Plainfield, N.J.: Logos Internation, 1976), p. 18; Goldman, "Sizing Up Carter."

[38]Carter, *op. cit.*, p. 60; Goldman, "Sizing Up Carter"; Schram, *op. cit.*, p. 50; Carter, *op. cit.*, p. 61.

[39]Carter, *loc. cit.*; Goldman, "Sizing Up Carter."

[40]Carter, *op. cit.*, p. 65.

[41]Schram, *op. cit.*, p. 49; Goldman, *op. cit.*

[42]Carter, *op. cit.*, pp. 36–37; Goldman, *op. cit.*

[43]*Ibid.*

[44]*Ibid.*, Carter, *op. cit.*, p. 34; Goldman, *op. cit.*

[45]Carter, *op. cit.*, pp. 66, 37.

[46]Schram, *op. cit.*, p. 49; Turner, *op. cit.*, pp. 106, 20.

[47]Turner, *op. cit.*, p. 106; Carter, *op. cit.*, p. 67; Goldman, *op. cit.*

[48]*Ibid.*

[49]Wheeler, *op. cit.*, p. 32; Goldman, *op. cit.*

[50]Greider, "A Carter Album," p. A17; Carter, *op. cit.*, p. 9.

[51]*Ibid.*, p. 32.

[52]Wheeler, *op. cit.*, p. 29; Carter, *op. cit.*, p. 77.

[53]Wheeler, *op. cit.*, p. 29.

[54]Carter, *op. cit.*, p. 7.

[55]*Ibid.*, pp. 79–80.

[56]*Ibid.*, p. 80.

[57]William Greider, "A Carter Album," *Washington Post*, October 25, 1976, p. A12.

[58]*Ibid.*

[59]*Ibid.*

[60]*Ibid.*

[61]*Ibid.*

[62]*Ibid.*

[63]Carter, *op. cit.*, pp. 84–85.

[64]Goldman, *op. cit.*; Fred McMorrow, *Jimmy: The Candidacy of Carter* (N. p.: A Strawberry Hill Book, 1976), unpaged.

[65]Not even the factual details are as certain as they might be; for all the journalistic scrutiny Carter was subject to, this period, particularly his performance in the Senate, has, in the recounting of it, some gaps and variations.

[66]Carter, *op. cit.*, pp. 85–86.

[67]*Ibid.*, pp. 87–93, italics added.

[68]*Ibid.*, p. 139.

[69]*Ibid.*, p. 87.

[70]*Ibid.*, pp. 89, 93.

[71]Goldman, *op. cit.*

[72]Jack Bass and Walter DeVries, *The Transformation of Southern Politics: Social Change and Political Consequences Since 1945* (New York: Basic Books, 1976), p. 142.

[73]Carter, *op. cit.*, p. 97.

[74]William Greider, "A Carter Album," *Washington Post*, October 26, 1976, p. A6.

[75]Goldman, *op. cit.*

[76]Greider, "A Carter Album," October 26, 1976.

[77]*Ibid.*

[78]*Time*, January 10, 1976, p. 12.

[79]Turner, *op. cit.*; Carter, *op. cit.*, p. 99; Moyers interview transcript, p. 26.

[80]Goldman, *op. cit.*

[81]Wheeler, *op. cit.*, p. 137; Carter, *op. cit.*, pp. 132–33.

[82]Harry R. David and Robert C. Good, eds., *Reinhold Niebuhr on Politics: His Political Philosophy and Its Application to Our Age as Expressed in His Writings* (New York: Charles Scribner's Sons, 1960), pp. 153, 154, 162. In that book Niebuhr writes: "We must establish tentative harmonies and provisional equities in a world from which sin cannot be eliminated, and yet hold these provisional and tentative moral achievements under the perspective of the Kingdom of God. . . . The love commandment is thus a guide for the approximation of justice and love which

make up the warp and woof of everyday existence. . . . Human life is under obligation not only to perfect every moral attitude in the direction of perfect love, but to extend it in the direction of universal love. . . . The love commandment is, in short, immediately relevant to every moral action."

[83]David Kucharsky, *The Man from Plains: The Mind and Spirit of Jimmy Carter* (New York: Harper and Row, 1976), p. 19.

[84]*Playboy,* November 1976.

[85]Carter, *op. cit.,* pp. 132, 133.

[86]*Ibid.,* p. 134; Wheeler, *op. cit.,* p. 139.

[87]*The Poems of Dylan Thomas.* Copyright 1946 by New Directions Publishing Corporation. Reprinted by permission of New Directions Publishing Corporation, J M Dent & Sons, and the trustees for the copyrights of the late Dylan Thomas.

[88]Schram, *op. cit.,* pp. 50–51.

[89]Mazlish and Diamond, *op. cit.,* p. 28; Greider, "A Carter Album."

[90]Carter, *op. cit.,* p. 130; Goldman, *op. cit.;* Revelations 3:20.

[91]"Our Savior has hands which are very gentle, and he cannot do much with a man who is hard." Carter, *op. cit.,* pp. 131–32.

[92]Schram, *op. cit.,* p. 112.

[93]Moyers interview transcript, p. 10.

[94]Carter, *op. cit.,* p. 61; Kucharsky, *op. cit.,* p. 26; Moyers interview transcript, p. 37.

[95]*The Presbyterian Hymnal* (Richmond, Va., Presbyterian Committee of Publication, 1927).

[96]Wheeler, *op. cit.,* p. 45; Goldman, *op. cit.;* Bass and DeVries, *op. cit.,* p. 144; Greider, "A Carter Album"; Carter, *op. cit.,* p. 106.

[97]Jimmy Carter, *A State in Action: Georgia 1971–75* (State Report); Goldman, *op. cit.*

[98]Wheeler, *op. cit.,* p. 83; Goldman, *op. cit.*

[99]Turner, *op. cit.,* p. 35.

[100]Schram, *op. cit.,* p. 19.

[101]Carter, *Why Not the Best?* pp. 9–10; *Playboy,* November 1976.

[102]*Time,* January 3, 1977, p. 13.

[103]Andrist, Ralph K., ed., *George Washington: A Biography in His Own Words,* Volume 2. (*Newsweek,* New York, 1972), pp. 302–3.

[104]Jimmy Carter, *Keeping Faith: Memoirs of a President* (New York: Bantam, 1982), p. 118.

[105]Charles Peters, "How to be a One-term President," *Harper's,* December, 1982, p. 17.

[106]Hamilton Jordan, *Crisis: The Last Year of the Carter Presidency* (New York: Putnam's, 1982), p. 318.

[107]Haynes Johnson, *In the Absence of Power: Governing America* (New York: Viking, 1980), p. 295.

[108]Carter, *Keeping Faith, op. cit.,* p. 65.

[109]*Ibid.,* p. 66.

[110]Robert Shogan, *Promises to Keep: Carter's First Hundred Days* (New York: Thomas Y. Crowell, 1977), p. 242.

[111]*Ibid.,* p. 226.

[112]Johnson, *op. cit.,* p. 297.

[113]Carter, *Keeping Faith, op. cit.,* p. 87.

[114]*Ibid.,* p. 575.

[115]Godfrey Hodgson, *All Things To All Men: The False Promise of the Modern American Presidency* (New York: Simon and Schuster, 1980), p. 23.

[116]Carter, *Keeping Faith, op. cit.,* p. 126.

[117]Jordan, *op. cit.,* p. 378. See Theodore White on "that shifting menagerie of cold-eyed money men and hot-eyed moralists who shuffle through the marble anterooms of the Capitol, who slink or stalk through the corridors of Senate and House office buildings." Theodore White, *America in Search of Itself: The Making of the President 1956–1980* (New York: Harper and Row, 1982), p. 203.

[118]Johnson, *op. cit.,* p. 48.

[119]Shogan, *op. cit.,* p. 125.

[120]*Ibid.*

[121]White, *op. cit.,* p. 269.

[122]*Ibid.,* pp. 208–9.

[123]Johnson, *op. cit.,* p. 20.

[124]*Ibid.,* p. 156.

[125]Shogan, *op. cit.,* p. 209.

[126]Carter, *Keeping Faith, op. cit.,* p. 67.

[127]Johnson, *op. cit.,* p. 234–242.

[128]*Ibid.,* p. 538.

[129]Shogan, *op. cit.,* p. 6.

[130]*Ibid.,* p. 35.

[131]White, *op. cit.,* p. 260.

[132]Germond and Witcover, *op. cit.,* p. 41.

[133]Betty Glad, *Jimmy Carter: In Search of the Great White House* (New York: W. W. Norton, 1980), pp. 423–24.

[134]Hodgson, *op. cit.,* p. 24; Glad, *op. cit.,* p. 433.

[135]Johnson, *op. cit.,* p. 265.

[136]Carter, *Keeping Faith, op. cit.,* p. 282.

[137]*Ibid.,* p. 399.

[138]I leave to the psychoanalytically oriented this aside in Carter's memoirs: "I had had to prepare the speech hurriedly, and in the car on the way to the Capitol, I had decided to add a Bible verse from the Sermon on the Mount: 'Blessed are the peacemakers: for—

?' I could not remember whether 'they shall be called the children of God' or 'theirs is the kingdom of heaven.' Luckily, I guessed right, and made them God's children. That quote got most of the headlines." Carter, *Keeping Faith*, p. 405. Carter the Sunday school teacher must have read the Sermon on the Mount many times and perhaps memorized the Beatitudes as a child. The first of the Beatitudes, Matthew 5:3, is "Blessed are the poor in spirit, for theirs is the kingdom of heaven."

[139]Jordan, *op. cit.*, p. 88.

[140]Carter, *Keeping Faith, op. cit.*, p. 210.

[141]*Ibid.*, p. 257.

[142]*Ibid.*, p. 417.

[143]*Ibid.*, p. 89.

[144]Shogan, *op. cit.*, p. 132.

[145]Germond and Witcover, *op. cit.*, p. 44.

[146]Roy Blount, Jr., *Crackers: This Whole Many-Angled Thing of Jimmy, More Carters, Ominous Little Animals, Sad-Singing Women, My Daddy and Me* (New York: Knopf, 1980), p. 84.

[147]From Schiller's "Ode to Joy," put to music in Beethoven's Ninth Symphony: "All Men Become Brothers Where Your Gentle Wing Rests."

[148]Jordan, *op. cit.*, p. 326.

[149]*Ibid.*, p. 330.

[150]Johnson, *op. cit.*, p. 197; Carter, *Keeping Faith, op. cit.*, p. 57; and Jordan, *op. cit.*, p. 71.

[151]James David Barber, *The Presidential Character: Predicting Performance in the White House* (Englewood Cliffs, N.J.: Prentice-Hall, 1972), p. 535.

[152]Jordan, *op. cit.*, p. 7.

[153]Shogan, *op. cit.*, p. 108; Carter, *Keeping Faith, op. cit.*, pp. 19, 84, 108, 178, 402, 514, and 544. Carter's sister Ruth told a Chicago reporter about a conversation she and her brother had, Jimmy asking Ruth how she would use Barber's types. Ruth recalls: "He would say, 'How about Kennedy?' And I would say, 'He was probably active-positive.' And he said, 'Yeah, that's right.' Then he asked about Nixon, and I said he was 'active-negative.' And he said, 'Yeah, you're right. How do you know so much about psychology?' I said, 'Oh, you know. It's just that I'm smart.'" Quoted in Betty Glad, *Jimmy Carter*, p. 487.

[154]Fallows, James, "The Passionless Presidency: The Trouble with Jimmy Carter's Administration," *The Atlantic*, May, 1976, p. 34. Fallows is a Washington editor of *The Atlantic*.

[155]Shogan, *op. cit.*, p. 133.

[156]Carter, *Keeping Faith, op. cit.*, p. 24.

[157]*Ibid.*, p. 533.

[158]*Ibid.*, p. 66.

[159]*Ibid.*, p. 62.

[160]Germond and Witcover, *op. cit.*, p. 457; Carter, *Keeping Faith, op. cit.*, p. 457.

[161]Carter, *Keeping Faith, op. cit.*, p. 457.

[162]Jordan, *op. cit.*, p. 34.

[163]Carter, *Keeping Faith, op. cit.*, p. 458.

[164]*Ibid.*, p. 465.

[165]*Ibid.*, p. 459.

[166]*Ibid.*, pp. 458–59.

[167]Germond and Witcover, *op. cit.*, pp. 88–89.

[168]Carter, *Keeping Faith, op. cit.*, p. 484.

[169]*Ibid.*, p. 509; Jordan, *op. cit.*, pp. 278, 260–62.

[170]Jordan, *op. cit.*, p. 264.

[171]*Ibid.*, p. 405.

[172]Johnson, *op. cit.*, p. 291.

[173]Carter, *Keeping Faith, op. cit.*, p. 591.

[174]*Ibid.*, p. 539.

[175]White, *op. cit.*, p. 225.

[176]*Ibid.*, p. 536.

[177]Carter, *Keeping Faith, op. cit.*, p. 143.

[178]*Ibid.*, p. 144.

[179]*Ibid.*, p. 151.

CHAPTER 14

[1]James David Barber, "Character in the Chief," Newsday, Nov. 29, 1987.

[2]Frye Gaillard, "Barber on the Presidency," The Charlotte Observer, July 3, 1988.

[3]George Bush, with Victor Gold, LOOKING FORWARD (New York: Bantam Books, 1988).

[4]George E. Condon, Jr., "Bush Learned He Had to Overcome Wealth," The San Diego Union, October 4, 1987.

[5]Fitzhugh Green, *George Bush: An Intimate Portrait* (New York: Hippocrene Books, 1989).

[6]Walt Harrington, "Born to Run," The Washington Post Magazine, September 28, 1986, p. 20.

[7]Bush with Gold, *op. cit.*, p. 26.

[8]Donald Morrison, ed., *The Winning of the White House* 1988 (New York: Time, Inc., 1988), p. 84.

[9]Bush with Gold, *op. cit.*, p. 26.

[10]Harrington, *op. cit.*, p. 20.

[11]Bush with Gold, *op. cit.*, p. 26.

[12]Nicholas King, GEORGE BUSH: A BIOGRAPHY (New York: Dodd, Mead, 1980), p. 11.

[13]*Ibid.*, p. 1.

[14]Harry Hurt III, "George Bush, Plucky Lad," Texas Monthly, June 1983, pp. 141–2.

[15]Bob Woodward and Walter Pincus, of the Post, quoted in Timothy Noah, "Old Blanddad," The New Republic, April 3, 1989, p. 17.

[16]Hurt, *op. cit.*, p. 208.

[17]Morrison, *op. cit.*, p. 81.

[18]*Ibid.*, p. 82.

[19]Hurt, *op. cit.*, p. 142.

[20]Gail Sheehy, "Is George Bush Too Nice to be President?", Vanity Fair, February 1987, p. 119.

[21]Garry Wills, "The Ultimate Loyalist," Time Magazine, August 22, 1988, p. 23.

[22]Green, *op. cit.*, p. 50.

[23]*Ibid.*, p. 208.

[24]*Ibid.*, p. 2.

[25]*Ibid.*, p. 79.

[26]cf. King, p. 16.

[27]Morrison, *op. cit.*, pp. 87–88.

[28]Gerald M. Boyd, "Bush Presidential Campaign is Nagged by Doubts," The New York Times, April 27, 1987.

[29]*Whose Broad Stripes and Bright Stars?: The Trivial Pursuit of the Presidency 1988* (New York: Warner Books, 1989), p. 467.

[30]Texas Monthly 207–8.

[31]Green, *op. cit.*, pp. 255–256.

[32]Morrison, *op. cit.*, pp. 78–79.

[33]Walt Harrington, *op. cit.*

[34]*Ibid.*, 20.

[35]Green, *op. cit.*, p. 28.

[36]Doug Wead, *George Bush: Man of Integrity* (Eugene, Oregon: Harvest House Publishers, 1988), pp. 8–9, italics added.

[37]Harrington, *op. cit.*, p. 20, italics added.

[38]Joe Hyams, "Bush's Own War Story," U.S. News, Dec 31, 1990/Jan 7, 1991, p. 26, italics added.

[39]*Ibid.*, p. 28.

[40]*Ibid.*, p. 23, italics added.

[41]Harrington, *op. cit.*, p. 20–21.

[42]Green, *op. cit.*, p. 52.

[43]Michael Kramer, "George Bush: A Republican For All Factions," New York, January 21, 1980, p. 43, italics added.

[44]Bush with Gold, *op. cit.*, p. 42.

[45]*Ibid.*

[46]Hurt, *op. cit.*, p. 143.

[47]Bush with Gold, *op. cit.*, p. 47, italics added.

[48]Hurt, *op. cit.*, p. 143, italics added.

[49]Donnie Radcliffe, *Simply Barbara Bush: A Portrait of America's Candid First Lady* (New York, Warner Books, 1989) p. 105.

[50]Hurt, *op. cit.*, pp. 143, 192.

[51]*Ibid.*, p. 53.

[52]*Ibid.*, p. 55.

[53]*Ibid.*, pp. 43, 41.

[54]*Ibid.*, p. 86.

[55]Bush with Gold, *op. cit.*, p. 11.

[56]*Ibid.*, p. 64, italics added.

[57]*Ibid.*, p. 193.

[58]*Ibid.*, p. 81, italics added.

[59]Timothy Noah, "Old Bland-dad," The New Republic, April 3, 1989, p. 18.

[60]King, *op. cit.*, p. 45, italics added.

[61]Bush with Gold, *op. cit.*, pp. 82–83.

[62]Noah, *op. cit.*, p. 18.

[63]Bush with Gold, *op. cit.*, p. 83, italics added.

[64]Hurt, *op. cit.*, p. 196.

[65]King, *op. cit.*, p. 53.

[66]Bush with Gold, *op. cit.*, p. 83.

[67]Harrington, *op. cit.*, p. 48.

[68]Bush with Gold, *op. cit.*, p. 92.

[69]Hurt, *op. cit.*, p. 198.

[70]Bush with Gold, *op. cit.*, p. 92.

[71]Gail Sheehy, *Character: America's Search for Leadership* (New York: Morrow, 1989), p. 174.

[72]*Ibid.*; cf. Green, p. 111.

[73]*Ibid.*, p. 200.

[74]*Ibid.*

[75]Bush with Gold, *op. cit.*, p. 116.

[76]Wead, *op. cit.*, p. 27.

[77]Green, *op. cit.*, p. 126.

[78]King, *op. cit.*, p. 84.

[79]Bush with Gold, *op. cit.*, pp. 127–128, italics added.

[80]Wead, *op. cit.*, p. 22.

[81]Hurt, *op. cit.*, p. 208.

[82]Current Biography, 1983, p. 40.

[83]Germond and Witcover, *op. cit.*, p. 111.

[84]Garry Wills, "The Power Populist," Time magazine, Nov 21, 1988, p. 55.

[85]Noah, *op. cit.*, p. 17.

[86]Michael Kramer, "What Does Bush Stand For?", U.S. News and World Report, August 22, 1988, p. 20, p. 15.

[87]"I've Been Underestimated," Time Magazine August 22, 1988, p. 20.

[88]Bush with Gold, *op. cit.*, p. xvii.

[89]Andrew Rosenthal, "Bush Claims Role In Hostage Rescue in Salvador Hotel," New York Times press release, November 23, 1989.

[90]*Ibid.*

[91]"A Party Derided," New York Times, March 10, 1991, p. 15.

[92]Don Oberdorfer, "The War No One Saw Coming," The Washington Post National Weekly Edition, March 18–24, 1991, p. 7.

[93]*Ibid.*, p. 7.

[94]*Ibid.*, p. 8.

[95]*Ibid.*, p. 8.

[96]*Ibid.*, p. 8.

[97]*Ibid.*, p. 9.

[98]*Ibid.*, p. 9.

[99]Alexander Cockburn, "Suddenly, Last Summer," Utne Reader, March/April 1991, p. 105.

[100]Oberdorfer, *op. cit.*, p. 10.

[101]Stuart Auerback, "Made in America, Used by Iraq," The Washington Post National Weekly Edition, March 18–24, p. 11.

[102]Thomas L. Friedman and Patrick E. Tyler, "From the First U.S. Resolve to Fight," New York Times, March 3, 1991, p. 1.

[103]Oberdorfer, *op. cit.*, p. 7.

[104]Friedman and Tyler, *op. cit.*, p. 12.

[105]"The Talk of the Town," The New Yorker, August 20, 1990, p. 25, italics added.

[106]Friedman and Tyler, *op. cit.*, p. 12.

[107]Dan Schorr, "On the Way to War," The New Leader, January 14, 1991, p. 3.

[108]Bruce W. Jentleson, "The Domestic Politics of Desert Shield," The Brookings Review, Winter 1990/91.

[109]ACLU News release, December 13, 1990, p. 1, quoting Kate Martin, Director of ACLU National Security.

[110]Bruce Jentleson, *op. cit.*

[111]*Ibid.*

[112]"Shutting Out Sam Nunn," Newsweek, February 4, 1991, p. 9.

[113]*Ibid.*

[114]Newsweek, November 26, 1990, pp. 28–29.

[115]Mortin Halperin and Gary Stein, "Task Force for a National Debate on the Persian Gulf Crisis," ACLU, December 7, 1990.

[116]Newsweek, January 2, 1991.

[117]Manning Marable, "The Bitter Fruits of War," *The Witness*, March 1991, p. 7.

[118]"What They're Saying About the War," *The Witness*, March 1991, p. 5.

[119]*Ibid.*

[120]*Ibid.*

[121]George Will, "Once Again Ike Was Right," Newsweek, January 14, 1991, p. 60.

[122]Chapel Hill Herald, January 12, 1991.

[123]James Bennet, "The Senate's Lame Doves," The Washington Monthly, March 1991, pp. 43–46.

[124]"News Conference," Washington Post, January 13, 1991.

[125]Edward Keynes, *Undeclared War: Twilight Zone of Constitutional Power* (University Park, Pennsylvania: Pennsylvania State University Press, 1991), pp. 2–3.

[126]*Ibid.*, p. xvi.

[127]"Bush has 'gut feeling' Iraq will pull back," December 30, 1990, Durham Morning Herald.

[128]"The Iraqi Nightmare," New York Times, Nov. 6, 1990, A 15.

[129]"War Shatters What Remains of Rational Discourse," The Chapel Hill Herald, February 4, 1991.

[130]Dan Goodgame, "What If We Do Nothing?", Time Magazine, January 7, 1991, p. 23.

[131]Time, *Ibid.*, p. 26.

[132]Robin Toner, "Discreet Maneuvers Over War Issue," New York Times, Washington Talk, February 21, 1991.

[133]John G. Healey, "Amnesty International USA Response to President Bush's Letter to Campus Newspapers," January 15, 1991.

[134]Colman McCarthy, "When the Media Danced to Jingo Bells," Washington Post, March 17, 1991.

[135]Vincent Carroll, "The Scarcity of Anti-War Editorial Voices," Washington Journalism Review, January/February 1991.

[136]Wall Street Journal, August 29, 1990.

[137]Katherine Boo, "Wham, Bam, Thanks Saddam," Washington Monthly, April 1991, p. 16; David Lamb, "Pentagon Hardball," Washington Journalism Review, April 1991.

[138]Dennis Bernstein, "Networks Under Pressure to Put Out Pro-War News," Chapel Hill Herald, March 21, 1991.

[139]Prime Time Live, ABC News, April 25, 1991.

[140]Steven Erlanger, "Church Convocation Calls for Cease-Fire in Persian Gulf War," New York Times, February 21, 1991.

[141]David Zucchino, "Bush Kept Control by Raising the Stakes After Each Iraqi Bluff,"

Philadelphia Inquirer, February 27, 1991, p. 14a.

[142]Garry Wills, "Congress Holds Coat for Bush's Immoral Duel," Chapel Hill Herald, January 15, 1991.

[143]Newsletter of the Commission on the Bicentennial of the United States Constitution, January 1991, Volume 7, Number 1.

[144]Jack Nelson, Los Angeles Times press release, February 16, 1991.

[145]Margaret Garrard Warner, "Bush Battles the 'Wimp Factor'", Newsweek, October 19, 1987, p. 32.

[146]Jack Nelson, *op. cit.,* italics added.

Index